# The
# GREAT BOOKS
# READER

JOHN MARK REYNOLDS

General Editor

*The*

# GREAT BOOKS
# READER

EXCERPTS AND ESSAYS *on the* MOST
INFLUENTIAL BOOKS *in* WESTERN CIVILIZATION

BETHANY HOUSE PUBLISHERS

*Minneapolis, Minnesota*

© 2011 by John Mark Reynolds

Published by Bethany House Publishers
11400 Hampshire Avenue South
Bloomington, Minnesota 55438
www.bethanyhouse.com

Bethany House Publishers is a division of
Baker Publishing Group, Grand Rapids, Michigan

Printed in the United States of America

Library of Congress Cataloging-in-Publication Data
  The Great Books reader : excerpts and essays on the most influential books in western civilization / John Mark Reynolds, general editor.
    p.  cm.
  Summary: "This anthology includes excerpts from thirty of the greatest works in western literature, and essays about those works written by distinguished professors, lecturers, and authors"—Provided by publisher.
  Includes bibliographical references.
  ISBN 978-0-7642-0852-2 (alk. paper)
  1. Best books. 2. Literature—Collections. 3. Christians—Books and reading. I. Reynolds, John Mark, 1963–
Z1035.9.G77  2011
011'.73—dc23                                                                        2011017513

Scripture quotations are from the King James Version of the Bible.

Cover design by Chris Gilbert/Studio Gearbox

11  12  13  14  15  16  17      7  6  5  4  3  2  1

# CONTENTS

Introduction   9

**1. Homer**   *17*
Introduction • Selection from *The Odyssey* • Essay by Al Geier

**2. Plato**   *33*
Introduction • Selection from the *Republic* • Essay by Gary Hartenburg

**3. Aristotle**   *57*
Introduction • Selection from *Nicomachean Ethics* • Essay by Jeff Lehman

**4. Virgil**   *77*
Introduction • Selection from the *Aeneid* • Essay by Jeff Lehman

**5. Augustine**   *103*
Introduction • Selection from *Confessions* • Essay by Peter Kreeft

**6. Boethius**   *125*
Introduction • Selection from *Consolation of Philosophy* • Essay by Michael Fatigati

**7. Thomas Aquinas**   *145*
Introduction • Selection from *Summa Theologica* • Essay by Peter Kreeft

**8. Dante Alighieri**  *167*

Introduction • Selection from the *Divine Comedy* • Essay by Anthony Esolen

**9. Geoffrey Chaucer**  *189*

Introduction • Selection from *The Canterbury Tales* • Essay by Diane Vincent

**10. Desiderius Erasmus**  *219*

Introduction • Selection from *In Praise of Folly* • Essay by Greg Peters

**11. John Calvin**  *237*

Introduction • Selection from *Institutes of the Christian Religion* • Essay by Russell D. Moore

**12. Edmund Spenser**  *255*

Introduction • Selection from *The Faerie Queene* • Essay by John Mark Reynolds

**13. Miguel de Cervantes**  *287*

Introduction • Selection from *Don Quixote* • Essay by RT Llizo

**14. William Shakespeare**  *313*

Introduction • Selection from *Much Ado About Nothing* • Essay by Melissa Schubert

**15. René Descartes**  *339*

Introduction • Selection from *Meditations* • Essay by Thomas Ward

**16. John Milton**  *357*

Introduction • Selection from *Paradise Lost* • Essay by Frederica Mathewes-Green

**17. Blaise Pascal** *379*

Introduction • Selection from *Pensées* • Essay by Peter Kreeft

**18. John Locke, Part One** *407*

Introduction • Selection (on Epistemology) from *An Essay Concerning Human Understanding* • Essay by Janelle Klapausak

**19. John Locke, Part Two** *427*

Introduction • Selection (on Politics) from *Two Treatises on Government: Second Treatise* • Essay by Jamie Campbell

**20. Isaac Newton** *449*

Introduction • Selection from *Mathematical Principles of Natural Philosophy* • Essay by William A. Dembski

**21. John Wesley** *469*

Introduction • Selection from *Sermons* • Essay by Joe Henderson

**22. Jane Austen** *487*

Introduction • Selection from *Pride and Prejudice* • Essay by John Mark Reynolds

**23. Alexis de Tocqueville** *499*

Introduction • Selection from *Democracy in America* • Essay by Hugh Hewitt

**24. Karl Marx (and Friedrich Engels)** *513*

Introduction • Selection from the *Communist Manifesto* • Essay by Hunter Baker

**25. Charles Darwin** *537*

Introduction • Selection from *On the Origin of Species* • Essay by Phil Johnson

**26. Leo Tolstoy**  *557*

Introduction • Selection from *Anna Karenina* • Essay by Frederica Mathewes-Green • Essay by Amy Obrist

**27. Fyodor Dostoevsky**  *585*

Introduction • Selection from *The Brothers Karamazov* • Essay by John Granger

**28. Friedrich Nietzsche**  *609*

Introduction • Selection from *Genealogy of Morals* • Essay by Fred Sanders

**29. G. K. Chesterton**  *627*

Introduction • Selection from *Orthodoxy* • Essay by Dale Ahlquist

Translation Credits   649
Contributors   653

# ON READING EXCERPTS
# OF GREAT BOOKS

You are reading a book that intends to introduce you to a better life. It does not intend to save your soul, as there is a greater collection of books in sacred Scripture to do that, but it does hope to help improve your mind. If we want to love the Lord God with our mind, it's best to make that mind as sharp and attractive as possible.

Christians look forward to a better kingdom, the perfect kingdom of God, but on this side of its full manifestation, we go on living. Our goal is to become fit subjects of that civilization, and while all of us were born human, created in God's image, this heritage only grants us the potential to become civilized. Virtuous practices—for example, reading and following an argument—help us to get there.

*Great Books Reader* is a useful first handbook for facilitating one important virtue: being well-read. Being well-read is not sufficient, and it isn't the highest virtue to which we can strive, but it is both necessary and practical. We are, after all, people of a Great Book; no Christian leader ought to choose illiteracy or intentionally fail to develop the intellectual skills needed to read well.

9

## Brief Defense of a (Nearly) Indefensible Project

Building a book of excerpts from great writers has risks. What if readers stop their exploration? What if instead of using their thoughts to join the discussion, to think for themselves, students simply adopt our opinions about the texts? What if this becomes the kind of volume that's purchased by home decorators to give a living room shelf a touch of class?

Reading only a bit of a great book (e.g., Plato's *Republic*) is like getting engaged but never marrying. The initial experience is pleasurable but can become frustrating if prolonged. Some things are only good in anticipation of a higher good that's coming. Following four consecutive lost Super Bowls, Buffalo Bills fans understand that getting to the big game is not the same as winning it. I'm told that being a bridesmaid (and not a bride) loses its savor sometime around the third wedding.

————

Let us warn you, then, away from these misuses of this book.

Do not use this text to avoid reading the books featured here in their entirety. This would twist the intentions of the authors, because though *Great Books Reader* is an introduction to writers you will love, it is not a full courtship. The best writers are approachable, but really getting to know them isn't cheap or easy. Each reflects God's grace in powerful ways—even when they have tried to reject Him. Knowing them will require a lifetime of effort; this book is a start at some literary matchmaking.

Reading an essay about a writer like Shakespeare always risks another sort of silliness. Time spent understanding a piece on *Hamlet* is usually better spent reading *Hamlet*. If the introductions here become a substitute for reading the real things, then this book will have failed. An appetizer will have become the main course!

Some time-pressed soul might question why Christians should bother reading these books at all. Why not just read the Bible? Well, there are solid reasons we should read great books. Again, we are a people of a Great Book and so should have a vested interest in literature in general.

Real love may be exclusive in its devotion, but any particular love creates the possibilities of other loves. In my experience, loving my wife better helps me love my friends better. Higher loves empower lower loves, and lower loves are practice for higher loves. If I love my neighbor as myself, then loving my country, an accumulation of neighbors, generally will follow.

Growing up loving the Bible made me apt to love other books. I don't love them in the same way I love the Bible, but a lesser love came easily. The splendor of sunlight does not take away from the glory of the stars.

Most important, any reader can fight with the lesser books, great though they may be, without risk of impiety. In contrast, sacred Scriptures are God's Word, and an attitude of reverence is appropriate when touching them; reverence can make it hard to hone skills. Generally, a man should not learn to box with his mother.

A tough great book is a perfect proving ground to become ready and able to read the Book of Books. All good books reflect God, but not all good books are about Him any more than every good song needs to be a praise song. A good person probably cannot *just* read the Bible . . . even after he has learned to read well.

Man needs more than God; he needs other men. Before the fall, when man walked with God alone in the Garden, God said it was not good for him to be alone. He created family so that men and women could cleave to each other and find natural community. Ideally this community would stretch over the ages, and we could ask Father Adam for advice from his store of wisdom gained over the millennia.

Death has cut us off from some of that community. We cannot ask Michelangelo his view of art deco, or request that Aristotle comment on *Till We Have Faces*. This loneliness is not good for us, yet books lessen it a bit. By reading older books we get a taste of the conversations of heaven.

Furthermore, separation from our ancestors has made us prejudiced. It's easy to love the familiar, but past ages come to us in new ways. For instance, they bore or disturb us. The dead say things we would or could not say and in ways that appall, bless, and startle us.

Reading them is a part of diversity. The easiest voices to ignore are those of the dead; nevertheless, they often are the ones we need most. We don't hear from the Christians of the sixteenth century on television, or the ancient Romans on our radio. We must turn to books and be willing to have open minds as we do so. They're like us in their humanity but different in their time. This difference sometimes will make no difference, but at other moments it will allow them to speak prophetically. The best revelation of men as they are today often comes from men long dead.

---

So this book of excerpts is a guide to the voices we will hear when we open the pages of the greatest books. Nobody *must* read it, but most of us *should*, if we have no other guides.

Why?

For one thing, like losing weight, reading the classics is a goal many of us fail to achieve. Each January I set out to weigh less, but too often I don't succeed because I try to do too much too quickly. Returning to the gym tempts me to start where I left off, but my body isn't ready. Strain or soreness sets in, and I quit without gaining any good from my pain.

Moderation is as important in the life of the mind as it is in the body. Readers lead, but the surrounding world does not encourage us to take the time to read. It has never been easier to get books but never harder to find the quiet needed to study them. Even colleges are full of events where reading gets in the way of floor activities.

We know we should read more, and the temptation is to get a complete "great books set" and plunge into it. This rarely works, though, because few of us are ready for that level of challenge. This book is a chance for the rest of us to begin where we can.

*Great Books Reader* also provides guides that most of us don't have in our neighborhoods. When Socrates was searching for truth, he practiced it in a community of students. Nobody should learn alone, and it's usually not too difficult to find someone to read with us. But who will teach us?

Of course, fundamentally, believers do not need a teacher for the deepest truths. Jesus lives within us, and the image of God abides in every human being. Based on common grace, there is no person who can fail to find God if God wishes to be found. *But even though we need no gurus, we may need guides.*

Most of us simply do not pursue the Way, the dialectic, "the Great Conversation" long enough. What do we mean by the Way? Reasoned discourse in a community. The path of knowledge. Following the argument moved by love in pursuit of God. Embracing anything that is good, true, and beautiful, and thinking on those things. While you may not *need* a guide in this journey, a good guide is helpful.

Accordingly, this book tries to fill the role of a good tutor in a great books discussion. The tutor does not tell the student what to think but instead learns with the student. Still, he or she has been reading the books for years and can, for example, ask important first questions. Even if the student comes to reject the opinions of the guiding tutor, the Conversation has been aided. View the essays in this volume as guides in your reading of the excerpts that these wise people have chosen. They are all following—and are committed to—the Way.

Some are experts on the books they're commenting on, recognized by the academic community for their scholarship on these particular works. On the other hand, I picked some amateur essay writers who are wise in the Way but are not scholars of the particular book on which they write. They come to the texts with love and experience but without dogmas to defend.

The essay writers are fellow students of the real guides: the authors whose works form the bulk of this book. Spend most of your time poring over Virgil or Aquinas and then watch your fellow students, perhaps further down the Way, as they too wrestle with these guides. The real teachers in this book are the great writers, and you get to listen in to the conversation between them and the bright fellow students in the subsequent essays.

Ultimately, this book presents an immediate overview of the Great Conversation. In the West of the world, this conversation has being going on for three thousand years or more. We have chosen to follow this thread not because it is the only or even the best conversation, but because it is the discussion into which we were born. Other books could introduce other texts and other traditions; even so, regardless of the starting point, the Way will be the same.

## Making the "Barely Okay" a Friend of the Good: How to Use This Book

The perfect can be the enemy of the good, because striving for better than the possible can prevent any achievement at all. Turning up our noses at the barely okay can also be the enemy of the good, because it can prevent necessary growth in ourselves or in our students. This book recognizes that all of us are lucky to have avoided Victorian corsets and collars but unlucky to have missed out on the good parts of a Victorian education. Our Latin and Greek are poor or nonexistent, and we've found long chapters hard.

For those of us raised on (or become accustomed to) reading blogs, *Great Books Reader* is a start at reading great books. You can follow the Way reading blogs, because anything that provokes a discussion among a group of friends is valuable. Sadly, however, most blogs do not have the depth or beauty of the great books. You can learn how to start *better* conversations through being introduced to the best topics and guides.

---

Here are five tips on how to use *GBR* in starting or going further along on the Way.

*First*, after the brief introduction, read the text—the excerpt—quickly; then, read it carefully a second time. Consider taking a moment to write about three hundred words on what you think the author is saying. (If writing is hard for you, record your ideas.) Only then turn to the essay by one of your fellow students and discover what he or she has to say.

*Second*, read charitably. Don't look for problems in the ideas on the first read. Great men and women have patterned their lives on the books you are reading. Why? What's good about it? What's true? What's beautiful? Try to get inside the world of Homer and see what it would be like to think with his view of reality. Only then can you begin to judge it, because only then do you really understand it.

*Third*, read argumentatively. Charity does not preclude being opinionated! After your second reading, compare, and bring into line, every thought with God's Word. Then realize that you have only brought those thoughts into line with *your thoughts about* God's Word! Ask yourself: are you right in your comprehension of that Word? Have you rightly understood the author, and the Author?

Embrace a point of view, and argue for it forcefully, but be meek enough to realize you might need to change your ideas. Commit yourself, and then see what you find.

Don't make the mistake of hiding any idea from the Way. Every thought must be examined by God—the Word, the Logos—including our beliefs about Him.

Also, don't make the secondary mistake of starting over all the time

14

in the vain belief that this shows humility. Ask the questions you really have, not ones you think you should have.

If you come to wonder about God's existence while reading this book, enjoy the wonder. But don't try to force yourself to doubt His existence if you truly do not. A double-minded and unstable man uses "reason" to undermine things he really knows to be true in order to justify his folly or sin. The single-minded man pursues the Logos knowing it's the only choice he actually has.

*Fourth*, don't try to get a "last word" on any of the authors. There is no harm—and much value—in ending with tentative conclusions. It's highly unlikely any of us will ever fathom all the depths of any of these writers before we get to continue the Discussion in the real City of God. Spend some time with each, wrestle honestly, and then move on to the next. Come back another time and try again.

As with physical fitness, mental fitness is a lifetime project.

*Fifth*, pick at least one author and go read the entire work found in partial form here. I would recommend starting with Homer, because he is accessible and there are many good translations of his great works. If America does become a post-Christian society, then something like his view of reality may prevail.

One more thing: Avoid secondary sources, and don't try to master all the details about an author. Most of us have loved something or other to death—like the *Star Trek* fan who watches all the episodes and movies too many times and eventually ruins the fun. Being an "expert" on Shakespeare is not the same thing as enjoying and learning from his plays. There's a place for the expert, but most of us will remain happy amateurs. Embrace that status.

---

This book is *not* Wikipedia for Christians. If you want to know more about the writer's life, check the Internet, but do so modestly. You're being introduced to the Great Conversation: a dozens-of-centuries-long dialogue between reasonable people. Don't lose the flow of ideas through time by becoming overly focused on details.

It's generally more important to listen to Plato than to know biographical facts about him. Treat the authors as if they were alive and speaking to you. Context is significant for a deeper understanding of them, but first try to grasp what endures in their work. What do they say that causes their words to speak to most people at most places at most times?

———

Note: Each excerpt is preceded by a short introduction to help you form good questions while you read. Different scholars and intellectuals will then respond to the piece in an essay and offer some insights. I'll often intentionally broach different issues than the essay writers. Try to hear the two of us dialogue with the great author.

Once again: Follow the argument, what Plato would call the logos, and keep an open mind. This pursuit is good for your soul and cannot harm you *unless you stop being a follower*.

That might feel scary or tiring: scary because you might think it implies there is no truth, or tiring because it possibly sets up an endless journey. Rather, the passionate pursuit of the argument is *hopeful*—it assumes that wondering can be wonderful and that humankind can continue making progress toward finding the truth. And the journey is not, so far as we know, endless; death brings us to the as-yet "undiscovered country" where, reports suggest, we will find full rest.

It's crucial to grasp that not all the authors in this book are in (or near) the same place in their pursuit of the Logos. Most are Christians, but not all. We represent many traditions within Christendom, though most of the Christian authors are evangelical in practice and in conviction, and most of them resonate with more traditional forms of the faith. I am convinced with Justin Martyr that none of us can follow the argument, the logos, without following the Logos (the Word).

If Christianity is true, then every argument will, if pursued to the end, lead to Jesus.

Of the making of books there is no end, especially if one is allowed to make books out of excerpts of other books. But there is an end to our time, indeed to our lives. We had better prepare for the one certainty of that life: death. These excerpts will demonstrate how to live well and show how to die well.

John Mark N. Reynolds
Torrey Honors Institute, 2011

## CHAPTER ONE

# HOMER

## Ancient Greek (c. 850 BC)

**B**efore the dialectical way was discovered (i.e., using reasoned argument in community with others), men told stories to find the truth. There *is* a place for storytelling in the dialect, but these ancient men *only* had the stories. Short of divine revelation, men walked blindly and tried to make sense of the world in the best way they knew.

In the earth's "West," the blind poet Homer was the first known great storyteller. He wove an epic around the fall of the magnificent city of Troy, and he penned a second massive story around the return home of one of the war's victors, Odysseus.

These tales are the epitome of centuries of thought, put together by genius, into a coherent worldview. These storytellers understood the futility of life and the nature of evil. Homer begins his *Iliad* in a war that does not end with the close of the text. His hero, Odysseus, wants only to come home; he recognizes that the life of the Greek gods was not suitable for men.

Hope, in Homer, is less a virtue than a cheat imposed on humanity by the gods to keep us going. His deities are whimsical, and many are wicked.

There is no fundamental order or pattern to the universe, and if Homer is right, then philosophy and science would be impossible.

Homer was so great that Greek culture became imaginatively captive to him. This was a good thing up to a point, because his works were spectacularly wise. They had limits, however, and when those were reached, the Greek religious establishment refused to change. Homer made powerful men slavish devotees of idols unfit for a free man's worship.

Socrates died for his failure to defeat the Homeric idols, and even Plato could not remove Homer's evils from the Western imagination. It fell to a Jewish rabbi named Paul to begin the process, on the Areopagus in Athens, centuries after Socrates died.

Christians are left with a Homer lacking the power of an establishment religion. The wisdom and beauty in the poet remains for us without the great peril. Polytheism may return in the post-Christian parts of the West, but if it does, it would do well to read the *Iliad* and the *Odyssey*, because this is the best of paganism.

There is more virtue in Homer, and less danger, than in a prosperity gospel preacher, after all.

<br>

## ⊂⊂ FROM ⊃⊃

# *The Odyssey*

<br>

## Book IX

<br>

And Ulysses answered, "King Alcinous, it is a good thing to hear a bard with such a divine voice as this man has. There is nothing better or more delightful than when a whole people make merry together, with the guests sitting orderly to listen, while the table is loaded with bread and meats, and the cup-bearer draws wine and fills his cup for every man. This is indeed as fair a sight as a man can see. Now, however, since you are inclined to ask the story of my sorrows, and rekindle my own sad memories in respect of them, I do not know how to begin, nor yet how to continue and conclude my tale, for the hand of heaven has been laid heavily upon me.

"Firstly, then, I will tell you my name that you too may know it, and one day, if I outlive this time of sorrow, may become my guests though I live so far away from all of you. I am Ulysses son of Laertes, reknowned among mankind for all manner of subtlety, so that my fame ascends to heaven. I live in Ithaca, where there is a high mountain called Neritum, covered with forests; and not far from it there is a group of islands very near to one another—Dulichium, Same, and the wooded island of Zacynthus. It lies squat on the horizon, all highest up in the sea towards the sunset, while the others lie away from it towards dawn. It is a rugged island, but it breeds brave men, and my eyes know none that they better love to look upon. The goddess Calypso kept me with her in her cave, and wanted me to marry her, as did also the cunning Aeaean goddess Circe; but they could neither of them persuade me, for there is nothing dearer to a man than his own country and his parents, and however splendid a home he may have in a foreign country, if it be far from father or mother, he does not care about it. Now, however, I will tell you of the many hazardous adventures which by Jove's will I met with on my return from Troy.

"When I had set sail thence the wind took me first to Ismarus, which is the city of the Cicons. There I sacked the town and put the people to the sword. We took their wives and also much booty, which we divided equitably amongst us, so that none might have reason to complain. I then said that we had better make off at once, but my men very foolishly would not obey me, so they stayed there drinking much wine and killing great numbers of sheep and oxen on the sea shore. Meanwhile the Cicons cried out for help to other Cicons who lived inland. These were more in number, and stronger, and they were more skilled in the art of war, for they could fight, either from chariots or on foot as the occasion served; in the morning, therefore, they came as thick as leaves and bloom in summer, and the hand of heaven was against us, so that we were hard pressed. They set the battle in array near the ships, and the hosts aimed their bronze-shod spears at one another. So long as the day waxed and it was still morning, we held our own against them, though they were more in number than we; but as the sun went down, towards the time when men loose their oxen, the Cicons got the better of us, and we lost half a dozen men from every ship we had; so we got away with those that were left.

"Thence we sailed onward with sorrow in our hearts, but glad to have escaped death though we had lost our comrades, nor did we leave till we had thrice invoked each one of the poor fellows who had perished by the hands of the Cicons. Then Jove raised the North wind against us till it blew a hurricane, so that land and sky were hidden in thick clouds, and night sprang forth out of the heavens. We let the ships run before the gale, but the force of the wind tore our sails to tatters, so we took them down for fear of shipwreck, and rowed our hardest towards the land. There we lay two days and two nights suffering much alike from toil and distress of mind, but on the morning of the third day we again raised our masts, set sail, and took our places, letting the wind and steersmen direct our ship. I should have got home at that time unharmed had not the North wind and the currents been against me as I was doubling Cape Malea, and set me off my course hard by the island of Cythera.

"I was driven thence by foul winds for a space of nine days upon the sea, but on the tenth day we reached the land of the Lotus-eaters, who live on a food that comes from a kind of flower. Here we landed to take in fresh water, and our crews got their mid-day meal on the shore near the ships. When they had eaten and drunk I sent two of my company to see what manner of men the people of the place might be, and they had a third man under them. They started at once, and went about among the Lotus-eaters, who did them no hurt, but gave them to eat of the lotus, which was so delicious that those who ate of it left off caring about home, and did not even want to go back and say what had happened to them, but were for staying and munching lotus with the Lotus-eater without thinking further of their return; nevertheless, though they wept bitterly I forced them back to the ships and made them fast under the benches. Then I told the rest to go on board at once, lest any of them should taste of the lotus and leave off wanting to get home, so they took their places and smote the grey sea with their oars.

"We sailed hence, always in much distress, till we came to the land of the lawless and inhuman Cyclopes. Now the Cyclopes neither plant nor plough, but trust in providence, and live on such wheat, barley, and grapes as grow wild without any kind of tillage, and their wild grapes yield them wine as the sun and the rain may grow them. They have no laws nor assemblies of the people, but live in caves on the tops of high mountains; each is lord and master in his family, and they take no account of their neighbours.

"Now off their harbour there lies a wooded and fertile island not quite close to the land of the Cyclopes, but still not far. It is overrun with wild goats, that breed there in great numbers and are never disturbed by foot of man; for sportsmen—who as a rule will suffer so much hardship in forest or among mountain precipices—do not go there, nor yet again is it ever ploughed or fed down, but it lies a wilderness untilled and unsown from year to year, and has no living thing upon it but only goats. For the Cyclopes have no ships, nor yet shipwrights who could make ships for them; they cannot therefore go from city to city, or sail over the sea to one another's country as people who have ships can do; if they had had these they would have colonized the island, for it is a very good one, and would yield everything in due season. There are meadows that in some places come right down to the sea shore, well watered and full of luscious grass; grapes would do there excellently; there is level land for ploughing, and it would always yield heavily at harvest time, for the soil is deep. There is a good harbour where no cables are wanted, nor yet anchors, nor need a ship be moored, but all one has to do is to beach one's vessel and stay there till the wind becomes fair for putting out to sea again. At the head of the harbour there is a spring of clear water coming out of a cave, and there are poplars growing all round it.

"Here we entered, but so dark was the night that some god must have brought us in, for there was nothing whatever to be seen. A thick mist hung all round our ships; the moon was hidden behind a mass of clouds so that no one could have seen the island if he had looked for it, nor were there any breakers to tell us we were close in shore before we found ourselves upon the land itself; when, however, we had beached the ships, we took down the sails, went ashore and camped upon the beach till daybreak.

"When the child of morning, rosy-fingered Dawn, appeared, we admired the island and wandered all over it, while the nymphs Jove's daughters roused the wild goats that we might get some meat for our dinner. On this we fetched our spears and bows and arrows from the ships, and dividing ourselves into three bands began to shoot the goats. Heaven sent us excellent sport; I had twelve ships with me, and each ship got nine goats, while my own ship had ten; thus through the livelong day to the going down of the sun we ate and drank our fill—and we had plenty of wine left, for each one of us had taken many jars full when we sacked the city of the Cicons, and this had not yet run out. While we were feasting we kept turning our eyes towards the land of the Cyclopes, which was hard by, and saw the smoke of their stubble fires. We could almost fancy we heard their voices and the bleating of their sheep and goats, but when the sun went down and it came on dark, we camped down upon the beach, and next morning I called a council.

"'Stay here, my brave fellows,' said I, 'all the rest of you, while I go with my ship and exploit these people myself: I want to see if they are uncivilized savages, or a hospitable and humane race.'

"I went on board, bidding my men to do so also and loose the hawsers; so they took their places and smote the grey sea with their oars. When we got to the land, which was not far, there, on the face of a cliff near the sea, we saw a great cave overhung with laurels. It was a station for a great many sheep and goats, and outside there was a large yard, with a high wall round it made of stones built into the ground and of trees both pine and oak. This was the abode of a huge monster who was then away from home shepherding his flocks. He would have nothing to do with other people, but led the life of an outlaw. He was a horrid creature, not like a human being at all, but resembling rather some crag that stands out boldly against the sky on the top of a high mountain.

"I told my men to draw the ship ashore, and stay where they were, all but the twelve best among them, who were to go along with myself. I also took a goatskin of sweet black wine which had been given me by Maron, Apollo son of Euanthes, who was priest of Apollo the patron god of Ismarus, and lived within the wooded precincts of the temple. When we were sacking the city we respected him, and spared his life, as also his wife and child; so he made me some presents of great value—seven talents of fine gold, and a bowl of silver, with twelve jars of sweet wine, unblended, and of the most exquisite flavour. Not a man nor maid in the house knew about it, but only himself, his wife, and one housekeeper: when he drank it he mixed twenty parts of water to one of wine, and yet the fragrance from the mixing-bowl was so exquisite that it was impossible to refrain from drinking. I filled a large skin with this wine, and took a wallet full of provisions with me, for my mind misgave me that I might have to deal with some savage who would be of great strength, and would respect neither right nor law.

"We soon reached his cave, but he was out shepherding, so we went inside and took stock of all that we could see. His cheese-racks were loaded with cheeses, and he had more lambs and kids than his pens could hold. They were kept in separate flocks; first there were the hoggets, then the oldest of the younger lambs and lastly the very young ones all kept apart from one another; as for his dairy, all the vessels, bowls, and milk pails into which he milked, were swimming with whey. When they saw all this, my men begged me to let them first steal some cheeses, and make off with them to the ship; they would then return, drive down the lambs and kids, put them on board and sail away with them. It would have been indeed better if we had done so but I would not listen to them, for I wanted to see the owner himself, in the hope that he might give me a present. When, however, we saw him my poor men found him ill to deal with.

"We lit a fire, offered some of the cheeses in sacrifice, ate others of them, and then sat waiting till the Cyclops should come in with his sheep. When he came, he brought in with him a huge load of dry firewood to light the fire for his supper, and this he flung with such a noise on to the floor of his cave that we hid ourselves for fear at the far end of the cavern. Meanwhile he drove all the ewes inside, as well as the she-goats that he was going to milk, leaving the males, both rams and he-goats, outside in the yards. Then he rolled a huge stone to the mouth of the cave—so huge that two and twenty strong four-wheeled waggons would not be enough to draw it from its place against the doorway. When he had so done he sat down and milked his ewes and goats, all in due course, and then let each of them have her own young. He curdled half the milk and set it aside in wicker strainers, but the other half he poured into bowls that he might drink it for his supper. When he had got through with all his work, he lit the fire, and then caught sight of us, whereon he said:

"'Strangers, who are you? Where do sail from? Are you traders, or do you sail the sea as rovers, with your hands against every man, and every man's hand against you?'

"We were frightened out of our senses by his loud voice and monstrous form, but I managed to say, 'We are Achaeans on our way home from Troy, but by the will of Jove, and stress of weather, we have been driven far out of our course. We are the people of Agamemnon, son of Atreus, who has won infinite renown throughout the whole world, by sacking so great a city and killing so many people. We therefore humbly pray you to show us some hospitality, and otherwise make us such presents as visitors may reasonably expect. May your excellency fear the wrath of heaven, for we are your suppliants, and Jove takes all respectable travellers under his protection, for he is the avenger of all suppliants and foreigners in distress.'

"To this he gave me but a pitiless answer, 'Stranger,' said he, 'you are a fool, or else you know nothing of this country. Talk to me, indeed, about fearing the gods or shunning their anger? We Cyclopes do not care about Jove or any of your blessed gods, for we are ever so much stronger than they. I shall not spare either yourself or your companions out of any regard for Jove, unless I am in the humour for doing so. And now tell me where you made your ship fast when you came on shore. Was it round the point, or is she lying straight off the land?'

"He said this to draw me out, but I was too cunning to be caught in that way, so I answered with a lie; 'Neptune,' said I, 'sent my ship on to the rocks at the far end of your country, and wrecked it. We were driven on to them from the open sea, but I and those who are with me escaped the jaws of death.'

"The cruel wretch vouchsafed me not one word of answer, but with a sudden clutch he gripped up two of my men at once and dashed them down upon the ground as though they had been puppies. Their brains were shed upon the ground, and the earth was wet with their blood. Then he tore them limb from limb and supped upon them. He gobbled them up like a lion in the wilderness, flesh, bones, marrow, and entrails, without leaving anything uneaten. As for us, we wept and lifted up our hands to heaven on seeing such a horrid sight, for we did not know what else to do; but when the Cyclops had filled his huge paunch, and had washed down his meal of human flesh with a drink of neat milk, he stretched himself full length upon the ground among his sheep, and went to sleep. I was at first inclined to seize my sword, draw it, and drive it into his vitals, but I reflected that if I did we should all certainly be lost, for we should never be able to shift the stone which the monster had put in front of the door. So we stayed sobbing and sighing where we were till morning came.

"When the child of morning, rosy-fingered Dawn, appeared, he again lit his fire, milked his goats and ewes, all quite rightly, and then let each have her own young one; as soon as he had got through with all his work, he clutched up two more of my men, and began eating them for his morning's meal. Presently, with the utmost ease, he rolled the stone away from the door and drove out his sheep, but he at once put it back again—as easily as though he were merely clapping the lid on to a quiver full of arrows. As soon as he had done so he shouted, and cried 'Shoo, shoo,' after his sheep to drive them on to the mountain; so I was left to scheme some way of taking my revenge and covering myself with glory.

"In the end I deemed it would be the best plan to do as follows. The Cyclops had a great club which was lying near one of the sheep pens; it was of green olive wood, and he had cut it intending to use it for a staff as soon as it should be dry. It was so huge that we could only compare it to the mast of a twenty-oared merchant vessel of large burden, and able to venture out into open sea. I went up to this club and cut off about six feet of it; I then gave this piece to the men and told them to fine it evenly off at one end, which they proceeded to do, and lastly I brought it to a point myself, charring the end in the fire to make it harder. When I had done this I hid it under dung, which was lying about all over the cave, and told the men to cast lots which of them should venture along with myself to lift it and bore it into the monster's eye while he was asleep. The lot fell upon the very four whom I should have chosen, and I myself made five. In the evening the wretch came back from shepherding, and drove his flocks into the cave—this time driving them all inside, and not leaving any in the yards; I suppose some fancy must have taken him, or a god must have prompted him to do so. As soon as he had put the stone back to its place against the door, he sat down, milked his ewes and his goats all quite rightly, and then let each have her own young one; when he had got through with all this work, he gripped up two more of my men, and made his supper off them. So I went up to him with an ivy-wood bowl of black wine in my hands:

"'Look here, Cyclops,' said I, 'you have been eating a great deal of man's flesh, so take this and drink some wine, that you may see what kind of liquor we had on board my ship. I was bringing it to you as a drink-offering, in the hope that you would take compassion upon me and further me on my way home, whereas all you do is to go on ramping and raving most intolerably. You ought to be ashamed yourself; how can you expect people to come see you any more if you treat them in this way?'

"He then took the cup and drank. He was so delighted with the taste of the wine that he begged me for another bowl full. 'Be so kind,' he said, 'as to give me some more, and tell me your name at once. I want to make you a present that you will be glad to have. We have wine even in this country, for our soil grows grapes and the sun ripens them, but this drinks like nectar and ambrosia all in one.'

"I then gave him some more; three times did I fill the bowl for him, and three times did he drain it without thought or heed; then, when I saw that the wine had got into his head, I said to him as plausibly as I could: 'Cyclops, you ask my name and I will tell it you; give me, therefore, the present you promised me; my name is Noman; this is what my father and mother and my friends have always called me.'

"But the cruel wretch said, 'Then I will eat all Noman's comrades before Noman himself, and will keep Noman for the last. This is the present that I will make him.'

"As he spoke he reeled, and fell sprawling face upwards on the ground. His great neck hung heavily backwards and a deep sleep took hold upon him. Presently he turned sick, and threw up both wine and the gobbets of human flesh on which he had been gorging, for he was very drunk. Then I thrust the beam of wood far into the embers to heat it, and encouraged my men lest any of them should turn faint-hearted. When the wood, green though it was, was about to blaze, I drew it out of the fire glowing with heat, and my men gathered round me, for heaven had filled their hearts with courage. We drove the sharp end of the beam into the monster's eye, and bearing upon it with all my weight I kept turning it round and round as though I were boring a hole in a ship's plank with an auger, which two men with a wheel and strap can keep on turning as long as they choose. Even thus did we bore the red hot beam into his eye, till the boiling blood bubbled all over it as we worked it round and round, so that the steam from the burning eyeball scalded his eyelids and eyebrows, and the roots of the eye sputtered in the fire. As a blacksmith plunges an axe or hatchet into cold water to temper it—for it is this that gives strength to the iron—and it makes a great hiss as he does so, even thus did the Cyclops' eye hiss round the beam of olive wood, and his hideous yells made the cave ring again. We ran away in a fright, but he plucked the beam all besmirched with gore from his eye, and hurled it from him in a frenzy of rage and pain, shouting as he did so to the other Cyclopes who lived on the bleak headlands near him; so they gathered from all quarters round his cave when they heard him crying, and asked what was the matter with him.

"'What ails you, Polyphemus,' said they, 'that you make such a noise, breaking the stillness of the night, and preventing us from being able to sleep? Surely no man is carrying off your sheep? Surely no man is trying to kill you either by fraud or by force?'

"But Polyphemus shouted to them from inside the cave, 'Noman is killing me by fraud! Noman is killing me by force!'

"'Then,' said they, 'if no man is attacking you, you must be ill; when Jove makes people ill, there is no help for it, and you had better pray to your father Neptune.'

"Then they went away, and I laughed inwardly at the success of my clever stratagem, but the Cyclops, groaning and in an agony of pain, felt about with his hands till he found the stone and took it from the door; then he sat in the doorway and stretched his hands in front of it to catch anyone going out with the sheep, for he thought I might be foolish enough to attempt this.

"As for myself I kept on puzzling to think how I could best save my own life and those of my companions; I schemed and schemed, as one who knows that his life depends upon it, for the danger was very great. In the end I deemed that this plan would be the best. The male sheep were well grown, and carried a heavy black fleece, so I bound them noiselessly in threes together, with some of the withies on which the wicked monster used to sleep. There was to be a man under the middle sheep, and the two on either side were to cover him, so that there were three sheep to each man. As for myself there was a ram finer than any of the others, so I caught hold of him by the back, esconced myself in the thick wool under his belly, and flung on patiently to his fleece, face upwards, keeping a firm hold on it all the time.

"Thus, then, did we wait in great fear of mind till morning came, but when the child of morning, rosy-fingered Dawn, appeared, the male sheep hurried out to feed, while the ewes remained bleating about the pens waiting to be milked, for their udders were full to bursting; but their master in spite of all his pain felt the backs of all the sheep as they stood upright, without being sharp enough to find out that the men were underneath their bellies. As the ram was going out, last of all, heavy with its fleece and with the weight of my crafty self; Polyphemus laid hold of it and said:

"'My good ram, what is it that makes you the last to leave my cave this morning? You are not wont to let the ewes go before you, but lead the mob with a run whether to flowery mead or bubbling fountain, and are the first to come home again at night; but now you lag last of all. Is it because you know your master has lost his eye, and are sorry because that wicked Noman and his horrid crew have got him down in his drink and blinded him? But I will have his life yet. If you could understand and talk, you would tell me where the wretch is hiding, and I would dash his brains upon the ground till they flew all over the cave. I should thus have some satisfaction for the harm this no-good Noman has done me.'

"As he spoke he drove the ram outside, but when we were a little way out from the cave and yards, I first got from under the ram's belly, and then freed my comrades; as for the sheep, which were very fat, by constantly heading them in the right direction we managed to drive them down to the ship. The crew rejoiced greatly at seeing those of us who had escaped death, but wept for the others whom the Cyclops had killed. However, I made signs to them by nodding and frowning that they were to hush their crying, and told them to get all the sheep on board at once and put out to sea; so they went aboard, took their places, and smote the grey sea with their oars. Then, when I had got as far out as my voice would reach, I began to jeer at the Cyclops.

"'Cyclops,' said I, 'you should have taken better measure of your man before eating up his comrades in your cave. You wretch, eat up your visitors in your own house? You might have known that your sin would find you out, and now Jove and the other gods have punished you.'

"He got more and more furious as he heard me, so he tore the top from off a high mountain, and flung it just in front of my ship so that it was within a little of hitting the end of the rudder. The sea quaked as the rock fell into it, and the wash of the wave it raised carried us back towards the mainland, and forced us towards the shore. But I snatched up a long pole and kept the ship off, making signs to my men by nodding my head, that they must row for their lives, whereon they laid out with a will. When we had got twice as far as we were before, I was for jeering at the Cyclops again, but the men begged and prayed of me to hold my tongue.

"'Do not,' they exclaimed, 'be mad enough to provoke this savage creature further; he has thrown one rock at us already which drove us back again to the mainland, and we made sure it had been the death of us; if he had then heard any further sound of voices he would have pounded our heads and our ship's timbers into a jelly with the rugged rocks he would have heaved at us, for he can throw them a long way.'

"But I would not listen to them, and shouted out to him in my rage, 'Cyclops, if any one asks you who it was that put your eye out and spoiled your beauty, say it was the valiant warrior Ulysses, son of Laertes, who lives in Ithaca.'

"On this he groaned, and cried out, 'Alas, alas, then the old prophecy about me is coming true. There was a prophet here, at one time, a man both brave and of great stature, Telemus son of Eurymus, who was an excellent seer, and did all the prophesying for the Cyclopes till he grew old; he told me that all this would happen to me some day, and said I should lose my sight by the hand of Ulysses. I have been all along expecting some one of imposing presence and superhuman strength, whereas he turns out to be a little insignificant weakling, who has managed to blind my eye by taking advantage of me in my drink; come here, then, Ulysses, that I may make you presents to show my hospitality, and urge Neptune to help you forward on your journey—for Neptune and I are father and son. He, if he so will, shall heal me, which no one else neither god nor man can do.'

"Then I said, 'I wish I could be as sure of killing you outright and sending you down to the house of Hades, as I am that it will take more than Neptune to cure that eye of yours.'

"On this he lifted up his hands to the firmament of heaven and prayed, saying, 'Hear me, great Neptune; if I am indeed your own true-begotten son, grant that Ulysses may never reach his home alive; or if he must get back to his friends at last, let him do so late and in sore plight after losing all his men [let him reach his home in another man's ship and find trouble in his house.']

"Thus did he pray, and Neptune heard his prayer. Then he picked up a rock much larger than the first, swung it aloft and hurled it with prodigious force. It fell just short of the ship, but was within a little of hitting the end of the rudder. The sea quaked as the rock fell into it, and the wash of the wave it raised drove us onwards on our way towards the shore of the island.

"When at last we got to the island where we had left the rest of our ships, we found our comrades lamenting us, and anxiously awaiting our return. We ran our vessel upon the sands and got out of her on to the sea shore; we also landed the Cyclops' sheep, and divided them equitably amongst us so that none might have reason to complain. As for the ram, my companions agreed that I should have it as an extra share; so I sacrificed it on the sea shore, and burned its thigh bones to Jove, who is the lord of all. But he heeded not my sacrifice, and only thought how he might destroy my ships and my comrades.

"Thus through the livelong day to the going down of the sun we feasted our fill on meat and drink, but when the sun went down and it came on dark, we camped upon the beach. When the child of morning, rosy-fingered Dawn, appeared, I bade my men on board and loose the hawsers. Then they took their places and smote the grey sea with their oars; so we sailed on with sorrow in our hearts, but glad to have escaped death though we had lost our comrades."

*Translated by Samuel Butler, 1900*


## ODYSSEUS A CHRISTIAN?

### Al Geier


When Cyclops devours two of his men, Odysseus, their warrior leader, immediately is inclined to take revenge, draw his sword, and slay—or try to slay—the monster. But just at that moment, it is said, a different kind of spiritedness (*heteros thymos*) prevails. Odysseus realizes that if he kills Cyclops, he and his men will be unable to move the boulder that guards the entrance to the cave they're in; they'll be trapped forever. Odysseus's restraint here is not an act of virtue but rather, under the circumstances, a completely pragmatic act.

A little later, Odysseus suffers a relapse. When he and his men are departing, he cannot keep himself from boasting to the now blinded Cyclops that it was he, Odysseus from Ithaca, who took his sight. Cyclops, provoked, hurls a boulder and almost destroys the ship. This boast is neither virtuous nor pragmatic, but foolish.

We are reminded of a similar foolishness in *The Iliad* by Achilles, the supposed best of the Achaians. As he is drawing his sword to slay Agamemnon, Athena comes down from Olympus and checks Achilles; she tells him to not draw his sword and to put aside his anger. Achilles does cease from drawing his sword but, in flagrant disregard of the command and the authority of the wise goddess, he does not put aside his anger, with terrible consequences developing.

Odysseus, on the other hand, eventually recovers from his failure and, by the end, has become transformed. When Athena commands Odysseus to cease from anger toward the kin of the slain suitors, "he yielded to her, and his heart was glad." Thus, unlike Achilles, Odysseus shows a proper regard for wisdom. Furthermore, his gladness suggests that here his restraint is not only pragmatic but that of a virtuous man. The first word of *The Odyssey* is "man" (*andra*). After all is said and done, it is Odysseus who's the real man, *and* the best of the Achaians.

"I say unto you, that ye resist not evil: but whosoever shall smite thee on thy right cheek, turn to him the other also" (Matthew 5:39). The response of he who is smitten is not at all pragmatic, but neither is mere self-restraint virtuous. Nor is it "goodness" simply not to seek revenge. The only way the evil of smiting can be acknowledged is if it is not denied. And the only way it cannot be denied is if it is affirmed. Offering the other cheek, therefore, is a denial of the goodness of retaliation, of "getting even." Getting even is not just; it is the repetition and increase of evil.

On the other hand, offering the other cheek is the ending of any further evil. It too is a "different kind of spiritedness," where the virtue of not getting even prevails over evening the score.

What Odysseus refrained from doing was the manly thing to do. But it was *also* the Christian thing.

## CHAPTER TWO

# PLATO

## Classical Greek (428/427–348/347 BC)

Certain critics of great-books education fear that the books will replace the Book. They understand that not everyone who loves wisdom falls into vanity, but they know that some of us do. They are right to worry, because certain authors are so good, so true, and so beautiful that they can appear to be sufficient. Plato is one of these.

Plato is almost enough.

We have every word Plato ever wrote—a sure sign of the regard every culture, from pagan to Muslim, had for the creator of written philosophy. Nobody burned Plato, because reading his work is the clearest introduction to the dialectic, the way of the Logos. In addition, there have always been disciples ready and willing to protect the texts that taught them the best of earthly practices and some glimpses of heavenly truths.

Three things must be kept in mind when reading Plato.

*First*, he wrote in dialogue form. He believed certain things, but those beliefs were less important to him than the process of reaching those beliefs. He wrote in a way that would provoke argument. Don't be afraid to be bored . . . and then ask why Plato is going on and on. Ask, and you find an answer.

This is because Plato wrote with great care. He was interested in numbers and grew up on the measured poetry of Homer. Perhaps the highest difficulty in reading Plato is knowing when to stop examining a page, a paragraph, a sentence, a word. The first word of *Republic* says Socrates is "going down," and the rest of the book contains a series of upward and downward motions.

*Second*, Plato does not speak in his own dialogues. Socrates is the main character in most (and certainly in *Republic*), but that does not mean Socrates is always speaking for Plato. The historic Socrates, like Jesus, wrote nothing, and like Jesus, he died for his virtues. Unlike Jesus, though, Socrates was not the perfect son of God. Be willing to argue with Socrates or question the persuasiveness of his arguments. Note that his best students do so at the start of *Republic*'s Book II.

*Third*, many Christians, from Justin Martyr through Augustine to C. S. Lewis and J. R. R. Tolkien, have found useful philosophy in Plato. His works contain ideas that are not only compatible with Christianity but can also be used to understand the faith. He anticipated many Jewish and Christian ideas.

Plato did not, however, foresee the Incarnation. In Book VII, he pictures humankind trapped in a cave. He imagines what would happen if one man escaped the trap of our captivity, but he never explains how this miracle might occur.

Christmas is the answer, but Plato only saw winter and never Christmas. Plato, like any man without special revelation, could not reason enough to see the history that would be made at Bethlehem when his beloved Logos came down and revealed himself to us, full of grace and truth.

&#95;&#95;&#95; FROM &#95;&#95;&#95;

# *The Republic*

## 2.II

### Socrates—Glaucon

With these words I was thinking that I had made an end of the discussion; but the end, in truth, proved to be only a beginning. For Glaucon, who is always the most pugnacious of men, was dissatisfied at Thrasymachus' retirement; he wanted to have the battle out. So he said to me: Socrates, do you wish really to persuade us, or only to seem to have persuaded us, that to be just is always better than to be unjust?

I should wish really to persuade you, I replied, if I could.

Then you certainly have not succeeded. Let me ask you now: How would you arrange goods—are there not some which we welcome for their own sakes, and independently of their consequences, as, for example, harmless pleasures and enjoyments, which delight us at the time, although nothing follows from them?

I agree in thinking that there is such a class, I replied.

Is there not also a second class of goods, such as knowledge, sight, health, which are desirable not only in themselves, but also for their results?

Certainly, I said.

And would you not recognize a third class, such as gymnastic, and the care of the sick, and the physician's art; also the various ways of money-making—these do us good but we regard them as disagreeable; and no one would choose them for their own sakes, but only for the sake of some reward or result which flows from them?

There is, I said, this third class also. But why do you ask?

Because I want to know in which of the three classes you would place justice?

In the highest class, I replied—among those goods which he who would be happy desires both for their own sake and for the sake of their results.

Then the many are of another mind; they think that justice is to be reckoned in the troublesome class, among goods which are to be pursued for the sake of rewards and of reputation, but in themselves are disagreeable and rather to be avoided.

I know, I said, that this is their manner of thinking, and that this was the thesis which Thrasymachus was maintaining just now, when he censured justice and praised injustice. But I am too stupid to be convinced by him.

I wish, he said, that you would hear me as well as him, and then I shall see whether you and I agree. For Thrasymachus seems to me, like a snake, to have been charmed by your voice sooner than he ought to have been; but to my mind the nature of justice and injustice have not yet been made clear. Setting aside their rewards and results, I want to know what they are in themselves, and how they inwardly work in the soul. If you please, then, I will revive the argument of Thrasymachus. And first I will speak of the nature and origin of justice according to the common view of them. Secondly, I will show that all men who practise justice do so against their will, of necessity, but not as a good. And thirdly, I will argue that there is reason in this view, for the life of the unjust is after all better far than the life of the just—if what they say is true, Socrates, since I myself am not of their opinion. But still I acknowledge that I am perplexed when I hear the voices of Thrasymachus and myriads of others dinning in my ears; and, on the other hand, I have never yet heard the superiority of justice to injustice maintained by any one in a satisfactory way. I want to hear justice praised in respect of itself; then I shall be satisfied, and you are the person from whom I think that I am most likely to hear this; and therefore I will praise the unjust life to the utmost of my power, and my manner of speaking will indicate the manner in which I desire to hear you too praising justice and censuring injustice. Will you say whether you approve of my proposal?

Indeed I do; nor can I imagine any theme about which a man of sense would oftener wish to converse.

I am delighted, he replied, to hear you say so, and shall begin by speaking, as I proposed, of the nature and origin of justice.

## Glaucon

They say that to do injustice is, by nature, good; to suffer injustice, evil; but that the evil is greater than the good. And so when men have both done and suffered injustice and have had experience of both, not being able to avoid the one and obtain the other, they think that they had better agree among themselves to have neither; hence there arise laws and mutual covenants; and that which is ordained by law is termed by them lawful and just. This they affirm to be the origin and nature of justice—it is a mean or compromise, between the best of all, which is to do injustice and not be punished, and the worst of all, which is to suffer injustice without the power of retaliation; and justice, being at a middle point between the two, is tolerated not as a good, but as the lesser evil, and honoured by reason of the inability of men to do injustice. For no man who is worthy to be called a man would ever submit to such an agreement if he were able to resist; he would be mad if he did. Such is the received account, Socrates, of the nature and origin of justice.

Now that those who practise justice do so involuntarily and because they have not the power to be unjust will best appear if we imagine something of this kind: having given both to the just and the unjust power to do what they will, let us watch and see whither desire will lead them; then we shall discover in the very act the just and unjust man to be proceeding along the same road, following their interest, which all natures deem to be their good, and are only diverted into the path of justice by the force of law. The liberty which we are supposing may be most completely given to them in the form of such a power as is said to have been possessed by Gyges the ancestor of Croesus the Lydian. According to the tradition, Gyges was a shepherd in the service of the king of Lydia; there was a great storm, and an earthquake made an opening in the earth at the place where he was feeding his flock. Amazed at the sight, he descended into the opening, where, among other marvels, he beheld a hollow brazen horse, having doors, at which he stooping and looking in saw a dead body of stature, as appeared to him, more than human, and having nothing on but a gold ring; this he took from the finger of the dead and reascended. Now the shepherds met together, according to custom, that they might send their monthly report about the flocks to the king; into their assembly he came having the ring on his finger, and as he was sitting among them he chanced to turn the collet of the ring inside his hand, when instantly he became invisible to the rest of the company and they began to speak of him as if he were no longer present. He was astonished at this, and again touching the ring he turned the collet outwards and reappeared; he made several trials of the ring, and always with the same result—when he turned the collet inwards he became invisible, when outwards he reappeared. Whereupon he contrived to be chosen one of the messengers who were sent to the court; where as soon as he arrived he seduced the queen, and with her help conspired against the king and slew him, and took the kingdom. Suppose now that there were two such magic rings, and the just put on one of them and the unjust the other; no man can be imagined to be of such an iron nature that he would stand fast in justice. No man would keep his hands off what was not his own when he could safely take what he liked out of the market, or go into houses and lie with any one at his pleasure, or kill or release from prison whom he would, and in all respects be like a God among men. Then the actions of the just would be as the actions of the unjust; they would both come at last to the same point. And this we may truly affirm to be a great proof that a man is just, not willingly or because he thinks that justice is any good to him individually, but of necessity, for wherever any one thinks that he can safely be unjust, there he is unjust. For all men believe in their hearts that injustice is far more profitable to the individual than justice, and he who argues as I have been supposing, will say that they are right. If you could imagine any one obtaining this power of becoming invisible, and never doing any wrong or touching what was another's, he would be thought by the lookers-on to be a most wretched idiot, although they would praise him to one another's faces, and keep up appearances with one another from a fear that they too might suffer injustice. Enough of this.

Now, if we are to form a real judgment of the life of the just and unjust, we must isolate them; there is no other way; and how is the isolation to be effected? I answer: Let the unjust man be entirely unjust, and the just man entirely just; nothing is to be taken away from either of them, and both are to be perfectly furnished for the work of their respective lives. First, let the unjust be like other distinguished masters of craft; like the skilful pilot or physician, who knows intuitively his own powers and keeps within their limits, and who, if he fails at any point, is able to recover himself. So let the unjust make his unjust attempts in the right way, and lie hidden if he means to be great in his injustice (he who is found out is nobody): for the highest reach of injustice is: to be deemed just when you are not. Therefore I say that in the perfectly unjust man we must assume the most perfect injustice; there is to be no deduction, but we must allow him, while doing the most unjust acts, to have acquired the greatest reputation for justice. If he have taken a false step he must be able to recover himself; he must be one who can speak with effect, if any of his deeds come to light, and who can force his way where force is required his courage and strength, and command of money and friends. And at his side let us place the just man in his nobleness and simplicity, wishing, as Aeschylus says, to be and not to seem good. There must be no seeming, for if he seem to be just he will be honoured and rewarded, and then we shall not know whether he is just for the sake of justice or for the sake of honours and rewards; therefore, let him be clothed in justice only, and have no other covering; and he must be imagined in a state of life the opposite of the former. Let him be the best of men, and let him be thought the worst; then he will have been put to the proof; and we shall see whether he will be affected by the fear of infamy and its consequences. And let him continue thus to the hour of death; being just and seeming to be unjust. When both have reached the uttermost extreme, the one of justice and the other of injustice, let judgment be given which of them is the happier of the two.

### Socrates—Glaucon

Heavens! my dear Glaucon, I said, how energetically you polish them up for the decision, first one and then the other, as if they were two statues.

I do my best, he said. And now that we know what they are like there is no difficulty in tracing out the sort of life which awaits either of them. This I will proceed to describe; but as you may think the description a little too coarse, I ask you to suppose, Socrates, that the words which follow are not mine. Let me put them into the mouths of the eulogists of injustice: They will tell you that the just man who is thought unjust will be scourged, racked, bound—will have his eyes burnt out; and, at last, after suffering every kind of evil, he will be impaled: Then he will understand that he ought to seem only, and not to be, just; the words of Aeschylus may be more truly spoken of the unjust than of the just. For the unjust is pursuing a reality; he does not live with a view to appearances—he wants to be really unjust and not to seem only:

His mind has a soil deep and fertile,

Out of which spring his prudent counsels.

In the first place, he is thought just, and therefore bears rule in the city; he can marry whom he will, and give in marriage to whom he will; also he can trade and deal where he likes, and always to his own advantage, because he has no misgivings about injustice and at every contest, whether in public or private, he gets the better of his antagonists, and gains at their expense, and is rich, and out of his gains he can benefit his friends, and harm his enemies; moreover, he can offer sacrifices, and dedicate gifts to the gods abundantly and magnificently, and can honour the gods or any man whom he wants to honour in a far better style than the just, and therefore he is likely to be dearer than they are to the gods. And thus, Socrates, gods and men are said to unite in making the life of the unjust better than the life of the just.

### Adeimantus—Socrates

I was going to say something in answer to Glaucon, when Adeimantus, his brother, interposed: Socrates, he said, you do not suppose that there is nothing more to be urged?

Why, what else is there? I answered.

The strongest point of all has not been even mentioned, he replied.

Well, then, according to the proverb, 'Let brother help brother'—if he fails in any part do you assist him; although I must confess that Glaucon has already said quite enough to lay me in the dust, and take from me the power of helping justice.

### Adeimantus

Nonsense, he replied. But let me add something more: There is another side to Glaucon's argument about the praise and censure of justice and injustice, which is equally required in order to bring out what I believe to be his meaning. Parents and tutors are always telling their sons and their wards that they are to be just; but why? not for the sake of justice, but for the sake of character and reputation; in the hope of obtaining for him who is reputed just some of those offices, marriages, and the like which Glaucon has enumerated among the advantages accruing to the unjust from the reputation of justice. More, however, is made of appearances by this class of persons than by the others; for they throw in the good opinion of the gods, and will tell you of a shower of benefits which the heavens, as they say, rain upon the pious; and this accords with the testimony of the noble Hesiod and Homer, the first of whom says, that the gods make the oaks of the just—

> To hear acorns at their summit, and bees in the middle;
> And the sheep are bowed down with the weight of their fleeces.

and many other blessings of a like kind are provided for them. And Homer has a very similar strain; for he speaks of one whose fame is—

> As the fame of some blameless king who, like a god,
> Maintains justice to whom the black earth brings forth
> Wheat and barley, whose trees are bowed with fruit,
> And his sheep never fail to bear, and the sea gives him fish.

Still grander are the gifts of heaven which Musaeus and his son vouchsafe to the just; they take them down into the world below, where they have the saints lying on couches at a feast, everlastingly drunk, crowned with garlands; their idea seems to be that an immortality of drunkenness is the highest meed of virtue. Some extend their rewards yet further; the posterity, as they say, of the faithful and just shall survive to the third and fourth generation. This is the style in which they praise justice. But about the wicked there is another strain; they bury them in a slough in Hades, and make them carry water in a sieve; also while they are yet living they bring them to infamy, and inflict upon them the punishments which Glaucon described as the portion of the just who are reputed to be unjust; nothing else does their invention supply. Such is their manner of praising the one and censuring the other.

Once more, Socrates, I will ask you to consider another way of speaking about justice and injustice, which is not confined to the poets, but is found in prose writers. The universal voice of mankind is always declaring that justice and virtue are honourable, but grievous and toilsome; and that the pleasures of vice and injustice are easy of attainment, and are only censured by law and opinion. They say also that honesty is for the most part less profitable than dishonesty; and they are quite ready to call wicked men happy, and to honour them both in public and private when they are rich or in any other way influential, while they despise and overlook those who may be weak and poor, even though acknowledging them to be better than the others. But most extraordinary of all is their mode of speaking about virtue and the gods: they say that the gods apportion calamity and misery to many good men, and good and happiness to the wicked. And mendicant prophets go to rich men's doors and persuade them that they have a power committed to them by the gods of making an atonement for a man's own or his ancestor's sins by sacrifices or charms, with rejoicings and feasts; and they promise to harm an enemy, whether just or unjust, at a small cost; with magic arts and incantations binding heaven, as they say, to execute their will. And the poets are the authorities to whom they appeal, now smoothing the path of vice with the words of Hesiod—

> Vice may be had in abundance without trouble; the way is
>    smooth and her dwelling-place is near. But before virtue the
>    gods have set toil, and a tedious and uphill road:

Then citing Homer as a witness that the gods may be influenced by men; for he also says:

> The gods, too, may be turned from their purpose; and men pray
>    to them and avert their wrath by sacrifices and soothing
>    entreaties, and by libations and the odour of fat, when they
>    have sinned and transgressed.

And they produce a host of books written by Musaeus and Orpheus, who were children of the Moon and the Muses—that is what they say—according to which they perform their ritual, and persuade not only individuals, but whole cities, that expiations and atonements for sin may be made by sacrifices and amusements which fill a vacant hour, and are equally at the service of the living and the dead; the latter sort they call mysteries, and they redeem us from the pains of hell, but if we neglect them no one knows what awaits us.

He proceeded: And now when the young hear all this said about virtue and vice, and the way in which gods and men regard them, how are their minds likely to be affected, my dear Socrates—those of them, I mean, who are quickwitted, and, like bees on the wing, light on every flower, and from all that they hear are prone to draw conclusions as to what manner of persons they should be and in what way they should walk if they would make the best of life? Probably the youth will say to himself in the words of Pindar—

> Can I by justice or by crooked ways of deceit ascend a loftier
> tower which may be a fortress to me all my days?

For what men say is that, if I am really just and am not also thought just profit there is none, but the pain and loss on the other hand are unmistakable. But if, though unjust, I acquire the reputation of justice, a heavenly life is promised to me. Since then, as philosophers prove, appearance tyrannizes over truth and is lord of happiness, to appearance I must devote myself. I will describe around me a picture and shadow of virtue to be the vestibule and exterior of my house; behind I will trail the subtle and crafty fox, as Archilochus, greatest of sages, recommends. But I hear some one exclaiming that the concealment of wickedness is often difficult; to which I answer, Nothing great is easy. Nevertheless, the argument indicates this, if we would be happy, to be the path along which we should proceed. With a view to concealment we will establish secret brotherhoods and political clubs. And there are professors of rhetoric who teach the art of persuading courts and assemblies; and so, partly by persuasion and partly by force, I shall make unlawful gains and not be punished. Still I hear a voice saying that the gods cannot be deceived, neither can they be compelled. But what if there are no gods? or, suppose them to have no care of human things—why in either case should we mind about concealment? And even if there are gods, and they do care about us, yet we know of them only from tradition and the genealogies of the poets; and these are the very persons who say that they may be influenced and turned by 'sacrifices and soothing entreaties and by offerings.' Let us be consistent then, and believe both or neither. If the poets speak truly, why then we had better be unjust, and offer of the fruits of injustice; for if we are just, although we may escape the vengeance of heaven, we shall lose the gains of injustice; but, if we are unjust, we shall keep the gains, and by our sinning and praying, and praying and sinning, the gods will be propitiated, and we shall not be punished. 'But there is a world below in which either we or our posterity will suffer for our unjust deeds.' Yes, my friend, will be the reflection, but there are mysteries and atoning deities, and these have great power. That is what mighty cities declare; and the children of the gods, who were their poets and prophets, bear a like testimony.

On what principle, then, shall we any longer choose justice rather than the worst injustice? when, if we only unite the latter with a deceitful regard to appearances, we shall fare to our mind both with gods and men, in life and after death, as the most numerous and the highest authorities tell us. Knowing all this, Socrates, how can a man who has any superiority of mind or person or rank or wealth, be willing to honour justice; or indeed to refrain from laughing when he hears justice praised? And even if there should be some one who is able to disprove the truth of my words, and who is satisfied that justice is best, still he is not angry with the unjust, but is very ready to forgive them, because he also knows that men are not just of their own free will; unless, peradventure, there be some one whom the divinity within him may have inspired with a hatred of injustice, or who has attained knowledge of the truth—but no other man. He only blames injustice who, owing to cowardice or age or some weakness, has not the power of being unjust. And this is proved by the fact that when he obtains the power, he immediately becomes unjust as far as he can be.

The cause of all this, Socrates, was indicated by us at the beginning of the argument, when my brother and I told you how astonished we were to find that of all the professing panegyrists of justice—beginning with the ancient heroes of whom any memorial has been preserved to us, and ending with the men of our own time—no one has ever blamed injustice or praised justice except with a view to the glories, honours, and benefits which flow from them. No one has ever adequately described either in verse or prose the true essential nature of either of them abiding in the soul, and invisible to any human or divine eye; or shown that of all the things of a man's soul which he has within him, justice is the greatest good, and injustice the greatest evil. Had this been the universal strain, had you sought to persuade us of this from our youth upwards, we should not have been on the watch to keep one another from doing wrong, but every one would have been his own watchman, because afraid, if he did wrong, of harbouring in himself the greatest of evils. I dare say that Thrasymachus and others would seriously hold the language which I have been merely repeating, and words even stronger than these about justice and injustice, grossly, as I conceive, perverting their true nature. But I speak in this vehement manner, as I must frankly confess to you, because I want to hear from you the opposite side; and I would ask you to show not only the superiority which justice has over injustice, but what effect they have on the possessor of them which makes the one to be a good and the other an evil to him. And please, as Glaucon requested of you, to exclude reputations; for unless you take away from each of them his true reputation and add on the false, we shall say that you do not praise justice, but the appearance of it; we shall think that you are only exhorting us to keep injustice dark, and that you really agree with Thrasymachus in thinking that justice is another's good and the interest of the stronger, and that injustice is a man's own profit and interest, though injurious to the weaker. Now as you have admitted that justice is one of that highest class of goods which are desired indeed for their results, but in a far greater degree for their own sakes—like sight or hearing or knowledge or health, or any other real and natural and not merely conventional good—I would ask you in your praise of justice to regard one point only: I mean the essential good and evil which justice and injustice work in the possessors of them. Let others praise justice and censure injustice, magnifying the rewards and honours of the one and abusing the other; that is a manner of arguing which, coming from them, I am ready to tolerate, but from you who have spent your whole life in the consideration of this question, unless I hear the contrary from your own lips, I expect something better. And therefore, I say, not only prove to us that justice is better than injustice, but show what they either of them do to the possessor of them, which makes the one to be a good and the other an evil, whether seen or unseen by gods and men.

**Socrates—Adeimantus**

I had always admired the genius of Glaucon and Adeimantus, but on hearing these words I was quite delighted, and said: Sons of an illustrious father, that was not a bad beginning of the Elegiac verses which the admirer of Glaucon made in honour of you after you had distinguished yourselves at the battle of Megara—

> "Sons of Ariston," he sang, "divine offspring of an illustrious hero."

The epithet is very appropriate, for there is something truly divine in being able to argue as you have done for the superiority of injustice, and remaining unconvinced by your own arguments. And I do believe that you are not convinced—this I infer from your general character, for had I judged only from your speeches I should have mistrusted you. But now, the greater my confidence in you, the greater is my difficulty in knowing what to say. For I am in a strait between two; on the one hand I feel that I am unequal to the task; and my inability is brought home to me by the fact that you were not satisfied with the answer which I made to Thrasymachus, proving, as I thought, the superiority which justice has over injustice. And yet I cannot refuse to help, while breath and speech remain to me; I am afraid that there would be an impiety in being present when justice is evil spoken of and not lifting up a hand in her defence. And therefore I had best give such help as I can.

Glaucon and the rest entreated me by all means not to let the question drop, but to proceed in the investigation. They wanted to arrive at the truth, first, about the nature of justice and injustice, and secondly, about their relative advantages. I told them, what I really thought, that the enquiry would be of a serious nature, and would require very good eyes. Seeing then, I said, that we are no great wits, I think that we had better adopt a method which I may illustrate thus; suppose that a short-sighted person had been asked by some one to read small letters from a distance; and it occurred to some one else that they might be found in another place which was larger and in which the letters were larger—if they were the same and he could read the larger letters first, and then proceed to the lesser—this would have been thought a rare piece of good fortune.

Very true, said Adeimantus; but how does the illustration apply to our enquiry?

I will tell you, I replied; justice, which is the subject of our enquiry, is, as you know, sometimes spoken of as the virtue of an individual, and sometimes as the virtue of a State.

True, he replied.

And is not a State larger than an individual?

It is.

Then in the larger the quantity of justice is likely to be larger and more easily discernible. I propose therefore that we enquire into the nature of justice and injustice, first as they appear in the State, and secondly in the individual, proceeding from the greater to the lesser and comparing them.

That, he said, is an excellent proposal.

And if we imagine the State in process of creation, we shall see the justice and injustice of the State in process of creation also.

I dare say.

When the State is completed there may be a hope that the object of our search will be more easily discovered.

Yes, far more easily.

But ought we to attempt to construct one? I said; for to do so, as I am inclined to think, will be a very serious task. Reflect therefore.

I have reflected, said Adeimantus, and am anxious that you should proceed.

A State, I said, arises, as I conceive, out of the needs of mankind; no one is self-sufficing, but all of us have many wants. Can any other origin of a State be imagined?

There can be no other.

Then, as we have many wants, and many persons are needed to supply them, one takes a helper for one purpose and another for another; and when these partners and helpers are gathered together in one habitation the body of inhabitants is termed a State.

True, he said.

And they exchange with one another, and one gives, and another receives, under the idea that the exchange will be for their good.

Very true.

Then, I said, let us begin and create in idea a State; and yet the true creator is necessity, who is the mother of our invention.

Of course, he replied.

Now the first and greatest of necessities is food, which is the condition of life and existence.

Certainly.

The second is a dwelling, and the third clothing and the like.

True.

And now let us see how our city will be able to supply this great demand: We may suppose that one man is a husbandman, another a builder, some one else a weaver—shall we add to them a shoemaker, or perhaps some other purveyor to our bodily wants?

Quite right.

The barest notion of a State must include four or five men.

Clearly.

And how will they proceed? Will each bring the result of his labours into a common stock?—the individual husbandman, for example, producing for four, and labouring four times as long and as much as he need in the provision of food with which he supplies others as well as himself; or will he have nothing to do with others and not be at the trouble of producing for them, but provide for himself alone a fourth of the food in a fourth of the time, and in the remaining three-fourths of his time be employed in making a house or a coat or a pair of shoes, having no partnership with others, but supplying himself all his own wants?

Adeimantus thought that he should aim at producing food only and not at producing everything.

Probably, I replied, that would be the better way; and when I hear you say this, I am myself reminded that we are not all alike; there are diversities of natures among us which are adapted to different occupations.

Very true.

And will you have a work better done when the workman has many occupations, or when he has only one?

When he has only one.

Further, there can be no doubt that a work is spoilt when not done at the right time?

No doubt.

For business is not disposed to wait until the doer of the business is at leisure; but the doer must follow up what he is doing, and make the business his first object.

He must.

And if so, we must infer that all things are produced more plentifully and easily and of a better quality when one man does one thing which is natural to him and does it at the right time, and leaves other things.

Undoubtedly.

Then more than four citizens will be required; for the husbandman will not make his own plough or mattock, or other implements of agriculture, if they are to be good for anything. Neither will the builder make his tools—and he too needs many; and in like manner the weaver and shoemaker.

. . .

And so, I said, we may consider three out of the four virtues to have been discovered in our State. The last of those qualities which make a state virtuous must be justice, if we only knew what that was.

The inference is obvious.

The time then has arrived, Glaucon, when, like huntsmen, we should surround the cover, and look sharp that justice does not steal away, and pass out of sight and escape us; for beyond a doubt she is somewhere in this country: watch therefore and strive to catch a sight of her, and if you see her first, let me know.

Would that I could! but you should regard me rather as a follower who has just eyes enough to see what you show him—that is about as much as I am good for.

Offer up a prayer with me and follow.

I will, but you must show me the way.

Here is no path, I said, and the wood is dark and perplexing; still we must push on.

Let us push on.

Here I saw something: Halloo! I said, I begin to perceive a track, and I believe that the quarry will not escape.

Good news, he said.

Truly, I said, we are stupid fellows.

Why so?

Why, my good sir, at the beginning of our enquiry, ages ago, there was justice tumbling out at our feet, and we never saw her; nothing could be more ridiculous. Like people who go about looking for what they have in their hands—that was the way with us—we looked not at what we were seeking, but at what was far off in the distance; and therefore, I suppose, we missed her.

What do you mean?

I mean to say that in reality for a long time past we have been talking of justice, and have failed to recognise her.

I grow impatient at the length of your exordium.

Well then, tell me, I said, whether I am right or not: You remember the original principle which we were always laying down at the foundation of the State, that one man should practise one thing only, the thing to which his nature was best adapted; now justice is this principle or a part of it.

Yes, we often said that one man should do one thing only.

Further, we affirmed that justice was doing one's own business, and not being a busybody; we said so again and again, and many others have said the same to us.

Yes, we said so.

Then to do one's own business in a certain way may be assumed to be justice. Can you tell me whence I derive this inference?

I cannot, but I should like to be told.

Because I think that this is the only virtue which remains in the State when the other virtues of temperance and courage and wisdom are abstracted; and, that this is the ultimate cause and condition of the existence of all of them, and while remaining in them is also their preservative; and we were saying that if the three were discovered by us, justice would be the fourth or remaining one.

That follows of necessity.

If we are asked to determine which of these four qualities by its presence contributes most to the excellence of the State, whether the agreement of rulers and subjects, or the preservation in the soldiers of the opinion which the law ordains about the true nature of dangers, or wisdom and watchfulness in the rulers, or whether this other which I am mentioning, and which is found in children and women, slave and freeman, artisan, ruler, subject—the quality, I mean, of every one doing his own work, and not being a busybody, would claim the palm—the question is not so easily answered.

Certainly, he replied, there would be a difficulty in saying which.

Then the power of each individual in the State to do his own work appears to compete with the other political virtues, wisdom, temperance, courage.

Yes, he said.

And the virtue which enters into this competition is justice?

Exactly.

Let us look at the question from another point of view: Are not the rulers in a State those to whom you would entrust the office of determining suits at law?

Certainly.

And are suits decided on any other ground but that a man may neither take what is another's, nor be deprived of what is his own?

Yes; that is their principle.

Which is a just principle?

Yes.

Then on this view also justice will be admitted to be the having and doing what is a man's own, and belongs to him?

Very true.

Think, now, and say whether you agree with me or not. Suppose a carpenter to be doing the business of a cobbler, or a cobbler of a carpenter; and suppose them to exchange their implements or their duties, or the same person to be doing the work of both, or whatever be the change; do you think that any great harm would result to the State?

Not much.

But when the cobbler or any other man whom nature designed to be a trader, having his heart lifted up by wealth or strength or the number of his followers, or any like advantage, attempts to force his way into the class of warriors, or a warrior into that of legislators and guardians, for which he is unfitted, and either to take the implements or the duties of the other; or when one man is trader, legislator, and warrior all in one, then I think you will agree with me in saying that this interchange and this meddling of one with another is the ruin of the State.

Most true.

Seeing then, I said, that there are three distinct classes, any meddling of one with another, or the change of one into another, is the greatest harm to the State, and may be most justly termed evil-doing?

Precisely.

And the greatest degree of evil-doing to one's own city would be termed by you injustice?

Certainly.

This then is injustice; and on the other hand when the trader, the auxiliary, and the guardian each do their own business, that is justice, and will make the city just.

I agree with you.

We will not, I said, be over-positive as yet; but if, on trial, this conception of justice be verified in the individual as well as in the State, there will be no longer any room for doubt; if it be not verified, we must have a fresh enquiry. First let us complete the old investigation, which we began, as you remember, under the impression that, if we could previously examine justice on the larger scale, there would be less difficulty in discerning her in the individual. That larger example appeared to be the State, and accordingly we constructed as good a one as we could, knowing well that in the good State justice would be found. Let the discovery which we made be now applied to the individual—if they agree, we shall be satisfied; or, if there be a difference in the individual, we will come back to the State and have another trial of the theory. The friction of the two when rubbed together may possibly strike a light in which justice will shine forth, and the vision which is then revealed we will fix in our souls.

That will be in regular course; let us do as you say.

I proceeded to ask: When two things, a greater and less, are called by the same name, are they like or unlike in so far as they are called the same?

Like, he replied.

The just man then, if we regard the idea of justice only, will be like the just State?

He will.

And a State was thought by us to be just when the three classes in the State severally did their own business; and also thought to be temperate and valiant and wise by reason of certain other affections and qualities of these same classes?

True, he said.

And so of the individual; we may assume that he has the same three principles in his own soul which are found in the State; and he may be rightly described in the same terms, because he is affected in the same manner?

Certainly, he said.

Once more then, O my friend, we have alighted upon an easy question—whether the soul has these three principles or not?

An easy question! Nay, rather, Socrates, the proverb holds that hard is the good.

*Translated by Benjamin Jowett and Lewis Campbell, 1894*

## ON JUSTICE IN THE REPUBLIC

### Gary Hartenburg

The *Republic,* Plato's masterpiece of philosophical writing, challenges readers by asking us to examine both our notions of justice and our motivations for just living. The dialogue—while treating subjects that range from ethics, metaphysics, and epistemology to politics, psychology, education, music, theology, art, and mathematics—is centrally a discussion of the nature of justice. In particular, Plato, through the literary lens of Socrates' first-person point of view, poses three questions about justice:

1. What is justice?
2. Is justice a virtue?
3. Is justice better than injustice?

To unify and oversimplify his answers, we can say that justice is the virtue that organizes the capacities of the soul into a stable, harmonious whole and that, since stability and harmony are objectively better than instability and discord, justice is preferable to injustice.

Plato investigates the nature of justice through an analogy between the soul and the *polis*. Although the discussion of politics is at the forefront of the *Republic*, the true purpose of that discussion is not political: Its point is to get a better view of the human soul (see 368e–369a), which in itself is very difficult to apprehend. Hence, when Plato argues (in a section not included here) that rulers must expunge immoral poetry from their communities, the reader must remember that Plato's concern is not so much with cities or nations but with individuals. His lesson is that it would be better for us if we did not allow ourselves to accept immoral art as a teacher and an authority. Whether such censorship becomes public law is another, secondary, matter.

The concept of the tripartite soul, which has fairly distinct rational, spirited, and desirous elements, is one of Plato's legacies to Western thought. In the *Republic*, the account of the tripartite soul is essentially connected to the account of justice: justice is present in the soul when each part of the soul is doing the work it is best suited to do.

Reason should be in charge of the soul, because it is the only aspect with both the foresight needed for long-term planning and the insight needed for knowing what is good. Desire does not know what is best because it "knows" only what it wants, which is whatever will satisfy it in the moment. Because desire is by nature insatiable, reason's capitulation of its ruling office to desire is the primary way through which most people's souls become disordered.

According to Plato, there is nothing wrong with desire itself. Desire, though, causes problems when it is put in charge of choosing. All the same, reason is too weak to maintain order by itself. It needs the assistance of the spirited element, which, as the seat of anger and courage, rouses individuals to action. Because this element of the soul can be aligned with either reason or desire, it must work with the rational part to maintain the soul's order—otherwise, disorder ensues.

A number of Protestant, Catholic, and Orthodox Christians throughout history have adopted this notion of the soul's harmony because it makes sense of the Christian doctrines of sin and sanctification, and it provides a model of Christian education. According to C. S. Lewis, for example, sanctification is a matter of *integrating* the dimensions of the human person by repairing the *disintegrating* effects of sin and advancing the soul's capacities into greater harmony with itself and unity with God.

Of course, Lewis does not think such sanctification can be accomplished without divine grace. Lewis also argues that, because a person's character is set largely by whether the spirited element sides with reason or desire, a central goal of education is to instruct students' sentiments in ways that align them with reason. According to the Christian Platonism of Lewis, education that does not train the sentiments, which are seated in the spirited element, creates students "without chests" who are unable to do what is good even if they have true opinions about it.

It is noteworthy that Plato, living before the time of Christ and probably without any exposure to Jewish Scriptures or teachings, was able to apprehend so clearly the nature of justice. That he was able to maintain his commitment to justice in the face of significant pressure to lend approval to the less scrupulous cultural and political élite of Athens is even more impressive.

Furthermore, Plato defends the goodness of justice without recourse to any utilitarian motivation, including the motivation of rewards in either this life or in the afterlife. A gripping picture of the perfectly just person given in the *Republic* is of a man who, while being completely just, is thought by everyone to be unjust and is persecuted and killed because of it. Plato argues that if this man is just, it is better for him to suffer these things than to be unjust, and not because he will be rewarded in the afterlife.

From what we can tell from his writings, Plato did not believe in a final end to history. The cosmos simply continues forever, and within the cosmos our souls pass from our bodies at our deaths until they take on temporary homes in other bodies and begin embodied life again. This means that although Plato tells a story at the very end of the *Republic* about individuals who face postmortem judgment, he does not think such judgment is either irremediable if one has lived unjustly or irrevocable if one has lived justly. Thus, it is remarkable that Plato does not think a person should be just simply because the just person will fare well in the afterlife.

As contemporary readers of the *Republic*, then, we are left to ponder on a personal level whether we love justice and goodness for their own sakes or only for the benefit of just living promises for the afterlife. Plato seems to have thought that being just so things turn out well after death is pitiful utilitarianism. In his view, we only love goodness when we love it for its own sake. In pressing for this conclusion, Plato did not know the true nature of what he was arguing for, though surely we can marvel at the fact that he bent all his powers to plead for as much as he did.

## CHAPTER THREE

# ARISTOTLE

## Classical Greek (384–322 BC)

**A**ristotle is a father to anyone who wishes to know.

He was a student of Plato, and Plato introduced him to the Way, but it was Aristotle who outlined the knowledge project for the rest of us. It was Aristotle who discovered the first rules of logic, and it was Aristotle who began the systematic examination of the natural world in order to understand it.

Aristotle wanted people to be happy, and he understood that a man cannot be happy unless he can flourish as a man. For people to flourish, we must have our physical needs met, be emotionally mature and satisfied, be virtuous, and—most of all—be able to think freely and rigorously. Aristotle knew a just society would not only allow the pursuit of happiness but, through reasonable social structures, would make happiness likely. Yet Aristotle lived in dangerous times, when politics, ethics, and science were all conspiring against the world into which Socrates and Plato had been born.

Aristotle's student, Alexander, became "the Great" in the eyes of history but not by the standards of Aristotle. Alexander was good at everything he tried *except* flourishing as a man. Conquering the world turned out to be easier for the godlike Alexander than vanquishing his inner demons and learning to control his excesses and passions.

57

The *Ethics* would have prevented Alexander's failure as a man, if he had been willing to listen to his teacher's ethics. Aristotle would have pointed his brilliant student to mastery of the soul instead of mastery of nations. The teacher assumed the superiority of the small community for human happiness, but Alexander preferred grandiose palaces and great empires. Aristotle urged men to be moderate; Alexander lived large.

Technology has given most of us more entertainment options and access to information than Alexander could ever have dreamed. We are godlike in our choices, and immoderation will amuse us to death just as surely as too much alcohol was bad for Alexander. Some will be tempted to tune out and flee all such choices.

Aristotle's *Ethics* offers us the "golden mean" between excess and defect. He teaches the civilized art of prudence. All of this is accomplished within a theistic framework, but one broadly compatible with any form of monotheism.

Christians will have untold opportunities to talk with non-Christians, and Aristotle gives us a moral language in which to carry on at least some of the conversation. Start getting those resources by reading his *Ethics*.

 FROM

# *Nicomachean Ethics*

## Books I & II

### I.1

Every art and every inquiry, and similarly every action and pursuit, is thought to aim at some good; and for this reason the good has rightly been declared to be that at which all things aim. But a certain difference is found among ends; some are activities, others are products apart from the activities that produce them. Where there are ends apart from the actions, it is the nature of the products to be better than the activities. Now, as there are many actions, arts, and sciences, their ends also are many; the end of the medical art is health, that of shipbuilding a vessel, that of strategy victory, that of economics wealth. But where such arts fall under a single capacity . . . in all of these the ends of the master arts are to be preferred to all the subordinate ends; for it is for the sake of the former that the latter are pursued. It makes no difference whether the activities themselves are the ends of the actions, or something else apart from the activities, as in the case of the sciences just mentioned.

## I.2

If, then, there is some end of the things we do, which we desire for its own sake (everything else being desired for the sake of this), and if we do not choose everything for the sake of something else (for at that rate the process would go on to infinity, so that our desire would be empty and vain), clearly this must be the good and the chief good. Will not the knowledge of it, then, have a great influence on life? Shall we not, like archers who have a mark to aim at, be more likely to hit upon what is right? If so, we must try, in outline at least, to determine what it is, and of which of the sciences or capacities it is the object. It would seem to belong to the most authoritative art and that which is most truly the master art. And politics appears to be of this nature; for it is this that ordains which of the sciences should be studied in a state, and which each class of citizens should learn and up to what point they should learn them; and we see even the most highly esteemed of capacities to fall under this, e.g. strategy, economics, rhetoric; now, since politics uses the rest of the sciences, and since, again, it legislates as to what we are to do and what we are to abstain from, the end of this science must include those of the others, so that this end must be the good for man. For even if the end is the same for a single man and for a state, that of the state seems at all events something greater and more complete whether to attain or to preserve; though it is worth while to attain the end merely for one man, it is finer and more godlike to attain it for a nation or for city-states. These, then, are the ends at which our inquiry aims, since it is political science, in one sense of that term.

## I.3

Our discussion will be adequate if it has as much clearness as the subject-matter admits of, for precision is not to be sought for alike in all discussions, any more than in all the products of the crafts. Now fine and just actions, which political science investigates, admit of much variety and fluctuation of opinion, so that they may be thought to exist only by convention, and not by nature. And goods also give rise to a similar fluctuation because they bring harm to many people; for before now men have been undone by reason of their wealth, and others by reason of their courage. We must be content, then, in speaking of such subjects and with such premises to indicate the truth roughly and in outline, and in speaking about things which are only for the most part true and with premises of the same kind to reach conclusions that are no better. In the same spirit, therefore, should each type of statement be received; for it is the mark of an educated man to look for precision in each class of things just so far as the nature of the subject admits; it is evidently equally foolish to accept probable reasoning from a mathematician and to demand from a rhetorician scientific proofs. . . .

## I.4

Let us resume our inquiry and state, in view of the fact that all knowledge and every pursuit aims at some good, what it is that we say political science aims at and what is the highest of all goods achievable by action. Verbally there is very general agreement; for both the general run of men and people of superior refinement say that it is happiness, and identify living well and doing well with being happy; but with regard to what happiness is they differ, and the many do not give the same account as the wise. For the former think it is some plain and obvious thing, like pleasure, wealth, or honour; they differ, however, from one another—and often even the same man identifies it with different things, with health when he is ill, with wealth when he is poor; but, conscious of their ignorance, they admire those who proclaim some great ideal that is above their comprehension. Now some thought that apart from these many goods there is another which is self-subsistent and causes the goodness of all these as well. To examine all the opinions that have been held were perhaps somewhat fruitless; enough to examine those that are most prevalent or that seem to be arguable.

Let us not fail to notice, however, that there is a difference between arguments from and those to the first principles. For Plato, too, was right in raising this question and asking, as he used to do, "are we on the way from or to the first principles?" There is a difference, as there is in a race-course between the course from the judges to the turning-point and the way back. For, while we must begin with what is known, things are objects of knowledge in two senses—some to us, some without qualification. Presumably, then, we must begin with things known to us. Hence any one who is to listen intelligently to lectures about what is noble and just, and generally, about the subjects of political science must have been brought up in good habits. For the fact is the starting-point, and if this is sufficiently plain to him, he will not at the start need the reason as well; and the man who has been well brought up has or can easily get starting points.

. . .

## I.7

Let us again return to the good we are seeking, and ask what it can be. It seems different in different actions and arts; it is different in medicine, in strategy, and in the other arts likewise. What then is the good of each? Surely that for whose sake everything else is done. In medicine this is health, in strategy victory, in architecture a house, in any other sphere something else, and in every action and pursuit the end; for it is for the sake of this that all men do whatever else they do. Therefore, if there is an end for all that we do, this will be the good achievable by action, and if there are more than one, these will be the goods achievable by action.

. . . Since there are evidently more than one end, and we choose some of these (e.g. wealth, flutes, and in general instruments) for the sake of something else, clearly not all ends are final ends; but the chief good is evidently something final. Therefore, if there is only one final end, this will be what we are seeking, and if there are more than one, the most final of these will be what we are seeking. Now we call that which is in itself worthy of pursuit more final than that which is worthy of pursuit for the sake of something else, and that which is never desirable for the sake of something else more final than the things that are desirable both in themselves and for the sake of that other thing, and therefore we call final without qualification that which is always desirable in itself and never for the sake of something else.

Now such a thing happiness, above all else, is held to be; for this we choose always for itself and never for the sake of something else, but honour, pleasure, reason, and every virtue we choose indeed for themselves . . . but we choose them also for the sake of happiness, judging that by means of them we shall be happy. Happiness, on the other hand, no one chooses for the sake of these, nor, in general, for anything other than itself.

From the point of view of self-sufficiency the same result seems to follow; for the final good is thought to be self-sufficient. Now by self-sufficient we do not mean that which is sufficient for a man by himself, for one who lives a solitary life, but also for parents, children, wife, and in general for his friends and fellow citizens, since man is born for citizenship. But some limit must be set to this; for if we extend our requirement to ancestors and descendants and friends' friends we are in for an infinite series. Let us examine this question, however, on another occasion; the self-sufficient we now define as that which when isolated makes life desirable and lacking in nothing; and such we think happiness to be; and further we think it most desirable of all things, without being counted as one good thing among others—if it were so counted it would clearly be made more desirable by the addition of even the least of goods; for that which is added becomes an excess of goods, and of goods the greater is always more desirable. Happiness, then, is something final and self-sufficient, and is the end of action.

Presumably, however, to say that happiness is the chief good seems a platitude, and a clearer account of what it is still desired. This might perhaps be given, if we could first ascertain the function of man. For just as for a flute-player, a sculptor, or an artist, and, in general, for all things that have a function or activity, the good and the "well" is thought to reside in the function, so would it seem to be for man, if he has a function. Have the carpenter, then, and the tanner certain functions or activities, and has man none? Is he born without a function? Or as eye, hand, foot, and in general each of the parts evidently has a function, may one lay it down that man similarly has a function apart from all these? What then can this be? Life seems to be common even to plants, but we are seeking what is peculiar to man. Let us exclude, therefore, the life of nutrition and growth. Next there would be a life of perception, but it also seems to be common even to the horse, the ox, and every animal. There remains, then, an active life of the element that has a rational principle; of this, one part has such a principle in the sense of being obedient to one, the other in the sense of possessing one and exercising thought. And, as "life of the rational element" also has two meanings, we must state that life in the sense of activity is what we mean; for this seems to be the more proper sense of the term. Now if the function of man is an activity of soul which follows or implies a rational principle, and if we say "so-and-so" and "a good so-and-so" have a function which is the same in kind, e.g. a lyre, and a good lyre-player, and so without qualification in all cases, eminence in respect of goodness being added to the name of the function . . . : if this is the case, and we state the function of man to be a certain kind of life, and this to be an activity or actions of the soul implying a rational principle, and the function of a good man to be the good and noble performance of these, and if any action is well performed when it is performed in accordance with the appropriate excellence: if this is the case, human good turns out to be activity of soul in accordance with virtue, and if there are more than one virtue, in accordance with the best and most complete. But we must add "in a complete life." For one swallow does not make a summer, nor does one day; and so too one day, or a short time, does not make a man blessed and happy.

. . .

## I.13

Since happiness is an activity of soul in accordance with perfect virtue, we must consider the nature of virtue. . . . [C]learly the virtue we must study is human virtue; for the good we were seeking was human good and the happiness human happiness. By human virtue we mean not that of the body but that of the soul; and happiness also we call an activity of soul. But if this is so, clearly the student of politics must know somehow the facts about soul. . . .

Some things are said about it, adequately enough . . . and we must use these, e.g. that one element in the soul is irrational and one has a rational principle. . . . Of the irrational element one division seems to be widely distributed, and vegetative in its nature, I mean that which causes nutrition and growth. . . . Now the excellence of this seems to be common to all species and not specifically human. . . . [L]et us leave the nutritive faculty alone, since it has by its nature no share in human excellence.

There seems to be also another irrational element in the soul—one which in a sense, however, shares in a rational principle. For we praise the rational principle of the continent man and of the incontinent, and the part of their soul that has such a principle, since it urges them aright and towards the best objects; but there is found in them also another element naturally opposed to the rational principle, which fights against and resists that principle. For exactly as paralysed limbs when we intend to move them to the right turn on the contrary to the left, so is it with the soul; the impulses of incontinent people move in contrary directions. But while in the body we see that which moves astray, in the soul we do not. No doubt, however, we must none the less suppose that in the soul too there is something contrary to the rational principle, resisting and opposing it. In what sense it is distinct from the other elements does not concern us. Now even this seems to have a share in a rational principle, as we said; at any rate in the continent man it obeys the rational principle and presumably in the temperate and brave man it is still more obedient; for in him it speaks, on all matters, with the same voice as the rational principle.

Therefore the irrational element also appears to be two-fold. For the vegetative element in no way shares in a rational principle, but the appetitive and in general the desiring element in a sense shares in it, in so far as it listens to and obeys it; this is the sense in which we speak of "taking account" of one's father or one's friends, not that in which we speak of "accounting for a mathematical property." That the irrational element is in some sense persuaded by a rational principle is indicated also by the giving of advice and by all reproof and exhortation. And if this element also must be said to have a rational principle, that which has a rational principle (as well as that which has not) will be twofold, one subdivision having it in the strict sense and in itself, and the other having a tendency to obey as one does one's father.

Virtue too is distinguished into kinds in accordance with this difference; for we say that some of the virtues are intellectual and others moral, philosophic wisdom and understanding and practical wisdom being intellectual, liberality and temperance moral. For in speaking about a man's character we do not say that he is wise or has understanding but that he is good-tempered or temperate; yet we praise the wise man also with respect to his state of mind; and of states of mind we call those which merit praise virtues.

## II.1

Virtue, then, being of two kinds, intellectual and moral, intellectual virtue in the main owes both its birth and its growth to teaching (for which reason it requires experience and time), while moral virtue comes about as a result of habit, whence also its name (*ethike*) is one that is formed by a slight variation from the word ethos (habit). From this it is also plain that none of the moral virtues arises in us by nature; for nothing that exists by nature can form a habit contrary to its nature. For instance the stone which by nature moves downwards cannot be habituated to move upwards, not even if one tries to train it by throwing it up ten thousand times; nor can fire be habituated to move downwards, nor can anything else that by nature behaves in one way be trained to behave in another. Neither by nature, then, nor contrary to nature do the virtues arise in us; rather we are adapted by nature to receive them, and are made perfect by habit.

Again, of all the things that come to us by nature we first acquire the potentiality and later exhibit the activity (this is plain in the case of the senses; for it was not by often seeing or often hearing that we got these senses, but on the contrary we had them before we used them, and did not come to have them by using them); but the virtues we get by first exercising them, as also happens in the case of the arts as well. For the things we have to learn before we can do them, we learn by doing them, e.g. men become builders by building and lyre-players by playing the lyre; so too we become just by doing just acts, temperate by doing temperate acts, brave by doing brave acts.

This is confirmed by what happens in states; for legislators make the citizens good by forming habits in them, and this is the wish of every legislator, and those who do not effect it miss their mark, and it is in this that a good constitution differs from a bad one.

Again, it is from the same causes and by the same means that every virtue is both produced and destroyed, and similarly every art; for it is from playing the lyre that both good and bad lyre-players are produced. And the corresponding statement is true of builders and of all the rest. . . . For if this were not so, there would have been no need of a teacher, but all men would have been born good or bad at their craft. This, then, is the case with the virtues also; by doing the acts that we do in our trans-actions with other men we become just or unjust, and by doing the acts that we do in the presence of danger, and being habituated to feel fear or confidence, we become brave or cowardly. The same is true of appetites and feelings of anger; some men become temperate and good-tempered, others self-indulgent and irascible, by behaving in one way or the other in the appropriate circumstances. Thus, in one word, states of character arise out of like activities. This is why the activities we exhibit must be of a certain kind; it is because the states of character correspond to the differences between these. It makes no small difference, then, whether we form habits of one kind or of another from our very youth; it makes a very great difference, or rather all the difference.

## II.2

Since, then, the present inquiry does not aim at theoretical knowledge . . . we must examine the nature of actions, namely how we ought to do them; for these determine also the nature of the states of character that are produced, as we have said. Now, that we must act according to the right rule is a common principle and must be assumed—it will be discussed later, i.e. both what the right rule is, and how it is related to the other virtues. But this must be agreed upon beforehand, that the whole account of matters of conduct must be given in outline and not precisely, as we said at the very beginning that the accounts we demand must be in accordance with the subject-matter; matters concerned with conduct and questions of what is good for us have no fixity, any more than matters of health. The general account being of this nature, the account of particular cases is yet more lacking in exactness; for they do not fall under any art or precept but the agents themselves must in each case consider what is appropriate to the occasion, as happens also in the art of medicine or of navigation.

But though our present account is of this nature we must give what help we can. First, then, let us consider this, that it is the nature of such things to be destroyed by defect and excess, as we see in the case of strength and of health ... both excessive and defective exercise destroys the strength, and similarly drink or food which is above or below a certain amount destroys the health, while that which is proportionate both produces and increases and preserves it. So too is it, then, in the case of temperance and courage and the other virtues. For the man who flies from and fears everything and does not stand his ground against anything becomes a coward, and the man who fears nothing at all but goes to meet every danger becomes rash; and similarly the man who indulges in every pleasure and abstains from none becomes self-indulgent, while the man who shuns every pleasure, as boors do, becomes in a way insensible; temperance and courage, then, are destroyed by excess and defect, and preserved by the mean.

But not only are the sources and causes of their origination and growth the same as those of their destruction, but also the sphere of their actualization will be the same; for this is also true of the things which are more evident to sense, e.g. of strength; it is produced by taking much food and undergoing much exertion, and it is the strong man that will be most able to do these things. So too is it with the virtues; by abstaining from pleasures we become temperate, and it is when we have become so that we are most able to abstain from them; and similarly too in the case of courage; for by being habituated to despise things that are terrible and to stand our ground against them we become brave, and it is when we have become so that we shall be most able to stand our ground against them.

## II.3

We must take as a sign of states of character the pleasure or pain that ensues on acts; for the man who abstains from bodily pleasures and delights in this very fact is temperate, while the man who is annoyed at it is self-indulgent, and he who stands his ground against things that are terrible and delights in this or at least is not pained is brave, while the man who is pained is a coward. For moral excellence is concerned with pleasures and pains; it is on account of the pleasure that we do bad things, and on account of the pain that we abstain from noble ones. Hence we ought to have been brought up in a particular way from our very youth, as Plato says, so as both to delight in and to be pained by the things that we ought; for this is the right education.

Again, if the virtues are concerned with actions and passions, and every passion and every action is accompanied by pleasure and pain, for this reason also virtue will be concerned with pleasures and pains. This is indicated also by the fact that punishment is inflicted by these means; for it is a kind of cure, and it is the nature of cures to be effected by contraries.

Again, as we said but lately, every state of soul has a nature relative to and concerned with the kind of things by which it tends to be made worse or better; but it is by reason of pleasures and pains that men become bad, by pursuing and avoiding these—either the pleasures and pains they ought not or when they ought not or as they ought not, or by going wrong in one of the other similar ways that may be distinguished. Hence men even define the virtues as certain states of impassivity and rest; not well, however, because they speak absolutely, and do not say "as one ought" and "as one ought not" and "when one ought or ought not," and the other things that may be added. We assume, then, that this kind of excellence tends to do what is best with regard to pleasures and pains, and vice does the contrary. . . .

## II.4

The question might be asked, what we mean by saying that we must become just by doing just acts, and temperate by doing temperate acts; for if men do just and temperate acts, they are already just and temperate, exactly as, if they do what is in accordance with the laws of grammar and of music, they are grammarians and musicians.

Or is this not true even of the arts? It is possible to do something that is in accordance with the laws of grammar, either by chance or at the suggestion of another. A man will be a grammarian, then, only when he has both done something grammatical and done it grammatically; and this means doing it in accordance with the grammatical knowledge in himself.

Again, the case of the arts and that of the virtues are not similar; for the products of the arts have their goodness in themselves, so that it is enough that they should have a certain character, but if the acts that are in accordance with the virtues have themselves a certain character it does not follow that they are done justly or temperately. The agent also must be in a certain condition when he does them; in the first place he must have knowledge, secondly he must choose the acts, and choose them for their own sakes, and thirdly his action must proceed from a firm and unchangeable character. These are not reckoned in as conditions of the possession of the arts, except the bare knowledge; but as a condition of the possession of the virtues knowledge has little or no weight, while the other conditions count not for a little but for everything, i.e. the very conditions which result from often doing just and temperate acts.

Actions, then, are called just and temperate when they are such as the just or the temperate man would do; but it is not the man who does these that is just and temperate, but the man who also does them as just and temperate men do them. It is well said, then, that it is by doing just acts that the just man is produced, and by doing temperate acts the temperate man; without doing these no one would have even a prospect of becoming good.

But most people do not do these, but take refuge in theory and think they are being philosophers and will become good in this way, behaving somewhat like patients who listen attentively to their doctors, but do none of the things they are ordered to do. As the latter will not be made well in body by such a course of treatment, the former will not be made well in soul by such a course of philosophy.

## II.5

Next we must consider what virtue is. Since things that are found in the soul are of three kinds—passions, faculties, states of character—virtue must be one of these. By passions I mean appetite, anger, fear, confidence, envy, joy, friendly feeling, hatred, longing, emulation, pity, and in general the feelings that are accompanied by pleasure or pain; by faculties the things in virtue of which we are said to be capable of feeling these, e.g. of becoming angry or being pained or feeling pity; by states of character the things in virtue of which we stand well or badly with reference to the passions, e.g. with reference to anger we stand badly if we feel it violently or too weakly, and well if we feel it moderately; and similarly with reference to the other passions.

Now neither the virtues nor the vices are passions, because we are not called good or bad on the ground of our passions, but are so called on the ground of our virtues and our vices, and because we are neither praised nor blamed for our passions . . . but for our virtues and our vices we are praised or blamed.

Again, we feel anger and fear without choice, but the virtues are modes of choice or involve choice. Further, in respect of the passions we are said to be moved, but in respect of the virtues and the vices we are said not to be moved but to be disposed in a particular way.

For these reasons also they are not faculties; for we are neither called good nor bad, nor praised nor blamed, for the simple capacity of feeling the passions; again, we have the faculties by nature, but we are not made good or bad by nature; we have spoken of this before. If, then, the virtues are neither passions nor faculties, all that remains is that they should be states of character. . . .

## II.6

We must, however, not only describe virtue as a state of character, but also say what sort of state it is. We may remark, then, that every virtue or excellence both brings into good condition the thing of which it is the excellence and makes the work of that thing be done well; e.g. the excellence of the eye makes both the eye and its work good; for it is by the excellence of the eye that we see well. . . . Therefore, if this is true in every case, the virtue of man also will be the state of character which makes a man good and which makes him do his own work well.

How this is to happen we have stated already, but it will be made plain also by the following consideration of the specific nature of virtue. In every-thing that is continuous and divisible it is possible to take more, less, or an equal amount, and that either in terms of the thing itself or relatively to us; and the equal is an intermediate between excess and defect. By the intermediate in the object I mean that which is equidistant from each of the extremes, which is one and the same for all men; by the intermediate relatively to us that which is neither too much nor too little—and this is not one, nor the same for all. For instance, if ten is many and two is few, six is the intermediate, taken in terms of the object; for it exceeds and is exceeded by an equal amount; this is intermediate according to arithmetical proportion. But the intermediate relatively to us is not to be taken so; if ten pounds are too much for a particular person to eat and two too little, it does not follow that the trainer will order six pounds; for this also is perhaps too much for the person who is to take it, or too little—too little for Milo, too much for the beginner in athletic exercises. The same is true of running and wrestling. Thus a master of any art avoids excess and defect, but seeks the intermediate and chooses this—the intermediate not in the object but relatively to us.

If it is thus, then, that every art does its work well—by looking to the intermediate and judging its works by this standard . . . and if, further, virtue is more exact and better than any art, as nature also is, then virtue must have the quality of aiming at the intermediate. I mean moral virtue; for it is this that is concerned with passions and actions, and in these there is excess, defect, and the intermediate. For instance, both fear and confidence and appetite and anger and pity and in general pleasure and pain may be felt both too much and too little, and in both cases not well; but to feel them at the right times, with reference to the right objects, towards the right people, with the right motive, and in the right way, is what is both intermediate and best, and this is characteristic of virtue. Similarly with regard to actions also there is excess, defect, and the intermediate. Now virtue is concerned with passions and actions, in which excess is a form of failure, and so is defect, while the intermediate is praised and is a form of success; and being praised and being successful are both characteristics of virtue. Therefore virtue is a kind of mean, since, as we have seen, it aims at what is intermediate.

Again, it is possible to fail in many ways . . . while to succeed is pos-sible only in one way (for which reason also one is easy and the other difficult—to miss the mark easy, to hit it difficult); for these reasons also, then, excess and defect are characteristic of vice, and the mean of virtue; for men are good in but one way, but bad in many.

Virtue, then, is a state of character concerned with choice, lying in a mean, i.e. the mean relative to us, this being determined by a rational principle, and by that principle by which the man of practical wisdom would determine it. Now it is a mean between two vices, that which depends on excess and that which depends on defect; and again it is a mean because the vices respectively fall short of or exceed what is right in both passions and actions, while virtue both finds and chooses that which is intermediate. Hence in respect of its substance and the definition which states its essence virtue is a mean, with regard to what is best and right an extreme.

But not every action nor every passion admits of a mean; for some have names that already imply badness, e.g. spite, shamelessness, envy, and in the case of actions adultery, theft, murder; for all of these and suchlike things imply by their names that they are themselves bad, and not the excesses or deficiencies of them. It is not possible, then, ever to be right with regard to them; one must always be wrong.

. . .

## II.8

There are three kinds of disposition, then, two of them vices, involving excess and deficiency respectively, and one a virtue, viz. the mean, and all are in a sense opposed to all; for the extreme states are contrary both to the intermediate state and to each other, and the intermediate to the extremes; as the equal is greater relatively to the less, less relatively to the greater, so the middle states are excessive relatively to the deficiencies, deficient relatively to the excesses, both in passions and in actions. For the brave man appears rash relatively to the coward, and cowardly relatively to the rash man. . . . Hence also the people at the extremes push the intermediate man each over to the other, and the brave man is called rash by the coward, cowardly by the rash man, and correspondingly in the other cases.

These states being thus opposed to one another, the greatest contrariety is that of the extremes to each other, rather than to the intermediate; for these are further from each other than from the intermediate, as the great is further from the small and the small from the great than both are from the equal. Again, to the intermediate some extremes show a certain likeness, as that of rashness to courage and that of prodigality to liberality; but the extremes show the greatest unlikeness to each other; now contraries are defined as the things that are furthest from each other, so that things that are further apart are more contrary.

To the mean in some cases the deficiency, in some the excess is more opposed; e.g. it is not rashness, which is an excess, but cowardice, which is a deficiency, that is more opposed to courage, and not insensibility, which is a deficiency, but self-indulgence, which is an excess, that is more opposed to temperance. . . . We describe as contrary to the mean, then, rather the directions in which we more often go to great lengths; and therefore self-indulgence, which is an excess, is the more contrary to temperance.

## II.9

. . . Hence . . . it is no easy task to be good. For in everything it is no easy task to find the middle, e.g. to find the middle of a circle is not for every one but for him who knows; so, too, any one can get angry . . . or give or spend money; but to do this to the right person, to the right extent, at the right time, with the right motive, and in the right way, that is not for every one, nor is it easy; wherefore goodness is both rare and laudable and noble.

Hence he who aims at the intermediate must first depart from what is the more contrary to it. . . . For of the extremes one is more erroneous, one less so; therefore, since to hit the mean is hard in the extreme, we must as a second best, as people say, take the least of the evils; and this will be done best in the way we describe. But we must consider the things towards which we ourselves also are easily carried away; for some of us tend to one thing, some to another; and this will be recognizable from the pleasure and the pain we feel. We must drag ourselves away to the contrary extreme; for we shall get into the intermediate state by drawing well away from error, as people do in straightening sticks that are bent.

Now in everything the pleasant or pleasure is most to be guarded against; for we do not judge it impartially. We ought, then, to feel towards pleasure as the elders of the people felt towards Helen, and in all circumstances repeat their saying; for if we dismiss pleasure thus we are less likely to go astray. It is by doing this, then . . . that we shall best be able to hit the mean.

But this is no doubt difficult, and especially in individual cases; for it is not easy to determine both how and with whom and on what provocation and how long one should be angry; for we too sometimes praise those who fall short and call them good-tempered, but sometimes we praise those who get angry and call them manly. The man, however, who deviates little from goodness is not blamed, whether he do so in the direction of the more or of the less, but only the man who deviates more widely; for he does not fail to be noticed. But up to what point and to what extent a man must deviate before he becomes blameworthy it is not easy to determine by reasoning, any more than anything else that is perceived by the senses; such things depend on particular facts, and the decision rests with perception. So much, then, is plain, that the intermediate state is in all things to be praised, but that we must incline sometimes towards the excess, sometimes towards the deficiency; for so shall we most easily hit the mean and what is right.

*Translated by W.D. Ross, 1908*

# ARISTOTLE'S NICOMACHEAN ETHICS

## Jeff Lehman

One of the founders of Western philosophy, Aristotle wrote many treatises on a wide variety of topics, including natural science, poetics, rhetoric, logic, and philosophy. Among these works, his *Nicomachean Ethics* has had a profound and enduring influence upon ethical reasoning in the Western tradition, as well as an incalculable influence on Christian moral thought in particular.

Like Socrates and Plato before him, Aristotle understood the moral life to consist in caring for one's soul. He sought to answer fundamental moral questions: What is the purpose of life? How do we become good? How do we determine what is right in any given situation? Aristotle's account is no ivory-tower philosophy, removed from common experience; rather, he engages our moral common sense from the beginning and uses it to come to solid, real-world conclusions about how we ought to live.

Aristotle begins the *Ethics* by determining the highest human good. In other words, what do we desire always for its own sake and never as a means to something else? He contends that man's highest good is *eudaimonia*, a Greek word typically translated "happiness." While this rendering is adequate, however, we should bear in mind that Aristotle's essential meaning is "complete well-being" or "human flourishing."

Now, while all people tend to agree that happiness is the highest good, there is certainly disagreement over that in which happiness consists. Is it pleasure? Honor? Wealth? Something else? In order to answer, Aristotle identifies man's "function"—i.e., the activity that is proper to his nature. The specific difference of human nature, or what distinguishes him from other species, is his rationality. Thus, happiness must consist in rational activity, which involves both knowing and choosing.

Aristotle defines *happiness* as "the activity of the soul in accordance with [complete] virtue." By "virtue" he means human excellence; since rational activity, again, involves both knowing and choosing, there are both intellectual and moral virtues.

After establishing the general context in Book I, Aristotle gives a more detailed account of moral virtue in Book II. A moral virtue is a deliberately chosen habit that's typically a "mean" between "extremes" of excess and deficiency; for example, the virtue of courage is the mean between the vices of rashness and cowardice. So, for Aristotle, it's not enough simply to act in accordance with reason once in a while. We must cultivate habits of virtue that develop into a firmly established moral character over a lifetime.

Furthermore, Aristotle is convinced that perfect moral virtue is difficult to acquire, at least in part because many particulars must be considered. As he puts it, "Anyone can get angry; but to do this to the right person, to the right extent, at the right time, with the right motive, and in the right way, that is not for every one, nor is it easy."

After spending the first half of Book III arguing that we're responsible for those actions we voluntarily choose, Aristotle begins an account of specific moral virtues (starting with courage and temperance) that continues through Books IV and V; he takes up intellectual virtues, such as wisdom, art, and prudence, in Book VI.

In Book VII, Aristotle addresses the reality of moral weakness in the struggle to do what is right. Unlike the Socrates of Plato's dialogues, Aristotle does not view moral failure as simply an intellectual mistake; even if we know what's right, we may still fail to do it. He concludes Book VII with a discussion of pleasure.

Books VIII and IX concern friendship, which Aristotle considers necessary for happiness. He identifies two imperfect kinds of friendship—those of pleasure and of utility—and a perfect kind, a friendship of virtue. In Book X he returns to a treatment of pleasure and then concludes by making a new claim regarding happiness, namely that the happiness involved in the life of contemplation is superior to the happiness of an active life. This is not to say, however, that the active life is unnecessary. We must live with others, and the life of moral virtue is an indispensable part of happiness.

*Nicomachean Ethics* is one of the few "great books" that's always near the top of anyone's list. Given its influence on the Western tradition, reading the *Ethics* is essential to understanding the Great Conversation that continues to unfold through the centuries. And as for Christian moral reasoning, there is certainly no other work by a non-Christian author that has had so profound an impact on the way we think about morality.

The *Ethics* is filled with pearls of ethical wisdom and provides a detailed, orderly account of what happiness is and how to pursue it. It's also invaluable for the questions it provokes: Is Aristotle's account of moral failure adequate? How does the difficulty of attaining virtue, of which he speaks, point to original sin (a primeval wounding of human nature) and to our need for grace to help us become good? Is his general account of human happiness true, as far as it goes? Is the contemplative life superior to the active life? How does the happiness of which Aristotle speaks relate to the happiness the Christian desires to enjoy in heaven?

## CHAPTER FOUR

# VIRGIL

## Classical Roman (70–19 BC)

**E**arly Christians were not sure what to make of Virgil.

The Roman sage was an obvious pagan, an apologist for the Roman Empire and its tyrant, Augustus, but he was also the most powerful epic poet since Homer. His work helped create the artistic justification for a new world order. The *Pax Romana* was based not just on law or the legions, but also on the imagination of Virgil.

The Romans were a strong power before Virgil, but the Greeks had captured their imaginations. While Rome conquered physical Greece, Greek mythology had enveloped Rome. The Empire could not be confident in itself until a Roman poet matched Homer and harmonized Greek civilization with Roman ideals.

Virgil took the Trojan War, the historic event at the center of Homer's works, and transformed it into the story of the arrival of Rome—victorious Rome as born from the defeat of Troy. The hero of Virgil's myth, Aeneas, fled a city sacked by the Greeks to build a city that would conquer Greece. Virgil, the poetic Aeneas, took Roman mythology, enthralled to Greek culture, and made it fully Roman again.

This triumph shaped a pattern for Christian intellectuals. They too

77

could take the best of a great culture (in this case Greece and Rome) and appropriate them for Christendom. The Romans might feed Christians to lions, but if Christians emulated Virgil, they might turn defeat into victory. The blood of the martyrs might become the faith's foundation.

Christians also considered evidence that Virgil may have been a prophet. Why? For one thing, Virgil wrote with divine-like command of his language and with wisdom regarding the human condition; his paganism is a step closer to the truth than Homer's. His description of the afterlife was helpful to Christian apologists, and his defense of many traditional Roman virtues compared favorably with the more decadent members of his culture. Augustus looked good to believers living under Nero, and the Pax Romana made the spread of the Gospel easier.

For another, Virgil seems to anticipate the coming of Jesus. Here's an excerpt:

> Sicilian Muses, let us take a loftier tone.
> Orchards and humble tamarisks don't give delight to all,
> and if we sing of woods, they should be worthy of a consul.
> Now comes the last age of the Cumaean song;
> the great order of the ages arises anew.
> Now the Virgin returns, and Saturn's reign returns;
> now a new generation is sent down from high heaven.
> Only, chaste Lucina, favor the child at his birth,
> by whom, first of all, the iron age will end
> and a golden race arise in all the world;
> now your Apollo reigns. (Eclogue IV)

The reason for the appearance of this seeming oracle in a series of pastoral poems—and its meaning to Virgil—is unknown. To early Christians facing persecution and denigrating attitudes without hope of powerful patrons, the temptation to perceive the greatest Roman poet as a pre-Christian prophet was profound.

This desire to befriend Virgil persisted as well. Even Dante, Christendom's most celebrated poet, picked Virgil as his guide through hell and his companion through purgatory. The American founders knew Virgil.

Literary fashions would change, and Homer would supplant Virgil in the twentieth-century mind. Many contemporary Christians no longer long for Rome, and they wish to root out any taint from its culture within Christendom.

What of Rome, Christendom's cradle? What of Virgil, its prophet and poet? Read this pagan man who almost lived to see Jesus, and decide for yourself.

⊙℮ FROM ℮⊙

# The Aeneid

## BOOK ONE

Arms, and the man I sing, who, forc'd by fate,
And haughty Juno's unrelenting hate,
Expell'd and exil'd, left the Trojan shore.
Long labors, both by sea and land, he bore,
And in the doubtful war, before he won
The Latian realm, and built the destin'd town;
His banish'd gods restor'd to rites divine,
And settled sure succession in his line,
From whence the race of Alban fathers come,
And the long glories of majestic Rome.

O Muse! the causes and the crimes relate;
What goddess was provok'd, and whence her hate;
For what offense the Queen of Heav'n began
To persecute so brave, so just a man;
Involv'd his anxious life in endless cares,
Expos'd to wants, and hurried into wars!
Can heav'nly minds such high resentment show,
Or exercise their spite in human woe?

Against the Tiber's mouth, but far away,
An ancient town was seated on the sea;
A Tyrian colony; the people made
Stout for the war, and studious of their trade:

Carthage the name; belov'd by Juno more
Than her own Argos, or the Samian shore.
Here stood her chariot; here, if Heav'n were kind,
The seat of awful empire she design'd.
Yet she had heard an ancient rumor fly,
(Long cited by the people of the sky,)
That times to come should see the Trojan race
Her Carthage ruin, and her tow'rs deface;
Nor thus confin'd, the yoke of sov'reign sway
Should on the necks of all the nations lay.
She ponder'd this, and fear'd it was in fate;
Nor could forget the war she wag'd of late
For conqu'ring Greece against the Trojan state.
Besides, long causes working in her mind,
And secret seeds of envy, lay behind;
Deep graven in her heart the doom remain'd
Of partial Paris, and her form disdain'd;
The grace bestow'd on ravish'd Ganymed,
Electra's glories, and her injur'd bed.
Each was a cause alone; and all combin'd
To kindle vengeance in her haughty mind.
For this, far distant from the Latian coast
She drove the remnants of the Trojan host;
And sev'n long years th' unhappy wand'ring train
Were toss'd by storms, and scatter'd thro' the main.
Such time, such toil, requir'd the Roman name,
Such length of labor for so vast a frame.

Now scarce the Trojan fleet, with sails and oars,
Had left behind the fair Sicilian shores,
Ent'ring with cheerful shouts the wat'ry reign,
And plowing frothy furrows in the main;
When, lab'ring still with endless discontent,
The Queen of Heav'n did thus her fury vent:

"Then am I vanquish'd? must I yield?" said she,
"And must the Trojans reign in Italy?
So Fate will have it, and Jove adds his force;
Nor can my pow'r divert their happy course.
Could angry Pallas, with revengeful spleen,
The Grecian navy burn, and drown the men?

80

She, for the fault of one offending foe,
The bolts of Jove himself presum'd to throw:
With whirlwinds from beneath she toss'd the ship,
And bare expos'd the bosom of the deep;
Then, as an eagle gripes the trembling game,
The wretch, yet hissing with her father's flame,
She strongly seiz'd, and with a burning wound
Transfix'd, and naked, on a rock she bound.
But I, who walk in awful state above,
The majesty of heav'n, the sister wife of Jove,
For length of years my fruitless force employ
Against the thin remains of ruin'd Troy!
What nations now to Juno's pow'r will pray,
Or off'rings on my slighted altars lay?"

Thus rag'd the goddess; and, with fury fraught.
The restless regions of the storms she sought,
Where, in a spacious cave of living stone,
The tyrant Aeolus, from his airy throne,
With pow'r imperial curbs the struggling winds,
And sounding tempests in dark prisons binds.
This way and that th' impatient captives tend,
And, pressing for release, the mountains rend.
High in his hall th' undaunted monarch stands,
And shakes his scepter, and their rage commands;
Which did he not, their unresisted sway
Would sweep the world before them in their way;
Earth, air, and seas thro' empty space would roll,
And heav'n would fly before the driving soul.
In fear of this, the Father of the Gods
Confin'd their fury to those dark abodes,
And lock'd 'em safe within, oppress'd with mountain loads;
Impos'd a king, with arbitrary sway,
To loose their fetters, or their force allay.
To whom the suppliant queen her pray'rs address'd,
And thus the tenor of her suit express'd:

"O Aeolus! for to thee the King of Heav'n
The pow'r of tempests and of winds has giv'n;
Thy force alone their fury can restrain,
And smooth the waves, or swell the troubled main—

A race of wand'ring slaves, abhorr'd by me,
With prosp'rous passage cut the Tuscan sea;
To fruitful Italy their course they steer,
And for their vanquish'd gods design new temples there.
Raise all thy winds; with night involve the skies;
Sink or disperse my fatal enemies.
Twice sev'n, the charming daughters of the main,
Around my person wait, and bear my train:
Succeed my wish, and second my design;
The fairest, Deiopeia, shall be thine,
And make thee father of a happy line."

To this the god: "'Tis yours, O queen, to will
The work which duty binds me to fulfil.
These airy kingdoms, and this wide command,
Are all the presents of your bounteous hand:
Yours is my sov'reign's grace; and, as your guest,
I sit with gods at their celestial feast;
Raise tempests at your pleasure, or subdue;
Dispose of empire, which I hold from you."

He said, and hurl'd against the mountain side
His quiv'ring spear, and all the god applied.
The raging winds rush thro' the hollow wound,
And dance aloft in air, and skim along the ground;
Then, settling on the sea, the surges sweep,
Raise liquid mountains, and disclose the deep.
South, East, and West with mix'd confusion roar,
And roll the foaming billows to the shore.
The cables crack; the sailors' fearful cries
Ascend; and sable night involves the skies;
And heav'n itself is ravish'd from their eyes.
Loud peals of thunder from the poles ensue;
Then flashing fires the transient light renew;
The face of things a frightful image bears,
And present death in various forms appears.
Struck with unusual fright, the Trojan chief,
With lifted hands and eyes, invokes relief;
And, "Thrice and four times happy those," he cried,
"That under Ilian walls before their parents died!
Tydides, bravest of the Grecian train!

Why could not I by that strong arm be slain,
And lie by noble Hector on the plain,
Or great Sarpedon, in those bloody fields
Where Simois rolls the bodies and the shields
Of heroes, whose dismember'd hands yet bear
The dart aloft, and clench the pointed spear!"

Thus while the pious prince his fate bewails,
Fierce Boreas drove against his flying sails,
And rent the sheets; the raging billows rise,
And mount the tossing vessels to the skies:
Nor can the shiv'ring oars sustain the blow;
The galley gives her side, and turns her prow;
While those astern, descending down the steep,
Thro' gaping waves behold the boiling deep.
Three ships were hurried by the southern blast,
And on the secret shelves with fury cast.
Those hidden rocks th' Ausonian sailors knew:
They call'd them Altars, when they rose in view,
And show'd their spacious backs above the flood.
Three more fierce Eurus, in his angry mood,
Dash'd on the shallows of the moving sand,
And in mid ocean left them moor'd aland.
Orontes' bark, that bore the Lycian crew,
(A horrid sight!) ev'n in the hero's view,
From stem to stern by waves was overborne:
The trembling pilot, from his rudder torn,
Was headlong hurl'd; thrice round the ship was toss'd,
Then bulg'd at once, and in the deep was lost;
And here and there above the waves were seen
Arms, pictures, precious goods, and floating men.
The stoutest vessel to the storm gave way,
And suck'd thro' loosen'd planks the rushing sea.
Ilioneus was her chief: Alethes old,
Achates faithful, Abas young and bold,
Endur'd not less; their ships, with gaping seams,
Admit the deluge of the briny streams.

. . .

He stood; and, while secure they fed below,
He took the quiver and the trusty bow

Achates us'd to bear: the leaders first
He laid along, and then the vulgar pierc'd;
Nor ceas'd his arrows, till the shady plain
Sev'n mighty bodies with their blood distain.
For the sev'n ships he made an equal share,
And to the port return'd, triumphant from the war.
The jars of gen'rous wine (Acestes' gift,
When his Trinacrian shores the navy left)
He set abroach, and for the feast prepar'd,
In equal portions with the ven'son shar'd.
Thus while he dealt it round, the pious chief
With cheerful words allay'd the common grief:
"Endure, and conquer! Jove will soon dispose
To future good our past and present woes.
With me, the rocks of Scylla you have tried;
Th' inhuman Cyclops and his den defied.
What greater ills hereafter can you bear?
Resume your courage and dismiss your care,
An hour will come, with pleasure to relate
Your sorrows past, as benefits of Fate.
Thro' various hazards and events, we move
To Latium and the realms foredoom'd by Jove.
Call'd to the seat (the promise of the skies)
Where Trojan kingdoms once again may rise,
Endure the hardships of your present state;
Live, and reserve yourselves for better fate."

These words he spoke, but spoke not from his heart;
His outward smiles conceal'd his inward smart.
The jolly crew, unmindful of the past,
The quarry share, their plenteous dinner haste.
Some strip the skin; some portion out the spoil;
The limbs, yet trembling, in the caldrons boil;
Some on the fire the reeking entrails broil.
Stretch'd on the grassy turf, at ease they dine,
Restore their strength with meat,
And cheer their souls with wine.
Their hunger thus appeas'd, their care attends
The doubtful fortune of their absent friends:
Alternate hopes and fears their minds possess,
Whether to deem 'em dead, or in distress.

84

Above the rest, Aeneas mourns the fate
Of brave Orontes, and th' uncertain state
Of Gyas, Lycus, and of Amycus.
The day, but not their sorrows, ended thus.

. . .

Some tale, some new pretense, he daily coin'd,
To soothe his sister, and delude her mind.
At length, in dead of night, the ghost appears
Of her unhappy lord: the specter stares,
And, with erected eyes, his bloody bosom bares.
The cruel altars and his fate he tells,
And the dire secret of his house reveals,
Then warns the widow, with her household gods,
To seek a refuge in remote abodes.
Last, to support her in so long a way,
He shows her where his hidden treasure lay.
Admonish'd thus, and seiz'd with mortal fright,
The queen provides companions of her flight:
They meet, and all combine to leave the state,
Who hate the tyrant, or who fear his hate.
They seize a fleet, which ready rigg'd they find;
Nor is Pygmalion's treasure left behind.
The vessels, heavy laden, put to sea
With prosp'rous winds; a woman leads the way.
I know not, if by stress of weather driv'n,
Or was their fatal course dispos'd by Heav'n;
At last they landed, where from far your eyes
May view the turrets of new Carthage rise;
There bought a space of ground, which (Byrsa call'd,
From the bull's hide) they first inclos'd, and wall'd.
"But whence are you? what country claims your birth?
What seek you, strangers, on our Libyan earth?"

To whom, with sorrow streaming from his eyes,
And deeply sighing, thus her son replies:
"Could you with patience hear, or I relate,
O nymph, the tedious annals of our fate!
Thro' such a train of woes if I should run,
The day would sooner than the tale be done!
From ancient Troy, by force expell'd, we came—

If you by chance have heard the Trojan name.
On various seas by various tempests toss'd,
At length we landed on your Libyan coast.
The good Aeneas am I call'd—a name,
While Fortune favor'd, not unknown to fame.
My household gods, companions of my woes,
With pious care I rescued from our foes.
To fruitful Italy my course was bent;
And from the King of Heav'n is my descent.
With twice ten sail I cross'd the Phrygian sea;
Fate and my mother goddess led my way.
Scarce sev'n, the thin remainders of my fleet,
From storms preserv'd, within your harbor meet.
Myself distress'd, an exile, and unknown,
Debarr'd from Europe, and from Asia thrown,
In Libyan desarts wander thus alone."

His tender parent could no longer bear;
But, interposing, sought to soothe his care.
"Whoe'er you are—not unbelov'd by Heav'n,
Since on our friendly shore your ships are driv'n—
Have courage: to the gods permit the rest,
And to the queen expose your just request.
Now take this earnest of success, for more:
Your scatter'd fleet is join'd upon the shore;
The winds are chang'd, your friends from danger free;
Or I renounce my skill in augury.
Twelve swans behold in beauteous order move,
And stoop with closing pinions from above;
Whom late the bird of Jove had driv'n along,
And thro' the clouds pursued the scatt'ring throng:
Now, all united in a goodly team,
They skim the ground, and seek the quiet stream.
As they, with joy returning, clap their wings,
And ride the circuit of the skies in rings;
Not otherwise your ships, and ev'ry friend,
Already hold the port, or with swift sails descend.
No more advice is needful; but pursue
The path before you, and the town in view."

Thus having said, she turn'd, and made appear
Her neck refulgent, and dishevel'd hair,
Which, flowing from her shoulders, reach'd the ground.
And widely spread ambrosial scents around:
In length of train descends her sweeping gown;
And, by her graceful walk, the Queen of Love is known.
The prince pursued the parting deity
With words like these: "Ah! whither do you fly?
Unkind and cruel! to deceive your son
In borrow'd shapes, and his embrace to shun;
Never to bless my sight, but thus unknown;
And still to speak in accents not your own."
Against the goddess these complaints he made,
But took the path, and her commands obey'd.
They march, obscure; for Venus kindly shrouds
With mists their persons, and involves in clouds,
That, thus unseen, their passage none might stay,
Or force to tell the causes of their way.
This part perform'd, the goddess flies sublime
To visit Paphos and her native clime;
Where garlands, ever green and ever fair,
With vows are offer'd, and with solemn pray'r:
A hundred altars in her temple smoke;
A thousand bleeding hearts her pow'r invoke.

They climb the next ascent, and, looking down,
Now at a nearer distance view the town.
The prince with wonder sees the stately tow'rs,
Which late were huts and shepherds' homely bow'rs,
The gates and streets; and hears, from ev'ry part,
The noise and busy concourse of the mart.
The toiling Tyrians on each other call
To ply their labor: some extend the wall;
Some build the citadel; the brawny throng
Or dig, or push unwieldly stones along.
Some for their dwellings choose a spot of ground,
Which, first design'd, with ditches they surround.
Some laws ordain; and some attend the choice
Of holy senates, and elect by voice.
Here some design a mole, while others there
Lay deep foundations for a theater;

From marble quarries mighty columns hew,
For ornaments of scenes, and future view.
Such is their toil, and such their busy pains,
As exercise the bees in flow'ry plains,
When winter past, and summer scarce begun,
Invites them forth to labor in the sun;
Some lead their youth abroad, while some condense
Their liquid store, and some in cells dispense;
Some at the gate stand ready to receive
The golden burthen, and their friends relieve;
All with united force, combine to drive
The lazy drones from the laborious hive:
With envy stung, they view each other's deeds;
The fragrant work with diligence proceeds.
"Thrice happy you, whose walls already rise!"
Aeneas said, and view'd, with lifted eyes,
Their lofty tow'rs; then, entiring at the gate,
Conceal'd in clouds (prodigious to relate)
He mix'd, unmark'd, among the busy throng,
Borne by the tide, and pass'd unseen along.

Full in the center of the town there stood,
Thick set with trees, a venerable wood.
The Tyrians, landing near this holy ground,
And digging here, a prosp'rous omen found:
From under earth a courser's head they drew,
Their growth and future fortune to foreshew.
This fated sign their foundress Juno gave,
Of a soil fruitful, and a people brave.
Sidonian Dido here with solemn state
Did Juno's temple build, and consecrate,
Enrich'd with gifts, and with a golden shrine;
But more the goddess made the place divine.
On brazen steps the marble threshold rose,
And brazen plates the cedar beams inclose:
The rafters are with brazen cov'rings crown'd;
The lofty doors on brazen hinges sound.
What first Aeneas this place beheld,
Reviv'd his courage, and his fear expell'd.
For while, expecting there the queen, he rais'd
His wond'ring eyes, and round the temple gaz'd,

Admir'd the fortune of the rising town,
The striving artists, and their arts' renown;
He saw, in order painted on the wall,
Whatever did unhappy Troy befall:
The wars that fame around the world had blown,
All to the life, and ev'ry leader known.
There Agamemnon, Priam here, he spies,
And fierce Achilles, who both kings defies.
He stopp'd, and weeping said: "O friend! ev'n here
The monuments of Trojan woes appear!
Our known disasters fill ev'n foreign lands:
See there, where old unhappy Priam stands!
Ev'n the mute walls relate the warrior's fame,
And Trojan griefs the Tyrians' pity claim."
He said (his tears a ready passage find),
Devouring what he saw so well design'd,
And with an empty picture fed his mind:
For there he saw the fainting Grecians yield,
And here the trembling Trojans quit the field,
Pursued by fierce Achilles thro' the plain,
On his high chariot driving o'er the slain.
The tents of Rhesus next his grief renew,
By their white sails betray'd to nightly view;
And wakeful Diomede, whose cruel sword
The sentries slew, nor spar'd their slumb'ring lord,
Then took the fiery steeds, ere yet the food
Of Troy they taste, or drink the Xanthian flood.
Elsewhere he saw where Troilus defied
Achilles, and unequal combat tried;
Then, where the boy disarm'd, with loosen'd reins,
Was by his horses hurried o'er the plains,
Hung by the neck and hair, and dragg'd around:
The hostile spear, yet sticking in his wound,
With tracks of blood inscrib'd the dusty ground.
Meantime the Trojan dames, oppress'd with woe,
To Pallas' fane in long procession go,
In hopes to reconcile their heav'nly foe.
They weep, they beat their breasts, they rend their hair,
And rich embroider'd vests for presents bear;
But the stern goddess stands unmov'd with pray'r.
Thrice round the Trojan walls Achilles drew

The corpse of Hector, whom in fight he slew.
Here Priam sues; and there, for sums of gold,
The lifeless body of his son is sold.
So sad an object, and so well express'd,
Drew sighs and groans from the griev'd hero's breast,
To see the figure of his lifeless friend,
And his old sire his helpless hand extend.
Himself he saw amidst the Grecian train,
Mix'd in the bloody battle on the plain;
And swarthy Memnon in his arms he knew,
His pompous ensigns, and his Indian crew.
Penthisilea there, with haughty grace,
Leads to the wars an Amazonian race:
In their right hands a pointed dart they wield;
The left, for ward, sustains the lunar shield.
Athwart her breast a golden belt she throws,
Amidst the press alone provokes a thousand foes,
And dares her maiden arms to manly force oppose.

Thus while the Trojan prince employs his eyes,
Fix'd on the walls with wonder and surprise,
The beauteous Dido, with a num'rous train
And pomp of guards, ascends the sacred fane.
Such on Eurotas' banks, or Cynthus' height,
Diana seems; and so she charms the sight,
When in the dance the graceful goddess leads
The choir of nymphs, and overtops their heads:
Known by her quiver, and her lofty mien,
She walks majestic, and she looks their queen;
Latona sees her shine above the rest,
And feeds with secret joy her silent breast.
Such Dido was; with such becoming state,
Amidst the crowd, she walks serenely great.
Their labor to her future sway she speeds,
And passing with a gracious glance proceeds;
Then mounts the throne, high plac'd before the shrine:
In crowds around, the swarming people join.
She takes petitions, and dispenses laws,
Hears and determines ev'ry private cause;
Their tasks in equal portions she divides,
And, where unequal, there by lots decides.

Another way by chance Aeneas bends
His eyes, and unexpected sees his friends,
Antheus, Sergestus grave, Cloanthus strong,
And at their backs a mighty Trojan throng,
Whom late the tempest on the billows toss'd,
And widely scatter'd on another coast.
The prince, unseen, surpris'd with wonder stands,
And longs, with joyful haste, to join their hands;
But, doubtful of the wish'd event, he stays,
And from the hollow cloud his friends surveys,
Impatient till they told their present state,
And where they left their ships, and what their fate,
And why they came, and what was their request;
For these were sent, commission'd by the rest,
To sue for leave to land their sickly men,
And gain admission to the gracious queen.
Ent'ring, with cries they fill'd the holy fane;
Then thus, with lowly voice, Ilioneus began:

"O queen! indulg'd by favor of the gods
To found an empire in these new abodes,
To build a town, with statutes to restrain
The wild inhabitants beneath thy reign,
We wretched Trojans, toss'd on ev'ry shore,
From sea to sea, thy clemency implore.
Forbid the fires our shipping to deface!
Receive th' unhappy fugitives to grace,
And spare the remnant of a pious race!
We come not with design of wasteful prey,
To drive the country, force the swains away:
Nor such our strength, nor such is our desire;
The vanquish'd dare not to such thoughts aspire.
A land there is, Hesperia nam'd of old;
The soil is fruitful, and the men are bold—
Th' Oenotrians held it once—by common fame
Now call'd Italia, from the leader's name.
To that sweet region was our voyage bent,
When winds and ev'ry warring element
Disturb'd our course, and, far from sight of land,
Cast our torn vessels on the moving sand:
The sea came on; the South, with mighty roar,

Dispers'd and dash'd the rest upon the rocky shore.
Those few you see escap'd the Storm, and fear,
Unless you interpose, a shipwreck here.
What men, what monsters, what inhuman race,
What laws, what barb'rous customs of the place,
Shut up a desart shore to drowning men,
And drive us to the cruel seas again?
If our hard fortune no compassion draws,
Nor hospitable rights, nor human laws,
The gods are just, and will revenge our cause.
Aeneas was our prince: a juster lord,
Or nobler warrior, never drew a sword;
Observant of the right, religious of his word.
If yet he lives, and draws this vital air,
Nor we, his friends, of safety shall despair;
Nor you, great queen, these offices repent,
Which he will equal, and perhaps augment.
We want not cities, nor Sicilian coasts,
Where King Acestes Trojan lineage boasts.
Permit our ships a shelter on your shores,
Refitted from your woods with planks and oars,
That, if our prince be safe, we may renew
Our destin'd course, and Italy pursue.
But if, O best of men, the Fates ordain
That thou art swallow'd in the Libyan main,
And if our young Iulus be no more,
Dismiss our navy from your friendly shore,
That we to good Acestes may return,
And with our friends our common losses mourn."
Thus spoke Ilioneus: the Trojan crew
With cries and clamors his request renew.

The modest queen a while, with downcast eyes,
Ponder'd the speech; then briefly thus replies:
"Trojans, dismiss your fears; my cruel fate,
And doubts attending an unsettled state,
Force me to guard my coast from foreign foes.
Who has not heard the story of your woes,
The name and fortune of your native place,
The fame and valor of the Phrygian race?
We Tyrians are not so devoid of sense,

Nor so remote from Phoebus' influence.
Whether to Latian shores your course is bent,
Or, driv'n by tempests from your first intent,
You seek the good Acestes' government,
Your men shall be receiv'd, your fleet repair'd,
And sail, with ships of convoy for your guard:
Or, would you stay, and join your friendly pow'rs
To raise and to defend the Tyrian tow'rs,
My wealth, my city, and myself are yours.
And would to Heav'n, the Storm, you felt, would bring
On Carthaginian coasts your wand'ring king.
My people shall, by my command, explore
The ports and creeks of ev'ry winding shore,
And towns, and wilds, and shady woods, in quest
Of so renown'd and so desir'd a guest."

Rais'd in his mind the Trojan hero stood,
And long'd to break from out his ambient cloud:
Achates found it, and thus urg'd his way:
"From whence, O goddess-born, this long delay?
What more can you desire, your welcome sure,
Your fleet in safety, and your friends secure?
One only wants; and him we saw in vain
Oppose the Storm, and swallow'd in the main.
Orontes in his fate our forfeit paid;
The rest agrees with what your mother said."
Scarce had he spoken, when the cloud gave way,
The mists flew upward and dissolv'd in day.

The Trojan chief appear'd in open sight,
August in visage, and serenely bright.
His mother goddess, with her hands divine,
Had form'd his curling locks, and made his temples shine,
And giv'n his rolling eyes a sparkling grace,
And breath'd a youthful vigor on his face;
Like polish'd ivory, beauteous to behold,
Or Parian marble, when enchas'd in gold:
Thus radiant from the circling cloud he broke,
And thus with manly modesty he spoke:

"He whom you seek am I; by tempests toss'd,
And sav'd from shipwreck on your Libyan coast;
Presenting, gracious queen, before your throne,
A prince that owes his life to you alone.
Fair majesty, the refuge and redress
Of those whom fate pursues, and wants oppress,
You, who your pious offices employ
To save the relics of abandon'd Troy;
Receive the shipwreck'd on your friendly shore,
With hospitable rites relieve the poor;
Associate in your town a wand'ring train,
And strangers in your palace entertain:
What thanks can wretched fugitives return,
Who, scatter'd thro' the world, in exile mourn?
The gods, if gods to goodness are inclin'd;
If acts of mercy touch their heav'nly mind,
And, more than all the gods, your gen'rous heart.
Conscious of worth, requite its own desert!
In you this age is happy, and this earth,
And parents more than mortal gave you birth.
While rolling rivers into seas shall run,
And round the space of heav'n the radiant sun;
While trees the mountain tops with shades supply,
Your honor, name, and praise shall never die.
Whate'er abode my fortune has assign'd,
Your image shall be present in my mind."
Thus having said, he turn'd with pious haste,
And joyful his expecting friends embrac'd:
With his right hand Ilioneus was grac'd,
Serestus with his left; then to his breast
Cloanthus and the noble Gyas press'd;
And so by turns descended to the rest.

The Tyrian queen stood fix'd upon his face,
Pleas'd with his motions, ravish'd with his grace;
Admir'd his fortunes, more admir'd the man;
Then recollected stood, and thus began:
"What fate, O goddess-born; what angry pow'rs
Have cast you shipwreck'd on our barren shores?
Are you the great Aeneas, known to fame,
Who from celestial seed your lineage claim?

The same Aeneas whom fair Venus bore
To fam'd Anchises on th' Idaean shore?
It calls into my mind, tho' then a child,
When Teucer came, from Salamis exil'd,
And sought my father's aid, to be restor'd:
My father Belus then with fire and sword
Invaded Cyprus, made the region bare,
And, conqu'ring, finish'd the successful war.
From him the Trojan siege I understood,
The Grecian chiefs, and your illustrious blood.
Your foe himself the Dardan valor prais'd,
And his own ancestry from Trojans rais'd.
Enter, my noble guest, and you shall find,
If not a costly welcome, yet a kind:
For I myself, like you, have been distress'd,
Till Heav'n afforded me this place of rest;
Like you, an alien in a land unknown,
I learn to pity woes so like my own."
She said, and to the palace led her guest;
Then offer'd incense, and proclaim'd a feast.
Nor yet less careful for her absent friends,
Twice ten fat oxen to the ships she sends;
Besides a hundred boars, a hundred lambs,
With bleating cries, attend their milky dams;
And jars of gen'rous wine and spacious bowls
She gives, to cheer the sailors' drooping souls.
Now purple hangings clothe the palace walls,
And sumptuous feasts are made in splendid halls:
On Tyrian carpets, richly wrought, they dine;
With loads of massy plate the sideboards shine,
And antique vases, all of gold emboss'd
(The gold itself inferior to the cost),
Of curious work, where on the sides were seen
The fights and figures of illustrious men,
From their first founder to the present queen.

The good Aeneas, paternal care
Iulus' absence could no longer bear,
Dispatch'd Achates to the ships in haste,
To give a glad relation of the past,
And, fraught with precious gifts, to bring the boy,

Snatch'd from the ruins of unhappy Troy:
A robe of tissue, stiff with golden wire;
An upper vest, once Helen's rich attire,
From Argos by the fam'd adultress brought,
With golden flow'rs and winding foliage wrought,
Her mother Leda's present, when she came
To ruin Troy and set the world on flame;
The scepter Priam's eldest daughter bore,
Her orient necklace, and the crown she wore
Of double texture, glorious to behold,
One order set with gems, and one with gold.
Instructed thus, the wise Achates goes,
And in his diligence his duty shows.

But Venus, anxious for her son's affairs,
New counsels tries, and new designs prepares:
That Cupid should assume the shape and face
Of sweet Ascanius, and the sprightly grace;
Should bring the presents, in her nephew's stead,
And in Eliza's veins the gentle poison shed:
For much she fear'd the Tyrians, double-tongued,
And knew the town to Juno's care belong'd.
These thoughts by night her golden slumbers broke,
And thus alarm'd, to winged Love she spoke:
"My son, my strength, whose mighty pow'r alone
Controls the Thund'rer on his awful throne,
To thee thy much-afflicted mother flies,
And on thy succor and thy faith relies.
Thou know'st, my son, how Jove's revengeful wife,
By force and fraud, attempts thy brother's life;
And often hast thou mourn'd with me his pains.
Him Dido now with blandishment detains;
But I suspect the town where Juno reigns.
For this 't is needful to prevent her art,
And fire with love the proud Phoenician's heart:
A love so violent, so strong, so sure,
As neither age can change, nor art can cure.
How this may be perform'd, now take my mind:
Ascanius by his father is design'd
To come, with presents laden, from the port,
To gratify the queen, and gain the court.

I mean to plunge the boy in pleasing sleep,
And, ravish'd, in Idalian bow'rs to keep,
Or high Cythera, that the sweet deceit
May pass unseen, and none prevent the cheat.
Take thou his form and shape. I beg the grace
But only for a night's revolving space:
Thyself a boy, assume a boy's dissembled face;
That when, amidst the fervor of the feast,
The Tyrian hugs and fonds thee on her breast,
And with sweet kisses in her arms constrains,
Thou may'st infuse thy venom in her veins."
The God of Love obeys, and sets aside
His bow and quiver, and his plumy pride;
He walks Iulus in his mother's sight,
And in the sweet resemblance takes delight.

The goddess then to young Ascanius flies,
And in a pleasing slumber seals his eyes:
Lull'd in her lap, amidst a train of Loves,
She gently bears him to her blissful groves,
Then with a wreath of myrtle crowns his head,
And softly lays him on a flow'ry bed.
Cupid meantime assum'd his form and face,
Foll'wing Achates with a shorter pace,
And brought the gifts. The queen already sate
Amidst the Trojan lords, in shining state,
High on a golden bed: her princely guest
Was next her side; in order sate the rest.
Then canisters with bread are heap'd on high;
Th' attendants water for their hands supply,
And, having wash'd, with silken towels dry.
Next fifty handmaids in long order bore
The censers, and with fumes the gods adore:
Then youths, and virgins twice as many, join
To place the dishes, and to serve the wine.
The Tyrian train, admitted to the feast,
Approach, and on the painted couches rest.
All on the Trojan gifts with wonder gaze,
But view the beauteous boy with more amaze,
His rosy-color'd cheeks, his radiant eyes,
His motions, voice, and shape, and all the god's disguise;

Nor pass unprais'd the vest and veil divine,
Which wand'ring foliage and rich flow'rs entwine.
But, far above the rest, the royal dame,
(Already doom'd to love's disastrous flame,)
With eyes insatiate, and tumultuous joy,
Beholds the presents, and admires the boy.
The guileful god about the hero long,
With children's play, and false embraces, hung;
Then sought the queen: she took him to her arms
With greedy pleasure, and devour'd his charms.
Unhappy Dido little thought what guest,
How dire a god, she drew so near her breast;
But he, not mindless of his mother's pray'r,
Works in the pliant bosom of the fair,
And molds her heart anew, and blots her former care.
The dead is to the living love resign'd;
And all Aeneas enters in her mind.

Now, when the rage of hunger was appeas'd,
The meat remov'd, and ev'ry guest was pleas'd,
The golden bowls with sparkling wine are crown'd,
And thro' the palace cheerful cries resound.
From gilded roofs depending lamps display
Nocturnal beams, that emulate the day.
A golden bowl, that shone with gems divine,
The queen commanded to be crown'd with wine:
The bowl that Belus us'd, and all the Tyrian line.
Then, silence thro' the hall proclaim'd, she spoke:
"O hospitable Jove! we thus invoke,
With solemn rites, thy sacred name and pow'r;
Bless to both nations this auspicious hour!
So may the Trojan and the Tyrian line
In lasting concord from this day combine.
Thou, Bacchus, god of joys and friendly cheer,
And gracious Juno, both be present here!
And you, my lords of Tyre, your vows address
To Heav'n with mine, to ratify the peace."
The goblet then she took, with nectar crown'd
(Sprinkling the first libations on the ground,)
And rais'd it to her mouth with sober grace;
Then, sipping, offer'd to the next in place.

'Twas Bitias whom she call'd, a thirsty soul;
He took challenge, and embrac'd the bowl,
With pleasure swill'd the gold, nor ceas'd to draw,
Till he the bottom of the brimmer saw.
The goblet goes around: Iopas brought
His golden lyre, and sung what ancient Atlas taught:
The various labors of the wand'ring moon,
And whence proceed th' eclipses of the sun;
Th' original of men and beasts; and whence
The rains arise, and fires their warmth dispense,
And fix'd and erring stars dispose their influence;
What shakes the solid earth; what cause delays
The summer nights and shortens winter days.
With peals of shouts the Tyrians praise the song:
Those peals are echo'd by the Trojan throng.
Th' unhappy queen with talk prolong'd the night,
And drank large draughts of love with vast delight;
Of Priam much enquir'd, of Hector more;
Then ask'd what arms the swarthy Memnon wore,
What troops he landed on the Trojan shore;
The steeds of Diomede varied the discourse,
And fierce Achilles, with his matchless force;
At length, as fate and her ill stars requir'd,
To hear the series of the war desir'd.
"Relate at large, my godlike guest," she said,
"The Grecian stratagems, the town betray'd:
The fatal issue of so long a war,
Your flight, your wand'rings, and your woes, declare;
For, since on ev'ry sea, on ev'ry coast,
Your men have been distress'd, your navy toss'd,
Sev'n times the sun has either tropic view'd,
The winter banish'd, and the spring renew'd."

*Translated by John Dryden, 1697*

# VIRGIL'S AENEID

## Jeff Lehman

**I**f through the *Iliad* and *Odyssey* Homer is teacher of the Greeks, through the *Aeneid* Virgil is teacher not only of the Romans but of the Western world. No epic poet could replace Homer, founder of the Western epic tradition; every later epic is, in one way or another, an acknowledgement of and response to him. Yet Virgil transcends Homer; the *Aeneid* is an epic not simply of city and home but of a world-embracing civilization that establishes universal peace under the rule of law. Many of our ideas about statesmanship and civic duty, our understanding of the relationship between public and private good, and our concern for the rule of law find expression in Virgil's tale of the wanderings and wars leading up to Rome's founding.

Two basic themes are identified in the opening line, which can be rendered:

> I sing of arms and the man . . .

In the *Aeneid* Virgil reworks the epic themes of Homer's poems in reverse order: the wanderings of Aeneas and his small band of exiles from Troy— taken up in the first six books—remind us of the wanderings of Odysseus, "the man of many ways"; the battles of the remaining six books call to mind the war outside the walls of Troy, the context for Homer's tale of the wrath of Achilles.

What Homer sings in two poems Virgil sings in one; from the first book we get a clear sense that the scope of the *Aeneid* is all-encompassing. Jupiter prophesies of the Romans,

> I've fixed no limits or duration to their possessions:
> I've given them empire without end.

This prophecy of Rome's future greatness sets the stage for Virgil's epic; every *Aeneid* reader lives in a world in which this divine promise has come to fruition.

In the above excerpt from Book I, we are introduced to the story of Aeneas. Essentially, the poem relates the journey of Aeneas and his fellow Trojans as they endeavor to found a new city. Aeneas is a man of many sorrows, duty-bound to lead the remnant of his people to a new fatherland

> hurled about endlessly by land and sea,
> by the will of the gods, by cruel Juno's remorseless anger,
> long suffering also in war, until he founded a city
> and brought his gods to Latium.

The poem's action begins with a furious storm at sea brought on by Juno, queen of the gods, enemy of the Trojans. The ships of Aeneas are devastated, but thanks to the aid of other deities, he and most of his men make it to shore, seeking refuge in Carthage.

The significance of the encounter with Dido and the Carthaginians would be lost on no Roman reader: Carthage was the greatest of Rome's adversaries in her competition for dominance of the Mediterranean; in Aeneas's narrow escape (Book IV), we see a mythical prefiguring of Rome's narrow escape from Hannibal's invasion during the Second Punic War. Book I ends with Dido's request that Aeneas tell her of the fall of Troy and of his subsequent wanderings.

From the beginning, Virgil refers to "pious" Aeneas, who repeatedly faces suffering and sacrifice for the sake of his people and by the will of the gods. His piety is not perfect, we might argue, but it becomes more so as the epic unfolds. In his journey through the Underworld (Book VI), Aeneas gets a glimpse of Rome's future glory and receives what has come to be known as the Roman Mandate:

> Roman, remember by your strength to rule
> Earth's peoples—for your arts are to be these:
> To pacify, to impose the rule of law,
> To spare the conquered, battle down the proud. (Fitzgerald
> translation.)

Here the duty of Aeneas is linked to the duty of the Roman people. One way to read the *Aeneid*'s last six books is as a progressive realization of this mandate in preparation for Rome's founding.

For the sake of universal peace under the rule of law, Aeneas and his men must engage in war to "battle down the proud." This brings us to the epic's final scene, where Aeneas is in single combat with Turnus, the fierce leader of the native Italians resisting the Trojan newcomers. Although Turnus is overcome by Aeneas and makes a plea for mercy, Aeneas becomes enraged and "founds" [*condit*] his blade in Turnus's chest. This "founding" reminds us of the poem's opening lines, where we're told that Aeneas will at last "found" [*conderet*] a city. Is the killing of Turnus necessary for the founding of Rome? Is it in accord with the Roman Mandate?

--------

Throughout history, Virgil's *Aeneid* has been viewed as a bridge between the classical and Christian traditions. During the Middle Ages, Christian authors saw the conquests of Rome as part of God's plan to establish a universal peace in preparation for Messiah's coming. This peace under the rule of law secured the possibility of pursuing one's own salvation freely.

Furthermore, the *Aeneid* was vital to the development of the Christian epic tradition. Dante speaks of Virgil as *il nostro maggior poeta*, "our greatest poet," and, again, has him serve as the pilgrim's guide through the underworld in his *Commedia*. Dante presents Virgil as one who held a light behind himself for others to see the way to salvation.

## CHAPTER FIVE

# AUGUSTINE

## Late Roman/Early Medieval (354–430)

$B$y the time of Augustine, Christians had proven they could hold their own against pagan thinkers. In Paul, for instance, they had acquired a first-rate intellect from Judaism. Nonetheless, there remained an outstanding question: "Was Christianity capable of producing a first-rate thinker?"

Augustine proved we could.

Most of the writers in this book were amazing thinkers; many wrote well, and a few did great deeds in their communities. Augustine did all three and did them at the highest level. In the time up to Augustine, the conversation in the West mostly had been a Christian reaction to outside ideas. After Augustine, the Great Conversation would be about *his* ideas for centuries.

Some Christians believe that the harder one thinks, the colder faith will grow. Augustine grew more brilliant as he grew more pious, more creative as he became more orthodox. His period of heresy was imitative, but his traditional Christianity took mental risks.

Augustine wrote so much, so well, for so long that he always is capable of surprising us. Moderns, and even some Christians who should know better, like to blame anything they don't like in Western culture on Augustine, but most of their accusations are oversimplifications of his complicated thought.

Augustine stood at the moment when all of civilization in the West might have vanished. He placed the weight of his mind, his heart, and his actions into creating a new Christendom on the wreckage.

Any man who would dare write learned works in Latin as the barbarians sacked the Empire had hope in the future. His titanic achievement was to create a lifeboat to save Christians, and the Church, from ruin and decay for the West as it slipped into the depths of a darker age.

What can this pastor for the ages teach us today?

## FROM

# Confessions

**(The beginning)**

"Great art thou, O Lord, and greatly to be praised . . . And man desires to praise thee, for he is a part of thy creation . . . Still he desires to praise thee . . . Thou hast prompted him, that he should delight to praise thee, for thou hast made us for thyself and restless is our heart until it comes to rest in thee.

Grant me, O Lord, to know and understand whether first to invoke thee or to praise thee; whether first to know thee or call upon thee. But who can invoke thee, knowing thee not? For he who knows thee not may invoke thee as another than thou art. It may be that we should invoke thee in order that we may come to know thee . . .

And how shall I call upon my God—my God and my Lord? For when I call on him I ask him to come into me. And what place is there in me into which my God can come? How could God, the God who made both heaven and earth, come into me? Is there anything in me, O Lord my God, that can contain thee? Do even the heaven and the earth, which thou hast made, and in which thou didst make me, contain thee? Is it possible that, since without thee nothing would be which does exist, thou didst make it so that whatever exists has some capacity to receive thee? Why, then, do I ask thee to come into me, since I also am and could not be if thou wert not in me? . . . Therefore I would not exist—I would simply not be at all—unless I exist in thee, from whom and by whom and in whom all things are. Even so, Lord; even so. Where do I call thee to, when I am already in thee? Or from whence wouldst thou come into me? . . .

Since, then, thou dost fill the heaven and earth, do they contain thee? Or, dost thou fill and overflow them, because they cannot contain thee? And where dost thou pour out what remains of thee after heaven and earth are full? Or, indeed, is there no need that thou, who dost contain all things, shouldst be contained by any, since those things which thou dost fill thou fillest by containing them? . . . Do greater things contain more of thee, and smaller things less? Or, is it not rather that thou art wholly present everywhere, yet in such a way that nothing contains thee wholly? . . .

What, therefore, is my God? . . . most merciful and most just; most secret and most truly present . . . unchangeable, yet changing all things; never new, never old; making all things new . . . always working, ever at rest . . . seeking, and yet possessing all things. Thou dost love, but without passion . . . Yet, O my God, my life, my holy Joy, what is this that I have said? What can any man say when he speaks of thee? But woe to them that keep silence—since even those who say most are dumb . . . "Hear me, O God! Woe to the sins of men!" When a man cries thus, thou showest him mercy, for thou didst create the man but not the sin in him.

### (Infancy)

Who brings to remembrance the sins of my infancy? For in thy sight there is none free from sin, not even the infant who has lived but a day upon this earth. Who brings this to my remembrance? Does not each little one, in whom I now observe what I no longer remember of myself? In what ways, in that time, did I sin? Was it that I cried for the breast? If I should now so cry—not indeed for the breast, but for food suitable to my condition—I should be most justly laughed at and rebuked. What I did then deserved rebuke but, since I could not understand those who rebuked me, neither custom nor common sense permitted me to be rebuked. As we grow we root out and cast away from us such childish habits. Yet I have not seen anyone who is wise who cast away the good when trying to purge the bad. Nor was it good, even in that time, to strive to get by crying what, if it had been given me, would have been hurtful; or to be bitterly indignant at those who, because they were older—not slaves, either, but free—and wiser than I, would not indulge my capricious desires. Was it a good thing for me to try, by struggling as hard as I could, to harm them for not obeying me, even when it would have done me harm to have been obeyed? Thus, the infant's innocence lies in the weakness of his body and not in the infant mind . . .

### (Boyhood)

For I did not, O Lord, lack memory or capacity, for, by thy will, I possessed enough for my age. However, my mind was absorbed only in play, and I was punished for this by those who were doing the same things themselves. But the idling of our elders is called business; the idling of boys, though quite like it, is punished by those same elders, and no one pities either the boys or the men. For will any common sense observer agree that I was rightly punished as a boy for playing ball—just because this hindered me from learning more quickly those lessons by means of which, as a man, I could play at more shameful games? . . . I disobeyed them, not because I had chosen a better way, but from a sheer love of play. I loved the vanity of victory, and I loved to have my ears tickled with lying fables, which made them itch even more ardently, and a similar curiosity glowed more and more in my eyes for the shows and sports of my elders. Yet those who put on such shows are held in such high repute that almost all desire the same for their children. They are therefore willing to have them beaten, if their childhood games keep them from the studies by which their parents desire them to grow up to be able to give such shows. Look down on these things with mercy, O Lord, and deliver us who now call upon thee; deliver those also who do not call upon thee, that they may call upon thee, and thou mayest deliver them. . . . I was compelled to learn about the wanderings of a certain Aeneas, oblivious of my own wanderings, and to weep for Dido dead, who slew herself for love. And all this while I bore with dry eyes my own wretched self dying to thee, O God, my life, in the midst of these things . . .

But woe unto you, O torrent of human custom! Who shall stay your course? When will you ever run dry? . . . Do I not read in you the stories of Jove the thunderer—and the adulterer? How could he be both? But so it says, and the sham thunder served as a cloak for him to play at real adultery . . . Yet which of our gowned masters will give a tempered hearing to a man trained in their own schools who cries out and says: "These were Homer's fictions; he transfers things human to the gods. I could have wished that he would transfer divine things to us." . . .

But in this time of childhood—which was far less dreaded for me than my adolescence—I had no love of learning, and hated to be driven to it. Yet I was driven to it just the same, and good was done for me, even though I did not do it well, for I would not have learned if I had not been forced to it. For no man does well against his will, even if what he does is a good thing . . . from this it is sufficiently clear that a free curiosity is more effective in learning than a discipline based on fear. Yet, by thy ordinance, O God, discipline is given to restrain the excesses of freedom . . .

Actually, was not all that smoke and wind? . . . But it was no wonder that I was thus carried toward vanity and was estranged from thee, O my God, when men were held up as models to me who, when relating a deed of theirs—not in itself evil—were covered with confusion if found guilty of a barbarism or a solecism; but who could tell of their own licentiousness and be applauded for it, so long as they did it in a full and ornate oration of well-chosen words. . . . Look down, O Lord God, and see patiently, as thou art wont to do, how diligently the sons of men observe the conventional rules of letters and syllables, taught them by those who learned their letters beforehand, while they neglect the eternal rules of everlasting salvation taught by thee. They carry it so far that if he who practices or teaches the established rules of pronunciation should speak (contrary to grammatical usage) without aspirating the first syllable of "hominem" ["ominem," and thus make it "a 'uman being"], he will offend men more than if he, a human being, were to hate another human being contrary to thy commandments . . . It is as if he should feel that there is an enemy who could be more destructive to himself than that hatred which excites him against his fellow man; or that he could destroy him whom he hates more completely than he destroys his own soul by this same hatred. Now, obviously, there is no knowledge of letters more innate than the writing of conscience—against doing unto another what one would not have done to himself. . . .

Is this the innocence of childhood? It is not, O Lord, it is not. I entreat thy mercy, O my God, for these same sins as we grow older are transferred from tutors and masters; they pass from nuts and balls and sparrows, to magistrates and kings, to gold and lands and slaves, just as the rod is succeeded by more severe chastisements. . . . However, O Lord, to thee most excellent and most good, thou Architect and Governor of the universe, thanks would be due thee, O our God, even if thou hadst not willed that I should survive my boyhood. For I existed even then; I lived and felt and was solicitous about my own well-being—a trace of that most mysterious unity from whence I had my being. . . .

## (Adolescence)

But what was it that delighted me save to love and to be loved? Still I did not keep the moderate way of the love of mind to mind—the bright path of friendship. Instead, the mists of passion steamed up out of the puddly concupiscence of the flesh, and the hot imagination of puberty, and they so obscured and overcast my heart that I was unable to distinguish pure affection from unholy desire. Both boiled confusedly within me, and dragged my unstable youth down over the cliffs of unchaste desires and plunged me into a gulf of infamy . . .

Theft is punished by thy law, O Lord, and by the law written in men's hearts, which not even ingrained wickedness can erase. For what thief will tolerate another thief stealing from him? . . . There was a pear tree close to our own vineyard, heavily laden with fruit, which was not tempting either for its color or for its flavor . . . We carried off a huge load of pears . . . Doing this pleased us all the more because it was forbidden . . . When, therefore, we inquire why a crime was committed, we do not accept the explanation unless it appears that there was the desire to obtain some of those values which we designate inferior, or else a fear of losing them . . . A man has murdered another man—what was his motive? Either he desired his wife or his property or else he would steal to support himself . . . What was it in you, O theft of mine, that I, poor wretch, doted on—you deed of darkness—in that sixteenth year of my age? Beautiful you were not, for you were a theft . . .

. . . And now, O Lord my God, I ask what it was in that theft of mine that caused me such delight; for behold it had no beauty of its own—certainly not the sort of beauty that exists in justice and wisdom, nor such as is in the mind, memory senses, and the animal life of man; nor yet the kind that is the glory and beauty of the stars in their courses; nor the beauty of the earth, or the sea—teeming with spawning life, replacing in birth that which dies and decays. Indeed, it did not have that false and shadowy beauty which attends the deceptions of vice.

For thus we see pride wearing the mask of high-spiritedness, although only thou, O God, art high above all. Ambition seeks honor and glory, whereas only thou shouldst be honored above all, and glorified forever. The powerful man seeks to be feared, because of his cruelty; but who ought really to be feared but God only? . . . The enticements of the wanton claim the name of love; and yet nothing is more enticing than thy love, nor is anything loved more healthfully than thy truth, bright and beautiful above all. . . . Indeed, ignorance and foolishness themselves go masked under the names of simplicity and innocence; yet there is no being that has true simplicity like thine, and none is innocent as thou art. Thus it is that by a sinner's own deeds he is himself harmed. Human sloth pretends to long for rest, but what sure rest is there save in the Lord? Luxury would fain be called plenty and abundance; but thou art the fullness and unfailing abundance of unfading joy. Prodigality presents a show of liberality; but thou art the most lavish giver of all good things. Covetousness desires to possess much; but thou art already the possessor of all things. Envy contends that its aim is for excellence; but what is so excellent as thou? Anger seeks revenge; but who avenges more justly than thou? . . . All things thus imitate thee—but pervertedly—when they separate themselves far from thee and raise themselves up against thee. . . .

. . . What was it, then, that I loved in that theft? And wherein was I imitating my Lord, even in a corrupted and perverted way? Did I wish, if only by gesture, to rebel against thy law even though I had no power to do so actually—so that, even as a captive, I might produce a sort of counterfeit liberty, by doing with impunity deeds that were forbidden, in a deluded sense of omnipotence? Behold this servant of thine, fleeing from his Lord and following a shadow! . . .

———

And, as the theft itself was nothing, I was all the more wretched in that I loved it so. Yet by myself alone I would not have done it—I still recall how I felt about this then—I could not have done it alone. I loved it then because of the companionship of my accomplices with whom I did it . . . when they say, "Let's go, let's do it," we are ashamed not to be shameless.

## ('College' at Carthage)

I came to Carthage, where a caldron of unholy loves was seething and bubbling all around me. I was not in love as yet, but I was in love with love . . . I was looking for something to love, for I was in love with loving . . . Within me I had a dearth of that inner food which is thyself, my God—although that dearth caused me no hunger . . . My God, my mercy, with how much bitterness didst thou, out of thy infinite goodness, flavor that sweetness for me! For I was not only beloved but also I secretly reached the climax of enjoyment; and yet I was joyfully bound with troublesome tics, so that I could be scourged with the burning iron rods of jealousy, suspicion, fear, anger, and strife . . .

———

Stage plays also captivated me, with their sights full of the images of my own miseries: fuel for my own fire. Now, why does a man like to be made sad by viewing doleful and tragic scenes, which he himself could not by any means endure? Yet, as a spectator, he wishes to experience from them a sense of grief, and in this very sense of grief his pleasure consists . . . But what kind of compassion is it that arises from viewing fictitious and unreal sufferings? The spectator is not expected to aid the sufferer but merely to grieve for him. . . . This is the reason for my love of griefs: that they would not probe into me too deeply (for I did not love to suffer in myself such things as I loved to look at), and they were the sort of grief which came from hearing those fictions, which affected only the surface of my emotion. . . .

——————

In the ordinary course of study I came upon a certain book of Cicero's, whose language almost all admire, though not his heart. This particular book of his contains an exhortation to philosophy and was called Hortensius. Now it was this book which quite definitely changed my whole attitude and turned my prayers toward thee, O Lord, and gave me new hope and new desires. Suddenly every vain hope became worthless to me, and with an incredible warmth of heart I yearned for an immortality of wisdom and began now to arise that I might return to thee . . . For with thee is wisdom. In Greek the love of wisdom is called "philosophy," and it was with this love that that book inflamed me . . . Since at that time, as thou knowest, O Light of my heart, the words of the apostle were unknown to me, I was delighted with Cicero's exhortation, at least enough so that I was stimulated by it, and enkindled and inflamed to love, to seek, to obtain, to hold, and to embrace, not this or that sect, but wisdom itself, wherever it might be. . . .

——————

I resolved, therefore, to direct my mind to the Holy Scriptures, that I might see what they were . . . Yet I was not of the number of those who could enter into it or bend my neck to follow its steps . . . When I then turned toward the Scriptures, they appeared to me to be quite unworthy to be compared with the dignity of Tully. For my inflated pride was repelled by their style, nor could the sharpness of my wit penetrate their inner meaning.

——————

Thus I fell among men, delirious in their pride, carnal and voluble, whose mouths were the snares of the devil . . . I was hungering and thirsting, not even after those first works of thine, but after thyself the Truth, "with whom is no variableness, neither shadow of turning." . . . Yet they still served me glowing fantasies in those dishes. And yet because I supposed the illusions to be from thee I fed on them—not with avidity, for thou didst not taste in my mouth as thou art, and thou wast not these empty fictions. Neither was I nourished by them, but was instead exhausted. Food in dreams appears like our food awake; yet the sleepers are not nourished by it, for they are asleep. . . .

----

For I was ignorant of that other reality, true Being. And so it was that I was subtly persuaded to agree with these foolish deceivers when they put their questions to me: "Whence comes evil?" and, "Is God limited by a bodily shape, and has he hairs and nails?" and, "Are those patriarchs to be esteemed righteous who had many wives at one time, and who killed men and who sacrificed living creatures?" In my ignorance I was much disturbed over these things and, though I was retreating from the truth, I appeared to myself to be going toward it, because I did not yet know that evil was nothing but a privation of good (that, indeed, it has no being) . . . And I did not know that God is a spirit who has no parts extended in length and breadth, whose being has no mass—for every mass is less in a part than in a whole—and if it be an infinite mass it must be less in such parts as are limited by a certain space than in its infinity. It cannot therefore be wholly everywhere as Spirit is, as God is . . . Nor did I know that true inner righteousness—which does not judge according to custom but by the measure of the most perfect law of God Almighty . . . by which the mores of various places and times were adapted to those places and times . . . as if, in a house, he sees a servant handle something that the butler is not permitted to touch, or when something is done behind a stable that would be prohibited in a dining room, and then a person should be indignant that in one house and one family the same things are not allowed to every member of the household . . . Is justice, then, variable and changeable? No, but the times over which she presides are not all alike because they are different times. . . .

----

. . . And now thou didst "stretch forth thy hand from above" and didst draw up my soul out of that profound darkness [of Manicheism] because my mother, thy faithful one, wept to thee on my behalf more than mothers are accustomed to weep for the bodily deaths of their children . . . And thou didst hear her, O Lord . . . But thou gavest her then another answer, by a priest of thine, a certain bishop reared in thy Church and well versed in thy books. When that woman had begged him to agree to have some discussion with me, to refute my errors . . . he answered that I was still unteachable, being inflated with the novelty of that heresy. . . . When he had said this she was not satisfied, but repeated more earnestly her entreaties, and shed copious tears, still beseeching him to see and talk with me. Finally the bishop, a little vexed at her importunity, exclaimed, "Go your way; as you live, it cannot be that the son of these tears should perish." As she often told me afterward, she accepted this answer as though it were a voice from heaven. . . .

And what did it profit me that, when I was scarcely twenty years old, a book of Aristotle's entitled The Ten Categories fell into my hands? . . . What did all this profit me, since it actually hindered me when I imagined that whatever existed was comprehended within those ten categories? I tried to interpret them, O my God, so that even thy wonderful and unchangeable unity could be understood as subjected to thy own magnitude or beauty, as if they existed in thee as their Subject—as they do in corporeal bodies—whereas thou art thyself thy own magnitude and beauty. A body is not great or fair because it is a body, because, even if it were less great or less beautiful, it would still be a body. . . . Yet, O Lord God of Truth, is any man pleasing to thee because he knows these things? No, for surely that man is unhappy who knows these things and does not know thee. And that man is happy who knows thee, even though he does not know these things. . . .

And because my piety—such as it was—still compelled me to believe that the good God never created any evil substance, I formed the idea of two masses, one opposed to the other, both infinite but with the evil more contracted and the good more expansive . . . Furthermore, the things they censured in thy Scriptures I thought impossible to be defended. And yet, occasionally, I desired to confer on various matters with someone well learned in those books, to test what he thought of them. For already the words of one Elpidius, who spoke and disputed face to face against these same Manicheans, had begun to impress me, even when I was at Carthage; because he brought forth things out of the Scriptures that were not easily withstood, to which their answers appeared to me feeble. One of their answers they did not give forth publicly, but only to us in private—when they said that the writings of the New Testament had been tampered with by unknown persons who desired to ingraft the Jewish law into the Christian faith. But they themselves never brought forward any uncorrupted copies. . . .

... I was now half inclined to believe that those philosophers whom they call "The Academics" were wiser than the rest in holding that we ought to doubt everything, and in maintaining that man does not have the power of comprehending any certain truth, for, although I had not yet understood their meaning, I was fully persuaded that they thought just as they are commonly reputed to do.

... I heard him (Ambrose), indeed, every Lord's Day, "rightly dividing the word of truth" among the people. And I became all the more convinced that all those knots of crafty calumnies which those deceivers of ours had knit together against the divine books could be unraveled ... Still rejoicing, I blushed that for so many years I had bayed, not against the Catholic faith, but against the fables of fleshly imagination. ...

### (Problem of Evil Answered)

Being thus gross-hearted and not clear even to myself, I then held that whatever had neither length nor breadth nor density nor solidity, and did not or could not receive such dimensions, was absolutely nothing. For at that time my mind dwelt only with ideas, which resembled the forms with which my eyes are still familiar, nor could I see that the act of thought, by which I formed those ideas, was itself immaterial ... And I kept seeking for an answer to the question, Whence is evil? And I sought it in an evil way ... Where, then, is evil, and whence does it come and how has it crept in? ... Has it no being at all? Why, then, do we fear and shun what has no being? Or if we fear it needlessly, then surely that fear is evil by which the heart is unnecessarily stabbed and tortured—and indeed a greater evil since we have nothing real to fear, and yet do fear. Therefore, either that is evil which we fear, or the act of fearing is in itself evil ...

... And it was made clear to me that all things are good even if they are corrupted. They could not be corrupted if they were supremely good; but unless they were good they could not be corrupted. If they were supremely good, they would be incorruptible; if they were not good at all, there would be nothing in them to be corrupted. For corruption harms; but unless it could diminish goodness, it could not harm ... So long as they are, therefore, they are good. Therefore, whatsoever is, is good. ... There is no sanity in those whom anything in creation displeases ... And I asked what wickedness was, and I found that it was no substance, but a perversion of the will bent aside from thee, O God ...

## (Christ the Way)

And I marveled that I now loved thee, and no fantasm in thy stead, and yet I was not stable enough to enjoy my God steadily. Instead I was transported to thee by thy beauty, and then presently torn away from thee by my own weight, sinking with grief into these lower things. This weight was carnal habit. But thy memory dwelt with me, and I never doubted in the least that there was One for me to cleave to; but I was not yet ready to cleave to thee firmly. ... I lapsed again into my accustomed ways, carrying along with me nothing but a loving memory of my vision, and an appetite for what I had, as it were, smelled the odor of, but was not yet able to eat. ...

I sought, therefore, some way to acquire the strength sufficient to enjoy thee; but I did not find it until I embraced that "Mediator between God and man, the man Christ Jesus" ... And, as yet, I was not humble enough to hold the humble Jesus; nor did I understand what lesson his weakness was meant to teach us ... in this lower world, he built for himself a humble habitation of our own clay, so that he might pull down from themselves and win over to himself those whom he is to bring subject to him; lowering their pride and heightening their love, to the end that they might go on no farther in self-confidence—but rather should become weak, seeing at their feet the Deity made weak by sharing our coats of skin—so that they might cast themselves, exhausted, upon him and be uplifted by his rising. ... I now believe that it was thy pleasure that I should ... distinguish what a difference there is between presumption and confession—between those who saw where they were to go even if they did not see the way, and the Way which leads, not only to the observing, but also the inhabiting of the blessed country. ...

With great eagerness, then, I fastened upon the venerable writings of thy Spirit and principally upon the apostle Paul. . . . And I saw that those pure words had but one face, and I learned to rejoice with trembling. . . .

### (The Conversion)

Then, as this vehement quarrel, which I waged with my soul in the chamber of my heart, was raging inside my inner dwelling, agitated both in mind and countenance, I seized upon Alypius and exclaimed: "What is the matter with us?" . . . The uninstructed start up and take heaven, and we—with all our learning but so little heart—see where we wallow in flesh and blood! Because others have gone before us, are we ashamed to follow, and not rather ashamed at our not following?" I scarcely knew what I said, and in my excitement I flung away from him, while he gazed at me in silent astonishment. For I did not sound like myself: my face, eyes, color, tone expressed my meaning more clearly than my words.

There was a little garden belonging to our lodging, of which we had the use—as of the whole house—for the master, our landlord, did not live there. The tempest in my breast hurried me out into this garden. . . . I fled into the garden, with Alypius following step by step; for I had no secret in which he did not share, and how could he leave me in such distress? . . . I sent up these sorrowful cries: "How long, how long? Tomorrow and tomorrow? Why not now? Why not this very hour make an end to my uncleanness?". . . . I was saying these things and weeping in the most bitter contrition of my heart, when suddenly I heard the voice of a boy or a girl I know not which—coming from the neighboring house, chanting over and over again, "Pick it up, read it; pick it up, read it." Immediately I ceased weeping and began most earnestly to think whether it was usual for children in some kind of game to sing such a song, but I could not remember ever having heard the like. So, damming the torrent of my tears, I got to my feet, for I could not but think that this was a divine command to open the Bible and read the first passage I should light upon. For I had heard how Anthony, accidentally coming into church while the gospel was being read, received the admonition as if what was read had been addressed to him: "Go and sell what you have and give it to the poor, and you shall have treasure in heaven; and come and follow me." By such an oracle he was forthwith converted to thee.

So I quickly returned to the bench where Alypius was sitting, for there I had put down the apostle's book when I had left there. I snatched it up, opened it, and in silence read the paragraph on which my eyes first fell: "Not in rioting and drunkenness, not in chambering and wantonness, not in strife and envying, but put on the Lord Jesus Christ, and make no provision for the flesh to fulfill the lusts thereof." I wanted to read no further, nor did I need to. For instantly, as the sentence ended, there was infused in my heart something like the light of full certainty and all the gloom of doubt vanished away. Closing the book, then, and putting my finger or something else for a mark I began—now with a tranquil countenance—to tell it all to Alypius. And he in turn disclosed to me what had been going on in himself, of which I knew nothing. He asked to see what I had read. I showed him, and he looked on even further than I had read. I had not known what followed. But indeed it was this, "Him that is weak in the faith, receive." This he applied to himself, and told me so. By these words of warning he was strengthened, and by exercising his good resolution and purpose—all very much in keeping with his character, in which, in these respects, he was always far different from and better than I—he joined me in full commitment without any restless hesitation . . . Then we went in to my mother, and told her what happened, to her great joy. We explained to her how it had occurred—and she leaped for joy triumphant; and she blessed thee, who art "able to do exceedingly abundantly above all that we ask or think." For she saw that thou hadst granted her far more than she had ever asked for. . . .

### (Death of Monica)

As the day now approached on which she was to depart this life—a day which thou knewest, but which we did not—it happened (though I believe it was by thy secret ways arranged) that she and I stood alone, leaning in a certain window from which the garden of the house we occupied at Ostia could be seen. Here in this place, removed from the crowd, we were resting ourselves for the voyage after the fatigues of a long journey. We were conversing alone very pleasantly and "forgetting those things which are past, and reaching forward toward those things which are future." We were in the present—and in the presence of Truth (which thou art)—discussing together what is the nature of the eternal life of the saints: which eye has not seen, nor ear heard, neither has entered into the heart of man. We opened wide the mouth of our heart, thirsting for those supernal streams of thy fountain, "the fountain of life" which is with thee, that we might be sprinkled with its waters according to our capacity and might in some measure weigh the truth of so profound a mystery. And when our conversation had brought us to the point where the very highest of physical sense and the most intense illumination of physical light seemed, in comparison with the sweetness of that life to come, not worthy of comparison, nor even of mention, we lifted ourselves with a more ardent love toward the Selfsame, and we gradually passed through all the levels of bodily objects, and even through the heaven itself, where the sun and moon and stars shine on the earth. Indeed, we soared higher yet by an inner musing, speaking and marveling at thy works. And we came at last to our own minds and went beyond them, that we might climb as high as that region of unfailing plenty where thou feedest Israel forever with the food of truth . . .

What we said went something like this: "If to any man the tumult of the flesh were silenced; and the phantoms of earth and waters and air were silenced; and the poles were silent as well; indeed, if the very soul grew silent to herself, and went beyond herself by not thinking of herself; if fancies and imaginary revelations were silenced; if every tongue and every sign and every transient thing—for actually if any man could hear them, all these would say, 'We did not create ourselves, but were created by Him who abides forever'—and if, having uttered this, they too should be silent, having stirred our ears to hear him who created them; and if then he alone spoke, not through them but by himself, that we might hear his word, not in fleshly tongue or angelic voice, nor sound of thunder, nor the obscurity of a parable, but might hear him—him for whose sake we love these things . . . And if this could be sustained, and other visions of a far different kind be taken away, and this one should so ravish and absorb and envelop its beholder in these inward joys that his life might be eternally like that one moment of knowledge which we now sighed after—would not this be the reality of the saying, 'Enter into the joy of thy Lord'?" ...

Then my mother said: "Son, for myself I have no longer any pleasure in anything in this life. Now that my hopes in this world are satisfied, I do not know what more I want here or why I am here. There was indeed one thing for which I wished to tarry a little in this life, and that was that I might see you a Catholic Christian before I died. My God hath answered this more than abundantly, so that I see you now made his servant and spurning all earthly happiness. What more am I to do here?" ... However, it was scarcely five days later ... I closed her eyes; and there flowed in a great sadness on my heart. ...

### (Concluding Address)

Let me know thee, O my Knower; let me know thee even as I am known. ... And what is there in me that could be hidden from thee, Lord, to whose eyes the abysses of man's conscience are naked, even if I were unwilling to confess it to thee? In doing so I would only hide thee from myself, not myself from thee ... What is it to me that men should hear my confessions as if it were they who were going to cure all my infirmities? People are curious to know the lives of others, but slow to correct their own. Why are they anxious to hear from me what I am, when they are unwilling to hear from thee what they are? ... Some have heard about me or from me, but their ear is not close to my heart, where I am whatever it is that I am. ... Now I ask all men whether they would rather rejoice in truth or in falsehood. They will no more hesitate to answer, "In truth," than to say that they wish to be happy. For a happy life is joy in the truth. Yet this is joy in thee, who art the Truth ... All wish for this happy life; all wish for this life which is the only happy one: joy in the truth is what all men wish ... I have had experience with many who wished to deceive, but not one who wished to be deceived ...

Why, then, does truth generate hatred, and why does thy servant who preaches the truth come to be an enemy to them who also love the happy life, which is nothing else than joy in the truth—unless it be that truth is loved in such a way that those who love something else besides her wish that to be the truth which they do love. Since they are unwilling to be deceived, they are unwilling to be convinced that they have been deceived. Therefore, they hate the truth for the sake of whatever it is that they love in place of the truth. They love truth when she shines on them; and hate her when she rebukes them. And since they are not willing to be deceived, but do wish to deceive, they love truth when she reveals herself and hate her when she reveals them. On this account, she will so repay them that those who are unwilling to be exposed by her she will indeed expose against their will, and yet will not disclose herself to them. . . .

———

It is not with a doubtful consciousness, but one fully certain that I love thee, O Lord. Thou hast smitten my heart with thy Word, and I have loved thee . . . But what is it that I love in loving thee? Not physical beauty, nor the splendor of time, nor the radiance of the light—so pleasant to our eyes—nor the sweet melodies of the various kinds of songs, nor the fragrant smell of flowers and ointments and spices; not manna and honey, not the limbs embraced in physical love—it is not these I love when I love my God. Yet it is true that I love a certain kind of light and sound and fragrance and food and embrace in loving my God, who is the light and sound and fragrance and food and embracement of my inner man—where that light shines into my soul which no place can contain, where time does not snatch away the lovely sound, where no breeze disperses the sweet fragrance, where no eating diminishes the food there provided, and where there is an embrace that no satiety comes to sunder. This is what I love when I love my God . . .

———

Belatedly I loved thee, O Beauty so ancient and so new, belatedly I loved thee. For see, thou wast within and I was without, and I sought thee out there. Unlovely, I rushed heedlessly among the lovely things thou hast made. Thou wast with me, but I was not with thee. These things kept me far from thee; even though they were not at all unless they were in thee. Thou didst call and cry aloud, and didst force open my deafness. Thou didst gleam and shine, and didst chase away my blindness. Thou didst breathe fragrant odors and I drew in my breath; and now I pant for thee.

I tasted, and now I hunger and thirst. Thou didst touch me, and I burned for thy peace.

*Translated by Albert C. Outler, 1955*

# THE INFLUENCE
# OF SAINT AUGUSTINE

## Peter Kreeft

Every person now living would be very different, or would not be at all, if Augustine had been different, or had not been. No Christian in history since the apostle Paul has had more influence. Almost single-handedly, Augustine forged the medieval Christian mind. Since the Reformation, he is the only extra-biblical writer whom both Roman Catholics and Protestant Reformers have loved, appealed to, and claimed as their own.

Augustine lived during the troubled times at the end of one age (the ancient Roman) and the beginning of another (the medieval Christian). He lived through the fall of Rome in AD 410, and he died as the smoke and fires of the barbarians were burning his native North African city. Rome was not just a city but "the eternal city"; not just an empire but civilization itself. The equivalent of a nuclear winter was descending.

To such a powerful crisis, Augustine did one of the most powerful things a man can do: he wrote books, very many of them, but especially two of the greatest, most popular, and most influential ever written.

One, the 1,500-page *The City of God*, is the world's first philosophy of history. It interprets all of the human story, from Creation to the Last Judgment, as the drama of divine providence and human free choice (both of which Augustine strongly defended), especially the choice between the two most fundamental options of membership in one or the other of the "two cities." The City of God is the invisible community of all who love

God as God; the City of the World is all those who love the world and themselves as their God.

*"Two loves have made two cities."* This produces history's central plotline and drama, culminating in heaven and hell. (*Nothing* is more dramatic than that.)

---

The other book, the *Confessions*, is the very same dramatic story in Augustine's own soul and life. It is the most beloved and influential book ever written by a Christian, next to the Bible, and it begins with the most frequently quoted Christian sentence outside the Bible, which summarizes both this book and the fundamental meaning of every human life: "Thou hast made us for Thyself, and [therefore] our hearts are restless until they rest in Thee." It's the gospel of the restless heart.

Augustine wrote *Confessions* in the form of a prayer. Like Job's speeches, it is addressed *to God*; we human readers are only eavesdroppers. This accounts for its ruthless, searing, Job-like honesty: it's written face-to-face with the One who knows all. That's also why it contains more questions, more interrogative sentences, than any other great book that isn't in literal dialogue format. Augustine simply could not stop asking searching questions, with both his mind and his heart.

*Confessions* is laced with scriptural quotations, literally hundreds of them. Scripture was more than an object of Augustine's gaze; it was in the heart of the gazer; it was not merely a book but the eyes through which all books, and life, were read. And this was done as naturally and spontaneously as breathing.

No author who ever lived has had both a more brilliant and searching mind *and* a more burning, passionate heart. These two qualities, which can tear other souls in two, united Augustine's. Medieval statuary almost always has him holding an open Bible in one hand and a burning heart in the other.

Yet, paradoxically, it is this very uniqueness and distinctiveness of Augustine, the combination of great mind/great heart, that makes him *Everyman writ large*. These are the two deepest facets in each of us, the two powers that flow from the fact that we are made in the finite image of infinite intelligence and infinite love.

Intelligence, reason, truth—this is of absolute value for Augustine.

But it is the heart that is the deepest. *Heart*, in Augustine, as in Scripture, does not essentially mean sentiment or emotion; it means love. *Amor meus, pondus meum*, he says: My love is my weight, my gravity, my destiny. I go where my love draws me. To love is to will, to choose, to take one fork in life's road rather than another.

The *Confessions* is the story, both inner and outer, of the twofold journey of Augustine's mind and heart. Again, like Job, it is apparently the story of man's search for God, but it's really the story of God's search for man. And in the case of Augustine, God's finding him was momentous. This is the story of the making of that man.

The *Confessions* must be read thoughtfully, not swallowed quickly like a pill but slowly chewed like gum. It is not water; it is rich, fine wine.

It's full of poetic beauties. It sings. It cries. It shouts. It bleeds. So does your soul, if you dare to set it down here in the lines of this book.

These excerpts are just short samples, snippets, "highlights." Please find and read the whole work, and be sure to get Frank Sheed's translation; no other comes close to doing justice to *Confessions'* beauty.

## CHAPTER SIX

# BOETHIUS

## Late Roman/Early Medieval (c. 480–524/525)

Boethius was at the end of the world as he knew it, and he felt horrible. Rome was fading away in the West, and Boethius had been educated to be a Roman gentleman, but the political future looked barbaric. Worse, he was facing personal annihilation and feared for the future of his family. Boethius had placed the power of his writing in service to the Christian Church, Rome, and his children; none of them were doing very well.

If the cable news networks are depressing you, then the last literate Roman may be the cure.

As civilization slowly collapsed around him, Boethius faced a time when the next day was measurably worse than the day before. The buildings going up were always inferior to the ruins around him. What was the future?

It could have been a dark era; instead it became a middle age that produced the bedrock ideas for representative government, international law, and the scientific revolution.

Boethius's little book *Consolation of Philosophy* has never stopped selling since he wrote it, even in ages when books were rare and each copy cost a fortune. Men paid the price for his book because it gives a real answer to human suffering. Boethius faced his own death but, more important, the death of everything he loved. He was miserable, and only "Lady Philosophy" offered him any consolation. Tough love, but it helped him.

In *Consolation of Philosophy*, Boethius moved from considering history from an actor's point of view to a "timeless" eternal view. From that divine perspective, nothing is ever utterly lost, because all of life is possessed by God in an eternal now.

Though time was gnawing away at Boethius and stealing all he valued, God was beyond time and loss. Gaining this philosophical vantage allowed the last Roman to become one of the first men of the Middle Ages.

The future would belong to Christians who could save what was best from Greek and Roman philosophy. Boethius found consolation in philosophy and helped secure that future from his prison cell. I find this very consoling.

⊂∉ FROM ⨾⊃

# Consolation of Philosophy

## Book I

*To pleasant songs my work was erstwhile given, and bright were all my labours then; but now in tears to sad refrains am I compelled to turn. Thus my maimed Muses guide my pen, and gloomy songs make no feigned tears bedew my face. Then could no fear so overcome to leave me companionless upon my way. They were the pride of my earlier bright-lived days: in my later gloomy days they are the comfort of my fate; for hastened by unhappiness has age come upon me without warning, and grief hath set within me the old age of her gloom. White hairs are scattered untimely on my head, and the skin hangs loosely from my worn-out limbs.*

*Happy is that death which thrusts not itself upon men in their pleasant years, yet comes to them at the oft-repeated cry of their sorrow. Sad is it how death turns away from the unhappy with so deaf an ear, and will not close, cruel, the eyes that weep. Ill is it to trust to Fortune's fickle bounty, and while yet she smiled upon me, the hour of gloom had well-nigh overwhelmed my head. Now has the cloud put off its alluring face, wherefore without scruple my life drags out its wearying delays.*

"Why, O my friends, did ye so often puff me up, telling me that I was fortunate? For he that is fallen low did never firmly stand."

While I was pondering thus in silence, and using my pen to set down so tearful a complaint, there appeared standing over my head a woman's form, whose countenance was full of majesty, whose eyes shone as with fire and in power of insight surpassed the eyes of men, whose colour was full of life, whose strength was yet intact though she was so full of years that none would ever think that she was subject to such age as ours. One could but doubt her varying stature, for at one moment she repressed it to the common measure of a man, at another she seemed to touch with her crown the very heavens: and when she had raised higher her head, it pierced even the sky and baffled the sight of those who would look upon it. Her clothing was wrought of the finest thread by subtle workmanship brought to an indivisible piece. This had she woven with her own hands, as I afterwards did learn by her own shewing. Their beauty was somewhat dimmed by the dullness of long neglect, as is seen in the smoke-grimed masks of our ancestors. On the border below was inwoven the symbol $\pi$, on that above was to be read a $\theta$. And between the two letters there could be marked degrees, by which, as by the rungs of a ladder, ascent might be made from the lower principle to the higher. Yet the hands of rough men had torn this garment and snatched such morsels as they could therefrom. In her right hand she carried books, in her left was a sceptre brandished.

When she saw that the Muses of poetry were present by my couch giving words to my lamenting, she was stirred a while; her eyes flashed fiercely, and said she, "Who has suffered these seducing mummers to approach this sick man? Never do they support those in sorrow by any healing remedies, but rather do ever foster the sorrow by poisonous sweets. These are they who stifle the fruit-bearing harvest of reason with the barren briars of the passions: they free not the minds of men from disease, but accustom them thereto. I would think it less grievous if your allurements drew away from me some uninitiated man, as happens in the vulgar herd. In such an one my labours would be naught harmed, but this man has been nourished in the lore of Eleatics and Academics; and to him have ye reached? Away

127

with you, Sirens, seductive unto destruction! leave him to my Muses to be cared for and to be healed."

Their band thus rated cast a saddened glance upon the ground, confessing their shame in blushes, and passed forth dismally over the threshold. For my part, my eyes were dimmed with tears, and I could not discern who was this woman of such commanding power. I was amazed, and turning my eyes to the ground I began in silence to await what she should do. Then she approached nearer and sat down upon the end of my couch: she looked into my face heavy with grief and cast down by sorrow to the ground, and then she raised her complaint over the trouble of my mind in these words.

*"Ah me! how blunted grows the mind when sunk below the o'erwhelming flood! Its own true light no longer burns within, and it would break forth to outer darknesses. How often care, when fanned by earthly winds, grows to a larger and unmeasured bane. This man has been free to the open heaven: his habit has it been to wander into the paths of the sky: his to watch the light of the bright sun, his to inquire into the brightness of the chilly moon; he, like a conqueror, held fast bound in its order every star that makes its wandering circle, turning its peculiar course. Nay, more, deeply has he searched into the springs of nature, whence came the roaring blasts that ruffle the ocean's bosom calm: what is the spirit that makes the firmament revolve; wherefore does the evening star sink into the western wave but to rise from the radiant East; what is the cause which so tempers the season of Spring that it decks the earth with rose-blossoms; whence comes it to pass that Autumn is prolific in the years of plenty and overflows with teeming vines: deeply to search these causes was his wont, and to bring forth secrets deep in Nature hid.*

"Now he lies there; extinct his reason's light, his neck in heavy chains thrust down, his countenance with grievous weight downcast; ah! the brute earth is all he can behold.

"But now," said she, "is the time for the physician's art, rather than for complaining." Then fixing her eyes wholly on me, she said, "Are you the man who was nourished upon the milk of my learning, brought up with my food until you had won your way to the power of a manly soul? Surely I had given you such weapons as would keep you safe, and your strength unconquered; if you had not thrown them away. Do you know me? Why do you keep silence? Are you dumb from shame or from dull amazement? I would it were from shame, but I see that amazement has overwhelmed you."

When she saw that I was not only silent, but utterly tongue-tied and dumb, she put her hand gently upon my breast, and said, "There is no danger: he is suffering from drowsiness, that disease which attacks so many minds which have been deceived. He has forgotten himself for a moment and will quickly remember, as soon as he recognises me. That he may do so, let me brush away from his eyes the darkening cloud of thoughts of matters perishable." So saying, she gathered her robe into a fold and dried my swimming eyes.

> *Then was dark night dispelled, the shadows fled away, and my eyes received returning power as before. 'Twas just as when the heavenly bodies are enveloped by the west wind's rush, and the sky stands thick with watery clouds; the sun is hidden and the stars are not yet come into the sky, and night descending from above o'erspreads the earth: but if the north wind smites this scene, launched forth from the Thracian cave, it unlocks the imprisoned daylight; the sun shines forth, and thus sparkling Phoebus smites with his rays our wondering eyes.*

In such a manner were the clouds of grief scattered. Then I drew breath again and engaged my mind in taking knowledge of my physician's countenance. So when I turned my eyes towards her and fixed my gaze upon her, I recognised my nurse, Philosophy, in whose chambers I had spent my life from earliest manhood. And I asked her, "Wherefore have you, mistress of all virtues, come down from heaven above to visit my lonely place of banishment? Is it that you, as well as I, may be harried, the victim of false charges?" "Should I," said she, "desert you, my nursling? Should I not share and bear my part of the burden which has been laid upon you from spite against my name? Surely Philosophy never allowed herself to let the innocent go upon their journey unbefriended. Think you I would fear calumnies? that I would be terrified as though they were a new misfortune? Think you that this is the first time that wisdom has been harassed by dangers among men of shameless ways? In ancient days before the time of my child, Plato, have we not as well as nowadays fought many a mighty battle against the recklessness of folly? And though Plato did survive, did not his master, Socrates, win his victory of an unjust death, with me present at his side? When after him the followers of Epicurus, and in turn the Stoics, and then others did all try their utmost to seize his legacy, they dragged me, for all my cries and struggles, as though to share me as plunder; they tore my robe which I had woven with mine own hands, and snatched away the fragments thereof: and when they thought I had altogether yielded myself to them, they departed.

. . .

"Are such your experiences, and do they sink into your soul?" she asked. "Do you listen only as 'the dull ass to the lyre'? Why do you weep? Wherefore flow your tears? 'Speak, nor keep secret in thine heart.' If you expect a physician to help you, you must lay bare your wound." Then did I rally my spirit till it was strong again, and answered, "Does the savage bitterness of my fortune still need recounting? Does it not stand forth plainly enough of itself? Does not the very aspect of this place strike you? Is this the library which you had chosen for yourself as your sure resting-place in my house? Is this the room in which you would so often tarry with me expounding the philosophy of things human and divine? Was my condition like this, or my countenance, when I probed with your aid the secrets of nature, when you marked out with a wand the courses of the stars, when you shaped our habits and the rule of all our life by the pattern of the universe? Are these the rewards we reap by yielding ourselves to you? Nay, you yourself have established this saying by the mouth of Plato, that commonwealths would be blessed if they were guided by those who made wisdom their study, or if those who guided them would make wisdom their study. By the mouth of that same great man did you teach that this was the binding reason why a commonwealth should be governed by philosophers, namely that the helm of government should not be left to unscrupulous or criminal citizens lest they should bring corruption and ruin upon the good citizens. Since, then, I had learned from you in quiet and inaction of this view, I followed it further, for I desired to practise it in public government. You and God Himself, who has grafted you in the minds of philosophers, are my witnesses that never have I applied myself to any office of state except that I might work for the common welfare of all good men. Thence followed bitter quarrels with evil men which could not be appeased, and, for the sake of preserving justice, contempt of the enmity of those in power, for this is the result of a free and fearless conscience."

. . .

But you see what end has fallen upon my innocency. In the place of the rewards of honest virtue, I am suffering the punishments of an ill deed that was not mine. And did ever any direct confession of a crime find its judges so well agreed upon exercising harshness, that neither the liability of the human heart to err, nor the changeableness of the fortune of all mankind, could yield one dissentient voice? If it had been said that I had wished to burn down temples, to murder with sacrilegious sword their priests, that I had planned the massacre of all good citizens, even so I should have been present to plead guilty or to be convicted, before the sentence was executed. But here am I, nearly five hundred-miles away, without the opportunity of defending myself, condemned to death and the confiscation of my property because of my too great zeal for the Senate. Ah! well have they deserved that none should ever be liable to be convicted on such a charge! Even those who laid information have seen the honour of this accusation, for, that they might blacken it with some criminal ingredient, they had need to lie, saying that I had violated my conscience by using unholy means to obtain offices corruptly. But you, by being planted within me, dispelled from the chamber of my soul all craving for that which perishes, and where your eyes were looking there could be no place for any such sacrilege. For you instilled into my ears, and thus into my daily thoughts, that saying of Pythagoras, "Follow after God." Nor was it seemly that I, whom you had built up to such excellence that you made me as a god, should seek the support of the basest wills of men. Yet, further, the innocent life within my home, my gathering of most honourable friends, my father-in-law Symmachus, a man esteemed no less in his public life than for his private conscientiousness, these all put far from me all suspicion of this crime. But—O the shame of it!—it is from you that they think they derive the warrant for such a charge, and we seem to them to be allied to ill-doing from this very fact that we are steeped in the principles of your teaching, and trained in your manners of life. Thus it is not enough that my deep respect for you has profited me nothing, but you yourself have received wanton contumely from the hatred that had rather fallen on me.

. . .

While I grieved thus in long-drawn pratings, Philosophy looked on with a calm countenance, not one whit moved by my complaints Then said she, "When I saw you in grief and in tears I knew thereby that you were unhappy and in exile, but I knew not how distant was your exile until your speech declared it. But you have not been driven so far from your home; you have wandered thence yourself: or if you would rather hold that you have been driven, you have been driven by yourself rather than by any other. No other could have done so to you. For if you recall your true native country, you know that it is not under the rule of the many-headed people, as was Athens of old, but there is one Lord, one King, who rejoices in the greater number of his subjects, not in their banishment. To be guided by his reins, to bow to his justice, is the highest liberty. Know you not that sacred and ancient law of your own state by which it is enacted that no man, who would establish a dwelling-place for himself therein, may lawfully be put forth? For there is no fear that any man should merit exile, if he be kept safe therein by its protecting walls. But any man that may no longer wish to dwell there, does equally no longer deserve to be there. Wherefore it is your looks rather than the aspect of this place which disturb me. It is not the walls of your library, decked with ivory and glass, that I need, but rather the resting-place in your heart, wherein I have not stored books, but I have of old put that which gives value to books, a store of thoughts from books of mine. As to your services to the common weal, you have spoken truly, though but scantily, if you consider your manifold exertions. Of all wherewith you have been charged either truthfully or falsely, you have but recorded what is well known. As for the crimes and wicked lies of the informers, you have rightly thought fit to touch but shortly thereon, for they are better and more fruitfully made common in the mouth of the crowd that discusses all matters. You have loudly and strongly upbraided the unjust ingratitude of the Senate: you have grieved over the charges made against myself, and shed tears over the insult to my fair fame: your last outburst of wrath was against Fortune, when you complained that she paid no fair rewards according to deserts: finally, you have prayed with passionate Muse that the same peace and order, that are seen in the heavens, might also rule the earth. But you are overwhelmed by this variety of mutinous passions: grief, rage, and gloom tear your mind asunder, and so in this present mood stronger measures cannot yet come nigh to heal you. Let us therefore use gentler means, and since, just as matter in the body hardens into a swelling, so have these disquieting influences, let these means soften by kindly handling the unhealthy spot, until it will bear a sharper remedy.

. . .

"First then," she continued, "will you let me find out and make trial of the state of your mind by a few small questions, that so I may understand what should be the method of your treatment?"

"Ask," said I, "what your judgment would have you ask, and I will answer you."

Then said she, "Think you that this universe is guided only at random and by mere chance? or think you there is any rule of reason constituted in it?"

"No, never would I think it could be so, nor believe that such sure motions could be made at random or by chance. I know that God, the founder of the universe, does overlook His work; nor ever may that day come which shall drive me to abandon this belief as untrue."

"So is it," she said, "and even so you cried just now, and only mourned that mankind alone has no part in this divine guardianship: you were fixed in your belief that all other things are ruled by reason. Yet, how strange! how much I wonder how it is that you can be so sick though you are set in such a health-giving state of mind! But let us look deeper into it: I cannot but think there is something lacking. Since you are not in doubt that the universe is ruled by God, tell me by what method you think that government is guided?"

"I scarcely know the meaning of your question; much less can I answer it."

"Was I wrong," said she, "to think that something was lacking, that there was some opening in your armour, some way by which this distracting disease has crept into your soul? But tell me, do you remember what is the aim and end of all things? what the object to which all nature tends?"

"I have heard indeed, but grief has blunted my memory."

"But do you not some how know whence all things have their source?"

"Yes," I said; "that source is God."

"Is it possible that you, who know the beginning of all things, should not know their end? But such are the ways of these distractions, such is

133

their power, that though they can move a man's position, they cannot pluck him from himself or wrench him from his roots. But this question would I have you answer: do you remember that you are a man?"

"How can I but remember that?"

"Can you then say what is a man?"

"Need you ask? I know that he is an animal, reasoning and mortal; that I know, and that I confess myself to be."

"Know you naught else that you are?" asked Philosophy.

"Naught," said I.

"Now," said she, "I know the cause, or the chief cause, of your sickness. You have forgotten what you are. Now therefore I have found out to the full the manner of your sickness, and how to attempt the restoring of your health. You are overwhelmed by this forgetfulness of yourself: hence you have been thus sorrowing that you are exiled and robbed of all your possessions. You do not know the aim and end of all things; hence you think that if men are worthless and wicked, they are powerful and fortunate. You have forgotten by what methods the universe is guided; hence you think that the chances of good and bad fortune are tossed about with no ruling hand. These things may lead not to disease only, but even to death as well. But let us thank the Giver of all health, that your nature has not altogether left you. We have yet the chief spark for your health's fire, for you have a true knowledge of the hand that guides the universe: you do believe that its government is not subject to random chance, but to divine reason. Therefore have no fear. From this tiny spark the fire of life shall forthwith shine upon you. But it is not time to use severer remedies, and since we know that it is the way of all minds to clothe themselves ever in false opinions as they throw off the true, and these false ones breed a dark distraction which confuses the true insight, therefore will I try to lessen this darkness for a while with gentle applications of easy remedies, that so the shadows of deceiving passions may be dissipated, and you may have power to perceive the brightness of true light."

*"When the stars are hidden by black clouds, no light can they afford. When the boisterous south wind rolls along the sea and stirs the surge, the water, but now as clear as glass, bright as the fair sun's light, is dark, impenetrable to sight, with stirred and scattered sand. The stream, that wanders down the mountain's*

*side, must often find a stumbling-block, a stone within its path torn from the hill's own rock. So too shalt thou: if thou wouldst see the truth in undimmed light, choose the straight road, the beaten path; away with passing joys! away with fear! put vain hopes to flight! and grant no place to grief! Where these distractions reign, the mind is clouded o'er, the soul is bound in chains."*

## Book II

Then for a while she held her peace. But when her silence, so discreet, made my thoughts to cease from straying, she thus began to speak: "If I have thoroughly learned the causes and the manner of your sickness, your former good fortune has so affected you that you are being consumed by longing for it. The change of one of her this alone has overturned your peace of mind through your own imagination. I understand the varied disguises of that unnatural state. I know how Fortune is ever most friendly and alluring to those whom she strives to deceive, until she overwhelms them with grief beyond bearing, by deserting them when least expected. If you recall her nature, her ways, or her deserts, you will see that you never had in her, nor have lost with her, aught that was lovely. Yet, I think, I shall not need great labour to recall this to your memory. For then too, when she was at your side with all her flattery, you were wont to reproach her in strong and manly terms; and to revile her with the opinions that you had gathered in worship of me with my favoured ones. But no sudden change of outward affairs can ever come without some upheaval in the mind. Thus has it followed that you, like others, have fallen somewhat away from your calm peace of mind. But it is time now for you to make trial of some gentle and pleasant draught, which by reaching your inmost parts shall prepare the way for yet stronger healing draughts. Try therefore the assuring influence of gentle argument which keeps its straight path only when it holds fast to my instructions. And with this art of orators let my handmaid, the art of song, lend her aid in chanting light or weighty harmonies as we desire.

"What is it, mortal man, that has cast you down into grief and mourning? You have seen something unwonted, it would seem, something strange to you. But if you think that Fortune has changed towards you, you are wrong. These are ever her ways: this is her very nature. She has with you preserved her own constancy by her very change. She was ever changeable at the time when she smiled upon you, when she was mocking you with the allurements of false good fortune. You have discovered both the different faces of the blind goddess. To the eyes of others she is veiled in part: to you she has made herself wholly known. If you find her welcome, make use of her ways, and so make no complaining. If she fills you with horror by her treachery, treat her with despite; thrust her away from you, for she tempts you to your ruin. For though she is the cause of this great trouble for you, she ought to have been the subject of calmness and peace. For no man can ever make himself sure that she will never desert him, and thus has she deserted you. Do you reckon such happiness to be prized, which is sure to pass away? Is good fortune dear to you, which is with you for a time and is not sure to stay, and which is sure to bring you unhappiness when it is gone? But seeing that it cannot be stayed at will, and that when it flees away it leaves misery behind, what is such a fleeting thing but a sign of coming misery? Nor should it ever satisfy any man to look only at that which is placed before his eyes. Prudence takes measure of the results to come from all things. The very changeableness of good and bad makes Fortune's threats no more fearful, nor her smiles to be desired. And lastly, when you have once put your neck beneath the yoke of Fortune, you must with steadfast heart bear whatever comes to pass within her realm. But if you would dictate the law by which she whom you have freely chosen to be your mistress must stay or go, surely you will be acting without justification; and your very impatience will make more bitter a lot which you cannot change. If you set your sails before the wind, will you not move forward whither the wind drives you, not whither your will may choose to go? If you intrust your seed to the furrow, will you not weigh the rich years and the barren against each other? You have given yourself over to Fortune's rule, and you must bow yourself to your mistress's ways. Are you trying to stay the force of her turning wheel? Ah! dull-witted mortal, if Fortune begin to stay still, she is no longer Fortune.

*"As thus she turns her wheel of chance with haughty hand, and presses on like the surge of Euripus's tides, fortune now tramples fiercely on a fearsome king, and now deceives no less a conquered man by raising from the ground his humbled face. She hears no wretch's cry, she heeds no tears, but wantonly*

136

*she mocks the sorrow which her cruelty has made. This is her sport: thus she proves her power; if in the selfsame hour one man is raised to happiness, and cast down in despair, 'tis thus she shews her might.*

"Now would I argue with you by these few words which Fortune herself might use: and do you consider whether her demands are fair 'Why, O man,' she might say, 'do you daily accuse me with your complainings? What injustice have I wrought upon you? Of what good things have I robbed you? Choose your judge whom you will, and before him strive with me for the right to hold your wealth and honours. If you can prove that any one of these does truly belong to any mortal man, readily will I grant that these you seek to regain were yours. When nature brought you forth from your mother's womb, I received you in my arms naked and bare of all things; I cherished you with my gifts, and I brought you up all too kindly with my favouring care, wherefore now you cannot bear with me, and I surrounded you with glory and all the abundance that was mine to give. Now it pleases me to withdraw my hand: be thankful, as though you had lived upon my loans. You have no just cause of complaint, as though you had really lost what was once your own. Why do you rail against me? I have wrought no violence towards you. Wealth, honours, and all such are within my rights. They are my handmaids; they know their mistress; they come with me and go when I depart. Boldly will I say that if these, of whose loss you complain, were ever yours, you would never have lost them at all. Am I alone to be stayed from using my rightful power? The heavens may grant bright sunlit days, and hide the same beneath the shade of night. The year may deck the earth's countenance with flowers and fruits, and again wrap it with chilling clouds. The sea may charm with its smoothed surface, but no less justly it may soon bristle in storms with rough waves. Is the insatiate discontent of man to bind me to a constancy which belongs not to my ways? Herein lies my very strength; this is my unchanging sport. I turn my wheel that spins its circle fairly; I delight to make the lowest turn to the top, the highest to the bottom. Come you to the top if you will, but on this condition, that you think it no unfairness to sink when the rule of my game demands it. Do you not know my ways?'"

. . .

## Book III

When [Lady Philosophy] finished her lay, its soothing tones left me spell-bound with my ears alert in my eagerness to listen. So a while afterwards I said, "Greatest comforter of weary minds, how have you cheered me with your deep thoughts and sweet singing too! No more shall I doubt my power to meet the blows of Fortune. So far am I from terror at the remedies which you did lately tell me were sharper, that I am longing to hear them, and eagerly I beg you for them."

Then said she, "I knew it when you laid hold upon my words in silent attention, and I was waiting for that frame of mind in you, or more truly, I brought it about in you. They that remain are indeed bitter to the tongue, but sweet to the inner man. But as you say you are eager to hear, how ardently you would be burning, if you knew whither I am attempting to lead you!"

"Whither is that?" I asked.

"To the true happiness, of which your soul too dreams; but your sight is taken up in imaginary views thereof, so that you cannot look upon itself."

Then said I, "I pray you shew me what that truly is, and quickly."

"I will do so," she said, "for your sake willingly. But first I will try to picture in words and give you the form of the cause, which is already better known to you, that so, when that picture is perfect and you turn your eyes to the other side, you may recognise the form of true happiness.

*"When a man would sow in virgin soil, first he clears away the bushes, cuts the brambles and the ferns, that the corn-goddess may go forth laden with her new fruit. The honey, that the bee has toiled to give us, is sweeter when the mouth has tasted bitter things. The stars shine with more pleasing grace when a storm has ceased to roar and pour down rain. After the morning star has dispersed the shades of night, the day in all its beauty drives its rosy chariot forth. So thou hast looked upon false happiness first; now draw thy neck from under her yoke: so shall true happiness now come into thy soul."*

She lowered her eyes for a little while as though searching the inner-most recesses of her mind; and then she continued: "The trouble of the many and various aims of mortal men bring them much care, and herein they go forward by different paths but strive to reach one end, which is happiness. And that good is that, to which if any man attain, he can desire nothing further. It is that highest of all good things, and it embraces in itself all good things: if any good is lacking, it cannot be the highest good, since then there is left outside it something which can be desired. Wherefore happiness is a state which is made perfect by the union of all good things. This end all men seek to reach, as I said, though by different paths. For there is implanted by nature in the minds of men a desire for the true good; but error leads them astray towards false goods by wrong paths.

"Some men believe that the highest good is to lack nothing, and so they are at pains to possess abundant riches. Others consider the true good to be that which is most worthy of admiration, and so they strive to attain to places of honour, and to be held by their fellow-citizens in honour thereby. Some determine that the highest good lies in the highest power; and so they either desire to reign themselves, or try to cleave to those who do reign. Others think that renown is the greatest good, and they therefore hasten to make a famous name by the arts of peace or of war. But more than all measure the fruit of good by pleasure and enjoyment, and these think that the happiest man is abandoned to pleasure.

"Further, there are those who confuse the aims and the causes of these good things: as those who desire riches for the sake of power or of pleasure, or those who seek power for the sake of money or celebrity. In these, then, and other things like to them, lies the aim of men's actions and prayers, such as renown and popularity, which seem to afford some fame, or wife and children, which are sought for the pleasure they give. On the other hand, the good of friends, which is the most honourable and holy of all, lies not in Fortune's but in Virtue's realm. All others are adopted for the sake of power or enjoyment.

"Again, it is plain that the good things of the body must be accounted to those false causes which we have mentioned; for bodily strength and stature seem to make men more able and strong; beauty and swiftness seem to give renown; health seems to give pleasure. By all these happiness alone is plainly desired. For each man holds that to be the highest good, which he seeks before all others. But we have defined the highest good to be happiness. Wherefore what each man desires above all others, he holds to be a state of happiness.

"Wherefore you have each of these placed before you as the form of human happiness: wealth, honours, power, glory, and pleasure. Epicurus considered these forms alone, and accordingly determined upon pleasure as the highest good, because all the others seemed but to join with it in bringing enjoyment to the mind.

"But to return to the aims of men: their minds seem to seek to regain the highest good, and their memories seem to dull their powers. It is as though a drunken man were seeking his home, but could not remember the way thither. Can those people be altogether wrong whose aim it is to lack nothing? No, there is nothing which can make happiness so perfect as an abundant possession of good things, needing naught that belongs to others, but in all ways sufficing for itself. Surely those others too are not mistaken who think that what is best is also most worthy of reverence and respect. It cannot be any cheap or base thing, to attain which almost all men aim and strive. And is power not to be accounted a good thing? Surely it is: can that be a weak thing or forceless, which is allowed in all cases to excel? Is renown of no value? We cannot surrender this; that whatever is most excellent, has also great renown. It is hardly worth saying that happiness has no torturing cares or gloom, and is not subject to grief and trouble; for even in small things, the aim is to find that which it is a delight to have and to enjoy. These, then, are the desires of men: they long for riches, places of honour, kingdoms, glory, and pleasure; and they long for them because they think that thereby they will find satisfaction, veneration, power, renown, and happiness. It is the good then which men seek by their different desires; and it is easy to shew how great a force nature has put therein, since in spite of such varying and discordant opinions, they are all agreed in the goal they seek, that of the highest good."

*Translated by W. V. Cooper, 1902*

# LADY PHILOSOPHY

## A TRUE SELF-HELP GUIDE FOR HAPPINESS

### Michael Fatigati

If, when you hear the word *philosophy,* you do not jump to the edge of your seat, eagerly expecting your life to be changed in one sonorous, rhetorical sweep, then you're not alone. Much of the philosophical tradition is marked by careful, nuanced distinctions, more often soporific than salvific.

So we might be surprised when Boethius, in his hour of need—tired, distressed, chained—is greeted by Lady Philosophy. What is more, though Boethius is a Christian, with all the host of heaven supposedly by his side, he is provided with an earthly guide in a tattered robe.

Boethius's *Consolation of Philosophy* is not what we would expect, but it is what humans, Christians included, oftentimes need. When we are grieving, depressed, or anxious, our culture either tells us to placate our wounds by escaping into entertainment or deceives us into thinking there is an easy solution. Lady Philosophy does not discount his pains, but she, the "physician," asks him to "lay bare [his] wound" so that she can clear his tear-shrouded eyes and get to the bottom of things. The *Consolation* is indeed a self-help book, but one without compromise.

In terms of literary merit, it's Boethius's masterpiece, weaving together poetry and prose, Christian and non-Christian allusions, into a graciously didactic narrative. Historically, it has been read by scholars, clergy, and laymen alike. In terms of morality, it is realistic but staunch. Lady Philosophy believes that the truest goods are internal (not found in the accoutrements of this world), so she will not let Boethius think he has lost the ability to be happy merely by being enslaved.

And this is the central question of the *Consolation*: How can we obtain happiness?

One easy way *not* to obtain happiness is by following Boethius's example at the outset. We come upon him reciting a poem that may appear artful to modern ears, but his call for the "maimed Muses to guide [his] pen" is the ancient equivalent of an emo-pop angst-ridden melody.

Boethius attributes the pride of his earlier days to these Muses, and now he sees them as his only comfort. The Muses can be taken to represent any kind of overbearing sentimental force, and it's clear what Lady Philosophy thinks of them: "Sirens, seductive unto destruction!"

He has sunk so low that he not only looks to the Muses for comfort in distress, but he sees his journey from bliss to exile as due to nothing more than the Muses and "Fortune's fickle bounty."

---

If Boethius is going to obtain happiness, he needs to break free from the influence of the Muses and find a way to guard himself from the shrapnel of fortune's whims. Lady Philosophy eventually probes him with two further questions: "What is the object to which all nature tends?" and "What is a man?" His failure to answer these interrelated queries properly shows Lady Philosophy the "chief cause" of his sickness.

Boethius remembers that all things were *created* by God, but he cannot name God as the *end* to which all things tend. Without an overarching sense of providence guiding the world, all we're left with is fickle fortune at the reins, and there's no telling whether good will lead to good, or vice versa. As an aside, this is the same predicament in which today's popular naturalistic, materialistic worldview seems often to land.

But even if Boethius could name God as the cause *and* end of all things, he could not obtain true happiness while still holding that man is merely an "animal, reasoning and mortal." This was the standard ancient definition of humanness, but the only powers of the soul it delineates are the passions (which we share with animals) and rationality.

Now, someone who has reason guiding his passions is better off than someone whose passions run wild, but logic cannot give access to true happiness. Boethius, even in his prison cell, has not forgotten the arguments of his predecessors for why the universe had a Creator. This logical truth is the "tiny spark" from which Lady Philosophy will fan the flames of his soul's health. But he needs to go beyond logic if he is to be happy—he needs to possess the divine.

As Lady Philosophy catalogues the variety of things humans pursue in order to be happy, she notes that they all dissipate, run out, and require other goods to be sustained. This constant quest for new goods to fill in the gaps leads her to conclude that what all humans really want is "an abundant possession of good things . . . in all ways sufficing for itself." We pursue happiness in various and misguided ways, but the intended end is always the same: a condition of self-sufficiency.

Truly, the only good thing that's entirely self-sufficient is the divine itself, so the divine is the only thing that truly *is* happiness. In the *Consolation*, as is shown in later sections, the divine, goodness, and happiness are all different ways of referring to the same thing.

This means that if we're to obtain happiness, we must *possess* the divine. We must have some way of literally having supreme goodness inside us and of transforming into little gods ourselves.

———

Many scholars conclude that Lady Philosophy never completely answers the questions of *how* we can possess the divine. She does offer some thoughts, and they are robust enough to be well worth reading, but in the end, Boethius (the author, not the character) seems to suggest that while philosophy can set us on the right track—performing the invaluable task of reigning in our passions and pointing us in the direction of the divine—more, ultimately, will be necessary.

Even so, since most of us, on introspection, are likely still shrouded by our own particular clouds of grief, we would do well to sit at the feet of Lady Philosophy, whatever her shortcomings.

## CHAPTER SEVEN

# THOMAS AQUINAS

## High Middle Ages (1225–1274)

Thomas Aquinas is a phenomenal gift to the entire church. He served a saintly king in a fabulous court in an age that had moved out from the shadow of pagan Rome. A new and high Christian civilization, a fascinating expression of Christendom, flourished at this time, and it culminated in the glories of the cathedrals, the rise of international law and scholarship, the divine poetry of Dante, and the philosophy of Thomas.

Here is a mind that prepared the way for the scientific and industrial revolutions.

Here is a mind that was Catholic enough to embrace any good idea, from wherever it came.

Thomas, of all men, knew that sacred and secular must come together in the beating heart of man as created in the image of God. He lived as he thought, and his hymns are as beautiful as his philosophy is profound.

Argue with Thomas, because that is what he wants you to do, but follow his argument carefully, for it is very subtle. Few readers, perhaps, will agree with everything he says—even the Church of Rome does not—but it's *always* worth considering.

Once you get the trick of reading Thomas, he is easy to "get" but also hard to exhaust. His argument is clear, but it's also subtle, and what seems like an obvious problem will be filled in later or is anticipated in his careful wording.

Unfortunately, most of us are not as careful in our reading as he was in his writing! Some Christian academics have misunderstood Thomas either by appropriating his "arguments" out of context or by being critical of ideas they've misunderstood. It is the work of devils to demonize, but some believers have demonized Thomas Aquinas.

He will endure their misunderstandings. He's still more than capable of teaching us important truths about relating divine things, mystery unseen, to earthly things.

CRE FROM ᵭᵕᵔ

# *Summa Theologica*

### Whether God exists? (I.2.3)

*Objection 1.* It seems that God does not exist; because if one of two contraries be infinite, the other would be altogether destroyed. But the word "God" means that He is infinite goodness. If, therefore, God existed, there would be no evil discoverable; but there is evil in the world. Therefore God does not exist.

*Objection 2.* Further, it is superfluous to suppose that what can be accounted for by a few principles has been produced by many. But it seems that everything we see in the world can be accounted for by other principles, supposing God did not exist. For all natural things can be reduced to one principle which is nature; and all voluntary things can be reduced to one principle which is human reason, or will. Therefore there is no need to suppose God's existence.

*On the contrary,* It is said in the person of God: "I am Who I am" (Ex. 3:14).

*I answer that,* The existence of God can be proved in five ways.

The first and more manifest way is the argument from motion. It is certain, and evident to our senses, that in the world some things are in motion. Now whatever is in motion is put in motion by another, for nothing can be in motion except it is in potentiality to that towards which it is in motion; whereas a thing moves inasmuch as it is in act. For motion is nothing else than the reduction of something from potentiality to actuality. But nothing can be reduced from potentiality to actuality, except by something in a state of actuality. Thus that which is actually hot, as fire, makes wood, which is potentially hot, to be actually hot, and thereby moves and changes it. Now it is not possible that the same thing should be at once in actuality and potentiality in the same respect, but only in different respects. For what is actually hot cannot simultaneously be potentially hot; but it is simultaneously potentially cold. It is therefore impossible that in the same respect and in the same way a thing should be both mover and moved, i.e. that it should move itself. Therefore, whatever is in motion must be put in motion by another. If that by which it is put in motion be itself put in motion, then this also must needs be put in motion by another, and that by another again. But this cannot go on to infinity, because then there would be no first mover, and, consequently, no other mover; seeing that subsequent movers move only inasmuch as they are put in motion by the first mover; as the staff moves only because it is put in motion by the hand. Therefore it is necessary to arrive at a first mover, put in motion by no other; and this everyone understands to be God.

The second way is from the nature of the efficient cause. In the world of sense we find there is an order of efficient causes. There is no case known (neither is it, indeed, possible) in which a thing is found to be the efficient cause of itself; for so it would be prior to itself, which is impossible. Now in efficient causes it is not possible to go on to infinity, because in all efficient causes following in order, the first is the cause of the intermediate cause, and the intermediate is the cause of the ultimate cause, whether the intermediate cause be several, or only one. Now to take away the cause is to take away the effect. Therefore, if there be no first cause among efficient causes, there will be no ultimate, nor any intermediate cause. But if in efficient causes it is possible to go on to infinity, there will be no first efficient cause, neither will there be an ultimate effect, nor any intermediate efficient causes; all of which is plainly false. Therefore it is necessary to admit a first efficient cause, to which everyone gives the name of God.

The third way is taken from possibility and necessity, and runs thus. We find in nature things that are possible to be and not to be, since they are found to be generated, and to corrupt, and consequently, they are possible to be and not to be. But it is impossible for these always to exist, for that which is possible not to be at some time is not. Therefore, if everything is possible not to be, then at one time there could have been nothing in existence. Now if this were true, even now there would be nothing in existence, because that which does not exist only begins to exist by something already existing. Therefore, if at one time nothing was in existence, it would have been impossible for anything to have begun to exist; and thus even now nothing would be in existence—which is absurd. Therefore, not all beings are merely possible, but there must exist something the existence of which is necessary. But every necessary thing either has its necessity caused by another, or not. Now it is impossible to go on to infinity in necessary things which have their necessity caused by another, as has been already proved in regard to efficient causes. Therefore we cannot but postulate the existence of some being having of itself its own necessity, and not receiving it from another, but rather causing in others their necessity. This all men speak of as God.

The fourth way is taken from the gradation to be found in things. Among beings there are some more and some less good, true, noble and the like. But "more" and "less" are predicated of different things, according as they resemble in their different ways something which is the maximum, as a thing is said to be hotter according as it more nearly resembles that which is hottest; so that there is something which is truest, something best, something noblest and, consequently, something which is uttermost being; for those things that are greatest in truth are greatest in being.... Now the maximum in any genus is the cause of all in that genus; as fire, which is the maximum heat, is the cause of all hot things. Therefore there must also be something which is to all beings the cause of their being, goodness, and every other perfection; and this we call God.

The fifth way is taken from the governance of the world. We see that things which lack intelligence, such as natural bodies, act for an end, and this is evident from their acting always, or nearly always, in the same way, so as to obtain the best result. Hence it is plain that not fortuitously, but designedly, do they achieve their end. Now whatever lacks intelligence cannot move towards an end, unless it be directed by some being endowed with knowledge and intelligence; as the arrow is shot to its mark by the archer. Therefore some intelligent being exists by whom all natural things are directed to their end; and this being we call God.

*Reply to Objection 1.* As Augustine says (Enchir. xi): "Since God is the highest good, He would not allow any evil to exist in His works, unless His omnipotence and goodness were such as to bring good even out of evil." This is part of the infinite goodness of God, that He should allow evil to exist, and out of it produce good.

*Reply to Objection 2.* Since nature works for a determinate end under the direction of a higher agent, whatever is done by nature must needs be traced back to God, as to its first cause. So also whatever is done voluntarily must also be traced back to some higher cause other than human reason or will, since these can change or fail; for all things that are changeable and capable of defect must be traced back to an immovable and self-necessary first principle, as was shown in the body of the Article.

## Of those things in which man's happiness consists. (I–II.2)

*Article 1. Whether man's happiness consists in wealth?*

*Objection 1.* It would seem that man's happiness consists in wealth. For since happiness is man's last end, it must consist in that which has the greatest hold on man's affections. Now this is wealth: for it is written (Eccl. 10:19): "All things obey money." Therefore man's happiness consists in wealth.

*Objection 2.* Further, according to Boethius (De Consol. iii), happiness is "a state of life made perfect by the aggregate of all good things." Now money seems to be the means of possessing all things: for, as the Philosopher says (Ethic. v, 5), money was invented, that it might be a sort of guarantee for the acquisition of whatever man desires. Therefore happiness consists in wealth.

*Objection 3.* Further, since the desire for the sovereign good never fails, it seems to be infinite. But this is the case with riches more than anything else; since "a covetous man shall not be satisfied with riches" (Eccl. 5:9). Therefore happiness consists in wealth.

*On the contrary,* Man's good consists in retaining happiness rather than in spreading it. But as Boethius says (De Consol. ii), "wealth shines in giving rather than in hoarding: for the miser is hateful, whereas the generous man is applauded." Therefore man's happiness does not consist in wealth.

*I answer that,* It is impossible for man's happiness to consist in wealth. For wealth is twofold, as the Philosopher says (Polit. i, 3), viz. natural and artificial. Natural wealth is that which serves man as a remedy for his natural wants: such as food, drink, clothing, cars, dwellings, and such like, while artificial wealth is that which is not a direct help to nature, as money, but is invented by the art of man, for the convenience of exchange, and as a measure of things salable.

Now it is evident that man's happiness cannot consist in natural wealth. For wealth of this kind is sought for the sake of something else, viz. as a support of human nature: consequently it cannot be man's last end, rather is it ordained to man as to its end. Wherefore in the order of nature, all such things are below man, and made for him, according to Ps. 8:8: "Thou hast subjected all things under his feet."

And as to artificial wealth, it is not sought save for the sake of natural wealth; since man would not seek it except because, by its means, he procures for himself the necessaries of life. Consequently much less can it be considered in the light of the last end. Therefore it is impossible for happiness, which is the last end of man, to consist in wealth.

*Reply to Objection 1.* All material things obey money, so far as the multitude of fools is concerned, who know no other than material goods, which can be obtained for money. But we should take our estimation of human goods not from the foolish but from the wise: just as it is for a person whose sense of taste is in good order, to judge whether a thing is palatable.

*Reply to Objection 2.* All things salable can be had for money: not so spiritual things, which cannot be sold. Hence it is written (Prov. 17:16): "What doth it avail a fool to have riches, seeing he cannot buy wisdom."

*Reply to Objection 3.* The desire for natural riches is not infinite: because they suffice for nature in a certain measure. But the desire for artificial wealth is infinite, for it is the servant of disordered concupiscence, which is not curbed, as the Philosopher makes clear (Polit. i, 3). Yet this desire for wealth is infinite otherwise than the desire for the sovereign good. For the more perfectly the sovereign good is possessed, the more it is loved, and other things despised: because the more we possess it, the more we know it. Hence it is written (Sir. 24:29): "They that eat me shall yet hunger." Whereas in the desire for wealth and for whatsoever temporal goods, the contrary is the case: for when we already possess them, we despise them, and seek others: which is the sense of Our Lord's words (Jn. 4:13): "Whosoever drinketh of this water," by which temporal goods are signified, "shall thirst again." The reason of this is that we realize more their insufficiency when we possess them: and this very fact shows that they are imperfect, and the sovereign good does not consist therein.

*Article 2. Whether man's happiness consists in honors?*

*Objection 1.* It would seem that man's happiness consists in honors. For happiness or bliss is "the reward of virtue," as the Philosopher says (Ethic. i, 9). But honor more than anything else seems to be that by which virtue is rewarded, as the Philosopher says (Ethic. iv, 3). Therefore happiness consists especially in honor.

*Objection 2.* Further, that which belongs to God and to persons of great excellence seems especially to be happiness, which is the perfect good. But that is honor, as the Philosopher says (Ethic. iv, 3). Moreover, the Apostle says (1 Tim. 1:17): "To . . . the only God be honor and glory." Therefore happiness consists in honor.

*Objection 3.* Further, that which man desires above all is happiness. But nothing seems more desirable to man than honor: since man suffers loss in all other things, lest he should suffer loss of honor. Therefore happiness consists in honor.

*On the contrary,* Happiness is in the happy. But honor is not in the honored, but rather in him who honors, and who offers deference to the person honored, as the Philosopher says (Ethic. i, 5). Therefore happiness does not consist in honor.

*I answer that,* It is impossible for happiness to consist in honor. For honor is given to a man on account of some excellence in him; and consequently it is a sign and attestation of the excellence that is in the person honored. Now a man's excellence is in proportion, especially to his happiness, which is man's perfect good; and to its parts, i.e. those goods by which he has a certain share of happiness. And therefore honor can result from happiness, but happiness cannot principally consist therein.

*Reply to Objection 1.* As the Philosopher says (Ethic. i, 5), honor is not that reward of virtue, for which the virtuous work: but they receive honor from men by way of reward, "as from those who have nothing greater to offer." But virtue's true reward is happiness itself, for which the virtuous work: whereas if they worked for honor, it would no longer be a virtue, but ambition.

*Reply to Objection 2.* Honor is due to God and to persons of great excellence as a sign of attestation of excellence already existing: not that honor makes them excellent.

*Reply to Objection 3.* That man desires honor above all else, arises from his natural desire for happiness, from which honor results, as stated above. Wherefore man seeks to be honored especially by the wise, on whose judgment he believes himself to be excellent or happy.

*Article 3. Whether man's happiness consists in fame or glory?*

*Objection 1.* It would seem that man's happiness consists in glory. For happiness seems to consist in that which is paid to the saints for the trials they have undergone in the world. But this is glory: for the Apostle says (Rom. 8:18): "The sufferings of this time are not worthy to be compared with the glory to come, that shall be revealed in us." Therefore happiness consists in glory.

*Objection 2.* Further, good is diffusive of itself, as stated by Dionysius (Div. Nom. iv). But man's good is spread abroad in the knowledge of others by glory more than by anything else: since, according to Ambrose . . . glory consists "in being well known and praised." Therefore man's happiness consists in glory.

*Objection 3.* Further, happiness is the most enduring good. Now this seems to be fame or glory; because by this men attain to eternity after a fashion. Hence Boethius says (De Consol. ii): "You seem to beget unto yourselves eternity, when you think of your fame in future time." Therefore man's happiness consists in fame or glory.

*On the contrary,* Happiness is man's true good. But it happens that fame or glory is false: for as Boethius says (De Consol. iii), "many owe their renown to the lying reports spread among the people. Can anything be more shameful? For those who receive false fame, must needs blush at their own praise." Therefore man's happiness does not consist in fame or glory.

*I answer that*, Man's happiness cannot consist in human fame or glory. For glory consists "in being well known and praised," as Ambrose . . . says. Now the thing known is related to human knowledge otherwise than to God's knowledge: for human knowledge is caused by the things known, whereas God's knowledge is the cause of the things known. Wherefore the perfection of human good, which is called happiness, cannot be caused by human knowledge: but rather human knowledge of another's happiness proceeds from, and, in a fashion, is caused by, human happiness itself, inchoate or perfect. Consequently man's happiness cannot consist in fame or glory. On the other hand, man's good depends on God's knowledge as its cause. And therefore man's beatitude depends, as on its cause, on the glory which man has with God; according to Ps. 90:15–16: "I will deliver him, and I will glorify him; I will fill him with length of days, and I will show him my salvation."

Furthermore, we must observe that human knowledge often fails, especially in contingent singulars, such as are human acts. For this reason human glory is frequently deceptive. But since God cannot be deceived, His glory is always true; hence it is written (2 Cor. 10:18): "He . . . is approved . . . whom God commendeth."

*Reply to Objection 1.* The Apostle speaks, then, not of the glory which is with men, but of the glory which is from God, with His Angels. Hence it is written (Mk. 8:38): "The Son of Man shall confess him in the glory of His Father, before His angels" [St. Thomas joins Mk. 8:38 with Lk. 12:8 owing to a possible variant in his text, or to the fact that he was quoting from memory].

*Reply to Objection 2.* A man's good which, through fame or glory, is in the knowledge of many, if this knowledge be true, must needs be derived from good existing in the man himself: and hence it presupposes perfect or inchoate happiness. But if the knowledge be false, it does not harmonize with the thing: and thus good does not exist in him who is looked upon as famous. Hence it follows that fame can nowise make man happy.

*Reply to Objection 3.* Fame has no stability; in fact, it is easily ruined by false report. And if sometimes it endures, this is by accident. But happiness endures of itself, and for ever.

*Article 4. Whether man's happiness consists in power?*

*Objection 1.* It would seem that happiness consists in power. For all things desire to become like to God, as to their last end and first beginning. But men who are in power, seem, on account of the similarity of power, to be most like to God: hence also in Scripture they are called "gods" (Ex. 22:28), "Thou shalt not speak ill of the gods." Therefore happiness consists in power.

*Objection 2.* Further, happiness is the perfect good. But the highest perfection for man is to be able to rule others; which belongs to those who are in power. Therefore happiness consists in power.

*Objection 3.* Further, since happiness is supremely desirable, it is contrary to that which is before all to be shunned. But, more than aught else, men shun servitude, which is contrary to power. Therefore happiness consists in power.

*On the contrary,* Happiness is the perfect good. But power is most imperfect. For as Boethius says (De Consol. iii), "the power of man cannot relieve the gnawings of care, nor can it avoid the thorny path of anxiety": and further on: "Think you a man is powerful who is surrounded by attendants, whom he inspires with fear indeed, but whom he fears still more?"

*I answer that,* It is impossible for happiness to consist in power; and this for two reasons. First because power has the nature of principle . . . whereas happiness has the nature of last end. Secondly, because power has relation to good and evil: whereas happiness is man's proper and perfect good. Wherefore some happiness might consist in the good use of power, which is by virtue, rather than in power itself.

Now four general reasons may be given to prove that happiness consists in none of the foregoing external goods. First, because, since happiness is man's supreme good, it is incompatible with any evil. Now all the foregoing can be found both in good and in evil men. Secondly, because, since it is the nature of happiness to "satisfy of itself" . . . having gained happiness, man cannot lack any needful good. But after acquiring any one of the foregoing, man may still lack many goods that are necessary to him; for instance, wisdom, bodily health, and such like. Thirdly, because, since happiness is the perfect good, no evil can accrue to anyone therefrom. This cannot be said of the foregoing: for it is written (Eccl. 5:12) that "riches" are sometimes "kept to the hurt of the owner"; and the same may be said of the other three. Fourthly, because man is ordained to happiness through principles that are in him; since he is ordained thereto naturally. Now the four goods mentioned above are due rather to external causes, and in most cases to fortune; for which reason they are called goods of fortune. Therefore it is evident that happiness nowise consists in the foregoing.

*Reply to Objection 1.* God's power is His goodness: hence He cannot use His power otherwise than well. But it is not so with men. Consequently it is not enough for man's happiness, that he become like God in power, unless he become like Him in goodness also.

*Reply to Objection 2.* Just as it is a very good thing for a man to make good use of power in ruling many, so is it a very bad thing if he makes a bad use of it. And so it is that power is towards good and evil.

*Reply to Objection 3.* Servitude is a hindrance to the good use of power: therefore is it that men naturally shun it; not because man's supreme good consists in power.

*Article 5. Whether man's happiness consists in any bodily good?*

*Objection 1.* It would seem that man's happiness consists in bodily goods. For it is written (Sir. 30:16): "There is no riches above the riches of the health of the body." But happiness consists in that which is best. Therefore it consists in the health of the body.

*Objection 2.* Further, Dionysius says (Div. Nom. v) that "to be" is better than "to live," and "to live" is better than all that follows. But for man's being and living, the health of the body is necessary. Since, therefore, happiness is man's supreme good, it seems that health of the body belongs more than anything else to happiness.

*Objection 3.* Further, the more universal a thing is, the higher the principle from which it depends; because the higher a cause is, the greater the scope of its power. Now just as the causality of the efficient cause consists in its flowing into something, so the causality of the end consists in its drawing the appetite. Therefore, just as the First Cause is that which flows into all things, so the last end is that which attracts the desire of all. But being itself is that which is most desired by all. Therefore man's happiness consists most of all in things pertaining to his being, such as the health of the body.

*On the contrary*, Man surpasses all other animals in regard to happiness.

But in bodily goods he is surpassed by many animals; for instance, by the elephant in longevity, by the lion in strength, by the stag in fleetness. Therefore man's happiness does not consist in goods of the body.

*I answer that,* It is impossible for man's happiness to consist in the goods of the body; and this for two reasons. First, because, if a thing be ordained to another as to its end, its last end cannot consist in the preservation of its being. Hence a captain does not intend as a last end, the preservation of the ship entrusted to him, since a ship is ordained to something else as its end, viz. to navigation. Now just as the ship is entrusted to the captain that he may steer its course, so man is given over to his will and reason: "God made man from the beginning and left him in the hand of his own counsel" (Sir. 15:14). Now it is evident that man is ordained to something as his end: since man is not the supreme good. Therefore the last end of man's reason and will cannot be the preservation of man's being.

Secondly, because, granted that the end of man's will and reason be the preservation of man's being, it could not be said that the end of man is some good of the body. For man's being consists in soul and body; and though the being of the body depends on the soul, yet the being of the human soul depends not on the body, as shown above (I, 75, 2); and the very body is for the soul, as matter for its form, and the instruments for the man that puts them into motion, that by their means he may do his work. Wherefore all goods of the body are ordained to the goods of the soul, as to their end. Consequently happiness, which is man's last end, cannot consist in goods of the body.

*Reply to Objection 1.* Just as the body is ordained to the soul, as its end, so are external goods ordained to the body itself. And therefore it is with reason that the good of the body is preferred to external goods, which are signified by "riches," just as the good of the soul is preferred to all bodily goods.

*Reply to Objection 2.* Being taken simply, as including all perfection of being, surpasses life and all that follows it; for thus being itself includes all these. And in this sense Dionysius speaks. But if we consider being itself as participated in this or that thing, which does not possess the whole perfection of being, but has imperfect being, such as the being of any creature; then it is evident that being itself together with an additional perfection is more excellent. Hence in the same passage Dionysius says that things that live are better than things that exist, and intelligent better than living things.

*Reply to Objection 3.* Since the end corresponds to the beginning; this argument proves that the last end is the first beginning of being, in Whom every perfection of being is: Whose likeness, according to their proportion, some desire as to being only, some as to living being, some as to being which is living, intelligent and happy. And this belongs to few.

*Article 6. Whether man's happiness consists in pleasure?*

*Objection 1.* It would seem that man's happiness consists in pleasure. For since happiness is the last end, it is not desired for something else, but other things for it. But this answers to pleasure more than to anything else: "for it is absurd to ask anyone what is his motive in wishing to be pleased" (Ethic. x, 2). Therefore happiness consists principally in pleasure and delight.

*Objection 2.* Further, "the first cause goes more deeply into the effect than the second cause" (De Causis i). Now the causality of the end consists in its attracting the appetite. Therefore, seemingly that which moves most the appetite, answers to the notion of the last end. Now this is pleasure: and a sign of this is that delight so far absorbs man's will and reason, that it causes him to despise other goods. Therefore it seems that man's last end, which is happiness, consists principally in pleasure.

*Objection 3.* Further, since desire is for good, it seems that what all desire is best. But all desire delight; both wise and foolish, and even irrational creatures. Therefore delight is the best of all. Therefore happiness, which is the supreme good, consists in pleasure.

*On the contrary,* Boethius says (De Consol. iii): "Any one that chooses to look back on his past excesses, will perceive that pleasures had a sad ending: and if they can render a man happy, there is no reason why we should not say that the very beasts are happy too."

*I answer that,* Because bodily delights are more generally known, "the name of pleasure has been appropriated to them" (Ethic. vii, 13), although other delights excel them: and yet happiness does not consist in them. Because in every thing, that which pertains to its essence is distinct from its proper accident: thus in man it is one thing that he is a mortal rational animal, and another that he is a risible animal. We must therefore consider that every delight is a proper accident resulting from happiness, or from some part of happiness; since the reason that a man is delighted is that he has some fitting good, either in reality, or in hope, or at least in memory. Now a fitting good, if indeed it be the perfect good, is precisely man's happiness: and if it is imperfect, it is a share of happiness, either proximate, or remote, or at least apparent. Therefore it is evident that neither is delight, which results from the perfect good, the very essence of happiness, but something resulting therefrom as its proper accident.

But bodily pleasure cannot result from the perfect good even in that way. For it results from a good apprehended by sense, which is a power of the soul, which power makes use of the body. Now good pertaining to the body, and apprehended by sense, cannot be man's perfect good. For since the rational soul excels the capacity of corporeal matter, that part of the soul which is independent of a corporeal organ, has a certain infinity in regard to the body and those parts of the soul which are tied down to the body: just as immaterial things are in a way infinite as compared to material things, since a form is, after a fashion, contracted and bounded by matter, so that a form which is independent of matter is, in a way, infinite. Therefore sense, which is a power of the body, knows the singular, which is determinate through matter: whereas the intellect, which is a power independent of matter, knows the universal, which is abstracted from matter, and contains an infinite number of singulars. Consequently it is evident that good which is fitting to the body, and which causes bodily delight through being apprehended by sense, is not man's perfect good, but is quite a trifle as compared with the good of the soul. Hence it is written (Wis. 7:9) that "all gold in comparison of her, is as a little sand." And therefore bodily pleasure is neither happiness itself, nor a proper accident of happiness.

*Reply to Objection 1.* It comes to the same whether we desire good, or desire delight, which is nothing else than the appetite's rest in good: thus it is owing to the same natural force that a weighty body is borne downwards and that it rests there. Consequently just as good is desired for itself, so delight is desired for itself and not for anything else, if the preposition "for" denote the final cause. But if it denote the formal or rather the motive cause, thus delight is desirable for something else, i.e. for the good, which is the object of that delight, and consequently is its principle, and gives it its form: for the reason that delight is desired is that it is rest in the thing desired.

*Reply to Objection 2.* The vehemence of desire for sensible delight arises from the fact that operations of the senses, through being the principles of our knowledge, are more perceptible. And so it is that sensible pleasures are desired by the majority.

*Reply to Objection 3.* All desire delight in the same way as they desire good: and yet they desire delight by reason of the good and not conversely, as stated above (ad 1). Consequently it does not follow that delight is the supreme and essential good, but that every delight results from some good, and that some delight results from that which is the essential and supreme good.

*Article 7. Whether some good of the soul constitutes man's happiness?*

*Objection 1.* It would seem that some good of the soul constitutes man's happiness. For happiness is man's good. Now this is threefold: external goods, goods of the body, and goods of the soul. But happiness does not consist in external goods, nor in goods of the body, as shown above (4, 5). Therefore it consists in goods of the soul.

*Objection 2.* Further, we love that for which we desire good, more than the good that we desire for it: thus we love a friend for whom we desire money, more than we love money. But whatever good a man desires, he desires it for himself. Therefore he loves himself more than all other goods. Now happiness is what is loved above all: which is evident from the fact that for its sake all else is loved and desired. Therefore happiness consists in some good of man himself: not, however, in goods of the body; therefore, in goods of the soul.

*Objection 3.* Further, perfection is something belonging to that which is perfected. But happiness is a perfection of man. Therefore happiness is something belonging to man. But it is not something belonging to the body, as shown above (Art. 5). Therefore it is something belonging to the soul; and thus it consists in goods of the soul.

*On the contrary,* As Augustine says (De Doctr. Christ. i, 22), "that which constitutes the life of happiness is to be loved for its own sake." But man is not to be loved for his own sake, but whatever is in man is to be loved for God's sake. Therefore happiness consists in no good of the soul.

*I answer that,* As stated above (Q. 1, A. 8), the end is twofold: namely, the thing itself, which we desire to attain, and the use, namely, the attainment or possession of that thing. If, then, we speak of man's last end, it is impossible for man's last end to be the soul itself or something belonging to it. Because the soul, considered in itself, is as something existing in potentiality: for it becomes knowing actually, from being potentially knowing; and actually virtuous, from being potentially virtuous. Now since potentiality is for the sake of act as for its fulfillment, that which in itself is in potentiality cannot be the last end. Therefore the soul itself cannot be its own last end.

In like manner neither can anything belonging to it, whether power, habit, or act. For that good which is the last end, is the perfect good fulfilling the desire. Now man's appetite, otherwise the will, is for the universal good. And any good inherent to the soul is a participated good, and consequently a portioned good. Therefore none of them can be man's last end.

But if we speak of man's last end, as to the attainment or possession thereof, or as to any use whatever of the thing itself desired as an end, thus does something of man, in respect of his soul, belong to his last end: since man attains happiness through his soul. Therefore the thing itself which is desired as end, is that which constitutes happiness, and makes man happy; but the attainment of this thing is called happiness. Consequently we must say that happiness is something belonging to the soul; but that which constitutes happiness is something outside the soul.

*Reply to Objection 1.* Inasmuch as this division includes all goods that man can desire, thus the good of the soul is not only power, habit, or act, but also the object of these, which is something outside. And in this way nothing hinders us from saying that what constitutes happiness is a good of the soul.

*Reply to Objection 2.* As far as the proposed objection is concerned, happiness is loved above all, as the good desired; whereas a friend is loved as that for which good is desired; and thus, too, man loves himself. Consequently it is not the same kind of love in both cases. As to whether man loves anything more than himself with the love of friendship there will be occasion to inquire when we treat of Charity.

*Reply to Objection 3.* Happiness, itself, since it is a perfection of the soul, is an inherent good of the soul; but that which constitutes happiness, viz. which makes man happy, is something outside his soul, as stated above.

*Article 8. Whether any created good constitutes man's happiness?*

*Objection 1.* It would seem that some created good constitutes man's happiness. For Dionysius says (Div. Nom. vii) that Divine wisdom "unites the ends of first things to the beginnings of second things," from which we may gather that the summit of a lower nature touches the base of the higher nature. But man's highest good is happiness. Since then the angel is above man in the order of nature (I, 111, 1), it seems that man's happiness consists in man somehow reaching the angel.

*Objection 2.* Further, the last end of each thing is that which, in relation to it, is perfect: hence the part is for the whole, as for its end. But the universe of creatures which is called the macrocosm, is compared to man who is called the microcosm (Phys. viii, 2), as perfect to imperfect. Therefore man's happiness consists in the whole universe of creatures.

*Objection 3.* Further, man is made happy by that which lulls his natural desire. But man's natural desire does not reach out to a good surpassing his capacity. Since then man's capacity does not include that good which surpasses the limits of all creation, it seems that man can be made happy by some created good. Consequently some created good constitutes man's happiness.

*On the contrary,* Augustine says (De Civ. Dei xix, 26): "As the soul is the life of the body, so God is man's life of happiness: of Whom it is written: 'Happy is that people whose God is the Lord' (Ps. 143:15)."

*I answer that,* It is impossible for any created good to constitute man's happiness. For happiness is the perfect good, which lulls the appetite altogether; else it would not be the last end, if something yet remained to be desired. Now the object of the will, i.e. of man's appetite, is the universal good; just as the object of the intellect is the universal true. Hence it is evident that naught can lull man's will, save the universal good. This is to be found, not in any creature, but in God alone; because every creature has goodness by participation. Wherefore God alone can satisfy the will of man, according to the words of Ps. 102:5: "Who satisfieth thy desire with good things." Therefore God alone constitutes man's happiness.

*Reply to Objection 1.* The summit of man does indeed touch the base of the angelic nature, by a kind of likeness; but man does not rest there as in his last end, but reaches out to the universal fount itself of good, which is the common object of happiness of all the blessed, as being the infinite and perfect good.

*Reply to Objection 2.* If a whole be not the last end, but ordained to a further end, then the last end of a part thereof is not the whole itself, but something else. Now the universe of creatures, to which man is compared as part to whole, is not the last end, but is ordained to God, as to its last end. Therefore the last end of man is not the good of the universe, but God himself.

*Reply to Objection 3.* Created good is not less than that good of which man is capable, as of something intrinsic and inherent to him: but it is less than the good of which he is capable, as of an object, and which is infinite. And the participated good which is in an angel, and in the whole universe, is a finite and restricted good.

## Whether Providence imposes any necessity on things foreseen? (I.22.4)

*Objection 1:* It seems that divine providence imposes necessity upon things foreseen . . . for divine providence cannot be frustrated.

*On the contrary,* Dionysius says that "to corrupt nature is not the work of providence." But it is in the nature of some things to be contingent. Divine providence does not therefore impose any necessity upon things so as to destroy their contingency.

*I answer that,* divine providence imposes necessity upon some things, not upon all, as some formerly believed. For to providence it belongs to order things towards an end. Now after the divine goodness, which is an extrinsic end to all things, the principal good in things themselves is the perfection of the universe, which would not be were not all grades of being found in things. Whence it pertains to providence to produce every grade of being. And thus it has prepared for some things necessary causes, so that they happen by necessity; for others contingent causes, that they may happen by contingency, according to the nature of their proximate causes.

*Reply to Objection 1:* The effect of divine providence is not only that things should happen somehow, but that they should happen either by necessity or contingency. Therefore whatsoever divine providence ordains to happen infallibly and of necessity, happens infallibly and of necessity; and that happens from contingency which the plan of divine providence conceives to happen from contingency.

*Translated by the Fathers of the English Dominican Province, 1920*

# THE TRUTH
# OF SAINT THOMAS AQUINAS

## Peter Kreeft

I am totally convinced that Saint Thomas Aquinas was the greatest, wisest, most intelligent merely human theologian who ever lived.

Why? Let the first reason be that he told the truth. Nothing trumps that.

Second, he's the master of common sense. What he says is always what sound reason says, even though he says it in his difficult, technical, medieval-Aristotelian vocabulary. G. K. Chesterton's *Saint Thomas Aquinas: The Dumb Ox* proves this brilliantly.

Third, he was not just a head but a heart: a saint and a practical man. Kings, peasants, and popes wrote to him for advice and always got back sound wisdom. (Example: his cure for depression—a hot bath, a glass of wine, and a good night's sleep.)

Fourth, he combined the two essential goals of thinking better than anyone else: profundity and clarity. He wrote about the most difficult and profound questions a man can ask: God and man, good and evil, life and death, virtue and vice, soul and body, intellect and will, predestination and free will, nature and grace—and he did it clearly and simply. Though at first he seems difficult, he becomes amazingly straightforward and simple on subsequent readings, once the vocabulary obstacle is overcome. He is a transparent window; there are no impositions of his personality, no rhetorical tricks, no extra words, no digressions, all bottom-line, right-to-the-point answers, and always with compelling logical reasons.

Fifth, he fulfilled more than anyone else the essential medieval program of a marriage of faith and reason, revelation and philosophy, the biblical and the classical inheritances. He "baptized" philosophy, especially Aristotle. He did not turn the Christian faith into a purely rational philosophy; he turned Aristotle's purely rational philosophy into a servant of Christian faith.

Sixth, he also combined elaborate, careful detail with "the big picture," his cosmic perspective, which is breathtakingly big.

Thomas Aquinas wrote many thousands of pages in addition to his unfinished four-thousand-page masterpiece, the *Summa Theologiae*, which he dictated to four secretaries at once, sentence by sentence, never changing a word. Then he stopped writing and called everything he had ever written "straw" compared with "what has been revealed to me" (or, in another account, "what I have seen"). His fellow monks heard a heavenly voice ask him, "You have written well of Me, Thomas, what will you have as your reward," and heard his absolutely perfect, absolutely simple answer: "Only Thyself, Lord." Never was more said in fewer words.

By the way, Protestants and Anglicans and even agnostics often love and respect Thomas as much as Catholics do. Certainly, there was no greater thinker for two thousand years between the death of Aristotle and the publication of Descartes' *Discourse on Method* (except perhaps Augustine). Whoever you are, your mind will get a wonderful workout in clarity and logic, as well as orthodox theology, by reading him.

Reading Thomas Aquinas is like eating spinach. It tastes strange at first, but it makes you stronger. His habits of clarity and order rub off on you, even when you disagree with him.

Nevertheless, read him slowly. The *Summa* is not a novel but a reference book.

Furthermore, *Summa* is an ordered summary, not a closed system. Its structural outline is a mirror of reality. It begins in God, "in the beginning," then proceeds to the act of Creation and God's continuing providence in dealing with creatures, centering on man, who alone is created in God's image; it ends with man's return to God, his end, through his moral and religious life, and finally man's means to this end of salvation, namely Christ, who saves man through His body and His church (which *is* His body). It's the universal drama of God as Alpha and Omega of all time and change. God pumps the blood of being through the arteries of creation into the body of the universe, which wears a human face, and receives it back through the veins of man's life of free choice of faith, hope, and love. This is a cosmic circulatory system.

It's good to be aware that, though logically outlined into many sub, sub-sub, and sub-sub-subdivisions, the basic unit of the *Summa* is the "article," typically a page or two long, which has five structural parts:

1. The *question* is formulated in a yes or no format, beginning with "*Whether . . .*"
2. *Objections* to his answer are given, fairly and clearly and completely, beginning with "*It seems that . . .*"
3. An argument from a past *authority* is given, with the formula "*On the contrary . . .*"
4. The body of the article, beginning with "*I answer that . . .*" is his main *proof* for his position, with explanations along the way.
5. Finally, each objection is answered, usually by distinguishing what is true and what is false in it.

This is no merely local and quaint medieval format. Not one of these steps can ever be omitted if we want to have good grounds for settling any controversial question.

Thomas Aquinas is scrupulously fair. Though his prosaic, literal, bottom-line logical style is an extreme contrast to Augustine's charming, rambling, and singing poetry, his single-minded, pure passion for truth is strikingly similar. Neither of them seems even *capable* of dishonesty.

If you were a CIA agent recruiting among philosophers for spies, no two would be more hopelessly inept than these.

## CHAPTER EIGHT

# DANTE ALIGHIERI

## Medieval (1265–1321)

**D**on't tell my Paris tour, but I once got lost in the cathedral of Notre Dame and never got back to the planned agenda. Nobody noticed because my body stayed with the group, but the complexity and splendor of the structure pulled my mind away from the noise and natter of an American tour group. I got lost trying to understand centuries of construction too quickly, and then the piety built into the stone refused to allow me to return to ugliness. Some part of me still sees the light through ancient glass: the color blue just is my wife's eyes seen in Notre Dame light.

Maybe I had been lost and the building found me, but the feeling was disorienting at first. The modern world is small and tidy, and the cosmos, as the Medievals truthfully saw it, was so much bigger than I imagined. It was tempting to return to modern simplicity because the shock of the vast cathedral was almost too much.

Realizing this makes me a bit sad, because I know that often big art has overwhelmed me, but I simply stayed on the tour. It was easier to be "bored" and look for the next WC stop than to let the weight of glory change me.

Dante's *Comedy* is risky in just that way. It's so big that the careful order and pattern is hard for our modern minds to discern. He's writing a big book, and we're used to stories that move simply from left to right. The *Comedy* has depth, and outside the Bible most of us aren't accustomed to dimensions.

The best advice I can give is to read quickly the first time. You will know you're missing more than you're gaining, but get what you can and then read the selection again. This time, look up some of the unfamiliar people and works. Third time, try reading the lines aloud and let the sound move you. Focus on a single line you want to understand the fourth time through, and read until you understand.

The *Comedy* is an entire Christian worldview. It isn't the only possible Christian worldview, because no human book could contain that whole, but it's a very good one. It combines the best science, theology, poetry, politics, and psychology from the age in which it was written. That means parts of it are wrong, but even where wrong, it stimulated in others the thinking that produced modernity.

Dante may get details incorrect, but as a Christian he gets the big picture gloriously right. He knows history is tragic but that it ends in a wedding between Christ and His church.

History is, therefore, truly a *comedy*. In this dark and tragic world, we sometimes forget the good news: it is love that moves the heavens and the farthest stars.

Get lost in Dante, and let Love find you.

 FROM

# The Divine Comedy's "Inferno"

## Canto I

> Midway upon the journey of our life
> I found myself within a forest dark,
> For the straight-forward pathway had been lost.

Ah me! how hard a thing it is to say
    What was this forest savage, rough, and stern,
    Which in the very thought renews the fear.

So bitter is it, death is little more;
    But of the good to treat, which there I found,
    Speak will I of the other things I saw there.

I cannot well repeat how there I entered,
    So full was I of slumber at the moment
    In which I had abandoned the true way.

But after I had reached a mountain's foot,
    At that point where the valley terminated,
    Which had with consternation pierced my heart,

Upward I looked, and I beheld its shoulders,
    Vested already with that planet's rays
    Which leadeth others right by every road.

Then was the fear a little quieted
    That in my heart's lake had endured throughout
    The night, which I had passed so piteously.

And even as he, who, with distressful breath,
    Forth issued from the sea upon the shore,
    Turns to the water perilous and gazes;

So did my soul, that still was fleeing onward,
    Turn itself back to re-behold the pass
    Which never yet a living person left.

After my weary body I had rested,
    The way resumed I on the desert slope,
    So that the firm foot ever was the lower.

And lo! almost where the ascent began,
    A panther light and swift exceedingly,
    Which with a spotted skin was covered o'er!

And never moved she from before my face,
    Nay, rather did impede so much my way,
    That many times I to return had turned.

The time was the beginning of the morning,
 And up the sun was mounting with those stars
 That with him were, what time the Love Divine

At first in motion set those beauteous things;
 So were to me occasion of good hope,
 The variegated skin of that wild beast,

The hour of time, and the delicious season;
 But not so much, that did not give me fear
 A lion's aspect which appeared to me.

He seemed as if against me he were coming
 With head uplifted, and with ravenous hunger,
 So that it seemed the air was afraid of him;

And a she-wolf, that with all hungerings
 Seemed to be laden in her meagreness,
 And many folk has caused to live forlorn!

She brought upon me so much heaviness,
 With the affright that from her aspect came,
 That I the hope relinquished of the height.

And as he is who willingly acquires,
 And the time comes that causes him to lose,
 Who weeps in all his thoughts and is despondent,

E'en such made me that beast withouten peace,
 Which, coming on against me by degrees
 Thrust me back thither where the sun is silent.

While I was rushing downward to the lowland,
 Before mine eyes did one present himself,
 Who seemed from long-continued silence hoarse.

When I beheld him in the desert vast,
 "Have pity on me," unto him I cried,
 "Whiche'er thou art, or shade or real man!"

He answered me: "Not man; man once I was,
 And both my parents were of Lombardy,
 And Mantuans by country both of them.

'Sub Julio' was I born, though it was late,
 And lived at Rome under the good Augustus,
 During the time of false and lying gods.

A poet was I, and I sang that just
 Son of Anchises, who came forth from Troy,
 After that Ilion the superb was burned.

But thou, why goest thou back to such annoyance?
 Why climb'st thou not the Mount Delectable,
 Which is the source and cause of every joy?"

"Now, art thou that Virgilius and that fountain
 Which spreads abroad so wide a river of speech?"
 I made response to him with bashful forehead.

"O, of the other poets honour and light,
 Avail me the long study and great love
 That have impelled me to explore thy volume!

Thou art my master, and my author thou,
 Thou art alone the one from whom I took
 The beautiful style that has done honour to me.

Behold the beast, for which I have turned back;
 Do thou protect me from her, famous Sage,
 For she doth make my veins and pulses tremble."

"Thee it behoves to take another road,"
 Responded he, when he beheld me weeping,
 "If from this savage place thou wouldst escape;

Because this beast, at which thou criest out,
 Suffers not any one to pass her way,
 But so doth harass him, that she destroys him;

And has a nature so malign and ruthless,
 That never doth she glut her greedy will,
 And after food is hungrier than before.

Many the animals with whom she weds,
 And more they shall be still, until the Greyhound
 Comes, who shall make her perish in her pain.

He shall not feed on either earth or pelf,
    But upon wisdom, and on love and virtue;
    'Twixt Feltro and Feltro shall his nation be;

Of that low Italy shall he be the saviour,
    On whose account the maid Camilla died,
    Euryalus, Turnus, Nisus, of their wounds;

Through every city shall he hunt her down,
    Until he shall have driven her back to Hell,
    There from whence envy first did let her loose.

Therefore I think and judge it for thy best
    Thou follow me, and I will be thy guide,
    And lead thee hence through the eternal place,

Where thou shalt hear the desperate lamentations,
    Shalt see the ancient spirits disconsolate,
    Who cry out each one for the second death;

And thou shalt see those who contented are
    Within the fire, because they hope to come,
    Whene'er it may be, to the blessed people;

To whom, then, if thou wishest to ascend,
    A soul shall be for that than I more worthy;
    With her at my departure I will leave thee;

Because that Emperor, who reigns above,
    In that I was rebellious to his law,
    Wills that through me none come into his city.

He governs everywhere, and there he reigns;
    There is his city and his lofty throne;
    O happy he whom thereto he elects!"

And I to him: "Poet, I thee entreat,
    By that same God whom thou didst never know,
    So that I may escape this woe and worse,

Thou wouldst conduct me there where thou hast said,
    That I may see the portal of Saint Peter,
    And those thou makest so disconsolate."

Then he moved on, and I behind him followed.

## Canto II

Day was departing, and the embrowned air
    Released the animals that are on earth
    From their fatigues; and I the only one

Made myself ready to sustain the war,
    Both of the way and likewise of the woe,
    Which memory that errs not shall retrace.

O Muses, O high genius, now assist me!
    O memory, that didst write down what I saw,
    Here thy nobility shall be manifest!

And I began: "Poet, who guidest me,
    Regard my manhood, if it be sufficient,
    Ere to the arduous pass thou dost confide me.

Thou sayest, that of Silvius the parent,
    While yet corruptible, unto the world
    Immortal went, and was there bodily.

But if the adversary of all evil
    Was courteous, thinking of the high effect
    That issue would from him, and who, and what,

To men of intellect unmeet it seems not;
    For he was of great Rome, and of her empire
    In the empyreal heaven as father chosen;

The which and what, wishing to speak the truth,
    Were stablished as the holy place, wherein
    Sits the successor of the greatest Peter.

Upon this journey, whence thou givest him vaunt,
    Things did he hear, which the occasion were
    Both of his victory and the papal mantle.

Thither went afterwards the Chosen Vessel,
    To bring back comfort thence unto that Faith,
    Which of salvation's way is the beginning.

But I, why thither come, or who concedes it?
    I not Aeneas am, I am not Paul,
    Nor I, nor others, think me worthy of it.

Therefore, if I resign myself to come,
    I fear the coming may be ill-advised;
    Thou'rt wise, and knowest better than I speak."

And as he is, who unwills what he willed,
    And by new thoughts doth his intention change,
    So that from his design he quite withdraws,

Such I became, upon that dark hillside,
    Because, in thinking, I consumed the emprise,
    Which was so very prompt in the beginning.

"If I have well thy language understood,"
    Replied that shade of the Magnanimous,
    "Thy soul attainted is with cowardice,

Which many times a man encumbers so,
    It turns him back from honoured enterprise,
    As false sight doth a beast, when he is shy.

That thou mayst free thee from this apprehension,
    I'll tell thee why I came, and what I heard
    At the first moment when I grieved for thee.

Among those was I who are in suspense,
    And a fair, saintly Lady called to me
    In such wise, I besought her to command me.

Her eyes where shining brighter than the Star;
    And she began to say, gentle and low,
    With voice angelical, in her own language:

'O spirit courteous of Mantua,
    Of whom the fame still in the world endures,
    And shall endure, long-lasting as the world;

A friend of mine, and not the friend of fortune,
    Upon the desert slope is so impeded
    Upon his way, that he has turned through terror,

And may, I fear, already be so lost,
    That I too late have risen to his succour,
    From that which I have heard of him in Heaven.

Bestir thee now, and with thy speech ornate,
    And with what needful is for his release,
    Assist him so, that I may be consoled.

Beatrice am I, who do bid thee go;
    I come from there, where I would fain return;
    Love moved me, which compelleth me to speak.

When I shall be in presence of my Lord,
    Full often will I praise thee unto him.'
    Then paused she, and thereafter I began:

'O Lady of virtue, thou alone through whom
    The human race exceedeth all contained
    Within the heaven that has the lesser circles,

So grateful unto me is thy commandment,
    To obey, if 'twere already done, were late;
    No farther need'st thou ope to me thy wish.

But the cause tell me why thou dost not shun
    The here descending down into this centre,
    From the vast place thou burnest to return to.'

'Since thou wouldst fain so inwardly discern,
    Briefly will I relate,' she answered me,
    'Why I am not afraid to enter here.

Of those things only should one be afraid
    Which have the power of doing others harm;
    Of the rest, no; because they are not fearful.

God in his mercy such created me
    That misery of yours attains me not,
    Nor any flame assails me of this burning.

A gentle Lady is in Heaven, who grieves
    At this impediment, to which I send thee,
    So that stern judgment there above is broken.

In her entreaty she besought Lucia,
    And said, "Thy faithful one now stands in need
    Of thee, and unto thee I recommend him."

Lucia, foe of all that cruel is,
    Hastened away, and came unto the place
    Where I was sitting with the ancient Rachel.

"Beatrice" said she, "the true praise of God,
    Why succourest thou not him, who loved thee so,
    For thee he issued from the vulgar herd?

Dost thou not hear the pity of his plaint?
    Dost thou not see the death that combats him
    Beside that flood, where ocean has no vaunt?"

Never were persons in the world so swift
    To work their weal and to escape their woe,
    As I, after such words as these were uttered,

Came hither downward from my blessed seat,
    Confiding in thy dignified discourse,
    Which honours thee, and those who've listened to it.'

After she thus had spoken unto me,
    Weeping, her shining eyes she turned away;
    Whereby she made me swifter in my coming;

And unto thee I came, as she desired;
    I have delivered thee from that wild beast,
    Which barred the beautiful mountain's short ascent.

What is it, then? Why, why dost thou delay?
    Why is such baseness bedded in thy heart?
    Daring and hardihood why hast thou not,

Seeing that three such Ladies benedight
    Are caring for thee in the court of Heaven,
    And so much good my speech doth promise thee?"

Even as the flowerets, by nocturnal chill,
   Bowed down and closed, when the sun whitens them,
   Uplift themselves all open on their stems;

Such I became with my exhausted strength,
   And such good courage to my heart there coursed,
   That I began, like an intrepid person:

"O she compassionate, who succoured me,
   And courteous thou, who hast obeyed so soon
   The words of truth which she addressed to thee!

Thou hast my heart so with desire disposed
   To the adventure, with these words of thine,
   That to my first intent I have returned.

Now go, for one sole will is in us both,
   Thou Leader, and thou Lord, and Master thou."
   Thus said I to him; and when he had moved,

I entered on the deep and savage way.

## Canto III

"Through me the way into the suffering city,
   Through me the way to the eternal pain,
   Through me the way that runs among the lost.

Justice urged on my high artificer;
   My maker was divine authority,
   The highest wisdom, and the primal love.

Before me nothing but eternal things were made,
   And I endure eternally.
   Abandon every hope, ye who enter here."

These words in sombre colour I beheld
   Written upon the summit of a gate;
   Whence I: "Their sense is, Master, hard to me!"

177

And he to me, as one experienced:
    "Here all suspicion needs must be abandoned,
    All cowardice must needs be here extinct.

We to the place have come, where I have told thee
    Thou shalt behold the people dolorous
    Who have foregone the good of intellect."

And after he had laid his hand on mine
    With joyful mien, whence I was comforted,
    He led me in among the secret things.

There sighs, complaints, and ululations loud
    Resounded through the air without a star,
    Whence I, at the beginning, wept thereat.

Languages diverse, horrible dialects,
    Accents of anger, words of agony,
    And voices high and hoarse, with sound of hands,

Made up a tumult that goes whirling on
    For ever in that air for ever black,
    Even as the sand doth, when the whirlwind breathes.

And I, who had my head with horror bound,
    Said: "Master, what is this which now I hear?
    What folk is this, which seems by pain so vanquished?"

And he to me: "This miserable mode
    Maintain the melancholy souls of those
    Who lived withouten infamy or praise.

Commingled are they with that caitiff choir
    Of Angels, who have not rebellious been,
    Nor faithful were to God, but were for self.

The heavens expelled them, not to be less fair;
    Nor them the nethermore abyss receives,
    For glory none the damned would have from them."

And I: "O Master, what so grievous is
    To these, that maketh them lament so sore?"
    He answered: "I will tell thee very briefly.

These have no longer any hope of death;
    And this blind life of theirs is so debased,
    They envious are of every other fate.

No fame of them the world permits to be;
    Misericord and Justice both disdain them.
    Let us not speak of them, but look, and pass."

And I, who looked again, beheld a banner,
    Which, whirling round, ran on so rapidly,
    That of all pause it seemed to me indignant;

And after it there came so long a train
    Of people, that I ne'er would have believed
    That ever Death so many had undone.

When some among them I had recognised,
    I looked, and I beheld the shade of him
    Who made through cowardice the great refusal.

Forthwith I comprehended, and was certain,
    That this the sect was of the caitiff wretches
    Hateful to God and to his enemies.

These miscreants, who never were alive,
    Were naked, and were stung exceedingly
    By gadflies and by hornets that were there.

These did their faces irrigate with blood,
    Which, with their tears commingled, at their feet
    By the disgusting worms was gathered up.

And when to gazing farther I betook me.
    People I saw on a great river's bank;
    Whence said I: "Master, now vouchsafe to me,

That I may know who these are, and what law
    Makes them appear so ready to pass over,
    As I discern athwart the dusky light."

And he to me: "These things shall all be known
    To thee, as soon as we our footsteps stay
    Upon the dismal shore of Acheron."

Then with mine eyes ashamed and downward cast,
    Fearing my words might irksome be to him,
    From speech refrained I till we reached the river.

And lo! towards us coming in a boat
    An old man, hoary with the hair of eld,
    Crying: "Woe unto you, ye souls depraved!

Hope nevermore to look upon the heavens;
    I come to lead you to the other shore,
    To the eternal shades in heat and frost.

And thou, that yonder standest, living soul,
    Withdraw thee from these people, who are dead!"
    But when he saw that I did not withdraw,

He said: "By other ways, by other ports
    Thou to the shore shalt come, not here, for passage;
    A lighter vessel needs must carry thee."

And unto him the Guide: "Vex thee not, Charon;
    It is so willed there where is power to do
    That which is willed; and farther question not."

Thereat were quieted the fleecy cheeks
    Of him the ferryman of the livid fen,
    Who round about his eyes had wheels of flame.

But all those souls who weary were and naked
    Their colour changed and gnashed their teeth together,
    As soon as they had heard those cruel words.

God they blasphemed and their progenitors,
    The human race, the place, the time, the seed
    Of their engendering and of their birth!

Thereafter all together they drew back,
    Bitterly weeping, to the accursed shore,
    Which waiteth every man who fears not God.

Charon the demon, with the eyes of glede,
    Beckoning to them, collects them all together,
    Beats with his oar whoever lags behind.

As in the autumn-time the leaves fall off,
  First one and then another, till the branch
  Unto the earth surrenders all its spoils;

In similar wise the evil seed of Adam
  Throw themselves from that margin one by one,
  At signals, as a bird unto its lure.

So they depart across the dusky wave,
  And ere upon the other side they land,
  Again on this side a new troop assembles.

"My son," the courteous Master said to me,
  "All those who perish in the wrath of God
  Here meet together out of every land;

And ready are they to pass o'er the river,
  Because celestial Justice spurs them on,
  So that their fear is turned into desire.

This way there never passes a good soul;
  And hence if Charon doth complain of thee,
  Well mayst thou know now what his speech imports."

This being finished, all the dusk champaign
  Trembled so violently, that of that terror
  The recollection bathes me still with sweat.

The land of tears gave forth a blast of wind,
  And fulminated a vermilion light,
  Which overmastered in me every sense,

And as a man whom sleep hath seized I fell.

. . .

## Canto V

Thus I descended out of the first circle
  Down to the second, that less space begirds,
  And so much greater dole, that goads to wailing.

There standeth Minos horribly, and snarls;
    Examines the transgressions at the entrance;
    Judges, and sends according as he girds him.

I say, that when the spirit evil-born
    Cometh before him, wholly it confesses;
    And this discriminator of transgressions

Seeth what place in Hell is meet for it;
    Girds himself with his tail as many times
    As grades he wishes it should be thrust down.

Always before him many of them stand;
    They go by turns each one unto the judgment;
    They speak, and hear, and then are downward hurled.

"O thou, that to this dolorous hostelry
    Comest," said Minos to me, when he saw me,
    Leaving the practice of so great an office,

"Look how thou enterest, and in whom thou trustest;
    Let not the portal's amplitude deceive thee."
    And unto him my Guide: "Why criest thou too?

Do not impede his journey fate-ordained;
    It is so willed there where is power to do
    That which is willed; and ask no further question."

And now begin the dolesome notes to grow
    Audible unto me; now am I come
    There where much lamentation strikes upon me.

I came into a place mute of all light,
    Which bellows as the sea does in a tempest,
    If by opposing winds 't is combated.

The infernal hurricane that never rests
    Hurtles the spirits onward in its rapine;
    Whirling them round, and smiting, it molests them.

When they arrive before the precipice,
    There are the shrieks, the plaints, and the laments,
    There they blaspheme the puissance divine.

I understood that unto such a torment
  The carnal malefactors were condemned,
  Who reason subjugate to appetite.

And as the wings of starlings bear them on
  In the cold season in large band and full,
  So doth that blast the spirits maledict;

It hither, thither, downward, upward, drives them;
  No hope doth comfort them for evermore,
  Not of repose, but even of lesser pain.

And as the cranes go chanting forth their lays,
  Making in air a long line of themselves,
  So saw I coming, uttering lamentations,

Shadows borne onward by the aforesaid stress.
  Whereupon said I: "Master, who are those
  People, whom the black air so castigates?"

"The first of those, of whom intelligence
  Thou fain wouldst have," then said he unto me,
  "The empress was of many languages.

To sensual vices she was so abandoned,
  That lustful she made licit in her law,
  To remove the blame to which she had been led.

She is Semiramis, of whom we read
  That she succeeded Ninus, and was his spouse;
  She held the land which now the Sultan rules.

The next is she who killed herself for love,
  And broke faith with the ashes of Sichaeus;
  Then Cleopatra the voluptuous."

Helen I saw, for whom so many ruthless
  Seasons revolved; and saw the great Achilles,
  Who at the last hour combated with Love.

Paris I saw, Tristan; and more than a thousand
  Shades did he name and point out with his finger,
  Whom Love had separated from our life.

After that I had listened to my Teacher,
  Naming the dames of eld and cavaliers,
  Pity prevailed, and I was nigh bewildered.

And I began: "O Poet, willingly
  Speak would I to those two, who go together,
  And seem upon the wind to be so light."

And, he to me: "Thou'lt mark, when they shall be
  Nearer to us; and then do thou implore them
  By love which leadeth them, and they will come."

Soon as the wind in our direction sways them,
  My voice uplift I: "O ye weary souls!
  Come speak to us, if no one interdicts it."

As turtle-doves, called onward by desire,
  With open and steady wings to the sweet nest
  Fly through the air by their volition borne,

So came they from the band where Dido is,
  Approaching us athwart the air malign,
  So strong was the affectionate appeal.

"O living creature gracious and benignant,
  Who visiting goest through the purple air
  Us, who have stained the world incarnadine,

If were the King of the Universe our friend,
  We would pray unto him to give thee peace,
  Since thou hast pity on our woe perverse.

Of what it pleases thee to hear and speak,
  That will we hear, and we will speak to you,
  While silent is the wind, as it is now.

Sitteth the city, wherein I was born,
  Upon the sea-shore where the Po descends
  To rest in peace with all his retinue.

Love, that on gentle heart doth swiftly seize,
  Seized this man for the person beautiful
  That was ta'en from me, and still the mode offends me.

Love, that exempts no one beloved from loving,
    Seized me with pleasure of this man so strongly,
    That, as thou seest, it doth not yet desert me;

Love has conducted us unto one death;
    Caina waiteth him who quenched our life!"
    These words were borne along from them to us.

As soon as I had heard those souls tormented,
    I bowed my face, and so long held it down
    Until the Poet said to me: "What thinkest?"

When I made answer, I began: "Alas!
    How many pleasant thoughts, how much desire,
    Conducted these unto the dolorous pass!"

Then unto them I turned me, and I spake,
    And I began: "Thine agonies, Francesca,
    Sad and compassionate to weeping make me.

But tell me, at the time of those sweet sighs,
    By what and in what manner Love conceded,
    That you should know your dubious desires?"

And she to me: "There is no greater sorrow
    Than to be mindful of the happy time
    In misery, and that thy Teacher knows.

But, if to recognise the earliest root
    Of love in us thou hast so great desire,
    I will do even as he who weeps and speaks.

One day we reading were for our delight
    Of Launcelot, how Love did him enthral.
    Alone we were and without any fear.

Full many a time our eyes together drew
    That reading, and drove the colour from our faces;
    But one point only was it that o'ercame us.

When as we read of the much-longed-for smile
    Being by such a noble lover kissed,
    This one, who ne'er from me shall be divided,

Kissed me upon the mouth all palpitating.
    Galeotto was the book and he who wrote it.
    That day no farther did we read therein."

And all the while one spirit uttered this,
    The other one did weep so, that, for pity,
    I swooned away as if I had been dying,

And fell, even as a dead body falls.

*Translated by Henry Wadsworth Longfellow, 1867*


## ON ANGUISH AND BEAUTY

### Anthony Esolen


**H**ow does one begin to praise the greatness of Dante's *Divine Comedy*?

It is as wildly various as the flora and fauna that sport across the capitals of an illuminated manuscript.

It is as theologically ordered and precise, in its own way, as the *Summa Theologica* of Saint Thomas Aquinas, Dante's leading light in matters of the intellect, the virtues, the church, and the nature of God.

It is as delightful as a romance with Lancelot and Guenevere, as terrifying as the apocalypse of John, and as wondrous as the seraphic vision that came to Saint Francis and marked him with the marks of Christ.

What moment in all of literature can surpass the profound anguish of an Ugolino who looks into the faces of his children, all prisoners on his account, and all, with him, about to starve to death, and who says, in a few stunning words, "I did not weep, I had so turned to stone"?

But then, what moment can surpass the wonder of Piccarda, who has become more human precisely because she has immersed herself in the divine Love? "In His will is our peace," says she.

If we say it's hard to find a single human moment, or a single one of the wonders of God as made manifest to man, that does not find its place in Dante's poem, we say no more than the truth, and yet we still fail to grasp the excellence here. For it's one thing to find these moments—to find, in the excerpt above, the grim blasphemy of sinners who wish, far more than that they had never been born, that their parents and the whole human race and the time and place of their begetting had never existed; a universal curse. Or to find the paradox that love, that sweetest of desires, had brought disaster and condemnation—as Francesca the gentle-spoken adulteress says, "Love led us to one death."

What astonishes more than all is to find all these things ordered in an artistic, philosophical, and theological whole, so that Virgil's encounter with Beatrice is meant to anticipate Dante's encounter with Francesca, and then with other lovers and indeed other writers of love poetry in the *Purgatory*, before the pilgrim poet finally meets Beatrice herself; she in turn leads him to Paradise, where he will enjoy at the last a vision of "the Love that moves the sun and the other stars."

Such an achievement in poetry had no precedent.

Dante could have done as Milton would do, centuries later, and adapt the meter, narrative techniques, and epic apparatus of Virgil's *Aeneid* to his own language. He did not.

He could have written in the style of the romancers of his own day, like the prodigious and remarkably original Chrétien de Troyes. He did not.

The *Divine Comedy* is of its own kind, even as it gathers to itself all the Christian and classical learning Dante had inherited. It's as if a man should study all the paintings of the dramatic Caravaggio and the brooding Rembrandt, and then, inspired by them, compose the *Saint Matthew Passion*—when, to boot, nothing of that sort had ever been composed before, and nothing quite of that sort would ever be composed again.

---

All of this is to insist that when we read Dante, even in the few cantos above, we bring to our reading more than the habits we have acquired in reading other poets. We must read as composers, as sculptors, as architects, as theologians.

Take, for example, the appearance of Beatrice to Virgil. We understand the necessity of the conversation. Dante the pilgrim is having second thoughts about entering hell—naturally. But instead of giving him an eminently practical reason for trusting him, as, for instance, that if Dante remains in the dark wilderness he will be lost for certain, but if he accompanies Virgil he at least has a chance, the Roman poet becomes for him and for us a courtly lover, swept into obedient service by a vision of a beautiful woman such as had no counterpart in anything he had ever written.

Now, if we conclude that this is just a fine quirk of poetic adaptation, we miss the deep humanity and theology both. Dante expects us to think—that is the object of reason—and to begin to see—that is the object of the intellect. This is, after all, the same Virgil who has just revealed to Dante that he will never enjoy the sight of God, and who has burst into an exclamation of longing and hopelessness: "Happy the man He chooses for His house!" *That* is the man who now tells Dante he has seen Beatrice, and, even before she gives her name, indeed before she speaks a word, "begged her for the grace of a command." The ancient pagan is a man like all men, made to be fulfilled only by the vision of holiness itself, the vision of God.

I hope, then, dear reader, that you will not approach this poem as if it were a mere artistic artifact. Such would be to sin against any work of truly great art, but it would be all the more disordered in the case of Dante. That is because Dante himself summons us to a deeper engagement with the world of man and the being and goodness of God.

If we were present on that dread day, under the blank staring of the Mediterranean sun, when, amid those who loved Him and those who plotted His destruction, Jesus raised Lazarus from the dead, would we confine our thoughts to the picturesque scene, or to the eloquence of the Master? No, *we would long to look upon the reality itself.* The only human thing to do, the only rational thing, would be to press beyond the human, in love. We would—or at least we should—take upon ourselves the ultimate task of our poet: to seek the face of God.

## CHAPTER NINE

# GEOFFREY CHAUCER

Middle Ages (1343–1400)

**R**eading a book that caused its author pangs of conscience as he died, and some measure of repentance for what he wrote, is an interesting project for a Christian. It reminds us that a work of genius does not justify all the contents; beauty of expression does not negate ethical ugliness.

Still, Chaucer stands at the beginning of literary English and firmly in the Christian faith. My grandfather died able to quote, in original rhyme, the start of *Canterbury Tales*, because the West Virginia teachers in his one-room schoolhouse recognized that Chaucer was a creator of their language.

Chaucer, like Homer, writes about a journey, but as a Christian he has a different goal. Homer wanted to go home, but Chaucer's pilgrims want a piece of man's true home: paradise. The pilgrim is heading for a piece of heaven on earth, the shrine with its relics, but he must pass through the cities of man and through the wilderness.

Homer's hero, Odysseus, is a storyteller, and so are Chaucer's pilgrims. Homer's stories bring him glory, but the stories of the pilgrims entertain and educate men on the Way. Chaucer is a pioneer of edutainment, and no story in *Canterbury Tales* is so bawdy as to lack a moral—even if a mistaken one.

Chaucer's pilgrims know the tension between what is and what should be. The pilgrims seek the prayers of Thomas à Beckett, the man who defied an English king in favor of his God. The pilgrims themselves need the prayers of Thomas, because their stories show that the world is still so much a part of them. Chaucer presents them, and his own culture, as it is and not as piety wishes it were.

He does not, thereby, justify folly or evil, but he does recognize that Christendom has not banished it with pagan idols. Against writers who would create unreal goody-goodies like Elsie Dinsmore or Rebecca of Sunnybrook Farm, Chaucer presents recognizable characters and comments on them. They're on the Way, not at the end of it!

Literary prudery is impossible for a Christian who must accept any book as violent as Judges or as erotic as the Song of Songs. Chaucer pushes the boundaries, and even he thought some of his tales "tend towards sin." He chose to be readable, but he may have become risible and risqué, using his Christian liberty to become a bit of a literary libertine.

> *"Here ends the book of the Tales of Canterbury,*
> *compiled by Geoffrey Chaucer,*
> *of whose soul, Jesus Christ, have mercy. Amen."*

 FROM

# The Canterbury Tales

## "THE FRANKLIN'S TALE"

### The Prologue

"In faith, Squier, thou hast thee well acquit,
And gentilly; I praise well thy wit,"
Quoth the Franklin; "considering thy youthe

So feelingly thou speak'st, Sir, I aloue thee,
As to my doom, there is none that is here
Of eloquence that shall be thy peer,
If that thou live; God give thee goode chance,
And in virtue send thee continuance,
For of thy speaking I have great dainty.
I have a son, and, by the Trinity;
It were me lever than twenty pound worth land,
Though it right now were fallen in my hand,
He were a man of such discretion
As that ye be: fy on possession,
But if a man be virtuous withal.
I have my sone snibbed and yet shall,
For he to virtue listeth not t'intend,
But for to play at dice, and to dispend,
And lose all that he hath, is his usage;
And he had lever talke with a page,
Than to commune with any gentle wight,
There he might learen gentilless aright."

"Straw for your gentillesse!" quoth our Host.
"What? Frankelin, pardie, Sir, well thou wost
That each of you must tellen at the least
A tale or two, or breake his behest."
"That know I well, Sir," quoth the Frankelin;
"I pray you have me not in disdain,
Though I to this man speak a word or two."
"Tell on thy tale, withoute wordes mo'."
"Gladly, Sir Host," quoth he, "I will obey
Unto your will; now hearken what I say;
I will you not contrary in no wise,
As far as that my wittes may suffice.
I pray to God that it may please you,
Then wot I well that it is good enow.

"These olde gentle Bretons, in their days,
Of divers aventures made lays,
Rhymeden in their firste Breton tongue;
Which layes with their instruments they sung,
Or elles reade them for their pleasance;
And one of them have I in remembrance,

Which I shall say with good will as I can.
But, Sirs, because I am a borel man,
At my beginning first I you beseech
Have me excused of my rude speech.
I learned never rhetoric, certain;
Thing that I speak, it must be bare and plain.
I slept never on the mount of Parnasso,
Nor learned Marcus Tullius Cicero.
Coloures know I none, withoute dread,
But such colours as growen in the mead,
Or elles such as men dye with or paint;
Colours of rhetoric be to me quaint;
My spirit feeleth not of such mattere.
But, if you list, my tale shall ye hear."

## The Tale

In Armoric', that called is Bretagne,
There was a knight, that lov'd and did his pain
To serve a lady in his beste wise;
And many a labour, many a great emprise,
He for his lady wrought, ere she were won:
For she was one the fairest under sun,
And eke thereto come of so high kindred,
That well unnethes durst this knight for dread,
Tell her his woe, his pain, and his distress
But, at the last, she for his worthiness,
And namely for his meek obeisance,
Hath such a pity caught of his penance,
That privily she fell of his accord
To take him for her husband and her lord
(Of such lordship as men have o'er their wives);
And, for to lead the more in bliss their lives,
Of his free will he swore her as a knight,
That never in all his life he day nor night
Should take upon himself no mastery
Against her will, nor kithe her jealousy,
But her obey, and follow her will in all,
As any lover to his lady shall;
Save that the name of sovereignety

That would he have, for shame of his degree.
She thanked him, and with full great humbless
She saide; "Sir, since of your gentleness
Ye proffer me to have so large a reign,
Ne woulde God never betwixt us twain,
As in my guilt, were either war or strife:
Sir, I will be your humble true wife,
Have here my troth, till that my hearte brest."
Thus be they both in quiet and in rest.

For one thing, Sires, safely dare I say,
That friends ever each other must obey,
If they will longe hold in company.
Love will not be constrain'd by mastery.
When mast'ry comes, the god of love anon
Beateth his wings, and, farewell, he is gone.
Love is a thing as any spirit free.
Women of kind desire liberty,
And not to be constrained as a thrall,
And so do men, if soothly I say shall.
Look who that is most patient in love,
He is at his advantage all above.
Patience is a high virtue certain,
For it vanquisheth, as these clerkes sayn,
Thinges that rigour never should attain.
For every word men may not chide or plain.
Learne to suffer, or, so may I go,
Ye shall it learn whether ye will or no.
For in this world certain no wight there is,
That he not doth or saith sometimes amiss.
Ire, or sickness, or constellation,
Wine, woe, or changing of complexion,
Causeth full oft to do amiss or speaken:
On every wrong a man may not be wreaken.
After the time must be temperance
To every wight that can of governance.
And therefore hath this worthy wise knight
(To live in ease) sufferance her behight;
And she to him full wisly gan to swear
That never should there be default in her.
Here may men see a humble wife accord;

Thus hath she ta'en her servant and her lord,
Servant in love, and lord in marriage.
Then was he both in lordship and servage?
Servage? nay, but in lordship all above,
Since he had both his lady and his love:
His lady certes, and his wife also,
The which that law of love accordeth to.
And when he was in this prosperity,
Home with his wife he went to his country,
Not far from Penmark, where his dwelling was,
And there he liv'd in bliss and in solace.
Who coulde tell, but he had wedded be,
The joy, the ease, and the prosperity,
That is betwixt a husband and his wife?
A year and more lasted this blissful life,
Till that this knight, of whom I spake thus,
That of Cairrud was call'd Arviragus,
Shope him to go and dwell a year or twain
In Engleland, that call'd was eke Britain,
To seek in armes worship and honour
(For all his lust he set in such labour);
And dwelled there two years; the book saith thus.

Now will I stint of this Arviragus,
And speak I will of Dorigen his wife,
That lov'd her husband as her hearte's life.
For his absence weepeth she and siketh,
As do these noble wives when them liketh;
She mourneth, waketh, waileth, fasteth, plaineth;
Desire of his presence her so distraineth,
That all this wide world she set at nought.
Her friendes, which that knew her heavy thought,
Comforte her in all that ever they may;
They preache her, they tell her night and day,
That causeless she slays herself, alas!
And every comfort possible in this case
They do to her, with all their business,
And all to make her leave her heaviness.
By process, as ye knowen every one,
Men may so longe graven in a stone,
Till some figure therein imprinted be:

194

So long have they comforted her, till she
Received hath, by hope and by reason,
Th' imprinting of their consolation,
Through which her greate sorrow gan assuage;
She may not always duren in such rage.
And eke Arviragus, in all this care,
Hath sent his letters home of his welfare,
And that he will come hastily again,
Or elles had this sorrow her hearty-slain.
Her friendes saw her sorrow gin to slake,
And prayed her on knees for Godde's sake
To come and roamen in their company,
Away to drive her darke fantasy;
And finally she granted that request,
For well she saw that it was for the best.

Now stood her castle faste by the sea,
And often with her friendes walked she,
Her to disport upon the bank on high,
There as many a ship and barge sigh,
Sailing their courses, where them list to go.
But then was that a parcel of her woe,
For to herself full oft, "Alas!" said she,
"Is there no ship, of so many as I see,
Will bringe home my lord? then were my heart
All warish'd of this bitter paine's smart."
Another time would she sit and think,
And cast her eyen downward from the brink;
But when she saw the grisly rockes blake,
For very fear so would her hearte quake,
That on her feet she might her not sustene
Then would she sit adown upon the green,
And piteously into the sea behold,
And say right thus, with careful sikes cold:
"Eternal God! that through thy purveyance
Leadest this world by certain governance,
In idle, as men say, ye nothing make;
But, Lord, these grisly fiendly rockes blake,
That seem rather a foul confusion
Of work, than any fair creation
Of such a perfect wise God and stable,

195

Why have ye wrought this work unreasonable?
For by this work, north, south, or west, or east,
There is not foster'd man, nor bird, nor beast:
It doth no good, to my wit, but annoyeth.
See ye not, Lord, how mankind it destroyeth?
A hundred thousand bodies of mankind
Have rockes slain, all be they not in mind;
Which mankind is so fair part of thy work,
Thou madest it like to thine owen mark.
Then seemed it ye had a great cherte
Toward mankind; but how then may it be
That ye such meanes make it to destroy?
Which meanes do no good, but ever annoy.
I wot well, clerkes will say as them lest,
By arguments, that all is for the best,
Although I can the causes not y-know;
But thilke God that made the wind to blow,
As keep my lord, this is my conclusion:
To clerks leave I all disputation:
But would to God that all these rockes blake
Were sunken into helle for his sake
These rockes slay mine hearte for the fear."
Thus would she say, with many a piteous tear.

Her friendes saw that it was no disport
To roame by the sea, but discomfort,
And shope them for to playe somewhere else.
They leade her by rivers and by wells,
And eke in other places delectables;
They dancen, and they play at chess and tables.
So on a day, right in the morning-tide,
Unto a garden that was there beside,
In which that they had made their ordinance
Of victual, and of other purveyance,
They go and play them all the longe day:
And this was on the sixth morrow of May,
Which May had painted with his softe showers
This garden full of leaves and of flowers:
And craft of manne's hand so curiously
Arrayed had this garden truely,
That never was there garden of such price,

But if it were the very Paradise.
Th'odour of flowers, and the freshe sight,
Would have maked any hearte light
That e'er was born, but if too great sickness
Or too great sorrow held it in distress;
So full it was of beauty and pleasance.
And after dinner they began to dance
And sing also, save Dorigen alone
Who made alway her complaint and her moan,
For she saw not him on the dance go
That was her husband, and her love also;
But natheless she must a time abide
And with good hope let her sorrow slide.

Upon this dance, amonge other men,
Danced a squier before Dorigen
That fresher was, and jollier of array
As to my doom, than is the month of May.
He sang and danced, passing any man,
That is or was since that the world began;
Therewith he was, if men should him descrive,
One of the beste faring men alive,
Young, strong, and virtuous, and rich, and wise,
And well beloved, and holden in great price.
And, shortly if the sooth I telle shall,
Unweeting of this Dorigen at all,
This lusty squier, servant to Venus,
Which that y-called was Aurelius,
Had lov'd her best of any creature
Two year and more, as was his aventure;
But never durst he tell her his grievance;
Withoute cup he drank all his penance.
He was despaired, nothing durst he say,
Save in his songes somewhat would he wray
His woe, as in a general complaining;
He said, he lov'd, and was belov'd nothing.
Of suche matter made he many lays,
Songes, complaintes, roundels, virelays
How that he durste not his sorrow tell,
But languished, as doth a Fury in hell;
And die he must, he said, as did Echo

For Narcissus, that durst not tell her woe.
In other manner than ye hear me say,
He durste not to her his woe bewray,
Save that paraventure sometimes at dances,
Where younge folke keep their observances,
It may well be he looked on her face
In such a wise, as man that asketh grace,
But nothing wiste she of his intent.
Nath'less it happen'd, ere they thennes went,
Because that he was her neighebour,
And was a man of worship and honour,
And she had knowen him of time yore,
They fell in speech, and forth aye more and more
Unto his purpose drew Aurelius;
And when he saw his time, he saide thus:
"Madam," quoth he, "by God that this world made,
So that I wist it might your hearte glade,
I would, that day that your Arviragus
Went over sea, that I, Aurelius,
Had gone where I should never come again;
For well I wot my service is in vain.
My guerdon is but bursting of mine heart.
Madame, rue upon my paine's smart,
For with a word ye may me slay or save.
Here at your feet God would that I were grave.
I have now no leisure more to say:
Have mercy, sweet, or you will do me dey."

She gan to look upon Aurelius;
"Is this your will," quoth she, "and say ye thus?
Ne'er erst," quoth she, "I wiste what ye meant:
But now, Aurelius, I know your intent.
By thilke God that gave me soul and life,
Never shall I be an untrue wife
In word nor work, as far as I have wit;
I will be his to whom that I am knit;
Take this for final answer as of me."
But after that in play thus saide she.
"Aurelius," quoth she, "by high God above,
Yet will I grante you to be your love
(Since I you see so piteously complain);

Looke, what day that endelong Bretagne
Ye remove all the rockes, stone by stone,
That they not lette ship nor boat to gon,
I say, when ye have made this coast so clean
Of rockes, that there is no stone seen,
Then will I love you best of any man;
Have here my troth, in all that ever I can;
For well I wot that it shall ne'er betide.
Let such folly out of your hearte glide.
What dainty should a man have in his life
For to go love another manne's wife,
That hath her body when that ever him liketh?"
Aurelius full often sore siketh;
"Is there none other grace in you?" quoth he,
"No, by that Lord," quoth she, "that maked me."
Woe was Aurelius when that he this heard,
And with a sorrowful heart he thus answer'd.
"Madame," quoth he, "this were an impossible.
Then must I die of sudden death horrible."
And with that word he turned him anon.

Then came her other friends many a one,
And in the alleys roamed up and down,
And nothing wist of this conclusion,
But suddenly began to revel new,
Till that the brighte sun had lost his hue,
For th' horizon had reft the sun his light
(This is as much to say as it was night);
And home they go in mirth and in solace;
Save only wretch'd Aurelius, alas
He to his house is gone with sorrowful heart.
He said, he may not from his death astart.
Him seemed, that he felt his hearte cold.
Up to the heav'n his handes gan he hold,
And on his knees bare he set him down.
And in his raving said his orisoun.
For very woe out of his wit he braid;
He wist not what he spake, but thus he said;
With piteous heart his plaint hath he begun
Unto the gods, and first unto the Sun.
He said; "Apollo God and governour

Of every plante, herbe, tree, and flower,
That giv'st, after thy declination,
To each of them his time and his season,
As thine herberow changeth low and high;
Lord Phoebus: cast thy merciable eye
On wretched Aurelius, which that am but lorn.
Lo, lord, my lady hath my death y-sworn,
Withoute guilt, but thy benignity
Upon my deadly heart have some pity.
For well I wot, Lord Phoebus, if you lest,
Ye may me helpe, save my lady, best.
Now vouchsafe, that I may you devise
How that I may be holp, and in what wise.
Your blissful sister, Lucina the sheen,
That of the sea is chief goddess and queen,—
Though Neptunus have deity in the sea,
Yet emperess above him is she;—
Ye know well, lord, that, right as her desire
Is to be quick'd and lighted of your fire,
For which she followeth you full busily,
Right so the sea desireth naturally
To follow her, as she that is goddess
Both in the sea and rivers more and less.
Wherefore, Lord Phoebus, this is my request,
Do this miracle, or do mine hearte brest;
That flow, next at this opposition,
Which in the sign shall be of the Lion,
As praye her so great a flood to bring,
That five fathom at least it overspring
The highest rock in Armoric Bretagne,
And let this flood endure yeares twain:
Then certes to my lady may I say,
'Holde your hest,' the rockes be away.
Lord Phoebus, this miracle do for me,
Pray her she go no faster course than ye;
I say this, pray your sister that she go
No faster course than ye these yeares two:
Then shall she be even at full alway,
And spring-flood laste bothe night and day.
And but she vouchesafe in such mannere
To grante me my sov'reign lady dear,

Pray her to sink every rock adown
Into her owen darke regioun
Under the ground, where Pluto dwelleth in
Or nevermore shall I my lady win.
Thy temple in Delphos will I barefoot seek.
Lord Phoebus! see the teares on my cheek
And on my pain have some compassioun."
And with that word in sorrow he fell down,
And longe time he lay forth in a trance.
His brother, which that knew of his penance,
Up caught him, and to bed he hath him brought,.
Despaired in this torment and this thought
Let I this woeful creature lie;
Choose he for me whe'er he will live or die.

Arviragus with health and great honour
(As he that was of chivalry the flow'r)
Is come home, and other worthy men.
Oh, blissful art thou now, thou Dorigen!
Thou hast thy lusty husband in thine arms,
The freshe knight, the worthy man of arms,
That loveth thee as his own hearte's life:
Nothing list him to be imaginatif
If any wight had spoke, while he was out,
To her of love; he had of that no doubt;
He not intended to no such mattere,
But danced, jousted, and made merry cheer.
And thus in joy and bliss I let them dwell,
And of the sick Aurelius will I tell
In languor and in torment furious
Two year and more lay wretch'd Aurelius,
Ere any foot on earth he mighte gon;
Nor comfort in this time had he none,
Save of his brother, which that was a clerk.
He knew of all this woe and all this work;
For to none other creature certain
Of this matter he durst no worde sayn;
Under his breast he bare it more secree
Than e'er did Pamphilus for Galatee.
His breast was whole withoute for to seen,
But in his heart aye was the arrow keen,

And well ye know that of a sursanure
In surgery is perilous the cure,
But men might touch the arrow or come thereby.
His brother wept and wailed privily,
Till at the last him fell in remembrance,
That while he was at Orleans in France,—
As younge clerkes, that be likerous—
To readen artes that be curious,
Seeken in every halk and every hern
Particular sciences for to learn,—
He him remember'd, that upon a day
At Orleans in study a book he say
Of magic natural, which his fellaw,
That was that time a bachelor of law
All were he there to learn another craft,
Had privily upon his desk y-laft;
Which book spake much of operations
Touching the eight and-twenty mansions
That longe to the Moon, and such folly
As in our dayes is not worth a fly;
For holy church's faith, in our believe,
Us suff'reth none illusion to grieve.
And when this book was in his remembrance
Anon for joy his heart began to dance,
And to himself he saide privily;
"My brother shall be warish'd hastily
For I am sicker that there be sciences,
By which men make divers apparences,
Such as these subtle tregetoures play.
For oft at feaste's have I well heard say,
That tregetours, within a halle large,
Have made come in a water and a barge,
And in the halle rowen up and down.
Sometimes hath seemed come a grim lioun,
And sometimes flowers spring as in a mead;
Sometimes a vine, and grapes white and red;
Sometimes a castle all of lime and stone;
And, when them liked, voided it anon:
Thus seemed it to every manne's sight.
Now then conclude I thus; if that I might
At Orleans some olde fellow find,

That hath these Moone's mansions in mind,
Or other magic natural above.
He should well make my brother have his love.
For with an appearance a clerk may make,
To manne's sight, that all the rockes blake
Of Bretagne were voided every one,
And shippes by the brinke come and gon,
And in such form endure a day or two;
Then were my brother warish'd of his woe,
Then must she needes holde her behest,
Or elles he shall shame her at the least."
Why should I make a longer tale of this?
Unto his brother's bed he comen is,
And such comfort he gave him, for to gon
To Orleans, that he upstart anon,
And on his way forth-ward then is he fare,
In hope for to be lissed of his care.

When they were come almost to that city,
But if it were a two furlong or three,
A young clerk roaming by himself they met,
Which that in Latin thriftily them gret.
And after that he said a wondrous thing;
"I know," quoth he, "the cause of your coming;"
Aud ere they farther any foote went,
He told them all that was in their intent.
The Breton clerk him asked of fellaws
The which he hadde known in olde daws,
And he answer'd him that they deade were,
For which he wept full often many a tear.
Down off his horse Aurelius light anon,
And forth with this magician is be gone
Home to his house, and made him well at ease;
Them lacked no vitail that might them please.
So well-array'd a house as there was one,
Aurelius in his life saw never none.
He shewed him, ere they went to suppere,
Forestes, parkes, full of wilde deer.
There saw he hartes with their hornes high,
The greatest that were ever seen with eye.
He saw of them an hundred slain with hounds,

And some with arrows bleed of bitter wounds.
He saw, when voided were the wilde deer,
These falconers upon a fair rivere,
That with their hawkes have the heron slain.
Then saw he knightes jousting in a plain.
And after this he did him such pleasance,
That he him shew'd his lady on a dance,
In which himselfe danced, as him thought.
And when this master, that this magic wrought,
Saw it was time, he clapp'd his handes two,
And farewell, all the revel is y-go.
And yet remov'd they never out of the house,
While they saw all the sightes marvelous;
But in his study, where his bookes be,
They satte still, and no wight but they three.
To him this master called his squier,

And said him thus, "May we go to supper?
Almost an hour it is, I undertake,
Since I you bade our supper for to make,
When that these worthy men wente with me
Into my study, where my bookes be."
"Sir," quoth this squier, "when it liketh you.
It is all ready, though ye will right now."
"Go we then sup," quoth he, "as for the best;
These amorous folk some time must have rest."
At after supper fell they in treaty
What summe should this master's guerdon be,
To remove all the rockes of Bretagne,
And eke from Gironde to the mouth of Seine.
He made it strange, and swore, so God him save,
Less than a thousand pound he would not have,
Nor gladly for that sum he would not gon.
Aurelius with blissful heart anon
Answered thus; "Fie on a thousand pound!
This wide world, which that men say is round,
I would it give, if I were lord of it.
This bargain is full-driv'n, for we be knit;
Ye shall be payed truly by my troth.
But looke, for no negligence or sloth,
Ye tarry us here no longer than to-morrow."

"Nay," quoth the clerk, "have here my faith to borrow."
To bed is gone Aurelius when him lest,
And well-nigh all that night he had his rest,
What for his labour, and his hope of bliss,
His woeful heart of penance had a liss.

Upon the morrow, when that it was day,
Unto Bretagne they took the righte way,
Aurelius and this magician beside,
And be descended where they would abide:
And this was, as the bookes me remember,
The colde frosty season of December.
Phoebus wax'd old, and hued like latoun,
That in his hote declinatioun
Shone as the burned gold, with streames bright;
But now in Capricorn adown he light,
Where as he shone full pale, I dare well sayn.
The bitter frostes, with the sleet and rain,
Destroyed have the green in every yard.
Janus sits by the fire with double beard,
And drinketh of his bugle horn the wine:
Before him stands the brawn of tusked swine
And "nowel" crieth every lusty man
Aurelius, in all that ev'r he can,
Did to his master cheer and reverence,
And prayed him to do his diligence
To bringe him out of his paines smart,
Or with a sword that he would slit his heart.
This subtle clerk such ruth had on this man,
That night and day he sped him, that he can,
To wait a time of his conclusion;
This is to say, to make illusion,
By such an appearance of jugglery
(I know no termes of astrology),
That she and every wight should ween and say,
That of Bretagne the rockes were away,
Or else they were sunken under ground.
So at the last he hath a time found
To make his japes and his wretchedness
Of such a superstitious cursedness.
His tables Toletanes forth he brought,

Full well corrected, that there lacked nought,
Neither his collect, nor his expanse years,
Neither his rootes, nor his other gears,
As be his centres, and his arguments,
And his proportional convenients
For his equations in everything.
And by his eighte spheres in his working,
He knew full well how far Alnath was shove
From the head of that fix'd Aries above,
That in the ninthe sphere consider'd is.
Full subtilly he calcul'd all this.
When he had found his firste mansion,
He knew the remnant by proportion;
And knew the rising of his moone well,
And in whose face, and term, and every deal;
And knew full well the moone's mansion
Accordant to his operation;
And knew also his other observances,
For such illusions and such meschances,
As heathen folk used in thilke days.
For which no longer made he delays;
But through his magic, for a day or tway,
It seemed all the rockes were away.

Aurelius, which yet despaired is
Whe'er he shall have his love, or fare amiss,
Awaited night and day on this miracle:
And when he knew that there was none obstacle,
That voided were these rockes every one,
Down at his master's feet he fell anon,
And said; "I, woeful wretch'd Aurelius,
Thank you, my Lord, and lady mine Venus,
That me have holpen from my cares cold."
And to the temple his way forth hath he hold,
Where as he knew he should his lady see.
And when he saw his time, anon right he
With dreadful heart and with full humble cheer
Saluteth hath his sovereign lady dear.
"My rightful Lady," quoth this woeful man,
"Whom I most dread, and love as I best can,
And lothest were of all this world displease,

Were't not that I for you have such disease,
That I must die here at your foot anon,
Nought would I tell how me is woebegone.
But certes either must I die or plain;
Ye slay me guilteless for very pain.
But of my death though that ye have no ruth,
Advise you, ere that ye break your truth:
Repente you, for thilke God above,
Ere ye me slay because that I you love.
For, Madame, well ye wot what ye have hight;
Not that I challenge anything of right
Of you, my sovereign lady, but of grace:
But in a garden yond', in such a place,
Ye wot right well what ye behighte me,
And in mine hand your trothe plighted ye,
To love me best; God wot ye saide so,
Albeit that I unworthy am thereto;
Madame, I speak it for th' honour of you,
More than to save my hearte's life right now;
I have done so as ye commanded me,
And if ye vouchesafe, ye may go see.
Do as you list, have your behest in mind,
For, quick or dead, right there ye shall me find;
In you hes all to do me live or dey;
But well I wot the rockes be away."

He took his leave, and she astonish'd stood;
In all her face was not one drop of blood:
She never ween'd t'have come in such a trap.
"Alas!" quoth she, "that ever this should hap!
For ween'd I ne'er, by possibility,
That such a monster or marvail might be;
It is against the process of nature."
And home she went a sorrowful creature;
For very fear unnethes may she go.
She weeped, wailed, all a day or two,
And swooned, that it ruthe was to see:
But why it was, to no wight tolde she,
For out of town was gone Arviragus.
But to herself she spake, and saide thus,
With face pale, and full sorrowful cheer,

In her complaint, as ye shall after hear.
"Alas!" quoth she, "on thee, Fortune, I plain,
That unware hast me wrapped in thy chain,
From which to scape, wot I no succour,
Save only death, or elles dishonour;
One of these two behoveth me to choose.
But natheless, yet had I lever lose
My life, than of my body have shame,
Or know myselfe false, or lose my name;
And with my death I may be quit y-wis.
Hath there not many a noble wife, ere this,
And many a maiden, slain herself, alas!
Rather than with her body do trespass?
Yes, certes; lo, these stories bear witness.
When thirty tyrants full of cursedness
Had slain Phidon in Athens at the feast,
They commanded his daughters to arrest,
And bringe them before them, in despite,
All naked, to fulfil their foul delight;
And in their father's blood they made them dance
Upon the pavement,—God give them mischance.
For which these woeful maidens, full of dread,
Rather than they would lose their maidenhead,
They privily be start into a well,
And drowned themselves, as the bookes tell.
They of Messene let inquire and seek
Of Lacedaemon fifty maidens eke,
On which they woulde do their lechery:
But there was none of all that company
That was not slain, and with a glad intent
Chose rather for to die, than to assent
To be oppressed of her maidenhead.
Why should I then to dien be in dread?
Lo, eke the tyrant Aristoclides,
That lov'd a maiden hight Stimphalides,
When that her father slain was on a night,
Unto Diana's temple went she right,
And hent the image in her handes two,
From which image she woulde never go;
No wight her handes might off it arace,
Till she was slain right in the selfe place.

208

Now since that maidens hadde such despite
To be defouled with man's foul delight,
Well ought a wife rather herself to sle,
Than be defouled, as it thinketh me.
What shall I say of Hasdrubale's wife,
That at Carthage bereft herself of life?
For, when she saw the Romans win the town,
She took her children all, and skipt adown
Into the fire, and rather chose to die,
Than any Roman did her villainy.
Hath not Lucretia slain herself, alas!
At Rome, when that she oppressed was
Of Tarquin? for her thought it was a shame
To live, when she hadde lost her name.
The seven maidens of Milesie also
Have slain themselves for very dread and woe,
Rather than folk of Gaul them should oppress.
More than a thousand stories, as I guess,
Could I now tell as touching this mattere.
When Abradate was slain, his wife so dear
Herselfe slew, and let her blood to glide
In Abradate's woundes, deep and wide,
And said, 'My body at the leaste way
There shall no wight defoul, if that I may.'
Why should I more examples hereof sayn?
Since that so many have themselves slain,
Well rather than they would defouled be,
I will conclude that it is bet for me
To slay myself, than be defouled thus.
I will be true unto Arviragus,
Or elles slay myself in some mannere,
As did Demotione's daughter dear,
Because she woulde not defouled be.
O Sedasus, it is full great pity
To reade how thy daughters died, alas!
That slew themselves for suche manner cas.
As great a pity was it, or well more,
The Theban maiden, that for Nicanor
Herselfe slew, right for such manner woe.
Another Theban maiden did right so;
For one of Macedon had her oppress'd,

She with her death her maidenhead redress'd.
What shall I say of Niceratus' wife,
That for such case bereft herself her life?
How true was eke to Alcibiades
His love, that for to dien rather chese,
Than for to suffer his body unburied be?
Lo, what a wife was Alceste?" quoth she.
"What saith Homer of good Penelope?
All Greece knoweth of her chastity.
Pardie, of Laedamia is written thus,
That when at Troy was slain Protesilaus,
No longer would she live after his day.
The same of noble Porcia tell I may;
Withoute Brutus coulde she not live,
To whom she did all whole her hearte give.
The perfect wifehood of Artemisie
Honoured is throughout all Barbarie.
O Teuta queen, thy wifely chastity
To alle wives may a mirror be."

Thus plained Dorigen a day or tway,
Purposing ever that she woulde dey;
But natheless upon the thirde night
Home came Arviragus, the worthy knight,
And asked her why that she wept so sore.
And she gan weepen ever longer more.
"Alas," quoth she, "that ever I was born!
Thus have I said," quoth she; "thus have I sworn."
And told him all, as ye have heard before:
It needeth not rehearse it you no more.
This husband with glad cheer, in friendly wise,
Answer'd and said, as I shall you devise.
"Is there aught elles, Dorigen, but this?"
"Nay, nay," quoth she, "God help me so, as wis
This is too much, an it were Godde's will."
"Yea, wife," quoth he, "let sleepe what is still,
It may be well par'venture yet to-day.
Ye shall your trothe holde, by my fay.
For, God so wisly have mercy on me,
I had well lever sticked for to be,
For very love which I to you have,

210

But if ye should your trothe keep and save.
Truth is the highest thing that man may keep."
But with that word he burst anon to weep,
And said; "I you forbid, on pain of death,
That never, while you lasteth life or breath,
To no wight tell ye this misaventure;
As I may best, I will my woe endure,
Nor make no countenance of heaviness,
That folk of you may deeme harm, or guess."
And forth he call'd a squier and a maid.
"Go forth anon with Dorigen," he said,
"And bringe her to such a place anon."
They take their leave, and on their way they gon:
But they not wiste why she thither went;
He would to no wight telle his intent.

This squier, which that hight Aurelius,
On Dorigen that was so amorous,
Of aventure happen'd her to meet
Amid the town, right in the quickest street,
As she was bound to go the way forthright
Toward the garden, there as she had hight.
And he was to the garden-ward also;
For well he spied when she woulde go
Out of her house, to any manner place;
But thus they met, of aventure or grace,
And he saluted her with glad intent,
And asked of her whitherward she went.
And she answered, half as she were mad,
"Unto the garden, as my husband bade,
My trothe for to hold, alas! alas!"
Aurelius gan to wonder on this case,
And in his heart had great compassion
Of her, and of her lamentation,
And of Arviragus, the worthy knight,
That bade her hold all that she hadde hight;
So loth him was his wife should break her truth
And in his heart he caught of it great ruth,
Considering the best on every side,
That from his lust yet were him lever abide,
Than do so high a churlish wretchedness

Against franchise, and alle gentleness;
For which in fewe words he saide thus;
"Madame, say to your lord Arviragus,
That since I see the greate gentleness
Of him, and eke I see well your distress,
That him were lever have shame (and that were ruth)
Than ye to me should breake thus your truth,
I had well lever aye to suffer woe,
Than to depart the love betwixt you two.
I you release, Madame, into your hond,
Quit ev'ry surement and ev'ry bond,
That ye have made to me as herebeforn,
Since thilke time that ye were born.
Have here my truth, I shall you ne'er repreve
Of no behest; and here I take my leave,
As of the truest and the beste wife
That ever yet I knew in all my life.
But every wife beware of her behest;
On Dorigen remember at the least.
Thus can a squier do a gentle deed,
As well as can a knight, withoute drede."

She thanked him upon her knees bare,
And home unto her husband is she fare,
And told him all, as ye have hearde said;
And, truste me, he was so well apaid,
That it were impossible me to write.
Why should I longer of this case indite?
Arviragus and Dorigen his wife
In sov'reign blisse ledde forth their life;
Ne'er after was there anger them between;
He cherish'd her as though she were a queen,
And she was to him true for evermore;
Of these two folk ye get of me no more.

Aurelius, that his cost had all forlorn,
Cursed the time that ever he was born.
"Alas!" quoth he, "alas that I behight
Of pured gold a thousand pound of weight
To this philosopher! how shall I do?
I see no more, but that I am fordo.

Mine heritage must I needes sell,
And be a beggar; here I will not dwell,
And shamen all my kindred in this place,
But I of him may gette better grace.
But natheless I will of him assay
At certain dayes year by year to pay,
And thank him of his greate courtesy.
My trothe will I keep, I will not he."
With hearte sore he went unto his coffer,
And broughte gold unto this philosopher,
The value of five hundred pound, I guess,
And him beseeched, of his gentleness,
To grant him dayes of the remenant;
And said; "Master, I dare well make avaunt,
I failed never of my truth as yet.
For sickerly my debte shall be quit
Towardes you how so that e'er I fare
To go a-begging in my kirtle bare:
But would ye vouchesafe, upon surety,
Two year, or three, for to respite me,
Then were I well, for elles must I sell
Mine heritage; there is no more to tell."

This philosopher soberly answer'd,
And saide thus, when he these wordes heard;
"Have I not holden covenant to thee?"
"Yes, certes, well and truely," quoth he.
"Hast thou not had thy lady as thee liked?"
"No, no," quoth he, and sorrowfully siked.
"What was the cause? tell me if thou can."
Aurelius his tale anon began,
And told him all as ye have heard before,
It needeth not to you rehearse it more.
He said, "Arviragus of gentleness
Had lever die in sorrow and distress,
Than that his wife were of her trothe false."
The sorrow of Dorigen he told him als',
How loth her was to be a wicked wife,
And that she lever had lost that day her life;
And that her troth she swore through innocence;
She ne'er erst had heard speak of apparence

That made me have of her so great pity,
And right as freely as he sent her to me,
As freely sent I her to him again:
This is all and some, there is no more to sayn."

The philosopher answer'd; "Leve brother,
Evereach of you did gently to the other;
Thou art a squier, and he is a knight,
But God forbidde, for his blissful might,
But if a clerk could do a gentle deed
As well as any of you, it is no drede
Sir, I release thee thy thousand pound,
As thou right now were crept out of the ground,
Nor ever ere now haddest knowen me.
For, Sir, I will not take a penny of thee
For all my craft, nor naught for my travail;
Thou hast y-payed well for my vitaille;
It is enough; and farewell, have good day."
And took his horse, and forth he went his way.
Lordings, this question would I aske now,
Which was the moste free, as thinketh you?
Now telle me, ere that ye farther wend.
I can no more, my tale is at an end.

# ON IDEALISM AND LIMITATIONS

## Diane Vincent

**H**appily-ever-after is where "The Franklin's Tale" begins. Hardly thirty lines are devoted to Arveragus and Dorigen's embodiment of late-medieval romantic ideals: the lady's beauty and nobility, the knight's many quests and feats, his long suffering of love-pangs and devoted service to her, and finally her realization of his worth and pity for him.

Once married, Dorigen and Arveragus attempt to keep some of the core romantic ideals of the medieval code of courtly love in conjugal love.

Arveragus, freely and unprompted, promises to remain her lover insofar as he rejects the "mastery" often thought the husband's due and promises instead to continue his service of his beloved by following Dorigen's will in all things. She, in response to his generosity, pledges to be his true wife, who will never willfully grieve him. Their marriage is established not by a contract or exchange of services—though we do see such a contract define the relationship between Aurelius and the magician—but by the *utterly gratuitous* gift of the lover and the free response of his beloved.

Thus, as the Franklin comments, Arveragus succeeds in having both his lady *and* his love. By contrast, that famous medieval lover Lancelot could only ever have his love, since Guenevere was Arthur's lady, and while he may be praised for his devotion to her, his passion could only ever attain to the temporary fulfillment of sex, rather than the lasting union of a happy marriage.

Elsewhere in *The Canterbury Tales*, too, romantic idealism does not fare well. We laugh or cry over the pilgrims' cynical views of marriage, in which any mutual love has disappeared and one spouse dominates or deceives the other. But the Franklin emphasizes repeatedly that Dorigen and Arveragus are faithful spouses *and* passionately devoted lovers. Their ability to remain lovers and spouses is, in part, what the tale puts to the test. And as much as the plot of "The Franklin's Tale" relies on exaggeration and elements of fantasy, the lovers' endeavor to translate their romance into their married life had real-life implications, because the behavior of English lovers was actually influenced by the ideals of the courtly lover's humble service and courtesy as well as of the ennobling power of love.

Of course, the best way to test the romance of a marriage is to send one spouse away for a long time (and include the risk of death for good measure) and to present the other with a seemingly perfect substitute lover. In Aurelius, we have all the outward trappings of the ideal courtly lover. He sings and dances better than any man alive (ever). He is also the handsomest man alive, young, rich, strong, popular, a prolific poet, and, conveniently, a near neighbor. Like Lancelot, he goes mad when rejected and is willing to sacrifice everything to attain his lady. "A servant in the game of Venus," he is love-sick, without question, but it's also clear that love is a game—however deadly—that he's playing.

His rhetoric is almost perfect, but beneath the veneer of courtesy he reveals the churlish heart he only owns up to later. Chaucer is careful to make it clear that Aurelius only achieves the illusion of satisfying Dorigen's condition, just as he only achieves a barely coherent illusion of humble service when he confronts Dorigen with his claim on her. "You know what you promised. Not that I challenge anything of you by right, sovereign lady, but by your grace" is a far cry from Arveragus's gift of freedom to her. Aurelius's shallow commitment to courtly love only becomes ennobling when he gives up the vulgar passion that had lain hidden beneath the elegant flourishes of love's game. What's more, in renouncing his ill-gotten power to constrain Dorigen's affection, he gives himself the gift of freedom from Venus's rule, from the passion that has been dominating his life for years to his detriment, to the sorrow of his brother, and to the deep distress of Dorigen and Arveragus.

Though a far nobler lover than Aurelius, Dorigen also suffers from play of courtly love. It is when the scene is set for love—after a jolly dance in a garden in the springtime of Love—that she playfully adds the impossible task to her refusal of Aurelius's advances. She intends her words to reinforce her emphatic rejection of his plea, since she knows her condition "will never happen." But by rhetorically playing Venus's game and giving the lover an impossible quest to achieve, she has implicitly agreed to abide by Venus's rules.

As much as her marriage to Arveragus successfully realizes the ideals of courtly love—service, humility, faithfulness in spite of suffering, and generosity—their marriage is no game. Dorigen understands and embraces the exclusive claims of conjugal love, but her careless play puts her in the impossible bind of having to choose between honor of word and honor of body. Her dilemma is impossible not only because failing in "truth" attends either choice, but also because it is precisely in conjugal love that honor of word and body are inextricably linked; to lose either is to lose both, and thereby to lose herself.

No wonder death is such an attractive option. Though we might protest that such an empty vow couldn't be binding, no one in the tale rejects its force. That ultimately her truth can be preserved only in the context of forgiveness shows the limits of our ability to speak and fulfill the truth of our words. Our promises, even when freely and consciously made, are subject to our limitations as much as to our wills.

---

What makes Geoffrey Chaucer such compelling reading is his creation of a riveting conversation between the ideal and the everyday: can Dorigen and Arveragus remain lovers and spouses when confronted with not just their temptations but also with their limitations? Such tensions are the root of much of Chaucer's well-known, and often biting, satire, but it's likewise the root of his insight into human relationships.

Here, in "The Franklin's Tale," we see the ennobling pursuit of an ideal lived out in the strains and trials that the world can place on even the most ideal of relationships. While it may be hard to be faithfully married to an ideal, it's impossible to stay passionately married without one. Arveragus's generosity to Dorigen and to Aurelius, though shocking, is as he says, "well-paid," and not only by the faithful love of his wife and by Aurelius's sacrifice. More than that, he is well-paid insofar as his and Dorigen's pursuit of a passionate conjugal love offers a chance for a boorish faker to abandon Venus's empty game and finally begin to become a noble man.

## CHAPTER TEN

# DESIDERIUS ERASMUS

Renaissance/Reformation (1466–1536)

Western Christendom once spoke with a united voice and, as Erasmus grew old, he witnessed the end of that era. He protested Church abuses but rejected Protestantism; he was a reformer but never Reformed.

Erasmus also defied the modernist conviction that a combination of increased learning and of comprehending the world's problems will inevitably lead to secularism. He was a pious man without ignoring hypocrisy, and he was fabulously learned without thinking that the intellect was everything.

Erasmus is a challenge to anyone too simplistically critical of the Roman Church as it was in the late Middle Ages. Erasmus saw many of the Church's abuses, and he attacked those misdeeds harshly, but he remained a faithful and well-regarded member of that flock. One reason the Roman Catholic Church endured the turmoil of the Renaissance-and-Reformation period was that she allowed room for critics. (The rest of us should take notice and allow for our own Erasmus.)

A better Bible was Erasmus's great gift to the Church of his time; it made the Reformation possible. Yet it also created a better Roman church. Such is the power of the Book on the minds of men, and such is the power of an intellect that harnesses itself to God's Word.

———————

Erasmus also is a model for the man of faith who would follow reason. *In Praise of Folly* must be understood as the product of Erasmus's Bible-saturated mind. His was a mind too broad for fundamentalism, which rejects reason, and too honest for intellectualism, which rejects revelation.

The fundamentalist burns with anti-intellectual zeal, and in reaction sophists are often swollen up with intellectualism. The fundamentalist and the sophist justify their excesses by the sin of their opposite. Fundamentalism and sophistry give piety and philosophy bad reputations with society.

Desiderius Erasmus, the great scholar, could never be described as anti-intellectual, but he did not worship worldly intellect. *Folly* walks the pathway of virtue between the two. Because Erasmus was a true scholar and intellectual, *Folly* concentrates on the temptations of intellectualism and the virtues in simple piety.

This is a good reminder for all of us involved with books like this one.

Read Erasmus and let his genius stimulate you, knowing that the man himself could not predict the ways his labors would be used by God. Like all great authors, he attracted brilliant readers (e.g., Luther) who took his work in unexpected directions.

Allow yourself to be provoked by Erasmus, and see where he takes you.

## FROM

# *In Praise of Folly*

### "AN ORATION . . . SPOKEN BY FOLLY . . ."

At what rate soever the world talks of me (for I am not ignorant what an ill report Folly has got, even among the most foolish), yet that I am that she, that only she, whose deity recreates both gods and men, even this is a sufficient argument, that I no sooner stepped up to speak to this full assembly than all your faces put on a kind of new and unwonted pleasantness. So suddenly have you cleared your brows, and with so frolic and hearty a laughter given me your applause, that in truth as many of you as I behold on every side of me seem to me no less than Homer's gods drunk with nectar and nepenthe; whereas before, you sat as lumpish and pensive as if you had come from consulting an oracle. And as it usually happens when the sun begins to show his beams, or when after a sharp winter the spring breathes afresh on the earth, all things immediately get a new face, new color, and recover as it were a certain kind of youth again: in like manner by but beholding me you have in an instant gotten another kind of countenance; and so what the otherwise great rhetoricians with their tedious and long-studied orations can hardly effect, to wit, to remove the trouble of the mind, I have done it at once with my single look. . . .

So provident has that great parent of mankind, Nature, been that there should not be anything without its mixture and, as it were, seasoning of Folly. For since according to the definition of the Stoics, wisdom is nothing else than to be governed by reason, and on the contrary Folly, to be given up to the will of our passions, that the life of man might not be altogether disconsolate and hard to away with, of how much more passion than reason has Jupiter composed us? putting in, as one would say, "scarce half an ounce to a pound." Besides, he has confined reason to a narrow corner of the brain and left all the rest of the body to our passions; has also set up, against this one, two as it were, masterless tyrants—anger, that possesses the region of the heart, and consequently the very fountain of life, the heart itself; and lust, that stretches its empire everywhere. Against which double force how powerful reason is let common experience declare, inasmuch as she, which yet is all she can do, may call out to us till she be hoarse again and tell us the rules of honesty and virtue; while they give up the reins to their governor and make a hideous clamor, till at last being wearied, he suffer himself to be carried whither they please to hurry him. . . .

But perhaps there are some that neglect this way of pleasure and rest satisfied in the enjoyment of their friends, calling friendship the most desirable of all things, more necessary than either air, fire, or water; so delectable that he that shall take it out of the world had as good put out the sun; and, lastly, so commendable, if yet that make anything to the matter, that neither the philosophers themselves doubted to reckon it among their chiefest good. But what if I show you that I am both the beginning and end of this so great good also? Nor shall I go about to prove it by fallacies, sorites, dilemmas, or other the like subtleties of logicians, but after my blunt way point out the thing as clearly as it were with my finger.

And now tell me if to wink, slip over, be blind at, or deceived in the vices of our friends, nay, to admire and esteem them for virtues, be not at least the next degree to folly? What is it when one kisses his mistress' freckle neck, another the wart on her nose? When a father shall swear his squint-eyed child is more lovely than Venus? What is this, I say, but mere folly? And so, perhaps you'll cry it is; and yet 'tis this only that joins friends together and continues them so joined. I speak of ordinary men, of whom none are born without their imperfections, and happy is he that is pressed with the least: for among wise princes there is either no friendship at all, or if there be, 'tis unpleasant and reserved, and that too but among a very few 'twere a crime to say none. For that the greatest part of mankind are fools, nay there is not anyone that dotes not in many things; and friendship, you know, is seldom made but among equals. And yet if it should so happen that there were a mutual good will between them, it is in no wise firm nor very long lived; that is to say, among such as are morose and more circumspect than needs, as being eagle-sighted into his friends' faults, but so blear-eyed to their own that they take not the least notice of the wallet that hangs behind their own shoulders.

Since then the nature of man is such that there is scarce anyone to be found that is not subject to many errors, add to this the great diversity of minds and studies, so many slips, oversights, and chances of human life, and how is it possible there should be any true friendship between those Argus, so much as one hour, were it not for that which the Greeks excellently call *euetheian*? And you may render it by folly or good nature, choose you whether. But what? Is not the author and parent of all our love, Cupid, as blind as a beetle? And as with him all colors agree, so from him is it that everyone likes his own sweeterkin best, though never so ugly, and "that an old man dotes on his old wife, and a boy on his girl." These things are not only done everywhere but laughed at too; yet as ridiculous as they are, they make society pleasant, and, as it were, glue it together.

And what has been said of friendship may more reasonably be presumed of matrimony, which in truth is no other than an inseparable conjunction of life. Good God! What divorces, or what not worse than that, would daily happen were not the converse between a man and his wife supported and cherished by flattery, apishness, gentleness, ignorance, dissembling, certain retainers of mine also! Whoop holiday! how few marriages should we have, if the husband should but thoroughly examine how many tricks his pretty little mop of modesty has played before she was married! And how fewer of them would hold together, did not most of the wife's actions escape the husband's knowledge through his neglect or sottishness! And for this also you are beholden to me, by whose means it is that the husband is pleasant to his wife, the wife to her husband, and the house kept in quiet.

A man is laughed at, when seeing his wife weeping he licks up her tears. But how much happier is it to be thus deceived than by being troubled with jealousy not only to torment himself but set all things in a hubbub! In fine, I am so necessary to the making of all society and manner of life both delightful and lasting, that neither would the people long endure their governors, nor the servant his master, nor the master his footman, nor the scholar his tutor, nor one friend another, nor the wife her husband, nor the usurer the borrower, nor a soldier his commander, nor one companion another, unless all of them had their interchangeable failings, one while flattering, other while prudently conniving, and generally sweetening one another with some small relish of folly.

And now you'd think I had said all, but you shall hear yet greater things. Will he, I pray, love anyone that hates himself? Or ever agree with another who is not at peace with himself? Or beget pleasure in another that is troublesome to himself? I think no one will say it that is not more foolish than Folly. And yet, if you should exclude me, there's no man but would be so far from enduring another that he would stink in his own nostrils, be nauseated with his own actions, and himself become odious to himself; forasmuch as Nature, in too many things rather a stepdame than a parent to us, has imprinted that evil in men, especially such as have least judgment, that everyone repents him of his own condition and admires that of others. Whence it comes to pass that all her gifts, elegancy, and graces corrupt and perish. For what benefit is beauty, the greatest blessing of heaven, if it be mixed with affectation? What youth, if corrupted with the severity of old age?

Lastly, what is that in the whole business of a man's life he can do with any grace to himself or others—for it is not so much a thing of art, as the very life of every action, that it be done with a good mien—unless this my friend and companion, Self-love, be present with it? Nor does she without cause supply me the place of a sister, since her whole endeavors are to act my part everywhere. For what is more foolish than for a man to study nothing else than how to please himself? To make himself the object of his own admiration? And yet, what is there that is either delightful or taking, nay rather what not the contrary, that a man does against the hair? Take away this salt of life, and the orator may even sit still with his action, the musician with all his division will be able to please no man, the player be hissed off the stage, the poet and all his Muses ridiculous, the painter with his art contemptible, and the physician with all his slip-slops go a-begging. . . .

You will be taken for an ugly fellow instead of youthful, and a beast instead of a wise man, a child instead of eloquent, and instead of a well-bred man, a clown. So necessary a thing it is that everyone flatter himself and commend himself to himself before he can be commended by others. Lastly, since it is the chief point of happiness "that a man is willing to be what he is," you have further abridged in this my Self-love, that no man is ashamed of his own face, no man of his own wit, no man of his own parentage, no man of his own house, no man of his manner of living, not any man of his own country; so that a Highlander has no desire to change with an Italian, a Thracian with an Athenian, not a Scythian for the Fortunate Islands. O the singular care of Nature, that in so great a variety of things has made all equal! Where she has been sometimes sparing of her gifts she has recompensed it with the mote of self-love; though here, I must confess, I speak foolishly, it being the greatest of all other her gifts: to say nothing that no great action was ever attempted without my motion, or art brought to perfection without my help. . . .

Yet why this? will someone say. Have patience, and I'll show you what I drive at. If anyone seeing a player acting his part on a stage should go about to strip him of his disguise and show him to the people in his true native form, would he not, think you, not only spoil the whole design of the play, but deserve himself to be pelted off with stones as a phantastical fool and one out of his wits? But nothing is more common with them than such changes; the same person one while impersonating a woman, and another while a man; now a youngster, and by and by a grim seignior; now a king, and presently a peasant; now a god, and in a trice again an ordinary fellow. But to discover this were to spoil all, it being the only thing that entertains the eyes of the spectators. And what is all this life but a kind of comedy, wherein men walk up and down in one another's disguises and act their respective parts, till the property-man brings them back to the attiring house. And yet he often orders a different dress, and makes him that came but just now off in the robes of a king put on the rags of a beggar. Thus are all things represented by counterfeit, and yet without this there was no living.

And here if any wise man, as it were dropped from heaven, should start up and cry, this great thing whom the world looks upon for as a god and I know not what is not so much as a man, for that like a beast he is led by his passions, but the worst of slaves, inasmuch as he gives himself up willingly to so many and such detestable masters. Again if he should bid a man that were bewailing the death of his father to laugh, for that he now began to live by having got an estate, without which life is but a kind of death; or call another that were boasting of his family ill begotten or base, because he is so far removed from virtue that is the only fountain of nobility; and so of the rest: what else would he get by it but be thought himself mad and frantic? For as nothing is more foolish than preposterous wisdom, so nothing is more unadvised than a forward unseasonable prudence. And such is his that does not comply with the present time "and order himself as the market goes," but forgetting that law of feasts, "either drink or begone," undertakes to disprove a common received opinion. Whereas on the contrary, 'tis the part of a truly prudent man not to be wise beyond his condition, but either to take no notice of what the world does, or run with it for company. But this is foolish, you'll say; nor shall I deny it, provided always you be so civil on the other side as to confess that this is to act a part in that world.

But, O you gods, "shall I speak or hold my tongue?" But why should I be silent in a thing that is more true than truth itself? However it might not be amiss perhaps in so great an affair to call forth the Muses from

Helicon, since the poets so often invoke them upon every foolish occasion. Be present then awhile, and assist me, you daughters of Jupiter, while I make it out that there is no way to that so much famed wisdom, nor access to that fortress as they call it of happiness, but under the banner of Folly. And first, 'tis agreed of all hands that our passions belong to Folly; inasmuch as we judge a wise man from a fool by this, that the one is ordered by them, the other by reason; and therefore the Stoics remove from a wise man all disturbances of mind as so many diseases. But these passions do not only the office of a tutor to such as are making towards the port of wisdom, but are in every exercise of virtue as it were spurs and incentives, nay and encouragers to well doing. . . .

But 'tis a sad thing, they say, to be mistaken. Nay rather, he is most miserable that is not so. For they are quite beside the mark that place the happiness of men in things themselves, since it only depends upon opinion. For so great is the obscurity and variety of human affairs that nothing can be clearly known, as it is truly said by our academics, the least insolent of all the philosophers; or if it could, it would but obstruct the pleasure of life. Lastly, the mind of man is so framed that it is rather taken with the false colors than truth; of which if anyone has a mind to make the experiment, let him go to church and hear sermons, in which if there be anything serious delivered, the audience is either asleep, yawning, or weary of it; but if the preacher—pardon my mistake, I would have said declaimer—as too often it happens, fall but into an old wives' story, they're presently awake, prick up their ears and gape after it. . . .

But perhaps I had better pass over our divines in silence and not stir this pool or touch this fair but unsavory plant, as a kind of men that are supercilious beyond comparison, and to that too, implacable; lest setting them about my ears, they attack me by troops and force me to a recantation sermon, which if I refuse, they straight pronounce me a heretic. For this is the thunderbolt with which they fright those whom they are resolved not to favor. And truly, though there are few others that less willingly acknowledge the kindnesses I have done them, yet even these too stand fast bound to me upon no ordinary accounts; while being happy in their own opinion, and as if they dwelt in the third heaven, they look with haughtiness on all others as poor creeping things and could almost find in their hearts to pity them; while hedged in with so many magisterial definitions, conclusions, corollaries, propositions explicit and implicit, they abound with so many starting-holes that Vulcan's net cannot hold them so fast, but they'll slip through with their distinctions, with which they so easily cut all knots asunder that a hatchet could not have done it better, so plentiful are they in their new-found words and prodigious terms. Besides, while they explicate the most hidden mysteries according to their own fancy—as how the world was first made; how original sin is derived to posterity; in what manner, how much room, and how long time Christ lay in the Virgin's womb; how accidents subsist in the Eucharist without their subject.

But these are common and threadbare; these are worthy of our great and illuminated divines, as the world calls them! At these, if ever they fall athwart them, they prick up—as whether there was any instant of time in the generation of the Second Person; whether there be more than one filiation in Christ; whether it be a possible proposition that God the Father hates the Son; or whether it was possible that Christ could have taken upon Him the likeness of a woman, or of the devil, or of an ass, or of a stone, or of a gourd; and then how that gourd should have preached, wrought miracles, or been hung on the cross; and what Peter had consecrated if he had administered the Sacrament at what time the body of Christ hung upon the cross; or whether at the same time he might be said to be man; whether after the Resurrection there will be any eating and drinking, since we are so much afraid of hunger and thirst in this world. There are infinite of these subtle trifles, and others more subtle than these, of notions, relations, instants, formalities, quiddities, haecceities, which no one can perceive without a Lynceus whose eyes could look through a stone wall and discover those things through the thickest darkness that never were.

Add to this those their other determinations, and those too so contrary to common opinion that those oracles of the Stoics, which they call paradoxes, seem in comparison of these but blockish and idle—as 'tis a lesser crime to kill a thousand men than to set a stitch on a poor man's shoe on the Sabbath day; and that a man should rather choose that the whole world with all food and raiment, as they say, should perish, than tell a lie, though never so inconsiderable. And these most subtle subtleties are rendered yet more subtle by the several methods of so many Schoolmen, that one might sooner wind himself out of a labyrinth than the entanglements of the realists, nominalists, Thomists, Albertists, Occamists, Scotists. Nor have I named all the several sects, but only some of the chief; in all which there is so much doctrine and so much difficulty that I may well conceive the apostles, had they been to deal with these new kind of divines, had needed to have prayed in aid of some other spirit.

Paul knew what faith was, and yet when he said, "Faith is the substance of things hoped for, and the evidence of things not seen," he did not define it doctor-like. And as he understood charity well himself, so he did as illogically divide and define it to others in his first Epistle to the Corinthians, Chapter the thirteenth. And devoutly, no doubt, did the apostles consecrate the Eucharist; yet, had they been asked the question touching the "terminus a quo," and the "terminus ad quem" of transubstantiation; of the manner how the same body can be in several places at one and the same time; of the difference the body of Christ has in heaven from that of the cross, or this in the Sacrament; in what point of time transubstantiation is, whereas prayer, by means of which it is, as being a discrete quantity, is transient; they would not, I conceive, have answered with the same subtlety as the Scotists dispute and define it.

They knew the mother of Jesus, but which of them has so philosophically demonstrated how she was preserved from original sin as have done our divines? Peter received the keys, and from Him too that would not have trusted them with a person unworthy; yet whether he had understanding or no, I know not, for certainly he never attained to that subtlety to determine how he could have the key of knowledge that had no knowledge himself. They baptized far and near, and yet taught nowhere what was the formal, material, efficient, and final cause of baptism, nor made the least mention of delible and indelible characters. They worshipped, 'tis true, but in spirit, following herein no other than that of the Gospel, "God is a Spirit, and they that worship, must worship him in spirit and truth;" yet it does not appear it was at that time revealed to them that an image sketched on the wall with a coal was to be worshipped with the same worship as Christ Himself, if at least the two forefingers be stretched out, the hair long and uncut, and have three rays about the crown of the head. For who can conceive these things, unless he has spent at least six and thirty years in the philosophical and supercelestial whims of Aristotle and the Schoolmen?

In like manner, the apostles press to us grace; but which of them distinguishes between free grace and grace that makes a man acceptable? They exhort us to good works, and yet determine not what is the work working, and what a resting in the work done. They incite us to charity, and yet make no difference between charity infused and charity wrought in us by our own endeavors. Nor do they declare whether it be an accident or a substance, a thing created or uncreated. They detest and abominate sin, but let me not live if they could define according to art what that is which we call sin, unless perhaps they were inspired by the spirit of the Scotists. . . .

And next these come those that commonly call themselves the religious and monks, most false in both titles, when both a great part of them are farthest from religion, and no men swarm thicker in all places than themselves. Nor can I think of anything that could be more miserable did not I support them so many several ways. For whereas all men detest them to that height, that they take it for ill luck to meet one of them by chance, yet such is their happiness that they flatter themselves. For first, they reckon it one of the main points of piety if they are so illiterate that they can't so much as read. And then when they run over their offices, which they carry about them, rather by tale than understanding, they believe the gods more than ordinarily pleased with their braying. And some there are among them that put off their trumperies at vast rates, yet rove up and down for the bread they eat; nay, there is scarce an inn, wagon, or ship into which they intrude not, to the no small damage of the commonwealth of beggars. And yet, like pleasant fellows, with all this vileness, ignorance, rudeness, and impudence, they represent to us, for so they call it, the lives of the apostles.

Yet what is more pleasant than that they do all things by rule and, as it were, a kind of mathematics, the least swerving from which were a crime beyond forgiveness—as how many knots their shoes must be tied with, of what color everything is, what distinction of habits, of what stuff made, how many straws broad their girdles and of what fashion, how many bushels wide their cowl, how many fingers long their hair, and how many hours sleep; which exact equality, how disproportionate it is, among such variety of bodies and tempers, who is there that does not perceive it? And yet by reason of these fooleries they not only set slight by others, but each different order, men otherwise professing apostolical charity, despise one another, and for the different wearing of a habit, or that 'tis of darker color, they put all things in combustion. And among these there are some so rigidly religious that their upper garment is haircloth, their inner of the finest linen; and, on the contrary, others wear linen without and hair next their skins. Others, again, are as afraid to touch money as poison, and yet neither forbear wine nor dallying with women. In a word, 'tis their only care that none of them come near one another in their manner of living, nor do they endeavor how they may be like Christ, but how they may differ among themselves. . . .

And for popes, that supply the place of Christ, if they should endeavor to imitate His life, to wit His poverty, labor, doctrine, cross, and contempt of life, or should they consider what the name pope, that is father, or holiness, imports, who would live more disconsolate than themselves? or who would purchase that chair with all his substance? or defend it, so purchased, with swords, poisons, and all force imaginable? so great a profit would the access of wisdom deprive him of—wisdom did I say? nay, the least corn of that salt which Christ speaks of: so much wealth, so much honor, so much riches, so many victories, so many offices, so many dispensations, so much tribute, so many pardons; such horses, such mules, such guards, and so much pleasure would it lose them. You see how much I have comprehended in a little: instead of which it would bring in watchings, fastings, tears, prayers, sermons, good endeavors, sighs, and a thousand the like troublesome exercises. Nor is this least considerable: so many scribes, so many copying clerks, so many notaries, so many advocates, so many promoters, so many secretaries, so many muleteers, so many grooms, so many bankers: in short, that vast multitude of men that overcharge the Roman See—I mistook, I meant honor—might beg their bread.

A most inhuman and economical thing, and more to be execrated, that those great princes of the Church and true lights of the world should be reduced to a staff and a wallet. Whereas now, if there be anything that requires their pains, they leave that to Peter and Paul that have leisure enough; but if there be anything of honor or pleasure, they take that to themselves. By which means it is, yet by my courtesy, that scarce any kind of men live more voluptuously or with less trouble; as believing that Christ will be well enough pleased if in their mystical and almost mimical pontificality, ceremonies, titles of holiness and the like, and blessing and cursing, they play the parts of bishops. To work miracles is old and antiquated, and not in fashion now; to instruct the people, troublesome; to interpret the Scripture, pedantic; to pray, a sign one has little else to do; to shed tears, silly and womanish; to be poor, base; to be vanquished, dishonorable and little becoming him that scarce admits even kings to kiss his slipper; and lastly, to die, uncouth; and to be stretched on a cross, infamous.

Theirs are only those weapons and sweet blessings which Paul mentions, and of these truly they are bountiful enough: as interdictions, hangings, heavy burdens, reproofs, anathemas, executions in effigy, and that terrible thunderbolt of excommunication, with the very sight of which they sink men's souls beneath the bottom of hell: which yet these most holy fathers in Christ and His vicars hurl with more fierceness against none than against such as, by the instigation of the devil, attempt to lessen or rob them of Peter's patrimony. When, though those words in the Gospel, "We have left all, and followed Thee," were his, yet they call his patrimony lands, cities, tribute, imposts, riches; for which, being enflamed with the love of Christ, they contend with fire and sword, and not without loss of much Christian blood, and believe they have then most apostolically defended the Church, the spouse of Christ, when the enemy, as they call them, are valiantly routed. As if the Church had any deadlier enemies than wicked prelates, who not only suffer Christ to run out of request for want of preaching him, but hinder his spreading by their multitudes of laws merely contrived for their own profit, corrupt him by their forced expositions, and murder him by the evil example of their pestilent life.

Nay, further, whereas the Church of Christ was founded in blood, confirmed by blood, and augmented by blood, now, as if Christ, who after his wonted manner defends his people, were lost, they govern all by the sword. And whereas war is so savage a thing that it rather befits beasts than men, so outrageous that the very poets feigned it came from the Furies, so pestilent that it corrupts all men's manners, so unjust that it is best executed by the worst of men, so wicked that it has no agreement with Christ; and yet, omitting all the other, they make this their only business. Here you'll see decrepit old fellows acting the parts of young men, neither troubled at their costs, nor wearied with their labors, nor discouraged at anything, so they may have the liberty of turning laws, religion, peace, and all things else quite topsy-turvy. Nor are they destitute of their learned flatterers that call that palpable madness zeal, piety, and valor, having found out a new way by which a man may kill his brother without the least breach of that charity which, by the command of Christ, one Christian owes another. And here, in troth, I'm a little at a stand whether the ecclesiastical German electors gave them this example, or rather took it from them; who, laying aside their habit, benedictions, and all the like ceremonies, so act the part of commanders that they think it a mean thing, and least beseeming a bishop, to show the least courage to Godward unless it be in a battle.

And as to the common herd of priests, they account it a crime to degenerate from the sanctity of their prelates. Heidah! How soldier-like they bustle about the *jus divinum* of titles, and how quicksighted they are to pick the least thing out of the writings of the ancients wherewith they may fright the common people and convince them, if possible, that more than a tenth is due! Yet in the meantime it least comes in their heads how many things are everywhere extant concerning that duty which they owe the people. Nor does their shorn crown in the least admonish them that a priest should be free from all worldly desires and think of nothing but heavenly things. Whereas on the contrary, these jolly fellows say they have sufficiently discharged their offices if they but anyhow mumble over a few odd prayers, which, so help me, Hercules! I wonder if any god either hear or understand, since they do neither themselves, especially when they thunder them out in that manner they are wont. But this they have in common with those of the heathens, that they are vigilant enough to the harvest of their profit, nor is there any of them that is not better read in those laws than the Scripture. Whereas if there be anything burdensome, they prudently lay that on other men's shoulders and shift it from one to the other, as men toss a ball from hand to hand, following herein the example of lay princes who commit the government of their kingdoms to their grand ministers, and they again to others, and leave all study of piety to the common people.

In like manner the common people put it over to those they call ecclesiastics, as if themselves were no part of the Church, or that their vow in baptism had lost its obligation. Again, the priests that call themselves secular, as if they were initiated to the world, not to Christ, lay the burden on the regulars; the regulars on the monks; the monks that have more liberty on those that have less; and all of them on the mendicants; the mendicants on the Carthusians, among whom, if anywhere, this piety lies buried, but yet so close that scarce anyone can perceive it. In like manner the popes, the most diligent of all others in gathering in the harvest of money, refer all their apostolical work to the bishops, the bishops to the parsons, the parsons to the vicars, the vicars to their brother mendicants, and they again throw back the care of the flock on those that take the wool.

But it is not my business to sift too narrowly the lives of prelates and priests for fear I seem to have intended rather a satire than an oration, and be thought to tax good princes while I praise the bad. And therefore, what I slightly taught before has been to no other end but that it might appear that there's no man can live pleasantly unless he be initiated to my rites and have me propitious to him. For how can it be otherwise when Fortune, the great directress of all human affairs, and myself are so all one that she was always an enemy to those wise men, and on the contrary so favorable to fools and careless fellows that all things hit luckily to them? . . .

But I forget myself and run beyond my bounds. Though yet, if I shall seem to have spoken anything more boldly or impertinently than I ought, be pleased to consider that not only Folly but a woman said it; remembering in the meantime that Greek proverb, "Sometimes a fool may speak a word in season," unless perhaps you expect an epilogue, but give me leave to tell you you are mistaken if you think I remember anything of what I have said, having foolishly bolted out such a hodgepodge of words. 'Tis an old proverb, "I hate one that remembers what's done over the cup." This is a new one of my own making: I hate a man that remembers what he hears. Wherefore farewell, clap your hands, live and drink lustily, my most excellent disciples of Folly.

*Translated by John Wilson, 1688*

# ERASMUS'S IN PRAISE OF FOLLY

## Greg Peters

Desiderius Erasmus was born in Rotterdam, Netherlands. As a well-educated man (he studied in Belgium, France, Italy, and England), Erasmus became one of the leading lights of the European Renaissance and was a frequent critic of the late medieval Catholic Church, though, once more, he remained in the Church until his death and did not become a Protestant. He is often thought of as the intellectual father of the Protestant Reformation.

Beginning in 1505, Erasmus set out to translate the New Testament into Latin. This endeavor helped him realize the unreliability of the existing edition of the Greek New Testament, so he set out to edit a new Greek edition. This was published in 1516 and has come to be known as the *Textus Receptus* ("Received Text"); it was the edition used by the translators of the King James Version. His best-known literary work, though, is *In Praise of Folly*, a critique of Church abuses and the world, published in 1511.

This is an oration in which Folly, personified as a woman, claims that what appears to be Folly outwardly, actually, is wise inwardly. Folly rails against that which she judges to be foolish in the areas of politics and society.

Erasmus's biting satire is also used to level criticisms against the Church, including theologians, monks, and clergymen. He makes vitriolic comments about contemporary political leaders and members of the learned professions. The work is highly rhetorical as well, so that Erasmus may express his opinions (through Folly) on a wide range of topics without having to offer grounded support.

For the Christian, it's the latter sections of this work that are most interesting. Here Erasmus turns his attention to a simpler biblical Christianity, over against the highly philosophical and scholastic theology of the later Middle Ages. For Erasmus, Jesus Christ was foolish for taking on human nature and dying on the cross; as well, he commended the foolish lifestyle to his disciples. That is, rejecting all worldly notions of the "good life" in order to chase after holiness and that which is spiritual: "this happiness of Christians, which they pursue with so much toil, is nothing else but a kind of madness and folly."

In fact, for Erasmus, "all Christian religion seems to have a kind of alliance with folly and in no respect to have any accord with wisdom." This being the case, the folly must be praised and must be sought after, since it is the very essence of the Christian religion. In Erasmus's estimation, "folly is more excellent than wisdom."

*In Praise of Folly* is a brilliant play on the Pauline interplay of wisdom and foolishness:

> Where is the one who is wise? Where is the scribe? Where is the debater of this age? Has not God made foolish the wisdom of the world? . . . For the foolishness of God is wiser than men, and the weakness of God is stronger than men. . . . But God chose what is foolish in the world to shame the wise; God chose what is weak in the world to shame the strong. (1 Corinthians 1:20, 25, 27)

Erasmus's work elaborates on this theme by showing that the truly wise are utterly foolish; those who think they are wise are the true fools. Given that we continue to live in a post-Christian culture that highly prizes so-called "learning" and the primacy of reason, Erasmus's text is a reminder that there is more to the life of the mind than simply learning for learning's sake. Though Christians must always be diligent to pursue truth and receive the wisdom offered by God, we must bear in mind that our knowledge is a kind of folly. That is to say, not only is it considered folly by the "world's" standards but, further, in the Erasmian and Pauline sense, we *are* fools, by extension, for Jesus: "We are fools for Christ's sake, but you are wise in Christ" (1 Corinthians 4:10). Reading the entire *In Praise of Folly* drives this point home—persuasively.

Desiderius Erasmus was a prolific author, so much so that his collected works, translated into English, fill approximately ninety volumes (published by the University of Toronto Press). Though a humanist in his learning and a Roman Catholic in ecclesial confession, Erasmus's work also contains spiritual and pastoral treatises, including *On Praying to God, An Explanation of the Apostles Creed,* and *Preparing for Death.*

235

Though *In Praise of Folly* is an excellent introduction to Erasmus and his central concerns, the reader who delves further into his literary corpus will not be disappointed. Erasmus is not only a voice of his time or a representative of the Roman Catholic Church; he also is a believer whose works deserve more attention from Christians of all churches and denominations.

## CHAPTER ELEVEN

# JOHN CALVIN

Renaissance/Reformation (1509–1564)

The United States of America is a footnote to John Calvin's ministry.

Calvin is not, of course, an American Founder, or even the direct source of many of our political ideas, but the very shape of the American colonies came in reaction to this Reformer's genius. New England was awash in Calvinism straight up, but even Anglican Virginia used a prayer book partly shaped by interactions with his thought. Imitation is not the only form of flattery; spirited opposition demonstrates potency too, and early American Christians who were not Calvinists often are best defined as "not Calvinists."

The ideas of the Genius of Geneva spread globally. Knowledge of Calvin is necessary to understand regions from southern Africa to northern Europe. Calvinism is one of the most fully developed cultural and theological alternatives to Orthodoxy or Catholic Christian thought amongst millions of Christians globally.

Oddly, despite his influence, few who aren't theologians read Calvin. He doesn't appear on the curriculum of many "great books" programs. If my students are not Calvinists, the few things they think they know about Calvin are often false and almost always negative. Simultaneously, Calvin is being revived in conservative evangelical circles hoping to deepen their intellectual and theological rigor. Too frequently these students know Calvin but have never thought critically about his ideas.

Both Calvinist and non-Calvinist students are often shocked when they read Calvin, because as with any seminal thinker, he often is more flexible than later creedal formulations in the Reformed communities. Calvin may be a Calvinist, but he's not a narrow one!

Calvin also had a classical and professional education that allowed him to draw on a diversity of sources. He thought his views biblical, but he did not think they were foreign to church history. Calvin wrote a rigorous, readable, systematic theology with the resources to sustain cultures in a diversity of people groups.

John Calvin clarifies ideas, and he challenges me every time I read him. His passion for Jesus has blessed me devotionally and points me to God. Even if we never become Calvinists, he is worth our time, every time. There are few enough writers about which that can be said.

CFROM 꼬

# Institutes of the Christian Religion

## Chapter 1:

### The Knowledge of God and of Ourselves Mutually Connected— Nature of This Connection

*Sections:*

1. The sum of true wisdom—viz. the knowledge of God and of ourselves. Effects of the latter.
2. Effects of the knowledge of God, in humbling our pride, unveiling our hypocrisy, demonstrating the absolute perfections of God, and our own utter helplessness.

3. Effects of the knowledge of God illustrated by the examples:
   1) of holy patriarchs;
   2) of holy angels;
   3) of the sun and moon.

1. Our wisdom, in so far as it ought to be deemed true and solid Wisdom, consists almost entirely of two parts: the knowledge of God and of ourselves. But as these are connected together by many ties, it is not easy to determine which of the two precedes and gives birth to the other. For, in the first place, no man can survey himself without forthwith turning his thoughts towards the God in whom he lives and moves; because it is perfectly obvious, that the endowments which we possess cannot possibly be from ourselves; nay, that our very being is nothing else than subsistence in God alone. In the second place, those blessings which unceasingly distil to us from heaven, are like streams conducting us to the fountain. Here, again, the infinitude of good which resides in God becomes more apparent from our poverty. In particular, the miserable ruin into which the revolt of the first man has plunged us, compels us to turn our eyes upwards; not only that while hungry and famishing we may thence ask what we want, but being aroused by fear may learn humility. For as there exists in man something like a world of misery, and ever since we were stript of the divine attire our naked shame discloses an immense series of disgraceful properties every man, being stung by the consciousness of his own unhappiness, in this way necessarily obtains at least some knowledge of God. Thus, our feeling of ignorance, vanity, want, weakness, in short, depravity and corruption, reminds us . . . that in the Lord, and none but He, dwell the true light of wisdom, solid virtue, exuberant goodness. We are accordingly urged by our own evil things to consider the good things of God; and, indeed, we cannot aspire to Him in earnest until we have begun to be displeased with ourselves. For what man is not disposed to rest in himself? Who, in fact, does not thus rest, so long as he is unknown to himself; that is, so long as he is contented with his own endowments, and unconscious or unmindful of his misery? Every person, therefore, on coming to the knowledge of himself, is not only urged to seek God, but is also led as by the hand to find him.

2. On the other hand, it is evident that man never attains to a true

self-knowledge until he has previously contemplated the face of God, and come down after such contemplation to look into himself. For (such is our innate pride) we always seem to ourselves just, and upright, and wise, and holy, until we are convinced, by clear evidence, of our injustice, vileness, folly, and impurity. Convinced, however, we are not, if we look to ourselves only, and not to the Lord also—He being the only standard by the application of which this conviction can be produced. For, since we are all naturally prone to hypocrisy, any empty semblance of righteousness is quite enough to satisfy us instead of righteousness itself. And since nothing appears within us or around us that is not tainted with very great impurity, so long as we keep our mind within the confines of human pollution, anything which is in some small degree less defiled delights us as if it were most pure just as an eye, to which nothing but black had been previously presented, deems an object of a whitish, or even of a brownish hue, to be perfectly white. Nay, the bodily sense may furnish a still stronger illustration of the extent to which we are deluded in estimating the powers of the mind. If, at mid-day, we either look down to the ground, or on the surrounding objects which lie open to our view, we think ourselves endued with a very strong and piercing eyesight; but when we look up to the sun, and gaze at it unveiled, the sight which did excellently well for the earth is instantly so dazzled and confounded by the refulgence, as to oblige us to confess that our acuteness in discerning terrestrial objects is mere dimness when applied to the sun. Thus too, it happens in estimating our spiritual qualities. So long as we do not look beyond the earth, we are quite pleased with our own righteousness, wisdom, and virtue; we address ourselves in the most flattering terms, and seem only less than demigods. But should we once begin to raise our thoughts to God, and reflect what kind of Being he is, and how absolute the perfection of that righteousness, and wisdom, and virtue, to which, as a standard, we are bound to be conformed, what formerly delighted us by its false show of righteousness will become polluted with the greatest iniquity; what strangely imposed upon us under the name of wisdom will disgust by its extreme folly; and what presented the appearance of virtuous energy will be condemned as the most miserable impotence. So far are those qualities in us, which seem most perfect, from corresponding to the divine purity.

3. Hence that dread and amazement with which as Scripture uniformly

relates, holy men were struck and overwhelmed whenever they beheld the presence of God. When we see those who previously stood firm and secure so quaking with terror, that the fear of death takes hold of them, nay, they are, in a manner, swallowed up and annihilated, the inference to be drawn is that men are never duly touched and impressed with a conviction of their insignificance, until they have contrasted themselves with the majesty of God. Frequent examples of this consternation occur both in the Book of Judges and the Prophetical Writings; so much so, that it was a common expression among the people of God, "We shall die, for we have seen the Lord." Hence the Book of Job, also, in humbling men under a conviction of their folly, feebleness, and pollution, always derives its chief argument from descriptions of the Divine wisdom, virtue, and purity. Nor without cause: for we see Abraham the readier to acknowledge himself but dust and ashes the nearer he approaches to behold the glory of the Lord, and Elijah unable to wait with unveiled face for His approach; so dreadful is the sight. And what can man do, man who is but rottenness and a worm, when even the Cherubim themselves must veil their faces in very terror? To this, undoubtedly, the Prophet Isaiah refers, when he says (Isa. 24:23), "The moon shall be confounded, and the sun ashamed, when the Lord of Hosts shall reign;" i.e., when he shall exhibit his refulgence, and give a nearer view of it, the brightest objects will, in comparison, be covered with darkness.

But though the knowledge of God and the knowledge of ourselves are bound together by a mutual tie, due arrangement requires that we treat of the former in the first place, and then descend to the latter.

## Chapter 2:

### What It Is to Know God—Tendency of This Knowledge

*Sections:*

1. The knowledge of God the Creator defined. The substance of this knowledge, and the use to be made of it.
2. Further illustration of the use, together with a necessary reproof of vain curiosity, and refutation of the Epicureans. The character

of God as it appears to the pious mind, contrasted with the absurd views of the Epicureans. Religion defined.

1. By the knowledge of God, I understand that by which we not only conceive that there is some God, but also apprehend what it is for our interest, and conducive to his glory, what, in short, it is befitting to know concerning him. For, properly speaking, we cannot say that God is known where there is no religion or piety. I am not now referring to that species of knowledge by which men, in themselves lost and under curse, apprehend God as a Redeemer in Christ the Mediator. I speak only of that simple and primitive knowledge, to which the mere course of nature would have conducted us, had Adam stood upright. For although no man will now, in the present ruin of the human race, perceive God to be either a father, or the author of salvation, or propitious in any respect, until Christ interpose to make our peace; still it is one thing to perceive that God our Maker supports us by his power, rules us by his providence, fosters us by his goodness, and visits us with all kinds of blessings, and another thing to embrace the grace of reconciliation offered to us in Christ. Since, then, the Lord first appears, as well in the creation of the world as in the general doctrine of Scripture, simply as a Creator, and afterwards as a Redeemer in Christ, a twofold knowledge of him hence arises: of these the former is now to be considered, the latter will afterwards follow in its order.

But although our mind cannot conceive of God, without rendering some worship to him, it will not, however, be sufficient simply to hold that he is the only being whom all ought to worship and adore, unless we are also persuaded that he is the fountain of all goodness, and that we must seek everything in him, and in none but him. My meaning is: we must be persuaded not only that as he once formed the world, so he sustains it by his boundless power, governs it by his wisdom, preserves it by his goodness, in particular, rules the human race with justice and judgment, bears with them in mercy, shields them by his protection; but also that not a particle of light, or wisdom, or justice, or power, or rectitude, or genuine truth, will anywhere be found, which does not flow from him, and of which he is not the cause; in this way we must learn to expect and ask all things from him, and thankfully ascribe to him whatever we receive. For this sense of the divine perfections is the proper master to teach us piety, out of which religion springs. By piety I mean that union of reverence and love to God which the knowledge of his benefits inspires. For, until men feel that they owe everything to God, that they are cherished by his paternal care, and that he is the author of all their blessings, so that nought is to be looked for away from him, they will never submit to him in voluntary obedience; nay, unless they place their entire happiness in him, they will never yield up their whole selves to him in truth and sincerity.

2. Those, therefore, who, in considering this question, propose to inquire what the essence of God is, only delude us with frigid speculations, it being much more our interest to know what kind of being God is, and what things are agreeable to his nature. For, of what use is it to join Epicurus in acknowledging some God who has cast off the care of the world, and only delights himself in ease? What avails it, in short, to know a God with whom we have nothing to do? The effect of our knowledge rather ought to be, first, to teach us reverence and fear; and, secondly, to induce us, under its guidance and teaching, to ask every good thing from him, and, when it is received, ascribe it to him. For how can the idea of God enter your mind without instantly giving rise to the thought, that since you are his workmanship, you are bound, by the very law of creation, to submit to his authority?—that your life is due to him?—that whatever you do ought to have reference to him? If so, it undoubtedly follows that your life is sadly corrupted, if it is not framed in obedience to him, since his will ought to be the law of our lives. On the other hand, your idea of his nature is not clear unless you acknowledge him to be the origin and fountain of all goodness. Hence would arise both confidence in him, and a desire of cleaving to him, did not the depravity of the human mind lead it away from the proper course of investigation.

For, first of all, the pious mind does not devise for itself any kind of God, but looks alone to the one true God; nor does it feign for him any character it pleases, but is contented to have him in the character in which he manifests himself, always guarding, with the utmost diligence, against transgressing his will, and wandering, with daring presumption, from the right path. He by whom God is thus known, perceiving how he governs all things, confides in him as his guardian and protector, and casts himself entirely upon his faithfulness—perceiving him to be the source of every blessing, if he is in any strait or feels any want, he instantly recurs to his protection and trusts to his aid—persuaded that he is good and merciful, he reclines upon him with sure confidence, and doubts not that, in the divine clemency, a remedy will be provided for his every time of need—acknowledging him as his Father and his Lord, he considers himself bound to have respect to his authority in all things, to reverence his majesty, aim at the advancement of his glory, and obey his commands—regarding him as a just judge, armed with severity to punish crimes, he keeps the judgment-seat always in his view. Standing in awe of it, he curbs himself, and fears to provoke his anger. Nevertheless, he is not so terrified by an apprehension of judgment as to wish he could withdraw himself, even if the means of escape lay before him; nay, he embraces him not less as the avenger of wickedness than as the rewarder of the righteous; because he perceives that it equally appertains to his glory to store up punishment for the one, and eternal life for the other. Besides, it is not the mere fear of punishment that restrains him from sin. Loving and revering God as his father, honouring and obeying him as his master, although there were no hell, he would revolt at the very idea of offending him.

Such is pure and genuine religion, namely, confidence in God coupled with serious fear—fear, which both includes in it willing reverence, and brings along with it such legitimate worship as is prescribed by the law. And it ought to be more carefully considered, that all men promiscuously do homage to God, but very few truly reverence him. On all hands there is abundance of ostentatious ceremonies, but sincerity of heart is rare.

## Chapter 3:

## The Knowledge of God Naturally Implanted in the Human Mind

*Sections:*

1. The knowledge of God being manifested to all makes the repro-bate without excuse. Universal belief and acknowledgement of the existence of God.
2. Objection—that religion and the belief of a Deity are the inventions of crafty politicians. Refutation of the objection. This universal belief confirmed by the examples of wicked men and Atheists.

3. Confirmed also by the vain endeavours of the wicked to banish all fear of God from their minds. Conclusion, that the knowledge of God is naturally implanted in the human mind.

1. That there exists in the human minds and indeed by natural instinct, some sense of Deity, we hold to be beyond dispute, since God himself, to prevent any man from pretending ignorance, has endued all men with some idea of his Godhead, the memory of which he constantly renews and occasionally enlarges, that all to a man being aware that there is a God, and that he is their Maker, may be condemned by their own conscience when they neither worship him nor consecrate their lives to his service. Certainly, if there is any quarter where it may be supposed that God is unknown, the most likely for such an instance to exist is among the dullest tribes farthest removed from civilisation. But, as a heathen tells us, there is no nation so barbarous, no race so brutish, as not to be imbued with the conviction that there is a God. Even those who, in other respects, seem to differ least from the lower animals, constantly retain some sense of religion; so thoroughly has this common conviction possessed the mind, so firmly is it stamped on the breasts of all men. Since, then, there never has been, from the very first, any quarter of the globe, any city, any household even, without religion, this amounts to a tacit confession, that a sense of Deity is inscribed on every heart.

Nay, even idolatry is ample evidence of this fact. For we know how reluctant man is to lower himself, in order to set other creatures above him. Therefore, when he chooses to worship wood and stone rather than be thought to have no God, it is evident how very strong this impression of a Deity must be; since it is more difficult to obliterate it from the mind of man, than to break down the feelings of his nature—these certainly being broken down, when, in opposition to his natural haughtiness, he spontaneously humbles himself before the meanest object as an act of reverence to God.

2. It is most absurd, therefore, to maintain, as some do, that religion was devised by the cunning and craft of a few individuals, as a means of keeping the body of the people in due subjection, while there was nothing which those very individuals, while teaching others to worship God, less believed than the existence of a God. I readily acknowledge, that designing

men have introduced a vast number of fictions into religion, with the view of inspiring the populace with reverence or striking them with terror, and thereby rendering them more obsequious; but they never could have succeeded in this, had the minds of men not been previously imbued with that uniform belief in God, from which, as from its seed, the religious propensity springs. And it is altogether incredible that those who, in the matter of religion, cunningly imposed on their ruder neighbours, were altogether devoid of a knowledge of God. For though in old times there were some, and in the present day not a few are found who deny the being of a God, yet, whether they will or not, they occasionally feel the truth which they are desirous not to know. We do not read of any man who broke out into more unbridled and audacious contempt of the Deity than C. Caligula, and yet none showed greater dread when any indication of divine wrath was manifested. Thus, however unwilling, he shook with terror before the God whom he professedly studied to condemn. You may every day see the same thing happening to his modern imitators. The most audacious despiser of God is most easily disturbed, trembling at the sound of a falling leaf. How so, unless in vindication of the divine majesty, which smites their consciences the more strongly the more they endeavour to flee from it. They all, indeed, look out for hiding-places where they may conceal themselves from the presence of the Lord, and again efface it from their mind; but after all their efforts they remain caught within the net. Though the conviction may occasionally seem to vanish for a moment, it immediately returns, and rushes in with new impetuosity, so that any interval of relief from the gnawing of conscience is not unlike the slumber of the intoxicated or the insane, who have no quiet rest in sleep, but are continually haunted with dire horrific dreams. Even the wicked themselves, therefore, are an example of the fact that some idea of God always exists in every human mind.

3. All men of sound Judgment will therefore hold, that a sense of Deity is indelibly engraven on the human heart. And that this belief is naturally engendered in all, and thoroughly fixed as it were in our very bones, is strikingly attested by the contumacy of the wicked, who, though they struggle furiously, are unable to extricate themselves from the fear of God. Though Diagoras, and others of like stamps make themselves merry with whatever has been believed in all ages concerning religion, and Dionysus scoffs at the Judgment of heaven, it is but a Sardonian grin; for the worm of conscience,

keener than burning steel, is gnawing them within. I do not say with Cicero, that errors wear out by age, and that religion increases and grows better day by day. For the world (as will be shortly seen) labours as much as it can to shake off all knowledge of God, and corrupts his worship in innumerable ways. I only say, that, when the stupid hardness of heart, which the wicked eagerly court as a means of despising God, becomes enfeebled, the sense of Deity, which of all things they wished most to be extinguished, is still in vigour, and now and then breaks forth. Whence we infer, that this is not a doctrine which is first learned at school, but one as to which every man is, from the womb, his own master; one which nature herself allows no individual to forget, though many, with all their might, strive to do so.

Moreover, if all are born and live for the express purpose of learning to know God, and if the knowledge of God, in so far as it fails to produce this effect, is fleeting and vain, it is clear that all those who do not direct the whole thoughts and actions of their lives to this end fail to fulfill the law of their being. This did not escape the observation even of philosophers. For it is the very thing which Plato meant . . . when he taught, as he often does, that the chief good of the soul consists in resemblance to God; i.e., when, by means of knowing him, she is wholly transformed into him. Thus Gryllus, also, in Plutarch . . . , reasons most skillfully, when he affirms that, if once religion is banished from the lives of men, they not only in no respect excel, but are, in many respects, much more wretched than the brutes, since, being exposed to so many forms of evil, they continually drag on a troubled and restless existence: that the only thing, therefore, which makes them superior is the worship of God, through which alone they aspire to immortality.

## Chapter 4:

### The Knowledge of God Stifled or Corrupted, Ignorantly or Maliciously

*Sections:*

1. The knowledge of God suppressed by ignorance, many falling away into superstition. Such persons, however, inexcusable, because their error is accompanied with pride and stubbornness.

2. Stubbornness the companion of impiety.

3. No pretext can justify superstition. This proved, first, from reason; and, secondly, from Scripture.

4. The wicked never willingly come into the presence of God. Hence their hypocrisy. Hence, too, their sense of Deity leads to no good result.

1. But though experience testifies that a seed of religion is divinely sown in all, scarcely one in a hundred is found who cherishes it in his heart, and not one in whom it grows to maturity, so far is it from yielding fruit in its season. Moreover, while some lose themselves in superstitious observances, and others, of set purpose, wickedly revolt from God, the result is that, in regard to the true knowledge of him, all are so degenerate, that in no part of the world can genuine godliness be found. In saying that some fall away into superstition, I mean not to insinuate that their excessive absurdity frees them from guilt; for the blindness under which they labour is almost invariably accompanied with vain pride and stubbornness. Mingled vanity and pride appear in this, that when miserable men do seek after God, instead of ascending higher than themselves, as they ought to do, they measure him by their own carnal stupidity, and, neglecting solid inquiry, fly off to indulge their curiosity in vain speculation. Hence, they do not conceive of him in the character in which he is manifested, but imagine him to be whatever their own rashness has devised. This abyss standing open, they cannot move one footstep without rushing headlong to destruction. With such an idea of God, nothing which they may attempt to offer in the way of worship or obedience can have any value in his sight, because it is not him they worship, but, instead of him, the dream and figment of their own heart. This corrupt procedure is admirably described by Paul, when he says, that "thinking to be wise, they became fools" (Rom. 1:22). He had previously said that "they became vain in their imaginations," but lest any should suppose them blameless, he afterwards adds, that they were deservedly blinded, because, not contented with sober inquiry, because, arrogating to themselves more than they have any title to do, they of their own accord court darkness, nay, bewitch themselves with perverse, empty show. Hence it is that their folly, the result not only of vain curiosity, but of licentious desire and overweening confidence in the pursuit of forbidden knowledge, cannot be excused.

2. The expression of David (Ps. 14:1, 53:1), "The fool hath said in his heart, There is no God," is primarily applied to those who, as will shortly farther appear, stifle the light of nature, and intentionally stupefy themselves. We see many, after they have become hardened in a daring course of sin, madly banishing all remembrance of God, though spontaneously suggested to them from within, by natural sense. To show how detestable this madness is, the Psalmist introduces them as distinctly denying that there is a God, because, although they do not disown his essence, they rob him of his justice and providence, and represent him as sitting idly in heaven. Nothing being less accordant with the nature of God than to cast off the government of the world, leaving it to chance, and so to wink at the crimes of men that they may wanton with impunity in evil courses; it follows, that every man who indulges in security, after extinguishing all fear of divine judgment, virtually denies that there is a God. As a just punishment of the wicked, after they have closed their own eyes, God makes their hearts dull and heavy, and hence, seeing, they see not. David, indeed, is the best interpreter of his own meaning, when he says elsewhere, the wicked has "no fear of God before his eyes" (Ps. 36:1); and, again, "He hath said in his heart, God hath forgotten; he hideth his face; he will never see it."

Thus, although they are forced to acknowledge that there is some God, they however, rob him of his glory by denying his power. For, as Paul declares, "If we believe not, he abideth faithful, he cannot deny himself" (2 Tim. 2:13); so those who feign to themselves a dead and dumb idol, are truly said to deny God. It is, moreover, to be observed, that though they struggle with their own convictions, and would fain not only banish God from their minds, but from heaven also, there stupefaction is never so complete as to secure them from being occasionally dragged before the divine tribunal. Still, as no fear restrains them from rushing violently in the face of God, so long as they are hurried on by that blind impulse, it cannot be denied that their prevailing state of mind in regard to him is brutish oblivion.

3. In this way, the vain pretext which many employ to clothe their superstition is overthrown. They deem it enough that they have some kind of zeal for religion, how preposterous soever it may be, not observing that true religion must be conformable to the will of God as its unerring standard; that he can never deny himself, and is no spectre or phantom, to be metamorphosed at each individual's caprice. It is easy to see how

superstition, with its false glosses, mocks God, while it tries to please him. Usually fastening merely on things on which he has declared he sets no value, it either contemptuously overlooks, or even undisguisedly rejects, the things which he expressly enjoins, or in which we are assured that he takes pleasure. Those, therefore, who set up a fictitious worship, merely worship and adore their own delirious fancies; indeed, they would never dare so to trifle with God, had they not previously fashioned him after their own childish conceits. Hence that vague and wandering opinion of Deity is declared by an apostle to be ignorance of God: "Howbeit, then, when ye knew not God, ye did service unto them which by nature are no gods." And he elsewhere declares, that the Ephesians were "without God" (Eph. 2:12) at the time when they wandered without any correct knowledge of him. It makes little difference, at least in this respect, whether you hold the existence of one God, or a plurality of gods, since, in both cases alike, by departing from the true God, you have nothing left but an execrable idol. It remains, therefore, to conclude with Lactantius . . . , "No religion is genuine that is not in accordance with truth."

4. To this fault they add a second—viz. that when they do think of God it is against their will; never approaching him without being dragged into his presence, and when there, instead of the voluntary fear flowing from reverence of the divine majesty, feeling only that forced and servile fear which divine judgment extorts—judgment which, from the impossibility of escape, they are compelled to dread, but which, while they dread, they at the same time also hate. To impiety, and to it alone, the saying of Statius properly applies: "Fear first brought gods into the world". . . . Those whose inclinations are at variance with the justice of God, knowing that his tribunal has been erected for the punishment of transgression, earnestly wish that that tribunal were overthrown. Under the influence of this feeling they are actually warring against God, justice being one of his essential attributes. Perceiving that they are always within reach of his power, that resistance and evasion are alike impossible, they fear and tremble. Accordingly, to avoid the appearance of contemning a majesty by which all are overawed, they have recourse to some species of religious observance, never ceasing meanwhile to defile themselves with every kind of vice, and add crime to crime, until they have broken the holy law of the Lord in every one of its requirements, and set his whole righteousness at nought; at all events, they

are not so restrained by their semblance of fear as not to luxuriate and take pleasure in iniquity, choosing rather to indulge their carnal propensities than to curb them with the bridle of the Holy Spirit.

But since this shadow of religion (it scarcely even deserves to be called a shadow) is false and vain, it is easy to infer how much this confused knowledge of God differs from that piety which is instilled into the breasts of believers, and from which alone true religion springs. And yet hypocrites would fain, by means of tortuous windings, make a show of being near to God at the very time they are fleeing from him. For while the whole life ought to be one perpetual course of obedience, they rebel without fear in almost all their actions, and seek to appease him with a few paltry sacrifices; while they ought to serve him with integrity of heart and holiness of life, they endeavour to procure his favour by means of frivolous devices and punctilios of no value.

Nay, they take greater license in their groveling indulgencies, because they imagine that they can fulfill their duty to him by preposterous expiations; in short, while their confidence ought to have been fixed upon him, they put him aside, and rest in themselves or the creatures. At length they bewilder themselves in such a maze of error, that the darkness of ignorance obscures, and ultimately extinguishes, those sparks which were designed to show them the glory of God. Still, however, the conviction that there is some Deity continues to exist, like a plant which can never be completely eradicated, though so corrupt that it is only capable of producing the worst of fruit. Nay, we have still stronger evidence of the proposition for which I now contend—viz. that a sense of Deity is naturally engraven on the human heart, in the fact, that the very reprobate are forced to acknowledge it. When at their ease, they can jest about God, and talk pertly and loquaciously in disparagement of his power; but should despair, from any cause, overtake them, it will stimulate them to seek him, and dictate ejaculatory prayers, proving that they were not entirely ignorant of God, but had perversely suppressed feelings which ought to have been earlier manifested.

*Translated by Henry Beveridge, Esq., 1845*

# John Calvin's Institutes
# of the Christian Religion

## Russell D. Moore

If today John Calvin were discovered alive and in suspended animation, frozen in a block of ice somewhere in the French Alps, most people probably wouldn't consider this good news. After all, the unfrozen Calvinist lawgiver rarely is thought of as the kind of figure modern audiences would want to drag back up.

His writings don't have the wink-of-the-eye, puckish grin that even his contemporary Martin Luther seems to sometimes convey in his many writings. Moreover, Calvin, although associated with some bland but commendable features such as hard work and thrift, is mostly known for awful things, such as burnings at the stake and the predestination of people to hell.

Calvin is too important, though, to leave him frozen in caricature, and he's too significant to leave him simply to his tribe of theological partisans. John Calvin—most significantly in his *Institutes of the Christian Religion*—offers insight to all in the Christian tradition, including those who consider themselves the furthest away from "Calvinism."

The *Institutes* was written first in 1536, with the final version completed in Latin in 1559. Calvin, a French convert from Catholicism to the ideas of the Protestant Reformation, quickly established himself as the early protest movement's most influential theologian. While those who have never read Calvin firsthand often assume the volume is obsessed with speculative notions about divine sovereignty and the order of God's decrees of election and reprobation, the excerpt here better represents something of the broader tone and substance of the Reformer's thought.

The tome's initial sentence establishes a core theme in Calvin's work: "Nearly all the wisdom we possess, that is to say, true and sound wisdom, consists of two parts: the knowledge of God and of ourselves." At first glance, this statement might seem to be exactly what we might expect from one so often associated with coldly cerebral Christian rationalism and abstract speculation. But the discussion Calvin begins on "knowledge" is far more complex, and far more engaging, than that.

First of all, Calvin here is setting the context for a vision of all of life as theological. By this, I don't mean merely that Calvin believes there is what some would call a Christian "worldview," a theologically informed way of thinking about all aspects of existence. Calvin means more than this. He means that every human being is, by definition, a theologian. Every "word"—that is, every means a person has for making sense of his reality—is inescapably a "word about God," a theology.

In addition, this truth is grounded above all in the creaturely nature of humanity. Referencing the apostle Paul's speech to the Athenians at Mars Hill, Calvin notes that it is in Creator God, by necessity, that every human person "lives and moves" (Acts 17:28). For Calvin, the universal impulse of humanity to worship gods or ideologies or themselves is hardly a coincidence of evolution. The sense of the divine is embedded in all human persons, as part of God's image itself. This awareness is activated by the icon of God's glory present in the created cosmos all around us. If we do not acknowledge this primal reality, we simply cannot apprehend ourselves as we really are, or the universe as it really is.

Further, it is not simply that all persons *ought* to be able to realize there is a God, if only they were to pay careful enough attention to the evidences for His existence. It is instead that all persons *do*, immediately, recognize this. Moreover, they recognize not only God's existence, but they also recognize, personally, the God who is. So why is there not a universal worship of the God in whom Calvin believes, the God of the Jewish and Christian Scriptures, the God of Jesus of Nazareth?

This is where John Calvin's view of sin emerges. Again, he's oft-misrepresented as having a gloomy, world-denying pessimism about humanity. Some of his followers throughout the centuries have yielded to this caricature. But Calvin's view of sin isn't censorious or cranky. Instead, this doctrine explains why worship is so difficult for humanity as it is. It is not, in Calvin's view, that we sin because we believe the wrong things; it is, rather, that *we believe the wrong things because we sin.*

In other words, human persons, in our fallenness, crave our own autonomy—the illusion that we are gods to ourselves. In order to protect this delusion and remain "free" from our Creator, we convince ourselves of what deep in our consciences we cannot deny—the reality of God, His moral law, the coming judgment.

Calvin here, echoing Paul, anticipates some of the psychological theories of later centuries in presenting a picture of the role the affections play in shaping the way we think. Sigmund Freud may have been quite wrong about many things, yet who can deny that human persons are motivated by more than merely rational impulses but additionally by an often dark and nearly incomprehensible psychic undertow? Calvin would root this in the fallen nature of the human condition. In order to know God and to know ourselves, Calvin insists, we must face this truth.

This is *hardly* a "pessimistic" picture, though, in the larger mosaic of Calvin's thought. Human persons can rightly read the cosmos, and ourselves, through the revelation God has disclosed in the person of Jesus Christ and in the "spectacles" of the Scriptures.

Calvin's view of revelation, and of knowledge as fundamentally a question of worship, grounds the importance in Protestant Christianity of preaching and widespread reading and study of the Bible in the languages of the people. This tradition, as it expanded in missionary movements and revivalist awakenings, shaped much of the trajectory of modern European and American thought.

Reading John Calvin's *Institutes*, you'll likely find points of disagreement, perhaps even major disagreements. But also you'll probably—whatever your religious communion—find the insights of a mind shaped by immersion in the Scriptures, in the church fathers, in Western classical thought. And, behind this, you'll discover a man who recognized something of what it meant (1) to be a creature, and (2) to look in worship and humility for the Creator in whom he lived and moved.

## CHAPTER TWELVE

# EDMUND SPENSER

## Early Modern (1552–1599)

If Christians did not invent romance, we at least perfected it in the West, and Spenser is a high point of that hard task. Plato understood love as a powerful engine that can destroy mankind or turn us to the good. Christ made that turn possible, and Spenser shows what can be done in the human soul if we take it.

For most contemporary people, holiness is a negation. Holy people *don't*. The "holy" student will *not* go to the bacchanalia of Spring Break; the secular kid will have all the fun. Being virtuous has become all about "not sinning."

Reading Spenser should remind Christians that virtue is empowering. Holy people *can*.

What can they do? For one thing, they can go on meaningful adventures. The difference between a quest and Spring Break is that the former can lead to romance and continued civilization, while the latter is parasitical on both. Having a baby at the end of Spring Break is bad news; by contrast, all truly great quests end in marriage that assists in producing the next generation.

Romance is painful, fecund, and joyous.

What is more, Spenser will teach a good reader that virtue is active and not passive. Faith works and kills dragons. The godly Christian should be going on adventures at any age, because there is always murder to be prevented, poverty to be alleviated, slavery to be abolished. There is also beauty to be created, lovers to be wooed, and children to be raised. While virtue is not intrinsically fun, it does enable humans to pursue happiness. Happiness is found when head, heart, and hands all work together in a flourishing and wonder-filled life.

<br><br>

⌨ FROM ⌨

# *The Faerie Queene*

<br>

CANTO I

*The Patron of true Holinesse,*
*Foule Errour doth defeate:*
*Hypocrisie him to entrape,*
*Doth to his home entreate.*

**i**

A Gentle Knight was pricking on the plaine,
Y cladd in mightie armes and silver shielde,
Wherein old dints of deepe wounds did remaine,
The cruell markes of many a bloudy fielde;
Yet armes till that time did he never wield:
His angry steede did chide his foming bitt,
As much disdayning to the curbe to yield:
Full jolly knight he seemd, and faire did sitt,
As one for knightly giusts and fierce encounters fitt.

**ii**

But on his brest a bloudie Crosse he bore,
The deare remembrance of his dying Lord,

For whose sweete sake that glorious badge he wore,
And dead as living ever him ador'd:
Upon his shield the like was also scor'd,
For soveraine hope, which in his helpe he had:
Right faithfull true he was in deede and word,
But of his cheere did seeme too solemne sad;
Yet nothing did he dread, but ever was ydrad.

iii

Upon a great adventure he was bond,
That greatest Gloriana to him gave,
That greatest Glorious Queene of Faerie lond,
To winne him worship, and her grace to have,
Which of all earthly things he most did crave;
And ever as he rode, his hart did earne
To prove his puissance in battell brave
Upon his foe, and his new force to learne;
Upon his foe, a Dragon horrible and stearne.

iv

A lovely Ladie rode him faire beside,
Upon a lowly Asse more white then snow,
Yet she much whiter, but the same did hide
Under a vele, that wimpled was full low,
And over all a blacke stole she did throw,
As one that inly mournd: so was she sad,
And heavie sat upon her palfrey slow;
Seemed in heart some hidden care she had,
And by her in a line a milke white lambe she lad.

v

So pure an innocent, as that same lambe,
She was in life and every vertuous lore,
And by descent from Royall lynage came
Of ancient Kings and Queenes, that had of yore
Their scepters stretcht from East to Westerne shore,

And all the world in their subjection held;
Till that infernall feend with foule uprore
Forwasted all their land, and them expeld:
Whom to avenge, she had this Knight from far compeld.

vi

Behind her farre away a Dwarfe did lag,
That lasie seemd in being ever last,
Or wearied with bearing of her bag
Of needments at his backe. Thus as they past,
The day with cloudes was suddeine overcast,
And angry Jove an hideous storme of raine
Did poure into his Lemans lap so fast,
That every wight to shrowd it did constrain,
And this faire couple eke to shroud themselves were fain.

vii

Enforst to seeke some covert nigh at hand,
A shadie grove not far away they spide,
That promist ayde the tempest to withstand:
Whose loftie trees yclad with sommers pride,
Did spred so broad, that heavens light did hide,
Not perceable with power of any starre:
And all within were pathes and alleies wide,
With footing worne, and leading inward farre:
Faire harbour that them seemes; so in they entred arre.

viii

And foorth they passe, with pleasure forward led,
Joying to heare the birdes sweete harmony,
Which therein shrouded from the tempest dred,
Seemd in their song to scorne the cruell sky.
Much can they prayse the trees so straight and hy,
The sayling Pine, the Cedar proud and tall,
The vine-prop Elme, the Poplar never dry,
The builder Oake, sole king of forrests all,
The Aspine good for staves, the Cypresse funerall.

**ix**

The Laurell, meed of mightie Conquerours
And Poets sage, the Firre that weepeth still,
The Willow worne of forlorne Paramours,
The Eugh obedient to the benders will,
The Birch for shaftes, the Sallow for the mill,
The Mirrhe sweete bleeding in the bitter wound,
The warlike Beech, the Ash for nothing ill,
The fruitfull Olive, and the Platane round,
The carver Holme, the Maple seeldom inward sound.

**x**

Led with delight, they thus beguile the way,
Untill the blustring storme is overblowne;
When weening to returne, whence they did stray,
They cannot find that path, which first was showne,
But wander too and fro in wayes unknowne,
Furthest from end then, when they neerest weene,
That makes them doubt, their wits be not their owne:
So many pathes, so many turnings seene,
That which of them to take, in diverse doubt they been.

**xi**

At last resolving forward still to fare,
Till that some end they finde or in or out,
That path they take, that beaten seemd most bare,
And like to lead the labyrinth about;
Which when by tract they hunted had throughout,
At length it brought them to a hollow cave,
Amid the thickest woods. The Champion stout
Eftsoones dismounted from his courser brave,
And to the Dwarfe a while his needlesse spere he gave.

**xii**

Be well aware, quoth then that Ladie milde,
Least suddaine mischiefe ye too rash provoke:

The danger hid, the place unknowne and wilde,
Breeds dreadfull doubts: Oft fire is without smoke,
And perill without show: therefore your stroke
Sir knight with-hold, till further triall made.
Ah Ladie (said he) shame were to revoke
The forward footing for an hidden shade:
Vertue gives her selfe light, through darkenesse for to wade.

**xiii**

Yea but (quoth she) the perill of this place
I better wot then you, though now too late
To wish you backe returne with foule disgrace,
Yet wisedome warnes, whilest foot is in the gate,
To stay the steppe, ere forced to retrate.
This is the wandring wood, this Errours den,
A monster vile, whom God and man does hate:
Therefore I read beware. Fly fly (quoth then
The fearefull Dwarfe:) this is no place for living men.

**xiv**

But full of fire and greedy hardiment,
The youthfull knight could not for ought be staide,
But forth unto the darksome hole he went,
And looked in: his glistring armor made
A litle glooming light, much like a shade,
By which he saw the ugly monster plaine,
Halfe like a serpent horribly displaide,
But th'other halfe did womans shape retaine,
Most lothsom, filthie, foule, and full of vile disdaine.

**xv**

And as she lay upon the durtie ground,
Her huge long taile her den all overspred,
Yet was in knots and many boughtes upwound,
Pointed with mortall sting. Of her there bred
A thousand yong ones, which she dayly fed,

Sucking upon her poisonous dugs, eachone
Of sundry shapes, yet all ill favored:
Soone as that uncouth light upon them shone,
Into her mouth they crept, and suddain all were gone.


## xvi

Their dam upstart, out of her den effraide,
And rushed forth, hurling her hideous taile
About her cursed head, whose folds displaid
Were stretcht now forth at length without entraile.
She lookt about, and seeing one in mayle
Armed to point, sought backe to turne againe;
For light she hated as the deadly bale,
Ay wont in desert darknesse to remaine,
Where plaine none might her see, nor she see any plaine.


## xvii

Which when the valiant Elfe perceiv'd, he lept
As Lyon fierce upon the flying pray,
And with his trenchand blade her boldly kept
From turning backe, and forced her to stay:
Therewith enrag'd she loudly gan to bray,
And turning fierce, her speckled taile advaunst,
Threatning her angry sting, him to dismay:
Who nought aghast, his mightie hand enhaunst:
The stroke down from her head unto her shoulder glaunst.


## xviii

Much daunted with that dint, her sence was dazd,
Yet kindling rage, her selfe she gathered round,
And all attonce her beastly body raizd
With doubled forces high above the ground:
Tho wrapping up her wrethed sterne arownd,
Lept fierce upon his shield, and her huge traine
All suddenly about his body wound,
That hand or foot to stirre he strove in vaine:
God helpe the man so wrapt in Errours endlesse traine.

**xix**

His Lady sad to see his sore constraint,
Cride out, Now now Sir knight, shew what ye bee,
Add faith unto your force, and be not faint:
Strangle her, else she sure will strangle thee.
That when he heard, in great perplexitie,
His gall did grate for griefe and high disdaine,
And knitting all his force got one hand free,
Wherewith he grypt her gorge with so great paine,
That soone to loose her wicked bands did her constraine.

**xx**

Therewith she spewd out of her filthy maw
A floud of poyson horrible and blacke,
Full of great lumpes of flesh and gobbets raw,
Which stunck so vildly, that it forst him slacke
His grasping hold, and from her turne him backe:
Her vomit full of bookes and papers was,
With loathly frogs and toades, which eyes did lacke,
And creeping sought way in the weedy gras:
Her filthy parbreake all the place defiled has.

**xxi**

As when old father Nilus gins to swell
With timely pride above the Aegyptian vale,
His fattie waves do fertile slime outwell,
And overflow each plaine and lowly dale:
But when his later spring gins to avale,
Huge heapes of mudd he leaves, wherein there breed
Ten thousand kindes of creatures, partly male
And partly female of his fruitfull seed;
Such ugly monstrous shapes elsewhere may no man reed.

**xxii**

The same so sore annoyed has the knight,
That welnigh choked with the deadly stinke,

His forces faile, ne can no longer fight.
Whose corage when the feend perceiv'd to shrinke,
She poured forth out of her hellish sinke
Her fruitfull cursed spawne of serpents small,
Deformed monsters, fowle, and blacke as inke,
Which swarming all about his legs did crall,
And him encombred sore, but could not hurt at all.

**xxiii**

As gentle Shepheard in sweete even-tide,
When ruddy Phoebus gins to welke in west,
High on an hill, his flocke to vewen wide,
Markes which do byte their hasty supper best;
A cloud of combrous gnattes do him molest,
All striving to infixe their feeble stings,
That from their noyance he no where can rest,
But with his clownish hands their tender wings
He brusheth oft, and oft doth mar their murmurings.

**xxiv**

Thus ill bestedd, and fearefull more of shame,
Then of the certaine perill he stood in,
Halfe furious unto his foe he came,
Resolv'd in minde all suddenly to win,
Or soone to lose, before he once would lin;
And strooke at her with more then manly force,
That from her body full of filthie sin
He raft her hatefull head without remorse;
A streame of cole black bloud forth gushed from her corse.

**xxv**

Her scattred brood, soone as their Parent deare
They saw so rudely falling to the ground,
Groning full deadly, all with troublous feare,
Gathred themselves about her body round,
Weening their wonted entrance to have found

At her wide mouth: but being there withstood
They flocked all about her bleeding wound,
And sucked up their dying mothers blood,
Making her death their life, and eke her hurt their good.

**xxvi**

That detestable sight him much amazde,
To see th'unkindly Impes of heaven accurst,
Devoure their dam; on whom while so he gazd,
Having all satisfide their bloudy thurst,
Their bellies swolne he saw with fulnesse burst,
And bowels gushing forth: well worthy end
Of such as drunke her life, the which them nurst;
Now needeth him no lenger labour spend,
His foes have slaine themselves, with whom he should contend.

**xxvii**

His Ladie seeing all, that chaunst, from farre
Approcht in hast to greet his victorie,
And said, Faire knight, borne under happy starre,
Who see your vanquisht foes before you lye:
Well worthy be you of that Armorie,
Wherein ye have great glory wonne this day,
And proov'd your strength on a strong enimie,
Your first adventure: many such I pray,
And henceforth ever wish, that like succeed it may.

**xxviii**

Then mounted he upon his Steede againe,
And with the Lady backward sought to wend;
That path he kept, which beaten was most plame,
Ne ever would to any by-way bend,
But still did follow one unto the end,
The which at last out of the wood them brought.
So forward on his way (with God to frend)
He passed forth, and new adventure sought;
Long way he travelled, before he heard of ought.

### xxix

At length they chaunst to meet upon the way
An aged Sire, in long blacke weedes yclad,
His feete all bare, his beard all hoarie gray,
And by his belt his booke he hanging had;
Sober he seemde, and very sagely sad,
And to the ground his eyes were lowly bent,
Simple in shew, and voyde of malice bad,
And all the way he prayed, as he went,
And often knockt his brest, as one that did repent.

### xxx

He faire the knight saluted, louting low,
Who faire him quited, as that courteous was:
And after asked him, if he did know
Of straunge adventures, which abroad did pas.
Ah my deare Sonne (quoth he) how should, alas,
Silly old man, that lives in hidden cell,
Bidding his beades all day for his trespas,
Tydings of warre and worldly trouble tell?
With holy father sits not with such things to mell.

### xxxi

But if of daunger which hereby doth dwell,
And homebred evill ye desire to heare,
Of a straunge man I can you tidings tell,
That wasteth all this countrey farre and neare.
Of such (said he) I chiefly do inquere,
And shall you well reward to shew the place,
In which that wicked wight his dayes doth weare:
For to all knighthood it is foule disgrace,
That such a cursed creature lives so long a space.

### xxxii

Far hence (quoth he) in wastfull wildernesse
His dwelling is, by which no living wight

May ever passe, but thorough great distresse.
Now (sayd the Lady) draweth toward night,
And well I wote, that of your later fight
Ye all forwearied be: for what so strong,
But wanting rest will also want of might?
The Sunne that measures heaven all day long,
At night doth baite his steedes the Ocean waves emong.


**xxxiii**

Then with the Sunne take Sir, your timely rest,
And with new day new worke at once begin:
Untroubled night they say gives counsell best.
Right well Sir knight ye have advised bin,
(Quoth then that aged man;) the way to win
Is wisely to advise: now day is spent;
Therefore with me ye may take up your In
For this same night. The knight was well content:
So with that godly father to his home they went.


**xxxiv**

A little lowly Hermitage it was,
Downe in a dale, hard by a forests side,
Far from resort of people, that did pas
In travell to and froe: a little wyde
There was an holy Chappell edifyde,
Wherein the Hermite dewly wont to say
His holy things each morne and eventyde:
Thereby a Christall streame did gently play,
Which from a sacred fountaine welled forth alway.


**xxxv**

Arrived there, the little house they fill,
Ne looke for entertainement, where none was:
Rest is their feast, and all things at their will;
The noblest mind the best contentment has.
With faire discourse the evening so they pas:

For that old man of pleasing wordes had store,
And well could file his tongue as smooth as glas;
He told of Saintes and Popes, and evermore
He strowd an Ave-Mary after and before.

## xxxvi

The drouping Night thus creepeth on them fast,
And the sad humour loading their eye liddes,
As messenger of Morpheus on them cast
Sweet slombring deaw, the which to sleepe them biddes.
Unto their lodgings then his guestes he riddes:
Where when all drownd in deadly sleepe he findes,
He to his study goes, and there amiddes
His Magick bookes and artes of sundry kindes,
He seekes out mighty charmes, to trouble sleepy mindes.

## xxxvii

Then choosing out few wordes most horrible,
(Let none them read) thereof did verses frame,
With which and other spelles like terrible,
He bad awake blacke Plutoes griesly Dame,
And cursed heaven, and spake reprochfull shame
Of highest God, the Lord of life and light;
A bold bad man, that dar'd to call by name
Great Gorgon, Prince of darknesse and dead night,
At which Cocytus quakes, and Styx is put to flight.

## xxxviii

And forth he cald out of deepe darknesse dred
Legions of Sprights, the which like little flyes
Fluttring about his ever damned hed,
A-waite whereto their service he applyes,
To aide his friends, or fray his enimies:
Of those he chose out two, the falsest twoo,
And fittest for to forge true-seeming lyes;
The one of them he gave a message too,
The other by him selfe staide other worke to doo.

**xxxix**

> He making speedy way through spersed ayre,
> And through the world of waters wide and peepe,
> To Morpheus house doth hastily repaire.
> Amid the bowels of the earth full steepe,
> And low, where dawning day doth never peepe,
> His dwelling is; there Tethys his wet bed
> Doth ever wash, and Cynthia still doth steepe
> In silver deaw his ever-drouping hed,
> Whiles sad Night over him her mantle black doth spred.

**xl**

> Whose double gates he findeth locked fast,
> The one faire fram'd of burnisht Yvory,
> The other all with silver overcast;
> And wakefull dogges before them farre do lye
> Watching to banish Care their enimy,
> Who oft is wont to trouble gentle Sleepe.
> By them the Sprite doth passe in quietly,
> And unto Morpheus comes, whom drowned deepe
> In drowsie fit he findes: of nothing he takes keepe.

**xli**

> And more, to lulle him in his slumber soft,
> A trickling streame from high rocke tumbling downe
> And ever-drizling raine upon the loft,
> Mixt with a murmuring winde, much like the sowne
> Of swarming Bees, did cast him in a swowne:
> No other noyse, nor peoples troublous cryes,
> As still are wont t'annoy the walled towne,
> Might there be heard: but carelesse Quiet lyes,
> Wrapt in eternall silence farre from enemyes.

**xlii**

> The messenger approching to him spake,
> But his wast wordes returnd to him in vaine:

So sound he slept, that nought mought him awake.
Then rudely he him thrust, and pusht with paine,
Whereat he gan to stretch: but he againe
Shooke him so hard, that forced him to speake.
As one then in a dreame, whose dryer braine
In tost with troubled sights and fancies weake,
He mumbled soft, but would not all his silence breake.

**xliii**

The Sprite then gan more boldly him to wake,
And threatned unto him the dreaded name
Of Hecate: whereat he gan to quake,
And lifting up his lumpish head, with blame
Halfe angry asked him, for what he came.
Hither (quoth he) me Archimago sent,
He that the stubborne Sprites can wisely tame,
He bids thee to him send for his intent
A fit false dreame, that can delude the sleepers sent.

**xliv**

The God obayde, and calling forth straight way
A diverse dreame out of his prison darke,
Delivered it to him, and downe did lay
His heavie head, devoide of carefull carke,
Whose sences all were straight benumbed and starke.
He backe returning by the Yvorie dore,
Remounted up as light as chearefull Larke,
And on his litle winges the dreame he bore
In hast unto his Lord, where he him left afore.

**xlv**

Who all this while with charmes and hidden artes,
Had made a Lady of that other Spright,
And fram'd of liquid ayre her tender partes
So lively, and so like in all mens sight,
That weaker sence it could have ravisht quight:

The maker selfe for all his wondrous witt,
Was nigh beguiled with so goodly sight:
Her all in white he clad, and over it
Cast a blacke stole, most like to seeme for Una fit.


## xlvi

Now when that ydle dreame was to him brought,
Unto that Elfin knight he bad him fly,
Where he slept soundly void of evill thought
And with false shewes abuse his fantasy,
In sort as he him schooled privily:
And that new creature borne without her dew,
Full of the makers guile, with usage sly
He taught to imitate that Lady trew,
Whose semblance she did carrie under feigned hew.


## xlvii

Thus well instructed, to their worke they hast,
And comming where the knight in slomber lay,
The one upon his hardy head him plast,
And made him dreame of loves and lustfull play,
That nigh his manly hart did melt away,
Bathed in wanton blis and wicked joy:
Then seemed him his Lady by him lay,
And to him playnd, how that false winged boy,
Her chast hart had subdewd, to learne Dame pleasures toy.


## xlviii

And she her selfe of beautie soveraigne Queene,
Faire Venus seemde unto his bed to bring
Her, whom he waking evermore did weene,
To be the chastest flowre, that ay did spring
On earthly braunch, the daughter of a king,
Now a loose Leman to vile service bound:
And eke the Graces seemed all to sing,
*Hymen iō Hymen,* dauncing all around,
While freshest Flora her with Yvie girlond crownd.

## xlix

In this great passion of unwonted lust,
Or wonted feare of doing ought amis,
He started up, as seeming to mistrust
Some secret ill, or hidden foe of his:
Lo there before his face his Lady is,
Under blake stole hyding her bayted hooke,
And as halfe blushing offred him to kis,
With gentle blandishment and lovely looke,
Most like that virgin true, which for her knight him took.

## l

All cleane dismayd to see so uncouth sight,
And halfe enraged at her shamelesse guise,
He thought have slaine her in his fierce despight:
But hasty heat tempring with sufferance wise,
He stayde his hand, and gan himselfe advise
To prove his sense, and tempt her faigned truth.
Wringing her hands in wemens pitteous wise,
Tho can she weepe, to stirre up gentle ruth,
Both for her noble bloud, and for her tender youth.

## li

And said, Ah Sir, my liege Lord and my love,
Shall I accuse the hidden cruell fate,
And mightie causes wrought in heaven above,
Or the blind God, that doth me thus amate,
For hoped love to winne me certaine hate?
Yet thus perforce he bids me do, or die.
Die is my dew: yet rew my wretched state
You, whom my hard avenging destinie
Hath made judge of my life or death indifferently.

## lii

Your owne deare sake forst me at first to leave
My Fathers kingdome, There she stopt with teares;

Her swollen hart her speach seemd to bereave,
And then againe begun, My weaker yeares
Captiv'd to fortune and frayle worldly feares,
Fly to your faith for succour and sure ayde:
Let me not dye in languor and long teares.
Why Dame (quoth he) what hath ye thus dismayd?
What frayes ye, that were wont to comfort me affrayd?

**liii**

Love of your selfe, she said, and deare constraint
Lets me not sleepe, but wast the wearie night
In secret anguish and unpittied plaint,
Whiles you in carelesse sleepe are drowned quight.
Her doubtfull words made that redoubted knight
Suspect her truth: yet since no'untruth he knew,
Her fawning love with foule disdainefull spight
He would not shend, but said, Deare dame I rew,
That for my sake unknowne such griefe unto you grew.

**liv**

Assure your selfe, it fell not all to ground;
For all so deare as life is to my hart,
I deeme your love, and hold me to you bound;
Ne let vaine feares procure your needlesse smart,
Where cause is none, but to your rest depart.
Not all content, yet seemd she to appease
Her mournefull plaintes, beguiled of her art,
And fed with words, that could not chuse but please,
So slyding softly forth, she turnd as to her ease.

**lv**

Long after lay he musing at her mood,
Much griev'd to think that gentle Dame so light,
For whose defence he was to shed his blood.
At last dull wearinesse of former fight
Having yrockt a sleepe his irkesome spright,

That troublous dreame gan freshly tosse his braine,
With bowres, and beds, and Ladies deare delight:
But when he saw his labour all was vaine,
With that misformed spright he backe returnd againe. . . .

## Canto XI

**1**

Then gentle Una saw the second fall
Of her deare knight, who wearie of long fight,
And faint through losse of bloud, mov'd not at all,
But lay as in a dreame of deepe delight,
Besmeard with pretious Balme, whose vertuous might
Did heale his wounds, and scorching heat alay,
Againe she stricken was with sore affright,
And for his safetie gan devoutly pray;
And watch the noyous night, and wait for joyous day.

**li**

The joyous day gan early to appeare,
And faire Aurora from the deawy bed
Of aged Tithone gan her selfe to reare,
With rosie cheekes, for shame as blushing red;
Her golden lockes for haste were loosely shed
About her eares, when Una her did marke
Clymbe to her charet, all with flowers spred,
From heaven high to chase the chearelesse darke;
With merry note her loud salutes the mounting larke.

**lii**

Then freshly up arose the doughtie knight,
All healed of his hurts and woundes wide,
And did himselfe to battell readie dight;
Whose early foe awaiting him beside
To have devourd, so soone as day he spyde,

When now he saw himselfe so freshly reare,
As if late fight had nought him damnifyde,
He woxe dismayd, and gan his fate to feare;
Nathlesse with wonted rage he him advaunced neare.

### liii

And in his first encounter, gaping wide,
He thought attonce him to have swallowd quight,
And rusht upon him with outragious pride;
Who him r'encountring fierce, as hauke in flight,
Perforce rebutted backe. The weapon bright
Taking advantage of his open jaw,
Ran through his mouth with so importune might,
That deepe emperst his darksome hollow maw,
And back retyrd, his life bloud forth with all did draw.

### liv

So downe he fell, and forth his life did breath,
That vanisht into smoke and cloudes swift;
So downe he fell, that th'earth him underneath
Did grone, as feeble so great load to lift;
So downe he fell, as an huge rockie clift,
Whose false foundation waves have washt away,
With dreadfull poyse is from the mayneland rift,
And rolling downe, great Neptune doth dismay;
So downe he fell, and like an heaped mountaine lay.

### lv

The knight himselfe even trembled at his fall,
So huge and horrible a masse it seem'd;
And his deare Ladie, that beheld it all,
Durst not approch for dread, which she misdeem'd,
But yet at last, when as the direfull feend
She saw not stirre, off-shaking vaine affright,
She nigher drew, and saw that joyous end:
Then God she praysd, and thankt her faithfull knight,
That had atchiev'd so great a conquest by his might.

# Canto XII

*Faire Una to the Redcrosse knight*
*betrouthed is with joy:*
*Though false Duessa it to barre*
*her false sleights doe imploy.*

i

Behold I see the haven nigh at hand,
To which I meane my wearie course to bend;
Vere the maine shete, and beare up with the land,
The which afore is fairely to be kend,
And seemeth safe from stormes, that may offend;
There this faire virgin wearie of her way
Must landed be, now at her journeyes end:
There eke my feeble barke a while may stay,
Till merry wind and weather call her thence away.

ii

Scarsely had Phœbus in the glooming East
Yet harnessed his firie-footed teeme,
Ne reard aboue the earth his flaming creast,
When the last deadly smoke aloft did steeme,
That signe of last outbreathed life did seeme,
Unto the watchman on the castle wall;
Who thereby dead that balefull Beast did deeme,
And to his Lord and Ladie lowd gan call,
To tell, how he had seene the Dragons fatall fall, . . .

xxi

Then forth he called that his daughter faire,
The fairest Un' his onely daughter deare,
His onely daughter, and his onely heyre;
Who forth proceeding with sad sober cheare,
As bright as doth the morning starre appeare
Out of the East, with flaming lockes bedight,
To tell the dawning day is dawning [drawing] neare,

And to the world does bring long wished light;
So faire and fresh that Lady shewd her selfe in sight.

## xxii

So faire and fresh, as freshest flowre in May;
For she had layd her mournefull stole aside,
And widow-like sad wimple throwne away,
Wherewith her heavnly beautie she did hide,
Whiles on her wearie journey she did ride;
And on her now a garment she did weare,
All lilly white, withoutten spot, or pride,
That seemd like silke and silver woven neare,
But neither silke nor silver therein did appeare.

## xxiii

The blazing brightnesse of her beauties beame,
And glorious light of her sunshyny face
To tell, were as to strive against the streame.
My ragged rimes are all too rude and bace,
Her heavenly lineaments for to enchace.
Ne wonder; for her owne deare loved knight,
All were she dayly with himselfe in place,
Did wonder much at her celestiall sight:
Oft had he seene her faire, but never so faire dight.

## xxiv

So fairely dight, when she in presence came,
She to her Sire made humble reverence,
And bowed low, that her right well became,
And added grace unto her excellence:
Who with great wisedome, and grave eloquence
Thus gan to say. But eare he thus had said,
With flying speede, and seeming great pretence,
Came running in, much like a man dismaid,
A Messenger with letters, which his message said.

**xxv**

All in the open hall amazed stood,
At suddeinnesse of that unwarie sight,
And wondred at his breathlesse hastie mood.
But he for nought would stay his passage right,
Till fast before the king he did alight;
Where falling flat, great humblesse he did make,
And kist the ground, whereon his foot was pight;
Then to his hands that writ he did betake,
Which he disclosing, red thus, as the paper spake.

**xxvi**

To thee, most mighty king of Eden faire,
Her greeting sends in these sad lines addrest,
The wofull daughter, and forsaken heire
Of that great Emperour of all the West;
And bids thee be advized for the best,
Ere thou thy daughter linck in holy band
Of wedlocke to that new unknowen guest:
For he already plighted his right hand
Unto another love, and to another land.

**xxvii**

To me sad mayd, or rather widow sad,
He was affiaunced long time before,
And sacred pledges he both gave, and had,
False erraunt knight, infamous, and forswore:
Witnesse the burning Altars, which he swore,
And guiltie heauens of his bold perjury,
Which though he hath polluted oft of yore,
Yet I to them for judgement just do fly,
And them coniure t'avenge this shamefull injury.

**xxviii**

Therefore since mine he is, or free or bond,
Or false or trew, or living or else dead,

Withhold, O soveraine Prince, your hasty hond
From knitting league with him, I you aread;
Ne weene my right with strength adowne to tread,
Through weakenesse of my widowhed, or woe:
For truth is strong, her rightfull cause to plead,
And shall find friends, if need requireth soe,
So bids thee well to fare, Thy neither friend, nor foe, Fidessa.


xxix

When he these bitter byting words had red,
The tydings straunge did him abashed make,
That still he sate long time astonished
As in great muse, ne word to creature spake.
At last his solemne silence thus he brake,
With doubtfull eyes fast fixed on his guest;
Redoubted knight, that for mine onely sake
Thy life and honour late adventurest,
Let nought be hid from me, that ought to be exprest.


xxx

What meane these bloudy vowes, and idle threats,
Throwne out from womanish impatient mind?
What heavens? what altars? what enraged heates
Here heaped up with termes of love unkind,
My conscience cleare with guilty bands would bind?
High God be witnesse, that I guiltlesse ame.
But if your selfe, Sir knight, ye faultie find,
Or wrapped be in loves of former Dame,
With crime do not it cover, but disclose the same.


xxxi

To whom the Redcrosse knight this answere sent,
My Lord, my King, be nought hereat dismayd,
Till well ye wote by grave intendiment,
What woman, and wherefore doth me upbrayd
With breach of love, and loyalty betrayd.

It was in my mishaps, as hitherward
I lately traveild, that unwares I strayd
Out of my way, through perils straunge and hard;
That day should faile me, ere I had them all declard.

#### xxxii

There did I find, or rather I was found
Of this false woman, that Fidessa hight,
Fidessa hight the falsest Dame on ground,
Most false Duessa, royall richly dight,
That easie was t'invegle weaker sight:
Who by her wicked arts, and wylie skill,
Too false and strong for earthly skill or might,
Unwares me wrought unto her wicked will,
And to my foe betrayd, when least I feared ill.

#### xxxiii

Then stepped forth the goodly royall Mayd,
And on the ground her selfe prostrating low,
With sober countenaunce thus to him sayd;
O pardon me, my soveraigne Lord, to show
The secret treasons, which of late I know
To have bene wroght by that false sorceresse.
She onely she it is, that earst did throw
This gentle knight into so great distresse,
That death him did awaite in dayly wretchednesse.

#### xxxiv

And now it seemes, that she suborned hath
This craftie messenger with letters vaine,
To worke new woe and improvided scath,
By breaking of the band betwixt vs twaine;
Wherein she used hath the practicke paine
Of this false footman, clokt with simplenesse,
Whom if ye please for to discover plaine,
Ye shall him Archimago find, I ghesse,
The falsest man alive; who tries shall find no lesse.

**xxxv**

> The king was greatly moved at her speach,
> And all with suddein indignation fraight,
> Bad on that Messenger rude hands to reach.
> Eftsoones the Gard, which on his state did wait,
> Attacht that faitor false, and bound him strait:
> Who seeming sorely chauffed at his band,
> As chained Beare, whom cruell dogs do bait,
> With idle force did faine them to withstand,
> And often semblaunce made to scape out of their hand.

**xxxvi**

> But they him layd full low in dungeon deepe,
> And bound him hand and foote with yron chains.
> And with continuall watch did warely keepe;
> Who then would thinke, that by his subtile trains
> He could escape fowle death or deadly paines?
> Thus when that Princes wrath was pacifide,
> He gan renew the late forbidden banes,
> And to the knight his daughter deare he tyde,
> With sacred rites and vowes for ever to abyde.

**xxxvii**

> His owne two hands the holy knots did knit,
> That none but death for ever can devide;
> His owne two hands, for such a turne most fit,
> The housling fire did kindle and provide,
> And holy water thereon sprinckled wide;
> At which the bushy Teade a groome did light,
> And sacred lampe in secret chamber hide,
> Where it should not be quenched day nor night,
> For feare of evill fates, but burnen ever bright.

**xxxviii**

> Then gan they sprinckle all the posts with wine,
> And made great feast to solemnize that day;

They all perfumde with frankincense divine,
And precious odours fetcht from far away,
That all the house did sweat with great aray:
And all the while sweete Musicke did apply
Her curious skill, the warbling notes to play,
To drive away the dull Melancholy;
The whiles one sung a song of love and jollity.

**xxxix**

During the which there was an heavenly noise
Heard sound through all the Pallace pleasantly,
Like as it had bene many an Angels voice,
Singing before th'eternall majesty,
In their trinall triplicities on hye;
Yet wist no creature, whence that heavenly sweet
Proceeded, yet eachone felt secretly
Himselfe thereby reft of his sences meet,
And ravished with rare impression in his sprite.

**xl**

Great ioy was made that day of young and old,
And solemne feast proclaimd throughout the land,
That their exceeding merth may not be told:
Suffice it heare by signes to understand
The usuall joyes at knitting of loves band.
Thrise happy man the knight himselfe did hold,
Possessed of his Ladies hart and hand,
And ever, when his eye did her behold,
His heart did seeme to melt in pleasures manifold.

**xli**

Her joyous presence and sweet company
In full content he there did long enioy,
Ne wicked envie, ne vile gealosy
His deare delights were able to annoy:
Yet swimming in that sea of blisfull joy,

He nought forgot, how he whilome had sworne,
In case he could that monstrous beast destroy,
Unto his Faerie Queene backe to returne:
The which he shortly did, and Una left to mourne.

**xlii**

Now strike your sailes ye jolly Mariners,
For we be come unto a quiet rode,
Where we must land some of our passengers,
And light this wearie vessell of her lode.
Here she a while may make her safe abode,
Till she repaired have her tackles spent,
And wants supplide. And then againe abroad
On the long voyage whereto she is bent:
Well may she speede and fairely finish her intent.
*FINIS LIB. I.*


# ON FAITH AND ROMANTICISM

## John Mark Reynolds


I first read Edmund Spenser because I loved C. S. Lewis, and C. S. Lewis loved *The Faerie Queene*. Sadly, I never really recovered from the first line of the book. A knight "pricking on the plaine" didn't communicate to my junior high mind as Spenser intended.

The poetry required learning many new words and spellings, plus a boatload of history. The language made seventh-grade favorite *The Lord of the Rings* seem as simple as *Nancy Drew* by comparison.

I had to come to accept that *The Faerie Queene* was hard work without granting easy access to the beauty that seemed to drip from the Narnia books or was the heart of *Phantastes*. The plot was simple; the characters, contrived. The book did not seem worth the effort, and I quit.

Years of teaching *The Faerie Queene* suggests my first reaction is a common one. The plot and the good bits likely don't seem worth the labor it takes to reach them, while the constant sucking up to Queen Elizabeth is annoying when not risible. Rare is the student, and fortunate, who loves this book immediately. For the rest of us, there is only the promise that Lewis saw something in it.

That alone might not have been enough to get me to try again, but any reader of romantic literature, and every lover of *Faerie*, finds Spenser turning up as an inspiration for favorite writers. I was missing something, and I knew it.

It turned out for me, as it has for so many of my students, that we'd never been taught to read a poem like *The Faerie Queene*.

The story is about the Knights of the Round Table and King Arthur; so many of us expect Malory or Tennyson plotting. It is set in Faerie, so we hope for Narnia. Instead, we get simple tales "disguising" an allegory about topics like "holiness." Spenser strained my piety to the breaking point as I longed for swords and sorcery over sermons.

At least the allegory seems easy. Anyone named Sans Foy ("faithless") will not be a good guy, though on one occasion someone with a good name is a baddie in disguise.

Lest we be confused for a moment, Spenser clues the reader into the "secret" right away. Saint George seems likely to kill the dragon, since that is what Saint George famously does. Saint George is indeed (at least) a stand-in for England, and he does indeed learn the ways of holiness.

I had an epiphany at Disneyland. I was walking through Sleeping Beauty Castle, looking at dioramas, and I thought, *Still-life scenes like this are becoming rare in our CG special-effects world.* For some reason this "clicked," and I suddenly saw how to appreciate Spenser's effects. He presents me, the reader, with a series of images, set pieces, that as a whole (and in detail) are meant to convey an overriding effect. Lewis, of course, had made this point better in his scholarly work on Spenser, but somehow I'd missed it.

Spenser is like an old-fashioned parade, and his scenes are like floats. One enjoys the float as a discrete whole and then moves to the next one. The connection between any two floats may be slight, but both are connected to the theme of the parade.

So the connection between the parts is there, but Spenser's design is not like with a modern novel. Each "shot" or image in the text must first be enjoyed for itself and only then picked apart or joined to the whole.

Nevertheless, doing this also requires learning Spenser's iconic vocabulary. As Lewis and other commentators have pointed out, his images drew on the familiar church and classical literature of the educated class of his time. When Una, a woman symbolizing the unified truth of the orthodox Christian faith, is first seen with her lamb and a dwarf, the informed reader understands that "the image" is part of "the Image." We do not expect to keep hearing about the lamb or the dwarf, and if they simply "vanish" in the next few scenes, well, this is to be anticipated in a parade.

The plot gives the reader the bigger meaning of each scene, and the details unlock the inner teaching. Once I found this way of seeing Spenser— and educated myself in the language of stained glass and coats of arms—I fell in love with *The Faerie Queene* and never looked back.

---

The obvious allegory is still there: Spenser loves Elizabeth, Anglican Protestantism, and romantic life. However, those are the shallow concerns of the poem, which is connected with deeper and older streams of catholic (general) Christianity. He rebuilds the unified cathedral of Christian thought, Dante's vision, as a Saint Paul's in London and not as Saint Peter's in Rome.

Spenser's "effects" are more suited to Handel and Tudor science than to chant and scholasticism. There also is less mystery in Spenser than in Dante, but likewise there is a greater attempt to let in light at every turn. In his vision, the clutter of the medieval cathedral is cleared away. That images and relics are exposed as tricks (of Archimago) allows the Christian to see *true faerie* in nature and in orthodoxy without being deceived and distracted by false loves.

Further, Spenser sanctifies the English story. He places the classical tradition within the deep myths of England using the tale of Arthur and so allows the romantic heart to be as enchanted by the English countryside as by the Greek or Italian landscapes. Spenser claims, and uses, the vocabulary of fifteen hundred years of Christendom, proving poetically that this is just as much the heritage of the Church of England as the Church of Rome.

What is more, Spenser is very Protestant, and the Catholic Church comes in for all sorts of attacks, most of which are uncharitable or unfair. In his defense, we should remember Spenser was living in a world where a Catholic queen of England had recently roasted Protestant heroes at the behest of Rome. He lived in the era of religious wars, and his pope was not, for instance, the blessed John Paul II.

————

Does this work?

It did work for romantics like George MacDonald and C. S. Lewis, enabling them to remain content Protestants and still find themselves part of the greater catholic faith.

It did not work for G. K. Chesterton, who made his way back to Rome by way of *Faerie*.

So, Spenser makes it *possible* to be a romantically fulfilled orthodox and Protestant Christian . . . perhaps.

## CHAPTER THIRTEEN

# MIGUEL DE CERVANTES

## Early Modern (1547–1616)

Only a hero and a brave man has the right to mock chivalry as a kind of madness, and only a genius can make it work. Cervantes was all three: hero, brave man, and genius. His linguistic powers helped create modern Spanish, and his reflections on the knight Don Quixote anticipate conversations and conclusions the rest of us are only coming to in recent years.

Perhaps the alternative to modernity is not postmodernity but an Age of Cervantes.

Cervantes fought and bled in one of history's great conflicts, the Battle of Lepanto, to defend Christendom against conquest by Islam. He justly was proud of his wounds and of the victory he and many like him had secured for his faith. As he mocks his culture and his church, it's important to remember that this is the mockery of a man who loved the Catholic faith enough to bleed for it. He lived in a world less parochial and more international than our own, one where the Pope could lead a multinational coalition whose relative power the U.N. could never muster.

Cervantes is witty, first of all. Laugh with him before becoming too serious about his knight. After all, it is absurd to tilt at windmills, and his knight does just that. And yet Don Quixote is more likable than the sane people around him.

Our own era sees people disappear into TV-episode fandom, role-playing games, and their mother's basements for long periods of time. We can relate to the idea that fictional worlds may be better than the world as it is. Fiction is sort of real, and if the options are living in Middle Earth or plodding through convention in a gray office cubicle, then many of us are off to find Gandalf.

"Should be" and "is" do not match up, this side of paradise, and so "is" can easily be less attractive than a madness that dreams the impossible. Still, the world exists, and our fictions do not, at least with the same power. Tragically, in a real world, Quixote must die, whatever his ambitions.

Cervantes did great deeds in difficult times. He lived a romantic life while others realistically slogged through historic events. Read his book to see Quixote and his critics, but also look for the genius of a real man, Cervantes, who resolves the tension in a Christian life imperfectly but fully lived.

CC FROM ⊃C

# Don Quixote

### Part I, Chapter I:

### Which Treats of the Character and Pursuits of the Famous Gentleman Don Quixote of La Mancha

In a village of La Mancha, the name of which I have no desire to call to mind, there lived not long since one of those gentlemen that keep a lance in the lance-rack, an old buckler, a lean hack, and a greyhound for coursing. An olla of rather more beef than mutton, a salad on most nights, scraps on Saturdays, lentils on Fridays, and a pigeon or so extra on Sundays, made away with three-quarters of his income. The rest of it went in a doublet of fine cloth and velvet breeches and shoes to match for holidays, while on week-days he made a brave figure in his best homespun.

He had in his house a housekeeper past forty, a niece under twenty, and a lad for the field and market-place, who used to saddle the hack as well as handle the bill-hook. The age of this gentleman of ours was bordering on fifty; he was of a hardy habit, spare, gaunt-featured, a very early riser and a great sportsman. They will have it his surname was Quixada or Quesada (for here there is some difference of opinion among the authors who write on the subject), although from reasonable conjectures it seems plain that he was called Quexana. This, however, is of but little importance to our tale; it will be enough not to stray a hair's breadth from the truth in the telling of it.

You must know, then, that the above-named gentleman whenever he was at leisure (which was mostly all the year round) gave himself up to reading books of chivalry with such ardour and avidity that he almost entirely neglected the pursuit of his field-sports, and even the management of his property; and to such a pitch did his eagerness and infatuation go that he sold many an acre of tillageland to buy books of chivalry to read, and brought home as many of them as he could get. But of all there were none he liked so well as those of the famous Feliciano de Silva's composition, for their lucidity of style and complicated conceits were as pearls in his sight, particularly when in his reading he came upon courtships and cartels, where he often found passages like "the reason of the unreason with which my reason is afflicted so weakens my reason that with reason I murmur at your beauty;" or again, "the high heavens, that of your divinity divinely fortify you with the stars, render you deserving of the desert your greatness deserves."

Over conceits of this sort the poor gentleman lost his wits, and used to lie awake striving to understand them and worm the meaning out of them; what Aristotle himself could not have made out or extracted had he come to life again for that special purpose. He was not at all easy about the wounds which Don Belianis gave and took, because it seemed to him that, great as were the surgeons who had cured him, he must have had his face and body covered all over with seams and scars. He commended, however, the author's way of ending his book with the promise of that interminable adventure, and many a time was he tempted to take up his pen and finish it properly as is there proposed, which no doubt he would have done, and made a successful piece of work of it too, had not greater and more absorbing thoughts prevented him.

Many an argument did he have with the curate of his village (a learned man, and a graduate of Siguenza) as to which had been the better knight, Palmerin of England or Amadis of Gaul. Master Nicholas, the village barber, however, used to say that neither of them came up to the Knight of Phoebus, and that if there was any that could compare with him it was Don Galaor, the brother of Amadis of Gaul, because he had a spirit that was equal to every occasion, and was no finikin knight, nor lachrymose like his brother, while in the matter of valour he was not a whit behind him. In short, he became so absorbed in his books that he spent his nights from sunset to sunrise, and his days from dawn to dark, poring over them; and what with little sleep and much reading his brains got so dry that he lost his wits. His fancy grew full of what he used to read about in his books, enchantments, quarrels, battles, challenges, wounds, wooings, loves, agonies, and all sorts of impossible nonsense; and it so possessed his mind that the whole fabric of invention and fancy he read of was true, that to him no history in the world had more reality in it.

He used to say the Cid Ruy Diaz was a very good knight, but that he was not to be compared with the Knight of the Burning Sword who with one back-stroke cut in half two fierce and monstrous giants. He thought more of Bernardo del Carpio because at Roncesvalles he slew Roland in spite of enchantments, availing himself of the artifice of Hercules when he strangled Antaeus the son of Terra in his arms. He approved highly of the giant Morgante, because, although of the giant breed which is always arrogant and ill-conditioned, he alone was affable and well-bred. But above all he admired Reinaldos of Montalban, especially when he saw him sallying forth from his castle and robbing everyone he met, and when beyond the seas he stole that image of Mahomet which, as his history says, was entirely of gold. To have a bout of kicking at that traitor of a Ganelon he would have given his housekeeper, and his niece into the bargain.

In short, his wits being quite gone, he hit upon the strangest notion that ever madman in this world hit upon, and that was that he fancied it was right and requisite, as well for the support of his own honour as for the service of his country, that he should make a knight-errant of himself, roaming the world over in full armour and on horseback in quest of adventures, and putting in practice himself all that he had read of as being the usual practices of knights-errant; righting every kind of wrong, and exposing himself to peril and danger from which, in the issue, he was to reap eternal renown and fame. Already the poor man saw himself crowned by the might of his arm Emperor of Trebizond at least; and so, led away by the intense enjoyment he found in these pleasant fancies, he set himself forthwith to put his scheme into execution.

The first thing he did was to clean up some armour that had belonged to his great-grandfather, and had been for ages lying forgotten in a corner eaten with rust and covered with mildew. He scoured and polished it as best he could, but he perceived one great defect in it, that it had no closed helmet, nothing but a simple morion. This deficiency, however, his ingenuity supplied, for he contrived a kind of half-helmet of pasteboard which, fitted on to the morion, looked like a whole one. It is true that, in order to see if it was strong and fit to stand a cut, he drew his sword and gave it a couple of slashes, the first of which undid in an instant what had taken him a week to do. The ease with which he had knocked it to pieces disconcerted him somewhat, and to guard against that danger he set to work again, fixing bars of iron on the inside until he was satisfied with its strength; and then, not caring to try any more experiments with it, he passed it and adopted it as a helmet of the most perfect construction.

He next proceeded to inspect his hack, which, with more quartos than a real and more blemishes than the steed of Gonela, that "tantum pellis et ossa fuit," surpassed in his eyes the Bucephalus of Alexander or the Babieca of the Cid. Four days were spent in thinking what name to give him, because (as he said to himself) it was not right that a horse belonging to a knight so famous, and one with such merits of his own, should be without some distinctive name, and he strove to adapt it so as to indicate what he had been before belonging to a knight-errant, and what he then was; for it was only reasonable that, his master taking a new character, he should take a new name, and that it should be a distinguished and full-sounding one, befitting the new order and calling he was about to follow. And so, after having composed, struck out, rejected, added to, unmade, and remade a multitude of names out of his memory and fancy, he decided upon calling him Rocinante, a name, to his thinking, lofty, sonorous, and significant of his condition as a hack before he became what he now was, the first and foremost of all the hacks in the world.

Having got a name for his horse so much to his taste, he was anxious to get one for himself, and he was eight days more pondering over this point, till at last he made up his mind to call himself "Don Quixote," whence, as has been already said, the authors of this veracious history have inferred that his name must have been beyond a doubt Quixada, and not Quesada as others would have it. Recollecting, however, that the valiant Amadis was not content to call himself curtly Amadis and nothing more, but added the name of his kingdom and country to make it famous, and called himself Amadis of Gaul, he, like a good knight, resolved to add on the name of his, and to style himself Don Quixote of La Mancha, whereby, he considered, he described accurately his origin and country, and did honour to it in taking his surname from it.

So then, his armour being furbished, his morion turned into a helmet, his hack christened, and he himself confirmed, he came to the conclusion that nothing more was needed now but to look out for a lady to be in love with; for a knight-errant without love was like a tree without leaves or fruit, or a body without a soul. As he said to himself, "If, for my sins, or by my good fortune, I come across some giant hereabouts, a common occurrence with knights-errant, and overthrow him in one onslaught, or cleave him asunder to the waist, or, in short, vanquish and subdue him, will it not be well to have some one I may send him to as a present, that he may come in and fall on his knees before my sweet lady, and in a humble, submissive voice say, 'I am the giant Caraculiambro, lord of the island of Malindrania, vanquished in single combat by the never sufficiently extolled knight Don Quixote of La Mancha, who has commanded me to present myself before your Grace, that your Highness dispose of me at your pleasure'?"

Oh, how our good gentleman enjoyed the delivery of this speech, especially when he had thought of some one to call his Lady! There was, so the story goes, in a village near his own a very good-looking farm-girl with whom he had been at one time in love, though, so far as is known, she never knew it nor gave a thought to the matter. Her name was Aldonza Lorenzo, and upon her he thought fit to confer the title of Lady of his Thoughts; and after some search for a name which should not be out of harmony with her own, and should suggest and indicate that of a princess and great lady, he decided upon calling her Dulcinea del Toboso—she being of El Toboso—a name, to his mind, musical, uncommon, and significant, like all those he had already bestowed upon himself and the things belonging to him.

. . .

## Part I, Chapter III:

## Wherein Is Related the Droll Way in Which Don Quixote Had Himself Dubbed a Knight

. . ."From this spot I rise not, valiant knight, until your courtesy grants me the boon I seek, one that will redound to your praise and the benefit of the human race." The landlord, seeing his guest at his feet and hearing a speech of this kind, stood staring at him in bewilderment, not knowing what to do or say, and entreating him to rise, but all to no purpose until he had agreed to grant the boon demanded of him. "I looked for no less, my lord, from your High Magnificence," replied Don Quixote, "and I have to tell you that the boon I have asked and your liberality has granted is that you shall dub me knight to-morrow morning, and that to-night I shall watch my arms in the chapel of this your castle; thus tomorrow, as I have said, will be accomplished what I so much desire, enabling me lawfully to roam through all the four quarters of the world seeking adventures on behalf of those in distress, as is the duty of chivalry and of knights-errant like myself, whose ambition is directed to such deeds."

The landlord, who, as has been mentioned, was something of a wag, and had already some suspicion of his guest's want of wits, was quite convinced of it on hearing talk of this kind from him, and to make sport for the night he determined to fall in with his humour. So he told him he was quite right in pursuing the object he had in view, and that such a motive was natural and becoming in cavaliers as distinguished as he seemed and his gallant bearing showed him to be; and that he himself in his younger days had followed the same honourable calling, roaming in quest of adventures in various parts of the world, among others the Curing-grounds of

Malaga, the Isles of Riaran, the Precinct of Seville, the Little Market of Segovia, the Olivera of Valencia, the Rondilla of Granada, the Strand of San Lucar, the Colt of Cordova, the Taverns of Toledo, and divers other quarters, where he had proved the nimbleness of his feet and the lightness of his fingers, doing many wrongs, cheating many widows, ruining maids and swindling minors, and, in short, bringing himself under the notice of almost every tribunal and court of justice in Spain; until at last he had retired to this castle of his, where he was living upon his property and upon that of others; and where he received all knights-errant of whatever rank or condition they might be, all for the great love he bore them and that they might share their substance with him in return for his benevolence.

He told him, moreover, that in this castle of his there was no chapel in which he could watch his armour, as it had been pulled down in order to be rebuilt, but that in a case of necessity it might, he knew, be watched anywhere, and he might watch it that night in a courtyard of the castle, and in the morning, God willing, the requisite ceremonies might be performed so as to have him dubbed a knight, and so thoroughly dubbed that nobody could be more so. He asked if he had any money with him, to which Don Quixote replied that he had not a farthing, as in the histories of knights-errant he had never read of any of them carrying any. On this point the landlord told him he was mistaken; for, though not recorded in the histories, because in the author's opinion there was no need to mention anything so obvious and necessary as money and clean shirts, it was not to be supposed therefore that they did not carry them, and he might regard it as certain and established that all knights-errant (about whom there were so many full and unimpeachable books) carried well-furnished purses in case of emergency, and likewise carried shirts and a little box of ointment to cure the wounds they received. For in those plains and deserts where they engaged in combat and came out wounded, it was not always that there was some one to cure them, unless indeed they had for a friend some sage magician to succour them at once by fetching through the air upon a cloud some damsel or dwarf with a vial of water of such virtue that by tasting one drop of it they were cured of their hurts and wounds in an instant and left as sound as if they had not received any damage whatever.

But in case this should not occur, the knights of old took care to see that their squires were provided with money and other requisites, such as lint and ointments for healing purposes; and when it happened that knights had no squires (which was rarely and seldom the case) they themselves carried everything in cunning saddle-bags that were hardly seen on the horse's croup, as if it were something else of more importance, because, unless for some such reason, carrying saddle-bags was not very favourably regarded among knights-errant. He therefore advised him (and, as his godson so soon to be, he might even command him) never from that time forth to travel without money and the usual requirements, and he would find the advantage of them when he least expected it.

Don Quixote promised to follow his advice scrupulously, and it was arranged forthwith that he should watch his armour in a large yard at one side of the inn; so, collecting it all together, Don Quixote placed it on a trough that stood by the side of a well, and bracing his buckler on his arm he grasped his lance and began with a stately air to march up and down in front of the trough, and as he began his march night began to fall.

The landlord told all the people who were in the inn about the craze of his guest, the watching of the armour, and the dubbing ceremony he contemplated. Full of wonder at so strange a form of madness, they flocked to see it from a distance, and observed with what composure he sometimes paced up and down, or sometimes, leaning on his lance, gazed on his armour without taking his eyes off it for ever so long; and as the night closed in with a light from the moon so brilliant that it might vie with his that lent it, everything the novice knight did was plainly seen by all.

Meanwhile one of the carriers who were in the inn thought fit to water his team, and it was necessary to remove Don Quixote's armour as it lay on the trough; but he seeing the other approach hailed him in a loud voice, "O thou, whoever thou art, rash knight that comest to lay hands on the armour of the most valorous errant that ever girt on sword, have a care what thou dost; touch it not unless thou wouldst lay down thy life as the penalty of thy rashness." The carrier gave no heed to these words (and he would have done better to heed them if he had been heedful of his health), but seizing it by the straps flung the armour some distance from him.

Seeing this, Don Quixote raised his eyes to heaven, and fixing his thoughts, apparently, upon his lady Dulcinea, exclaimed, "Aid me, lady mine, in this the first encounter that presents itself to this breast which thou holdest in subjection; let not thy favour and protection fail me in this first jeopardy;" and, with these words and others to the same purpose, dropping his buckler he lifted his lance with both hands and with it smote such a blow on the carrier's head that he stretched him on the ground, so stunned that had he followed it up with a second there would have been no need of a surgeon to cure him. This done, he picked up his armour and returned to his beat with the same serenity as before.

Shortly after this, another, not knowing what had happened (for the carrier still lay senseless), came with the same object of giving water to his mules, and was proceeding to remove the armour in order to clear the trough, when Don Quixote, without uttering a word or imploring aid from anyone, once more dropped his buckler and once more lifted his lance, and without actually breaking the second carrier's head into pieces, made more than three of it, for he laid it open in four. At the noise all the people of the inn ran to the spot, and among them the landlord. Seeing this, Don Quixote braced his buckler on his arm, and with his hand on his sword exclaimed, "O Lady of Beauty, strength and support of my faint heart, it is time for thee to turn the eyes of thy greatness on this thy captive knight on the brink of so mighty an adventure." By this he felt himself so inspired that he would not have flinched if all the carriers in the world had assailed him. The comrades of the wounded perceiving the plight they were in began from a distance to shower stones on Don Quixote, who screened himself as best he could with his buckler, not daring to quit the trough and leave his armour unprotected.

The landlord shouted to them to leave him alone, for he had already told them that he was mad, and as a madman he would not be account-able even if he killed them all. Still louder shouted Don Quixote, calling them knaves and traitors, and the lord of the castle, who allowed knights-errant to be treated in this fashion, a villain and a low-born knight whom, had he received the order of knighthood, he would call to account for his treachery. "But of you," he cried, "base and vile rabble, I make no account; fling, strike, come on, do all ye can against me, ye shall see what the reward of your folly and insolence will be." This he uttered with so much spirit and boldness that he filled his assailants with a terrible fear, and as much for this reason as at the persuasion of the landlord they left off stoning him, and he allowed them to carry off the wounded, and with the same calmness and composure as before resumed the watch over his armour.

But these freaks of his guest were not much to the liking of the landlord, so he determined to cut matters short and confer upon him at once the unlucky order of knighthood before any further misadventure could occur; so, going up to him, he apologised for the rudeness which, without his knowledge, had been offered to him by these low people, who, however, had been well punished for their audacity. As he had already told him, he said, there was no chapel in the castle, nor was it needed for what remained to be done, for, as he understood the ceremonial of the order, the whole point of being dubbed a knight lay in the accolade and in the slap on the shoulder, and that could be administered in the middle of a field; and that he had now done all that was needful as to watching the armour, for all requirements were satisfied by a watch of two hours only, while he had been more than four about it. Don Quixote believed it all, and told him he stood there ready to obey him, and to make an end of it with as much despatch as possible; for, if he were again attacked, and felt himself to be dubbed knight, he would not, he thought, leave a soul alive in the castle, except such as out of respect he might spare at his bidding.

Thus warned and menaced, the castellan forthwith brought out a book in which he used to enter the straw and barley he served out to the carriers, and, with a lad carrying a candle-end, and the two damsels already mentioned, he returned to where Don Quixote stood, and bade him kneel down. Then, reading from his account-book as if he were repeating some devout prayer, in the middle of his delivery he raised his hand and gave him a sturdy blow on the neck, and then, with his own sword, a smart slap on the shoulder, all the while muttering between his teeth as if he was saying his prayers. Having done this, he directed one of the ladies to gird on his sword, which she did with great self-possession and gravity, and not a little was required to prevent a burst of laughter at each stage of the ceremony; but what they had already seen of the novice knight's prowess kept their laughter within bounds. On girding him with the sword the worthy lady said to him, "May God make your worship a very fortunate knight, and grant you success in battle."

Don Quixote asked her name in order that he might from that time forward know to whom he was beholden for the favour he had received, as he meant to confer upon her some portion of the honour he acquired

by the might of his arm. She answered with great humility that she was
called La Tolosa, and that she was the daughter of a cobbler of Toledo who
lived in the stalls of Sanchobienaya, and that wherever she might be she
would serve and esteem him as her lord. Don Quixote said in reply that
she would do him a favour if thenceforward she assumed the "Don" and
called herself Dona Tolosa. She promised she would, and then the other
buckled on his spur, and with her followed almost the same conversation
as with the lady of the sword. He asked her name, and she said it was La
Molinera, and that she was the daughter of a respectable miller of Ante-
quera; and of her likewise Don Quixote requested that she would adopt
the "Don" and call herself Dona Molinera, making offers to her further
services and favours.

Having thus, with hot haste and speed, brought to a conclusion these
never-till-now-seen ceremonies, Don Quixote was on thorns until he saw
himself on horseback sallying forth in quest of adventures; and saddling
Rocinante at once he mounted, and embracing his host, as he returned
thanks for his kindness in knighting him, he addressed him in language so
extraordinary that it is impossible to convey an idea of it or report it. The
landlord, to get him out of the inn, replied with no less rhetoric though
with shorter words, and without calling upon him to pay the reckoning
let him go with a Godspeed.

. . .

**Part I, Chapter VII:**

**Of the Second Sally of Our Worthy Knight Don Quixote of La
Mancha**

At this instant Don Quixote began shouting out, "Here, here, valiant
knights! here is need for you to put forth the might of your strong arms,
for they of the Court are gaining the mastery in the tourney!" Called away
by this noise and outcry, they proceeded no farther with the scrutiny of the
remaining books, and so it is thought that "The Carolea," "The Lion of
Spain," and "The Deeds of the Emperor," written by Don Luis de Avila,
went to the fire unseen and unheard; for no doubt they were among those

that remained, and perhaps if the curate had seen them they would not have undergone so severe a sentence.

When they reached Don Quixote he was already out of bed, and was still shouting and raving, and slashing and cutting all round, as wide awake as if he had never slept.

They closed with him and by force got him back to bed, and when he had become a little calm, addressing the curate, he said to him, "Of a truth, Senor Archbishop Turpin, it is a great disgrace for us who call ourselves the Twelve Peers, so carelessly to allow the knights of the Court to gain the victory in this tourney, we the adventurers having carried off the honour on the three former days."

"Hush, gossip," said the curate; "please God, the luck may turn, and what is lost to-day may be won to-morrow; for the present let your worship have a care of your health, for it seems to me that you are over-fatigued, if not badly wounded."

"Wounded no," said Don Quixote, "but bruised and battered no doubt, for that bastard Don Roland has cudgelled me with the trunk of an oak tree, and all for envy, because he sees that I alone rival him in his achievements. But I should not call myself Reinaldos of Montalvan did he not pay me for it in spite of all his enchantments as soon as I rise from this bed. For the present let them bring me something to eat, for that, I feel, is what will be more to my purpose, and leave it to me to avenge myself."

They did as he wished; they gave him something to eat, and once more he fell asleep, leaving them marvelling at his madness.

That night the housekeeper burned to ashes all the books that were in the yard and in the whole house; and some must have been consumed that deserved preservation in everlasting archives, but their fate and the laziness of the examiner did not permit it, and so in them was verified the proverb that the innocent suffer for the guilty.

One of the remedies which the curate and the barber immediately applied to their friend's disorder was to wall up and plaster the room where the books were, so that when he got up he should not find them (possibly the cause being removed the effect might cease), and they might say that a magician had carried them off, room and all; and this was done with all despatch. Two days later Don Quixote got up, and the first thing he did was to go and look at his books, and not finding the room where he had left it, he wandered from side to side looking for it. He came to the place where the door used to be, and tried it with his hands, and turned and twisted his eyes in every direction without saying a word; but after a good while he asked his housekeeper whereabouts was the room that held his books.

The housekeeper, who had been already well instructed in what she was to answer, said, "What room or what nothing is it that your worship is looking for? There are neither room nor books in this house now, for the devil himself has carried all away."

"It was not the devil," said the niece, "but a magician who came on a cloud one night after the day your worship left this, and dismounting from a serpent that he rode he entered the room, and what he did there I know not, but after a little while he made off, flying through the roof, and left the house full of smoke; and when we went to see what he had done we saw neither book nor room: but we remember very well, the house-keeper and I, that on leaving, the old villain said in a loud voice that, for a private grudge he owed the owner of the books and the room, he had done mischief in that house that would be discovered by-and-by: he said too that his name was the Sage Munaton."

"He must have said Friston," said Don Quixote.

"I don't know whether he called himself Friston or Friton," said the housekeeper, "I only know that his name ended with 'ton.'"

"So it does," said Don Quixote, "and he is a sage magician, a great enemy of mine, who has a spite against me because he knows by his arts and lore that in process of time I am to engage in single combat with a knight whom he befriends and that I am to conquer, and he will be unable to prevent it; and for this reason he endeavours to do me all the ill turns that he can; but I promise him it will be hard for him to oppose or avoid what is decreed by Heaven."

"Who doubts that?" said the niece; "but, uncle, who mixes you up in these quarrels? Would it not be better to remain at peace in your own house instead of roaming the world looking for better bread than ever came of wheat, never reflecting that many go for wool and come back shorn?"

"Oh, niece of mine," replied Don Quixote, "how much astray art thou in thy reckoning: ere they shear me I shall have plucked away and stripped off the beards of all who dare to touch only the tip of a hair of mine."

The two were unwilling to make any further answer, as they saw that his anger was kindling.

In short, then, he remained at home fifteen days very quietly without showing any signs of a desire to take up with his former delusions, and during this time he held lively discussions with his two gossips, the curate and the barber, on the point he maintained, that knights-errant were what the world stood most in need of, and that in him was to be accomplished the revival of knight-errantry. The curate sometimes contradicted him, sometimes agreed with him, for if he had not observed this precaution he would have been unable to bring him to reason.

Meanwhile Don Quixote worked upon a farm labourer, a neighbour of his, an honest man (if indeed that title can be given to him who is poor), but with very little wit in his pate. In a word, he so talked him over, and with such persuasions and promises, that the poor clown made up his mind to sally forth with him and serve him as esquire. Don Quixote, among other things, told him he ought to be ready to go with him gladly, because any moment an adventure might occur that might win an island in the twinkling of an eye and leave him governor of it. On these and the like promises Sancho Panza (for so the labourer was called) left wife and children, and engaged himself as esquire to his neighbour. Don Quixote next set about getting some money; and selling one thing and pawning another, and making a bad bargain in every case, he got together a fair sum. He provided himself with a buckler, which he begged as a loan from a friend, and, restoring his battered helmet as best he could, he warned his squire Sancho of the day and hour he meant to set out, that he might provide himself with what he thought most needful.

Above all, he charged him to take alforjas with him. The other said he would, and that he meant to take also a very good ass he had, as he was not much given to going on foot. About the ass, Don Quixote hesitated a little, trying whether he could call to mind any knight-errant taking with him an esquire mounted on ass-back, but no instance occurred to his memory. For all that, however, he determined to take him, intending to furnish him with a more honourable mount when a chance of it presented itself, by appropriating the horse of the first discourteous knight he encountered. Himself he provided with shirts and such other things as he could, according to the advice the host had given him; all which being done, without taking leave, Sancho Panza of his wife and children, or Don Quixote of his housekeeper and niece, they sallied forth unseen by anybody from the village one night, and made such good way in the course of it that by daylight they held themselves safe from discovery, even should search be made for them.

Sancho rode on his ass like a patriarch, with his alforjas and bota, and longing to see himself soon governor of the island his master had promised him. Don Quixote decided upon taking the same route and road he had taken on his first journey, that over the Campo de Montiel, which he travelled with less discomfort than on the last occasion, for, as it was early morning and the rays of the sun fell on them obliquely, the heat did not distress them.

And now said Sancho Panza to his master, "Your worship will take care, Senor Knight-errant, not to forget about the island you have promised me, for be it ever so big I'll be equal to governing it."

To which Don Quixote replied, "Thou must know, friend Sancho Panza, that it was a practice very much in vogue with the knights-errant of old to make their squires governors of the islands or kingdoms they won, and I am determined that there shall be no failure on my part in so liberal a custom; on the contrary, I mean to improve upon it, for they sometimes, and perhaps most frequently, waited until their squires were old, and then when they had had enough of service and hard days and worse nights, they gave them some title or other, of count, or at the most marquis, of some valley or province more or less; but if thou livest and I live, it may well be that before six days are over, I may have won some kingdom that has others dependent upon it, which will be just the thing to enable thee to be crowned king of one of them. Nor needst thou count this wonderful, for things and chances fall to the lot of such knights in ways so unexampled and unexpected that I might easily give thee even more than I promise thee."

"In that case," said Sancho Panza, "if I should become a king by one of those miracles your worship speaks of, even Juana Gutierrez, my old woman, would come to be queen and my children infantes."

"Well, who doubts it?" said Don Quixote.

"I doubt it," replied Sancho Panza, "because for my part I am persuaded that though God should shower down kingdoms upon earth, not one of them would fit the head of Mari Gutierrez. Let me tell you, senor, she is not worth two maravedis for a queen; countess will fit her better, and that only with God's help."

"Leave it to God, Sancho," returned Don Quixote, "for he will give her what suits her best; but do not undervalue thyself so much as to come to be content with anything less than being governor of a province."

"I will not, senor," answered Sancho, "specially as I have a man of such quality for a master in your worship, who will know how to give me all that will be suitable for me and that I can bear."

. . .

## Part II, Chapter LXXIV:

## Of How Don Quixote Fell Sick, and of the Will He Made, and How He Died

As nothing that is man's can last for ever, but all tends ever downwards from its beginning to its end, and above all man's life, and as Don Quixote's enjoyed no special dispensation from heaven to stay its course, its end and close came when he least looked for it. For—whether it was of the dejection the thought of his defeat produced, or of heaven's will that so ordered it—a fever settled upon him and kept him in his bed for six days, during which he was often visited by his friends the curate, the bachelor, and the barber, while his good squire Sancho Panza never quitted his bedside. They, persuaded that it was grief at finding himself vanquished, and the object of his heart, the liberation and disenchantment of Dulcinea, unattained, that kept him in this state, strove by all the means in their power to cheer him up; the bachelor bidding him take heart and get up to begin his pastoral life, for which he himself, he said, had already composed an eclogue that would take the shine out of all Sannazaro had ever written, and had bought with his own money two famous dogs to guard the flock, one called Barcino and the other Butron, which a herdsman of Quintanar had sold him.

But for all this Don Quixote could not shake off his sadness. His friends called in the doctor, who felt his pulse and was not very well satisfied

303

with it, and said that in any case it would be well for him to attend to the health of his soul, as that of his body was in a bad way. Don Quixote heard this calmly; but not so his housekeeper, his niece, and his squire, who fell weeping bitterly, as if they had him lying dead before them. The doctor's opinion was that melancholy and depression were bringing him to his end. Don Quixote begged them to leave him to himself, as he had a wish to sleep a little. They obeyed, and he slept at one stretch, as the saying is, more than six hours, so that the housekeeper and niece thought he was going to sleep for ever. But at the end of that time he woke up, and in a loud voice exclaimed, "Blessed be Almighty God, who has shown me such goodness. In truth his mercies are boundless, and the sins of men can neither limit them nor keep them back!"

The niece listened with attention to her uncle's words, and they struck her as more coherent than what usually fell from him, at least during his illness, so she asked, "What are you saying, senor? Has anything strange occurred? What mercies or what sins of men are you talking of?"

"The mercies, niece," said Don Quixote, "are those that God has this moment shown me, and with him, as I said, my sins are no impediment to them. My reason is now free and clear, rid of the dark shadows of ignorance that my unhappy constant study of those detestable books of chivalry cast over it. Now I see through their absurdities and deceptions, and it only grieves me that this destruction of my illusions has come so late that it leaves me no time to make some amends by reading other books that might be a light to my soul. Niece, I feel myself at the point of death, and I would fain meet it in such a way as to show that my life has not been so ill that I should leave behind me the name of a madman; for though I have been one, I would not that the fact should be made plainer at my death. Call in to me, my dear, my good friends the curate, the bachelor Samson Carrasco, and Master Nicholas the barber, for I wish to confess and make my will."

But his niece was saved the trouble by the entrance of the three. The instant Don Quixote saw them he exclaimed, "Good news for you, good sirs, that I am no longer Don Quixote of La Mancha, but Alonso Quixano, whose way of life won for him the name of Good. Now am I the enemy of Amadis of Gaul and of the whole countless troop of his descendants; odious to me now are all the profane stories of knight-errantry; now I perceive my folly, and the peril into which reading them brought me; now, by God's mercy schooled into my right senses, I loathe them."

When the three heard him speak in this way, they had no doubt whatever that some new craze had taken possession of him; and said Samson, "What? Senor Don Quixote! Now that we have intelligence of the lady Dulcinea being disenchanted, are you taking this line; now, just as we are on the point of becoming shepherds, to pass our lives singing, like princes, are you thinking of turning hermit? Hush, for heaven's sake, be rational and let's have no more nonsense."

"All that nonsense," said Don Quixote, "that until now has been a reality to my hurt, my death will, with heaven's help, turn to my good. I feel, sirs, that I am rapidly drawing near death; a truce to jesting; let me have a confessor to confess me, and a notary to make my will; for in extremities like this, man must not trifle with his soul; and while the curate is confessing me let some one, I beg, go for the notary."

They looked at one another, wondering at Don Quixote's words; but, though uncertain, they were inclined to believe him, and one of the signs by which they came to the conclusion he was dying was this so sudden and complete return to his senses after having been mad; for to the words already quoted he added much more, so well expressed, so devout, and so rational, as to banish all doubt and convince them that he was sound of mind. The curate turned them all out, and left alone with him confessed him. The bachelor went for the notary and returned shortly afterwards with him and with Sancho, who, having already learned from the bachelor the condition his master was in, and finding the housekeeper and niece weeping, began to blubber and shed tears.

The confession over, the curate came out saying, "Alonso Quixano the Good is indeed dying, and is indeed in his right mind; we may now go in to him while he makes his will."

This news gave a tremendous impulse to the brimming eyes of the housekeeper, niece, and Sancho Panza his good squire, making the tears burst from their eyes and a host of sighs from their hearts; for of a truth, as has been said more than once, whether as plain Alonso Quixano the Good, or as Don Quixote of La Mancha, Don Quixote was always of a gentle disposition and kindly in all his ways, and hence he was beloved, not only by those of his own house, but by all who knew him.

The notary came in with the rest, and as soon as the preamble of the will had been set out and Don Quixote had commended his soul to God with all the devout formalities that are usual, coming to the bequests, he said, "Item, it is my will that, touching certain moneys in the hands of Sancho Panza (whom in my madness I made my squire), inasmuch as between him and me there have been certain accounts and debits and credits, no claim be made against him, nor any account demanded of him in respect of them; but that if anything remain over and above, after he has paid himself what I owe him, the balance, which will be but little, shall be his, and much good may it do him; and if, as when I was mad I had a share in giving him the government of an island, so, now that I am in my senses, I could give him that of a kingdom, it should be his, for the simplicity of his character and the fidelity of his conduct deserve it." And then, turning to Sancho, he said, "Forgive me, my friend, that I led thee to seem as mad as myself, making thee fall into the same error I myself fell into, that there were and still are knights-errant in the world."

"Ah!" said Sancho weeping, "don't die, master, but take my advice and live many years; for the foolishest thing a man can do in this life is to let himself die without rhyme or reason, without anybody killing him, or any hands but melancholy's making an end of him. Come, don't be lazy, but get up from your bed and let us take to the fields in shepherd's trim as we agreed. Perhaps behind some bush we shall find the lady Dulcinea disenchanted, as fine as fine can be. If it be that you are dying of vexation at having been vanquished, lay the blame on me, and say you were over-thrown because I had girthed Rocinante badly; besides you must have seen in your books of chivalry that it is a common thing for knights to upset one another, and for him who is conquered to-day to be conqueror tomorrow."

"Very true," said Samson, "and good Sancho Panza's view of these cases is quite right."

"Sirs, not so fast," said Don Quixote, "'in last year's nests there are no birds this year.' I was mad, now I am in my senses; I was Don Quixote of La Mancha, I am now, as I said, Alonso Quixano the Good; and may my repentance and sincerity restore me to the esteem you used to have for me; and now let Master Notary proceed.

"Item, I leave all my property absolutely to Antonia Quixana my niece, here present, after all has been deducted from the most available portion of it that may be required to satisfy the bequests I have made. And the first disbursement I desire to be made is the payment of the wages I owe for the time my housekeeper has served me, with twenty ducats, over and above, for a gown. The curate and the bachelor Samson Carrasco, now present, I appoint my executors.

"Item, it is my wish that if Antonia Quixana, my niece, desires to marry, she shall marry a man of whom it shall be first of all ascertained by information taken that he does not know what books of chivalry are; and if it should be proved that he does, and if, in spite of this, my niece insists upon marrying him, and does marry him, then that she shall forfeit the whole of what I have left her, which my executors shall devote to works of charity as they please.

"Item, I entreat the aforesaid gentlemen my executors, that, if any happy chance should lead them to discover the author who is said to have written a history now going about under the title of 'Second Part of the Achievements of Don Quixote of La Mancha,' they beg of him on my behalf as earnestly as they can to forgive me for having been, without intending it, the cause of his writing so many and such monstrous absurdities as he has written in it; for I am leaving the world with a feeling of compunction at having provoked him to write them."

With this he closed his will, and a faintness coming over him he stretched himself out at full length on the bed. All were in a flutter and made haste to relieve him, and during the three days he lived after that on which he made his will he fainted away very often. The house was all in confusion; but still the niece ate and the housekeeper drank and Sancho Panza enjoyed himself; for inheriting property wipes out or softens down in the heir the feeling of grief the dead man might be expected to leave behind him.

At last Don Quixote's end came, after he had received all the sacraments, and had in full and forcible terms expressed his detestation of books of chivalry. The notary was there at the time, and he said that in no book of chivalry had he ever read of any knight-errant dying in his bed so calmly and so like a Christian as Don Quixote, who amid the tears and lamentations of all present yielded up his spirit, that is to say died. On perceiving it the curate begged the notary to bear witness that Alonso Quixano the Good, commonly called Don Quixote of La Mancha, had passed away from this present life, and died naturally; and said he desired this testimony in order to remove the possibility of any other author save Cide Hamete Benengeli bringing him to life again falsely and making interminable stories out of his achievements.

Such was the end of the Ingenious Gentleman of La Mancha, whose village Cide Hamete would not indicate precisely, in order to leave all the towns and villages of La Mancha to contend among themselves for the right to adopt him and claim him as a son, as the seven cities of Greece contended for Homer. The lamentations of Sancho and the niece and housekeeper are omitted here, as well as the new epitaphs upon his tomb; Samson Carrasco, however, put the following lines:

> A doughty gentleman lies here;
> A stranger all his life to fear;
> Nor in his death could Death prevail,
> In that last hour, to make him quail.
> He for the world but little cared;
> And at his feats the world was scared;
> A crazy man his life he passed,
> But in his senses died at last.

And said most sage Cide Hamete to his pen, "Rest here, hung up by this brass wire, upon this shelf, O my pen, whether of skilful make or clumsy cut I know not; here shalt thou remain long ages hence, unless presumptuous or malignant story-tellers take thee down to profane thee. But ere they touch thee warn them, and, as best thou canst, say to them:

> Hold off! ye weaklings; hold your hands!
>     Adventure it let none,
>     For this emprise, my lord the king,
>     Was meant for me alone.

"For me alone was Don Quixote born, and I for him; it was his to act, mine to write; we two together make but one, notwithstanding and in spite of that pretended Tordesillesque writer who has ventured or would venture with his great, coarse, ill-trimmed ostrich quill to write the achievements of my valiant knight; no burden for his shoulders, nor subject for his frozen wit: whom, if perchance thou shouldst come to know him, thou shalt warn to leave at rest where they lie the weary mouldering bones of Don Quixote, and not to attempt to carry him off, in opposition to all the privileges of death, to Old Castile, making him rise from the grave where in reality and truth he lies stretched at full length, powerless to make any third expedition or new sally; for the two that he has already made, so much to the enjoyment and approval of everybody to whom they have become known, in this as well as in foreign countries, are quite sufficient for the purpose of turning into ridicule the whole of those made by the whole set of the knights-errant; and so doing shalt thou discharge thy Christian calling, giving good counsel to one that bears ill-will to thee.

"And I shall remain satisfied, and proud to have been the first who has ever enjoyed the fruit of his writings as fully as he could desire; for my desire has been no other than to deliver over to the detestation of mankind the false and foolish tales of the books of chivalry, which, thanks to that of my true Don Quixote, are even now tottering, and doubtless doomed to fall for ever. Farewell."

*Translated by John Ormsby, 1885*

# ON MADNESS AND REALITY

## RT Llizo

**M**iguel de Cervantes y Saavedra's "Sorrowful Knight" strikes us, at the outset, as a buffoon, a loveable fool who's easy to scorn.

He's a *hidalgo*, the equivalent of what might be known in England as a country squire, which means, as the second or third son of nobility, he cannot inherit his father's title, but he can't engage in business either, so he runs his estate (at least, what's left of it) while selling several of its parcels in order to buy books on knight-errantry.

Then he leaves the care of his estate in order to pursue foolish fantasies, all culled from silly books. After reading Ariosto's *Orlando Furioso* and other tales, he's convinced that the world of knight-errantry is the best way to lead one's life, and he decides to do something about it. He sallies forth in search of "adventures," seeing giants and castles that turn out to be merely windmills and taverns.

As his sidekick, or, shall we say, his squire, we have Sancho Panza, who believes promises of a governorship of distant islands and castles. The plain facts of the matter, however, are plain to Sancho as he constantly tries to remind Don Quixote that the objects he's charging toward are actually common structures.

Don Quixote, undaunted, continues in his insistence that these are indeed giants and that they must be slain. When the matter is made clear to the Sorrowful Knight after a round with the windmills—which ends with him on his back—he blames his delusion on "enchantment" and continues his noble quest.

———

It's easy to write off Don Quixote as a deranged nutcase, but as we read through the novel, something begins to evolve. We laugh in the beginning, but then we gradually become caught up in his world; we begin to see it from his eyes, and we end up enjoying it.

We grieve with Sancho for his death, for the vision of a world where he is more than a worthless ne'er-do-well—an important governor and lord—will die with him. The barmaid weeps, and we weep with her, for in Don Quixote's eyes, she's more than a mere barmaid; she's a noble lady named Dulcinea.

What's happened? How is it that we chuckle at him at the onset but now are caught up in his "madness"?

But this is where Cervantes has caught us in our own folly. *Is* it madness?

In the course of the tale, we begin with a self-assured notion that the world Don Quixote imagines makes him unable to live in the true milieu of "reality," yet increasingly our own assumptions about the nature of that reality come under question.

In Part II we're moved by statements like these:

All I aim at is, to convince the world of its error in not reviving those happy times [of chivalry], in which the order of the knight-errant flourished. . . . But nowadays, sloth triumphs over diligence, idleness over labour, vice over virtue, arrogance over bravery, the theory over the practice of arms, which only lived and flourished in those golden ages, and in those knights-errant. (From the Oxford World's Classics, 528.)

One can hear the quintessential Christ-like question coming through in the following passage:

> In the meantime, tell me, friend Sancho, what do folks say of me about this town? What opinion has the common people of me? What think the gentlemen, and what the cavaliers? What is said of my prowess, what of my exploits, and what of my courtesy? What discourse is there of the design I have engaged in, to revive and restore to the world the long-forgotten order of chivalry? (ibid., 535)

Sancho's answer is quite expected: "The common people take your worship for a downright madman" (ibid.). But what can be said of Don Quixote's stated desire to "revive and restore" the chivalric order?

———

Reality is a complex phenomenon, filled with dimensions, not the least of which are two that Christians affirm and understand: the physical and the spiritual. We are invited by Cervantes to enter into Don Quixote's imaginary world and reflect on these layers.

We're to ignore no points of view: neither the idealism of Don Quixote nor the realism/literalism of Sancho Panza. The point that comes across is this: We must not have a reductionist attitude toward reality.

While we must not fall into the gnosticizing trap of seeing the world as only ideal, without any reference to the physical and tangible universe we inhabit, neither should we commit to a crass literalism devoid of imagination and poetry.

Poetry in the soul ennobles the insignificant. Something in us does yearn for the ideal Don Quixote envisions, and yet his failed efforts to actualize it should give us pause, for however noble his vision, it cannot be established here and now without any reference to the needs of the here and now.

Cervantes' masterpiece, then, cautions the literalist/materialist against a world (and a future) devoid of enchantment, just as it challenges the idealist who gazes toward heaven to remember that the coming reality is "not yet."

Laugh at the beginning, if you will. In the end, the Sorrowful Knight has the last laugh.

## CHAPTER FOURTEEN

# WILLIAM SHAKESPEARE

## Early Modern (1564–1616)

I came to love William Shakespeare as a grown-up, but I felt guilty for not liking him as a kid.

One deterrent to loving him was thinking I had to do so. So many fans of the Bard were insufferable. Once, nearly in the grip of a Shakespeare play, my experience was ruined by a loud "expert" picking apart the performance with a fanboy's insider language.

Finally, Shakespeare is written in English, but not English that was easily accessible. Nothing ever made brought on theatrical shame faster than to hear something I could almost understand, knew I should understand, but could not comprehend.

Unfortunately, years of teaching suggest my early experiences are not totally unique. Nor did "hip" teachers help in trying to make Shakespeare relevant by shouting out all the naughty bits (or putting his characters in "modern" costumes). They ended up making timeless plays seem as dated as the word *hip*.

One advantage most of us have is that we know Shakespeare is good.

We know that most films or plays we actually like have stolen a line or an idea from Shakespeare. There's no pop cultural facet in which the Bard cannot make an appearance.

My own passion for Shakespeare came after I worked on the language. I had to stop being embarrassed for not knowing older English and simply work to learn the vocabulary and speech patterns as if it were a foreign tongue. Looked at this way, Shakespearean English is the easiest "second language" most of us will ever learn!

It is hard to enjoy a comedy when you can't understand the jokes.

Next I remembered that Shakespeare's plays were plays, not philosophy texts with swordfights. Watch them live in a theater when you can. Good actors will help interpret the tricky parts. If you cannot go to the play, get a video performance. Watch the play with the text in hand, then read the text again.

William Shakespeare presents a Christian worldview that is deeply biblical. As a result, it's no more afraid of the body than the Song of Solomon, no more violent than Judges, and just like Esther, it sometimes doesn't directly mention God's name. Of course, Shakespeare is not inerrant, but he is a culturally confident believer.

He's given me a better vocabulary to woo my wife, insight into politics, and wisdom about living and dying well. Shakespeare isn't "cool," but he's excellent. For most of us he's not easy, but he's worthwhile. And when seen in a good production, he can reveal as much beauty as a man can safely see this side of paradise.

Look for yourself.

⊂⊄ FROM ⊃⊃

# From Much Ado About Nothing

## ACT II, SCENE I

### A hall in *Leonato's* house

*Enter LEONATO, ANTONIO, HERO, BEATRICE, and others*

LEONATO: Was not Count John here at supper?

ANTONIO: I saw him not.

BEATRICE: How tartly that gentleman looks! I never can see him but I am heart-burned an hour after.

HERO: He is of a very melancholy disposition.

BEATRICE: He were an excellent man that were made just in the mid-way between him and Benedick: the one is too like an image and says nothing, and the other too like my lady's eldest son, evermore tattling.

LEONATO: Then half Signior Benedick's tongue in Count John's mouth, and half Count John's melancholy in Signior Benedick's face,—

BEATRICE: With a good leg and a good foot, uncle, and money enough in his purse, such a man would win any woman in the world, if a' could get her good-will.

LEONATO: By my troth, niece, thou wilt never get thee a husband, if thou be so shrewd of thy tongue.

ANTONIO: In faith, she's too curst.

BEATRICE: Too curst is more than curst: I shall lessen God's sending that way; for it is said, "God sends a curst cow short horns;" but to a cow too curst he sends none.

LEONATO: So, by being too curst, God will send you no horns.

BEATRICE: Just, if he send me no husband; for the which blessing I am at him upon my knees every morning and evening. Lord, I could not endure a husband with a beard on his face: I had rather lie in the woollen.

LEONATO: You may light on a husband that hath no beard.

BEATRICE: What should I do with him? dress him in my apparel and make him my waiting-gentlewoman? He that hath a beard is more than a youth, and he that hath no beard is less than a man: and he that is more than a youth is not for me, and he that is less than a man, I am not for him: therefore, I will even take sixpence in earnest of the bear-ward, and lead his apes into hell.

LEONATO: Well, then, go you into hell?

BEATRICE: No, but to the gate; and there will the devil meet me, like an old cuckold, with horns on his head, and say "Get you to heaven, Beatrice, get you to heaven; here's no place for you maids:" so deliver I up my apes, and away to Saint Peter for the heavens; he shows me where the bachelors sit, and there live we as merry as the day is long.

ANTONIO: [To HERO] Well, niece, I trust you will be ruled by your father.

BEATRICE: Yes, faith; it is my cousin's duty to make curtsy and say "Father, as it please you." But yet for all that, cousin, let him be a handsome fellow, or else make another curtsy and say "Father, as it please me."

LEONATO: Well, niece, I hope to see you one day fitted with a husband.

BEATRICE: Not till God make men of some other metal than earth. Would it not grieve a woman to be overmastered with a pierce of valiant dust? to make an account of her life to a clod of wayward marl? No, uncle, I'll none: Adam's sons are my brethren; and, truly, I hold it a sin to match in my kindred.

LEONATO: Daughter, remember what I told you: if the prince do solicit you in that kind, you know your answer.

BEATRICE: The fault will be in the music, cousin, if you be not wooed in good time: if the prince be too important, tell him there is measure in every thing and so dance out the answer. For, hear me, Hero: wooing, wedding, and repenting, is as a Scotch jig, a measure, and a cinque pace: the first suit is hot and hasty, like a Scotch jig, and full as fantastical; the wedding, mannerly-modest, as a measure, full of state and ancientry; and then comes repentance and, with his bad legs, falls into the cinque pace faster and faster, till he sink into his grave.

LEONATO: Cousin, you apprehend passing shrewdly.

BEATRICE: I have a good eye, uncle; I can see a church by daylight.

LEONATO: The revellers are entering, brother: make good room.

*(All put on their masks)*


*Enter DON PEDRO, CLAUDIO, BENEDICK, BALTHASAR, DON JOHN,*
*BORACHIO, MARGARET, URSULA and others, masked*

DON PEDRO: Lady, will you walk about with your friend?
HERO: So you walk softly and look sweetly and say nothing, I am yours
    for the walk; and especially when I walk away.
DON PEDRO: With me in your company?
HERO: I may say so, when I please.
DON PEDRO: And when please you to say so?
HERO: When I like your favour; for God defend the lute should be like
    the case!
DON PEDRO: My visor is Philemon's roof; within the house is Jove.
HERO: Why, then, your visor should be thatched.
DON PEDRO: Speak low, if you speak love.

*(Drawing her aside)*

BALTHASAR: Well, I would you did like me.
MARGARET: So would not I, for your own sake; for I have many
    ill-qualities.
BALTHASAR: Which is one?
MARGARET: I say my prayers aloud.
BALTHASAR: I love you the better: the hearers may cry, Amen.
MARGARET: God match me with a good dancer!
BALTHASAR: Amen.
MARGARET: And God keep him out of my sight when the dance is
    done! Answer, clerk.
BALTHASAR: No more words: the clerk is answered.
URSULA: I know you well enough; you are Signior Antonio.
ANTONIO: At a word, I am not.
URSULA: I know you by the waggling of your head.

ANTONIO: To tell you true, I counterfeit him.

URSULA: You could never do him so ill-well, unless you were the very man. Here's his dry hand up and down: you are he, you are he.

ANTONIO: At a word, I am not.

URSULA: Come, come, do you think I do not know you by your excellent wit? can virtue hide itself? Go to, mum, you are he: graces will appear, and there's an end.

BEATRICE: Will you not tell me who told you so?

BENEDICK: No, you shall pardon me.

BEATRICE: Nor will you not tell me who you are?

BENEDICK: Not now.

BEATRICE: That I was disdainful, and that I had my good wit out of the "Hundred Merry Tales:"—well this was Signior Benedick that said so.

BENEDICK: What's he?

BEATRICE: I am sure you know him well enough.

BENEDICK: Not I, believe me.

BEATRICE: Did he never make you laugh?

BENEDICK: I pray you, what is he?

BEATRICE: Why, he is the prince's jester: a very dull fool; only his gift is in devising impossible slanders: none but libertines delight in him; and the commendation is not in his wit, but in his villany; for he both pleases men and angers them, and then they laugh at him and beat him. I am sure he is in the fleet: I would he had boarded me.

BENEDICK: When I know the gentleman, I'll tell him what you say.

BEATRICE: Do, do: he'll but break a comparison or two on me; which, peradventure not marked or not laughed at, strikes him into melancholy; and then there's a partridge wing saved, for the fool will eat no supper that night.

*(Music)*

We must follow the leaders.

BENEDICK: In every good thing.

BEATRICE: Nay, if they lead to any ill, I will leave them at the next turning.

*(Dance)*

*Then exeunt all except DON JOHN, BORACHIO, and CLAUDIO*

DON JOHN: Sure my brother is amorous on Hero and hath withdrawn her father to break with him about it. The ladies follow her and but one visor remains.

BORACHIO: And that is Claudio: I know him by his bearing.

DON JOHN: Are not you Signior Benedick?

CLAUDIO: You know me well; I am he.

DON JOHN: Signior, you are very near my brother in his love: he is enamoured on Hero; I pray you, dissuade him from her: she is no equal for his birth: you may do the part of an honest man in it.

CLAUDIO: How know you he loves her?

DON JOHN: I heard him swear his affection.

BORACHIO: So did I too; and he swore he would marry her to-night.

DON JOHN: Come, let us to the banquet.

*Exeunt DON JOHN and BORACHIO*

CLAUDIO: Thus answer I in the name of Benedick,
But hear these ill news with the ears of Claudio.
'Tis certain so; the prince wooes for himself.
Friendship is constant in all other things
Save in the office and affairs of love:
Therefore, all hearts in love use their own tongues;
Let every eye negotiate for itself
And trust no agent; for beauty is a witch
Against whose charms faith melteth into blood.
This is an accident of hourly proof,
Which I mistrusted not. Farewell, therefore, Hero!

*Re-enter BENEDICK*

BENEDICK: Count Claudio?

CLAUDIO: Yea, the same.

BENEDICK: Come, will you go with me?

CLAUDIO: Whither?

BENEDICK: Even to the next willow, about your own business, county.

What fashion will you wear the garland of? about your neck, like an usurer's chain? or under your arm, like a lieutenant's scarf? You must wear it one way, for the prince hath got your Hero.

CLAUDIO: I wish him joy of her.

BENEDICK: Why, that's spoken like an honest drovier: so they sell bullocks. But did you think the prince would have served you thus?

CLAUDIO: I pray you, leave me.

BENEDICK: Ho! now you strike like the blind man: 'twas the boy that stole your meat, and you'll beat the post.

CLAUDIO: If it will not be, I'll leave you.

*Exit*

BENEDICK: Alas, poor hurt fowl! now will he creep into sedges. But that my Lady Beatrice should know me, and not know me! The prince's fool! Ha? It may be I go under that title because I am merry. Yea, but so I am apt to do myself wrong; I am not so reputed: it is the base, though bitter, disposition of Beatrice that puts the world into her person and so gives me out. Well, I'll be revenged as I may.

*Re-enter DON PEDRO*

DON PEDRO: Now, signior, where's the count? did you see him?

BENEDICK: Troth, my lord, I have played the part of Lady Fame. I found him here as melancholy as a lodge in a warren: I told him, and I think I told him true, that your grace had got the good will of this young lady; and I offered him my company to a willow-tree, either to make him a garland, as being forsaken, or to bind him up a rod, as being worthy to be whipped.

DON PEDRO: To be whipped! What's his fault?

BENEDICK: The flat transgression of a schoolboy, who, being overjoyed with finding a birds' nest, shows it his companion, and he steals it.

DON PEDRO: Wilt thou make a trust a transgression? The transgression is in the stealer.

BENEDICK: Yet it had not been amiss the rod had been made, and the garland too; for the garland he might have worn himself, and the rod he might have bestowed on you, who, as I take it, have stolen his birds' nest.

DON PEDRO: I will but teach them to sing, and restore them to the owner.

BENEDICK: If their singing answer your saying, by my faith, you say honestly.

DON PEDRO: The Lady Beatrice hath a quarrel to you: the gentleman that danced with her told her she is much wronged by you.

BENEDICK: O, she misused me past the endurance of a block! an oak but with one green leaf on it would have answered her; my very visor began to assume life and scold with her. She told me, not thinking I had been myself, that I was the prince's jester, that I was duller than a great thaw; huddling jest upon jest with such impossible conveyance upon me that I stood like a man at a mark, with a whole army shooting at me. She speaks poniards, and every word stabs: if her breath were as terrible as her terminations, there were no living near her; she would infect to the north star. I would not marry her, though she were endowed with all that Adam had left him before he transgressed: she would have made Hercules have turned spit, yea, and have cleft his club to make the fire too. Come, talk not of her: you shall find her the infernal Ate in good apparel. I would to God some scholar would conjure her; for certainly, while she is here, a man may live as quiet in hell as in a sanctuary; and people sin upon purpose, because they would go thither; so, indeed, all disquiet, horror and perturbation follows her.

DON PEDRO: Look, here she comes.

*Enter CLAUDIO, BEATRICE, HERO, and LEONATO*

BENEDICK: Will your grace command me any service to the world's end? I will go on the slightest errand now to the Antipodes that you can devise to send me on; I will fetch you a tooth-picker now from the furthest inch of Asia, bring you the length of Prester John's foot, fetch you a hair off the great Cham's beard, do you any embassage to the Pigmies, rather than hold three words' conference with this harpy. You have no employment for me?

DON PEDRO: None, but to desire your good company.

BENEDICK: O God, sir, here's a dish I love not: I cannot endure my Lady Tongue.

*Exit*

DON PEDRO: Come, lady, come; you have lost the heart of Signior Benedick.

BEATRICE: Indeed, my lord, he lent it me awhile; and I gave him use for it, a double heart for his single one: marry, once before he won it of me with false dice, therefore your grace may well say I have lost it.

DON PEDRO: You have put him down, lady, you have put him down.

BEATRICE: So I would not he should do me, my lord, lest I should prove the mother of fools. I have brought Count Claudio, whom you sent me to seek.

DON PEDRO: Why, how now, count! wherefore are you sad?

CLAUDIO: Not sad, my lord.

DON PEDRO: How then? sick?

CLAUDIO: Neither, my lord.

BEATRICE: The count is neither sad, nor sick, nor merry, nor well; but civil count, civil as an orange, and something of that jealous complexion.

DON PEDRO: I' faith, lady, I think your blazon to be true; though, I'll be sworn, if he be so, his conceit is false. Here, Claudio, I have wooed in thy name, and fair Hero is won: I have broke with her father, and his good will obtained: name the day of marriage, and God give thee joy!

LEONATO: Count, take of me my daughter, and with her my fortunes: his grace hath made the match, and all grace say Amen to it.

BEATRICE: Speak, count, 'tis your cue.

CLAUDIO: Silence is the perfectest herald of joy: I were but little happy, if I could say how much. Lady, as you are mine, I am yours: I give away myself for you and dote upon the exchange.

BEATRICE: Speak, cousin; or, if you cannot, stop his mouth with a kiss, and let not him speak neither.

DON PEDRO: In faith, lady, you have a merry heart.

BEATRICE: Yea, my lord; I thank it, poor fool, it keeps on the windy side of care. My cousin tells him in his ear that he is in her heart.

CLAUDIO: And so she doth, cousin.

BEATRICE: Good Lord, for alliance! Thus goes every one to the world but I, and I am sunburnt; I may sit in a corner and cry heigh-ho for a husband!

DON PEDRO: Lady Beatrice, I will get you one.

BEATRICE: I would rather have one of your father's getting. Hath your grace ne'er a brother like you? Your father got excellent husbands, if a maid could come by them.

DON PEDRO: Will you have me, lady?

BEATRICE: No, my lord, unless I might have another for working-days: your grace is too costly to wear every day. But, I beseech your grace, pardon me: I was born to speak all mirth and no matter.

DON PEDRO: Your silence most offends me, and to be merry best becomes you; for, out of question, you were born in a merry hour.

BEATRICE: No, sure, my lord, my mother cried; but then there was a star danced, and under that was I born. Cousins, God give you joy!

LEONATO: Niece, will you look to those things I told you of?

BEATRICE: I cry you mercy, uncle. By your grace's pardon.

*Exit*

DON PEDRO: By my troth, a pleasant-spirited lady.

LEONATO: There's little of the melancholy element in her, my lord: she is never sad but when she sleeps, and not ever sad then; for I have heard my daughter say, she hath often dreamed of unhappiness and wake herself with laughing.

DON PEDRO: She cannot endure to hear tell of a husband.

LEONATO: O, by no means: she mocks all her wooers out of suit.

DON PEDRO: She were an excellent wife for Benedick.

LEONATO: O Lord, my lord, if they were but a week married, they would talk themselves mad.

DON PEDRO: County Claudio, when mean you to go to church?

CLAUDIO: To-morrow, my lord: time goes on crutches till love have all his rites.

LEONATO: Not till Monday, my dear son, which is hence a just seven-night; and a time too brief, too, to have all things answer my mind.

DON PEDRO: Come, you shake the head at so long a breathing: but, I warrant thee, Claudio, the time shall not go dully by us. I will in the interim undertake one of Hercules' labours; which is, to bring Signior Benedick and the Lady Beatrice into a mountain of affection the one with the other. I would fain have it a match, and I doubt not but to fashion it, if you three will but minister such assistance as I shall give you direction.

LEONATO: My lord, I am for you, though it cost me ten nights' watchings.

CLAUDIO: And I, my lord.

DON PEDRO: And you too, gentle Hero?

HERO: I will do any modest office, my lord, to help my cousin to a good husband.

DON PEDRO: And Benedick is not the unhopefullest husband that I know. Thus far can I praise him; he is of a noble strain, of approved valour and confirmed honesty. I will teach you how to humour your cousin, that she shall fall in love with Benedick; and I, with your two helps, will so practise on Benedick that, in despite of his quick wit and his queasy stomach, he shall fall in love with Beatrice. If we can do this, Cupid is no longer an archer: his glory shall be ours, for we are the only love-gods. Go in with me, and I will tell you my drift.

*Exeunt . . .*

## ACT II, SCENE III

### *Leonato's* orchard

*Enter BENEDICK*

BENEDICK: Boy!

*Enter Boy*

Boy: Signior?

BENEDICK: In my chamber-window lies a book: bring it hither to me in the orchard.

Boy: I am here already, sir.

BENEDICK: I know that; but I would have thee hence, and here again.

*Exit Boy*

I do much wonder that one man, seeing how much another man is a fool when he dedicates his behaviors to love, will, after he hath laughed at such shallow follies in others, become the argument of his own scorn by falling in love: and such a man is Claudio. I have known when there was no music with him but the drum and the fife; and now had he rather hear the tabour and the pipe: I have known when he would have walked ten mile a-foot to see a good armour; and now will he lie ten nights awake, carving the fashion of a new doublet. He was wont to speak plain and to the purpose, like an honest man and a soldier; and now is he turned orthography; his words are a very fantastical banquet, just so many strange dishes. May I be so converted and see with these eyes? I cannot tell; I think not: I will not be sworn, but love may transform me to an oyster; but I'll take my oath on it, till he have made an oyster of me, he shall never make me such a fool. One woman is fair, yet I am well; another is wise, yet I am well; another virtuous, yet I am well; but till all graces be in one woman, one woman shall not come in my grace. Rich she shall be, that's certain; wise, or I'll none; virtuous, or I'll never cheapen her; fair, or I'll never look on her; mild, or come not near me; noble, or not I for an angel; of good discourse, an excellent musician, and her hair shall be of what colour it please God. Ha! the prince and Monsieur Love! I will hide me in the arbour.

*Withdraws*

*Enter DON PEDRO, CLAUDIO, and LEONATO, followed by BALTHASAR and Musicians*

DON PEDRO: Come, shall we hear this music?
CLAUDIO: Yea, my good lord. How still the evening is,
As hush'd on purpose to grace harmony!
DON PEDRO: See you where Benedick hath hid himself?

CLAUDIO: O, very well, my lord: the music ended,
    We'll fit the kid-fox with a pennyworth.
DON PEDRO: Come, Balthasar, we'll hear that song again.
BALTHASAR: O, good my lord, tax not so bad a voice
    To slander music any more than once.
DON PEDRO: It is the witness still of excellency
    To put a strange face on his own perfection.
    I pray thee, sing, and let me woo no more.
BALTHASAR: Because you talk of wooing, I will sing;
    Since many a wooer doth commence his suit
    To her he thinks not worthy, yet he wooes,
    Yet will he swear he loves.
DON PEDRO: Now, pray thee, come;
    Or, if thou wilt hold longer argument,
    Do it in notes.
BALTHASAR: Note this before my notes;
    There's not a note of mine that's worth the noting.
DON PEDRO: Why, these are very crotchets that he speaks;
    Note, notes, forsooth, and nothing.

*Air*

BENEDICK: Now, divine air! now is his soul ravished! Is it not strange that sheeps' guts should hale souls out of men's bodies? Well, a horn for my money, when all's done.

*The Song*

BALTHASAR: Sigh no more, ladies, sigh no more,
    Men were deceivers ever,
    One foot in sea and one on shore,
    To one thing constant never:
    Then sigh not so, but let them go,
    And be you blithe and bonny,
    Converting all your sounds of woe
    Into Hey nonny, nonny.

Sing no more ditties, sing no more,
Of dumps so dull and heavy;
The fraud of men was ever so,
Since summer first was leafy:
Then sigh not so,
But let them go,
And be you blithe and bonny,
Converting all your sounds of woe
Into Hey nonny, nonny.

DON PEDRO: By my troth, a good song.

BALTHASAR: And an ill singer, my lord.

DON PEDRO: Ha, no, no, faith; thou singest well enough for a shift.

BENEDICK [*aside.*]: An he had been a dog that should have howled thus, they would have hanged him: and I pray God his bad voice bode no mischief. I had as lief have heard the night-raven, come what plague could have come after it.

DON PEDRO: Yea, marry, dost thou hear, Balthasar? I pray thee, get us some excellent music; for tomorrow night we would have it at the Lady Hero's chamber-window.

BALTHASAR: The best I can, my lord.

DON PEDRO: Do so: farewell.

*Exit BALTHASAR and Musicians*

Come hither, Leonato. What was it you told me of to-day, that your niece Beatrice was in love with Signior Benedick?

CLAUDIO: O, ay: [*aside to Don Pedro*] stalk on. stalk on; the fowl sits. I did never think that lady would have loved any man.

LEONATO: No, nor I neither; but most wonderful that she should so dote on Signior Benedick, whom she hath in all outward behaviors seemed ever to abhor.

BENEDICK [*aside*]: Is't possible? Sits the wind in that corner?

LEONATO: By my troth, my lord, I cannot tell what to think of it but that she loves him with an enraged affection: it is past the infinite of thought.

DON PEDRO: May be she doth but counterfeit.

CLAUDIO: Faith, like enough.

LEONATO: O God, counterfeit! There was never counterfeit of passion came so near the life of passion as she discovers it.

DON PEDRO: Why, what effects of passion shows she?

CLAUDIO [*aside*]: Bait the hook well; this fish will bite.

LEONATO: What effects, my lord? She will sit you; [*to Claudio*] you heard my daughter tell you how.

CLAUDIO: She did, indeed.

DON PEDRO: How, how, pray you? You amaze me: I would have thought her spirit had been invincible against all assaults of affection.

LEONATO: I would have sworn it had, my lord; especially against Benedick.

BENEDICK [*aside*]: I should think this a gull, but that the white-bearded fellow speaks it: knavery cannot, sure, hide himself in such reverence.

CLAUDIO [*aside*]: He hath ta'en the infection: hold it up.

DON PEDRO: Hath she made her affection known to Benedick?

LEONATO: No; and swears she never will: that's her torment.

CLAUDIO: 'Tis true, indeed; so your daughter says: "Shall I," says she, "that have so oft encountered him with scorn, write to him that I love him?"

LEONATO: This says she now when she is beginning to write to him; for she'll be up twenty times a night, and there will she sit in her smock till she have writ a sheet of paper: my daughter tells us all.

CLAUDIO: Now you talk of a sheet of paper, I remember a pretty jest your daughter told us of.

LEONATO: O, when she had writ it and was reading it over, she found Benedick and Beatrice between the sheet?

CLAUDIO: That.

LEONATO: O, she tore the letter into a thousand halfpence; railed at herself, that she should be so immodest to write to one that she knew would flout her; "I measure him," says she, "by my own spirit; for I should flout him, if he writ to me; yea, though I love him, I should."

CLAUDIO: Then down upon her knees she falls, weeps, sobs, beats her heart, tears her hair, prays, curses; "O sweet Benedick! God give me patience!"

LEONATO: She doth indeed; my daughter says so: and the ecstasy hath so much overborne her that my daughter is sometime afeared she will do a desperate outrage to herself: it is very true.

DON PEDRO: It were good that Benedick knew of it by some other, if she will not discover it.

CLAUDIO: To what end? He would make but a sport of it and torment the poor lady worse.

DON PEDRO: An he should, it were an alms to hang him. She's an excellent sweet lady; and, out of all suspicion, she is virtuous.

CLAUDIO: And she is exceeding wise.

DON PEDRO: In every thing but in loving Benedick.

LEONATO: O, my lord, wisdom and blood combating in so tender a body, we have ten proofs to one that blood hath the victory. I am sorry for her, as I have just cause, being her uncle and her guardian.

DON PEDRO: I would she had bestowed this dotage on me: I would have daffed all other respects and made her half myself. I pray you, tell Benedick of it, and hear what a' will say.

LEONATO: Were it good, think you?

CLAUDIO: Hero thinks surely she will die; for she says she will die, if he love her not, and she will die, ere she make her love known, and she will die, if he woo her, rather than she will bate one breath of her accustomed crossness.

DON PEDRO: She doth well: if she should make tender of her love, 'tis very possible he'll scorn it; for the man, as you know all, hath a contemptible spirit.

CLAUDIO: He is a very proper man.

DON PEDRO: He hath indeed a good outward happiness.

CLAUDIO: Before God! and, in my mind, very wise.

DON PEDRO: He doth indeed show some sparks that are like wit.

CLAUDIO: And I take him to be valiant.

DON PEDRO: As Hector, I assure you: and in the managing of quarrels you may say he is wise; for either he avoids them with great discretion, or undertakes them with a most Christian-like fear.

LEONATO: If he do fear God, a' must necessarily keep peace: if he break the peace, he ought to enter into a quarrel with fear and trembling.

DON PEDRO: And so will he do; for the man doth fear God, howsoever it seems not in him by some large jests he will make. Well I am sorry for your niece. Shall we go seek Benedick, and tell him of her love?

CLAUDIO: Never tell him, my lord: let her wear it out with good counsel.

LEONATO: Nay, that's impossible: she may wear her heart out first.

DON PEDRO: Well, we will hear further of it by your daughter: let it cool the while. I love Benedick well; and I could wish he would modestly examine himself, to see how much he is unworthy so good a lady.

LEONATO: My lord, will you walk? dinner is ready.

CLAUDIO [*aside*]: If he do not dote on her upon this, I will never trust my expectation.

DON PEDRO [*aside*]: Let there be the same net spread for her; and that must your daughter and her gentlewomen carry. The sport will be, when they hold one an opinion of another's dotage, and no such matter: that's the scene that I would see, which will be merely a dumb-show. Let us send her to call him in to dinner.

*Exeunt DON PEDRO, CLAUDIO, and LEONATO*

BENEDICK [*advancing from the arbour.*] This can be no trick: the conference was sadly borne. They have the truth of this from Hero. They seem to pity the lady: it seems her affections have their full bent. Love me! why, it must be requited. I hear how I am censured: they say I will bear myself proudly, if I perceive the love come from her; they say too that she will rather die than give any sign of affection. I did never think to marry: I must not seem proud: happy are they that hear their detractions and can put them to mending. They say the lady is fair; 'tis a truth, I can bear them witness; and virtuous; 'tis so, I cannot reprove it; and wise, but for loving me; by my troth, it is no addition to her wit, nor no great argument of her folly, for I will be horribly in love with her. I may chance have some odd quirks and remnants of wit broken on me, because I have railed so long against marriage: but doth not the appetite alter? a man loves the meat in his youth that he cannot endure in his age. Shall quips and sentences and these paper bullets of the brain awe a man from the career of his humour? No, the world must be peopled. When I said I would die a bachelor, I did not think I should live till I were married. Here comes Beatrice. By this day! she's a fair lady: I do spy some marks of love in her.

*Enter BEATRICE*

BEATRICE: Against my will I am sent to bid you come in to dinner.
BENEDICK: Fair Beatrice, I thank you for your pains.
BEATRICE: I took no more pains for those thanks than you take pains to thank me: if it had been painful, I would not have come.
BENEDICK: You take pleasure then in the message?
BEATRICE: Yea, just so much as you may take upon a knife's point and choke a daw withal. You have no stomach, signior: fare you well.

*Exit*

BENEDICK: Ha! "Against my will I am sent to bid you come in to dinner;" there's a double meaning in that "I took no more pains for those thanks than you took pains to thank me." that's as much as to say, Any pains that I take for you is as easy as thanks. If I do not take pity of her, I am a villain; if I do not love her, I am a Jew. I will go get her picture.

*Exit*

# ACT III, SCENE I

## *Leonato's* garden

*Enter HERO, MARGARET, and URSULA*

HERO: Good Margaret, run thee to the parlor;
    There shalt thou find my cousin Beatrice
    Proposing with the prince and Claudio:
    Whisper her ear and tell her, I and Ursula
    Walk in the orchard and our whole discourse
    Is all of her; say that thou overheard'st us;

And bid her steal into the pleached bower,
Where honeysuckles, ripen'd by the sun,
Forbid the sun to enter, like favourites,
Made proud by princes, that advance their pride
Against that power that bred it: there will she hide her,
To listen our purpose. This is thy office;
Bear thee well in it and leave us alone.

MARGARET: I'll make her come, I warrant you, presently.

*Exit*

HERO: Now, Ursula, when Beatrice doth come,
As we do trace this alley up and down,
Our talk must only be of Benedick.
When I do name him, let it be thy part
To praise him more than ever man did merit:
My talk to thee must be how Benedick
Is sick in love with Beatrice. Of this matter
Is little Cupid's crafty arrow made,
That only wounds by hearsay.

*Enter BEATRICE, behind*

Now begin;
For look where Beatrice, like a lapwing, runs
Close by the ground, to hear our conference.

URSULA: The pleasant'st angling is to see the fish
Cut with her golden oars the silver stream,
And greedily devour the treacherous bait:
So angle we for Beatrice; who even now
Is couched in the woodbine coverture.
Fear you not my part of the dialogue.

HERO: Then go we near her, that her ear lose nothing
Of the false sweet bait that we lay for it.

*[They approach the bower]*

No, truly, Ursula, she is too disdainful;
I know her spirits are as coy and wild
As haggerds of the rock.
URSULA: But are you sure
That Benedick loves Beatrice so entirely?
HERO: So says the prince and my new-trothed lord.
URSULA: And did they bid you tell her of it, madam?
HERO: They did entreat me to acquaint her of it;
But I persuaded them, if they loved Benedick,
To wish him wrestle with affection,
And never to let Beatrice know of it.
URSULA: Why did you so? Doth not the gentleman
Deserve as full as fortunate a bed
As ever Beatrice shall couch upon?
HERO: O god of love! I know he doth deserve
As much as may be yielded to a man:
But Nature never framed a woman's heart
Of prouder stuff than that of Beatrice;
Disdain and scorn ride sparkling in her eyes,
Misprising what they look on, and her wit
Values itself so highly that to her
All matter else seems weak: she cannot love,
Nor take no shape nor project of affection,
She is so self-endeared.
URSULA: Sure, I think so;
And therefore certainly it were not good
She knew his love, lest she make sport at it.
HERO: Why, you speak truth. I never yet saw man,
How wise, how noble, young, how rarely featured,
But she would spell him backward: if fair-faced,
She would swear the gentleman should be her sister;
If black, why, Nature, drawing of an antique,
Made a foul blot; if tall, a lance ill-headed;
If low, an agate very vilely cut;
If speaking, why, a vane blown with all winds;
If silent, why, a block moved with none.

So turns she every man the wrong side out
And never gives to truth and virtue that
Which simpleness and merit purchaseth.
URSULA: Sure, sure, such carping is not commendable.
HERO: No, not to be so odd and from all fashions
As Beatrice is, cannot be commendable:
But who dare tell her so? If I should speak,
She would mock me into air; O, she would laugh me
Out of myself, press me to death with wit.
Therefore let Benedick, like cover'd fire,
Consume away in sighs, waste inwardly:
It were a better death than die with mocks,
Which is as bad as die with tickling.
URSULA: Yet tell her of it: hear what she will say.
HERO: No; rather I will go to Benedick
And counsel him to fight against his passion.
And, truly, I'll devise some honest slanders
To stain my cousin with: one doth not know
How much an ill word may empoison liking.
URSULA: O, do not do your cousin such a wrong.
She cannot be so much without true judgment—
Having so swift and excellent a wit
As she is prized to have—as to refuse
So rare a gentleman as Signior Benedick.
HERO: He is the only man of Italy.
Always excepted my dear Claudio.
URSULA: I pray you, be not angry with me, madam,
Speaking my fancy: Signior Benedick,
For shape, for bearing, argument and valour,
Goes foremost in report through Italy.
HERO: Indeed, he hath an excellent good name.
URSULA: His excellence did earn it, ere he had it.
When are you married, madam?
HERO: Why, every day, to-morrow. Come, go in:
I'll show thee some attires, and have thy counsel
Which is the best to furnish me to-morrow.

URSULA: She's limed, I warrant you: we have caught her, madam.
HERO: If it proves so, then loving goes by haps:
    Some Cupid kills with arrows, some with traps.

*Exeunt HERO and URSULA*

BEATRICE [advancing]: What fire is in mine ears? Can this be true?
    Stand I condemn'd for pride and scorn so much?
    Contempt, farewell! and maiden pride, adieu!
    No glory lives behind the back of such.
    And, Benedick, love on; I will requite thee,
    Taming my wild heart to thy loving hand:
    If thou dost love, my kindness shall incite thee
    To bind our loves up in a holy band;
    For others say thou dost deserve, and I
    Believe it better than reportingly.

*Exit*

# ON MUCH ADO ABOUT NOTHING

## Melissa Schubert

Some of us can be tempted to dismiss comedy as taking reality too lightly. But here's why I take comedies seriously: they present and celebrate the world in which we survive our own and others' mistakes, follies, transgressions, and deep sins. However lightly, dimly, or bleakly, comedies revel in our survival—in the delaying of death and the staying of the curse. Comedies tell the story of ruined folk somehow avoiding ruin.

The world turns out to be sufficiently ample, elastic, wide, and often bountiful, even for we who've been exiled from paradise. Sometimes the happy vision is as meager an offering as the survival of the thwarted villain still mired in all his disdain for the universe. But its happiest pictures include long-awaited reunions, the practice of forgiveness, and weddings—festive unions between undeserving lovers that promise even more life for the community and love for the world.

And so we have Shakespeare's delightful play, *Much Ado About Nothing*. One primary subject (and a subject of all of his comedies) is love struggling toward marriage. Marriage is the goal of the lover's quartet (Beatrice and Benedick, Hero and Claudio) as well as the goal of the community in Messina. Marriage is proposed, by the play, as a happy situation, not only for the characters of the play but also for the city. Benedick has it right when he proclaims, "The world must be peopled."

But the road to union is thick with obstacles, those present in the self and those presented by others. The self-identified "plain-dealing villain," Don John, sets himself against the formation of community both by refusing peace with his brother and by making himself an enemy to marriage. He takes his only pleasure in spoiling others' happiness.

Claudio, whose naiveté leaves him vulnerable to Don John's villainy, falls for the ruse that suggests Hero's infidelity because his knowledge of and faith in her is insubstantial. Hero is much more a victim of her own lover's mistake than of her own fault. She must—and what a profound task—forgive him his wrongs.

Beatrice, reluctant to submit to another in love, not wishing to be mastered, must learn to see Benedick as something besides a threat to her freedom. Benedick fears marriage, too, expressing anxiety about cuckoldry, so he postures himself as above it all.

The path for none of the four is smooth since, even in small and familiar ways, they stumble as they approach love and happiness. Thus they arrive at their happy ending not by the natural trajectory of character but by a series of delicate interventions.

Beatrice and Benedick's friends employ their very faults to steer them toward loving each other. Human creatures need one another's generous help. Often we're *most* helped when our community can witness our faults and offer gentle correctives.

The other chief trick of the play is Hero's feigned death for Claudio's real sins. Here is where we see most deeply the insistence that it's possible that, in the end, we will not get what we deserve, we will not suffer the full consequence of our sins, but we will be saved.

Notably, the redemption hinges on the luxury of time, a resource notably absent in Shakespeare's tragedies. In *Hamlet*, the time is out of joint. Macbeth's destruction seems wildly rapid. Bad timing governs both Romeo's and Juliet's deaths. But in *Much Ado*, there's enough time—time for mistakes, for discovery, for repentance, for repair, for forgiveness.

With the provision of time comes also a call to patience, the sort most admirably displayed in Hero's suffering. Here is a faithful image of life on earth: where we must sit and talk to clarify misunderstandings, where we abide winter's waiting for the spring, where it takes time for criminals to come to justice, where love buds long before it blossoms. Here is a summons to Christian hope in light of the world's story, this divine comedy, where, even in the face of the direst realities, we look for the resurrection of the dead and the blessed life of the glory to come.

## CHAPTER FIFTEEN

# RENÉ DESCARTES

## Early Modern (1596–1650)

René Descartes was the philosophical father of modernity. Before this turns the believing reader against Descartes, remind yourself that while modernity is not Christianity, modernity is the product of a Christian civilization. Lately the defects of modernity have been made plain to us while its virtues have been taken for granted.

Modernity brought humanity the fruits of applied science, including medicine, democratic forms of government, and a flourishing of the arts. Individual men and women all over the world have greater access to these good things than at any time in history. It would be tragic if Christianity allowed secularism to claim all modernity's laudable work while believers blamed themselves for the shortcomings.

Descartes demonstrated both the virtues and shortcomings of the age he helped create. He insisted, following orthodox tradition, that the faith must be reasonable. Against the growing din of skepticism, he defended a robust, supernatural version of Christianity. He also was willing to take risks in that defense and come to conclusions that didn't always work out. (This too was in the orthodox apologetical tradition.)

Descartes insisted that believers deal with the best science and the best critiques. He forced critics to come up to his level instead of lowering himself to theirs. His respect for dialectic, science, and critics are positive features of the modern age.

Previous centuries of Christianity had, perhaps, overemphasized the standing and initiative of the collective church over the journey and growth of the individual member. Descartes joined Augustine in expressing faith personally (while remaining, in some way, part of the larger catholic Christian tradition).

———

Modernity gone wrong has isolated humanity and made human reason autonomous of (and dismissive toward) revelation. Descartes may not have made these errors himself, but the tendencies are there in his writings. The world he helped create also developed disrespect for human experience: if an idea could not be "proven," then it was disreputable. The more chaotic elements of postmodern thought have been a natural counterreaction.

Read his work critically, but not overly critically. If one wishes to abandon the modern, one cannot take for granted that one will continue to enjoy all of the good it has produced. One thing is certain: René Descartes is admirably clear, persuasive, and faithful in suggesting the direction he believes we should take.

⊂⊂ FROM ⊃⊃

# Meditations

## Meditation One

## Of the Things of Which We May Doubt

1. Several years have now elapsed since I first became aware that I had accepted, even from my youth, many false opinions for true, and that consequently what I afterward based on such principles was highly doubtful; and from that time I was convinced of the necessity of undertaking

once in my life to rid myself of all the opinions I had adopted, and of commencing anew the work of building from the foundation, if I desired to establish a firm and abiding superstructure in the sciences. But as this enterprise appeared to me to be one of great magnitude, I waited until I had attained an age so mature as to leave me no hope that at any stage of life more advanced I should be better able to execute my design. On this account, I have delayed so long that I should henceforth consider I was doing wrong were I still to consume in deliberation any of the time that now remains for action. To-day, then, since I have opportunely freed my mind from all cares [and am happily disturbed by no passions], and since I am in the secure possession of leisure in a peaceable retirement, I will at length apply myself earnestly and freely to the general overthrow of all my former opinions.

2. But, to this end, it will not be necessary for me to show that the whole of these are false—a point, perhaps, which I shall never reach; but as even now my reason convinces me that I ought not the less carefully to withhold belief from what is not entirely certain and indubitable, than from what is manifestly false, it will be sufficient to justify the rejection of the whole if I shall find in each some ground for doubt. Nor for this purpose will it be necessary even to deal with each belief individually, which would be truly an endless labor; but, as the removal from below of the foundation necessarily involves the downfall of the whole edifice, I will at once approach the criticism of the principles on which all my former beliefs rested.

3. All that I have, up to this moment, accepted as possessed of the highest truth and certainty, I received either from or through the senses. I observed, however, that these sometimes misled us; and it is the part of prudence not to place absolute confidence in that by which we have even once been deceived.

4. But it may be said, perhaps, that, although the senses occasionally mislead us respecting minute objects, and such as are so far removed from us as to be beyond the reach of close observation, there are yet many other of their informations (presentations), of the truth of which it is manifestly impossible to doubt; as for example, that I am in this place, seated by the fire, clothed in a winter dressing gown, that I hold in my hands this piece of paper, with other intimations of the same nature. But how could I deny

that I possess these hands and this body, and withal escape being classed with persons in a state of insanity, whose brains are so disordered and clouded by dark bilious vapors as to cause them pertinaciously to assert that they are monarchs when they are in the greatest poverty; or clothed [in gold] and purple when destitute of any covering; or that their head is made of clay, their body of glass, or that they are gourds? I should certainly be not less insane than they, were I to regulate my procedure according to examples so extravagant.

5. Though this be true, I must nevertheless here consider that I am a man, and that, consequently, I am in the habit of sleeping, and representing to myself in dreams those same things, or even sometimes others less probable, which the insane think are presented to them in their waking moments. How often have I dreamt that I was in these familiar circumstances, that I was dressed, and occupied this place by the fire, when I was lying undressed in bed? At the present moment, however, I certainly look upon this paper with eyes wide awake; the head which I now move is not asleep; I extend this hand consciously and with express purpose, and I perceive it; the occurrences in sleep are not so distinct as all this. But I cannot forget that, at other times I have been deceived in sleep by similar illusions; and, attentively considering those cases, I perceive so clearly that there exist no certain marks by which the state of waking can ever be distinguished from sleep, that I feel greatly astonished; and in amazement I almost persuade myself that I am now dreaming.

6. Let us suppose, then, that we are dreaming, and that all these particulars—namely, the opening of the eyes, the motion of the head, the forth-putting of the hands—are merely illusions; and even that we really possess neither an entire body nor hands such as we see. Nevertheless it must be admitted at least that the objects which appear to us in sleep are, as it were, painted representations which could not have been formed unless in the likeness of realities; and, therefore, that those general objects, at all events, namely, eyes, a head, hands, and an entire body, are not simply imaginary, but really existent. For, in truth, painters themselves, even when they study to represent sirens and satyrs by forms the most fantastic and extraordinary, cannot bestow upon them natures absolutely new, but can only make a certain medley of the members of different animals; or if they chance to imagine something so novel that nothing at all similar has ever

been seen before, and such as is, therefore, purely fictitious and absolutely false, it is at least certain that the colors of which this is composed are real. And on the same principle, although these general objects, viz. [a body], eyes, a head, hands, and the like, be imaginary, we are nevertheless absolutely necessitated to admit the reality at least of some other objects still more simple and universal than these, of which, just as of certain real colors, all those images of things, whether true and real, or false and fantastic, that are found in our consciousness *(cogitatio),* are formed.

7. To this class of objects seem to belong corporeal nature in general and its extension; the figure of extended things, their quantity or magnitude, and their number, as also the place in, and the time during, which they exist, and other things of the same sort.

8. We will not, therefore, perhaps reason illegitimately if we conclude from this that Physics, Astronomy, Medicine, and all the other sciences that have for their end the consideration of composite objects, are indeed of a doubtful character; but that Arithmetic, Geometry, and the other sciences of the same class, which regard merely the simplest and most general objects, and scarcely inquire whether or not these are really existent, contain somewhat that is certain and indubitable: for whether I am awake or dreaming, it remains true that two and three make five, and that a square has but four sides; nor does it seem possible that truths so apparent can ever fall under a suspicion of falsity [or incertitude].

9. Nevertheless, the belief that there is a God who is all powerful, and who created me, such as I am, has, for a long time, obtained steady possession of my mind. How, then, do I know that he has not arranged that there should be neither earth, nor sky, nor any extended thing, nor figure, nor magnitude, nor place, providing at the same time, however, for [the rise in me of the perceptions of all these objects, and] the persuasion that these do not exist otherwise than as I perceive them? And further, as I sometimes think that others are in error respecting matters of which they believe themselves to possess a perfect knowledge, how do I know that I am not also deceived each time I add together two and three, or number the sides of a square, or form some judgment still more simple, if more simple indeed can be imagined? But perhaps Deity has not been willing that I should be thus deceived, for he is said to be supremely good. If, however, it were repugnant to the goodness of Deity to have created

me subject to constant deception, it would seem likewise to be contrary to his goodness to allow me to be occasionally deceived; and yet it is clear that this is permitted.

10. Some, indeed, might perhaps be found who would be disposed rather to deny the existence of a Being so powerful than to believe that there is nothing certain. But let us for the present refrain from opposing this opinion, and grant that all which is here said of a Deity is fabulous: nevertheless, in whatever way it be supposed that I reach the state in which I exist, whether by fate, or chance, or by an endless series of antecedents and consequents, or by any other means, it is clear (since to be deceived and to err is a certain defect) that the probability of my being so imperfect as to be the constant victim of deception, will be increased exactly in proportion as the power possessed by the cause, to which they assign my origin, is lessened. To these reasonings I have assuredly nothing to reply, but am constrained at last to avow that there is nothing of all that I formerly believed to be true of which it is impossible to doubt, and that not through thoughtlessness or levity, but from cogent and maturely considered reasons; so that henceforward, if I desire to discover anything certain, I ought not the less carefully to refrain from assenting to those same opinions than to what might be shown to be manifestly false.

11. But it is not sufficient to have made these observations; care must be taken likewise to keep them in remembrance. For those old and customary opinions perpetually recur—long and familiar usage giving them the right of occupying my mind, even almost against my will, and subduing my belief; nor will I lose the habit of deferring to them and confiding in them so long as I shall consider them to be what in truth they are, viz, opinions to some extent doubtful, as I have already shown, but still highly probable, and such as it is much more reasonable to believe than deny. It is for this reason I am persuaded that I shall not be doing wrong, if, taking an opposite judgment of deliberate design, I become my own deceiver, by supposing, for a time, that all those opinions are entirely false and imaginary, until at length, having thus balanced my old by my new prejudices, my judgment shall no longer be turned aside by perverted usage from the path that may conduct to the perception of truth. For I am assured that, meanwhile, there will arise neither peril nor error from this course, and

that I cannot for the present yield too much to distrust, since the end I now seek is not action but knowledge.

12. I will suppose, then, not that Deity, who is sovereignly good and the fountain of truth, but that some malignant demon, who is at once exceedingly potent and deceitful, has employed all his artifice to deceive me; I will suppose that the sky, the air, the earth, colors, figures, sounds, and all external things, are nothing better than the illusions of dreams, by means of which this being has laid snares for my credulity; I will consider myself as without hands, eyes, flesh, blood, or any of the senses, and as falsely believing that I am possessed of these; I will continue resolutely fixed in this belief, and if indeed by this means it be not in my power to arrive at the knowledge of truth, I shall at least do what is in my power, viz, [suspend my judgment], and guard with settled purpose against giving my assent to what is false, and being imposed upon by this deceiver, whatever be his power and artifice. But this undertaking is arduous, and a certain indolence insensibly leads me back to my ordinary course of life; and just as the captive, who, perchance, was enjoying in his dreams an imaginary liberty, when he begins to suspect that it is but a vision, dreads awakening, and conspires with the agreeable illusions that the deception may be prolonged; so I, of my own accord, fall back into the train of my former beliefs, and fear to arouse myself from my slumber, lest the time of laborious wakefulness that would succeed this quiet rest, in place of bringing any light of day, should prove inadequate to dispel the darkness that will arise from the difficulties that have now been raised.

## Meditation II

## Of the Nature of the Human Mind; and That It Is More Easily Known Than the Body

1. The Meditation of yesterday has filled my mind with so many doubts, that it is no longer in my power to forget them. Nor do I see, meanwhile, any principle on which they can be resolved; and, just as if I had fallen all of a sudden into very deep water, I am so greatly disconcerted as to be unable either to plant my feet firmly on the bottom or sustain myself by swimming on the surface. I will, nevertheless, make an effort, and try anew

the same path on which I had entered yesterday, that is, proceed by casting aside all that admits of the slightest doubt, not less than if I had discovered it to be absolutely false; and I will continue always in this track until I shall find something that is certain, or at least, if I can do nothing more, until I shall know with certainty that there is nothing certain. Archimedes, that he might transport the entire globe from the place it occupied to another, demanded only a point that was firm and immovable; so, also, I shall be entitled to entertain the highest expectations, if I am fortunate enough to discover only one thing that is certain and indubitable.

2. I suppose, accordingly, that all the things which I see are false (fictitious); I believe that none of those objects which my fallacious memory represents ever existed; I suppose that I possess no senses; I believe that body, figure, extension, motion, and place are merely fictions of my mind. What is there, then, that can be esteemed true? Perhaps this only, that there is absolutely nothing certain.

3. But how do I know that there is not something different altogether from the objects I have now enumerated, of which it is impossible to entertain the slightest doubt? Is there not a God, or some being, by whatever name I may designate him, who causes these thoughts to arise in my mind? But why suppose such a being, for it may be I myself am capable of producing them? Am I, then, at least not something? But I before denied that I possessed senses or a body; I hesitate, however, for what follows from that? Am I so dependent on the body and the senses that without these I cannot exist? But I had the persuasion that there was absolutely nothing in the world, that there was no sky and no earth, neither minds nor bodies; was I not, therefore, at the same time, persuaded that I did not exist? Far from it; I assuredly existed, since I was persuaded. But there is I know not what being, who is possessed at once of the highest power and the deepest cunning, who is constantly employing all his ingenuity in deceiving me. Doubtless, then, I exist, since I am deceived; and, let him deceive me as he may, he can never bring it about that I am nothing, so long as I shall be conscious that I am something. So that it must, in fine, be maintained, all things being maturely and carefully considered, that this proposition (pronunciatum) *I am, I exist*, is necessarily true each time it is expressed by me, or conceived in my mind.

4. But I do not yet know with sufficient clearness what I am, though

assured that I am; and hence, in the next place, I must take care, lest perchance I inconsiderately substitute some other object in room of what is properly myself, and thus wander from truth, even in that knowledge (cognition) which I hold to be of all others the most certain and evident. For this reason, I will now consider anew what I formerly believed myself to be, before I entered on the present train of thought; and of my previous opinion I will retrench all that can in the least be invalidated by the grounds of doubt I have adduced, in order that there may at length remain nothing but what is certain and indubitable.

5. What then did I formerly think I was? Undoubtedly I judged that I was a man. But what is a man? Shall I say a rational animal? Assuredly not; for it would be necessary forthwith to inquire into what is meant by animal, and what by rational, and thus, from a single question, I should insensibly glide into others, and these more difficult than the first; nor do I now possess enough of leisure to warrant me in wasting my time amid subtleties of this sort. I prefer here to attend to the thoughts that sprung up of themselves in my mind, and were inspired by my own nature alone, when I applied myself to the consideration of what I was. In the first place, then, I thought that I possessed a countenance, hands, arms, and all the fabric of members that appears in a corpse, and which I called by the name of body. It further occurred to me that I was nourished, that I walked, perceived, and thought, and all those actions I referred to the soul; but what the soul itself was I either did not stay to consider, or, if I did, I imagined that it was something extremely rare and subtile, like wind, or flame, or ether, spread through my grosser parts. As regarded the body, I did not even doubt of its nature, but thought I distinctly knew it, and if I had wished to describe it according to the notions I then entertained, I should have explained myself in this manner: By body I understand all that can be terminated by a certain figure; that can be comprised in a certain place, and so fill a certain space as therefrom to exclude every other body; that can be perceived either by touch, sight, hearing, taste, or smell; that can be moved in different ways, not indeed of itself, but by something foreign to it by which it is touched [and from which it receives the impression]; for the power of self-motion, as likewise that of perceiving and thinking, I held as by no means pertaining to the nature of body; on the contrary, I was somewhat astonished to find such faculties existing in some bodies.

6. But [as to myself, what can I now say that I am], since I suppose there exists an extremely powerful, and, if I may so speak, malignant being, whose whole endeavors are directed toward deceiving me? Can I affirm that I possess any one of all those attributes of which I have lately spoken as belonging to the nature of body? After attentively considering them in my own mind, I find none of them that can properly be said to belong to myself. To recount them were idle and tedious. Let us pass, then, to the attributes of the soul. The first mentioned were the powers of nutrition and walking; but, if it be true that I have no body, it is true likewise that I am capable neither of walking nor of being nourished. Perception is another attribute of the soul; but perception too is impossible without the body; besides, I have frequently, during sleep, believed that I perceived objects which I afterward observed I did not in reality perceive. Thinking is another attribute of the soul; and here I discover what properly belongs to myself. This alone is inseparable from me. I am—I exist: this is certain; but how often? As often as I think; for perhaps it would even happen, if I should wholly cease to think, that I should at the same time altogether cease to be. I now admit nothing that is not necessarily true. I am therefore, precisely speaking, only a thinking thing, that is, a mind *(mens sive animus)*, understanding, or reason, terms whose signification was before unknown to me. I am, however, a real thing, and really existent; but what thing? The answer was, a thinking thing.

. . .

## Meditation III

### Of God: That He Exists

1. I will now close my eyes, I will stop my ears, I will turn away my senses from their objects, I will even efface from my consciousness all the images of corporeal things; or at least, because this can hardly be accomplished, I will consider them as empty and false; and thus, holding converse only with myself, and closely examining my nature, I will endeavor to obtain by degrees a more intimate and familiar knowledge of myself. I am a thinking (conscious) thing, that is, a being who doubts, affirms, denies, knows

a few objects, and is ignorant of many—[who loves, hates], wills, refuses, who imagines likewise, and perceives; for, as I before remarked, although the things which I perceive or imagine are perhaps nothing at all apart from me [and in themselves], I am nevertheless assured that those modes of consciousness which I call perceptions and imaginations, in as far only as they are modes of consciousness, exist in me.

. . .

7. But among these ideas, some appear to me to be innate, others adventitious, and others to be made by myself (factitious); for, as I have the power of conceiving what is called a thing, or a truth, or a thought, it seems to me that I hold this power from no other source than my own nature; but if I now hear a noise, if I see the sun, or if I feel heat, I have all along judged that these sensations proceeded from certain objects existing out of myself; and, in fine, it appears to me that sirens, hippogryphs, and the like, are inventions of my own mind. But I may even perhaps come to be of opinion that all my ideas are of the class which I call adventitious, or that they are all innate, or that they are all factitious; for I have not yet clearly discovered their true origin.

. . .

13. But there is still another way of inquiring whether, of the objects whose ideas are in my mind, there are any that exist out of me. If ideas are taken in so far only as they are certain modes of consciousness, I do not remark any difference or inequality among them, and all seem, in the same manner, to proceed from myself; but, considering them as images, of which one represents one thing and another a different, it is evident that a great diversity obtains among them. For, without doubt, those that represent substances are something more, and contain in themselves, so to speak, more objective reality [that is, participate by representation in higher degrees of being or perfection], than those that represent only modes or accidents; and again, the idea by which I conceive a God [sovereign], eternal, infinite, [immutable], all-knowing, all-powerful, and the creator of all things that are out of himself, this, I say, has certainly in it more objective reality than those ideas by which finite substances are represented.

14. Now, it is manifest by the natural light that there must at least be as

much reality in the efficient and total cause as in its effect; for whence can the effect draw its reality if not from its cause? And how could the cause communicate to it this reality unless it possessed it in itself? And hence it follows, not only that what is cannot be produced by what is not, but likewise that the more perfect, in other words, that which contains in itself more reality, cannot be the effect of the less perfect; and this is not only evidently true of those effects, whose reality is actual or formal, but likewise of ideas, whose reality is only considered as objective. Thus, for example, the stone that is not yet in existence, not only cannot now commence to be, unless it be produced by that which possesses in itself, formally or eminently, all that enters into its composition, [in other words, by that which contains in itself the same properties that are in the stone, or others superior to them]; and heat can only be produced in a subject that was before devoid of it, by a cause that is of an order, [degree or kind], at least as perfect as heat; and so of the others. But further, even the idea of the heat, or of the stone, cannot exist in me unless it be put there by a cause that contains, at least, as much reality as I conceive existent in the heat or in the stone for although that cause may not transmit into my idea anything of its actual or formal reality, we ought not on this account to imagine that it is less real; but we ought to consider that, [as every idea is a work of the mind], its nature is such as of itself to demand no other formal reality than that which it borrows from our consciousness, of which it is but a mode [that is, a manner or way of thinking]. But in order that an idea may contain this objective reality rather than that, it must doubtless derive it from some cause in which is found at least as much formal reality as the idea contains of objective; for, if we suppose that there is found in an idea anything which was not in its cause, it must of course derive this from nothing. But, however imperfect may be the mode of existence by which a thing is objectively [or by representation] in the understanding by its idea, we certainly cannot, for all that, allege that this mode of existence is nothing, nor, consequently, that the idea owes its origin to nothing.

. . .

17. But, among these my ideas, besides that which represents myself, respecting which there can be here no difficulty, there is one that represents a God; others that represent corporeal and inanimate things; others angels; others animals; and, finally, there are some that represent men like myself.

18. But with respect to the ideas that represent other men, or animals, or angels, I can easily suppose that they were formed by the mingling and composition of the other ideas which I have of myself, of corporeal things, and of God, although they were, apart from myself, neither men, animals, nor angels.

19. And with regard to the ideas of corporeal objects, I never discovered in them anything so great or excellent which I myself did not appear capable of originating; for, by considering these ideas closely and scrutinizing them individually, in the same way that I yesterday examined the idea of wax, I find that there is but little in them that is clearly and distinctly perceived. As belonging to the class of things that are clearly apprehended, I recognize the following, viz, magnitude or extension in length, breadth, and depth; figure, which results from the termination of extension; situation, which bodies of diverse figures preserve with reference to each other; and motion or the change of situation; to which may be added substance, duration, and number. But with regard to light, colors, sounds, odors, tastes, heat, cold, and the other tactile qualities, they are thought with so much obscurity and confusion, that I cannot determine even whether they are true or false; in other words, whether or not the ideas I have of these qualities are in truth the ideas of real objects. For although I before remarked that it is only in judgments that formal falsity, or falsity properly so called, can be met with, there may nevertheless be found in ideas a certain material falsity, which arises when they represent what is nothing as if it were something. Thus, for example, the ideas I have of cold and heat are so far from being clear and distinct, that I am unable from them to discover whether cold is only the privation of heat, or heat the privation of cold; or whether they are or are not real qualities: and since, ideas being as it were images there can be none that does not seem to us to represent some object, the idea which represents cold as something real and positive will not improperly be called false, if it be correct to say that cold is nothing but a privation of heat; and so in other cases.

. . .

22. . . . . I must consider whether there is anything that cannot be supposed to originate with myself. By the name God, I understand a substance infinite, [eternal, immutable], independent, all-knowing, all-powerful, and by which I myself, and every other thing that exists, if any such there be,

were created. But these properties are so great and excellent, that the more attentively I consider them the less I feel persuaded that the idea I have of them owes its origin to myself alone. And thus it is absolutely necessary to conclude, from all that I have before said, that God exists.

. . .

26. But perhaps I am something more than I suppose myself to be, and it may be that all those perfections which I attribute to God, in some way exist potentially in me, although they do not yet show themselves, and are not reduced to act. Indeed, I am already conscious that my knowledge is being increased [and perfected] by degrees; and I see nothing to prevent it from thus gradually increasing to infinity, nor any reason why, after such increase and perfection, I should not be able thereby to acquire all the other perfections of the Divine nature; nor, in fine, why the power I possess of acquiring those perfections, if it really now exist in me, should not be sufficient to produce the ideas of them.

27. Yet, on looking more closely into the matter, I discover that this cannot be; for, in the first place, although it were true that my knowledge daily acquired new degrees of perfection, and although there were potentially in my nature much that was not as yet actually in it, still all these excellences make not the slightest approach to the idea I have of the Deity, in whom there is no perfection merely potentially [but all actually] existent; for it is even an unmistakable token of imperfection in my knowledge, that it is augmented by degrees. Further, although my knowledge increase more and more, nevertheless I am not, therefore, induced to think that it will ever be actually infinite, since it can never reach that point beyond which it shall be incapable of further increase. But I conceive God as actually infinite, so that nothing can be added to his perfection. And, in fine, I readily perceive that the objective being of an idea cannot be produced by a being that is merely potentially existent, which, properly speaking, is nothing, but only by a being existing formally or actually.

. . .

39. But before I examine this with more attention, and pass on to the consideration of other truths that may be evolved out of it, I think it proper to remain here for some time in the contemplation of God himself—that

I may ponder at leisure his marvelous attributes—and behold, admire, and adore the beauty of this light so unspeakably great, as far, at least, as the strength of my mind, which is to some degree dazzled by the sight, will permit. For just as we learn by faith that the supreme felicity of another life consists in the contemplation of the Divine majesty alone, so even now we learn from experience that a like meditation, though incomparably less perfect, is the source of the highest satisfaction of which we are susceptible in this life.

*Translated by John Veitch, 1901*

# "THE BEAUTY
# OF THIS IMMENSE LIGHT"

## THE PLACE OF GOD IN THE MEDITATIONS

### Thomas Ward

The *Meditations* of René Descartes is probably the most widely read philosophical text in the Western world. Not only is it rich and challenging, but it's also a work of literary brilliance. Not since Augustine's *Confessions* had there been a philosophical work so *personal*.

Written in the first-person singular, in a nontechnical idiom (for the most part), any reader can approach the work and begin immediately to grapple with weighty problems. But its brilliance as a piece of literature is most clearly evident in the way its ideas are reinforced through its literary form. In a first-person *meditation*, Descartes is articulating a philosophical position that places the individual thinker—the *meditator*—at the logical foundations of philosophical inquiry.

Descartes reserves a prominent role for God in his philosophy, but it might seem that the pride of place is actually reserved for the individual thinker attempting to reason his way out of his solitude, with God introduced merely to ensure that the reconstruction of knowledge can proceed. Indeed, the subsequent philosophical tradition has tended to characterize Descartes's philosophy in just this way, with him as a reluctant theist. Many echo the sentiments of his contemporary Blaise Pascal, who said, "I cannot forgive Descartes; in all his philosophy he did his best to dispense with God."

Like the *Confessions*, however, *Meditations* is a God-infused book. Most readers these days overlook this fact, tending to write off the more theological aspects and to focus on the meditator's skeptical arguments and subjective outlook. This is unfair. A proper appreciation of Descartes demands we take his theological thought seriously.

So, how does God enter the philosophical picture? Descartes's fundamental philosophical goal was to discover an absolutely certain foundation of knowledge, and he thought he'd made this discovery in one three-word Latin sentence:

*Cogito, ergo sum*; I think, therefore I am.

(Roughly the same thought is expressed in different terms in the *Meditations*; this version is found in *Principles of Philosophy*.) The idea is that you cannot doubt your own existence, because the act of doubting presupposes that there's something doing the doubting—the doubter.

Dissatisfied with what he'd been taught at school, Descartes set out to question everything, rejecting each belief that wasn't certain. In the First Meditation, he walks us through a gauntlet of skeptical arguments, offering reasons for doubting our beliefs in even the most ordinary and obvious things: that there's a physical world, that you have a body, that other people exist, that God exists, and that 2 + 2 = 4. By the close, it seems skepticism has swept everything aside, that there is nothing but "inextricable darkness."

However, in the Second Meditation, Descartes realizes there is one thing that simply cannot be doubted: that he exists.

From this single foundation of certainty, Descartes attempts a reconstruction of all our knowledge of the world and of God. Certain at least that he *is*, he wonders how, if he were the only existing thing, he should have an idea of a supremely perfect, infinite Being.

He first reasons that there is no way he himself could be the source of his idea of God, that God Himself must *be* and must have given Descartes the idea of Himself; in his beautiful portrayal, the idea of God is "the mark of the craftsman stamped on his work."

So, Descartes's world has gone from one to two; first him alone in the darkness, and now him together with God. From here he reflects on God's nature, in particular His goodness. He reasons it would be inconsistent with God's goodness that nearly all his beliefs should be utterly false; God, he says, is not a deceiver.

If we're sufficiently careful in our pursuit of knowledge, then, we can be assured we will reach it. With this argument, Descartes reopens the door to the external world. If we restrict ourselves to believing only those things that we can "clearly and distinctly" perceive, we will not err in our judgment.

―――――――

Perhaps now we can see, minimally, why Pascal's critique may not be sufficiently charitable. There definitely is a sense in which the self comes before God in Descartes's system, but there is equally, and arguably more importantly, a sense in which God is before everything else. Let me explain.

For Descartes, the *knowledge* of oneself comes before the knowledge of God. I don't mean "before" in a temporal sense, the way we might think of a child gaining self-awareness before she becomes aware of God. I do mean that in an explanation of the justification of our beliefs, knowledge of God (and of the world God has created) follows knowledge of oneself.

In the course of writing Descartes not only uses the *Cogito, ergo sum* argument to support his other beliefs, he also discovers some of the external conditions that make possible the activity of meditating in the first place. Most significantly, he discovers that his existence and activity must be sustained from moment to moment by God's continual conservation. Thus, for Descartes, the *existence* of oneself comes after the existence of God.

We might say that Descartes set out alone to discover God but learned that God was with him in the search.

## CHAPTER SIXTEEN

# JOHN MILTON

## Early Modern (1608–1674)

In the English Civil War, the king got Oxford, the rural poor, and most of the artists. Parliament had most of the Puritans, new money, and people who hated playing cards and celebrating Christmas. As a result, Oliver Cromwell took more battles, but the king looked better losing than the "Lord Protector" looked winning.

One might think that association with regicides destroyed the poetic temperament, were it not for one man: John Milton. He was so exceptional that he destroyed the rule. England had produced a great epic poet, and he sided with the Commonwealth.

Milton's famous *Paradise Lost* is a heterodox conflation of biblical history with classical images. He rejects biblical dualism, and his view of women is offensive by any standard, but his poetry is sublime, and some of his characters, particularly his devils, are unforgettable. While Dante's Satan is trapped at the bottom of God's hell, Milton's Satan gets all the good speeches. If his Satan is more appealing to moderns than his God, that may say more about moderns than Milton.

John Milton showed admirable personal courage in several ways.

First, he stuck to his republican beliefs even when most opted for a return to monarchy. Whatever the merits of his convictions, he held them even when it was dangerous to do so.

Second, he composed some of his greatest works after going blind.

Finally, he was willing to offend even his Puritan patrons by taking more liberal positions on divorce, religious freedom, and doctrine than most would contemplate.

Read his poetry looking for creative genius freely dealing with biblical history. Milton was willing to take creative liberties that other writers such as Shakespeare had avoided by ducking most direct allusions to scriptural stories. Compare his scope and style to that of Homer, and watch Milton do in English what Homer had done in Greek.

Milton was an able defender of the Commonwealth and, less attractively, of the tyrant Cromwell. The beauty of his poetry is not diminished by his support for questionable cause. Whether or not Milton was a wonderful person or an effective politician, he is one of the greatest English poets.

 FROM

# *Paradise Lost*

## Book I

> Of Mans First Disobedience, and the Fruit
> Of that Forbidden Tree, whose mortal taste
> Brought Death into the World, and all our woe,
> With loss of Eden, till one greater Man
> Restore us, and regain the blissful Seat, [5]
> Sing Heav'nly Muse, that on the secret top
> Of Oreb, or of Sinai, didst inspire
> That Shepherd, who first taught the chosen Seed,
> In the Beginning how the Heav'ns and Earth
> Rose out of Chaos: Or if Sion Hill [10]
> Delight thee more, and Siloa's Brook that flow'd

Fast by the Oracle of God; I thence
Invoke thy aid to my adventrous Song,
That with no middle flight intends to soar
Above th' Aonian Mount, while it pursues [15]
Things unattempted yet in Prose or Rhime.
And chiefly Thou O Spirit, that dost prefer
Before all Temples th' upright heart and pure,
Instruct me, for Thou know'st; Thou from the first
Wast present, and with mighty wings outspread [20]
Dove-like satst brooding on the vast Abyss
And mad'st it pregnant: What in me is dark
Illumin, what is low raise and support;
That to the highth of this great Argument
I may assert Eternal Providence, [25]
And justifie the wayes of God to men.

Say first, for Heav'n hides nothing from thy view
Nor the deep Tract of Hell, say first what cause
Mov'd our Grand Parents in that happy State,
Favour'd of Heav'n so highly, to fall off [30]
From their Creator, and transgress his Will
For one restraint, Lords of the World besides?
Who first seduc'd them to that foul revolt?
Th' infernal Serpent; he it was, whose guile
Stird up with Envy and Revenge, deceiv'd [35]
The Mother of Mankind, what time his Pride
Had cast him out from Heav'n, with all his Host
Of Rebel Angels, by whose aid aspiring
To set himself in Glory above his Peers,
He trusted to have equal'd the most High, [40]
If he oppos'd; and with ambitious aim
Against the Throne and Monarchy of God
Rais'd impious Warr in Heav'n and Battel proud
With vain attempt. Him the Almighty Power
Hurld headlong flaming from th' Ethereal Skie [45]
With hideous ruine and combustion down
To bottomless perdition, there to dwell
In Adamantine Chains and penal Fire,
Who durst defie th' Omnipotent to Arms.
Nine times the Space that measures Day and Night [50]
To mortal men, he with his horrid crew

Lay vanquisht, rowling in the fiery Gulfe
Confounded though immortal: But his doom
Reserv'd him to more wrath; for now the thought
Both of lost happiness and lasting pain [55]
Torments him; round he throws his baleful eyes
That witness'd huge affliction and dismay
Mixt with obdurate pride and stedfast hate:
At once as far as Angels kenn he views
The dismal Situation waste and wilde, [60]
A Dungeon horrible, on all sides round
As one great Furnace flam'd, yet from those flames
No light, but rather darkness visible
Serv'd onely to discover sights of woe,
Regions of sorrow, doleful shades, where peace [65]
And rest can never dwell, hope never comes
That comes to all; but torture without end
Still urges, and a fiery Deluge, fed
With ever-burning Sulphur unconsum'd:
Such place Eternal Justice had prepar'd [70]
For those rebellious, here their Prison ordain'd
In utter darkness, and their portion set
As far remov'd from God and light of Heav'n
As from the Center thrice to th' utmost Pole.
O how unlike the place from whence they fell! [75]
There the companions of his fall, o'rewhelm'd
With Floods and Whirlwinds of tempestuous fire,
He soon discerns, and weltring by his side
One next himself in power, and next in crime,
Long after known in Palestine, and nam'd [80]
Beelzebub. To whom th' Arch-Enemy,
And thence in Heav'n call'd Satan, with bold words
Breaking the horrid silence thus began.

If thou beest he; But O how fall'n! how chang'd
From him, who in the happy Realms of Light [85]
Cloth'd with transcendent brightness didst out-shine
Myriads though bright: If he Whom mutual league,
United thoughts and counsels, equal hope
And hazard in the Glorious Enterprize,
Joynd with me once, now misery hath joynd [90]
In equal ruin: into what Pit thou seest

From what highth fall'n, so much the stronger prov'd
He with his Thunder: and till then who knew
The force of those dire Arms? yet not for those,
Nor what the Potent Victor in his rage [95]
Can else inflict, do I repent or change,
Though chang'd in outward lustre; that fixt mind
And high disdain, from sence of injur'd merit,
That with the mightiest rais'd me to contend,
And to the fierce contention brought along [100]
Innumerable force of Spirits arm'd
That durst dislike his reign, and me preferring,
His utmost power with adverse power oppos'd
In dubious Battel on the Plains of Heav'n,
And shook his throne. What though the field be lost? [105]
All is not lost; the unconquerable Will,
And study of revenge, immortal hate,
And courage never to submit or yield:
And what is else not to be overcome?
That Glory never shall his wrath or might [110]
Extort from me. To bow and sue for grace
With suppliant knee, and deifie his power,
Who from the terrour of this Arm so late
Doubted his Empire, that were low indeed,
That were an ignominy and shame beneath [115]
This downfall; since by Fate the strength of Gods
And this Empyreal substance cannot fail,
Since through experience of this great event
In Arms not worse, in foresight much advanc't,
We may with more successful hope resolve [120]
To wage by force or guile eternal Warr
Irreconcileable, to our grand Foe,
Who now triumphs, and in th' excess of joy
Sole reigning holds the Tyranny of Heav'n.

So spake th' Apostate Angel, though in pain, [125]
Vaunting aloud, but rackt with deep despare:
And him thus answer'd soon his bold Compeer.

O Prince, O Chief of many Throned Powers,
That led th' imbattelld Seraphim to Warr
Under thy conduct, and in dreadful deeds [130]

361

Fearless, endanger'd Heav'ns perpetual King;
And put to proof his high Supremacy,
Whether upheld by strength, or Chance, or Fate,
Too well I see and rue the dire event,
That with sad overthrow and foul defeat [135]
Hath lost us Heav'n, and all this mighty Host
In horrible destruction laid thus low,
As far as Gods and Heav'nly Essences
Can perish: for the mind and spirit remains
Invincible, and vigour soon returns, [140]
Though all our Glory extinct, and happy state
Here swallow'd up in endless misery.
But what if he our Conquerour, (whom I now
Of force believe Almighty, since no less
Then such could hav orepow'rd such force as ours) [145]
Have left us this our spirit and strength intire
Strongly to suffer and support our pains,
That we may so suffice his vengeful ire,
Or do him mightier service as his thralls
By right of Warr, what e're his business be [150]
Here in the heart of Hell to work in Fire,
Or do his Errands in the gloomy Deep;
What can it then avail though yet we feel
Strength undiminisht, or eternal being
To undergo eternal punishment? [155]
Whereto with speedy words th' Arch-fiend reply'd.

Fall'n Cherube, to be weak is miserable
Doing or Suffering: but of this be sure,
To do ought good never will be our task,
But ever to do ill our sole delight, [160]
As being the contrary to his high will
Whom we resist. If then his Providence
Out of our evil seek to bring forth good,
Our labour must be to pervert that end,
And out of good still to find means of evil; [165]
Which oft times may succeed, so as perhaps
Shall grieve him, if I fail not, and disturb
His inmost counsels from their destind aim.
But see the angry Victor hath recall'd
His Ministers of vengeance and pursuit [170]

Back to the Gates of Heav'n: The Sulphurous Hail
Shot after us in storm, oreblown hath laid
The fiery Surge, that from the Precipice
Of Heav'n receiv'd us falling, and the Thunder,
Wing'd with red Lightning and impetuous rage, [175]
Perhaps hath spent his shafts, and ceases now
To bellow through the vast and boundless Deep.
Let us not slip th' occasion, whether scorn,
Or satiate fury yield it from our Foe.
Seest thou yon dreary Plain, forlorn and wilde, [180]
The seat of desolation, voyd of light,
Save what the glimmering of these livid flames
Casts pale and dreadful? Thither let us tend
From off the tossing of these fiery waves,
There rest, if any rest can harbour there, [185]
And reassembling our afflicted Powers,
Consult how we may henceforth most offend
Our Enemy, our own loss how repair,
How overcome this dire Calamity,
What reinforcement we may gain from Hope, [190]
If not what resolution from despare.

Thus Satan talking to his neerest Mate
With Head up-lift above the wave, and Eyes
That sparkling blaz'd, his other Parts besides
Prone on the Flood, extended long and large [195]
Lay floating many a rood, in bulk as huge
As whom the Fables name of monstrous size,
Titanian, or Earth-born, that warr'd on Jove,
Briareos or Typhon, whom the Den
By ancient Tarsus held, or that Sea-beast [200]
Leviathan, which God of all his works
Created hugest that swim th' Ocean stream:
Him haply slumbring on the Norway foam
The Pilot of some small night-founder'd Skiff,
Deeming some Island, oft, as Sea-men tell, [205]
With fixed Anchor in his skaly rind
Moors by his side under the Lee, while Night
Invests the Sea, and wished Morn delayes:
So stretcht out huge in length the Arch-fiend lay
Chain'd on the burning Lake, nor ever thence [210]

Had ris'n or heav'd his head, but that the will
And high permission of all-ruling Heaven
Left him at large to his own dark designs,
That with reiterated crimes he might
Heap on himself damnation, while he sought [215]
Evil to others, and enrag'd might see
How all his malice serv'd but to bring forth
Infinite goodness, grace and mercy shewn
On Man by him seduc't, but on himself
Treble confusion, wrath and vengeance pour'd. [220]
Forthwith upright he rears from off the Pool
His mighty Stature; on each hand the flames
Drivn backward slope their pointing spires, and rowld
In billows, leave i'th' midst a horrid Vale.
Then with expanded wings he stears his flight [225]
Aloft, incumbent on the dusky Air
That felt unusual weight, till on dry Land
He lights, if it were Land that ever burn'd
With solid, as the Lake with liquid fire;
And such appear'd in hue, as when the force [230]
Of subterranean wind transports a Hill
Torn from Pelorus, or the shatter'd side
Of thundring Ætna, whose combustible
And fewel'd entrals thence conceiving Fire,
Sublim'd with Mineral fury, aid the Winds, [235]
And leave a singed bottom all involv'd
With stench and smoak: Such resting found the sole
Of unblest feet. Him followed his next Mate,
Both glorying to have scap't the Stygian flood
As Gods, and by their own recover'd strength, [240]
Not by the sufferance of supernal Power.

Is this the Region, this the Soil, the Clime,
Said then the lost Arch-Angel, this the seat
That we must change for Heav'n, this mournful gloom
For that celestial light? Be it so, since he [245]
Who now is Sovran can dispose and bid
What shall be right: fardest from him is best
Whom reason hath equald, force hath made supream
Above his equals. Farewel happy Fields
Where Joy for ever dwells: Hail horrours, hail [250]

Infernal world, and thou profoundest Hell
Receive thy new Possessor: One who brings
A mind not to be chang'd by Place or Time.
The mind is its own place, and in it self
Can make a Heav'n of Hell, a Hell of Heav'n. [255]
What matter where, if I be still the same,
And what I should be, all but less then he
Whom Thunder hath made greater? Here at least
We shall be free; th' Almighty hath not built
Here for his envy, will not drive us hence: [260]
Here we may reign secure, and in my choyce
To reign is worth ambition though in Hell:
Better to reign in Hell, then serve in Heav'n.
But wherefore let we then our faithful friends,
Th' associates and copartners of our loss [265]
Lye thus astonisht on th' oblivious Pool,
And call them not to share with us their part
In this unhappy Mansion, or once more
With rallied Arms to try what may be yet
Regaind in Heav'n, or what more lost in Hell? [270]

So Satan spake, and him Beelzebub
Thus answer'd. Leader of those Armies bright,
Which but th' Onmipotent none could have foyld,
If once they hear that voyce, their liveliest pledge
Of hope in fears and dangers, heard so oft [275]
In worst extreams, and on the perilous edge
Of battel when it rag'd, in all assaults
Their surest signal, they will soon resume
New courage and revive, though now they lye
Groveling and prostrate on yon Lake of Fire, [280]
As we erewhile, astounded and amaz'd,
No wonder, fall'n such a pernicious highth.

He scarce had ceas't when the superiour Fiend
Was moving toward the shoar; his ponderous shield
Ethereal temper, massy, large and round, [285]
Behind him cast; the broad circumference
Hung on his shoulders like the Moon, whose Orb
Through Optic Glass the Tuscan Artist views
At Ev'ning from the top of Fesole,

Or in Valdarno, to descry new Lands, [290]
Rivers or Mountains in her spotty Globe.
His Spear, to equal which the tallest Pine
Hewn on Norwegian hills, to be the Mast
Of some great Ammiral, were but a wand,
He walkt with to support uneasie steps [295]
Over the burning Marle, not like those steps
On Heavens Azure, and the torrid Clime
Smote on him sore besides, vaulted with Fire;
Nathless he so endur'd, till on the Beach
Of that inflamed Sea, he stood and call'd [300]
His Legions, Angel Forms, who lay intrans't
Thick as Autumnal Leaves that strow the Brooks
In Vallombrosa, where th' Etrurian shades
High overarch't imbowr; or scatterd sedge
Afloat, when with fierce Winds Orion arm'd [305]
Hath vext the Red-Sea Coast, whose waves orethrew
Busiris and his Memphian Chivalry,
While with perfidious hatred they pursu'd
The Sojourners of Goshen, who beheld
From the safe shore their floating Carkases [310]
And broken Chariot Wheels, so thick bestrown
Abject and lost lay these, covering the Flood,
Under amazement of their hideous change.
He call'd so loud, that all the hollow Deep
Of Hell resounded. Princes, Potentates, [315]
Warriers, the Flowr of Heav'n, once yours, now lost,
If such astonishment as this can seize
Eternal spirits; or have ye chos'n this place
After the toyl of Battel to repose
Your wearied vertue, for the ease you find [320]
To slumber here, as in the Vales of Heav'n?
Or in this abject posture have ye sworn
To adore the Conquerour? who now beholds
Cherube and Seraph rowling in the Flood
With scatter'd Arms and Ensigns, till anon [325]
His swift pursuers from Heav'n Gates discern
Th' advantage, and descending tread us down
Thus drooping, or with linked Thunderbolts
Transfix us to the bottom of this Gulfe.
Awake, arise, or be for ever fall'n. [330] . . .

[At this point, the fallen angels rise and assemble, and their leaders are introduced in an epic catalogue. Satan rallies them and calls a council to decide how to proceed in their war against God. To house this council, the demons construct a magnificent palace named Pandemonium (a word of Milton's invention).

Book II presents the deliberation of the council. Moloch first proposes open war against heaven. Then Belial proposes doing nothing, in the hopes of avoiding further punishment. After the third speaker, Mammon, advises making improvements in hell to make it more livable, Beelzebub rises and delivers the following speech. (*Summary: Joe Henderson*)]

## Book II

>... Thrones and Imperial Powers, off-spring of heav'n [310]
>Ethereal Vertues; or these Titles now
>Must we renounce, and changing stile be call'd
>Princes of Hell? for so the popular vote
>Inclines, here to continue, and build up here
>A growing Empire; doubtless; while we dream, [315]
>And know not that the King of Heav'n hath doom'd
>This place our dungeon, not our safe retreat
>Beyond his Potent arm, to live exempt
>From Heav'ns high jurisdiction, in new League
>Banded against his Throne, but to remaine [320]
>In strictest bondage, though thus far remov'd,
>Under th' inevitable curb, reserv'd
>His captive multitude: For he, be sure
>In heighth or depth, still first and last will Reign
>Sole King, and of his Kingdom loose no part [325]
>By our revolt, but over Hell extend
>His Empire, and with Iron Scepter rule
>Us here, as with his Golden those in Heav'n.
>What sit we then projecting peace and Warr?
>Warr hath determin'd us, and foild with loss [330]
>Irreparable; tearms of peace yet none
>Voutsaf't or sought; for what peace will be giv'n
>To us enslav'd, but custody severe,
>And stripes, and arbitrary punishment
>Inflicted? and what peace can we return, [335]

But to our power hostility and hate,
Untam'd reluctance, and revenge though slow,
Yet ever plotting how the Conqueror least
May reap his conquest, and may least rejoyce
In doing what we most in suffering feel? [340]
Nor will occasion want, nor shall we need
With dangerous expedition to invade
Heav'n, whose high walls fear no assault or Siege,
Or ambush from the Deep. What if we find
Some easier enterprize? There is a place [345]
(If ancient and prophetic fame in Heav'n
Err not) another World, the happy seat
Of some new Race call'd Man, about this time
To be created like to us, though less
In power and excellence, but favour'd more [350]
Of him who rules above; so was his will
Pronounc'd among the Gods, and by an Oath,
That shook Heav'ns whol circumference, confirm'd.
Thither let us bend all our thoughts, to learn
What creatures there inhabit, of what mould, [355]
Or substance, how endu'd, and what their Power,
And where their weakness, how attempted best,
By force or suttlety: Though Heav'n be shut,
And Heav'ns high Arbitrator sit secure
In his own strength, this place may lye expos'd [360]
The utmost border of his Kingdom, left
To their defence who hold it: here perhaps
Som advantagious act may be achiev'd
By sudden onset, either with Hell fire
To waste his whole Creation, or possess [365]
All as our own, and drive as we were driven,
The punie habitants, or if not drive,
Seduce them to our Party, that their God
May prove their foe, and with repenting hand
Abolish his own works. This would surpass [370]
Common revenge, and interrupt his joy
In our Confusion, and our Joy upraise
In his disturbance; when his darling Sons
Hurl'd headlong to partake with us, shall curse
Their frail Original, and faded bliss, [375]
Faded so soon. Advise if this be worth

Attempting, or to sit in darkness here
Hatching vain Empires. Thus Beelzebub
Pleaded his devilish Counsel, first devis'd
By Satan, and in part propos'd: for whence, [380]
But from the Author of all ill could Spring
So deep a malice, to confound the race
Of mankind in one root, and Earth with Hell
To mingle and involve, done all to spite
The great Creatour? But their spite still serves [385]
His glory to augment. The bold design
Pleas'd highly those infernal States, and joy
Sparkl'd in all their eyes; with full assent
They vote: whereat his speech he thus renews.

Well have ye judg'd, well ended long debate, [390]
Synod of Gods, and like to what ye are,
Great things resolv'd; which from the lowest deep
Will once more lift us up, in spight of Fate,
Neerer our ancient Seat; perhaps in view
Of those bright confines, whence with neighbouring Arms [395]
And opportune excursion we may chance
Re-enter Heav'n; or else in some milde Zone
Dwell not unvisited of Heav'ns fair Light
Secure, and at the brightning Orient beam
Purge off this gloom; the soft delicious Air, [400]
To heal the scarr of these corrosive Fires
Shall breath her balme. But first whom shall we send
In search of this new world, whom shall we find
Sufficient? who shall tempt with wandring feet
The dark unbottom'd infinite Abyss [405]
And through the palpable obscure find out
His uncouth way, or spread his aerie flight
Upborn with indefatigable wings
Over the vast abrupt, ere he arrive
The happy Ile; what strength, what art can then [410]
Suffice, or what evasion bear him safe
Through the strict Senteries and Stations thick
Of Angels watching round? Here he had need
All circumspection, and we now no less
Choice in our suffrage; for on whom we send, [415]
The weight of all and our last hope relies.

This said, he sat; and expectation held
His look suspence, awaiting who appeer'd
To second, or oppose, or undertake
The perilous attempt; but all sat mute, [420]
Pondering the danger with deep thoughts; and each
In others count'nance read his own dismay
Astonisht: none among the choice and prime
Of those Heav'n-warring Champions could be found
So hardie as to proffer or accept [425]
Alone the dreadful voyage; till at last
Satan, whom now transcendent glory rais'd
Above his fellows, with Monarchal pride
Conscious of highest worth, unmov'd thus spake.

O Progeny of Heav'n, Empyreal Thrones, [430]
With reason hath deep silence and demurr
Seis'd us, though undismaid: long is the way
And hard, that out of Hell leads up to light;
Our prison strong, this huge convex of Fire,
Outrageous to devour, immures us round [435]
Ninefold, and gates of burning Adamant
Barr'd over us prohibit all egress.
These past, if any pass, the void profound
Of unessential Night receives him next
Wide gaping, and with utter loss of being [440]
Threatens him, plung'd in that abortive gulf.
If thence he scape into whatever world,
Or unknown Region, what remains him less
Then unknown dangers and as hard escape.
But I should ill become this Throne, O Peers, [445]
And this Imperial Sov'ranty, adorn'd
With splendor, arm'd with power, if aught propos'd
And judg'd of public moment, in the shape
Of difficulty or danger could deterr
Mee from attempting. Wherefore do I assume [450]
These Royalties, and not refuse to Reign,
Refusing to accept as great a share
Of hazard as of honour, due alike
To him who Reigns, and so much to him due
Of hazard more, as he above the rest [455]
High honourd sits? Go therefore mighty Powers,

Terror of Heav'n, though fall'n; intend at home,
While here shall be our home, what best may ease
The present misery, and render Hell
More tollerable; if there be cure or charm [460]
To respite or deceive, or slack the pain
Of this ill Mansion: intermit no watch
Against a wakeful Foe, while I abroad
Through all the Coasts of dark destruction seek
Deliverance for us all: this enterprize [465]
None shall partake with me. Thus saying rose
The Monarch, and prevented all reply,
Prudent, least from his resolution rais'd
Others among the chief might offer now
(Certain to be refus'd) what erst they fear'd; [470]
And so refus'd might in opinion stand
His Rivals, winning cheap the high repute
Which he through hazard huge must earn. But they
Dreaded not more th' adventure then his voice
Forbidding; and at once with him they rose; [475]
Their rising all at once was as the sound
Of Thunder heard remote. Towards him they bend
With awful reverence prone; and as a God
Extoll him equal to the highest in Heav'n:
Nor fail'd they to express how much they prais'd, [480]
That for the general safety he despis'd
His own: for neither do the Spirits damn'd
Loose all their vertue; least bad men should boast
Their specious deeds on earth, which glory excites,
Or clos ambition varnisht o're with zeal. [485]
Thus they their doubtful consultations dark
Ended rejoycing in their matchless Chief ...

[With the council ended, Satan begins his epic journey from hell to earth to carry out his plan. He encounters the monsters Sin and Death at hell's gate and is entertained in the court of Chaos and Night on his journey across the wide gulf that separates heaven from hell. He finally sees our universe shining like a tiny star, a "pendant world" hanging from heaven by a golden chain.

In Book III the scene changes to heaven, where God sees Satan's journey and foresees his success in tempting mankind. God clears himself of responsibility and declares His intention to have grace on man, even though His justice requires that someone must take man's punishment. In a scene parallel to Satan's acceptance of the mission to deceive, the Son of God accepts the mission to give himself as a ransom.

Meanwhile, Satan journeys from the convex shell of the universe to earth, where he perches on Mount Niphates. Here he sits, looking over Eden and pondering his mission, at the opening of Book IV. (*Summary: Joe Henderson*)]

## Book IV

> For that warning voice, which he who saw
> Th' Apocalyps, heard cry in Heaven aloud,
> Then when the Dragon, put to second rout,
> Came furious down to be reveng'd on men,
> Wo to the inhabitants on Earth! that now, [5]
> While time was, our first-Parents had bin warnd
> The coming of thir secret foe, and scap'd
> Haply so scap'd his mortal snare; for now
> Satan, now first inflam'd with rage, came down,
> The Tempter ere th' Accuser of man-kind, [10]
> To wreck on innocent frail man his loss
> Of that first Battel, and his flight to Hell:
> Yet not rejoycing in his speed, though bold,
> Far off and fearless, nor with cause to boast,
> Begins his dire attempt, which nigh the birth [15]
> Now rowling, boiles in his tumultuous brest,
> And like a devillish Engine back recoiles
> Upon himself; horror and doubt distract
> His troubl'd thoughts, and from the bottom stirr
> The Hell within him, for within him Hell [20]
> He brings, and round about him, nor from Hell
> One step no more then from himself can fly
> By change of place: Now conscience wakes despair
> That slumberd, wakes the bitter memorie
> Of what he was, what is, and what must be [25]
> Worse; of worse deeds worse sufferings must ensue.
> Sometimes towards Eden which now in his view
> Lay pleasant, his grievd look he fixes sad,

Sometimes towards Heav'n and the full-blazing Sun,
Which now sat high in his Meridian Towre: [30]
Then much revolving, thus in sighs began.

O thou that with surpassing Glory crownd,
Look'st from thy sole Dominion like the God
Of this new World; at whose sight all the Starrs
Hide their diminisht heads; to thee I call, [35]
But with no friendly voice, and add thy name
O Sun, to tell thee how I hate thy beams
That bring to my remembrance from what state
I fell, how glorious once above thy Spheare;
Till Pride and worse Ambition threw me down [40]
Warring in Heav'n against Heav'ns matchless King:
Ah wherefore! he deservd no such return
From me, whom he created what I was
In that bright eminence, and with his good
Upbraided none; nor was his service hard. [45]
What could be less then to afford him praise,
The easiest recompence, and pay him thanks,
How due! yet all his good prov'd ill in me,
And wrought but malice; lifted up so high
I 'sdeind subjection, and thought one step higher [50]
Would set me highest, and in a moment quit
The debt immense of endless gratitude,
So burthensome, still paying, still to ow;
Forgetful what from him I still receivd,
And understood not that a grateful mind [55]
By owing owes not, but still pays, at once
Indebted and dischargd; what burden then?
O had his powerful Destiny ordaind
Me some inferiour Angel, I had stood
Then happie; no unbounded hope had rais'd [60]
Ambition. Yet why not? som other Power
As great might have aspir'd, and me though mean
Drawn to his part; but other Powers as great
Fell not, but stand unshak'n, from within
Or from without, to all temptations arm'd. [65]
Hadst thou the same free Will and Power to stand?
Thou hadst: whom hast thou then or what to accuse,
But Heav'ns free Love dealt equally to all?

Be then his Love accurst, since love or hate,
To me alike, it deals eternal woe. [70]
Nay curs'd be thou; since against his thy will
Chose freely what it now so justly rues.
Me miserable! which way shall I flie
Infinite wrauth, and infinite despaire?
Which way I flie is Hell; my self am Hell; [75]
And in the lowest deep a lower deep
Still threatning to devour me opens wide,
To which the Hell I suffer seems a Heav'n.
O then at last relent: is there no place
Left for Repentance, none for Pardon left? [80]
None left but by submission; and that word
Disdain forbids me, and my dread of shame
Among the Spirits beneath, whom I seduc'd
With other promises and other vaunts
Then to submit, boasting I could subdue [85]
Th' Omnipotent. Ay me, they little know
How dearly I abide that boast so vaine,
Under what torments inwardly I groane:
While they adore me on the Throne of Hell,
With Diadem and Sceptre high advanc'd [90]
The lower still I fall, onely Supream
In miserie; such joy Ambition findes.
But say I could repent and could obtaine
By Act of Grace my former state; how soon
Would higth recall high thoughts, how soon unsay [95]
What feign'd submission swore: ease would recant
Vows made in pain, as violent and void.
For never can true reconcilement grow
Where wounds of deadly hate have peirc'd so deep:
Which would but lead me to a worse relapse [100]
And heavier fall: so should I purchase deare
Short intermission bought with double smart.
This knows my punisher; therefore as farr
From granting hee, as I from begging peace:
All hope excluded thus, behold in stead [105]
Of us out-cast, exil'd, his new delight,
Mankind created, and for him this World.
So farewel Hope, and with Hope farewel Fear,
Farewel Remorse: all Good to me is lost;

Evil be thou my Good; by thee at least [110]
Divided Empire with Heav'ns King I hold
By thee, and more then half perhaps will reigne;
As Man ere long, and this new World shall know.

# ON EVIL AND HEROISM

## Frederica Mathewes-Green

The magnificent opening lines of *Paradise Lost*, with their echoes of Homer, Virgil, and Ariosto, announce Milton's aim not only to equal but to soar above all previous epics. His hopes rest not only on his poetic powers, supported by his heavenly muse, but on the height of his chief argument. Whereas Virgil chose for his subject matter the foundation of the Roman Empire, and Homer told of the battle between East and West, Milton selected the creation of mankind and the opening battle of the war with their greatest enemy. Given his sublime subject matter—and, given that his story transcends all national limitations—Milton's challenge will be to find and maintain an "answerable style" (IX, 20) across the grand canvas of his twelve books.

After the trumpet fanfare of the prologue, *Paradise Lost* plunges directly into the middle of its story. Although beginning the narration *in medias res* may be conventional, Milton still delivers a shock by his choice of where in the tale to start; or, more precisely, with whom. Epics customarily begin at a critical point in the story of their heroes. *Paradise Lost* opens with the fall of the rebellious angels, the critical point in the account of Satan.

As the narrative unfolds, it becomes clear that Milton has chosen Satan as the central protagonist. Not only does Satan have more stage time and more lines than any other character, he also is the subject of the most conventions associated with epic heroes. It is Satan who goes on an epic journey, fights a momentous battle, faces off with monsters, rallies his troops with inspiring speeches, visits noble courts, employs cunning stratagems, and of course, descends to the underworld.

Another way to measure the centrality of Satan's role is to observe that *Paradise Lost* takes six (out of twelve) books to reach the point where the Genesis account of man's disobedience begins. The half of *Paradise Lost* Milton supplements to the biblical story is not about man but Satan, and the effect of adding prequels that portray the origins of the villain is to transform the entire saga into the story of the villain.

Giving the role of epic hero to Satan commits Milton to investing his character with the heroic qualities of strength, eloquence, resolution, and grandeur. These attributes are all on full display in the opening scenes of Satan lifting himself up from the fiery flood and rousing his fallen troops to action. However, if it's evident that Milton has found in Satan the virtues that will make him a compelling epic hero, it is less evident that his decision will allow him to craft a virtuous epic. A work of art can hardly be called virtuous if its effect is to create sympathy for the devil.

One way of discovering an acceptable moral is to disassociate Milton's Satan from the Satan of Christian tradition and belief. Perhaps his character doesn't represent enmity with the Creator, malice toward humanity, pernicious deception. Perhaps in *Paradise Lost* he stands for freedom from social conformity, fidelity to personal vision, opposition to entrenched power.

This understanding seems to lie behind William Blake's positive assessment of Milton as "of the Devil's party without knowing it." Blake, and other Romantic poets after him, saw in Milton's Satan a defender of liberty, parallel to Milton himself, a vigorous champion of freedom of speech and religion and a steadfast opponent of the tyranny of Charles I.

This Romantic reading is only possible if one radically underestimates how deeply ingrained the biblical drama was in the imaginations of Milton and his audience . . . *and* if one ignores sizable portions of the text. C. S. Lewis (in his *Preface to Paradise Lost*, 99) handily dispels the notion that Milton's Satan is intended to be admired or emulated. He observes that in the course of the poem, Satan undergoes a "progressive degradation": "From hero, to general . . . to politician . . . to secret service agent, [to peeping Tom], and thence to a toad, and finally to a snake."

However, it is unnecessary to read to the end of the epic to ascertain Milton's judgment. Even in Book I, where Satan is most impressive, he is introduced as an "infernal serpent" (I, 34) filled with the ugly vices of envy, hatred, and guile, and the narrator interrupts the account several times to remind the reader that Satan's plans are futile, serving only to bring on himself "treble confusion, wrath, and vengeance" (I, 220). From the outset, Milton's Satan is a fiend and fool.

Milton's design, which caused him to cast a fiend as his hero, becomes clearer when one recognizes that the association between Satan and epic heroes cuts both ways. It not only—dangerously—points out the possibility of heroic virtues in Satan, it also—discerningly—points out the possibility of satanic vices in the epic heroes. With his moral senses trained by Christian truth, Milton can detect more than a whiff of brimstone in Achilles' "sense of injur'd merit" (I, 98), in the guile of Odysseus, in Aeneas's lust for "Honour, Dominion, glorie, and renoune" (VI, 442). Although Milton can be said to be following the tradition of epic one-upmanship, he achieves it not by creating a more impressive hero (as Virgil does) but by creating a despicable and damnable hero who throws into doubt the whole concept of heroism.

Although Milton's approach to heroism in *Paradise Lost* is primarily critical, he does go on to offer glimpses of a greater heroism in God's Son, in Abdiel, and particularly in Adam, who demonstrates "the better fortitude of patience and heroic Martyrdom" (IX, 31–32). Adam's surprising heroism consists of patiently enduring his fallen state and accepting that his roles as husband and father will be his part in God's design to bruise the serpent's head. *Paradise Lost* also sets the stage for the Son of God's "deeds Above Heroic" in *Paradise Regained* (I, 14–15).

In the final account, Milton's epic transcends previous works not by its eloquent style or by its sublime imaginative creations but by its simple moral: trust and obey.

## CHAPTER SEVENTEEN

# BLAISE PASCAL

## Enlightenment (1623–1662)

Smart young adults often are tormented by the difference between what should be in the world and what is. The "is" regularly embitters adults in later life. Emo-poetry on the pain in our hearts gives way to elderly cynicism without any Pythonesque humour.

Scratch a bitter grown-up, and frequently you find a disappointed romantic, sick at heart and brutal in his judgments.

Pascal is an antidote. Like Jesus, Pascal was a brilliant man who died young. Also like Jesus, Pascal knew the gap between *is* and *ought*. Pascal, though, left a written record of his thoughts in the form of almost tweetable musings; these are tweets from a deep thinker and a lover of Christ. He was that rarity: a young man with an old soul.

He lived in yet another time when Christendom was failing; however, he was the rare man who understood the good, the bad, and the presumption in his epoch. He did so by using the new intellectual tools without falling for the guff that his was an age of special enlightenment. He was the best of his time because he appreciated the new wine of progress but also kept the finest old wines.

Pascal is easy to read and, in any given saying, easy to understand.

As with Proverbs, reading his words will pay off quickly. Like that Bible book, catching the deep coherence behind all the sayings is worth years of effort. Pascal is easy in the particulars and difficult in the generalities but rewarding in both.

Read Pascal with your understanding, but with a mind stirred up by your heart. Some of his argument is in the poetry of his words and in the emotions they arouse. Like Plato, Pascal knew that following the way of the dialectic was intellectual activity, but this mental movement was driven by a heart motivated by love.

If you think nobody gets it and that God and Christianity are stupid and ugly, Pascal is the response. Smarter than almost anyone, he also is utterly passionate about faith. He's what most of us longed to be as younglings, but additionally he became loving and wise. From Saint Lucy to Jim Elliot, the good often die young, but few leave a sage's record. Read Blaise Pascal and see what God can do with a precocious and a passionate piety.

### FROM

# *Pensées*

## (1) Outline

*First part: Misery of man without God.*
*Second part: Happiness of man with God.*
     (Or)
*First part: That nature is corrupt. Proved by nature itself.*
*Second part: That there is a Redeemer. Proved by Scripture.* (60)

## (2) Strategy

(Order:) Men despise religion; they hate it and fear it is true. To remedy this, we must begin by showing that religion is not contrary to reason; that it is venerable, to inspire respect for it; then we must make it lovable, to make good men hope it is true; finally, we must prove it is true.

Venerable, because it has perfect knowledge of man; lovable because it promises the true good. (187)

---

(Inconstancy:) We think we are playing on ordinary organs when playing upon man. Men are organs, it is true, but, odd, changeable, variable with pipes not arranged in proper order. Those who only know how to play on ordinary organs will not produce harmonies on these. We must know where the keys are. (111)

---

If he exalt himself, I humble him; if he humble himself, I exalt him; and I always contradict him, till he understands that he is an incomprehensible monster. (420)

---

Grace is indeed needed to turn a man into a saint; and he who doubts it does not know what a saint or a man is. (508)

## (3) Wretchedness

—We desire truth, and find within ourselves only uncertainty.

—We seek happiness, and find only misery and death.

—We cannot but desire truth and happiness, and are incapable of certainty or happiness. This desire is left to us, partly to punish us, partly to make us perceive wherefrom we are fallen. (437)

## (4) The Paradox of Greatness and Wretchedness

The more light we have, the more greatness and the more baseness we discover in man. . . .

Philosophers, they astonish ordinary men.

Christians, they astonish philosophers. (443)

---

Man is neither angel nor brute, and the unfortunate thing is that he who would act the angel acts the brute. (358)

It is dangerous to make man see too clearly his equality with the brutes without showing him his greatness. It is also dangerous to make him see his greatness too clearly, apart from his vileness. It is still more dangerous to leave him in ignorance of both. (418)

Man is but a reed, the most feeble thing in nature; but he is a thinking reed. The entire universe need not arm itself to crush him. A vapour, a drop of water suffices to kill him. But, if the universe were to crush him, man would still be more noble than that which killed him, because he knows that he dies and the advantage which the universe has over him; the universe knows nothing of this.

All our dignity consists, then, in thought. By it we must elevate ourselves, and not by space and time which we cannot fill. Let us endeavour, then, to think well; this is the principle of morality. (347)

(A thinking reed:) It is not from space that I must seek my dignity, but from the government of my thought. I shall have no more if I possess worlds. By space the universe encompasses and swallows me up like an atom; by thought I comprehend the world. (348)

The greatness of man is great in that he knows himself to be miserable. A tree does not know itself to be miserable. It is then being miserable to know oneself to be miserable; but it is also being great to know that one is miserable. (397)

All these same miseries prove man's greatness. They are the miseries of a great lord, of a deposed king. (398)

For who is unhappy at not being a king, except a deposed king? . . . Who is unhappy at only having one mouth? And who is not unhappy at having only one eye? Probably no man ever ventured to mourn at not having three eyes. But any one is inconsolable at having none. (409)

It is in vain, O men, that you seek within yourselves the remedy for your ills. . . . (430)

---

What astonishes me most is to see that all the world is not astonished at its own weakness. Men act seriously. . . . (374)

## (5) Why God Hides

He has willed to make himself quite recognisable by those; and thus, willing to appear openly to those who seek Him with all their heart, and to be hidden from those who flee from Him with all their heart, He so regulates the knowledge of Himself that He has given signs of Himself, visible to those who seek Him, and not to those who seek Him not. There is enough light for those who only desire to see, and enough obscurity for those who have a contrary disposition. (430)

## (6) Example of Vanity

We do not rest satisfied with the present. We anticipate the future as too slow in coming, as if in order to hasten its course; or we recall the past, to stop its too rapid flight.

—Let each one examine his thoughts, and he will find them all occupied with the past and the future. . . .

So we never live, but we hope to live; and, as we are always preparing to be happy, it is inevitable we should never be so. (172)

---

A mere trifle consoles us, for a mere trifle distresses us. (136)

---

It is natural for the mind to believe and for the will to love; so that, for want of true objects, they must attach themselves to false. (81)

---

What is the Ego? . . .

Does he who loves someone on account of beauty really love that person? No; for the small-pox, which will kill beauty without killing the person, will cause him to love her no more.

—And if one loves me for my judgment, memory, he does not love me, for I can lose these qualities without losing myself. Where, then, is this Ego, if it be neither in the body nor in the soul? (323)

---

He who will know fully the vanity of man has only to consider the causes and effects of love. The cause is a *je ne sais quoi* (["I know not what,"] Corneille), and the effects are dreadful. This *je ne sais quoi*, so small an object that we cannot recognise it, agitates a whole country, princes, armies, the entire world.

—Cleopatra's nose: had it been shorter, the whole aspect of the world would have been altered. (162)

---

Cromwell was about to ravage all Christendom; the royal family was undone, and his own for ever established, save for a little grain of sand which formed in his ureter. Rome herself was trembling under him; but this small piece of gravel having formed there, he is dead, his family cast down, all is peaceful, and the king is restored. (176)

---

The power of flies; they win battles, hinder our soul from acting, eat our body. (367)

## (7) Vanity of Human Justice

"Why do you kill me?"

"What! do you not live on the other side of the water? If you lived on this side, my friend, I should be an assassin, and it would be unjust to slay you in this manner. But since you live on the other side, I am a hero, and it is just." (293)

---

Being unable to cause might to obey justice, men have made it just to obey might. Unable to strengthen justice, they have justified might. (299)

---

When all tend to debauchery, none appears to do so. He who stops draws attention to the excess of others, like a fixed point. (382)

## (8) Vanity of Human Reason

(Imagination:) If the greatest philosopher in the world find himself upon a plank wider than actually necessary, but hanging over a precipice, his imagination will prevail, though his reason convince him of his safety. . . .

The tone of voice affects the wisest, and changes the force of a discourse or a poem. . . .

If the physicians had not their cassocks and their mules, if the doctors had not their square caps and their robes four times too wide, they would never have duped the world. . . . (82)

---

The imagination enlarges little objects so as to fill our souls with a fantastic estimate; and, with rash insolence, it belittles the great to its own measure, as when talking of God. (84)

## (9) Vanity of Dogmatism and Skepticism

(Instinct, reason:) We have an incapacity of proof, insurmountable by all dogmatism. We have an idea of truth, invincible to all scepticism. (395)

---

(Philosophers:) A fine thing to cry to a man who does not know himself, that he should come of himself to God! And a fine thing to say so to a man who does know himself! (509)

## (10) Alienation ("Lost in the Cosmos")

Let man then contemplate the whole of nature in her full and grand majesty . . . let our imagination pass beyond; it will sooner exhaust the power of conception than nature that of supplying material for conception. The whole visible world is only an imperceptible atom in the ample bosom of nature. No idea approaches it . . . we only produce atoms in comparison with the reality of things. It is an infinite sphere, the centre of which is everywhere, the circumference nowhere. In short, it is the greatest sensible mark of the almighty power of God that imagination loses itself in that thought. . . .

Returning to himself, let man consider what he is in comparison with all existence; let him regard himself as lost in this remote corner of nature; and from the little cell in which he finds himself lodged . . . let him estimate at their true value the earth, kingdoms, cities, and himself. What is a man in the Infinite? . . .

But to show him another prodigy equally astonishing, let him examine the most delicate things he knows. Let a mite be given him, with its minute body and parts incomparably more minute, limbs with their joints, veins in the limbs, blood in the veins, humours in the blood, drops in the humours, vapours in the drops. Dividing these last things again, let him exhaust his powers of conception, and let the last object at which he can arrive be now that of our discourse. Perhaps he will think that here is the smallest point in nature. I will let him see therein a new abyss. I will paint for him not only the visible universe, but all that he can conceive of nature's immensity in the womb of this abridged atom. Let him see therein an infinity of universes, each of which has its firmament, its planets, its earth . . . in each earth animals, and in the last mites, in which he will find again all that the first had. . . .

He who regards himself in this light will be afraid of himself, and observing himself sustained in the body given him by nature between those two abysses of the Infinite and Nothing, will tremble at the sight of these marvels; and I think that, as his curiosity changes into admiration, he will be more disposed to contemplate them in silence than to examine them with presumption. For, in fact, what is man in nature? A Nothing in comparison with the Infinite, an All in comparison with the Nothing, a mean between nothing and everything. Since he is infinitely removed from comprehending the extremes, the end of things and their beginning are hopelessly hidden from him in an impenetrable secret; he is equally incapable of seeing the Nothing from which he was made, and the Infinite in which he is swallowed up. . . .

This is our true state; this is what makes us incapable of certain knowledge and of absolute ignorance. We sail within a vast sphere, ever drifting in uncertainty, driven from end to end. When we think to attach ourselves to any point and to fasten to it, it wavers and leaves us; and if we follow it, it eludes our grasp, slips past us, and vanishes for ever. Nothing stays for us. This is our natural condition and yet most contrary to our inclination; we burn with desire to find solid ground and an ultimate sure foundation whereon to build a tower reaching to the Infinite. But our whole ground-work cracks, and the earth opens to abysses. (72)

---

The eternal silence of these infinite spaces frightens me. (206)

---

When I consider the short duration of my life, swallowed up in the eternity before and after, the little space which I fill and even can see, engulfed in the infinite immensity of spaces of which I am ignorant and which know me not, I am frightened and am astonished at being here rather than there; for there is no reason why here rather than there, why now rather than then. Who has put me here? By whose order and direction have this place and time been allotted to me? (205)

## (11) Death

And what crowns all this is prediction, so that it should not be said that it is chance which has done it?

—Now, if the passions had no hold on us, a week and a hundred years would amount to the same thing. (694)

---

Between us and heaven or hell there is only life, which is the frailest thing in the world. (213)

---

Let us imagine a number of men in chains and all condemned to death, where some are killed each day in the sight of the others, and those who remain see their own fate in that of their fellows and wait their turn, looking at each other sorrowfully and without hope. It is an image of the condition of men. (199)

---

We run carelessly to the precipice, after we have put something before us to prevent us seeing it. (183)

---

We are fools to depend upon the society of our fellow-men. Wretched as we are, powerless as we are, they will not aid us; we shall die alone. (211)

## (12) Sin, Selfishness

(Self-love:) The nature of self-love and of this human Ego is to love self only and consider self only. But what will man do? He cannot prevent this object that he loves from being full of faults and wants. He wants to be great, and he sees himself small. He wants to be happy, and he sees himself miserable. He wants to be perfect, and he sees himself full of imperfections. . . .

This embarrassment in which he finds himself produces in him the most unrighteous and criminal passion that can be imagined; for he conceives a mortal enmity against that truth which reproves him and which convinces him of his faults. He would annihilate it, but, unable to destroy it in its essence, he destroys it as far as possible in his own knowledge and in that of others; that is to say, he devotes all his attention to hiding his faults both from others and from himself, and he cannot endure either that others should point them out to him, or that they should see them. Truly it is an evil to be full of faults; but it is a still greater evil to be full of them and to be unwilling to recognise them, since that is to add the further fault of a voluntary illusion. . . .

There are different degrees in this aversion to truth; but all may perhaps be said to have it in some degree, because it is inseparable from self-love. (100)

---

From lust men have found and extracted excellent rules of policy, morality, and justice; but in reality this vile root of man, this *figmentum malum,* is only covered, it is not taken away. (453)

---

When we want to think of God, is there nothing which turns us away, and tempts us to think of something else? All this is bad, and is born in us. (478)

---

He who hates not in himself his self-love, and that instinct which leads him to make himself God, is indeed blinded. Who does not see that there is nothing so opposed to justice and truth? For it is false that we deserve this, and it is unfair and impossible to attain it, since all demand the same thing. It is, then, a manifest injustice which is innate in us, of which we cannot get rid, and of which we must get rid.

—Yet no religion has indicated that this was a sin; or that we were born in it; or that we were obliged to resist it; or has thought of giving us remedies for it. (492)

However, we are born with it; therefore born unjust, for all tends to self . . . and the propensity to self is the beginning of all disorder, in war, in politics, in economy. . . . We are, therefore, born unjust and depraved. (477)

No religion but our own has taught that man is born in sin. No sea of philosophers has said this. Therefore none have declared the truth.
—No sect or religion has always existed on earth, but the Christian religion. (606)

There are only two kinds of men: the righteous who believe themselves sinners; the rest, sinners, who believe themselves righteous. (534)

## (13) Diversion

As men are not able to fight against death, misery, ignorance, they have taken it into their heads, in order to be happy, not to think of them at all. (169)

If man were happy, he would be the more so, the less he was diverted, like the Saints and God. Yes; but is it not to be happy to have a faculty of being amused by diversion? No; for that comes from elsewhere and from without, and thus is dependent, and therefore subject to be disturbed by a thousand accidents, which bring inevitable griefs. (170)

Despite these miseries, man wishes to be happy, and only wishes to be happy, and cannot wish not to be so. But how will he set about it? To be happy he would have to make himself immortal; but, not being able to do so, it has occurred to him to prevent himself from thinking of death. (169)

(Diversion): When I have occasionally set myself to consider the different distractions of men, the pains and perils to which they expose themselves at court or in war, whence arise so many quarrels, passions, bold and often bad ventures, etc., I have discovered that all the unhappiness of men arises from one single fact, that they cannot stay quietly in their own chamber. . . . Hence it comes that men so much love noise and stir; hence it comes that the prison is so horrible a punishment; hence it comes that the pleasure of solitude is a thing incomprehensible. . . .

They have a secret instinct which impels them to seek amusement and occupation abroad, and which arises from the sense of their constant unhappiness. They have another secret instinct, a remnant of the greatness of our original nature, which teaches them that happiness in reality consists only in rest and not in stir. And of these two contrary instincts they form within themselves a confused idea, which hides itself from their view in the depths of their soul, inciting them to aim at rest through excitement, and always to fancy that the satisfaction which they have not will come to them, if, by surmounting whatever difficulties confront them, they can thereby open the door to rest.

—Thus passes away all man's life. Men seek rest in a struggle against difficulties; and when they have conquered these, rest becomes insufferable. . . .

—Thus so wretched is man that he would weary even without any cause for weariness from the peculiar state of his disposition; and so frivolous is he that, though full of a thousand reasons for weariness, the least thing, such as playing billiards or hitting a ball, is sufficient to amuse him.

—But will you say what object has he in all this? The pleasure of bragging tomorrow among his friends that he has played better than another. So others sweat in their own rooms to show to the learned that they have solved a problem in algebra, which no one had hitherto been able to solve. Many more expose themselves to extreme perils, in my opinion as foolishly, in order to boast afterwards that they have captured a town. Lastly, others wear themselves out in studying all these things, not in order to become wiser, but only in order to prove that they know them; and these are the most senseless of the band, since they are so knowingly. . . .

—This man spends his life without weariness in playing [gambling] every day for a small stake. Give him each morning the money he can win each day, on condition he does not play; you make him miserable. It will perhaps be said that he seeks the amusement of play and not the winnings. Make him, then, play for nothing; he will not become excited over it and will feel bored. It is, then, not the amusement alone that he seeks. . . . He must get excited over it and deceive himself by the fancy that he will be happy to win what he would not have as a gift on condition of not playing; and he must make for himself an object of passion, and excite over it his desire, his anger, his fear, to obtain his imagined end, as children are frightened at the face they have blackened. (139)

(Misery:) The only thing which consoles us for our miseries is diversion, and yet this is the greatest of our miseries. For it is this which principally hinders us from reflecting upon ourselves and which makes us insensibly ruin ourselves. Without this we should be in a state of weariness, and this weariness would spur us to seek a more solid means of escaping from it. But diversion amuses us, and leads us unconsciously to death. (171)

## (14) Indifference

The immortality of the soul is a matter which is of so great consequence to us and which touches us so profoundly that we must have lost all feeling to be indifferent as to knowing what it is. All our actions and thoughts must take such different courses, according as there are or are not eternal joys to hope for, that it is impossible to take one step with sense and judgment unless we regulate our course by our view of this point which ought to be our ultimate end.

—Thus our first interest and our first duty is to enlighten ourselves on this subject, whereon depends all our conduct. . . .

Therefore among those who do not believe, I make a vast difference between those who strive with all their power to inform themselves and those who live without troubling or thinking about it.

—I can have only compassion for those who sincerely bewail their doubt, who regard it as the greatest of misfortunes, and who, sparing no effort to escape it, make of this inquiry their principal and most serious occupation.

But as for those who pass their life without thinking of this ultimate end of life. . . . I look upon them in a manner quite different.

—This carelessness in a matter which concerns themselves, their eternity, their all, moves me more to anger than pity; it astonishes and shocks me; it is to me monstrous. I do not say this out of the pious zeal of a spiritual devotion. I expect, on the contrary, that we ought to have this feeling from principles of human interest and self-love.

What joy can we find in the expectation of nothing but hopeless misery? What reason for boasting that we are in impenetrable darkness? And how can it happen that the following argument occurs to a reasonable man?

"I know not who put me into the world, nor what the world is, nor what I myself am. . . . I see those frightful spaces of the universe which surround me, and I find myself tied to one corner of this vast expanse, without knowing why I am put in this place rather than in another, nor why the short time which is given me to live is assigned to me at this point rather than at another of the whole eternity which was before me or which shall come after me. . . . All I know is that I must soon die, but what I know least is this very death which I cannot escape.

"As I know not whence I come, so I know not whither I go. . . . And from all this I conclude that I ought to spend all the days of my life without caring to inquire into what must happen to me. Perhaps I might find some solution to my doubts, but I will not take the trouble, nor take a step to seek it; and after treating with scorn those who are concerned with this care, I will go without foresight and without fear to try the great event, and let myself be led carelessly to death, uncertain of the eternity of my future state."

Who would desire to have for a friend a man who talks in this fashion? Who would choose him out from others to tell him of his affairs? Who would have recourse to him in affliction? And indeed to what use in life could one put him?

—In truth, it is the glory of religion to have for enemies men so unreasonable . . . and thus it is not natural that there should be men indifferent to the loss of their existence, and to the perils of everlasting suffering. They are quite different with regard to all other things. They are afraid of mere trifles; they foresee them; they feel them. And this same man who spends so many days and nights in rage and despair for the loss of office, or for some imaginary insult to his honour, is the very one who knows without anxiety and without emotion that he will lose all by death. It is a monstrous thing to see in the same heart and at the same time this sensibility to trifles and this strange insensibility to the greatest objects. It is an incomprehensible enchantment, and a supernatural slumber, which indicates as its cause an all-powerful force. (194)

An heir finds the title-deeds of his house. Will he say, "Perhaps they are forged" and neglect to examine them? (217)

## (15) Passionate Truth-Seeking

There are only three kinds of persons; those who serve God, having found Him; others who are occupied in seeking Him, not having found Him; while the remainder live without seeking Him and without having found Him. The first are reasonable and happy, the last are foolish and unhappy; those between are unhappy and reasonable. (257)

Nature presents to me nothing which is not matter of doubt and concern. If I saw nothing there which revealed a Divinity, I would come to a negative conclusion; if I saw everywhere the signs of a Creator, I would remain peacefully in faith. But, seeing too much to deny and too little to be sure, I am in a state to be pitied; wherefore I have a hundred times wished that if a God maintains Nature, she should testify to Him unequivocally, and that, if the signs she gives are deceptive, she should suppress them altogether; that she should say everything or nothing, that I might see which cause I ought to follow. Whereas in my present state, ignorant of what I am or of what I ought to do, I know neither my condition nor my duty. My heart inclines wholly to know where is the true good, in order to follow it; nothing would be too dear to me for eternity. (229)

It is an astounding fact that no canonical writer has ever made use of nature to prove God. They all strive to make us believe in Him. (243)

Truth is so obscure in these times, and falsehood so established, that, unless we love the truth, we cannot know it. (864)

### (16) Three Levels of Reality to Search: Body, Mind, Heart

The infinite distance between body and mind is a symbol of the infinitely more infinite distance between mind and charity; for charity is supernatural. . . .

These are three orders differing in kind. . . .

—All bodies, the firmament, the stars, the earth and its kingdoms, are not equal to the lowest mind; for mind knows all these and itself; and these bodies nothing.

—All bodies together, and all minds together, and all their products, are not equal to the least feeling of charity. This is of an order infinitely more exalted.

—From all bodies together, we cannot obtain one little thought; this is impossible and of another order. From all bodies and minds, we cannot produce a feeling of true charity; this is impossible and of another and supernatural order. (793)

---

The vanity of the sciences: Physical science will not console me for the ignorance of morality in the time of affliction. But the science of ethics will always console me for the ignorance of the physical sciences. (67)

### (17) The Heart

The heart has its reasons, which reason does not know. We feel it in a thousand things. I say that the heart naturally loves the Universal Being, and also itself naturally, according as it gives itself to them; and it hardens itself against one or the other at its will. You have rejected the one and kept the other. Is it by reason that you love yourself? (277)

---

It is the heart which experiences God, and not the reason. This, then, is faith: God felt by the heart, not by the reason. (278)

### (18) Faith and Reason

(Submission:) We must know where to doubt, where to feel certain, where to submit. He who does not do so understands not the force of reason.

There are some who offend against these three rules, either by affirming everything as demonstrative, from want of knowing what demonstration is; or by doubting everything, from want of knowing where to submit; or by submitting in everything, from want of knowing where they must judge. (268)

Two extremes: to exclude reason, to admit reason only. (253)

[Paraphrasing] Saint Augustine: Reason would never submit, if it did not judge that there are some occasions on which it ought to submit. It is then right for it to submit, when it judges that it ought to submit. (270)

The last proceeding of reason is to recognise that there is an infinity of things which are beyond it. It is but feeble if it does not see so far as to know this. (267)

## (19) Why God Hides

God prefers rather to incline the will than the intellect. Perfect clearness would be of use to the intellect and would harm the will. To humble pride. (581)

If God had permitted only one religion, it has been too easily known; but when we look at it closely, we clearly discern the truth amidst this confusion. (578)

But it is at the same time true that He hides Himself from those who tempt Him, and that He reveals Himself to those who seek Him, because men are both unworthy and capable of God; unworthy by their corruption, capable by their original nature. (557)

If there were no obscurity, man would not be sensible of his corruption; if there were no light, man would not hope for a remedy. Thus, it is not only fair, but advantageous to us, that God be partly hidden and partly revealed; since it is equally dangerous to man to know God without knowing his own wretchedness, and to know his own wretchedness without knowing God. (586)

———

I admire the boldness with which these persons undertake to speak of God. In addressing their argument to infidels, their first chapter is to prove Divinity from the works of nature. I should not be astonished at their enterprise, if they were addressing their argument to the faithful; for it is certain that those who have the living faith in their hearts see at once that all existence is none other than the work of the God whom they adore. But for those in whom this light is extinguished, and in whom we purpose to rekindle it, persons destitute of faith and grace, who, seeking with all their light whatever they see in nature . . . is to give them ground for believing that the proofs of our religion are very weak. . . .

—It is not after this manner that Scripture speaks, which has a better knowledge of the things that are of God. It says, on the contrary, that God is a hidden God, and that, since the corruption of nature, He has left men in a darkness from which they can escape only through Jesus Christ, without whom all communion with God is cut off. *Nemo novit Patrem, nisi Filius, et cui voluerit Filius revelare.* [Mt. 11:27—"Neither knoweth any man the Father, save the Son, and he to whomsoever the Son will reveal him."]

This is what Scripture points out to us, when it says in so many places that those who seek God find Him. It is not of that light, "like the noonday sun," that this is said. We do not say that those who seek the noonday sun, or water in the sea, shall find them; and hence the evidence of God must not be of this nature. So it tells us elsewhere: *Vere tu es Deus absconditus.* [Is. 45:15—"Verily, thou art a God that hidest thyself."] (242)

———

There is enough light for those who only desire to see, and enough obscurity for those who have a contrary disposition. (430)

## (20) Why Scripture Is Obscure

God, in order to cause the Messiah to be known by the good and not to be known by the wicked, made Him to be foretold in this manner. If the manner of the Messiah had been clearly foretold, there would have been no obscurity, even for the wicked. If the time had been obscurely foretold, there would have been obscurity, even for the good. . . . But that time has been clearly foretold, and the manner in types.

By this means, the wicked, taking the promised blessings for material blessings, have fallen into error. . . . For the understanding of the promised blessings depends on the heart, which calls good that which it loves; but the understanding of the promised time does not depend on the heart. And thus the clear prediction of the time, and the obscure prediction of the blessings, deceive the wicked alone. (758)

---

When David foretold that the Messiah would deliver His people from their enemies, one can believe that in the flesh these would be the Egyptians. . . . But one can well believe also that the enemies would be their sins; for indeed the Egyptians were not their enemies, but their sins were so. (692)

## (21) Scriptural Clues

Proof of Jesus Christ: The supposition that the apostles were impostors is very absurd. Let us think it out. Let us imagine those twelve men, assembled after the death of Jesus Christ, plotting to say that He was risen. By this they attack all the powers. The heart of man is strangely inclined to fickleness, to change, to promises, to gain. However little any of them might have been led astray by all these attractions, nay more, by the fear of prisons, tortures, and death, they were lost. Let us follow up this thought. (801)

---

The apostles were either deceived or deceivers. Either supposition has difficulties; for it is not possible to mistake a man raised from the dead. . . .

While Jesus Christ was with them, He could sustain them. But, after that, if He did not appear to them, who inspired them to act? (802)

## (22) Jewish Clues

To meet with this people is astonishing to me, and seems to me worthy of attention. (619)

---

(On the Sincerity of the Jews:) They preserve lovingly and carefully the book in which Moses declares that they have been all their life ungrateful to God, and that he knows they will be still more so after his death; but that he calls heaven and earth to witness against them and that he has taught them enough. (631)

---

(To show that the true Jews and the true Christians have but the same religion:) The religion of the Jews seemed to consist essentially in the fatherhood of Abraham, in circumcision, in sacrifices, in ceremonies, in the Ark, in the temple, in Jerusalem, and, finally, in the law, and in the covenant with Moses.

—I say that it consisted in none of those things, but only in the love of God, and that God disregarded all the other things. (610)

## (23) Miracles

It is not possible to have a reasonable belief against miracles. (815)

---

How I hate these follies of not believing in the Eucharist, etc.! If the Gospel be true, if Jesus Christ be God, what difficulty is there? (224)

---

"Had I seen a miracle," say men, "I should become converted." How can they be sure they would do a thing of the nature of which they are ignorant? They imagine that this conversion consists in a worship of God which is like commerce, and in a communion such as they picture to themselves. True religion consists in annihilating self before that Universal Being, whom we have so often provoked, and who can justly destroy us at any time; in recognising that we can do nothing without Him, and have deserved nothing from Him but His displeasure. It consists in knowing that there is an unconquerable opposition between us and God, and that without a mediator there can be no communion with Him. (470)

## (24) The Two Essential Truths

Christianity is strange. It bids man recognise that he is vile, even abominable, and bids him desire to be like God. Without such a counterpoise, this dignity would make him horribly vain, or this humiliation would make him terribly abject. (537)

The knowledge of God without that of man's misery causes pride. The knowledge of man's misery without that of God causes despair. The knowledge of Jesus Christ constitutes the middle course, because in Him we find both God and our misery. (527)

Misery induces despair, pride induces presumption. The Incarnation shows man the greatness of his misery by the greatness of the remedy which he required. (526)

If man is not made for God, why is he only happy in God? If man is made for God, why is he so opposed to God? (438)

And on this ground they take occasion to revile the Christian religion, because they misunderstand it. They imagine that it consists simply in the worship of a God considered as great, powerful, and eternal; which is strictly deism, almost as far removed from the Christian religion as atheism. . . .

But let them conclude what they will against deism, they will conclude nothing against the Christian religion, which properly consists in the mystery of the Redeemer, who, uniting in Himself the two natures, human and divine, has redeemed men from the corruption of sin in order to reconcile them in His divine person to God.

The Christian religion, then, teaches men these two truths; that there is a God whom men can know, and that there is a corruption in their nature which renders them unworthy of Him. It is equally important to men to know both these points; and it is equally dangerous for man to know God without knowing his own wretchedness, and to know his own wretchedness without knowing the Redeemer who can free him from it. The knowledge of only one of these points gives rise either to the pride of philosophers, who have known God, and not their own wretchedness, or to the despair of atheists, who know their own wretchedness, but not the Redeemer. (556)

## (25) Christocentrism

Jesus Christ is end of all, and the centre to which all tends. Whoever knows Him knows the reason of everything. (556)

---

The metaphysical proofs of God are so remote from the reasoning of men, and so complicated, that they make little impression; and if they should be of service to some, it would be only during the moment that they see such demonstration; but an hour afterwards they fear they have been mistaken. . . . This is the result of the knowledge of God obtained without Jesus Christ. (543)

---

Jesus Christ is a God whom we approach without pride and before whom we humble ourselves without despair. (528)

---

Not only do we know God by Jesus Christ alone, but we know ourselves only by Jesus Christ. We know life and death only through Jesus Christ. Apart from Jesus Christ, we do not know what is our life, nor our death, nor God, nor ourselves. (548)

---

This religion, so great in miracles, saints, blameless Fathers, learned and great witnesses, martyrs, established kings . . . so great in science, after having displayed all her miracles and all her wisdom, rejects all this, and declares that she has neither wisdom nor signs, but only the cross. . . . (587)

## (26) The Wager

Order: I would have far more fear of being mistaken, and of finding that the Christian religion was true, than of not being mistaken in believing it true. (241)

---

"God is, or He is not." But to which side shall we incline? Reason can decide nothing here. There is an infinite chaos which separated us. A game is being played at the extremity of this infinite distance where heads or tails will turn up. What will you wager? According to reason, you can do neither the one thing nor the other; according to reason, you can defend neither of the propositions.

Do not, then, reprove for error those who have made a choice; for you know nothing about it.

"No, but I blame them for having made, not this choice, but a choice; for again both he who chooses heads and he who chooses tails are equally at fault, they are both in the wrong. The true course is not to wager at all."

—Yes; but you must wager. It is not optional. You are embarked. Which will you choose then? Let us see. Since you must choose, let us see which interests you least. You have two things to lose, the true and the good; and two things to stake, your reason and your will, your knowledge and your happiness; and your nature has two things to shun, error and misery. Your reason is no more shocked in choosing one rather than the other, since you must of necessity choose. This is one point settled. But your happiness? Let us weigh the gain and the loss in wagering that God is. Let us estimate these two chances. If you gain, you gain all; if you lose, you lose nothing. Wager, then, without hesitation that He is. . . . And so our proposition is of infinite force, when there is the finite to stake in a game where there are equal risks of gain and of loss, and the infinite to gain. This is demonstrable; and if men are capable of any truths, this is one.

"I confess it, I admit it. But, still, is there no means of seeing the faces of the cards?"

Yes, Scripture and the rest, etc.

"Yes, but I have my hands tied and my mouth closed; I am forced to wager, and am not free. I am not released, and am so made that I cannot believe. What, then, would you have me do?"

True. But at least learn your inability to believe, since reason brings you to this, and yet you cannot believe. Endeavour, then, to convince yourself, not by increase of proofs of God, but by the abatement of your passions. You would like to attain faith and do not know the way; you would like to cure yourself of unbelief and ask the remedy for it. Learn of those who have been bound like you, and who now stake all their possessions. These are people who know the way which you would follow, and who are cured of an ill of which you would be cured. Follow the way by which they began; by acting as if they believed. . . . Even this will naturally make you believe. . . .

"But this is what I am afraid of."

And why? What have you to lose? . . . Now, what harm will befall you in taking this side? You will be faithful, humble, grateful, generous, a sincere friend, truthful. . . . Certainly you will not have those poisonous pleasures, glory and luxury; but will you not have others? I will tell you that you will thereby gain in this life, and that, at each step you take on this road, you will see so great certainty of gain, so much nothingness in what you risk, that you will at last recognise that you have wagered for something certain and infinite, for which you have given nothing.

"Ah! This discourse transports me, charms me." . . .

If this discourse pleases you and seems impressive, know that it is made by a man who has knelt, both before and after it, in prayer to that Being, infinite and without parts, before whom he lays all he has, for you also to lay before Him all you have for your own good and for His glory, that so strength may be given to lowliness. (233)

## (27) The Body of Christ, the Church

The examples of the noble deaths of the Lacedaemonians and others scarce touch us. For what good is it to us? But the example of the death of the martyrs touches us; for they are "our members." . . .

There is nothing of this in the examples of the heathen. We have no tie with them; as we do not become rich by seeing a stranger who is so, but in fact by seeing a father or a husband who is so. (481)

---

To be a member is to have neither life, being, nor movement, except through the spirit of the body, and for the body.

The separate member, seeing no longer the body to which it belongs, has only a perishing and dying existence. . . .

It cannot by its nature love any other thing, except for itself and to subject it to self, because each thing loves itself more than all. But, in loving the body, it loves itself, because it only exists in it, by it, and for it. . . .

We love ourselves, because we are members of Jesus Christ. We love Jesus Christ, because He is the body of which we are members. All is one, one is in the other, like the Three Persons [of the Trinity]. (483)

---

The least movement affects all nature; the entire sea changes because of a rock. Thus, in grace, the least action affects everything by its consequences; therefore everything is important. (505)

---

Jesus will be in agony even to the end of the world. We must not sleep during that time. . . .

Do little things as though they were great, because of the majesty of Jesus Christ who does them in us and who lives our life; and do the greatest things as though they were little and easy, because of His omnipotence. (553)

---

I consider Jesus Christ in all persons . . . Jesus Christ as poor in the poor, Jesus Christ as rich in the rich. . . . (785)

## (28) Pascal's Conversion Experience

The year of grace 1654.
Monday, 23 November, feast of Saint Clement. . . .
From about half-past ten in the evening until about half-past midnight.

Fire.
The God of Abraham, the God of Isaac, the God of Jacob.
Not of the philosophers and intellectuals.
Certitude, certitude, feeling, joy, peace.
The God of Jesus Christ. . . .

*Translated by W. F. Trotter, 1910*

# PASCAL'S ARROWS

## Peter Kreeft

Unlike Augustine, who lived a long life and wrote hundreds of treatises, Blaise Pascal died young and wrote only one great book, the *Pensées*. Yet even that is not a book; it is almost a thousand scattered *notes* for a book he never finished. (*Pensées* means, simply, "thoughts.") Only nine or ten are finished chapters, two- to six-pages long; the rest are a few paragraphs or a few sentences or even a few words. One editor called them "a workshop in ruins."

I have organized the "big ideas" in a logical and psychological sequence, like events in a conversion story, and added headings or titles for each step. I think this is the sequence he had in mind, but he did not have time to arrange and classify most of them. They are just "thoughts": not a book but the unfinished raw material for a book.

However, they are more powerful in this unfinished condition than they would have been had Pascal lived to integrate them into a finished work. They're like raw pearls without a string. Pascal mercifully was struck dead before he could spoil his masterpiece.

I teach "great books," many of them Christian masterpieces—by St. John, St. Paul, St. Augustine, Boethius, St. Anselm, St. Thomas Aquinas, Dante, Shakespeare, Dostoyevsky, Tolstoy, Kierkegaard, Newman, Chesterton, Lewis, Tolkien. All are geniuses. But no Christian writer who ever lived speaks to my very modern and secular students more powerfully than Pascal. His "thoughts" are arrows shot straight into their hearts. He makes them get suddenly very quiet, even stop breathing for ten seconds. He *knows* them. He knows God. And he is a matchmaker.

He wrote as he was dying. It was to have been an argument for the truth of the Christian faith, one that appealed to the heart as much as the head. He wrote most of it after he had given away his entire large library except for two books, which he reread continually, and these two explain its power: the Bible and Augustine's *Confessions*. The first two you'd want to take to your desert island for the rest of your life.

---

The salient biographical facts can be summarized very briefly. Blaise Pascal was a seventeenth-century contemporary and acquaintance of Descartes, "the father of modern philosophy." But he was the only modern philosopher for two hundred years, until the existentialists, who didn't get on Descartes's rationalist, Enlightenment bandwagon of making science an idol.

Even so, he was a very great scientist himself. He did major work in physics (he was the first to prove the atmosphere has weight) and mathematics (he founded much of probability theory). A computer language is named after him because he invented the first working computer (calculator); he also invented the vacuum cleaner and the first public transportation system.

Pascal knew the power of science to make us clever and powerful, and he was also aware of its impotence to make us wise or good. Pascal knew *sin*.

## CHAPTER EIGHTEEN

# JOHN LOCKE, PART ONE

## Enlightenment (1632–1704)

**M**any Americans fear that philosophy will make them useless. They will start thinking about ideas, and soon that will lead to thinking about thinking.

They're right that the topic will quickly arise, but they shouldn't fear it. John Locke, the intellectual founder of most of the world's democracies, thought it necessary that free men and women should think about thinking. In fact, he believed bad thinking about thinking would undermine society.

John Locke lived in an age when every educated person was expected to have a coherent philosophy. This sensible expectation included having a view about what was "knowable" and how it could be "known." Questions about knowledge were part of the philosophical discipline called *epistemology*, and Locke's generation believed any person worthy of voting should have thought out how to make good decisions about that vote.

Men with a bad epistemology may be given a good constitution, but they will not know how to properly make choices under it. Free people need to know the truth, if it can be known, about knowing the truth!

John Locke had much faith in reason, and the profound and wonderful changes he witnessed went a long way toward justifying that faith. It is popular in some quarters to bewail "modernist" thought, but, once more, few wish to dispense with the innumerable blessings of modernity. Locke helped give us political liberty in his treatises on government, and he believed his epistemology was tied to his politics (see John Locke, Part Two). Those of us who love liberty should hesitate to quickly dismiss his epistemology.

As a faithful member of the Church of England and a Christian apologist, Locke supported the faith, but many later philosophers used his ideas about knowledge to undermine it. Partly, this was because they ignored or overlooked his more theological works and arguments as "less important." Locke, conversely, placed all his writings in a theological context after extensive biblical reflection. He took biblical history for granted; the existence of a first man and woman created in God's image did philosophical work for him.

This must be taken into account in order for us to understand the whole of Locke's labor and its impact on the dominantly Christian population of his day. Criticisms of modern epistemology may apply less to Locke and more to secularized versions of Locke.

A traditional believer reading Locke today may still wonder if the philosopher did have too much faith in the existence of "culturally neutral reason" and human access to it. At any rate, Locke would welcome us to the discussion.

CRITICAL

## ◌◌ FROM ◌◌

# An Essay Concerning Human Understanding

## Book 1

**A**n Inquiry into the understanding, pleasant and useful. Since it is the understanding that sets man above the rest of sensible beings, and gives him all the advantage and dominion which he has over them; it is certainly a subject, even for its nobleness, worth our labour to inquire into. The understanding, like the eye, whilst it makes us see and perceive all other things, takes no notice of itself; and it requires art and pains to set it at a distance and make it its own object. But whatever be the difficulties that lie in the way of this inquiry; whatever it be that keeps us so much in the dark to ourselves; sure I am that all the light we can let in upon our minds, all the acquaintance we can make with our own understandings, will not only be very pleasant, but bring us great advantage, in directing our thoughts in the search of other things.

. . .

*Method.* It is therefore worth while to search out the bounds between opinion and knowledge; and examine by what measures, in things whereof we have no certain knowledge, we ought to regulate our assent and moderate our persuasion. In order whereunto I shall pursue this following method:

First, I shall inquire into the original of those ideas, notions, or whatever else you please to call them, which a man observes, and is conscious to himself he has in his mind; and the ways whereby the understanding comes to be furnished with them.

Secondly, I shall endeavour to show what knowledge the understanding hath by those ideas; and the certainty, evidence, and extent of it.

Thirdly, I shall make some inquiry into the nature and grounds of faith or opinion: whereby I mean that assent which we give to any proposition as true, of whose truth yet we have no certain knowledge. And here we shall have occasion to examine the reasons and degrees of assent.

. . .

*The way shown how we come by any knowledge, sufficient to prove it not innate.* It is an established opinion, amongst some men, that there are in the understanding certain innate principles; some primary notions, koinai ennoiai ["common concept"], characters, as it were stamped upon the mind of man; which the soul receives in its very first being, and brings into the world with it. It would be sufficient to convince unprejudiced readers of the falseness of this supposition, if I should only show (as I hope I shall in the following parts of this Discourse) how men, barely by the use of their natural faculties, may attain to all the knowledge they have, without the help of any innate impressions; and may arrive at certainty, without any such original notions or principles. For I imagine any one will easily grant that it would be impertinent to suppose the ideas of colours innate in a creature to whom God hath given sight, and a power to receive them by the eyes from external objects: and no less unreasonable would it be to attribute several truths to the impressions of nature, and innate characters, when we may observe in ourselves faculties fit to attain as easy and certain knowledge of them as if they were originally imprinted on the mind.

But because a man is not permitted without censure to follow his own thoughts in the search of truth, when they lead him ever so little out of the common road, I shall set down the reasons that made me doubt of the truth of that opinion, as an excuse for my mistake, if I be in one; which I leave to be considered by those who, with me, dispose themselves to embrace truth wherever they find it.

. . .

*The steps by which the mind attains several truths.* The senses at first let in particular ideas, and furnish the yet empty cabinet, and the mind by degrees growing familiar with some of them, they are lodged in the memory, and names got to them. Afterwards, the mind proceeding further, abstracts them, and by degrees learns the use of general names. In this manner the mind comes to be furnished with ideas and language, the materials about which to exercise its discursive faculty. And the use of reason becomes daily more visible, as these materials that give it employment increase. But though the having of general ideas and the use of general words and reason usually grow together, yet I see not how this any way proves them innate. The knowledge of some truths, I confess, is very early in the mind but in a way that shows them not to be innate. For, if we will observe, we shall find it still to be about ideas, not innate, but acquired; it being about those first which are imprinted by external things, with which infants have earliest to do, which make the most frequent impressions on their senses. In ideas thus got, the mind discovers that some agree and others differ, probably as soon as it has any use of memory; as soon as it is able to retain and perceive distinct ideas. But whether it be then or no, this is certain, it does so long before it has the use of words; or comes to that which we commonly call "the use of reason." For a child knows as certainly before it can speak the difference between the ideas of sweet and bitter (i.e. that sweet is not bitter), as it knows afterwards (when it comes to speak) that wormwood and sugarplums are not the same thing.

. . .

*No moral principles so clear and so generally received as the forementioned speculative maxims.* If those speculative Maxims, whereof we discoursed in the foregoing chapter, have not an actual universal assent from all mankind, as we there proved, it is much more visible concerning practical Principles, that they come short of an universal reception: and I think it will be hard to instance any one moral rule which can pretend to so general and ready an assent as, "What is, is"; or to be so manifest a truth as this, that "It is impossible for the same thing to be and not to be." Whereby it is evident that they are further removed from a title to be innate; and the doubt of their being native impressions on the mind is stronger against those moral principles than the other. Not that it brings their truth at all in question. They are equally true, though not equally evident. Those speculative maxims carry their own evidence with them: but moral principles require reasoning and discourse, and some exercise of the mind, to discover the certainty of their truth. They lie not open as natural characters engraven on the mind; which, if any such were, they must needs be visible by themselves, and by their own light be certain and known to everybody. But this is no derogation to their truth and certainty; no more than it is to the truth or certainty of the three angles of a triangle being equal to two right ones: because it is not so evident as "the whole is bigger than a part," nor so apt to be assented to at first hearing. It may suffice that these moral rules are capable of demonstration: and therefore it is our own faults if we come not to a certain knowledge of them. But the ignorance wherein many men are of them, and the slowness of assent wherewith others receive them, are manifest proofs that they are not innate, and such as offer themselves to their view without searching.

*Faith and justice not owned as principles by all men.* Whether there be any such moral principles, wherein all men do agree, I appeal to any who have been but moderately conversant in the history of mankind, and looked abroad beyond the smoke of their own chimneys. Where is that practical truth that is universally received, without doubt or question, as it must be if innate? Justice, and keeping of contracts, is that which most men seem to agree in. This is a principle which is thought to extend itself to the dens of thieves, and the confederacies of the greatest villains; and they who have gone furthest towards the putting off of humanity itself, keep faith and rules of justice one with another. I grant that outlaws themselves do this one amongst another: but it is without receiving these as the innate laws of nature. They practise them as rules of convenience within their own communities: but it is impossible to conceive that he embraces justice as a practical principle, who acts fairly with his fellow-highwayman, and at the same time plunders or kills the next honest man he meets with. Justice and truth are the common ties of society; and therefore even outlaws and robbers, who break with all the world besides, must keep faith and rules of equity amongst themselves; or else they cannot hold together. But will any one say, that those that live by fraud or rapine have innate principles of truth and justice which they allow and assent to?

. . .

*Idea of God not innate.* If any idea can be imagined innate, the idea of God may, of all others, for many reasons, be thought so; since it is hard to conceive how there should be innate moral principles, without an innate idea of a Deity. Without a notion of a law-maker, it is impossible to have a notion of a law, and an obligation to observe it. Besides the atheists taken notice of amongst the ancients, and left branded upon the records of history, hath not navigation discovered, in these later ages, whole nations, at the bay of Soldania, in Brazil, [in Boranday,] and in the Caribbee islands, etc., amongst whom there was to be found no notion of a God, no religion? . . . [There] are instances of nations where uncultivated nature has been left to itself, without the help of letters and discipline, and the improvements of arts and sciences. But there are others to be found who have enjoyed these in a very great measure, who yet, for want of a due application of their thoughts this way, want the idea and knowledge of God. It will, I doubt not, be a surprise to others, as it was to me, to find the Siamites of this number. But for this, let them consult the King of France's late envoy thither, who gives no better account of the Chinese themselves. And if we will not believe La Loubere, the missionaries of China, even the Jesuits themselves, the great encomiasts of the Chinese, do all to a man agree, and will convince us, that the sect of the literari, or learned, keeping to the old religion of China, and the ruling party there, are all of them atheists. . . . And perhaps, if we should with attention mind the lives and discourses of people not so far off, we should have too much reason to fear, that many, in more civilized countries, have no very strong and clear impressions of a Deity upon their minds, and that the complaints of atheism made from the pulpit are not without reason. And though only some profligate wretches own it too barefacedly now; yet perhaps we should hear more than we do of it from others, did not the fear of the magistrate's sword, or their neighbour's censure, tie up people's tongues; which, were the apprehensions of punishment or shame taken away, would as openly proclaim their atheism as their lives do.

*The name of God not universal or obscure in meaning.* But had all mankind everywhere a notion of a God, (whereof yet history tells us the contrary,) it would not from thence follow, that the idea of him was innate. For, though no nation were to be found without a name, and some few dark notions of him, yet that would not prove them to be natural impressions on the mind; no more than the names of fire, or the sun, heat, or number, do prove the ideas they stand for to be innate; because the names of those things, and the ideas of them, are so universally received and known amongst mankind. Nor, on the contrary, is the want of such a name, or the absence of such a notion out of men's minds, any argument against the being of a

God; any more than it would be a proof that there was no loadstone in the world, because a great part of mankind had neither a notion of any such thing nor a name for it; or be any show of argument to prove that there are no distinct and various species of angels, or intelligent beings above us, because we have no ideas of such distinct species, or names for them. For, men being furnished with words, by the common language of their own countries, can scarce avoid having some kind of ideas of those things whose names those they converse with have occasion frequently to mention to them. And if they carry with it the notion of excellency, greatness, or something extraordinary; if apprehension and concernment accompany it; if the fear of absolute and irresistible power set it on upon the mind—the idea is likely to sink the deeper, and spread the further; especially if it be such an idea as is agreeable to the common light of reason, and naturally deducible from every part of our knowledge, as that of a God is. For the visible marks of extraordinary wisdom and power appear so plainly in all the works of the creation, that a rational creature, who will but seriously reflect on them, cannot miss the discovery of a Deity. And the influence that the discovery of such a Being must necessarily have on the minds of all that have but once heard of it is so great, and carries such a weight of thought and communication with it, that it seems stranger to me that a whole nation of men should be anywhere found so brutish as to want the notion of a God, than that they should be without any notion of numbers, or fire. . . .

## Book 2

*. . . All ideas come from sensation or reflection.* Let us then suppose the mind to be, as we say, white paper, void of all characters, without any ideas: How comes it to be furnished? Whence comes it by that vast store which the busy and boundless fancy of man has painted on it with an almost endless variety? Whence has it all the materials of reason and knowledge? To this I answer, in one word, from EXPERIENCE. In that all our knowledge is founded; and from that it ultimately derives itself. Our observation employed either, about external sensible objects, or about the internal operations of our minds perceived and reflected on by ourselves, is that

which supplies our understandings with all the materials of thinking. These two are the fountains of knowledge, from whence all the ideas we have, or can naturally have, do spring.

*The objects of sensation one source of ideas.* First, our Senses, conversant about particular sensible objects, do convey into the mind several distinct perceptions of things, according to those various ways wherein those objects do affect them. And thus we come by those ideas we have of yellow, white, heat, cold, soft, hard, bitter, sweet, and all those which we call sensible qualities; which when I say the senses convey into the mind, I mean, they from external objects convey into the mind what produces there those perceptions. This great source of most of the ideas we have, depending wholly upon our senses, and derived by them to the understanding, I call SENSATION.

*The operations of our minds, the other source of them.* Secondly, the other fountain from which experience furnisheth the understanding with ideas is—the perception of the operations of our own mind within us, as it is employed about the ideas it has got—which operations, when the soul comes to reflect on and consider, do furnish the understanding with another set of ideas, which could not be had from things without. And such are perception, thinking, doubting, believing, reasoning, knowing, willing, and all the different actings of our own minds; which we being conscious of, and observing in ourselves, do from these receive into our understandings as distinct ideas as we do from bodies affecting our senses. This source of ideas every man has wholly in himself; and though it be not sense, as having nothing to do with external objects, yet it is very like it, and might properly enough be called internal sense. But as I call the other SENSATION, so I call this REFLECTION, the ideas it affords being such only as the mind gets by reflecting on its own operations within itself. By reflection then, in the following part of this discourse, I would be understood to mean, that notice which the mind takes of its own operations, and the manner of them, by reason whereof there come to be ideas of these operations in the understanding. These two, I say, viz. external material things, as the objects of SENSATION, and the operations of our own minds within, as the objects of REFLECTION, are to me the only originals from whence all our ideas take their beginnings. The term operations here I use in a large sense, as comprehending not barely the actions of the mind about its ideas, but some sort of passions arising sometimes from them, such as is the satisfaction or uneasiness arising from any thought.

. . .

*The original of all our knowledge.* In time the mind comes to reflect on its own operations about the ideas got by sensation, and thereby stores itself with a new set of ideas, which I call ideas of reflection. These are the impressions that are made on our senses by outward objects that are extrinsical to the mind; and its own operations, proceeding from powers intrinsical and proper to itself, which, when reflected on by itself, become also objects of its contemplation—are, as I have said, the original of all knowledge. Thus the first capacity of human intellect is, that the mind is fitted to receive the impressions made on it; either through the senses by outward objects, or by its own operations when it reflects on them. This is the first step a man makes towards the discovery of anything, and the groundwork whereon to build all those notions which ever he shall have naturally in this world. All those sublime thoughts which tower above the clouds, and reach as high as heaven itself, take their rise and footing here: in all that great extent wherein the mind wanders, in those remote speculations it may seem to be elevated with, it stirs not one jot beyond those ideas which sense or reflection have offered for its contemplation.

. . .

*Our ideas and the qualities of bodies.* Whatsoever the mind perceives in itself, or is the immediate object of perception, thought, or understanding, that I call idea; and the power to produce any idea in our mind, I call quality of the subject wherein that power is. Thus a snowball having the power to produce in us the ideas of white, cold, and round—

the power to produce those ideas in us, as they are in the snowball, I call qualities; and as they are sensations or perceptions in our understandings, I call them ideas; which ideas, if I speak of sometimes as in the things themselves, I would be understood to mean those qualities in the objects which produce them in us.

*Primary qualities of bodies.* Qualities thus considered in bodies are, First, such as are utterly inseparable from the body, in what state soever it be; and such as in all the alterations and changes it suffers, all the force can be used upon it, it constantly keeps; and such as sense constantly finds in every particle of matter which has bulk enough to be perceived; and the mind finds inseparable from every particle of matter, though less than to make itself singly be perceived by our senses: [for example,] Take a grain of wheat, divide it into two parts; each part has still solidity, extension, figure, and mobility: divide it again, and it retains still the same qualities; and so divide it on, till the parts become insensible; they must retain still each of them all those qualities. For division (which is all that a mill, or pestle, or any other body, does upon another, in reducing it to insensible parts) can never take away either solidity, extension, figure, or mobility from any body, but only makes two or more distinct separate masses of matter, of that which was but one before; all which distinct masses, reckoned as so many distinct bodies, after division, make a certain number. These I call original or primary qualities of body, which I think we may observe to produce simple ideas in us, viz. solidity, extension, figure, motion or rest, and number.

*Secondary qualities of bodies.* Secondly, such qualities which in truth are nothing in the objects themselves but power to produce various sensations in us by their primary qualities, i.e. by the bulk, figure, texture, and motion of their insensible parts, as colours, sounds, tastes, etc. These I call secondary qualities. To these might be added a third sort, which are allowed to be barely powers; though they are as much real qualities in the subject as those which I, to comply with the common way of speaking, call qualities, but for distinction, secondary qualities. For the power in fire to produce a new colour, or consistency, in wax or clay, by its primary qualities, is as much a quality in fire, as the power it has to produce in me a new idea or sensation of warmth or burning, which I felt not before, by the same primary qualities, viz. the bulk, texture, and motion of its insensible parts.

. . .

*The ideas of the primary alone really exist.* The particular bulk, number, figure, and motion of the parts of fire or snow are really in them, whether any one's senses perceive them or no: and therefore they may be called real qualities, because they really exist in those bodies. But light, heat, whiteness, or coldness, are no more really in them than sickness or pain is in manna. Take away the sensation of them; let not the eyes see light

417

or colours, nor the ears hear sounds; let the palate not taste, nor the nose smell, and all colours, tastes, odours, and sounds, as they are such particular ideas, vanish and cease, and are reduced to their causes, i.e. bulk, figure, and motion of parts.

. . .

*[Complex ideas,] Made by the mind out of simple ones.* We have hitherto considered those ideas, in the reception whereof the mind is only passive, which are those simple ones received from sensation and reflection before mentioned, whereof the mind cannot make one to itself, nor have any idea which does not wholly consist of them. But as the mind is wholly passive in the reception of all its simple ideas, so it exerts several acts of its own, whereby out of its simple ideas, as the materials and foundations of the rest, the others are framed. The acts of the mind, wherein it exerts its power over its simple ideas, are chiefly these three: (1) Combining several simple ideas into one compound one; and thus all complex ideas are made. (2) The second is bringing two ideas, whether simple or complex, together, and setting them by one another, so as to take a view of them at once, without uniting them into one; by which way it gets all its ideas of relations. (3) The third is separating them from all other ideas that accompany them in their real existence: this is called abstraction: and thus all its general ideas are made. This shows man's power, and its ways of operation, to be much the same in the material and intellectual world. For the materials in both being such as he has no power over, either to make or destroy, all that man can do is either to unite them together, or to set them by one another, or wholly separate them. I shall here begin with the first of these in the consideration of complex ideas, and come to the other two in their due places. As simple ideas are observed to exist in several combinations united together, so the mind has a power to consider several of them united together as one idea; and that not only as they are united in external objects, but as itself has joined them together. Ideas thus made up of several simple ones put together, I call complex; such as are beauty, gratitude, a man, an army, the universe; which, though complicated of various simple ideas, or complex ideas made up of simple ones, yet are, when the mind pleases, considered each by itself, as one entire thing, and signified by one name.

. . .

*[Ideas of Duration and Expansion:] Both capable of greater and less. . . .* Distance or space, in its simple abstract conception, to avoid confusion, I call expansion, to distinguish it from extension, which by some is used to express this distance only as it is in the solid parts of matter, and so includes, or at least intimates, the idea of body: whereas the idea of pure distance includes no such thing. I prefer also the word expansion to space, because space is often applied to distance of fleeting successive parts, which never exist together, as well as to those which are permanent. In both these (viz. expansion and duration) the mind has this common idea of continued lengths, capable of greater or less quantities. For a man has as clear an idea of the difference of the length of an hour and a day, as of an inch and a foot.

*Expansion not bounded by matter.* The mind, having got the idea of the length of any part of expansion, let it be a span, or a pace, or what length you will, can, as has been said, repeat that idea, and so, adding it to the former, enlarge its idea of length, and make it equal to two spans, or two paces; and so, as often as it will, till it equals the distance of any parts of the earth one from another, and increase thus till it amounts to the distance of the sun or remotest star. By such a progression as this, setting out from the place where it is, or any other place, it can proceed and pass beyond all those lengths, and find nothing to stop its going on, either in or without body. It is true, we can easily in our thoughts come to the end of solid extension; the extremity and bounds of all body we have no difficulty to arrive at: but when the mind is there, it finds nothing to hinder its progress into this endless expansion; of that it can neither find nor conceive any end. Nor let any one say, that beyond the bounds of body, there is nothing at all; unless he will confine God within the limits of matter. Solomon, whose understanding was filled and enlarged with wisdom, seems to have other thoughts when he says, "Heaven, and the heaven of heavens, cannot contain thee." And he, I think, very much magnifies to himself the capacity of his own understanding, who persuades himself that he can extend his thoughts further than God exists, or imagine any expansion where He is not.

*Nor duration by motion.* Just so is it in duration. The mind having got the idea of any length of duration, can double, multiply, and enlarge it, not only beyond its own, but beyond the existence of all corporeal beings, and all the measures of time, taken from the great bodies of all the world and their motions. But yet every one easily admits that though we make duration boundless, as certainly it is, we cannot yet extend it beyond all being.

. . .

The now secondary qualities of bodies would disappear, if we could discover the primary ones of their minute parts. Had we senses acute enough to discern the minute particles of bodies, and the real constitution on which their sensible qualities depend, I doubt not but they would produce quite different ideas in us: and that which is now the yellow colour of gold, would then disappear, and instead of it we should see an admirable texture of parts, of a certain size and figure. This microscopes plainly discover to us; for what to our naked eyes produces a certain colour, is, by thus augmenting the acuteness of our senses, discovered to be quite a different thing; and the thus altering, as it were, the proportion of the bulk of the minute parts of a coloured object to our usual sight, produces different ideas from what it did before. Thus, sand or pounded glass, which is opaque, and white to the naked eye, is pellucid in a microscope; and a hair seen in this way, loses its former colour, and is, in a great measure, pellucid, with a mixture of some bright sparkling colours, such as appear from the refraction of diamonds, and other pellucid bodies. Blood, to the naked eye, appears all red; but by a good microscope, wherein its lesser parts appear, shows only some few globules of red, swimming in a pellucid liquor, and how these red globules would appear, if glasses could be found that could yet magnify them a thousand or ten thousand times more, is uncertain.

*Our faculties for discovery of the qualities and powers of substances suited to our state.* The infinite wise Contriver of us, and all things about us, hath fitted our senses, faculties, and organs, to the conveniences of life, and the business we have to do here. We are able, by our senses, to know and distinguish things: and to examine them so far as to apply them to our uses, and several ways to accommodate the exigences of this life. We have insight enough into their admirable contrivances and wonderful effects, to admire and magnify the wisdom, power, and goodness of their Author. Such a knowledge as this, which is suited to our present condition, we want not faculties to attain. But it appears not that God intended we should have a perfect, clear, and adequate knowledge of them: that perhaps is not in the comprehension of any finite being. We are furnished with faculties (dull and weak as they are) to discover enough in the creatures to lead us to the knowledge of the Creator, and the knowledge of our duty; and we are fitted well enough with abilities to provide for the conveniences of living: these are our business in this world. But were our senses altered, and made much quicker and acuter, the appearance and outward scheme of things would have quite another face to us; and, I am apt to think, would be inconsistent with our being, or at least well-being, in this part of the universe which we inhabit. He that considers how little our constitution is able to bear a remove into parts of this air, not much higher than that we commonly breath in, will have reason to be satisfied, that in this globe of earth allotted for our mansion, the all-wise Architect has suited our organs, and the bodies that are to affect them, one to another. If our sense of hearing were but a thousand times quicker than it is, how would a perpetual noise distract us. And we should in the quietest retirement be less able to sleep or meditate than in the middle of a sea-fight. Nay, if that most instructive of our senses, seeing, were in any man a thousand or a hundred thousand times more acute than it is by the best microscope, things several millions of times less than the smallest object of his sight now would then be visible to his naked eyes, and so he would come nearer to the discovery of the texture and motion of the minute parts of corporeal things; and in many of them, probably get ideas of their internal constitutions: but then he would be in a quite different world from other people: nothing would appear the same to him and others: the visible ideas of everything would be different. So that I doubt, whether he and the rest of men could discourse concerning the objects of sight, or have any communication about colours, their appearances being so wholly different. . . .

. . .

*We know nothing of things beyond our simple ideas of them.* Which we are not at all to wonder at, since we having but some few superficial ideas of things, discovered to us only by the senses from without, or by the mind, reflecting on what it experiments in itself within, have no knowledge beyond that, much less of the internal constitution, and true nature of things, being destitute of faculties to attain it. And therefore experimenting and discovering in ourselves knowledge, and the power of voluntary motion, as certainly as we experiment, or discover in things without us, the cohesion and separation of solid parts, which is the extension and motion of bodies; we have as much reason to be satisfied with our notion of immaterial spirit, as with our notion of body, and the existence of the one as well as the other. For it being no more a contradiction that thinking should exist separate and independent from solidity, than it is a contradiction that solidity should exist separate and independent from thinking, they being both but simple ideas, independent one from another: and having as clear and distinct ideas in us of thinking, as of solidity, I know not why we may not as well allow a thinking thing without solidity, i.e. immaterial, to exist, as a solid thing without thinking, i.e. matter, to exist; especially since it is not harder to conceive how thinking should exist without matter, than how matter should think. For whensoever we would proceed beyond these simple ideas we have from sensation and reflection, and dive further into the nature of things, we fall presently into darkness and obscurity, perplexedness and difficulties, and can discover nothing further but our own blindness and ignorance. But whichever of these complex ideas be clearest, that of body, or immaterial spirit, this is evident, that the simple ideas that make them up are no other than what we have received from sensation or reflection: and so is it of all our other ideas of substances, even of God himself.

*Our complex idea of God.* For if we examine the idea we have of the incomprehensible Supreme Being, we shall find that we come by it the same way; and that the complex ideas we have both of God, and separate spirits, are made of the simple ideas we receive from reflection: [for example,] having, from what we experiment in ourselves, got the ideas of existence and duration; of knowledge and power; of pleasure and happiness; and of several other qualities and powers, which it is better to have than to be without; when we would frame an idea the most suitable we can to the Supreme Being, we enlarge every one of these with our idea of infinity; and so putting them together, make our complex idea of God. For that the mind has such a power of enlarging some of its ideas, received from sensation and reflection, has been already shown.

*Our complex idea of God as infinite.* If I find that I know some few things, and some of them, or all, perhaps imperfectly, I can frame an idea of knowing twice as many; which I can double again, as often as I can add to number; and thus enlarge my idea of knowledge, by extending its comprehension to all things existing, or possible. The same also I can do of knowing them more perfectly; i.e. all their qualities, powers, causes, consequences, and relations, etc., till all be perfectly known that is in them, or can any way relate to them: and thus frame the idea of infinite or boundless knowledge. The same may also be done of power, till we come to that we call infinite; and also of the duration of existence, without beginning or end, and so frame the idea of an eternal being. The degrees or extent wherein we ascribe existence, power, wisdom, and all other perfections (which we can have any ideas of) to that sovereign Being, which we call God, being all boundless and infinite, we frame the best idea of him our minds are capable of: all which is done, I say, by enlarging those simple ideas we have taken from the operations of our own minds, by reflection; or by our senses, from exterior things, to that vastness to which infinity can extend them.

*God in his own essence incognisable.* For it is infinity, which, joined to our ideas of existence, power, knowledge, etc., makes that complex idea, whereby we represent to ourselves, the best we can, the Supreme Being. For, though in his own essence (which certainly we do not know, not knowing the real essence of a pebble, or a fly, or of our own selves) God be simple and uncompounded; yet I think I may say we have no other idea of him, but a complex one of existence, knowledge, power, happiness, etc., infinite and eternal: which are all distinct ideas, and some of them, being relative, are again compounded of others: all which being, as has been shown, originally got from sensation and reflection, go to make up the idea or notion we have of God.

# ON CERTAINTY

## Janelle Klapausak

John Locke's *Essay Concerning Human Understanding* begins with the stated project to "search out the bounds between opinion and knowledge." Like most early modern philosophers (writing from c. 1600–1800), Locke was fascinated by the question of certainty. He wanted to know what, of all we take for granted, is truly certain (knowledge) and what is merely opinion. This question was a natural one for Locke and his contemporaries to be asking after decades of profound change for Western Europe.

During the sixteenth century, two overhauls of thought had permeated the Continent. The first was the Protestant Reformation, which "began" with Luther's posting of his Ninety-Five Theses in 1517, and the second was the Scientific Revolution, which most scholars date to the publication of Copernicus's *On the Revolutions of the Celestial Spheres* in 1543. These two intellectual movements, different as they might have been in other ways, shared one crucial characteristic: both cast doubt on propositions that had been accepted for centuries. The Reformation called into question Roman ecclesial authority; the Revolution cast doubt on the authority of Aristotle's method of scientific inquiry.

The philosophers reacting to these revolutions in the early seventeenth century felt the foundations of knowledge shifting under their feet. Their understandable response was to try to find a way to sort through the list of things we all think we know and figure out which are true and which are false. They wanted to reestablish a solid foundation for knowledge by developing a method to discern that which is certainly true.

John Locke's first move in addressing this question was to reject the theory of *innate ideas*. In the preceding centuries, most philosophers had believed there are certain propositions with which we're "preprogrammed." These might include logical and mathematical concepts (like the idea that a proposition cannot be both true and false at the same time) but might also include ethical propositions (e.g., that murder is always wrong).

Locke rejects this doctrine that certain beliefs come "preprogrammed" in all people. Instead, he argues that the mind is a blank slate, or *tabula rasa*, at birth, and that every belief we have we get from observing the world around us.

This point is especially interesting because in René Descartes's *Meditations*, published forty years before Locke's *Essay*, he'd argued that our idea of God is one of these innate ideas, and that it is through this notion that we can be certain that God exists. Descartes believed that only God could cause this idea of God to exist in our minds; Locke maintained that we can get our concept of God from observing the world around us, whether or not God exists.

In a second important shift, Locke insisted that all knowledge comes from observing the world, but it's not the case that all the things we observe are actually *in* the world. Locke said the qualities we observe in the world can be split into two categories. Some qualities—like an object's solidity or its shape—are qualities in the object itself, what Locke calls *primary qualities*. However, in Locke's argument, sometimes when we're observing a quality of an object, what's actually happening is that the object is affecting *us* in some way. This is why, he said, the same water can feel hot on cold hands and cold on hot hands: the hotness or coldness isn't a quality the water itself has, but, instead, it's a power that the water has to affect us. It's not that an object *is* yellow, but, rather, that an object *produces* a yellow effect on us when we observe it.

The practical effect of these two propositions, taken together, is to create a gap between how we experience the world and how the world really is. The rejection of innate ideas means that our observations are the only way we can get knowledge about the world, and the distinction between primary and secondary qualities means our senses don't give us information about the world *as it is*. Instead, objects in the world cause us to have *impressions*, which may or may not be related to how those things actually are.

Locke deduced that the list of "things we can be sure about" is much shorter than we may have thought. The world presents us with impressions, and we have no way of getting at the world itself to discover whether or not the impressions are true.

This itself was a common story among early modern philosophers. The search for certainty did not lead to sure knowledge, as thinkers like Descartes hoped it would. Instead, it led to increasing skepticism about our ability to know anything for certain.

This may seem like a depressing conclusion, but it isn't one at which Christians should be too surprised. The "early modern project" was to ground certainty in human reason. If this project fails, it may be simply because human knowledge depends on something else for its certainty.

Discovering that we cannot trust in our reason alone, but, crucially, must trust that God has made our reason and our perceptions accurate, may be a substantial and necessary correction in our view both of ourselves and of our relationship to God—a correction we can thank Locke for revealing.

## CHAPTER NINETEEN

# JOHN LOCKE, PART TWO

## Enlightenment (1632–1704)

**A**merica exists because of John Locke. There are other reasons, of course, but this republic owes the larger part of the ideas behind it to the English philosopher. The Founders depended so much on his ideas and philosophic vocabulary that it's almost more fascinating to note where they deviated from him than where they agreed. When the Declaration says that "we hold these truths to be self-evident" and that humans have a right to "life, liberty, and pursuit of happiness," they were channeling Locke.

Understanding Locke goes a long way toward answering the popular question, "Is America a Christian nation?"

If by that one means that the United States is Christendom, then the answer is "Of course not." Christendom is vastly larger than any particular nation or people. If it means that only Christians (in some strong sense of the term) formed this nation, then the answer is "Don't be ridiculous." Even the Byzantine Empire, as overtly Christian a state as has ever existed, could not claim this. The U.S. Founders created a nation that assumed a believing majority but did not demand that individuals be believers.

In two ways, Christianity is essential to understanding America. For one, the vast majority of the population has always been Christian, so in that sense it has always been a nation of Christians.

Also, the founding philosopher of America, John Locke, was very much a Christian. Locke's language is scripturally permeated, his arguments assume the truth of the gospel, and he supported Christian ethics. He engaged in Christian apologetics, was intent on showing his Anglican bishop his ideas were orthodox, and quoted the Bible continuously.

Locke depended on biblical history to make his case. In his political work, he simply assumed the population of England to be Christian, and he could defend the right to revolution based on that idea.

The *Second Treatise of Government* implies to the not-even-careful reader that there must be a *First Treatise*. That earlier work by Locke was a devastating critique of the argument for an absolute monarch, based mostly on biblical history. Locke was careful to show that nothing in the Bible, or of Christianity, denies humans the right to revolt against a bad government; nothing gives the king absolute power.

Locke finished off serious defense of "divine right" in the English-speaking world, showing not only that philosophy can make progress but also that average citizens can notice that progress.

All the same, that he meant to build a Christian political philosophy does not mean he succeeded. Read Locke and ask yourself if he did. Or did he inadvertently help to bring on the toxic secularism of our own time?

## ⊂⊂ FROM ⊃⊃

# *Two Treatises on Government: Second Treatise*

### Chapter II:

### Of the State of Nature

*§. 4.*

To understand political power right, and derive it from its original, we must consider, what state all men are naturally in, and that is, a state of perfect freedom to order their actions, and dispose of their possessions and persons, as they think fit, within the bounds of the law of nature, without asking leave, or depending upon the will of any other man.

A state also of equality, wherein all the power and jurisdiction is reciprocal, no one having more than another; there being nothing more evident, than that creatures of the same species and rank, promiscuously born to all the same advantages of nature, and the use of the same faculties, should also be equal one amongst another without subordination or subjection, unless the lord and master of them all should, by any manifest declaration of his will, set one above another, and confer on him, by an evident and clear appointment, an undoubted right to dominion and sovereignty.

*§. 5.*

This equality of men by nature, the judicious Hooker looks upon as so evident in itself, and beyond all question, that he makes it the foundation of that obligation to mutual love amongst men, on which he builds the duties they owe one another, and from whence he derives the great maxims of justice and charity. His words are,

"The like natural inducement hath brought men to know that it is no less their duty, to love others than themselves; for seeing those things which are equal, must needs all have one measure; if I cannot but wish to receive good, even as much at every man's hands, as any man can wish unto his own soul, how should I look to have any part of my desire herein satisfied, unless myself be careful to satisfy the like desire, which is undoubtedly in other men, being of one and the same nature? To have any thing offered them repugnant to this desire, must needs in all respects grieve them as much as me; so that if I do harm, I must look to suffer, there being no reason that others should shew greater measure of love to me, than they have by me shewed unto them: my desire therefore to be loved of my equals in nature, as much as possible may be, imposeth upon me a natural duty of bearing to them-ward fully the like affection; from which relation of equality between ourselves and them that are as ourselves, what several rules and canons natural reason hath drawn, for direction of life, no man is ignorant." . . .

### §. 6.

But though this be a state of liberty, yet it is not a state of licence: though man in that state have an uncontroulable liberty to dispose of his person or possessions, yet he has not liberty to destroy himself, or so much as any creature in his possession, but where some nobler use than its bare preservation calls for it. The state of nature has a law of nature to govern it, which obliges every one: and reason, which is that law, teaches all mankind, who will but consult it, that being all equal and independent, no one ought to harm another in his life, health, liberty, or possessions: for men being all the workmanship of one omnipotent, and infinitely wise maker; all the servants of one sovereign master, sent into the world by his order, and about his business; they are his property, whose workmanship they are, made to last during his, not one another's pleasure: and being furnished with like faculties, sharing all in one community of nature, there cannot be supposed any such subordination among us, that may authorize us to destroy one another, as if we were made for one another's uses, as the inferior ranks of creatures are for our's. Every one, as he is bound to preserve himself, and not to quit his station willfully, so by the like reason, when his own preservation comes not in competition, ought he, as much as he can, to preserve the rest of mankind, and may not, unless it be to do justice on an offender, take away, or impair the life, or what tends to the preservation of the life, the liberty, health, limb, or goods of another.

## §. 7.

And that all men may be restrained from invading others rights, and from doing hurt to one another, and the law of nature be observed, which willeth the peace and preservation of all mankind, the execution of the law of nature is, in that state, put into every man's hands, whereby every one has a right to punish the transgressors of that law to such a degree, as may hinder its violation: for the law of nature would, as all other laws that concern men in this world, be in vain, if there were no body that in the state of nature had a power to execute that law, and thereby preserve the innocent and restrain offenders. And if any one in the state of nature may punish another for any evil he has done, every one may do so: for in that state of perfect equality, where naturally there is no superiority or jurisdiction of one over another, what any may do in prosecution of that law, every one must needs have a right to do.

## §. 8.

And thus, in the state of nature, one man comes by a power over another; but yet no absolute or arbitrary power, to use a criminal, when he has got him in his hands, according to the passionate heats, or boundless extravagancy of his own will; but only to retribute to him, so far as calm reason and conscience dictate, what is proportionate to his transgression, which is so much as may serve for reparation and restraint: for these two are the only reasons, why one man may lawfully do harm to another, which is that we call punishment. In transgressing the law of nature, the offender declares himself to live by another rule than that of reason and common equity, which is that measure God has set to the actions of men, for their mutual security; and so he becomes dangerous to mankind, the tye, which is to secure them from injury and violence, being slighted and broken by him. Which being a trespass against the whole species, and the peace and safety of it, provided for by the law of nature, every man upon this score, by the right he hath to preserve mankind in general, may restrain, or where it is necessary, destroy things noxious to them, and so may bring such evil on any one, who hath transgressed that law, as may make him repent the doing of it, and thereby deter him, and by his example others, from doing the like mischief. And in this case, and upon this ground, *every man hath a right to punish the offender, and be executioner of the law of nature.*

### §. 9.

I doubt not but this will seem a very strange doctrine to some men: but before they condemn it, I desire them to resolve me, by what right any prince or state can put to death, or punish an alien, for any crime he commits in their country. It is certain their laws, by virtue of any sanction they receive from the promulgated will of the legislative, reach not a stranger: they speak not to him, nor, if they did, is he bound to hearken to them. The legislative authority, by which they are in force over the subjects of that commonwealth, hath no power over him. Those who have the supreme power of making laws in England, France or Holland, are to an Indian, but like the rest of the world, men without authority: and therefore, if by the law of nature every man hath not a power to punish offences against it, as he soberly judges the case to require, I see not how the magistrates of any community can punish an alien of another country; since, in reference to him, they can have no more power than what every man naturally may have over another.

### §. 10.

Besides the crime which consists in violating the law, and varying from the right rule of reason, whereby a man so far becomes degenerate, and declares himself to quit the principles of human nature, and to be a noxious creature, there is commonly injury done to some person or other, and some other man receives damage by his transgression: in which case he who hath received any damage, has, besides the right of punishment common to him with other men, a particular right to seek reparation from him that has done it: and any other person, who finds it just, may also join with him that is injured, and assist him in recovering from the offender so much as may make satisfaction for the harm he has suffered.

. . .

## Chapter VIII:

## Of the Beginning of Political Societies

*§. 95.*

Men being, as has been said, by nature, all free, equal, and independent, no one can be put out of this estate, and subjected to the political power of another, without his own consent. The only way whereby any one divests himself of his natural liberty, and puts on the bonds of civil society, is by agreeing with other men to join and unite into a community, for their comfortable, safe, and peaceable living one amongst another, in a secure enjoyment of their properties, and a greater security against any, that are not of it. This any number of men may do, because it injures not the freedom of the rest; they are left as they were in the liberty of the state of nature. When any number of men have so consented to make one community or government, they are thereby presently incorporated, and make one body politic, wherein the majority have a right to act and conclude the rest.

*§. 96.*

For when any number of men have, by the consent of every individual, made a community, they have thereby made that community one body, with a power to act as one body, which is only by the will and determination of the majority. For that which acts any community, being only the consent of the individuals of it, and it being necessary to that which is one body to move one way; it is necessary the body should move that way whither the greater force carries it, which is the consent of the majority: or else it is impossible it should act or continue one body, one community, which the consent of every individual that united into it, agreed that it should; and so every one is bound by that consent to be concluded by the majority. And therefore we see, that in assemblies, impowered to act by positive laws, where no number is set by that positive law which impowers them, the act of the majority passes for the act of the whole, and of course determines, as having, by the law of nature and reason, the power of the whole.

### *§. 97.*

And thus every man, by consenting with others to make one body politic under one government, puts himself under an obligation, to every one of that society, to submit to the determination of the majority, and to be concluded by it; or else this original compact, whereby he with others incorporates into one society, would signify nothing, and be no compact, if he be left free, and under no other ties than he was in before in the state of nature. For what appearance would there be of any compact? What new engagement if he were no farther tied by any decrees of the society, than he himself thought fit, and did actually consent to? This would be still as great a liberty, as he himself had before his compact, or any one else in the state of nature hath, who may submit himself, and consent to any acts of it if he thinks fit.

### *§. 98.*

For if the consent of the majority shall not, in reason, be received as the act of the whole, and conclude every individual; nothing but the consent of every individual can make any thing to be the act of the whole: but such a consent is next to impossible ever to be had, if we consider the infirmities of health, and avocations of business, which in a number, though much less than that of a commonwealth, will necessarily keep many away from the public assembly. To which if we add the variety of opinions, and contrariety of interests, which unavoidably happen in all collections of men, the coming into society upon such terms would be only like Cato's coming into the theatre, only to go out again. Such a constitution as this would make the mighty Leviathan of a shorter duration, than the feeblest creatures, and not let it outlast the day it was born in: which cannot be supposed, till we can think, that rational creatures should desire and constitute societies only to be dissolved: for where the majority cannot conclude the rest, there they cannot act as one body, and consequently will be immediately dissolved again.

### *§. 99.*

Whosoever therefore out of a state of nature unite into a community, must be understood to give up all the power, necessary to the ends for which they unite into society, to the majority of the community, unless they expressly agreed in any number greater than the majority. And this is done by barely agreeing to unite into one political society, which is all the compact that is, or needs be, between the individuals, that enter into, or make up a commonwealth. And thus that, which begins and actually constitutes any political society, is nothing but the consent of any number of freemen capable of a majority to unite and incorporate into such a society. And this is that, and that only, which did, or could give beginning to any lawful government in the world.

. . .

### *§. 104.*

But to conclude, reason being plain on our side, that men are naturally free, and the examples of history shewing, that the governments of the world, that were begun in peace, had their beginning laid on that foundation, and were made by the consent of the people; there can be little room for doubt, either where the right is, or what has been the opinion, or practice of mankind, about the first erecting of governments.

. . .

### *§. 112.*

Thus we may see how probable it is, that people that were naturally free, and by their own consent either submitted to the government of their father, or united together out of different families to make a government, should generally put the rule into one man's hands, and chuse to be under the conduct of a single person, without so much as by express conditions limiting or regulating his power, which they thought safe enough in his honesty and prudence; though they never dreamed of monarchy being Jure Divino, which we never heard of among mankind, till it was revealed to us by the divinity of this last age; nor ever allowed paternal power to have a right to dominion, or to be the foundation of all government. And thus much may suffice to shew, that as far as we have any light from history, we have reason to conclude, that all peaceful beginnings of government have been laid in the consent of the people. I say peaceful, because I shall have occasion in another place to speak of conquest, which some esteem a way of beginning of governments.

The other objection I find urged against the beginning of polities, in the way I have mentioned, is this, viz.

### §. 113.

That all men being born under government, some or other, it is impossible any of them should ever be free, and at liberty to unite together, and begin a new one, or ever be able to erect a lawful government.

If this argument be good, I ask, how came so many lawful monarchies into the world? For if any body, upon this supposition, can shew me any one man in any age of the world free to begin a lawful monarchy, I will be bound to shew him ten other freemen at liberty, at the same time to unite and begin a new government under a regal, or any other form; it being demonstration, that if any one, born under the dominion of another, may be so free as to have a right to command others in a new and distinct empire, every one that is born under the dominion of another may be so free too, and may become a ruler, or subject, of a distinct separate government. And so by this their own principle, either all men, however born, are free, or else there is but one lawful prince, one lawful government in the world. And then they have nothing to do, but barely to shew us which that is; which when they have done, I doubt not but all mankind will easily agree to pay obedience to him.

### §. 114.

Though it be a sufficient answer to their objection, to shew that it involves them in the same difficulties that it doth those they use it against; yet I shall endeavour to discover the weakness of this argument a little farther.

All men, say they, are born under government, and therefore they cannot be at liberty to begin a new one. Every one is born a subject to his father, or his prince, and is therefore under the perpetual tie of subjection and allegiance. It is plain mankind never owned nor considered any such natural subjection that they were born in, to one or to the other that tied them, without their own consents, to a subjection to them and their heirs.

### §. 115.

For there are no examples so frequent in history, both sacred and profane, as those of men withdrawing themselves, and their obedience, from the jurisdiction they were born under, and the family or community they were bred up in, and setting up new governments in other places; from whence sprang all that number of petty commonwealths in the beginning of ages, and which always multiplied, as long as there was room enough, till the stronger, or more fortunate, swallowed the weaker; and those great ones again breaking to pieces, dissolved into lesser dominions. All which are so many testimonies against paternal sovereignty, and plainly prove, that it was not the natural right of the father descending to his heirs, that made governments in the beginning, since it was impossible, upon that ground, there should have been so many little kingdoms; all must have been but only one universal monarchy, if men had not been at liberty to separate themselves from their families, and the government, be it what it will, that was set up in it, and go and make distinct commonwealths and other governments, as they thought fit.

### §. 116.

This has been the practice of the world from its first beginning to this day; nor is it now any more hindrance to the freedom of mankind, that they are born under constituted and ancient polities, that have established laws, and set forms of government, than if they were born in the woods, amongst the unconfined inhabitants, that run loose in them: for those, who would persuade us, that by being born under any government, we are naturally subjects to it, and have no more any title or pretence to the freedom of the state of nature, have no other reason (bating that of paternal power, which we have already answered) to produce for it, but only, because our fathers or progenitors passed away their natural liberty, and thereby bound up themselves and their posterity to a perpetual subjection to the government, which they themselves submitted to. It is true, that whatever engagements or promises any one has made for himself, he is under the obligation of them, but cannot, by any compact whatsoever, bind his children or posterity: for his son, when a man, being altogether as free as the father, any act of the father can no more give away the liberty of the son, than it can of any body else: he may indeed annex such conditions to the land, he enjoyed as a subject of any commonwealth, as may oblige his son to be of that community, if he will enjoy those possessions which were his father's; because that estate being his father's property, he may dispose, or settle it, as he pleases.

### §. 117.

And this has generally given the occasion to mistake in this matter; because commonwealths not permitting any part of their dominions to be dismembered, nor to be enjoyed by any but those of their community, the son cannot ordinarily enjoy the possessions of his father, but under the same terms his father did, by becoming a member of the society; whereby he puts himself presently under the government he finds there established, as much as any other subject of that commonwealth. And thus the consent of freemen, born under government, which only makes them members of it, being given separately in their turns, as each comes to be of age, and not in a multitude together; people take no notice of it, and thinking it not done at all, or not necessary, conclude they are naturally subjects as they are men.

### §. 118.

But, it is plain, governments themselves understand it otherwise; they claim no power over the son, because of that they had over the father; nor look on children as being their subjects, by their fathers being so. If a subject of England have a child, by an English woman in France, whose subject is he? Not the king of England's; for he must have leave to be admitted to the privileges of it: nor the king of France's; for how then has his father a liberty to bring him away, and breed him as he pleases? And who ever was judged as a traytor or deserter, if he left, or warred against a country, for being barely born in it of parents that were aliens there? It is plain then, by the practice of governments themselves, as well as by

438

the law of right reason, that a child is born a subject of no country or government. He is under his father's tuition and authority, till he comes to age of discretion; and then he is a freeman, at liberty what government he will put himself under, what body politic he will unite himself to: for if an Englishman's son, born in France, be at liberty, and may do so, it is evident there is no tie upon him by his father's being a subject of this kingdom; nor is he bound up by any compact of his ancestors. And why then hath not his son, by the same reason, the same liberty, though he be born any where else? Since the power that a father hath naturally over his children, is the same, where-ever they be born, and the ties of natural obligations, are not bounded by the positive limits of kingdoms and commonwealths.

### *§. 119.*

Every man being, as has been shewed, naturally free, and nothing being able to put him into subjection to any earthly power, but only his own consent; it is to be considered, what shall be understood to be a sufficient declaration of a man's consent, to make him subject to the laws of any government. There is a common distinction of an express and a tacit consent, which will concern our present case. No body doubts but an express consent, of any man entering into any society, makes him a perfect member of that society, a subject of that government. The difficulty is, what ought to be looked upon as a tacit consent, and how far it binds, i.e. how far any one shall be looked on to have consented, and thereby submitted to any government, where he has made no expressions of it at all. And to this I say, that every man, that hath any possessions, or enjoyment, of any part of the dominions of any government, doth thereby give his tacit consent, and is as far forth obliged to obedience to the laws of that government, during such enjoyment, as any one under it; whether this his possession be of land, to him and his heirs for ever, or a lodging only for a week; or whether it be barely travelling freely on the highway; and in effect, it reaches as far as the very being of any one within the territories of that government.

. . .

### §. 122.

But submitting to the laws of any country, living quietly, and enjoying privileges and protection under them, makes not a man a member of that society: this is only a local protection and homage due to and from all those, who, not being in a state of war, come within the territories belonging to any government, to all parts whereof the force of its laws extends. But this no more makes a man a member of that society, a perpetual subject of that commonwealth, than it would make a man a subject to another, in whose family he found it convenient to abide for some time; though, whilst he continued in it, he were obliged to comply with the laws, and submit to the government he found there. And thus we see, that foreigners, by living all their lives under another government, and enjoying the privileges and protection of it, though they are bound, even in conscience, to submit to its administration, as far forth as any denison; yet do not thereby come to be subjects or members of that commonwealth. Nothing can make any man so, but his actually entering into it by positive engagement, and express promise and compact. This is that, which I think, concerning the beginning of political societies, and that consent which makes any one a member of any commonwealth.

. . .

## Chapter XIV:

### Prerogative

### §. 159.

Where the legislative and executive power are in distinct hands, (as they are in all moderated monarchies, and well-framed governments) there the good of the society requires, that several things should be left to the discretion of him that has the executive power: for the legislators not being able to foresee, and provide by laws, for all that may be useful to the community, the executor of the laws, having the power in his hands, has by the common law of nature a right to make use of it for the good of the society, in many cases, where the municipal law has given no direction, till the legislative can conveniently be assembled to provide for it. Many things there are, which the law can by no means provide for; and those must necessarily be left to the discretion of him that has the executive power in his hands, to be ordered by him as the public good and advantage shall require: nay, it is fit that the laws themselves should in some cases give way to the executive power, or rather to this fundamental law of nature and government, viz. That as much as may be, all the members of the society are to be preserved: for since many accidents may happen, wherein a strict and rigid observation of the laws may do harm; (as not to pull down an innocent man's house to stop the fire, when the next to it is burning) and a man may come sometimes within the reach of the law, which makes no distinction of persons, by an action that may deserve reward and pardon; 'tis fit the ruler should have a power, in many cases, to mitigate the severity of the law, and pardon some offenders: for the end of government being the preservation of all, as much as may be, even the guilty are to be spared, where it can prove no prejudice to the innocent.

### *§. 160.*

This power to act according to discretion, for the public good, without the prescription of the law, and sometimes even against it, is that which is called prerogative: for since in some governments the lawmaking power is not always in being, and is usually too numerous, and so too slow, for the dispatch requisite to execution; and because also it is impossible to foresee, and so by laws to provide for, all accidents and necessities that may concern the public, or to make such laws as will do no harm, if they are executed with an inflexible rigour, on all occasions, and upon all persons that may come in their way; therefore there is a latitude left to the executive power, to do many things of choice which the laws do not prescribe.

### *§. 161.*

This power, whilst employed for the benefit of the community, and suitably to the trust and ends of the government, is undoubted prerogative, and never is questioned: for the people are very seldom or never scrupulous or nice in the point; they are far from examining prerogative, whilst it is in any tolerable degree employed for the use it was meant, that is, for the good of the people, and not manifestly against it: but if there comes to be a question between the executive power and the people, about a thing claimed as a prerogative; the tendency of the exercise of such prerogative to the good or hurt of the people, will easily decide that question.

### §. 162.

It is easy to conceive, that in the infancy of governments, when commonwealths differed little from families in number of people, they differed from them too but little in number of laws: and the governors, being as the fathers of them, watching over them for their good, the government was almost all prerogative. A few established laws served the turn, and the discretion and care of the ruler supplied the rest. But when mistake or flattery prevailed with weak princes to make use of this power for private ends of their own, and not for the public good, the people were fain by express laws to get prerogative determined in those points wherein they found disadvantage from it: and thus declared limitations of prerogative were by the people found necessary in cases which they and their ancestors had left, in the utmost latitude, to the wisdom of those princes who made no other but a right use of it, that is, for the good of their people.

### §. 163.

And therefore they have a very wrong notion of government, who say, that the people have incroached upon the prerogative, when they have got any part of it to be defined by positive laws: for in so doing they have not pulled from the prince any thing that of right belonged to him, but only declared, that that power which they indefinitely left in his or his ancestors hands, to be exercised for their good, was not a thing which they intended him when he used it otherwise: for the end of government being the good of the community, whatsoever alterations are made in it, tending to that end, cannot be an incroachment upon any body, since no body in government can have a right tending to any other end: and those only are incroachments which prejudice or hinder the public good. Those who say otherwise, speak as if the prince had a distinct and separate interest from the good of the community, and was not made for it; the root and source from which spring almost all those evils and disorders which happen in

kingly governments. And indeed, if that be so, the people under his government are not a society of rational creatures, entered into a community
for their mutual good; they are not such as have set rulers over themselves,
to guard, and promote that good; but are to be looked on as an herd of
inferior creatures under the dominion of a master, who keeps them and
works them for his own pleasure or profit. If men were so void of reason,
and brutish, as to enter into society upon such terms, prerogative might
indeed be, what some men would have it, an arbitrary power to do things
hurtful to the people.

### §. 164.

But since a rational creature cannot be supposed, when free, to put
himself into subjection to another, for his own harm; (though, where he
finds a good and wise ruler, he may not perhaps think it either necessary
or useful to set precise bounds to his power in all things) prerogative can
be nothing but the people's permitting their rulers to do several things, of
their own free choice, where the law was silent, and sometimes too against
the direct letter of the law, for the public good; and their acquiescing in it
when so done: for as a good prince, who is mindful of the trust put into
his hands, and careful of the good of his people, cannot have too much
prerogative, that is, power to do good; so a weak and ill prince, who would
claim that power which his predecessors exercised without the direction
of the law, as a prerogative belonging to him by right of his office, which
he may exercise at his pleasure, to make or promote an interest distinct
from that of the public, gives the people an occasion to claim their right,
and limit that power, which, whilst it was exercised for their good, they
were content should be tacitly allowed.

### §. 165.

And therefore he that will look into the history of England, will
find, that prerogative was always largest in the hands of our wisest and
best princes; because the people, observing the whole tendency of their
actions to be the public good, contested not what was done without law
to that end: or, if any human frailty or mistake (for princes are but men,
made as others) appeared in some small declinations from that end; yet

'twas visible, the main of their conduct tended to nothing but the care of the public. The people therefore, finding reason to be satisfied with these princes, whenever they acted without, or contrary to the letter of the law, acquiesced in what they did, and, without the least complaint, let them inlarge their prerogative as they pleased, judging rightly, that they did nothing herein to the prejudice of their laws, since they acted conformable to the foundation and end of all laws, the public good.

### §. 166.

Such god-like princes indeed had some title to arbitrary power by that argument, that would prove absolute monarchy the best government, as that which God himself governs the universe by; because such kings partake of his wisdom and goodness. Upon this is founded that saying, That the reigns of good princes have been always most dangerous to the liberties of their people: for when their successors, managing the government with different thoughts, would draw the actions of those good rulers into precedent, and make them the standard of their prerogative, as if what had been done only for the good of the people was a right in them to do, for the harm of the people, if they so pleased; it has often occasioned contest, and sometimes public disorders, before the people could recover their original right, and get that to be declared not to be prerogative, which truly was never so; since it is impossible that any body in the society should ever have a right to do the people harm; though it be very possible, and reasonable, that the people should not go about to set any bounds to the prerogative of those kings, or rulers, who themselves transgressed not the bounds of the public good: for prerogative is nothing but the power of doing public good without a rule.

### §. 167.

The power of calling parliaments in England, as to precise time, place, and duration, is certainly a prerogative of the king, but still with this trust, that it shall be made use of for the good of the nation, as the exigencies of the times, and variety of occasions, shall require: for it being impossible to foresee which should always be the fittest place for them to assemble in, and what the best season; the choice of these was left with the executive power, as might be most subservient to the public good, and best suit the ends of parliaments.

### *§. 168.*

The old question will be asked in this matter of prerogative, But who shall be judge when this power is made a right use of? I answer: between an executive power in being, with such a prerogative, and a legislative that depends upon his will for their convening, there can be no judge on earth; as there can be none between the legislative and the people, should either the executive, or the legislative, when they have got the power in their hands, design, or go about to enslave or destroy them. The people have no other remedy in this, as in all other cases where they have no judge on earth, but to appeal to heaven: for the rulers, in such attempts, exercising a power the people never put into their hands, (who can never be supposed to consent that any body should rule over them for their harm) do that which they have not a right to do. And where the body of the people, or any single man, is deprived of their right, or is under the exercise of a power without right, and have no appeal on earth, then they have a liberty to appeal to heaven, whenever they judge the cause of sufficient moment. And therefore, though the people cannot be judge, so as to have, by the constitution of that society, any superior power, to determine and give effective sentence in the case; yet they have, by a law antecedent and paramount to all positive laws of men, reserved that ultimate determination to themselves which belongs to all mankind, where there lies no appeal on earth, viz. to judge, whether they have just cause to make their appeal to heaven. And this judgment they cannot part with, it being out of a man's power so to submit himself to another, as to give him a liberty to destroy him; God and nature never allowing a man so to abandon himself, as to neglect his own preservation: and since he cannot take away his own life, neither can he give another power to take it. Nor let any one think, this lays a perpetual foundation for disorder; for this operates not, till the inconveniency is so great, that the majority feel it, and are weary of it, and find a necessity to have it amended. But this the executive power, or wise princes, never need come in the danger of: and it is the thing, of all others, they have most need to avoid, as of all others the most perilous.

# NOTIONS OF THE PUBLIC GOOD

## THE POLITICAL POINT IN LOCKE

## Jamie Campbell

In modern American politics, everything is open for debate. The effi-cacy of a candidate, the impact of a tax measure, even the legitimacy of government itself is up for discussion. While valued, political debate often is taken for granted, an assumed privilege born out from the fundamental characteristics of a democratic republican government. Americans talk about government because they believe citizens play a fundamental role in making sure that the government fulfills its function.

The notion that humanity is capable of forming, reforming, and cri-tiquing political society is an idea that gained remarkable momentum in Western political thought during the Enlightenment. In particular, the works of John Locke, influential in the shaping of American political thought, sought to demonstrate that legitimate government comes from the people and operates for the public good.

Locke's political works begin, not with the rights man has, but with the fact that he was created. Thus, in the *Second Treatise*, he makes various assertions about man's political nature and the impact this nature has on the formation of government. Man's common creation informs man's essential and political nature. Locke's writings demonstrate that, at its best, political theorizing is an engagement with man as he is and not as he ought to be; a task of construction, not merely critique.

Published anonymously during his life, Locke's political writings largely grew out of his own observations of the unrest that plagued England dur-ing his lifetime.

[H]is life spanned one of the most tumultuous periods of English history. He was ten years old when England became divided by civil war and still at Westminster School when Charles I was executed nearby in 1649. He lived through the subsequent interregnum when various governments of the Commonwealth and Cromwell's Protectorate were in power, the subsequent Restoration of Charles II in 1660, and the radicalization of English politics in which he was sufficiently implicated so that he was forced into exile for most of the 1680s—returning only after the Glorious Revolution of 1688. (Introduction to *Two Treatises of Government and A Letter Concerning Toleration: John Locke,* ed. Ian Shapiro [New Haven/London: Yale University Press, 2003], x.)

———

As an empiricist, Locke valued the role of observation in the development of any fundamental idea. What he observed was that existing notions of government were insufficient to maintain peace and prosperity.

———

The volatility and instability of government during Locke's age led him, and many others, to generate commentary not only on how government should run but also on the essential elements of the beginning of political society in general. Many of these theorists turned to the Bible in support of their conclusions.

Locke respected the Scriptures, but he soundly rejected the arguments of political absolutism and divine right that many contemporaries argued were found there.

In his *First Treatise*, Locke discussed the significance of God having created Adam, and the type of political power and responsibilities this creation incurred. For Locke, man necessarily exists in a state of self and other—that is, all men are created by God, and no man exists without other men.

This common creation, then, results in equality of freedom. No man can claim any higher source for his existence than God; no man can claim any legitimate authority over any other man because all men are created. Similarly, common creation creates the "obligation to mutual love amongst men" (*Second Treatise,* §5). The rights or powers man has are an outgrowth of this reality.

According to Locke, man in the state of nature, prior to the formation of political society, has two basic powers (or rights): the power to preserve his own life and the life of others, and the power to punish someone who has caused harm. Within political society, man yields these powers, in varying extents, to the political community. Through express consent, man yields the power that is necessary for the formation of government.

Locke claimed that the purpose of all this power yielding is the public good, or "the good of every particular member of that society, as far as by common rules it can be provided for" (*First Treatise*, § 92). The concept of public good woven throughout most of the *Second Treatise* must be read in light of Locke's primary notions of man, of reason, and of freedom; all the foundational elements that contribute to his political theory are interconnected.

By establishing "public good" as the object of political society, Locke also placed it as a limit:

> [T]he power of society . . . can never be supposed to extend farther than the common good . . . to be directed to no other end but the peace, safety and public good of the people. (*Second Treatise*, §131)

Even Locke's axiom of majority rule in a political society stems from a desire to properly utilize the power that's been transferred from the individual to the society. It's not that the majority gets to decide what's best, based on their own interests against any minority political interests; rather, the majority is bound by the very responsibility of the public good.

In so far as *self* and *other* are interdependent for Locke, even in a state of nature, it's a rational conclusion that government's primary responsibilities, once formed, are aimed at maintaining and providing for the preservation and flourishing of the whole, not just the individual. For John Locke, the public good *is* the point of political society.

## CHAPTER TWENTY

# ISAAC NEWTON

## Enlightenment (1642–1727)

Plato left behind Platonism, Aristotle left Aristotelianism, and Thomas Aquinas left Thomism. Isaac Newton did not leave behind "Newtonism," and that marks a major break in the Great Discussion. It was not that Newton was ignored, reviled, or forced to drink hemlock. To the contrary, all his contemporaries knew he was a world-class genius; even so, he did not leave an all-embracing school of thought to answer all of life's questions.

The difference was that human thought had grown too complex for even an Isaac Newton to master most of it. He worked within the philosophical assumptions he inherited from the Middle Ages, the Renaissance, and the Reformation. Newton transformed science, and his work had serious philosophical and theological implications, but he himself never worked those out well.

Science, especially physics, made slow progress up to Newton, but he seemed to equal all of those centuries of gains by himself. For some time, there appeared little left to do scientifically but examine the implications of his ideas and work out the details. Newton confirmed that we live in a cosmos, an ordered structure. If anything, the structure seemed too airtight for free will or chance.

Poets like William Blake feared Newton had discovered a clockwork universe with no place for God or romance, though Newton himself remained a theist. Reformed Christians in particular had viewed science and the Scientific Revolution as an ally, but beginning with Newtonian physics the doubts began to grow.

While physics made huge strides through Newton's work, metaphysics seemed stuck in the past. Science provided humanity tangible gains that made life better while religious wars tore apart much of Europe. As a result, physics seemed more important to human progress than metaphysics.

In the popular imagination, Newton became a forerunner to an age when science might solve all our problems. His limitations were forgotten, but too often so were his actual writings. A great antidote to "scientism," the belief that science can solve everything, is to read the works of great scientists. Their genius in describing what *is* has been of much value; *however,* they have nothing to say about what *ought* to be.

And yet a better description of "is" *does* suggest possibilities and limits to what could be. Newton was no spectacular philosopher or theologian, but philosophers and theologians could not ignore his discoveries.

Isaac Newton did not speak the modern world into being, as some of his peers suspected, but he contributed much of material value and did almost no harm. Few great thinkers could make the same claim. Read Newton and look for both the genius and the limitations of the man.

CꙄ FROM ꙄꙄ

# Mathematical Principles
# of Natural Philosophy

## THE PRINCIPIA

## Author's Preface

Since the ancients (as we are told by *Pappus*), made great account of the science of mechanics in the investigation of natural things; and the moderns, laying aside substantial forms and occult qualities, have endeavoured to subject the phænomena of nature to the laws of mathematics, I have in this treatise cultivated mathematics so far as it regards philosophy. The ancients considered mechanics in a twofold respect; as rational, which proceeds accurately by demonstration: and practical. To practical mechanics all the manual arts belong, from which mechanics took its name. But as artificers do not work with perfect accuracy, it comes to pass that mechanics is so distinguished from geometry, that what is perfectly accurate is called geometrical, what is less so, is called mechanical. But the errors are not in the art, but in the artificers. He that works with less accuracy is an imperfect mechanic; and if any could work with perfect accuracy, he would be the most perfect mechanic of all; for the description of right lines and circles, upon which geometry is founded, belongs to mechanics. Geometry does not teach us to draw these lines, but requires them to be drawn; for it requires that the learner should first be taught to describe these accurately, before he enters upon geometry; then it shows how by these operations problems may be solved. To describe right lines and circles are problems, but not geometrical problems. The solution of these problems is required from mechanics; and by geometry the use of them, when so solved, is shown; and it is the glory of geometry that from those few principles, brought from without, it is able to produce so many things.

Therefore geometry is founded in mechanical practice, and is nothing but that part of universal mechanics which accurately proposes and demonstrates the art of measuring. But since the manual arts are chiefly conversant in the moving of bodies, it comes to pass that geometry is commonly referred to their magnitudes, and mechanics to their motion. In this sense rational mechanics will be the science of motions resulting from any forces whatsoever, and of the forces required to produce any motions, accurately proposed and demonstrated. This part of mechanics was cultivated by the ancients in the five powers which relate to manual arts, who considered gravity (it not being a manual power), no otherwise than as it moved weights by those powers. Our design not respecting arts, but philosophy, and our subject not manual but natural powers, we consider chiefly those things which relate to gravity, levity, elastic force, the resistance of fluids, and the like forces, whether attractive or impulsive; and therefore we offer this work as the mathematical principles of philosophy; for all the difficulty of philosophy seems to consist in this—from the phænomena of motions to investigate the forces of nature, and then from these forces to demonstrate the other phænomena; and to this end the general propositions in the first and second book are directed.

In the third book we give an example of this in the explication of the System of the World; for by the propositions mathematically demonstrated in the former books, we in the third derive from the celestial phenomena the forces of gravity with which bodies tend to the sun and the several planets. Then from these forces, by other propositions which are also mathematical, we deduce the motions of the planets, the comets, the moon, and the sea. I wish we could derive the rest of the phænomena of nature by the same kind of reasoning from mechanical principles; for I am induced by many reasons to suspect that they may all depend upon certain forces by which the particles of bodies, by some causes hitherto unknown, are either mutually impelled towards each other, and cohere in regular figures, or are repelled and recede from each other; which forces being unknown, philosophers have hitherto attempted the search of nature in vain; but I hope the principles here laid down will afford some light either to this or some truer method of philosophy.

In the publication of this work the most acute and universally learned Mr. Edmund Halley not only assisted me with his pains in correcting the press and taking care of the schemes, but it was to his solicitations that its becoming public is owing; for when he had obtained of me my demonstrations of the figure of the celestial orbits, he continually pressed me to communicate the same to the *Royal Society*, who afterwards, by their kind encouragement and entreaties, engaged me to think of publishing them. But after I had begun to consider the inequalities of the lunar motions, and had entered upon some other things relating to the laws and measures of gravity, and other forces: and the figures that would be described by bodies attracted according to given laws; and the motion of several bodies moving among themselves; the motion of bodies in resisting mediums; the forces, densities, and motions, of mediums; the orbits of the comets, and such like; deferred that publication till I had made a search into those matters, and could put forth the whole together.

What relates to the lunar motions (being imperfect), I have put all together in the corollaries of Prop. 66, to avoid being obliged to propose and distinctly demonstrate the several things there contained in a method more prolix than the subject deserved, and interrupt the series of the several propositions. Some things, found out after the rest, I chose to insert in places less suitable, rather than change the number of the propositions and the citations. I heartily beg that what I have here done may be read with candour; and that the defects in a subject so difficult be not so much reprehended as kindly supplied, and investigated by new endeavours of my readers.

ISAAC NEWTON
Cambridge, Trinity College, May 8, 1686

. . .

## SCHOLIUM

Hitherto I have laid down the definitions of such words as are less known, and explained the sense in which I would have them to be understood in the following discourse. I do not define time, space, place and motion, as being well known to all. Only I must observe, that the vulgar conceive those quantities under no other notions but from the relation they bear to sensible objects. And thence arise certain prejudices, for the removing of which, it will be convenient to distinguish them into absolute and relative, true and apparent, mathematical and common.

I. Absolute, true, and mathematical time, of itself, and from its own nature flows equably without regard to anything external, and by another name is called duration: relative, apparent, and common time, is some sensible and external (whether accurate or unequable) measure of duration by the means of motion, which is commonly used instead of true time; such as an hour, a day, a month, a year.

II. Absolute space, in its own nature, without regard to anything external, remains always similar and immovable. Relative space is some movable dimension or measure of the absolute spaces; which our senses determine by its position to bodies; and which is vulgarly taken for immovable space; such is the dimension of a subterraneous, an æreal, or celestial space, determined by its position in respect of the earth. Absolute and relative space, are the same in figure and magnitude; but they do not remain always numerically the same. For if the earth, for instance, moves, a space of our air, which relatively and in respect of the earth remains always the same, will at one time be one part of the absolute space into which the air passes; at another time it will be another part of the same, and so, absolutely understood, it will be perpetually mutable.

III. Place is a part of space which a body takes up, and is according to the space, either absolute or relative. I say, a part of space; not the situation, nor the external surface of the body. For the places of equal solids are always equal; but their superfices, by reason of their dissimilar figures, are often unequal. Positions properly have no quantity, nor are they so much the places themselves, as the properties of places. The motion of the whole is the same thing with the sum of the motions of the parts; that is, the translation of the whole, out of its place, is the same thing with the sum of the translations of the parts out of their places; and therefore the place of the whole is the same thing with the sum of the places of the parts, and for that reason, it is internal, and in the whole body.

IV. Absolute motion is the translation of a body from one absolute place into another; and relative motion, the translation from one relative place into another. Thus in a ship under sail, the relative place of a body is that part of the ship which the body possesses; or that part of its cavity which the body fills, and which therefore moves together with the ship: and relative rest is the continuance of the body in the same part of the ship, or of its cavity. But real, absolute rest, is the continuance of the body in the same part of that immovable space, in which the ship itself, its cavity, and all that it contains, is moved. Wherefore, if the earth is really at rest, the body, which relatively rests in the ship, will really and absolutely move with the same velocity which the ship has on the earth.

But if the earth also moves, the true and absolute motion of the body will arise, partly from the true motion of the earth, in immovable space; partly from the relative motion of the ship on the earth; and if the body moves also relatively in the ship; its true motion will arise, partly from the true motion of the earth, in immovable space, and partly from the relative motions as well of the ship on the earth, as of the body in the ship; and from these relative motions will arise the relative motion of the body on the earth. As if that part of the earth, where the ship is, was truly moved toward the east, with a velocity of 10010 parts; while the ship itself, with a fresh gale, and full sails, is carried towards the west, with a velocity expressed by 10 of those parts; but a sailor walks in the ship towards the east, with 1 part of the said velocity; then the sailor will be moved truly in immovable space towards the east, with a velocity of 10001 parts, and relatively on the earth towards the west, with a velocity of 9 of those parts.

Absolute time, in astronomy, is distinguished from relative, by the equation or correction of the vulgar time. For the natural days are truly unequal, though they are commonly considered as equal, and used for a measure of time; astronomers correct this inequality for their more accurate deducing of the celestial motions. It may be, that there is no such thing as an equable motion, whereby time may be accurately measured. All motions may be accelerated and retarded, but the true, or equable, progress of absolute time is liable to no change. The duration or perseverance of the existence of things remains the same, whether the motions are swift or slow, or none at all: and therefore it ought to be distinguished from what are only sensible measures thereof; and out of which we collect it, by means of the astronomical equation. The necessity of which equation, for determining the times of a phenomenon, is evinced as well from the experiments of the pendulum clock, as by eclipses of the satellites of *Jupiter*.

As the order of the parts of time is immutable, so also is the order of the parts of space. Suppose those parts to be moved out of their places, and they will be moved (if the expression may be allowed) out of themselves. For times and spaces are, as it were, the places as well of themselves as of all other things. All things are placed in time as to order of succession; and in space as to order of situation. It is from their essence or nature that they are places; and that the primary places of things should be moveable, is absurd. These are therefore the absolute places; and translations out of those places, are the only absolute motions.

But because the parts of space cannot be seen, or distinguished from one another by our senses, therefore in their stead we use sensible measures of them. For from the positions and distances of things from any body considered as immovable, we define all places; and then with respect to such places, we estimate all motions, considering bodies as transferred from some of those places into others. And so, instead of absolute places and motions, we use relative ones; and that without any inconvenience in common affairs; but in philosophical disquisitions, we ought to abstract from our senses, and consider things themselves, distinct from what are only sensible measures of them. For it may be that there is no body really at rest, to which the places and motions of others may be referred.

But we may distinguish rest and motion, absolute and relative, one from the other by their properties, causes and effects. It is a property of rest, that bodies really at rest do rest in respect to one another. And therefore as it is possible, that in the remote regions of the fixed stars, or perhaps far beyond them, there may be some body absolutely at rest; but impossible to know, from the position of bodies to one another in our regions whether any of these do keep the same position to that remote body; it follows that absolute rest cannot be determined from the position of bodies in our regions.

. . .

## AXIOMS, OR LAWS OF MOTION

### LAW I

*Every body perseveres in its state of rest, or of uniform motion in a right line, unless it is compelled to change that state by forces impressed thereon.*

Projectiles persevere in their motions, so far as they are not retarded by the resistance of the air, or impelled downwards by the force of gravity.

A top, whose parts by their cohesion are perpetually drawn aside from rectilinear motions, does not cease its rotation, otherwise than as it is retarded by the air. The greater bodies of the planets and comets, meeting with less resistance in more free spaces, preserve their motions both progressive and circular for a much longer time.

## LAW II

*The alteration of motion is ever proportional to the motive force impressed; and is made in the direction of the right line in which that force is impressed.*

If any force generates a motion, a double force will generate double the motion, a triple force triple the motion, whether that force be impressed altogether and at once, or gradually and successively. And this motion (being always directed the same way with the generating force), if the body moved before, is added to or subducted from the former motion, according as they directly conspire with or are directly contrary to each other; or obliquely joined, when they are oblique, so as to produce a new motion compounded from the determination of both.

## LAW III

*To every action there is always opposed an equal reaction: or the mutual actions of two bodies upon each other are always equal, and directed to contrary parts.*

Whatever draws or presses another is as much drawn or pressed by that other. If you press a stone with your finger, the finger is also pressed by the stone. If a horse draws a stone tied to a rope, the horse (if I may so say) will be equally drawn back towards the stone: for the distended rope, by the same endeavour to relax or unbend itself, will draw the horse as much towards the stone, as it does the stone towards the horse, and will obstruct the progress of the one as much as it advances that of the other. If a body impinge upon another, and by its force change the motion of the other, that body also (because of the equality of the mutual pressure) will undergo an equal change, in its own motion, towards the contrary part. The changes made by these actions are equal, not in the velocities but in the motions of bodies; that is to say, if the bodies are not hindered by any other impediments. For, because the motions are equally changed, the changes of the velocities made towards contrary parts are reciprocally proportional to the bodies. This law takes place also in attractions, as will be proved in the next scholium.

. . .

## RULES OF REASONING IN PHILOSOPHY

### RULE I

*We are to admit no more causes of natural things than such
as are both time and sufficient to explain their appearances.*

To this purpose the philosophers say that Nature does nothing in vain, and more is in vain when less will serve; for Nature is pleased with simplicity, and affects not the pomp of superfluous causes.

### RULE II

*Therefore to the same natural effects we must, as
far as possible, assign the same causes.*

As to respiration in a man and in a beast; the descent of stones in *Europe* and in *America*; the light of our culinary fire and of the sun; the reflection of light in the earth, and in the planets.

### RULE III

*The qualities of bodies, which admit neither intension nor remis-
sion of degrees, and which are found to belong to all bodies within the reach of our experiments, are to be esteemed
the universal qualities of all bodies whatsoever.*

For since the qualities of bodies are only known to us by experiments, we are to hold for universal all such as universally agree with experiments; and such as are not liable to diminution can never be quite taken away. We are certainly not to relinquish the evidence of experiments for the sake of dreams and vain fictions of our own devising; nor are we to recede from the analogy of Nature, which uses to be simple, and always consonant to itself. We no other way know the extension of bodies than by our senses, nor do these reach it in all bodies; but because we perceive extension in all that are sensible, therefore we ascribe it universally to all others also. That abundance of bodies are hard, we learn by experience; and because the hardness of the whole arises from the hardness of the parts, we therefore justly infer the hardness of the undivided particles not only of the bodies we feel but of all others. That all bodies are impenetrable, we gather not from reason, but from sensation. The bodies which we handle we find impenetrable, and thence conclude impenetrability to be an universal property of all bodies whatsoever. That all bodies are moveable, and endowed with certain powers (which we call the *vires inertiae*) of persevering in their motion, or in their rest, we only infer from the like properties observed in the bodies which we have seen. The extension, hardness, impenetrability, mobility, and *vis inertiae* of the whole, result from the extension, hardness, impenetrability, mobility, and *vires inertiae* of the parts; and thence we conclude the least particles of all bodies to be also all extended, and hard and impenetrable, and moveable, and endowed with their proper *vires inertia*. And this is the foundation of all philosophy.

Moreover, that the divided but contiguous particles of bodies may be separated from one another, is a matter of observation; and, in the particles that remain undivided, our minds are able to distinguish yet lesser parts, as is mathematically demonstrated. But whether the parts so distinguished, and not yet divided, may, by the powers of Nature, be actually divided and separated from one another, we cannot certainly determine. Yet, had we the proof of but one experiment that any undivided particle, in breaking a hard and solid body, suffered a division, we might by virtue of this rule conclude that the undivided as well as the divided particles may be divided and actually separated to infinity.

Lastly, if it universally appears, by experiments and astronomical observations, that all bodies about the earth gravitate towards the earth, and that in proportion to the quantity of matter which they severally contain;

that the moon likewise, according to the quantity of its matter, gravitates towards the earth; that, on the other hand, our sea gravitates towards the moon; and all the planets mutually one towards another; and the comets in like manner towards the sun; we must, in consequence of this rule, universally allow that all bodies whatsoever are endowed with a principle of mutual gravitation. For the argument from the appearances concludes with more force for the universal gravitation of all bodies than for their impenetrability; of which, among those in the celestial regions, we have no experiments, nor any manner of observation. Not that I affirm gravity to be essential to bodies: by their *vis insita* I mean nothing but their *vis inertiae*. This is immutable. Their gravity is diminished as they recede from the earth.

## RULE IV

*In experimental philosophy we are to look upon propositions collected by general induction from phaenomena as accurately or very nearly true, notwithstanding any contrary hypotheses that may be imagined, till such time as other phaenomena occur, by which they may either be made more accurate, or liable to exceptions.*

This rule we must follow, that the argument of induction may not be evaded by hypotheses.

. . .

## GENERAL SCHOLIUM

The hypothesis of vortices is pressed with many difficulties. That every planet by a radius drawn to the sun may describe areas proportional to the times of description, the periodic times of the several parts of the vortices should observe the duplicate proportion of their distances from the sun; but that the periodic times of the planets may obtain the sesquiplicate proportion of their distances from the sun, the periodic times of the parts of the vortex ought to be in the sesquiplicate proportion of their distances. That the smaller vortices may maintain their lesser revolutions about *Saturn*, *Jupiter*, and other planets, and swim quietly and undisturbed in the greater vortex of the sun, the periodic times of the parts of the sun's vortex should be equal; but the rotation of the sun and planets about their axes, which ought to correspond with the motions of their vortices, recede far from all these proportions. The motions of the comets are exceedingly regular, are governed by the same laws with the motions of the planets, and can by no means be accounted for by the hypothesis of vortices; for comets are carried with very eccentric motions through all parts of the heavens indifferently, with a freedom that is incompatible with the notion of a vortex.

Bodies projected in our air suffer no resistance but from the air. Withdraw the air, as is done in Mr. Boyle's vacuum, and the resistance ceases; for in this void a bit of line down and a piece of solid gold descend with equal velocity. And the parity of reason must take place in the celestial spaces above the earth's atmosphere; in which spaces, where there is no air to resist their motions, all bodies will move with the greatest freedom; and the planets and comets will constantly pursue their revolutions in orbits given in kind and position, according to the laws above explained; but though these bodies may, indeed, persevere in their orbits by the mere laws of gravity, yet they could by no means have at first derived the regular position of the orbits themselves from those laws.

The six primary planets are revolved about the sun in circles concentric with the sun, and with motions directed towards the same parts, and almost in the same plane. Ten moons are revolved about the earth, Jupiter and Saturn, in circles concentric with them, with the same direction of motion, and nearly in the planes of the orbits of those planets; but it is not to be conceived that mere mechanical causes could give birth to so many regular motions, since the comets range over all parts of the heavens in very eccentric orbits; for by that kind of motion they pass easily through the orbs of the planets, and with great rapidity; and in their aphelions, where they move the slowest, and are detained the longest, they recede to the greatest distances from each other, and thence suffer the least disturbance from their mutual attractions.

This most beautiful system of the sun, planets, and comets, could only proceed from the counsel and dominion of an intelligent and powerful Being. And if the fixed stars are the centres of other like systems, these, being formed by the like wise counsel, must be all subject to the dominion of One; especially since the light of the fixed stars is of the same nature with the light of the sun, and from every system light passes into all the other systems: and lest the systems of the fixed stars should, by their gravity, fall on each other mutually, he hath placed those systems at immense distances one from another.

This Being governs all things, not as the soul of the world, but as Lord over all; and on account of his dominion he is wont to be called *Lord God* παντοκράτωρ [*pantokratōr*], or *Universal Ruler*; for *God* is a relative word, and has a respect to servants; and *Deity* is the dominion of God not over his own body, as those imagine who fancy God to be the soul of the world, but over servants. The Supreme God is a Being eternal, infinite, absolutely perfect; but a being, however perfect, without dominion, cannot be said to be Lord God; for we say, my God, your God, the God of *Israel*, the God of Gods, and Lord of Lords; but we do not say, my Eternal, your Eternal, the Eternal of *Israel*, the Eternal of Gods; we do not say, my Infinite, or my Perfect: these are titles which have no respect to servants. The word *God* usually signifies *Lord*; but every lord is not a God. It is the dominion of a spiritual being which constitutes a God: a true, supreme, or imaginary dominion makes a true, supreme, or imaginary God. And from his true dominion it follows that the true God is a living, intelligent, and powerful Being; and, from his other perfections, that he is supreme, or most perfect. He is eternal and infinite, omnipotent and omniscient; that is, his duration reaches from eternity to eternity; his presence from infinity to infinity; he governs all things, and knows all things that are or can be done. He is not eternity or infinity, but eternal and infinite; he is not duration or space, but he endures and is present. He endures for ever, and is every where present; and by existing always and every where, he constitutes duration and space.

Since every particle of space is *always*, and every indivisible moment of duration is *every where*, certainly the Maker and Lord of all things cannot be *never* and *no where*. Every soul that has perception is, though in different times and in different organs of sense and motion, still the same indivisible person. There are given successive parts in duration, coexistent parts in space, but neither the one nor the other in the person of a man, or his thinking principle; and much less can they be found in the thinking substance of God. Every man, so far as he is a thing that has perception, is one and the same man during his whole life, in all and each of his organs of sense. God is the same God, always and every where. He

462

is omnipresent not *virtually* only, but also *substantially*; for virtue cannot subsist without substance. In him are all things contained and moved; yet neither affects the other: God suffers nothing from the motion of bodies; bodies find no resistance from the omnipresence of God.

It is allowed by all that the Supreme God exists necessarily; and by the same necessity he exists *always* and *every where*. Whence also he is all similar, all eye, all ear, all brain, all arm, all power to perceive, to understand, and to act; but in a manner not at all human, in a manner not at all corporeal, in a manner utterly unknown to us. As a blind man has no idea of colours, so have we no idea of the manner by which the all-wise God perceives and understands all things. He is utterly void of all body and bodily figure, and can therefore neither be seen, nor heard, nor touched; nor ought he to be worshipped under the representation of any corporeal thing. We have ideas of his attributes, but what the real substance of any thing is we know not. In bodies, we see only their figures and colours, we hear only the sounds, we touch only their outward surfaces, we smell only the smells, and taste the savours; but their inward substances are not to be known either by our senses, or by any reflex act of our minds: much less, then, have we any idea of the substance of God. We know him only by his most wise and excellent contrivances of things, and final causes: we admire him for his perfections; but we reverence and adore him on account of his dominion: for we adore him as his servants; and a god without dominion, providence, and final causes, is nothing else but Fate and Nature.

Blind metaphysical necessity, which is certainly the same always and every where, could produce no variety of things. All that diversity of natural things which we find suited to different times and places could arise from nothing but the ideas and will of a Being necessarily existing. But, by way of allegory, God is said to see, to speak, to laugh, to love, to hate, to desire, to give, to receive, to rejoice, to be angry, to fight, to frame, to work, to build; for all our notions of God are taken from the ways of mankind by a certain similitude, which, though not perfect, has some likeness, however. And thus much concerning God; to discourse of whom from the appearances of things, does certainly belong to Natural Philosophy.

Hitherto we have explained the phenomena of the heavens and of our sea by the power of gravity, but have not yet assigned the cause of this power. This is certain, that it must proceed from a cause that penetrates to the very centres of the sun and planets, without suffering the least diminution of its force; that operates not according to the quantity of the surfaces of the particles upon which it acts (as mechanical causes use to do), but according to the quantity of the solid matter which they contain, and propagates its virtue on all sides to immense distances, decreasing always in the duplicate proportion of the distances. Gravitation towards the sun is made up out of the gravitations towards the several particles of which the body of the sun is composed; and in receding from the sun decreases accurately in the duplicate proportion of the distances as far as the orb of Saturn, as evidently appears from the quiescence of the aphelions of the planets; nay, and even to the remotest aphelions of the comets, if those aphelions are also quiescent.

But hitherto I have not been able to discover the cause of those properties of gravity from phaenomena, and I frame no hypotheses; for whatever is not deduced from the phaenomena is to be called an hypothesis; and hypotheses, whether metaphysical or physical, whether of occult qualities or mechanical, have no place in experimental philosophy. In this philosophy particular propositions are inferred from the phenomena, and afterwards rendered general by induction. Thus it was that the impenetrability, the mobility, and the impulsive force of bodies, and the laws of motion and of gravitation, were discovered. And to us it is enough that gravity does really exist, and acts according to the laws which we have explained, and abundantly serves to account for all the motions of the celestial bodies, and of our sea.

And now we might add something concerning a certain most subtle Spirit which pervades and lies hid in all gross bodies; by the force and action of which Spirit the particles of bodies mutually attract one another at near distances, and cohere, if contiguous; and electric bodies operate to greater distances, as well repelling as attracting the neighbouring corpuscles; and light is emitted, reflected, refracted, inflected, and heats bodies; and all sensation is excited, and the members of animal bodies move at the command of the will, namely, by the vibrations of this Spirit, mutually propagated along the solid filaments of the nerves, from the outward organs of sense to the brain, and from the brain into the muscles. But these are things that cannot be explained in few words, nor are we furnished with that sufficiency

of experiments which is required to an accurate determination and demonstration of the laws by which this electric and elastic Spirit operates.

*Translated by Andrew Motte, 1729*

# Isaac Newton's Mathematical Principles of Natural Philosophy

## William A. Dembski

Isaac Newton is widely regarded as the greatest scientist of all time. His
claim to fame rests chiefly on this work. In it—or, the *Principia Mathematica,* as it is also called—Newton invents the infinitesimal calculus
and with it delineates the fundamental laws governing the structure and
dynamics of physical reality. From the motion of billiard balls to the motion
of planets and everything in between, Newton's *Principia* was thought to
give the final word.

Sometimes genius is underappreciated during the life of the genius.
Not so with Newton. His genius was evident and reverenced from the
start. Isaac Barrow, Newton's predecessor in the prestigious Lucasian Chair
of Mathematics at Cambridge, was so impressed with Newton that he
resigned and had Newton assume the chair (a professorship subsequently
held by such luminaries as Charles Babbage, Paul Dirac, and, presently,
Stephen Hawking).

Newton's contemporary Edmund Halley, the famed astronomer
remembered for the comet named for him, even wrote an ode to Newton.
It closes with the effusive praise,

> Come celebrate with me in song the name
> Of Newton, to the Muses dear; for he
> Unlocked the hidden treasuries of Truth:
> So richly through his mind had Phoebus cast

The radiance of his own divinity.
Nearer the gods no mortal may approach.

In the same spirit, Alexander Pope, a younger contemporary, wrote this epitaph:

Nature and Nature's laws lay hid in night:
God said, "Let Newton be!" and all was light.

Even the twentieth-century economist John Maynard Keynes recognized how profoundly Newton's genius had impacted seventeenth-century intellectual life, referring to him as "the last wonder-child to whom the Magi could do sincere and appropriate homage."

―――――――

Although *Principia Mathematica* is highly technical, it contains several extended passages of interest to the general reader. Thus, for instance, we find bold statements about God's role as a designing intelligence behind the world. Contemporary scientists who feel passionately about the religious significance of their scientific work may still offer up such statements, but usually they will keep them off to one side. Newton, by contrast, saw no contradiction in doing his best science and then immediately, in the same written work, giving it a theological interpretation.

Although we think of Newton as the preeminent scientist of his (and, indeed, any) age, it is remarkable that science was only one of the many professional hats he wore. His higher passion seems to have been theology, and he spent much time studying and writing about the Bible.

He was also an avid alchemist. Moreover, in the 1690s, he abruptly left his ivory-tower professorship at Cambridge to assume duties heading the government mint in London. (Imagine string-theorist Ed Witten leaving Princeton's Institute for Advanced Study to move to D.C. and head the U.S. Treasury.)

Yet for all the other hats Newton wore, he accomplished nothing like the distinction he achieved in science. There he was a soaring figure. In theology, by contrast, he was a well-read but self-schooled amateur. Also, his theological views were heterodox: Though accepting the Bible as largely factual (including the miracles ascribed to Jesus), Newton sided with Arius against Athanasius, rejecting the divinity of Christ.

In ancient Athens, Socrates would go about asking recognized experts in a given area broader philosophical questions: What is justice? What is truth? (etc.) He found that expertise in one area tends not to transfer to others, especially when these require wisdom. Newton seems to fit this mold. In the science of physics, he was preeminent. And yet when he delved into other areas, he was undistinguished and, at times, even a duffer.

What is Newton's legacy? He properly belongs to science, where he still ranks in the number one spot, though he has some close seconds and thirds (such as Albert Einstein and James Clerk Maxwell). In Newton's day, it was thought that he had once and for all nailed down the deep structure of the physical universe. With the revolutions in electromagnetism, general relativity, and quantum mechanics in the nineteenth and twentieth centuries, however, it's now obvious his physics was only part of the picture.

Newtonian physics captures the motion of medium-sized objects at medium speeds. That's why it's still the first thing beginning physics students learn. But it's clear that the scope of Newton's physics is strictly limited. The odes by Halley and Pope celebrating him and his achievements could no longer be written with a straight face.

In his day, he was, as John Locke said, "the incomparable Mr. Newton." Nowadays, he is a *primus inter pares*: He remains the greatest of scientists, but one who rubs shoulders with other great scientists and not as one who towers above the rest.

## CHAPTER TWENTY ONE

# JOHN WESLEY

Modern (1703–1791)

Evangelical students often wonder if, as evangelicals, they belong in the Great Conversation.

It's sad that they should have this fear, but it's a natural result of a culture that misunderstands and stereotypes them. The history of the movement is little taught and even less often sympathetically presented. This can be internalized into an anti-intellectualism that accepts the clichés and even tries to glory in them.

We are called to be fools for Christ's sake but not to be fools for the sake of foolish bigotry. Intellectualism, the belief that human intellect is enough for a good life, is a sin, but anti-intellectualism is no better. Anti-intellectualism is not merely opposed to intellectualism, a good thing, but opposed to the mind. Christians want good works based on good ideas, faith that works.

John Wesley, Oxford man, theologian, and preacher, was an evangelical with balance. He preached with evangelical zeal *and* with classical training. He wanted souls to be saved from hell forever but for men to become better subjects of Christendom today.

He was a social reformer who never preached merely a social gospel.

He burned to know God, but his passionate arguments likewise showed logical rigor. Though Wesley didn't despise education, he didn't worship it. He lived the Great Conversation in his deeds and writings, not just in a classroom.

It was an example that compelled evangelical ministers for centuries.

My own great-grandfather rode circuit, spreading the gospel, emulating the example of generations of preachers in America inspired by the Wesleyans. This country preacher worked with multiple Bible translations and tried to emulate the scriptural and thoughtful style that was at the heart of the best of American revivalism. The Wesleyan tradition demanded Great-Grandfather's best efforts: body, mind, and emotion.

———————

John Wesley also helped save England from a costly secular revolution like the one that nearly destroyed France. The great preacher gave all classes of Englishmen encouragement to live authentic Christian lives . . . and not just have the right ideas. He fought the infidel by increasing study of Scripture, through warm-hearted piety, and via passionate action. He encouraged the powerful to help the poor, and he motivated the poor to become worthy of the help.

Wesley's work inspired deathless poetry and music; his brother, Charles Wesley, is among the world's most celebrated and beloved hymnists.

You don't have to be a Wesleyan to be moved by his sermons or sing Wesleyan hymns. Wesley and his movement defended ideas worth considering, did deeds worth emulating, and wrote songs everyone in Christendom should be singing. John Wesley, evangelical hero, is part of the Great Conversation.

## ⊂⊘ FROM ⊘⊃

# *Sermons*

### Sermon 1: "Salvation by Faith"

*By grace are ye saved through faith. (Ephesians 2:8)*

1. All the blessings which God hath bestowed upon man are of his mere grace, bounty, or favour; his free, undeserved favour; favour altogether undeserved; man having no claim to the least of his mercies. It was free grace that "formed man of the dust of the ground, and breathed into him a living soul," and stamped on that soul the image of God, and "put all things under his feet." The same free grace continues to us, at this day, life, and breath, and all things. For there is nothing we are, or have, or do, which can deserve the least thing at God's hand. "All our works, Thou, O God, hast wrought in us." These, therefore, are so many more instances of free mercy: and whatever righteousness may be found in man, this is also the gift of God.

2. Wherewithal then shall a sinful man atone for any the least of his sins? With his own works? No. Were they ever so many or holy, they are not his own, but God's. But indeed they are all unholy and sinful themselves, so that every one of them needs a fresh atonement. Only corrupt fruit grows on a corrupt tree. And his heart is altogether corrupt and abominable; being "come short of the glory of God," the glorious righteousness at first impressed on his soul, after the image of his great Creator. Therefore, having nothing, neither righteousness nor works, to plead, his mouth is utterly stopped before God.

3. If then sinful men find favour with God, it is "grace upon grace!" If God vouchsafe still to pour fresh blessings upon us, yea, the greatest of all blessings, salvation; what can we say to these things, but, "Thanks be unto God for his unspeakable gift!" And thus it is. Herein "God commendeth his love toward us, in that, while we were yet sinners, Christ died" to save us. "By grace" then "are ye saved through faith." Grace is the source, faith the condition, of salvation.

Now, that we fall not short of the grace of God, it concerns us carefully to inquire:

I. What faith it is through which we are saved?
II. What is the salvation which is through faith?
III. How we may answer some objections?

## I.

1. *What faith it is through which we are saved.* And, first, it is not barely the faith of a heathen. Now, God requireth of a heathen to believe, "that God is; that he is a rewarder of them that diligently seek him;" and that he is to be sought by glorifying him as God, by giving him thanks for all things, and by a careful practice of moral virtue, of justice, mercy, and truth, toward their fellow creatures. A Greek or Roman, therefore, yea, a Scythian or Indian, was without excuse if he did not believe thus much: the being and attributes of God, a future state of reward and punishment, and the obligatory nature of moral virtue. For this is barely the faith of a heathen.

2. Nor, secondly, is it the faith of a devil, though this goes much farther than that of a heathen. For the devil believes, not only that there is a wise and powerful God, gracious to reward, and just to punish; but also, that Jesus is the Son of God, the Christ, the Saviour of the world. So we find him declaring, in express terms, "I know Thee who Thou art; the Holy One of God" (Lk. 4:34). Nor can we doubt but that unhappy spirit believes all those words which came out of the mouth of the Holy One, yea, and whatsoever else was written by those holy men of old, of two of whom he was compelled to give that glorious testimony, "These men are the servants of the most high God, who show unto you the way of salvation." Thus much, then, the great enemy of God and man believes, and trembles in believing—that God was made manifest in the flesh; that he will "tread all enemies under his feet;" and that "all Scripture was given by inspiration of God." Thus far goeth the faith of a devil.

3. Thirdly. The faith through which we are saved, in that sense of the word which will hereafter be explained, is not barely that which the Apostles themselves had while Christ was yet upon earth; though they so believed on him as to "leave all and follow him;" although they had then

power to work miracles, to "heal all manner of sickness, and all manner of disease;" yea, they had then "power and authority over all devils;" and, which is beyond all this, were sent by their Master to "preach the kingdom of God."

4. What faith is it then through which we are saved? It may be answered, first, in general, it is a faith in Christ: Christ, and God through Christ, are the proper objects of it. Herein, therefore, it is sufficiently, absolutely distinguished from the faith either of ancient or modern heathens. And from the faith of a devil it is fully distinguished by this: it is not barely a speculative, rational thing, a cold, lifeless assent, a train of ideas in the head; but also a disposition of the heart. For thus saith the Scripture, "With the heart man believeth unto righteousness;" and, "If thou shalt confess with thy mouth the Lord Jesus, and shalt believe in thy heart that God hath raised him from the dead, thou shalt be saved."

5. And herein does it differ from that faith which the Apostles themselves had while our Lord was on earth, that it acknowledges the necessity and merit of his death, and the power of his resurrection. It acknowledges his death as the only sufficient means of redeeming man from death eternal, and his resurrection as the restoration of us all to life and immortality; inasmuch as he "was delivered for our sins, and rose again for our justification." Christian faith is then, not only an assent to the whole gospel of Christ, but also a full reliance on the blood of Christ; a trust in the merits of his life, death, and resurrection; a recumbency upon him as our atonement and our life, as given for us, and living in us; and, in consequence hereof, a closing with him, and cleaving to him, as our "wisdom, righteousness, sanctification, and redemption," or, in one word, our salvation.


## II.

1. *What salvation it is,* which is through this faith, is the Second thing to be considered. And, First, whatsoever else it imply, it is a present salvation. It is something attainable, yea, actually attained, on earth, by those who are partakers of this faith. For thus saith the Apostle to the believers at Ephesus, and in them to the believers of all ages, not, *Ye shall be* (though that also is true), but, "*Ye are saved through faith.*"

2. *Ye are saved* (to comprise all in one word) from sin. This is the salvation which is through faith. This is that great salvation foretold by the angel, before God brought his First-begotten into the world: "Thou shalt call his name Jesus; for he shall save his people from their sins." And neither here, nor in other parts of holy writ, is there any limitation or restriction. All his people, or, as it is elsewhere expressed, "all that believe in him," he will save from all their sins; from original and actual, past and present sin, "of the flesh and of the spirit." Through faith that is in him, they are saved both from the guilt and from the power of it.

3. First. From the guilt of all past sin: for, whereas all the world is guilty before God, insomuch that should he "be extreme to mark what is done amiss, there is none that could abide it;" and whereas, "by the law is" only "the knowledge of sin," but no deliverance from it, so that, "by" fulfilling "the deeds of the law, no flesh can be justified in his sight": now, "the righteousness of God, which is by faith of Jesus Christ, is manifested unto all that believe." Now, "they are justified freely by his grace, through the redemption that is in Jesus Christ." "Him God hath set forth to be a propitiation through faith in his blood, to declare his righteousness for [or by] the remission of the sins that are past." Now hath Christ taken away "the curse of the law, being made a curse for us." He hath "blotted out the handwriting that was against us, taking it out of the way, nailing it to his cross." "There is therefore no condemnation now to them which" believe "in Christ Jesus."

4. And being saved from guilt, they are saved from fear. Not indeed from a filial fear of offending; but from all servile fear; from that fear which hath torment; from fear of punishment; from fear of the wrath of God, whom they now no longer regard as a severe Master, but as an indulgent Father. "They have not received again the spirit of bondage, but the Spirit of adoption, whereby they cry, Abba, Father: the Spirit itself also bearing witness with their spirits, that they are the children of God." They are also saved from the fear, though not from the possibility, of falling away from the grace of God, and coming short of the great and precious promises. Thus have they "peace with God through our Lord Jesus Christ. They rejoice in hope of the glory of God. And the love of God is shed abroad in their hearts, through the Holy Ghost, which is given unto them." And hereby they are persuaded (though perhaps not at all times, nor with the

same fullness of persuasion), that "neither death, nor life, nor things present, nor things to come, nor height, nor depth, nor any other creature, shall be able to separate them from the love of God, which is in Christ Jesus our Lord."

5. Again: through this faith they are saved from the power of sin, as well as from the guilt of it. So the Apostle declares, "Ye know that he was manifested to take away our sins; and in him is no sin. Whosoever abideth in him sinneth not" (1 Jn. 3:5ff.). Again, "Little children, let no man deceive you. He that committeth sin is of the devil. Whosoever believeth is born of God. And whosoever is born of God doth not commit sin; for his seed remaineth in him: and he cannot sin, because he is born of God." Once more: "We know that whosoever is born of God sinneth not; but he that is begotten of God keepeth himself, and that wicked one toucheth him not" (1 Jn. 5:18).

6. He that is, by faith, born of God sinneth not (1) by any habitual sin; for all habitual sin is sin reigning: But sin cannot reign in any that believeth. Nor (2) by any wilful sin: for his will, while he abideth in the faith, is utterly set against all sin, and abhorreth it as deadly poison. Nor (3) by any sinful desire; for he continually desireth the holy and perfect will of God, and any tendency to an unholy desire, he by the grace of God, stifleth in the birth. Nor (4) doth he sin by infirmities, whether in act, word, or thought; for his infirmities have no concurrence of his will; and without this they are not properly sins. Thus, "he that is born of God doth not commit sin"; and though he cannot say he hath not sinned, yet now "he sinneth not."

7. This then is the salvation which is through faith, even in the present world: a salvation from sin, and the consequences of sin, both often expressed in the word *justification*; which, taken in the largest sense, implies a deliverance from guilt and punishment, by the atonement of Christ actually applied to the soul of the sinner now believing on him, and a deliverance from the power of sin, through Christ *formed in his heart*. So that he who is thus justified, or saved by faith, is indeed *born again*. He is *born again of the Spirit* unto a new life, which "is hid with Christ in God." And as a new-born babe he gladly receives the *adolon*, "*sincere* milk of the word, and grows thereby;" going on in the might of the Lord his God, from faith to faith, from grace to grace, until at

length, he come unto "a perfect man, unto the measure of the stature of the fullness of Christ."

<h2 style="text-align:center">III.</h2>

1. The first usual *objection* to this is, that to preach salvation or justification, by faith only, is to preach against holiness and good works. To which a short answer might be given: "It would be so, if we spake, as some do, of a faith which was separate from these; but we speak of a faith which is not so, but productive of all good works, and all holiness."

2. But it may be of use to consider it more at large; especially since it is no new objection, but as old as St. Paul's time. For even then it was asked, "Do we not make void the law through faith?" We answer, First, all who preach not faith do manifestly make void the law; either directly and grossly, by limitations and comments that eat out all the spirit of the text; or indirectly, by not pointing out the only means whereby it is possible to perform it. Whereas, Secondly, "we establish the law," both by showing its full extent and spiritual meaning; and by calling all to that living way, whereby "the righteousness of the law may be fulfilled in them." These, while they trust in the blood of Christ alone, use all the ordinances which he hath appointed, do all the "good works which he had before prepared that they should walk therein," and enjoy and manifest all holy and heavenly tempers, even the same mind that was in Christ Jesus.

3. But does not preaching this faith lead men into pride? We answer, Accidentally it may: therefore ought every believer to be earnestly cautioned, in the words of the great Apostle. "Because of unbelief," the first branches "were broken off: and thou standest by faith. Be not high-minded, but fear. If God spared not the natural branches, take heed lest he spare not thee. Behold therefore the goodness and severity of God! On them which fell, severity; but towards thee, goodness, if thou continue in his goodness; otherwise thou also shalt be cut off." And while he continues therein, he will remember those words of St. Paul, foreseeing and answering this very objection (Rom. 3:27), "Where is boasting then? It is excluded. By what law? Of works? Nay: but by the law of faith." If a man were justified by his works, he would have whereof to glory. But there is no glorying for him

"that worketh not, but believeth on him that justifieth the ungodly" (Rom. 4:5). To the same effect are the words both preceding and following the text (Eph. 2:4ff.): "God, who is rich in mercy, even when we were dead in sins, hath quickened us together with Christ (by grace ye are saved), that he might show the exceeding riches of his grace in his kindness toward us through Christ Jesus. For by grace are ye saved through faith; and that not of yourselves." Of yourselves cometh neither your faith nor your salvation: "it is the gift of God;" the free, undeserved gift; the faith through which ye are saved, as well as the salvation which he of his own good pleasure, his mere favour, annexes thereto. That ye believe, is one instance of his grace; that believing ye are saved, another. "Not of works, lest any man should boast." For all our works, all our righteousness, which were before our believing, merited nothing of God but condemnation; so far were they from deserving faith, which therefore, whenever given, is not of works. Neither is salvation of the works we do when we believe, for it is then God that worketh in us: and, therefore, that he giveth us a reward for what he himself worketh, only commendeth the riches of his mercy, but leaveth us nothing whereof to glory.

4. "However, may not the speaking thus of the mercy of God, as saving or justifying freely by faith only, encourage men in sin?" Indeed, it may and will: Many will "continue in sin that grace may abound." But their blood is upon their own head. The goodness of God ought to lead them to repentance; and so it will those who are sincere of heart. When they know there is yet forgiveness with him, they will cry aloud that he would blot out their sins also, through faith which is in Jesus. And if they earnestly cry, and faint not, if they seek him in all the means he hath appointed; if they refuse to be comforted till he come; "he will come, and will not tarry." And he can do much work in a short time. Many are the examples, in the Acts of the Apostles, of God's working this faith in men's hearts, even like lightning falling from heaven. So in the same hour that Paul and Silas began to preach, the jailer repented, believed, and was baptized; as were three thousand, by St. Peter, on the day of Pentecost, who all repented and believed at his first preaching. And, blessed be God, there are now many living proofs that he is still "mighty to save."

5. Yet to the same truth, placed in another view, a quite contrary objection is made: "If a man cannot be saved by all that he can do, this will

drive men to despair." True, to despair of being saved by their own works, their own merits, or righteousness. And so it ought; for none can trust in the merits of Christ, till he has utterly renounced his own. He that "goeth about to stablish his own righteousness" cannot receive the righteousness of God. The righteousness which is of faith cannot be given him while he trusteth in that which is of the law.

6. But this, it is said, is an uncomfortable doctrine. The devil spoke like himself, that is, without either truth or shame, when he dared to suggest to men that it is such. It is the only comfortable one, it is "very full of comfort," to all self-destroyed, self-condemned sinners. That "whosoever believeth on him shall not be ashamed that the same Lord over all is rich unto all that call upon him": here is comfort, high as heaven, stronger than death! What! Mercy for all? For Zacchaeus, a public robber? For Mary Magdalene, a common harlot? Methinks I hear one say "Then I, even I, may hope for mercy!" And so thou mayest, thou afflicted one, whom none hath comforted! God will not cast out thy prayer. Nay, perhaps he may say the next hour, "Be of good cheer, thy sins are forgiven thee;" so forgiven, that they shall reign over thee no more; yea, and that "the Holy Spirit shall bear witness with thy spirit that thou art a child of God." O glad tidings! tidings of great joy, which are sent unto all people! "Ho, every one that thirsteth, come ye to the waters: Come ye, and buy, without money and without price." Whatsoever your sins be, "though red like crimson," though more than the hairs of your head, "return ye unto the Lord, and he will have mercy upon you, and to our God, for he will abundantly pardon."

7. When no more objections occur, then we are simply told that salvation by faith only ought not to be preached as the first doctrine, or, at least, not to be preached at all. But what saith the Holy Ghost? "Other foundation can no man lay than that which is laid, even Jesus Christ." So then, that "whosoever believeth on him shall be saved," is, and must be, the foundation of all our preaching; that is, must be preached first. "Well, but not to all." To whom, then are we not to preach it? Whom shall we except? The poor? Nay; they have a peculiar right to have the gospel preached unto them. The unlearned? No. God hath revealed these things unto unlearned and ignorant men from the beginning. The young? By no means. "Suffer these," in any wise, "to come unto Christ, and forbid them not." The sinners? Least of all. "He came not to call the righteous,

but sinners to repentance." Why then, if any, we are to except the rich, the learned, the reputable, the moral men. And, it is true, they too often except themselves from hearing; yet we must speak the words of our Lord. For thus the tenor of our commission runs, "Go and preach the gospel to every creature." If any man wrest it, or any part of it, to his destruction, he must bear his own burden. But still, "as the Lord liveth, whatsoever the Lord saith unto us, that we will speak."

8. At this time, more especially, will we speak, that "by grace are ye saved through faith": because, never was the maintaining this doctrine more seasonable than it is at this day. Nothing but this can effectually prevent the increase of the Romish delusion among us. It is endless to attack, one by one, all the errors of that Church. But salvation by faith strikes at the root, and all fall at once where this is established. It was this doctrine, which our Church justly calls *the strong rock and foundation of the Christian religion*, that first drove Popery out of these kingdoms; and it is this alone can keep it out. Nothing but this can give a check to that immorality which hath "overspread the land as a flood." Can you empty the great deep, drop by drop? Then you may reform us by dissuasives from particular vices. But let the "righteousness which is of God by faith" be brought in, and so shall its proud waves be stayed. Nothing but this can stop the mouths of those who "glory in their shame, and openly deny the Lord that bought them." They can talk as sublimely of the law, as he that hath it written by God in his heart. To hear them speak on this head might incline one to think they were not far from the kingdom of God: but take them out of the law into the gospel; begin with the righteousness of faith; with Christ, "the end of the law to every one that believeth;" and those who but now appeared almost, if not altogether, Christians, stand confessed the sons of perdition; as far from life and salvation (God be merciful unto them!) as the depth of hell from the height of heaven.

9. For this reason the adversary so rages whenever "salvation by faith" is declared to the world: for this reason did he stir up earth and hell, to destroy those who first preached it. And for the same reason, knowing that faith alone could overturn the foundations of his kingdom, did he call forth all his forces, and employ all his arts of lies and calumny, to affright Martin Luther from reviving it. Nor can we wonder threat; for, as that man of God observes, "How would it enrage a proud, strong man armed,

to be stopped and set at nought by a little child coming against him with a reed in his hand!" especially when he knew that little child would surely overthrow him, and tread him under foot. Even so, Lord Jesus! Thus hath Thy strength been ever "made perfect in weakness!" Go forth then, thou little child that believest in him, and his "right hand shall teach thee terrible things!" Though thou art helpless and weak as an infant of days, the strong man shall not be able to stand before thee. Thou shalt prevail over him, and subdue him, and overthrow him and trample him under thy feet. Thou shalt march on, under the great Captain of thy salvation, "conquering and to conquer," until all thine enemies are destroyed, and "death is swallowed up in victory."

Now, thanks be to God, which giveth us the victory through our Lord Jesus Christ; to whom, with the Father and the Holy Ghost, be blessing, and glory, and wisdom, and thanksgiving, and honour, and power, and might, for ever and ever. Amen.

### "And Can It Be," Charles Wesley (1738)

And can it be that I should gain
an interest in the Savior's blood!
Died he for me? who caused his pain!
For me? who him to death pursued?
Amazing love! How can it be
that thou, my God, shouldst die for me?
Amazing love! How can it be
that thou, my God, shouldst die for me?

'Tis mystery all: th' Immortal dies!
Who can explore his strange design?
In vain the firstborn seraph tries
to sound the depths of love divine.
'Tis mercy all! Let earth adore;
let angel minds inquire no more.
'Tis mercy all! Let earth adore;
let angel minds inquire no more.

He left his Father's throne above
(so free, so infinite his grace!),
emptied himself of all but love,
and bled for Adam's helpless race.
'Tis mercy all, immense and free,

for O my God, it found out me!
'Tis mercy all, immense and free,
for O my God, it found out me!

Long my imprisoned spirit lay,
fast bound in sin and nature's night;
thine eye diffused a quickening ray;
I woke, the dungeon flamed with light;
my chains fell off, my heart was free,
I rose, went forth, and followed thee.
My chains fell off, my heart was free,
I rose, went forth, and followed thee.

. . .

No condemnation now I dread;
Jesus, and all in him, is mine;
alive in him, my living Head,
and clothed in righteousness divine,
bold I approach th' eternal throne,
and claim the crown, through Christ my own.
Bold I approach th' eternal throne,
and claim the crown, through Christ my own.

### "O for a Thousand Tongues to Sing," Charles Wesley (1740)

. . . Glory to God, and praise and love
Be ever, ever given,
By saints below and saints above,
The church in earth and heaven.

On this glad day the glorious Sun
Of Righteousness arose;
On my benighted soul He shone
And filled it with repose.

Sudden expired the legal strife,
'Twas then I ceased to grieve;
My second, real, living life
I then began to live.

Then with my heart I first believed,
Believed with faith divine,
Power with the Holy Ghost received
To call the Savior mine.

I felt my Lord's atoning blood
Close to my soul applied;
Me, me He loved, the Son of God,
For me, for me He died!

I found and owned His promise true,
Ascertained of my part,
My pardon passed in heaven I knew
When written on my heart.

O for a thousand tongues to sing
My great Redeemer's praise,
The glories of my God and King,
The triumphs of His grace!

My gracious Master and my God,
Assist me to proclaim,
To spread through all the earth abroad
The honors of Thy name.

Jesus! the name that charms our fears,
That bids our sorrows cease;
'Tis music in the sinner's ears,
'Tis life, and health, and peace.

He breaks the power of canceled sin,
He sets the prisoner free;
His blood can make the foulest clean,
His blood availed for me.

He speaks, and, listening to His voice,
New life the dead receive,
The mournful, broken hearts rejoice,
The humble poor believe.

Hear Him, ye deaf; His praise, ye dumb,
Your loosened tongues employ;
Ye blind, behold your Savior come,
And leap, ye lame, for joy.

Look unto Him, ye nations, own
Your God, ye fallen race;
Look, and be saved through faith alone,
Be justified by grace.

See all your sins on Jesus laid:
The Lamb of God was slain,
His soul was once an offering made
For every soul of man. . . .

### "O for a Heart to Praise My God," Charles Wesley (1742)

O for a heart to praise my God,
A heart from sin set free,
A heart that always feels Thy blood
So freely shed for me.

A heart resigned, submissive, meek,
My great Redeemer's throne,
Where only Christ is heard to speak,
Where Jesus reigns alone.

A humble, lowly, contrite, heart,
Believing, true and clean,
Which neither life nor death can part
From Christ who dwells within.

A heart in every thought renewed
And full of love divine,
Perfect and right and pure and good,
A copy, Lord, of Thine.

My heart, Thou know'st, can never rest
Till Thou create my peace;
Till of mine Eden repossest,
From self, and sin, I cease.

Thy nature, gracious Lord, impart;
Come quickly from above;
Write Thy new name upon my heart,
Thy new, best name of Love. . . .

# ON SALVATION

## Joe Henderson

John Wesley's sermon "Salvation by Faith" stands at the head of his collection. Along with the Bible and the Methodist hymnbook (hymns mostly composed by his younger brother, Charles), the Standard Sermons were the basic equipment of the evangelists and circuit riders who proclaimed the message of salvation throughout England and America.

Wesley preached this sermon at St. Mary's, Oxford, on June 11, 1738. That year, when Wesley—the Oxford don and Anglican priest—turned thirty-five, was a turning point in his own life and in the life of the church. It was the year of Wesley's true personal conversion, which he described in his journal entry for May 24, 1738:

> In the evening I went very unwilling to a meeting of a society in Aldersgate street, where one was reading Luther's preface to the epistle to the Romans. About a quarter before nine, while he was describing the change which God works in the heart through faith in Christ, I felt my heart strangely warmed. I felt I did trust in Christ, Christ alone, for salvation; and an assurance was given me that he had taken away my sins, even mine, and saved me from the law of sin and death.

That year also saw the beginning of the evangelical awakening that has come to be called the Wesleyan Revival. John Wesley later reported that although his preaching in the thirteen years before 1738 had produced little fruit, after that year, "the word of God ran as fire among the stubble . . . multitudes crying out, 'What must we do to be saved?' and afterwards witnessing, 'By grace we are saved by faith.'"

"Salvation by Faith" thus can be seen both as Wesley's personal testimony of how salvation came to him and as the testimony of thousands who found salvation though his message. Of course, Wesley would insist that the message did not come from him but from the Bible. His work in the sermon is simply to explicate the statement, "By grace are ye saved by faith" (from Paul's letter to the Ephesians), by clarifying what Paul meant by "faith" and what he meant by "salvation."

*Faith*, explains Wesley, is "not barely a speculative, rational thing, a cold, lifeless assent." Instead it is a "disposition of the heart" in the context of a personal relationship, a "cleaving to [Christ]" best expressed in words like "trust," "confidence," "reliance," and even "recumbency." This understanding assumes but goes beyond the definition offered by Augustine and Aquinas: "thinking with assent." Although faith certainly includes mental assent to the propositional truths of the Gospel, Wesley maintains that it also includes a believer's trust in his or her personal significance.

Wesley defines faith by personalizing the words of an Anglican homily:

> It is a sure confidence which a man hath in God, that through the merits of Christ, *his* sins are forgiven, and *he* reconciled to the favour of God.

The repeated personal pronouns echo his account of his conversion: "He had taken away my sins, even mine, and saved me." They also echo Luther's message of trust in Christ's work, *"pro me, pro nobis,"* and of course Paul's profession of "faith in the one that loved me and gave himself for me."

---

Salvation, in Wesley's understanding, includes more than justification. Pardon from sin and deliverance from the fear of death and damnation are only the beginning. Salvation also entails transformation, or regeneration, that enables happy and holy living in the present. Wesley's striking affirmations of God's power to save the believer from the power of sin caused controversy in his own time and continue to be controversial today. However, Wesley could point to the teaching of the apostles, particularly (as he does in this sermon) the statement in 1 John that "those who are born of God do not sin."

Although Wesley's later sermons offer a more nuanced interpretation of this truth (arguing against the quietist claim that conversion frees Christians from sinful desires), he never wavered in his proclamation that Christ could save believers not only from the guilt of sin but also from its power. Wesley's message of salvation can be distinguished from his Protestant forebears chiefly in this: his presentation of the broad scope of salvation available in this life, that it makes possible victory over sin, conformity to the character of Christ, and perfection in holy love.

———

If John Wesley's preaching of salvation allowed multitudes to witness, "By grace we are saved through faith," Charles Wesley's hymns allowed them to sing their testimony. He wrote two of his best-known hymns, "And Can It Be" and "O for a Thousand Tongues," to help believers celebrate the day of their conversion, when God's grace and salvation reached them. (The latter was originally titled "For the Anniversary Day of One's Conversion.")

Charles, who experienced conversion a few days before his brother, sounds the same note of the Gospel brought home to the individual believer: Christ's atoning blood was "to my soul applied"; His infinite grace "found out me"; Christ is "my own." As in John's sermons, Charles's hymns celebrate freedom from both the guilt and the power of bondage: "He breaks the power of cancelled sin, he sets the prisoner free."

The hymn "O for a Heart to Praise my God" is a prayer for the holiness, or perfection in love, that John preached. Whereas John's affirmations about the kind or degree of holiness possible to attain in this life may excite debate, Charles's earnest supplications for a more Christ-like heart express the longings of believers across many different traditions. His words appear in the hymnbooks of many denominations so that the church can sing with one united voice, asking for renewed hearts "full of love divine."

# JANE AUSTEN

### Modern (1775–1817)

**H**orrific wars roiled Europe.

Napoleon, a great antichrist, destroyed the peace of Christendom.

Nelson. Trafalgar. Wellington. Waterloo. Those were the names and places of the day immortalized by the English nation in shrines and statues.

At least the English nation *tried* to immortalize them; traveling with American honor students makes plain that while one has to explain Wellington, he rarely must describe Mr. Darcy.

It was a lightly regarded novelist of manners who has endured best to our day. A few people noticed her genius, Sir Walter Scott in particular. Scott was the great writer of his day—now too little read—and he defended "light" novels as worthwhile. The spare prose of Austen found fewer readers then, but Scott was right that the realistic and plain portrayal of one portion of English life was an important trend in literature.

Jane Austen is abused by some English departments eager for a "great woman writer" and obsessed with making the same ideological points in every book read. Austen refuses to fit neat categories. She obviously opposed the reduction of women to mindless objects for male entertainment, but in a revolutionary age, one thoroughly roiled by notions of radical emancipation, Austen was no revolutionary. She was a progressive conservative . . . a Christian in the tradition of Saint Paul.

Paul undercut Roman slavery by insisting that all slaves be treated as part of the family of God; the system naturally died in the Christian West with a minimum of dislocation and social turmoil.

Jane Austen insisted that women are human, fully human, and have their own voice. Stupid restrictions on women could not survive those deeply Christian truths.

Austen saved what must be saved—what was good—about English Christian civilization, but she gently pointed it in better directions. Her works were read with pleasure in the Royal Family, but her attitudes toward chastity and family life would have been a beneficial check to the hedonism rampant in those circles. Liberation too often meant being libertine, and Austen would have nothing to do with moral breakdown.

Austen's characters are *good* in the most conventional Christian sense, but they are not prigs, bores, or prudes. Her women are *human* in the fullest sense, but they reflect that part of the image of God that is the sole preserve of the female.

Jane Austen, Christian, steered between feminism and misogyny to give readers a "middle way." Read and see if it works.

### FROM

# *Pride and Prejudice*

### Chapter I

It is a truth universally acknowledged, that a single man in possession of a good fortune must be in want of a wife.

However little known the feelings or views of such a man may be on his first entering a neighbourhood, this truth is so well fixed in the minds of the surrounding families, that he is considered as the rightful property of some one or other of their daughters.

"My dear Mr. Bennet," said his lady to him one day, "have you heard that Netherfield Park is let at last?"

Mr. Bennet replied that he had not.

"But it is," returned she; "for Mrs. Long has just been here, and she told me all about it."

Mr. Bennet made no answer.

"Do not you want to know who has taken it?" cried his wife impatiently.

"*You* want to tell me, and I have no objection to hearing it."

This was invitation enough.

"Why, my dear, you must know, Mrs. Long says that Netherfield is taken by a young man of large fortune from the north of England; that he came down on Monday in a chaise and four to see the place, and was so much delighted with it that he agreed with Mr. Morris immediately; that he is to take possession before Michaelmas, and some of his servants are to be in the house by the end of next week."

"What is his name?"

"Bingley."

"Is he married or single?"

"Oh! single, my dear, to be sure! A single man of large fortune; four or five thousand a year. What a fine thing for our girls!"

"How so? how can it affect them?"

"My dear Mr. Bennet," replied his wife, "how can you be so tiresome! You must know that I am thinking of his marrying one of them."

"Is that his design in settling here?"

"Design! nonsense, how can you talk so! But it is very likely that he *may* fall in love with one of them, and therefore you must visit him as soon as he comes."

"I see no occasion for that. You and the girls may go, or you may send them by themselves, which perhaps will be still better; for, as you are as handsome as any of them, Mr. Bingley might like you the best of the party."

"My dear, you flatter me. I certainly *have* had my share of beauty, but I do not pretend to be any thing extraordinary now. When a woman has five grown up daughters, she ought to give over thinking of her own beauty."

"In such cases, a woman has not often much beauty to think of."

"But, my dear, you must indeed go and see Mr. Bingley when he comes into the neighbourhood."

"It is more than I engage for, I assure you."

"But consider your daughters. Only think what an establishment it would be for one of them. Sir William and Lady Lucas are determined to go, merely on that account, for in general, you know they visit no new comers. Indeed you must go, for it will be impossible for us to visit him, if you do not."

"You are over-scrupulous, surely. I dare say Mr. Bingley will be very glad to see you; and I will send a few lines by you to assure him of my hearty consent to his marrying which ever he chooses of the girls; though I must throw in a good word for my little Lizzy."

"I desire you will do no such thing. Lizzy is not a bit better than the others; and I am sure she is not half so handsome as Jane, nor half so good humoured as Lydia. But you are always giving *her* the preference."

"They have none of them much to recommend them," replied he; "they are all silly and ignorant like other girls; but Lizzy has something more of quickness than her sisters."

"Mr. Bennet, how can you abuse your own children in such way? You take delight in vexing me. You have no compassion on my poor nerves."

"You mistake me, my dear. I have a high respect for your nerves. They are my old friends. I have heard you mention them with consideration these twenty years at least."

"Ah! you do not know what I suffer."

"But I hope you will get over it, and live to see many young men of four thousand a year come into the neighbourhood."

"It will be no use to us if twenty such should come, since you will not visit them."

"Depend upon it, my dear, that when there are twenty I will visit them all."

Mr. Bennet was so odd a mixture of quick parts, sarcastic humour, reserve, and caprice, that the experience of three and twenty years had been insufficient to make his wife understand his character. *Her* mind was less difficult to develop. She was a woman of mean understanding, little information, and uncertain temper. When she was discontented, she fancied herself nervous. The business of her life was to get her daughters married; its solace was visiting and news.

...

## Chapter XXXIV

When they were gone, Elizabeth, as if intending to exasperate herself as much as possible against Mr. Darcy, chose for her employment the examination of all the letters which Jane had written to her since her being in Kent. They contained no actual complaint, nor was there any revival of past occurrences, or any communication of present suffering. But in all, and in almost every line of each, there was a want of that cheerfulness which had been used to characterize her style, and which, proceeding from the serenity of a mind at ease with itself, and kindly disposed towards every one, had been scarcely ever clouded. Elizabeth noticed every sentence conveying the idea of uneasiness with an attention which it had hardly received on the first perusal. Mr. Darcy's shameful boast of what misery he had been able to inflict gave her a keener sense of her sister's sufferings. It was some consolation to think that his visit to Rosings was to end on the day after the next, and a still greater that in less than a fortnight she should herself be with Jane again, and enabled to contribute to the recovery of her spirits by all that affection could do. She could not think of Darcy's leaving Kent without remembering that his cousin was to go with him; but Colonel Fitzwilliam had made it clear that he had no intentions at all, and agreeable as he was, she did not mean to be unhappy about him.

While settling this point, she was suddenly roused by the sound of the door bell, and her spirits were a little fluttered by the idea of its being Colonel Fitzwilliam himself, who had once before called late in the evening, and might now come to enquire particularly after her. But this idea was soon banished, and her spirits were very differently affected, when, to her utter amazement, she saw Mr. Darcy walk into the room. In an hurried manner he immediately began an enquiry after her health, imputing his visit to a wish of hearing that she were better. She answered him with cold civility. He sat down for a few moments, and then getting up, walked about the room. Elizabeth was surprised, but said not a word. After a silence of several minutes, he came towards her in an agitated manner, and thus began,

"In vain have I struggled. It will not do. My feelings will not be repressed. You must allow me to tell you how ardently I admire and love you."

Elizabeth's astonishment was beyond expression. She stared, coloured, doubted, and was silent. This he considered sufficient encouragement, and the avowal of all that he felt and had long felt for her immediately followed. He spoke well, but there were feelings besides those of the heart to be detailed, and he was not more eloquent on the subject of tenderness than of pride. His sense of her inferiority—of its being a degradation—of the family obstacles which judgment had always opposed to inclination, were dwelt on with a warmth which seemed due to the consequence he was wounding, but was very unlikely to recommend his suit.

In spite of her deeply-rooted dislike, she could not be insensible to the compliment of such a man's affection, and though her intentions did not vary for an instant, she was at first sorry for the pain he was to receive; till, roused to resentment by his subsequent language, she lost all compassion in anger. She tried, however, to compose herself to answer him with patience, when he should have done. He concluded with representing to her the strength of that attachment which, in spite of all his endeavours, he had found impossible to conquer; and with expressing his hope that it would now be rewarded by her acceptance of his hand. As he said this, she could easily see that he had no doubt of a favourable answer. He spoke of apprehension and anxiety, but his countenance expressed real security. Such a circumstance could only exasperate farther, and when he ceased, the colour rose into her cheeks, and she said,

"In such cases as this, it is, I believe, the established mode to express a sense of obligation for the sentiments avowed, however unequally they may be returned. It is natural that obligation should be felt, and if I could feel gratitude, I would now thank you. But I cannot—I have never desired your good opinion, and you have certainly bestowed it most unwillingly. I am sorry to have occasioned pain to any one. It has been most unconsciously done, however, and I hope will be of short duration. The feelings which, you tell me, have long prevented the acknowledgment of your regard, can have little difficulty in overcoming it after this explanation."

Mr. Darcy, who was leaning against the mantle-piece with his eyes fixed on her face, seemed to catch her words with no less resentment than surprise. His complexion became pale with anger, and the disturbance of his mind was visible in every feature. He was struggling for the appearance of composure, and would not open his lips, till he believed himself to have attained it. The pause was to Elizabeth's feelings dreadful. At length, in a voice of forced calmness, he said,

"And this is all the reply which I am to have the honour of expecting! I might, perhaps, wish to be informed why, with so little endeavour at civility, I am thus rejected. But it is of small importance."

"I might as well enquire," replied she, "why, with so evident a design of offending and insulting me, you chose to tell me that you liked me against your will, against your reason, and even against your character? Was not this some excuse for incivility, if I was uncivil? But I have other provocations. You know I have. Had not my own feelings decided against you, had they been indifferent, or had they even been favourable, do you think that any consideration would tempt me to accept the man, who has been the means of ruining, perhaps for ever, the happiness of a most beloved sister?"

As she pronounced these words, Mr. Darcy changed colour; but the emotion was short, and he listened without attempting to interrupt her while she continued.

"I have every reason in the world to think ill of you. No motive can excuse the unjust and ungenerous part you acted there. You dare not, you cannot deny that you have been the principal, if not the only means of dividing them from each other, of exposing one to the censure of the world for caprice and instability, the other to its derision for disappointed hopes, and involving them both in misery of the acutest kind."

She paused, and saw with no slight indignation that he was listening with an air which proved him wholly unmoved by any feeling of remorse. He even looked at her with a smile of affected incredulity.

"Can you deny that you have done it?" she repeated.

With assumed tranquility he then replied, "I have no wish of denying that I did every thing in my power to separate my friend from your sister, or that I rejoice in my success. Towards him I have been kinder than towards myself."

Elizabeth disdained the appearance of noticing this civil reflection, but its meaning did not escape, nor was it likely to conciliate, her.

"But it is not merely this affair," she continued, "on which my dislike is founded. Long before it had taken place, my opinion of you was decided. Your character was unfolded in the recital which I received many months ago from Mr. Wickham. On this subject, what can you have to say? In what imaginary act of friendship can you here defend yourself? Or under what misrepresentation, can you here impose upon others?"

"You take an eager interest in that gentleman's concerns," said Darcy in a less tranquil tone, and with a heightened colour.

"Who that knows what his misfortunes have been, can help feeling an interest in him?"

"His misfortunes!'" repeated Darcy contemptuously; "Yes, his misfortunes have been great indeed."

"And of your infliction," cried Elizabeth with energy. "You have reduced him to his present state of poverty, comparative poverty. You have withheld the advantages, which you must know to have been designed for him. You have deprived the best years of his life, of that independence which was no less his due than his desert. You have done all this! and yet you can treat the mention of his misfortunes with contempt and ridicule."

"And this," cried Darcy, as he walked with quick steps across the room, "is your opinion of me! This is the estimation in which you hold me! I thank you for explaining it so fully. My faults, according to this calculation, are heavy indeed! But perhaps," added he, stopping in his walk, and turning towards her, "these offences might have been overlooked, had not your pride been hurt by my honest confession of the scruples that had long prevented my forming any serious design. These bitter accusations might have been suppressed, had I with greater policy concealed my struggles, and flattered you into the belief of my being impelled by unqualified, unalloyed inclination—by reason, by reflection, by every thing. But disguise of every sort is my abhorrence. Nor am I ashamed of the feelings I related. They were natural and just. Could you expect me to rejoice in the inferiority of your connections? To congratulate myself on the hope of relations, whose condition in life is so decidedly beneath my own?"

Elizabeth felt herself growing more angry every moment; yet she tried to the utmost to speak with composure when she said,

"You are mistaken, Mr. Darcy, if you suppose that the mode of your declaration affected me in any other way, than as it spared me the concern which I might have felt in refusing you, had you behaved in a more gentleman-like manner."

She saw him start at this, but he said nothing, and she continued,

"You could not have made me the offer of your hand in any possible way that would have tempted me to accept it."

Again his astonishment was obvious; and he looked at her with an expression of mingled incredulity and mortification. She went on.

"From the very beginning, from the first moment I may almost say, of my acquaintance with you, your manners, impressing me with the fullest belief of your arrogance, your conceit, and your selfish disdain of the feelings of others, were such as to form that ground-work of disapprobation, on which succeeding events have built so immoveable a dislike; and I had not known you a month before I felt that you were the last man in the world whom I could ever be prevailed on to marry."

"You have said quite enough, madam. I perfectly comprehend your feelings, and have now only to be ashamed of what my own have been. Forgive me for having taken up so much of your time, and accept my best wishes for your health and happiness."

And with these words he hastily left the room, and Elizabeth heard him the next moment open the front door and quit the house.

The tumult of her mind was now painfully great. She knew not how to support herself, and from actual weakness sat down and cried for half an hour. Her astonishment, as she reflected on what had passed, was increased by every review of it. That she should receive an offer of marriage from Mr. Darcy! that he should have been in love with her for so many months! so much in love as to wish to marry her in spite of all the objections which had made him prevent his friend's marrying her sister, and which must appear at least with equal force in his own case, was almost incredible! It was gratifying to have inspired unconsciously so strong an affection. But his pride, his abominable pride, his shameless avowal of what he had done with respect to Jane, his unpardonable assurance in acknowledging, though he could not justify it, and the unfeeling manner in which he had mentioned Mr. Wickham, his cruelty towards whom he had not attempted to deny, soon overcame the pity which the consideration of his attachment had for a moment excited.

She continued in very agitating reflections till the sound of Lady Catherine's carriage made her feel how unequal she was to encounter Charlotte's observation, and hurried her away to her room.

# TRUTHS UNIVERSALLY
# TO BE ACKNOWLEDGED

## ON PRIDE AND PREJUDICE

## John Mark Reynolds

It is a truth universally acknowledged, that a single man in possession of a good fortune must be in want of a wife."

A book full of universal truths begins with a claim about truth that isn't. As the novel will show, not all single rich men have thoughts of, or even are in very great need of, a wife. Is the long-suffering Mr. Bennet really better off married? Perhaps, but it is not obviously so, and certainly his is not a situation most men would envy.

In fact, Austen has written a book in which many such truths are exposed as the result of pride and/or more prejudice. Both pride and prejudice get in the way of love, and the universal truth she reveals is that both men and women of any fortune are in desperate need of love from someone other than themselves.

Austen argues by demonstration and by showing the folly of alternatives. If you have not read the whole book, please stop reading this essay, go get a copy, and finish *Pride and Prejudice*. It's a truth universally to be acknowledged that people who do not actually read all of a great book before discussing it spoil the power of the book when they return to it later.

My assumption is that these chapters have reminded you of the Bennet family—especially the nature of the daughters and of the tension that exists between Darcy and Elizabeth. They eventually marry (I warned you to stop reading if you didn't know the outcome), but only when both have been purged of a great deal of pride and prejudice.

All the Bennet daughters lack something, and that something is not a man. In Austen, marriage is *not* the coming together of two equals but the coming together of two human beings who are very different yet compatible. Men are not women; women are not men. It is the fusing of the two "others" that makes marriage explosively fruitful.

Two become one, and civilization gets three!

Austen knew nothing of our modern quest for equality. People are not numbers, and so they are never "equal." Some folk are higher placed than others, have more money, were more fortunate in their parents, or are brighter. These gifts do not come to us by merit but by the unfathomable providence of God.

At the same time, foolish people might confuse graces bestowed by God with actual merit. Mr. Collins, as odious and pitiable a man as one can imagine, makes this error. Wealthy patrons are better in their potency, but they may not have done anything with their graces. Abilities or gifts without works are worse than useless, and one who has been given much should be expected to do much. Mr. Darcy lives up to the expectations of his gifts; Mr. Collins's patron does not.

Austen didn't make the French Revolutionaries' mistake of assuming that the plumber could become a professor by legal declaration and wishing it to be so. On the other hand, she also does not make the pitiable error of the Old Regime and assume that all lords are lordly.

Instead she is deeply conservative, because she is an advocate of love. Love knows nothing of equality, because the lover always elevates the Beloved above all others. Nobody makes a lover cling only to his beloved and forsake all others. Passion demands it, at least at first. It is an essential feature of Christian civilization to insist that this love vow be cherished and honored.

Men and women aren't allowed to swear eternal fidelity and then forget. They must renew their vows and grow in love to each other. The trouble is that love, while necessary, isn't enough this side of paradise. Ideally, all Beloveds should be worthy of our love, but not all are fit objects of our passion.

Lydia, the passionate sister, makes the mistake of believing that love always reports truly on the character of the Beloved. Sadly, she has fixed her attentions on someone unworthy of her love. Her prejudice that a man who is lovely and should be good is worthy of love and good, will ruin her by the end of the book.

God bestows great gifts on human beings with perfect justice, but not all gifts we are given come from God. Some gifts come from society or culture, and it is here that problems develop. Civilization will stunt the progress of women so that marriage to Mr. Collins is more desirable than marriage to a fit man. Mr. Collins will be given social position he misuses and does not deserve while more fit men are passed over.

Austen didn't pretend this system is just; while it needed to be changed, it could only be changed slowly, or the revolution would cause more pain than it brought pleasure. She saw things as they were—didn't always like them but accepted what must be accepted. Elizabeth, on the other hand, is too demanding of life.

Elizabeth demands perfect justice and knowledge that justice has been done. This is ideal, but unrealistic. Charity, absolute romance, demands that in a fallen world we judge by the standard by which we wish to be judged. She misjudges Darcy, but that's not her only problem. She requires too much of the world, and she lacks mercy. Even with her friends she's too quick to assume she knows what's best.

It's a truth universally to be acknowledged that love between beings as different as men and women can *only* work when the men and women are fully human. It is their common humanity, the virtue of exhibiting God's image, that makes the dangerous fusion of two "others" fecund and not just explosive. Austen demonstrated a temporary truth, an ideal so valuable in our age, one that before Christ returns will never quite be realized. We will have to be charitable even to Mrs. Bennet and Mr. Collins, understanding that all have sinned and fallen short of the glory of God.

## CHAPTER TWENTY THREE

# ALEXIS DE TOCQUEVILLE

### Modern (1805–1859)

Conservative Americans tempted in recent decades to mock the French must read Alexis de Tocqueville to remind themselves that many of our best ideas and noblest defenders have come from France. The American Founders were overwhelmingly Englishmen, but more than a few thought about government with a strong French accent. Alexis de Tocqueville would remind the next generation after the founding what this mental combination had produced.

He was born into one of the finest families of France, but he spent his entire life advocating for liberty. The French Revolution had culminated in butchery and an empire. Tocqueville lived as a citizen of French republics, subject of a restored monarchy, and a foe of a second empire. The American Revolution turned out much differently, and Tocqueville suggested why.

Christians learned over the centuries the limits and role of government. Utopian schemes that associated Christendom too closely with any particular regime almost always led to tyranny and abuse. Too much freedom, however, could lead to social chaos and anarchy. Between tyranny and anarchy was the Christian commonwealth that could maximize public liberty because of the morality of the people.

Read carefully: Tocqueville reminds believers that the liberty of each human soul is of great value. He also reminds us that no earthly state is perfect and that humanity is not perfectible in this life. Tocqueville was a man with modest goals and realistic dreams.

Citizens of any constitutional state owe a debt to him. His support for liberty under law, for public liberty and private piety, persuaded many American readers. Every nation needs more people who love liberty, fear mob rule, and hate tyranny with the consistent logic and passion of Alexis de Tocqueville. He is still quoted by presidential candidates, but too often he's ignored by presidents, and therein lies the danger.

Tocqueville reads beautifully but governs even better.

<br>

⟨ FROM ⟩

# Democracy in America

### Chapter 5

### Of the Manner in Which Religion in the United States Avails Itself of Democratic Tendencies

I have laid it down in a preceding chapter that men cannot do without dogmatical belief; and even that it is very much to be desired that such belief should exist amongst them. I now add, that of all the kinds of dogmatical belief the most desirable appears to me to be dogmatical belief in matters of religion; and this is a very clear inference, even from no higher consideration than the interests of this world. There is hardly any human action, however particular a character be assigned to it, which does not originate in some very general idea men have conceived of the Deity, of his relation to mankind, of the nature of their own souls, and of their duties to their fellow-creatures. Nor can anything prevent these ideas from being the common spring from which everything else emanates. Men are therefore immeasurably interested in acquiring fixed ideas of God, of the soul, and of their common duties to their Creator and to their fellow-men; for doubt on these first principles would abandon all their actions to the impulse of chance, and would condemn them to live, to a certain extent, powerless and undisciplined.

This is then the subject on which it is most important for each of us to entertain fixed ideas; and unhappily it is also the subject on which it is most difficult for each of us, left to himself, to settle his opinions by the sole force of his reason. None but minds singularly free from the ordinary anxieties of life—minds at once penetrating, subtle, and trained by thinking—can even with the assistance of much time and care, sound the depth of these most necessary truths. And, indeed, we see that these philosophers are themselves almost always enshrouded in uncertainties; that at every step the natural light which illuminates their path grows dimmer and less secure; and that, in spite of all their efforts, they have as yet only discovered a small number of conflicting notions, on which the mind of man has been tossed about for thousands of years, without either laying a firmer grasp on truth, or finding novelty even in its errors. Studies of this nature are far above the average capacity of men; and even if the majority of mankind were capable of such pursuits, it is evident that leisure to cultivate them would still be wanting. Fixed ideas of God and human nature are indispensable to the daily practice of men's lives; but the practice of their lives prevents them from acquiring such ideas.

The difficulty appears to me to be without a parallel. Amongst the sciences there are some which are useful to the mass of mankind, and which are within its reach; others can only be approached by the few, and are not cultivated by the many, who require nothing beyond their more remote applications: but the daily practice of the science I speak of is indispensable to all, although the study of it is inaccessible to the far greater number.

General ideas respecting God and human nature are therefore the ideas above all others which it is most suitable to withdraw from the habitual action of private judgment, and in which there is most to gain and least to lose by recognizing a principle of authority. The first object and one of the principal advantages of religions, is to furnish to each of these fundamental questions a solution which is at once clear, precise, intelligible to the mass of mankind, and lasting. There are religions which are very false and very absurd; but it may be affirmed, that any religion which remains within the circle I have just traced, without aspiring to go beyond it (as many religions have attempted to do, for the purpose of enclosing on every side the free progress of the human mind), imposes a salutary restraint on the intellect; and it must be admitted that, if it do not save men in another world, such religion is at least very conducive to their happiness and their greatness in this.

This is more especially true of men living in free countries. When the religion of a people is destroyed, doubt gets hold of the highest portions of the intellect, and half paralyzes all the rest of its powers. Every man accustoms himself to entertain none but confused and changing notions on the subjects most interesting to his fellow-creatures and himself. His opinions are ill-defended and easily abandoned: and, despairing of ever resolving by himself the hardest problems of the destiny of man, he ignobly submits to think no more about them. Such a condition cannot but enervate the soul, relax the springs of the will, and prepare a people for servitude. Nor does it only happen, in such a case, that they allow their freedom to be wrested from them; they frequently themselves surrender it. When there is no longer any principle of authority in religion any more than in politics, men are speedily frightened at the aspect of this unbounded independence. The constant agitation of all surrounding things alarms and exhausts them. As everything is at sea in the sphere of the intellect, they determine at least that the mechanism of society should be firm and fixed; and as they cannot resume their ancient belief, they assume a master.

For my own part, I doubt whether man can ever support at the same time complete religious independence and entire public freedom. And I am inclined to think, that if faith be wanting in him, he must serve; and if he be free, he must believe.

Perhaps, however, this great utility of religions is still more obvious amongst nations where equality of conditions prevails than amongst others. It must be acknowledged that equality, which brings great benefits into the world, nevertheless suggests to men (as will be shown hereafter) some very dangerous propensities. It tends to isolate them from each other, to concentrate every man's attention upon himself; and it lays open the soul to an inordinate love of material gratification. The greatest advantage of religion is to inspire diametrically contrary principles. There is no religion which does not place the object of man's desires above and beyond the treasures of earth, and which does not naturally raise his soul to regions far above those of the senses. Nor is there any which does not impose on man some sort of duties to his kind, and thus draws him at times from the contemplation of himself. This occurs in religions the most false and dangerous. Religious nations are therefore naturally strong on the very point on which democratic nations are weak; which shows of what importance it is for men to preserve their religion as their conditions become more equal.

I have neither the right nor the intention of examining the supernatural means which God employs to infuse religious belief into the heart of man. I am at this moment considering religions in a purely human point of view: my object is to inquire by what means they may most easily retain their sway in the democratic ages upon which we are entering. It has been shown that, at times of general cultivation and equality, the human mind does not consent to adopt dogmatical opinions without reluctance, and feels their necessity acutely in spiritual matters only. This proves, in the first place, that at such times religions ought, more cautiously than at any other, to confine themselves within their own precincts; for in seeking to extend their power beyond religious matters, they incur a risk of not being believed at all. The circle within which they seek to bound the human intellect ought therefore to be carefully traced, and beyond its verge the mind should be left in entire freedom to its own guidance. Mahommed professed to derive from Heaven, and he has inserted in the Koran, not only a body of religious doctrines, but political maxims, civil and criminal laws, and theories of science. The gospel, on the contrary, only speaks of the general relations of men to God and to each other—beyond which it inculcates and imposes no point of faith. This alone, besides a thousand other reasons, would suffice to prove that the former of these religions will never long predominate in a cultivated and democratic age, whilst the latter is destined to retain its sway at these as at all other periods.

But in continuation of this branch of the subject, I find that in order for religions to maintain their authority, humanly speaking, in democratic ages, they must not only confine themselves strictly within the circle of spiritual matters: their power also depends very much on the nature of the belief they inculcate, on the external forms they assume, and on the obligations they impose. The preceding observation, that equality leads men to very general and very extensive notions, is principally to be understood as applied to the question of religion. Men living in a similar and equal condition in the world readily conceive the idea of the one God, governing every man by the same laws, and granting to every man future happiness on the same conditions. The idea of the unity of mankind constantly leads them back to the idea of the unity of the Creator; whilst, on the contrary, in a state of society where men are broken up into very unequal ranks, they are apt to devise as many deities as there are nations, castes, classes, or families, and to trace a thousand private roads to heaven.

It cannot be denied that Christianity itself has felt, to a certain extent, the influence which social and political conditions exercise on religious opinions. At the epoch at which the Christian religion appeared upon earth, Providence, by whom the world was doubtless prepared for its coming, had gathered a large portion of the human race, like an immense flock, under the sceptre of the Caesars. The men of whom this multitude was composed were distinguished by numerous differences; but they had thus much in common, that they all obeyed the same laws, and that every subject was so weak and insignificant in relation to the imperial potentate, that all appeared equal when their condition was contrasted with his.

This novel and peculiar state of mankind necessarily predisposed men to listen to the general truths which Christianity teaches, and may serve to explain the facility and rapidity with which they then penetrated into the human mind. The counterpart of this state of things was exhibited after the destruction of the empire. The Roman world being then as it were shattered into a thousand fragments, each nation resumed its pristine individuality. An infinite scale of ranks very soon grew up in the bosom of these nations; the different races were more sharply defined, and each nation was divided by castes into several peoples.

In the midst of this common effort, which seemed to be urging human society to the greatest conceivable amount of voluntary subdivision, Christianity did not lose sight of the leading general ideas which it had brought into the world. But it appeared, nevertheless, to lend itself, as much as was possible, to those new tendencies to which the fractional distribution of mankind had given birth. Men continued to worship an only God, the Creator and Preserver of all things; but every people, every city, and, so to speak, every man, thought to obtain some distinct privilege, and win the favor of an especial patron at the foot of the Throne of Grace. Unable to subdivide the Deity, they multiplied and improperly enhanced the importance of the divine agents. The homage due to saints and angels became an almost idolatrous worship amongst the majority of the Christian world; and apprehensions might be entertained for a moment lest the religion of Christ should retrograde towards the superstitions which it had subdued.

It seems evident, that the more the barriers are removed which separate nation from nation amongst mankind, and citizen from citizen amongst a people, the stronger is the bent of the human mind, as if by its own impulse, towards the idea of an only and all-powerful Being, dispensing equal laws in the same manner to every man. In democratic ages, then, it is more particularly important not to allow the homage paid to secondary agents to be confounded with the worship due to the Creator alone.

Another truth is no less clear—that religions ought to assume fewer external observances in democratic periods than at any others. In speaking of philosophical method among the Americans, I have shown that nothing is more repugnant to the human mind in an age of equality than the idea of subjection to forms. Men living at such times are impatient of figures; to their eyes symbols appear to be the puerile artifice which is used to conceal or to set off truths, which should more naturally be bared to the light of open day: they are unmoved by ceremonial observances, and they are predisposed to attach a secondary importance to the details of public worship. Those whose care it is to regulate the external forms of religion in a democratic age should pay a close attention to these natural propensities of the human mind, in order not unnecessarily to run counter to them.

I firmly believe in the necessity of forms, which fix the human mind in the contemplation of abstract truths, and stimulate its ardor in the pursuit of them, whilst they invigorate its powers of retaining them steadfastly. Nor do I suppose that it is possible to maintain a religion without external observances; but, on the other hand, I am persuaded that, in the ages upon which we are entering, it would be peculiarly dangerous to multiply them beyond measure; and that they ought rather to be limited to as much as is absolutely necessary to perpetuate the doctrine itself, which is the substance of religions of which the ritual is only the form. A religion which should become more minute, more peremptory, and more surcharged with small observances at a time in which men are becoming more equal, would soon find itself reduced to a band of fanatical zealots in the midst of an infidel people.

In all religions there are some ceremonies which are inherent in the substance of the faith itself, and in these nothing should, on any account, be changed. This is especially the case with Roman Catholicism, in which the doctrine and the form are frequently so closely united as to form one point of belief.

I anticipate the objection, that as all religions have general and eternal truths for their object, they cannot thus shape themselves to the shifting spirit of every age without forfeiting their claim to certainty in the eyes of mankind. To this I reply again, that the principal opinions which constitute belief, and which theologians call articles of faith, must be very carefully distinguished from the accessories connected with them. Religions are obliged to hold fast to the former, whatever be the peculiar spirit of the age; but they should take good care not to bind themselves in the same manner to the latter at a time when everything is in transition, and when the mind, accustomed to the moving pageant of human affairs, reluctantly endures the attempt to fix it to any given point. The fixity of external and secondary things can only afford a chance of duration when civil society is itself fixed; under any other circumstances I hold it to be perilous.

We shall have occasion to see that, of all the passions which originate in, or are fostered by, equality, there is one which it renders peculiarly intense, and which it infuses at the same time into the heart of every man: I mean the love of well-being. The taste for well-being is the prominent and indelible feature of democratic ages. It may be believed that a religion which should undertake to destroy so deep seated a passion, would meet its own destruction thence in the end; and if it attempted to wean men entirely from the contemplation of the good things of this world, in order to devote their faculties exclusively to the thought of another, it may be foreseen that the soul would at length escape from its grasp, to plunge into the exclusive enjoyment of present and material pleasures. The chief concern of religions is to purify, to regulate, and to restrain the excessive and exclusive taste for well-being which men feel at periods of equality; but they would err in attempting to control it completely or to eradicate it. They will not succeed in curing men of the love of riches: but they may still persuade men to enrich themselves by none but honest means.

This brings me to a final consideration, which comprises, as it were, all the others. The more the conditions of men are equalized and assimilated to each other, the more important is it for religions, whilst they carefully abstain from the daily turmoil of secular affairs, not needlessly to run counter to the ideas which generally prevail, and the permanent interests which exist in the mass of the people. For as public opinion grows to be more and more evidently the first and most irresistible of existing powers, the religious principle has no external support strong enough to enable it long to resist its attacks. This is not less true of a democratic people, ruled by a despot, than in a republic. In ages of equality, kings may often command obedience, but the majority always commands belief: to the majority, therefore, deference is to be paid in whatsoever is not contrary to the faith.

I showed in my former volumes how the American clergy stand aloof from secular affairs. This is the most obvious, but it is not the only, example of their self-restraint. In America religion is a distinct sphere, in which the priest is sovereign, but out of which he takes care never to go. Within its limits he is the master of the mind; beyond them, he leaves men to themselves, and surrenders them to the independence and instability which belong to their nature and their age. I have seen no country in which Christianity is clothed with fewer forms, figures, and observances than in the United States; or where it presents more distinct, more simple, or more general notions to the mind. Although the Christians of America are divided into a multitude of sects, they all look upon their religion in the same light.

This applies to Roman Catholicism as well as to the other forms of belief. There are no Romish priests who show less taste for the minute individual observances for extraordinary or peculiar means of salvation, or who cling more to the spirit, and less to the letter of the law, than the Roman Catholic priests of the United States. Nowhere is that doctrine of the Church, which prohibits the worship reserved to God alone from being offered to the saints, more clearly inculcated or more generally followed. Yet the Roman Catholics of America are very submissive and very sincere.

Another remark is applicable to the clergy of every communion. The American ministers of the gospel do not attempt to draw or to fix all the thoughts of man upon the life to come; they are willing to surrender a portion of his heart to the cares of the present; seeming to consider the goods of this world as important, although as secondary, objects. If they take no part themselves in productive labor, they are at least interested in its progression, and ready to applaud its results; and whilst they never cease to point to the other world as the great object of the hopes and fears of the believer, they do not forbid him honestly to court prosperity in this. Far from attempting to show that these things are distinct and contrary to one another, they study rather to find out on what point they are most nearly and closely connected.

All the American clergy know and respect the intellectual supremacy exercised by the majority; they never sustain any but necessary conflicts with it. They take no share in the altercations of parties, but they readily adopt the general opinions of their country and their age; and they allow themselves to be borne away without opposition in the current of feeling and opinion by which everything around them is carried along. They endeavor to amend their contemporaries, but they do not quit fellowship with them. Public opinion is therefore never hostile to them; it rather supports and protects them; and their belief owes its authority at the same time to the strength which is its own, and to that which they borrow from the opinions of the majority. Thus it is that, by respecting all democratic tendencies not absolutely contrary to herself, and by making use of several of them for her own purposes, religion sustains an advantageous struggle with that spirit of individual independence which is her most dangerous antagonist.

## Chapter 6

### Of the Progress of Roman Catholicism in the United States

America is the most democratic country in the world, and it is at the same time (according to reports worthy of belief) the country in which the Roman Catholic religion makes most progress. At first sight this is surprising. Two things must here be accurately distinguished: equality inclines men to wish to form their own opinions; but, on the other hand, it imbues them with the taste and the idea of unity, simplicity, and impartiality in the power which governs society. Men living in democratic ages are therefore very prone to shake off all religious authority; but if they consent to subject themselves to any authority of this kind, they choose at least that it should be single and uniform. Religious powers not radiating from a common centre are naturally repugnant to their minds; and they almost as readily conceive that there should be no religion, as that there should be several.

At the present time, more than in any preceding one, Roman Catholics are seen to lapse into infidelity, and Protestants to be converted to Roman Catholicism. If the Roman Catholic faith be considered within the pale of the church, it would seem to be losing ground; without that pale, to be gaining it. Nor is this circumstance difficult of explanation. The men of our days are naturally disposed to believe; but, as soon as they have any religion, they immediately find in themselves a latent propensity which urges them unconsciously towards Catholicism. Many of the doctrines and the practices of the Romish Church astonish them; but they feel a secret admiration for its discipline, and its great unity attracts them. If Catholicism could at length withdraw itself from the political animosities to which it has given rise, I have hardly any doubt but that the same spirit of the age, which appears to be so opposed to it, would become so favorable as to admit of its great and sudden advancement.

One of the most ordinary weaknesses of the human intellect is to seek to reconcile contrary principles, and to purchase peace at the expense of logic. Thus there have ever been, and will ever be, men who, after having submitted some portion of their religious belief to the principle of authority, will seek to exempt several other parts of their faith from its influence, and to keep their minds floating at random between liberty and obedience. But I am inclined to believe that the number of these thinkers will be less in democratic than in other ages; and that our posterity will tend more and more to a single division into two parts—some relinquishing Christianity entirely, and others returning to the bosom of the Church of Rome. . . .

*Translated by Henry Reeve, 1901*

# ON RELIGION IN AMERICA

## Hugh Hewitt

$\mathbf{A}$lexis de Tocqueville came to the United States from France in 1831 to observe and report, which he did in two volumes, published in 1835 and 1840. The above excerpt is from the second volume, and from the translation by Henry Reeves, which Tocqueville did not care for. Translations matter, of course, but we do not know if Tocqueville would have cared for any of the later translations either. Reeves well may have been less objectionable to Tocqueville than all the others.

It is good, perhaps, to use a translation criticized by the author of the original, as it should alert the reader to the fact that all translations are suspect. Be on guard, then, when you aren't reading the original.

Furthermore, be on guard whenever you read about religion from an author who is himself not a proponent of the beliefs being reported. How could such an account be fair when the premise on so important a matter isn't shared? Would you trust Richard Dawkins to write a report on American religious practices in 2010? Or Christopher Hitchens?

Well, Tocqueville actually was fair, in both volumes of his work. He may not have been more interested in religion in America than he was any other subject to which he turned his attention, but he was quite thorough in his recordings of how it operated forty years after the Founding.

As you think about the text above, ask yourself where Tocqueville is going. Here again is the last paragraph of the fifth chapter:

> All the American clergy know and respect the intellectual supremacy exercised by the majority; they never sustain any but necessary conflicts with it. They take no share in the altercations of parties, but they readily adopt the general opinions of their country and their age; and they allow themselves to be borne away without opposition in the current of feeling and opinion by which everything around them is carried along. They endeavor to amend their contemporaries, but they do not quit fellowship with them. Public opinion is therefore never hostile to them; it rather supports and protects them; and their belief owes its authority at

the same time to the strength which is its own, and to that which they borrow from the opinions of the majority. Thus it is that, by respecting all democratic tendencies not absolutely contrary to herself, and by making use of several of them for her own purposes, religion sustains an advantageous struggle with that spirit of individual independence which is her most dangerous antagonist.

---

So what in the world is he saying? Is he calling the clergy spineless? Or is he complimenting their flexibility in the face of majoritarian rule?

And what does he mean by the assertion—quite definite—that "the spirit of individual independence" is the most dangerous antagonist of religion?

Note as well that after raising your suspicions about the clergy generally, Tocqueville goes on (in a chapter as short and to the point as the preceding was long and twisting) to applaud the progress of Roman Catholicism on the new continent. He nearly declares the victory of Catholicism in America, and this just a few short years before fearsome anti-Catholic prejudice would sweep the land.

Perhaps, though, he was just being farsighted, for if anyone examines the present American religious landscape, which sect has held together more closely, and even greater prospered, than the Roman Catholic? Beset by problems after *Vatican II*, of course, and humbled by the child-abuse scandal, still the Roman Church has grown and grown, fueled by immigration but also renewed by two pontiffs who have seemed to understand what Tocqueville knew: People want guidance for their souls once they are convinced they have them.

And they want dogma. Particularly in a hyper-democratic age when all is being thrown down—even definitions of institutions as central to the society as marriage.

This is just a brief introduction to *Democracy in America*, but here's a guarantee. You'll be able to return again and again and be charmed by the language and always be startled by what's almost a prophetic voice. Given his uncanny instinct, read very carefully what Tocqueville has to say about faith generally in an age of equality.

## CHAPTER TWENTY FOUR

# KARL MARX

Modern (1818–1883)

$\mathbf{K}$arl Marx wanted the world to be better than it was. He wanted an end to poverty, hunger, and ignorance. He revered science and was well read. He looked at the modern West and rejected both the Greco-Roman and Judeo-Christian foundations of that culture. He believed history was inevitably moving past both and that secularism and Communism were the future.

Marx, at least philosophically, must be credited with good intentions, but his ideas have been applied badly. Any great idea can be perverted—Christians know this from experience—but Marxism has never been applied to a society without being perverted.

To many, this suggests that there's something deeply wrong at the heart of the project. The likely root of the problem was that an honest desire to make things better was pushed in Marx, as for many other men, to utopian extremes. Attempting to make a fallen world better than it can be will break things better left unbroken. It will empower men to do great deeds, but great men fit for such deeds may be too rare for the challenge.

Christians must read Marx knowing that millions of believers were slaughtered in his name. Of all the writers in this book, it might be Marx who will demand of us the greatest exercise of charity.

Jesus calls us to love our enemies, and so we must love Marx. You cannot pretend to love a man without understanding his ideas, and part of loving the man is to recognize his intentions, including his hostility to the faith. Christian love also can include learning why Marx rejected the Christendom he saw and what he hoped to achieve in his work.

We may hate many of the results of his work, reject his view of history, and criticize his faulty economic reasoning, but we can still learn from Karl Marx.

First, we must understand what caused millions and millions of people to be motivated to live and even to die for his vision.

Second, we must comprehend the failures that made his ideas possible, for most often they also are our own failures.

Finally, we must see what insights can be redeemed from within the Marxist worldview. Great genius is not so common that we can afford to let *any* truth go to waste.

Even Karl Marx was a subject of King Logos.

## FROM

# *The Communist Manifesto*

### Introduction

A spectre is haunting Europe—the spectre of Communism. All the Powers of old Europe have entered into a holy alliance to exorcise this spectre: Pope and Czar, Metternich and Guizot, French Radicals and German police-spies.

Where is the party in opposition that has not been decried as Communistic by its opponents in power? Where the Opposition that has not hurled back the branding reproach of Communism, against the more advanced opposition parties, as well as against its reactionary adversaries?

Two things result from this fact.

I. Communism is already acknowledged by all European Powers to be itself a Power.

II. It is high time that Communists should openly, in the face of the whole world, publish their views, their aims, their tendencies, and meet this nursery tale of the Spectre of Communism with a Manifesto of the party itself.

To this end, Communists of various nationalities have assembled in London, and sketched the following Manifesto, to be published in the English, French, German, Italian, Flemish and Danish languages.

## I. Bourgeois and Proletarians

The history of all hitherto existing societies is the history of class struggles.

Freeman and slave, patrician and plebeian, lord and serf, guild-master and journeyman, in a word, oppressor and oppressed, stood in constant opposition to one another, carried on an uninterrupted, now hidden, now open fight, a fight that each time ended, either in a revolutionary re-constitution of society at large, or in the common ruin of the contending classes.

In the earlier epochs of history, we find almost everywhere a complicated arrangement of society into various orders, a manifold gradation of social rank. In ancient Rome we have patricians, knights, plebeians, slaves; in the Middle Ages, feudal lords, vassals, guild-masters, journeymen, apprentices, serfs; in almost all of these classes, again, subordinate gradations.

The modern bourgeois society that has sprouted from the ruins of feudal society has not done away with clash antagonisms. It has but established new classes, new conditions of oppression, new forms of struggle in place of the old ones. Our epoch, the epoch of the bourgeoisie, possesses, however, this distinctive feature: it has simplified the class antagonisms: Society as a whole is more and more splitting up into two great hostile camps, into two great classes, directly facing each other: Bourgeoisie and Proletariat.

From the serfs of the Middle Ages sprang the chartered burghers of the earliest towns. From these burgesses the first elements of the bourgeoisie were developed.

The discovery of America, the rounding of the Cape, opened up fresh ground for the rising bourgeoisie. The East-Indian and Chinese markets, the colonisation of America, trade with the colonies, the increase in the means of exchange and in commodities generally, gave to commerce, to navigation, to industry, an impulse never before known, and thereby, to the revolutionary element in the tottering feudal society, a rapid development.

The feudal system of industry, under which industrial production was monopolised by closed guilds, now no longer sufficed for the growing wants of the new markets. The manufacturing system took its place. The guild-masters were pushed on one side by the manufacturing middle class; division of labour between the different corporate guilds vanished in the face of division of labour in each single workshop.

Meantime the markets kept ever growing, the demand ever rising. Even manufacture no longer sufficed. Thereupon, steam and machinery revolutionised industrial production. The place of manufacture was taken by the giant, Modern Industry, the place of the industrial middle class, by industrial millionaires, the leaders of whole industrial armies, the modern bourgeois.

Modern industry has established the world-market, for which the discovery of America paved the way. This market has given an immense development to commerce, to navigation, to communication by land. This development has, in its time, reacted on the extension of industry; and in proportion as industry, commerce, navigation, railways extended, in the same proportion the bourgeoisie developed, increased its capital, and pushed into the background every class handed down from the Middle Ages.

Now the modern bourgeoisie is itself the product of a long course of development, of a series of revolutions in the modes of production and of exchange.

Each step in the development of the bourgeoisie was accompanied by a corresponding political advance of that class. An oppressed class under the sway of the feudal nobility, an armed and self-governing association in the mediaeval commune; here independent urban republic (as in Italy and Germany), there taxable "third estate" of the monarchy (as in France), afterwards, in the period of manufacture proper, serving either the semi-feudal or the absolute monarchy as a counterpoise against the nobility, and, in fact, corner-stone of the great monarchies in general, the bourgeoisie has at last, since the establishment of Modern Industry and of the world-market, conquered for itself, in the modern representative State, exclusive political sway. The executive of the modern State is but a committee for managing the common affairs of the whole bourgeoisie.

The bourgeoisie, historically, has played a most revolutionary part.

The bourgeoisie, wherever it has got the upper hand, has put an end to all feudal, patriarchal, idyllic relations. It has pitilessly torn asunder the motley feudal ties that bound man to his "natural superiors," and has left remaining no other nexus between man and man than naked self-interest, than callous "cash payment." It has drowned the most heavenly ecstasies of religious fervour, of chivalrous enthusiasm, of philistine sentimentalism, in the icy water of egotistical calculation. It has resolved personal worth into exchange value. And in place of the numberless and feasible chartered freedoms, has set up that single, unconscionable freedom—Free Trade. In one word, for exploitation, veiled by religious and political illusions, naked, shameless, direct, brutal exploitation.

The bourgeoisie has stripped of its halo every occupation hitherto honoured and looked up to with reverent awe. It has converted the physician, the lawyer, the priest, the poet, the man of science, into its paid wage labourers.

The bourgeoisie has torn away from the family its sentimental veil, and has reduced the family relation to a mere money relation.

The bourgeoisie has disclosed how it came to pass that the brutal display of vigour in the Middle Ages, which Reactionists so much admire, found its fitting complement in the most slothful indolence. It has been the first to show what man's activity can bring about. It has accomplished wonders far surpassing Egyptian pyramids, Roman aqueducts, and Gothic cathedrals; it has conducted expeditions that put in the shade all former Exoduses of nations and crusades.

The bourgeoisie cannot exist without constantly revolutionising the instruments of production, and thereby the relations of production, and with them the whole relations of society. Conservation of the old modes of production in unaltered form, was, on the contrary, the first condition of existence for all earlier industrial classes. Constant revolutionising of production, uninterrupted disturbance of all social conditions, everlasting uncertainty and agitation distinguish the bourgeois epoch from all earlier ones. All fixed, fast-frozen relations, with their train of ancient and venerable prejudices and opinions, are swept away, all new-formed ones become antiquated before they can ossify. All that is solid melts into air, all that is holy is profaned, and man is at last compelled to face with sober senses, his real conditions of life, and his relations with his kind.

The need of a constantly expanding market for its products chases the bourgeoisie over the whole surface of the globe. It must nestle everywhere, settle everywhere, establish connexions everywhere.

The bourgeoisie has through its exploitation of the world-market given a cosmopolitan character to production and consumption in every country. To the great chagrin of Reactionists, it has drawn from under the feet of industry the national ground on which it stood. All old-established national industries have been destroyed or are daily being destroyed. They are dislodged by new industries, whose introduction becomes a life and death question for all civilised nations, by industries that no longer work up indigenous raw material, but raw material drawn from the remotest zones; industries whose products are consumed, not only at home, but in every quarter of the globe. In place of the old wants, satisfied by the productions of the country, we find new wants, requiring for their satisfaction the products of distant lands and climes. In place of the old local and national seclusion and self-sufficiency, we have intercourse in every direction, universal inter-dependence of nations. And as in material, so also in intellectual production. The intellectual creations of individual nations become common property. National one-sidedness and narrow-mindedness become more and more impossible, and from the numerous national and local literatures, there arises a world literature.

The bourgeoisie, by the rapid improvement of all instruments of production, by the immensely facilitated means of communication, draws all, even the most barbarian, nations into civilisation. The cheap prices of its commodities are the heavy artillery with which it batters down all Chinese walls, with which it forces the barbarians' intensely obstinate hatred of foreigners to capitulate. It compels all nations, on pain of extinction, to adopt the bourgeois mode of production; it compels them to introduce what it calls civilisation into their midst, i.e., to become bourgeois themselves. In one word, it creates a world after its own image.

The bourgeoisie has subjected the country to the rule of the towns. It has created enormous cities, has greatly increased the urban population as compared with the rural, and has thus rescued a considerable part of the population from the idiocy of rural life. Just as it has made the country dependent on the towns, so it has made barbarian and semi-barbarian countries dependent on the civilised ones, nations of peasants on nations of bourgeois, the East on the West.

The bourgeoisie keeps more and more doing away with the scattered state of the population, of the means of production, and of property. It has agglomerated production, and has concentrated property in a few hands. The necessary consequence of this was political centralisation. Independent, or but loosely connected provinces, with separate interests, laws, governments and systems of taxation, became lumped together into one nation, with one government, one code of laws, one national class-interest, one frontier and one customs-tariff. The bourgeoisie, during its rule of scarce one hundred years, has created more massive and more colossal productive forces than have all preceding generations together. Subjection of Nature's forces to man, machinery, application of chemistry to industry and agriculture, steam-navigation, railways, electric telegraphs, clearing of whole continents for cultivation, canalisation of rivers, whole populations conjured out of the ground—what earlier century had even a presentiment that such productive forces slumbered in the lap of social labour?

We see then: the means of production and of exchange, on whose foundation the bourgeoisie built itself up, were generated in feudal society. At a certain stage in the development of these means of production and of exchange, the conditions under which feudal society produced and exchanged, the feudal organisation of agriculture and manufacturing industry, in one word, the feudal relations of property became no longer compatible with the already developed productive forces; they became so many fetters. They had to be burst asunder; they were burst asunder.

Into their place stepped free competition, accompanied by a social and political constitution adapted to it, and by the economical and political sway of the bourgeois class.

. . .

At this stage the labourers still form an incoherent mass scattered over the whole country, and broken up by their mutual competition. If anywhere they unite to form more compact bodies, this is not yet the consequence of their own active union, but of the union of the bourgeoisie, which class, in order to attain its own political ends, is compelled to set the whole proletariat in motion, and is moreover yet, for a time, able to do so. At this stage, therefore, the proletarians do not fight their enemies, but the enemies of their enemies, the remnants of absolute monarchy, the landowners, the non-industrial bourgeois, the petty bourgeoisie. Thus the whole historical movement is concentrated in the hands of the bourgeoisie; every victory so obtained is a victory for the bourgeoisie.

But with the development of industry the proletariat not only increases in number; it becomes concentrated in greater masses, its strength grows, and it feels that strength more. The various interests and conditions of life within the ranks of the proletariat are more and more equalised, in proportion as machinery obliterates all distinctions of labour, and nearly everywhere reduces wages to the same low level. The growing competition among the bourgeois, and the resulting commercial crises, make the wages of the workers ever more fluctuating. The unceasing improvement of machinery, ever more rapidly developing, makes their livelihood more and more precarious; the collisions between individual workmen and individual bourgeois take more and more the character of collisions between two classes. Thereupon the workers begin to form combinations (Trade Unions) against the bourgeois; they club together in order to keep up the rate of wages; they found permanent associations in order to make provision beforehand for these occasional revolts. Here and there the contest breaks out into riots.

Now and then the workers are victorious, but only for a time. The real fruit of their battles lies, not in the immediate result, but in the ever-expanding union of the workers. This union is helped on by the improved means of communication that are created by modern industry and that place the workers of different localities in contact with one another. It was just this contact that was needed to centralise the numerous local struggles, all of the same character, into one national struggle between classes. But every class struggle is a political struggle. And that union, to attain which the burghers of the Middle Ages, with their miserable highways, required centuries, the modern proletarians, thanks to railways, achieve in a few years.

This organisation of the proletarians into a class, and consequently into a political party, is continually being upset again by the competition between the workers themselves. But it ever rises up again, stronger, firmer, mightier. It compels legislative recognition of particular interests of the workers, by taking advantage of the divisions among the bourgeoisie itself. Thus the ten-hours' bill in England was carried.

Altogether collisions between the classes of the old society further, in many ways, the course of development of the proletariat. The bourgeoisie finds itself involved in a constant battle. At first with the aristocracy; later on, with those portions of the bourgeoisie itself, whose interests have become antagonistic to the progress of industry; at all times, with the bourgeoisie of foreign countries. In all these battles it sees itself compelled to appeal to the proletariat, to ask for its help, and thus, to drag it into the political arena. The bourgeoisie itself, therefore, supplies the proletariat with its own instruments of political and general education, in other words, it furnishes the proletariat with weapons for fighting the bourgeoisie.

Further, as we have already seen, entire sections of the ruling classes are, by the advance of industry, precipitated into the proletariat, or are at least threatened in their conditions of existence. These also supply the proletariat with fresh elements of enlightenment and progress.

Finally, in times when the class struggle nears the decisive hour, the process of dissolution going on within the ruling class, in fact within the whole range of society, assumes such a violent, glaring character, that a small section of the ruling class cuts itself adrift, and joins the revolutionary class, the class that holds the future in its hands. Just as, therefore, at an earlier period, a section of the nobility went over to the bourgeoisie, so now a portion of the bourgeoisie goes over to the proletariat, and in particular, a portion of the bourgeois ideologists, who have raised themselves to the level of comprehending theoretically the historical movement as a whole.

Of all the classes that stand face to face with the bourgeoisie today, the proletariat alone is a really revolutionary class. The other classes decay and finally disappear in the face of Modern Industry; the proletariat is its special and essential product. The lower middle class, the small manufacturer, the shopkeeper, the artisan, the peasant, all these fight against the bourgeoisie, to save from extinction their existence as fractions of the middle class. They are therefore not revolutionary, but conservative. Nay more, they are reactionary, for they try to roll back the wheel of history. If by chance they are revolutionary, they are so only in view of their impending transfer into the proletariat, they thus defend not their present, but their future interests; they desert their own standpoint to place themselves at that of the proletariat.

The "dangerous class," the social scum, that passively rotting mass thrown off by the lowest layers of old society, may, here and there, be swept into the movement by a proletarian revolution; its conditions of life, however, prepare it far more for the part of a bribed tool of reactionary intrigue.

In the conditions of the proletariat, those of old society at large are already virtually swamped. The proletarian is without property; his relation to his wife and children has no longer anything in common with the bourgeois family-relations; modern industrial labour, modern subjection to capital, the same in England as in France, in America as in Germany, has stripped him of every trace of national character. Law, morality, religion, are to him so many bourgeois prejudices, behind which lurk in ambush just as many bourgeois interests.

All the preceding classes that got the upper hand, sought to fortify their already acquired status by subjecting society at large to their conditions of appropriation. The proletarians cannot become masters of the productive forces of society, except by abolishing their own previous mode of appropriation, and thereby also every other previous mode of appropriation. They have nothing of their own to secure and to fortify; their mission is to destroy all previous securities for, and insurances of, individual property.

All previous historical movements were movements of minorities, or in the interests of minorities. The proletarian movement is the self-conscious, independent movement of the immense majority, in the interests of the immense majority. The proletariat, the lowest stratum of our present society, cannot stir, cannot raise itself up, without the whole superincumbent strata of official society being sprung into the air.

Though not in substance, yet in form, the struggle of the proletariat with the bourgeoisie is at first a national struggle. The proletariat of each country must, of course, first of all settle matters with its own bourgeoisie.

In depicting the most general phases of the development of the proletariat, we traced the more or less veiled civil war, raging within existing society, up to the point where that war breaks out into open revolution, and where the violent overthrow of the bourgeoisie lays the foundation for the sway of the proletariat.

Hitherto, every form of society has been based, as we have already seen, on the antagonism of oppressing and oppressed classes. But in order to oppress a class, certain conditions must be assured to it under which it can, at least, continue its slavish existence. The serf, in the period of serfdom, raised himself to membership in the commune, just as the petty bourgeois, under the yoke of feudal absolutism, managed to develop into a bourgeois. The modern laborer, on the contrary, instead of rising with the progress of industry, sinks deeper and deeper below the conditions of existence of his own class. He becomes a pauper, and pauperism develops more rapidly than population and wealth. And here it becomes evident, that the bourgeoisie is unfit any longer to be the ruling class in society, and to impose its conditions of existence upon society as an over-riding law. It is unfit to rule because it is incompetent to assure an existence to its slave within his slavery, because it cannot help letting him sink into such a state, that it has to feed him, instead of being fed by him. Society can no longer live under this bourgeoisie, in other words, its existence is no longer compatible with society.

The essential condition for the existence, and for the sway of the bourgeois class, is the formation and augmentation of capital; the condition for capital is wage-labour. Wage-labour rests exclusively on competition between the laborers. The advance of industry, whose involuntary promoter is the bourgeoisie, replaces the isolation of the labourers, due to competition, by their revolutionary combination, due to association. The development of Modern Industry, therefore, cuts from under its feet the very foundation on which the bourgeoisie produces and appropriates products. What the bourgeoisie, therefore, produces, above all, is its own grave-diggers. Its fall and the victory of the proletariat are equally inevitable.

## II. Proletarians and Communists

In what relation do the Communists stand to the proletarians as a whole?

The Communists do not form a separate party opposed to other working-class parties.

They have no interests separate and apart from those of the proletariat as a whole.

They do not set up any sectarian principles of their own, by which to shape and mould the proletarian movement.

The Communists are distinguished from the other working-class parties by this only: (1) In the national struggles of the proletarians of the different countries, they point out and bring to the front the common interests of entire proletariat, independently of nationality. (2) In the various stages of development which the struggle of the working class against the bourgeoisie has to pass through, they always and everywhere represent the interests of the movement as a whole.

The Communists, therefore, are on the one hand, practically, the most advanced and resolute section of the working-class parties of every country, that section which pushes forward all others; on the other hand, theoretically, they have over the great mass of the proletariat the advantage of clearly understanding the line of march, the conditions, and the ultimate general results of the proletarian movement.

The immediate aim of the Communist is the same as that of all the other proletarian parties: formation of the proletariat into a class, overthrow of the bourgeois supremacy, conquest of political power by the proletariat.

The theoretical conclusions of the Communists are in no way based on ideas or principles that have been invented, or discovered, by this or that would-be universal reformer. They merely express, in general terms, actual relations springing from an existing class struggle, from a historical movement going on under our very eyes. The abolition of existing property relations is not at all a distinctive feature of Communism.

All property relations in the past have continually been subject to historical change consequent upon the change in historical conditions.

The French Revolution, for example, abolished feudal property in favour of bourgeois property.

The distinguishing feature of Communism is not the abolition of property generally, but the abolition of bourgeois property. But modern bourgeois private property is the final and most complete expression of the system of producing and appropriating products, that is based on class antagonisms, on the exploitation of the many by the few.

In this sense, the theory of the Communists may be summed up in the single sentence: Abolition of private property.

We Communists have been reproached with the desire of abolishing the right of personally acquiring property as the fruit of a man's own labour, which property is alleged to be the groundwork of all personal freedom, activity and independence.

Hard-won, self-acquired, self-earned property! Do you mean the property of the petty artisan and of the small peasant, a form of property that preceded the bourgeois form? There is no need to abolish that; the development of industry has to a great extent already destroyed it, and is still destroying it daily.

Or do you mean modern bourgeois private property?

But does wage-labour create any property for the labourer? Not a bit. It creates capital, i.e., that kind of property which exploits wage-labour, and which cannot increase except upon condition of begetting a new supply of wage-labour for fresh exploitation. Property, in its present form, is based on the antagonism of capital and wage-labour. Let us examine both sides of this antagonism.

To be a capitalist, is to have not only a purely personal, but a social status in production. Capital is a collective product, and only by the united action of many members, nay, in the last resort, only by the united action of all members of society, can it be set in motion.

Capital is, therefore, not a personal, it is a social power.

When, therefore, capital is converted into common property, into the property of all members of society, personal property is not thereby transformed into social property. It is only the social character of the property that is changed. It loses its class-character.

Let us now take wage-labour.

The average price of wage-labour is the minimum wage, i.e., that quantum of the means of subsistence, which is absolutely requisite in bare existence as a labourer. What, therefore, the wage-labourer appropriates by means of his labour, merely suffices to prolong and reproduce a bare existence. We by no means intend to abolish this personal appropriation of the products of labour, an appropriation that is made for the maintenance and reproduction of human life, and that leaves no surplus wherewith to command the labour of others. All that we want to do away with, is the miserable character of this appropriation, under which the labourer lives merely to increase capital, and is allowed to live only in so far as the interest of the ruling class requires it.

In bourgeois society, living labour is but a means to increase accumulated labour. In Communist society, accumulated labour is but a means to widen, to enrich, to promote the existence of the labourer.

In bourgeois society, therefore, the past dominates the present; in Communist society, the present dominates the past. In bourgeois society capital is independent and has individuality, while the living person is dependent and has no individuality.

And the abolition of this state of things is called by the bourgeois, abolition of individuality and freedom! And rightly so. The abolition of bourgeois individuality, bourgeois independence, and bourgeois freedom is undoubtedly aimed at.

By freedom is meant, under the present bourgeois conditions of production, free trade, free selling and buying. But if selling and buying disappears, free selling and buying disappears also. This talk about free selling and buying, and all the other "brave words" of our bourgeoisie about freedom in general, have a meaning, if any, only in contrast with restricted selling and buying, with the fettered traders of the Middle Ages, but have no meaning when opposed to the Communistic abolition of buying and selling, of the bourgeois conditions of production, and of the bourgeoisie itself.

You are horrified at our intending to do away with private property. But in your existing society, private property is already done away with for nine-tenths of the population; its existence for the few is solely due to its non-existence in the hands of those nine-tenths. You reproach us, therefore, with intending to do away with a form of property, the necessary condition for whose existence is the non-existence of any property for the immense majority of society.

In one word, you reproach us with intending to do away with your property. Precisely so; that is just what we intend.

From the moment when labour can no longer be converted into capital, money, or rent, into a social power capable of being monopolised, i.e., from the moment when individual property can no longer be transformed into bourgeois property, into capital, from that moment, you say individuality vanishes.

You must, therefore, confess that by "individual" you mean no other person than the bourgeois, than the middle-class owner of property. This person must, indeed, be swept out of the way, and made impossible.

Communism deprives no man of the power to appropriate the products of society; all that it does is to deprive him of the power to subjugate the labour of others by means of such appropriation.

It has been objected that upon the abolition of private property all work will cease, and universal laziness will overtake us.

According to this, bourgeois society ought long ago to have gone to the dogs through sheer idleness; for those of its members who work, acquire nothing, and those who acquire anything, do not work. The whole of this objection is but another expression of the tautology: that there can no longer be any wage-labour when there is no longer any capital.

All objections urged against the Communistic mode of producing and appropriating material products, have, in the same way, been urged against the Communistic modes of producing and appropriating intellectual products. Just as, to the bourgeois, the disappearance of class property is the disappearance of production itself, so the disappearance of class culture is to him identical with the disappearance of all culture.

That culture, the loss of which he laments, is, for the enormous majority, a mere training to act as a machine.

But don't wrangle with us so long as you apply, to our intended abolition of bourgeois property, the standard of your bourgeois notions of freedom, culture, law, etc. Your very ideas are but the outgrowth of the conditions of your bourgeois production and bourgeois property, just as your jurisprudence is but the will of your class made into a law for all, a will, whose essential character and direction are determined by the economical conditions of existence of your class.

The selfish misconception that induces you to transform into eternal laws of nature and of reason, the social forms springing from your present mode of production and form of property-historical relations that rise and disappear in the progress of production—this misconception you share with every ruling class that has preceded you. What you see clearly in the case of ancient property, what you admit in the case of feudal property, you are of course forbidden to admit in the case of your own bourgeois form of property.

Abolition of the family! Even the most radical flare up at this infamous proposal of the Communists.

On what foundation is the present family, the bourgeois family, based? On capital, on private gain. In its completely developed form this family exists only among the bourgeoisie. But this state of things finds its complement in the practical absence of the family among the proletarians, and in public prostitution.

The bourgeois family will vanish as a matter of course when its complement vanishes, and both will vanish with the vanishing of capital.

Do you charge us with wanting to stop the exploitation of children by their parents? To this crime we plead guilty.

But, you will say, we destroy the most hallowed of relations, when we replace home education by social.

And your education! Is not that also social, and determined by the social conditions under which you educate, by the intervention, direct or indirect, of society, by means of schools, etc.? The Communists have not invented the intervention of society in education; they do but seek to alter the character of that intervention, and to rescue education from the influence of the ruling class.

The bourgeois clap-trap about the family and education, about the hallowed co-relation of parent and child, becomes all the more disgusting, the more, by the action of Modern Industry, all family ties among the proletarians are torn asunder, and their children transformed into simple articles of commerce and instruments of labour.

But you Communists would introduce community of women, screams the whole bourgeoisie in chorus.

The bourgeois sees in his wife a mere instrument of production. He hears that the instruments of production are to be exploited in common, and, naturally, can come to no other conclusion than that the lot of being common to all will likewise fall to the women.

He has not even a suspicion that the real point is to do away with the status of women as mere instruments of production.

For the rest, nothing is more ridiculous than the virtuous indignation of our bourgeois at the community of women which, they pretend, is to be openly and officially established by the Communists. The Communists have no need to introduce community of women; it has existed almost from time immemorial.

Our bourgeois, not content with having the wives and daughters of their proletarians at their disposal, not to speak of common prostitutes, take the greatest pleasure in seducing each other's wives.

Bourgeois marriage is in reality a system of wives in common and thus, at the most, what the Communists might possibly be reproached with, is that they desire to introduce, in substitution for a hypocritically concealed, an openly legalised community of women. For the rest, it is self-evident that the abolition of the present system of production must bring with it the abolition of the community of women springing from that system, i.e., of prostitution both public and private.

The Communists are further reproached with desiring to abolish countries and nationality.

The working men have no country. We cannot take from them what they have not got. Since the proletariat must first of all acquire political supremacy, must rise to be the leading class of the nation, must constitute itself the nation, it is, so far, itself national, though not in the bourgeois sense of the word.

National differences and antagonisms between peoples are daily more and more vanishing, owing to the development of the bourgeoisie, to freedom of commerce, to the world-market, to uniformity in the mode of production and in the conditions of life corresponding thereto.

The supremacy of the proletariat will cause them to vanish still faster. United action, of the leading civilised countries at least, is one of the first conditions for the emancipation of the proletariat.

In proportion as the exploitation of one individual by another is put an end to, the exploitation of one nation by another will also be put an end to. In proportion as the antagonism between classes within the nation vanishes, the hostility of one nation to another will come to an end.

. . .

The Communist revolution is the most radical rupture with traditional property relations; no wonder that its development involves the most radical rupture with traditional ideas.

But let us have done with the bourgeois objections to Communism.

We have seen above, that the first step in the revolution by the working class, is to raise the proletariat to the position of ruling as to win the battle of democracy.

The proletariat will use its political supremacy to wrest, by degrees, all capital from the bourgeoisie, to centralise all instruments of production in the hands of the State, i.e., of the proletariat organised as the ruling class; and to increase the total of productive forces as rapidly as possible.

Of course, in the beginning, this cannot be effected except by means of despotic inroads on the rights of property, and on the conditions of bourgeois production; by means of measures, therefore, which appear economically insufficient and untenable, but which, in the course of the movement, outstrip themselves, necessitate further inroads upon the old social order, and are unavoidable as a means of entirely revolutionising the mode of production.

These measures will of course be different in different countries.

Nevertheless in the most advanced countries, the following will be pretty generally applicable.

1. Abolition of property in land and application of all rents of land to public purposes.
2. A heavy progressive or graduated income tax.
3. Abolition of all right of inheritance.
4. Confiscation of the property of all emigrants and rebels.
5. Centralisation of credit in the hands of the State, by means of a national bank with State capital and an exclusive monopoly.
6. Centralisation of the means of communication and transport in the hands of the State.
7. Extension of factories and instruments of production owned by the State; the bringing into cultivation of waste-lands, and the improvement of the soil generally in accordance with a common plan.
8. Equal liability of all to labour. Establishment of industrial armies, especially for agriculture.
9. Combination of agriculture with manufacturing industries; gradual abolition of the distinction between town and country, by a more equable distribution of the population over the country.
10. Free education for all children in public schools. Abolition of

children's factory labour in its present form. Combination of education with industrial production, etc., etc.

——————

When, in the course of development, class distinctions have disappeared, and all production has been concentrated in the hands of a vast association of the whole nation, the public power will lose its political character. Political power, properly so called, is merely the organised power of one class for oppressing another. If the proletariat during its contest with the bourgeoisie is compelled, by the force of circumstances, to organise itself as a class, if, by means of a revolution, it makes itself the ruling class, and, as such, sweeps away by force the old conditions of production, then it will, along with these conditions, have swept away the conditions for the existence of class antagonisms and of classes generally, and will thereby have abolished its own supremacy as a class.

In place of the old bourgeois society, with its classes and class antagonisms, we shall have an association, in which the free development of each is the condition for the free development of all.

. . .

## IV. Position of the Communists in Relation to the Various Existing Opposition Parties

Section II has made clear the relations of the Communists to the existing working-class parties, such as the Chartists in England and the Agrarian Reformers in America.

The Communists fight for the attainment of the immediate aims, for the enforcement of the momentary interests of the working class; but in the movement of the present, they also represent and take care of the future of that movement. In France the Communists ally themselves with the Social-Democrats, against the conservative and radical bourgeoisie, reserving, however, the right to take up a critical position in regard to phrases and illusions traditionally handed down from the great Revolution.

In Switzerland they support the Radicals, without losing sight of the fact that this party consists of antagonistic elements, partly of Democratic Socialists, in the French sense, partly of radical bourgeois.

In Poland they support the party that insists on an agrarian revolution as the prime condition for national emancipation, that party which fomented the insurrection of Cracow in 1846.

In Germany they fight with the bourgeoisie whenever it acts in a revolutionary way, against the absolute monarchy, the feudal squirearchy, and the petty bourgeoisie.

But they never cease, for a single instant, to instill into the working class the clearest possible recognition of the hostile antagonism between bourgeoisie and proletariat, in order that the German workers may straightaway use, as so many weapons against the bourgeoisie, the social and political conditions that the bourgeoisie must necessarily introduce along with its supremacy, and in order that, after the fall of the reactionary classes in Germany, the fight against the bourgeoisie itself may immediately begin.

The Communists turn their attention chiefly to Germany, because that country is on the eve of a bourgeois revolution that is bound to be carried out under more advanced conditions of European civilisation, and with a much more developed proletariat, than that of England was in the seventeenth, and of France in the eighteenth century, and because the bourgeois revolution in Germany will be but the prelude to an immediately following proletarian revolution.

In short, the Communists everywhere support every revolutionary movement against the existing social and political order of things.

In all these movements they bring to the front, as the leading question in each, the property question, no matter what its degree of development at the time.

Finally, they labour everywhere for the union and agreement of the democratic parties of all countries.

The Communists disdain to conceal their views and aims. They openly declare that their ends can be attained only by the forcible overthrow of all existing social conditions. Let the ruling classes tremble at a Communistic revolution. The proletarians have nothing to lose but their chains. They have a world to win.

## WORKING MEN OF ALL COUNTRIES, UNITE!

*Translated by Samuel Moore, 1888*

# REFLECTIONS
# ON THE COMMUNIST MANIFESTO

Hunter Baker

We sometimes have trouble convincing people that they should care about what luminaries like Plato, Aristotle, Augustine, and Aquinas wrote. Part of the trouble with being modern is that we have a prejudice against the old. I can recall listening to an atheist at a public meeting argue vociferously that today we're much more intelligent than men like the American Founders and, therefore, should not defer to them. With suitable rhetorical flourish, I would say it is "self-evident" that such a statement is untrue!

However, I write this short response to the *Communist Manifesto* by Karl Marx (and Friedrich Engels), not because of the profound insights that should be learned and made part of our own intellectual armamentarium, but instead because the work in question exerted a massive influence on recent history and arguably led to a half century of intense (yet "cold") conflict in which two huge portions of the globe glared at each other across a chasm of spiritual/ideological division and simmering nuclear conflagration.

The United States is a nation founded on the basis of certain strong political principles having to do with social contract, freedom, limited government, and exceptions to power brought together by the providential fusion of both Christian and classical sentiments. Approximately 130 years later, the Soviet Union was similarly founded on political ideals (though much different ones) as it rocketed along into a supposedly "inevitable" future on the vehicle of Marx's historical analysis of class struggle. For a long time, many—even those who loved America—feared that the Soviets would indeed triumph. Whittaker Chambers, who successfully exposed Alger Hiss (his former colleague in Soviet espionage), sadly wrote that he felt he had left the winning side for the losing one when he decided to turn his back on the Marxist cause.

What to say about this incredibly consequential document? In truth, Marx's analysis was reductive in the extreme as he boiled down the entirety of human history to the class struggle. Because the entire narrative is founded on this idea, it is vulnerable to questions about the premise. Is class really the most important aspect? What about race, ethnicity, family/clan, village, the nation-state? The Marxist revolution covered over these factors and held them in check through extraordinary coercion, only to see them spontaneously surge back into prominence when the Berlin Wall came down.

And what of his view of religion? His assumption that it's merely an "opiate of the people" was all too easy and dismissive. He completely disregarded the possibility that religious truth could arise from events in time, space, and history, such as the resurrection of Jesus Christ, which served as Paul's "proof" to the men of Athens that his assertions about God's character were grounded in reality.

Marx's greatest error of all may have had to do with his view of human sin. Ranging over the history of class struggle, this revolutionary thinker dwelt upon the injustice of the propertied group oppressing their dispossessed brethren. The inequities that developed so dramatically with the rapid progress of the Industrial Revolution inspired his rage. He saw man treating his fellowmen as though they were mere commodities, cogs in a machine to perform deadening, unskilled work in never-ending repetition. Yet, somehow, he was able to easily believe that human beings—those same creatures who'd *created* the systems he found so evil—would then turn around and employ state power magnitudes above what previously had been known to bring about a socialist paradise. The assumption that an enlightened vanguard would prove much more trustworthy with power than those who held it before now seems quite naïve.

The authors of the *Manifesto* declared that the transition to its society of the future would require a "dictatorship of the proletariat." But they imagined the period of dictatorship would come to an end as a new stage, the "withering away of the state," took hold. At that point, there would no longer be a need for much coercion, as men would no longer struggle against each other but would live in harmony while experiencing the necessary leisure to fully develop their interests.

The Soviet Union, the world state that served as the pioneering Marxist experiment and the most powerful exemplar of the species, featured increasingly onerous *dictatorship* without much *withering*. Looking back, disappointed Marxist/socialists lament that Russia was the wrong country, or that the methods were wrong, or that Stalin was wrong. But the insight such persons have missed, as Martin Malia pointed out in *The Soviet Tragedy*, is that "the Soviet experiment turned totalitarian not despite its being socialist, but *because* it was socialist." The domination of private property by the state radically undermines civil society and places individuals into such dependence that they're unable to stand up for the preservation of their freedoms.

It has been on this point that many leftists have been blind. They protest that Castro's Cubans may not have "civil rights," but "economic rights" instead. Do they, indeed, have those rights? Or are these rights merely the reward of subsistence in exchange for obedience?

So read this most potent *Manifesto* and gain insight into the struggle for the world that dominated the twentieth century.

## CHAPTER TWENTY FIVE

# CHARLES DARWIN

## Modern (1809–1882)

$S$ay "Charles Darwin" at a party and the reaction will go a long way to telling a man where he is. No reaction to Darwin indicates a gathering of the mentally or culturally comatose. Darwin made it possible for Richard Dawkins to be an intellectually fulfilled atheist and for Ken Ham to build a creationist think tank and a Creation Museum.

Darwin has been praised as a maker of the modern mind and damned for the same reason.

Sadly, most Americans debating Darwin are more likely to own a T-shirt or a mug with his iconic face than to have actually read his work. This is a travesty, as Darwin is still the best proponent of his remarkable hypothesis regarding the "origin of the species."

Charles Darwin provided a brilliant natural explanation for phenomenon that many believed could be explained only through supernatural creation. As a result, his work immediately was used and misused by people with opinions on God, creation, and the nature of humankind . . . meaning everybody.

This means Darwin's books, like the Bible or Marx, provoke many of us to be bad readers. Reading Darwin defensively obscures flaws in his original arguments. Those blemishes led to scientific discoveries that improved on his original ideas; missing the defects is a very bad idea. It also prevents seeing why a few thoughtful people still dissent from his general ideas.

Reading Darwin only to attack him continuously also is foolhardy.

First, it prevents following the argument where it leads. Not listening prevents learning.

Second, it avoids seeing where he is most persuasive. If Darwin is wrong, some of his ideas still have motivated much scientific and biological progress over the last century. Darwin is a man, not a devil, and he deserves his due.

So read this selection with an open mind; follow the presentation, and then analyze it. Charles Darwin cannot be read to get the best modern take on evolutionary mechanisms or the data now used to support biological evolution. Still, one can examine Darwin to see if one is persuaded that the *type of answer* he proposes is likely to succeed. Is he proposing a strong general strategy to the biological problems he faces? Is he ignoring important philosophical problems? Is he making tacit theological assumptions? Does he assume he knows what a Creator would and would not create?

Ask Darwin hard questions with an open mind. To his credit, that is the purpose for which he wrote his books.

⟢ FROM ⟣

# On the Origin of Species

## Chapter 14

As this whole volume is one long argument, it may be convenient to the reader to have the leading facts and inferences briefly recapitulated.

That many and grave objections may be advanced against the theory of descent with modification through natural selection, I do not deny. I have endeavoured to give to them their full force. Nothing at first can appear more difficult to believe than that the more complex organs and instincts should have been perfected not by means superior to, though analogous with, human reason, but by the accumulation of innumerable slight variations, each good for the individual possessor. Nevertheless, this difficulty, though appearing to our imagination insuperably great, cannot be considered real if we admit the following propositions, namely,—that gradations in the perfection of any organ or instinct, which we may consider, either do now exist or could have existed, each good of its kind,—that all organs and instincts are, in ever so slight a degree, variable,—and, lastly, that there is a struggle for existence leading to the preservation of each profitable deviation of structure or instinct. The truth of these propositions cannot, I think, be disputed.

. . .

As natural selection acts by competition, it adapts the inhabitants of each country only in relation to the degree of perfection of their associates; so that we need feel no surprise at the inhabitants of any one country, although on the ordinary view supposed to have been specially created and adapted for that country, being beaten and supplanted by the naturalised productions from another land. Nor ought we to marvel if all the contrivances in nature be not, as far as we can judge, absolutely perfect; and if some of them be abhorrent to our ideas of fitness. We need not marvel at the sting of the bee causing the bee's own death; at drones being produced in such vast numbers for one single act, and being then slaughtered by their sterile sisters; at the astonishing waste of pollen by our fir-trees; at the instinctive hatred of the queen bee for her own fertile daughters; at ichneumonidae feeding within the live bodies of caterpillars; and at other such cases. The wonder indeed is, on the theory of natural selection, that more cases of the want of absolute perfection have not been observed.

The complex and little known laws governing variation are the same, as far as we can see, with the laws which have governed the production of so-called specific forms. In both cases physical conditions seem to have produced but little direct effect; yet when varieties enter any zone, they occasionally assume some of the characters of the species proper to that zone. In both varieties and species, use and disuse seem to have produced some effect; for it is difficult to resist this conclusion when we look, for instance, at the logger-headed duck, which has wings incapable of flight, in nearly the same condition as in the domestic duck; or when we look at the burrowing tucutucu, which is occasionally blind, and then at certain moles, which are habitually blind and have their eyes covered with skin; or when we look at the blind animals inhabiting the dark caves of America and Europe. In both varieties and species correction of growth seems to have played a most important part, so that when one part has been modified other parts are necessarily modified. In both varieties and species reversions to long-lost characters occur. How inexplicable on the theory of creation is the occasional appearance of stripes on the shoulder and legs of the several species of the horse-genus and in their hybrids! How simply is this fact explained if we believe that these species have descended from a striped progenitor, in the same manner as the several domestic breeds of pigeon have descended from the blue and barred rock-pigeon!

On the ordinary view of each species having been independently created, why should the specific characters, or those by which the species of the same genus differ from each other, be more variable than the generic characters in which they all agree? Why, for instance, should the colour of a flower be more likely to vary in any one species of a genus, if the other species, supposed to have been created independently, have differently coloured flowers, than if all the species of the genus have the same coloured flowers? If species are only well-marked varieties, of which the characters have become in a high degree permanent, we can understand this fact; for they have already varied since they branched off from a common progenitor in certain characters, by which they have come to be specifically distinct from each other; and therefore these same characters would be more likely still to be variable than the generic characters which have been inherited without change for an enormous period.

It is inexplicable on the theory of creation why a part developed in a very unusual manner in any one species of a genus, and therefore, as we may naturally infer, of great importance to the species, should be eminently liable to variation; but, on my view, this part has undergone, since the several species branched off from a common progenitor, an unusual amount of variability and modification, and therefore we might expect this part generally to be still variable. But a part may be developed in the most unusual manner, like the wing of a bat, and yet not be more variable than any other structure, if the part be common to many subordinate forms, that is, if it has been inherited for a very long period; for in this case it will have been rendered constant by long-continued natural selection.

Glancing at instincts, marvelous as some are, they offer no greater difficulty than does corporeal structure on the theory of the natural selection of successive, slight, but profitable modifications. We can thus understand why nature moves by graduated steps in endowing different animals of the same class with their several instincts. I have attempted to show how much light the principle of gradation throws on the admirable architectural powers of the hive-bee. Habit no doubt sometimes comes into play in modifying instincts; but it certainly is not indispensable, as we see, in the case of neuter insects, which leave no progeny to inherit the effects of long-continued habit. On the view of all the species of the same genus having descended from a common parent, and having inherited much in common, we can understand how it is that allied species, when placed under considerably different conditions of life, yet should follow nearly the same instincts; why the thrush of South America, for instance, lines her nest with mud like our British species. On the view of instincts having been slowly acquired through natural selection we need not marvel at some instincts being apparently not perfect and liable to mistakes, and at many instincts causing other animals to suffer.

If species be only well-marked and permanent varieties, we can at once see why their crossed offspring should follow the same complex laws in their degrees and kinds of resemblance to their parents,—in being absorbed into each other by successive crosses, and in other such points,—as do the crossed offspring of acknowledged varieties. On the other hand, these would be strange facts if species have been independently created, and varieties have been produced by secondary laws.

If we admit that the geological record is imperfect in an extreme degree, then such facts as the record gives, support the theory of descent with modification. New species have come on the stage slowly and at successive intervals; and the amount of change, after equal intervals of time, is widely different in different groups. The extinction of species and of whole groups of species, which has played so conspicuous a part in the history of the organic world, almost inevitably follows on the principle of natural selection; for old forms will be supplanted by new and improved forms. Neither single species nor groups of species reappear when the chain of ordinary generation has once been broken. The gradual diffusion of dominant forms, with the slow modification of their descendants, causes the forms of life, after long intervals of time, to appear as if they had changed simultaneously throughout the world. The fact of the fossil remains of each formation being in some degree intermediate in character between the fossils in the formations above and below, is simply explained by their intermediate position in the chain of descent.

The grand fact that all extinct organic beings belong to the same system with recent beings, falling either into the same or into intermediate groups, follows from the living and the extinct being the offspring of common parents. As the groups which have descended from an ancient progenitor have generally diverged in character, the progenitor with its early descendants will often be intermediate in character in comparison with its later descendants; and thus we can see why the more ancient a fossil is, the oftener it stands in some degree intermediate between existing and allied groups.

Recent forms are generally looked at as being, in some vague sense, higher than ancient and extinct forms; and they are in so far higher as the later and more improved forms have conquered the older and less improved organic beings in the struggle for life. Lastly, the law of the long endurance of allied forms on the same continent,—of marsupials in Australia, of edentata in America, and other such cases,—is intelligible, for within a confined country, the recent and the extinct will naturally be allied by descent.

Looking to geographical distribution, if we admit that there has been during the long course of ages much migration from one part of the world to another, owing to former climatal and geographical changes and to the many occasional and unknown means of dispersal, then we can understand, on the theory of descent with modification, most of the great leading facts in Distribution.

We can see why there should be so striking a parallelism in the distribution of organic beings throughout space, and in their geological succession throughout time; for in both cases the beings have been connected by the bond of ordinary generation, and the means of modification have been the same. We see the full meaning of the wonderful fact, which must have struck every traveller, namely, that on the same continent, under the most diverse conditions, under heat and cold, on mountain and lowland, on deserts and marshes, most of the inhabitants within each great class are plainly related; for they will generally be descendants of the same progenitors and early colonists.

On this same principle of former migration, combined in most cases with modification, we can understand, by the aid of the Glacial period, the identity of some few plants, and the close alliance of many others, on the most distant mountains, under the most different climates; and likewise the close alliance of some of the inhabitants of the sea in the northern and southern temperate zones, though separated by the whole intertropical ocean. Although two areas may present the same physical conditions of life, we need feel no surprise at their inhabitants being widely different, if they have been for a long period completely separated from each other; for as the relation of organism to organism is the most important of all relations, and as the two areas will have received colonists from some third source or from each other, at various periods and in different proportions, the course of modification in the two areas will inevitably be different.

On this view of migration, with subsequent modification, we can see why oceanic islands should be inhabited by few species, but of these, that many should be peculiar. We can clearly see why those animals which cannot cross wide spaces of ocean, as frogs and terrestrial mammals, should not inhabit oceanic islands; and why, on the other hand, new and peculiar species of bats, which can traverse the ocean, should so often be found on islands far distant from any continent. Such facts as the presence of peculiar species of bats, and the absence of all other mammals, on oceanic islands, are utterly inexplicable on the theory of independent acts of creation.

The existence of closely allied or representative species in any two areas, implies, on the theory of descent with modification, that the same parents formerly inhabited both areas; and we almost invariably find that wherever many closely allied species inhabit two areas, some identical species common to both still exist. Wherever many closely allied yet distinct species occur, many doubtful forms and varieties of the same species likewise occur. It is a rule of high generality that the inhabitants of each area are related to the inhabitants of the nearest source whence immigrants might have been derived. We see this in nearly all the plants and animals of the Galapagos archipelago, of Juan Fernandez, and of the other American islands being related in the most striking manner to the plants and animals of the neighbouring American mainland; and those of the Cape de Verde archipelago and other African islands to the African mainland. It must be admitted that these facts receive no explanation on the theory of creation.

The fact, as we have seen, that all past and present organic beings constitute one grand natural system, with group subordinate to group, and with extinct groups often falling in between recent groups, is intelligible on the theory of natural selection with its contingencies of extinction and divergence of character. On these same principles we see how it is, that the mutual affinities of the species and genera within each class are so complex and circuitous. We see why certain characters are far more serviceable than others for classification;—why adaptive characters, though of paramount importance to the being, are of hardly any importance in classification; why characters derived from rudimentary parts, though of no service to the being, are often of high classificatory value; and why embryological characters are the most valuable of all. The real affinities of all organic beings are due to inheritance or community of descent. The natural system is a genealogical arrangement, in which we have to discover the lines of descent by the most permanent characters, however slight their vital importance may be.

The framework of bones being the same in the hand of a man, wing of a bat, fin of the porpoise, and leg of the horse,—the same number of vertebrae forming the neck of the giraffe and of the elephant,—and innumerable other such facts, at once explain themselves on the theory of descent with slow and slight successive modifications. The similarity of pattern in the wing and leg of a bat, though used for such different purposes,—in the jaws and legs of a crab,—in the petals, stamens, and pistils of a flower, is likewise intelligible on the view of the gradual modification of parts or organs, which were alike in the early progenitor of each class. On the principle of successive variations not always supervening at an early age, and being inherited at a corresponding not early period of life, we can clearly see why the embryos of mammals, birds, reptiles, and fishes should be so closely alike, and should be so unlike the adult forms. We may cease marveling at the embryo of an air-breathing mammal or bird having branchial slits and arteries running in loops, like those in a fish which has to breathe the air dissolved in water, by the aid of well-developed branchiae.

Disuse, aided sometimes by natural selection, will often tend to reduce an organ, when it has become useless by changed habits or under changed conditions of life; and we can clearly understand on this view the meaning of rudimentary organs. But disuse and selection will generally act on each creature, when it has come to maturity and has to play its full part in the struggle for existence, and will thus have little power of acting on an organ during early life; hence the organ will not be much reduced or rendered rudimentary at this early age.

The calf, for instance, has inherited teeth, which never cut through the gums of the upper jaw, from an early progenitor having well-developed teeth; and we may believe, that the teeth in the mature animal were reduced, during successive generations, by disuse or by the tongue and palate having been fitted by natural selection to browse without their aid; whereas in the calf, the teeth have been left untouched by selection or disuse, and on the principle of inheritance at corresponding ages have been inherited from a remote period to the present day. On the view of each organic being and each separate organ having been specially created, how utterly inexplicable it is that parts, like the teeth in the embryonic calf or like the shrivelled wings under the soldered wing-covers of some beetles, should thus so frequently bear the plain stamp of inutility! Nature may be said to have taken pains to reveal, by rudimentary organs and by homologous structures, her scheme of modification, which it seems that we willfully will not understand.

I have now recapitulated the chief facts and considerations which have thoroughly convinced me that species have changed, and are still slowly changing by the preservation and accumulation of successive slight favourable variations. Why, it may be asked, have all the most eminent living naturalists and geologists rejected this view of the mutability of species? It cannot be asserted that organic beings in a state of nature are subject to no variation; it cannot be proved that the amount of variation in the course of long ages is a limited quantity; no clear distinction has been, or can be, drawn between species and well-marked varieties. It cannot be maintained that species when intercrossed are invariably sterile, and varieties invariably fertile; or that sterility is a special endowment and sign of creation. The belief that species were immutable productions was almost unavoidable as long as the history of the world was thought to be of short duration; and now that we have acquired some idea of the lapse of time, we are too apt to assume, without proof, that the geological record is so perfect that it would have afforded us plain evidence of the mutation of species, if they had undergone mutation.

But the chief cause of our natural unwillingness to admit that one species has given birth to other and distinct species, is that we are always slow in admitting any great change of which we do not see the intermediate steps. The difficulty is the same as that felt by so many geologists, when Lyell first insisted that long lines of inland cliffs had been formed, and great valleys excavated, by the slow action of the coast-waves. The mind cannot possibly grasp the full meaning of the term of a hundred million years; it cannot add up and perceive the full effects of many slight variations, accumulated during an almost infinite number of generations.

Although I am fully convinced of the truth of the views given in this volume under the form of an abstract, I by no means expect to convince experienced naturalists whose minds are stocked with a multitude of facts all viewed, during a long course of years, from a point of view directly opposite to mine. It is so easy to hide our ignorance under such expressions as the "plan of creation," "unity of design," etc., and to think that we give an explanation when we only restate a fact. Any one whose disposition leads him to attach more weight to unexplained difficulties than to the explanation of a certain number of facts will certainly reject my theory. A few naturalists, endowed with much flexibility of mind, and who have already begun to doubt on the immutability of species, may be influenced by this volume; but I look with confidence to the future, to young and rising naturalists, who will be able to view both sides of the question with impartiality. Whoever is led to believe that species are mutable will do good service by conscientiously expressing his conviction; for only thus can the load of prejudice by which this subject is overwhelmed be removed.

Several eminent naturalists have of late published their belief that a multitude of reputed species in each genus are not real species; but that other species are real, that is, have been independently created. This seems to me a strange conclusion to arrive at. They admit that a multitude of forms, which till lately they themselves thought were special creations, and which are still thus looked at by the majority of naturalists, and which consequently have every external characteristic feature of true species,—they admit that these have been produced by variation, but they refuse to extend the same view to other and very slightly different forms. Nevertheless they do not pretend that they can define, or even conjecture, which are the created forms of life, and which are those produced by secondary laws. They admit variation as a *vera causa* in one case, they arbitrarily reject it in another, without assigning any distinction in the two cases. The day will come when this will be given as a curious illustration of the blindness of preconceived opinion.

These authors seem no more startled at a miraculous act of creation than at an ordinary birth. But do they really believe that at innumerable periods in the earth's history certain elemental atoms have been commanded suddenly to flash into living tissues? Do they believe that at each supposed act of creation one individual or many were produced? Were all the infinitely numerous kinds of animals and plants created as eggs or seed, or as full grown? and in the case of mammals, were they created bearing the false marks of nourishment from the mother's womb? Although naturalists very properly demand a full explanation of every difficulty from those who believe in the mutability of species, on their own side they ignore the whole subject of the first appearance of species in what they consider reverent silence.

It may be asked how far I extend the doctrine of the modification of species. The question is difficult to answer, because the more distinct the forms are which we may consider, by so much the arguments fall away in force. But some arguments of the greatest weight extend very far. All the members of whole classes can be connected together by chains of affinities, and all can be classified on the same principle, in groups subordinate to groups. Fossil remains sometimes tend to fill up very wide intervals between existing orders. Organs in a rudimentary condition plainly show that an early progenitor had the organ in a fully developed state; and this in some instances necessarily implies an enormous amount of modification in the descendants. Throughout whole classes various structures are formed on the same pattern, and at an embryonic age the species closely resemble each other. Therefore I cannot doubt that the theory of descent with modification embraces all the members of the same class. I believe that animals have descended from at most only four or five progenitors, and plants from an equal or lesser number.

Analogy would lead me one step further, namely, to the belief that all animals and plants have descended from some one prototype. But analogy may be a deceitful guide. Nevertheless all living things have much in common, in their chemical composition, their germinal vesicles, their cellular structure, and their laws of growth and reproduction. We see this even in so trifling a circumstance as that the same poison often similarly affects plants and animals; or that the poison secreted by the gall-fly produces monstrous growths on the wild rose or oak-tree. Therefore I should infer from analogy that probably all the organic beings which have ever lived on this earth have descended from some one primordial form, into which life was first breathed.

When the views entertained in this volume on the origin of species, or when analogous views are generally admitted, we can dimly foresee that there will be a considerable revolution in natural history. Systematists will be able to pursue their labours as at present; but they will not be incessantly haunted by the shadowy doubt whether this or that form be in essence a species. This I feel sure, and I speak after experience, will be no slight relief. The endless disputes whether or not some fifty species of British brambles are true species will cease. Systematists will have only to decide (not that this will be easy) whether any form be sufficiently constant and distinct from other forms, to be capable of definition; and if definable, whether the differences be sufficiently important to deserve a specific name. This latter point will become a far more essential consideration than it is at present; for differences, however slight, between any two forms, if not blended by intermediate gradations, are looked at by most naturalists as sufficient to raise both forms to the rank of species. Hereafter we shall be compelled to acknowledge that the only distinction between species and well-marked varieties is, that the latter are known, or believed, to be connected at the present day by intermediate gradations, whereas species were formerly thus connected.

Hence, without quite rejecting the consideration of the present existence of intermediate gradations between any two forms, we shall be led to weigh more carefully and to value higher the actual amount of difference between them. It is quite possible that forms now generally acknowledged to be merely varieties may hereafter be thought worthy of specific names, as with the primrose and cowslip; and in this case scientific and common

language will come into accordance. In short, we shall have to treat species in the same manner as those naturalists treat genera, who admit that genera are merely artificial combinations made for convenience. This may not be a cheering prospect; but we shall at least be freed from the vain search for the undiscovered and undiscoverable essence of the term species.

The other and more general departments of natural history will rise greatly in interest. The terms used by naturalists of affinity, relationship, community of type, paternity, morphology, adaptive characters, rudimentary and aborted organs, etc., will cease to be metaphorical, and will have a plain signification. When we no longer look at an organic being as a savage looks at a ship, as at something wholly beyond his comprehension; when we regard every production of nature as one which has had a history; when we contemplate every complex structure and instinct as the summing up of many contrivances, each useful to the possessor, nearly in the same way as when we look at any great mechanical invention as the summing up of the labour, the experience, the reason, and even the blunders of numerous workmen; when we thus view each organic being, how far more interesting, I speak from experience, will the study of natural history become!

A grand and almost untrodden field of inquiry will be opened, on the causes and laws of variation, on correlation of growth, on the effects of use and disuse, on the direct action of external conditions, and so forth. The study of domestic productions will rise immensely in value. A new variety raised by man will be a far more important and interesting subject for study than one more species added to the infinitude of already recorded species. Our classifications will come to be, as far as they can be so made, genealogies; and will then truly give what may be called the plan of creation. The rules for classifying will no doubt become simpler when we have a definite object in view. We possess no pedigrees or armorial bearings; and we have to discover and trace the many diverging lines of descent in our natural genealogies, by characters of any kind which have long been inherited. Rudimentary organs will speak infallibly with respect to the nature of long-lost structures. Species and groups of species, which are called aberrant, and which may fancifully be called living fossils, will aid us in forming a picture of the ancient forms of life. Embryology will reveal to us the structure, in some degree obscured, of the prototypes of each great class.

When we can feel assured that all the individuals of the same species, and all the closely allied species of most genera, have within a not very remote period descended from one parent, and have migrated from some one birthplace; and when we better know the many means of migration, then, by the light which geology now throws, and will continue to throw, on former changes of climate and of the level of the land, we shall surely be enabled to trace in an admirable manner the former migrations of the inhabitants of the whole world. Even at present, by comparing the differences of the inhabitants of the sea on the opposite sides of a continent, and the nature of the various inhabitants of that continent in relation to their apparent means of immigration, some light can be thrown on ancient geography.

The noble science of Geology loses glory from the extreme imperfection of the record. The crust of the earth with its embedded remains must not be looked at as a well-filled museum, but as a poor collection made at hazard and at rare intervals. The accumulation of each great fossiliferous formation will be recognised as having depended on an unusual concurrence of circumstances, and the blank intervals between the successive stages as having been of vast duration. But we shall be able to gauge with some security the duration of these intervals by a comparison of the preceding and succeeding organic forms. We must be cautious in attempting to correlate as strictly contemporaneous two formations, which include few identical species, by the general succession of their forms of life. As species are produced and exterminated by slowly acting and still existing causes, and not by miraculous acts of creation and by catastrophes; and as the most important of all causes of organic change is one which is almost independent of altered and perhaps suddenly altered physical conditions, namely, the mutual relation of organism to organism,—the improvement of one being entailing the improvement or the extermination of others; it follows, that the amount of organic change in the fossils of consecutive formations probably serves as a fair measure of the lapse of actual time. A number of species, however, keeping in a body might remain for a long period unchanged, whilst within this same period, several of these species, by migrating into new countries and coming into competition with foreign associates, might become modified; so that we must not overrate the accuracy of organic change as a measure of time.

During early periods of the earth's history, when the forms of life were probably fewer and simpler, the rate of change was probably slower; and at the first dawn of life, when very few forms of the simplest structure existed, the rate of change may have been slow in an extreme degree. The whole history of the world, as at present known, although of a length quite incomprehensible by us, will hereafter be recognised as a mere fragment of time, compared with the ages which have elapsed since the first creature, the progenitor of innumerable extinct and living descendants, was created.

In the distant future I see open fields for far more important researches. Psychology will be based on a new foundation, that of the necessary acquirement of each mental power and capacity by gradation. Light will be thrown on the origin of man and his history.

Authors of the highest eminence seem to be fully satisfied with the view that each species has been independently created. To my mind it accords better with what we know of the laws impressed on matter by the Creator, that the production and extinction of the past and present inhabitants of the world should have been due to secondary causes, like those determining the birth and death of the individual. When I view all beings not as special creations, but as the lineal descendants of some few beings which lived long before the first bed of the Silurian system was deposited, they seem to me to become ennobled. Judging from the past, we may safely infer that not one living species will transmit its unaltered likeness to a distant futurity. And of the species now living very few will transmit progeny of any kind to a far distant futurity; for the manner in which all organic beings are grouped, shows that the greater number of species of each genus, and all the species of many genera, have left no descendants, but have become utterly extinct.

We can so far take a prophetic glance into futurity as to foretell that it will be the common and widely-spread species, belonging to the larger and dominant groups, which will ultimately prevail and procreate new and dominant species. As all the living forms of life are the lineal descendants of those which lived long before the Silurian epoch, we may feel certain that the ordinary succession by generation has never once been broken, and that no cataclysm has desolated the whole world. Hence we may look with some confidence to a secure future of equally inappreciable length.

And as natural selection works solely by and for the good of each being, all corporeal and mental endowments will tend to progress towards perfection.

It is interesting to contemplate an entangled bank, clothed with many plants of many kinds, with birds singing on the bushes, with various insects flitting about, and with worms crawling through the damp earth, and to reflect that these elaborately constructed forms, so different from each other, and dependent on each other in so complex a manner, have all been produced by laws acting around us. These laws, taken in the largest sense, being Growth with Reproduction; inheritance which is almost implied by reproduction; Variability from the indirect and direct action of the external conditions of life, and from use and disuse; a Ratio of Increase so high as to lead to a Struggle for Life, and as a consequence to Natural Selection, entailing Divergence of Character and the Extinction of less-improved forms.

Thus, from the war of nature, from famine and death, the most exalted object which we are capable of conceiving, namely, the production of the higher animals, directly follows. There is grandeur in this view of life, with its several powers, having been originally breathed into a few forms or into one; and that, whilst this planet has gone cycling on according to the fixed law of gravity, from so simple a beginning endless forms most beautiful and most wonderful have been, and are being, evolved.


# ON NATURE AND SURVIVAL

## Phil Johnson


The concluding chapter of Darwin's masterpiece is exceptionally important because it provides an overview of the logic of the entire book, which Darwin frankly describes as "one long argument" in support of his theory. In brief, the gist is that the theory must be true because it could be true; it explains an immense number of facts; the objections to it either can be shown or will eventually be shown to be inconclusive or even groundless.

At the start, Darwin concedes that it may at first appear difficult to believe that the "complex organs and instincts of animals have been perfected" not by some intelligent oversight, "but by the accumulation of innumerable slight variations, each good for the possessor." The last phrase is important. Natural selection is a blind, purposeless process with no ability to preserve a presently useless innovation that might become useful for a descendant organism at a future time. Unless the innovation is immediately useful in empowering the organism possessing it to leave more offspring than another organism not possessing it, the innovation will not be passed on to the next generation.

Darwin continues, saying that the apparent difficulty in believing that an unintelligent process can perfect complex organs and instincts cannot be considered real, if we consider that there are many variations in these organs and instincts and there is a struggle for existence, leading to the preservation of profitable variations, and that gradations in the state of perfection of each organ may once have existed, each good of its kind. It may be difficult even to conjecture all the details of the process, and there are cases of particular difficulty, but Darwin has shown in other chapters how some of the difficulties can be overcome.

This brings us to a point of particular interest. It may be conceded that where there are heritable variations in any population, the variant forms best fitted to survive and reproduce will succeed in leaving descendents, and these descendents will resemble their successful parents. The difficulty is not in establishing that such a process occurs, but in testing whether it truly accounts for the transformation of a species into a basically different and more complex organism. On the contrary, it may be that natural selection so described is a conservative force, accounting for how a species can continue to thrive under different environmental conditions without undergoing any radical transformation. Critics have summarized the point by saying that, despite its title, Darwin's "Origin" describes the "survival of the species, but not the arrival of the species."

The creative natural selection required by Darwin's theory has never been observed in nature or in laboratory experiments. Supporters say this is because creative evolution occurred so long ago and over so long a time period. This is a reasonable explanation, if we presume the theory to be true, but maybe creative natural selection has not been observed because it has not occurred.

Three passages from this chapter are particularly thought-provoking:
(1) Darwin's struggle against entrenched orthodoxy.

Darwin wrote that: "Although I am fully convinced of the truth of the views given in this volume . . . I by no means expect to convince experienced naturalists whose minds are stocked with a multitude of facts all viewed, during the long course of years, from a point of view directly opposite to mine. . . ." Against such narrow partisans of the old school, Darwin could only appeal to a hoped-for new generation of scientists "who will be able to view both sides of the question with impartiality." This appeal from an old guard's orthodoxy to a new generation's more flexible mentality is ironic for later readers, because Darwinism is now itself the entrenched orthodoxy, and those who would present an alternative have to appeal to a later generation of scientists whom they hope will be more willing to consider their ideas.

(2) Darwin's theory versus the fossil record.

Darwin recognized that his doctrine of evolution by the accumulation of an immense number of small variations via natural selection implied that there must have been an infinitude of connecting links between the living and extinct inhabitants of the world. It puzzled him that the fossil record did not show the existence of the many fine gradations required by the theory. This absence of links, he thought, was the most obvious of the many objections that may be urged against the theory.

Darwin admitted that he could answer this objection only by supposing that the fossil record must be far more imperfect than most geologists believed at the time. He thought the imperfection stemmed from the fact that only a very small percentage of the fossil beds that must exist on the earth had been explored as of 1859.

Darwin's argument implied that future fossil discoveries would tend to confirm the presence of innumerable intermediate forms in the fossil record. Now that 150 years have passed since he published *On the Origin of Species,* the question is whether the enormous efforts that have been made to discover evidence that would validate his prediction have resolved the difficulty. On the contrary, fossil experts have observed that, especially where the fossils are most abundant, there is a consistent pattern of sudden emergence of new forms of life, followed by long periods of stasis, meaning the absence of significant change. The fossils show that, over time, there has been change in the kind of organisms living on the earth, but not that the change has occurred by the Darwinian method.

(3) Is there a place for God in Darwin's theory?

Darwin said: "I see no good reason why the views given in this volume should shock the religious feelings of anyone. A celebrated author and divine has written to me that he has 'gradually learnt to see that it is just as noble a conception of the deity to believe that He created a few original forms capable of self-development into other and needful forms as to believe that He required a fresh act of creation to supply the voids caused by the action of His laws.'"

There has been much speculation as to whether this reassurance was meant sincerely or whether Darwin merely hoped it would mollify some religious objectors, including his own wife. Some of his supporters objected to the reassurance as a failure of nerve, and Darwin dropped it from later editions of *The Origin*.

It may be that it's a noble conception of God to suppose He supplied the first organisms and equipped them with everything they would need to evolve into more complex forms. Darwin's objective, however, was not to support a noble view of God but rather to provide a scientific explanation of the history of life from which God was rigorously excluded. Subsequent Darwinists have made it a priority to extend this naturalistic explanation to the ultimate origin of life from non-living components. Any suggestion that God needed to intervene at any point in the process is derided as an attack on science itself.

The answer to the question, then, is no. There is no place for God in Darwin's theory, although many suppose they can reconcile belief in his theory with belief in the existence of God. If God does exist, it seems that, from a Darwinian standpoint, He is unnecessary, because the origin of all the many forms of life proceeds very well without the need for His participation.

## CHAPTER TWENTY SIX

# LEO TOLSTOY

## Modern (1828–1910)

Leo Tolstoy was a Christian, of a sort, a man with noble aspirations, to a point, but he also was a cad and politically irresponsible. He turned over the tables of the moneychangers, but he also managed to do quite well for himself in terms of literary reputation. Reading Tolstoy is a profound experience and can be enlightening, but the source of that light is often in question. He is an uncertain ally for a believer.

Tolstoy was the putative prophet honored in his own time. He rightly opposed corruption in the political establishment but was feted by the academic establishment. It was this establishment that was breeding the monsters who would destroy Old Russia.

Russia faced the same turmoil that came to many lands after successive revolutions: scientific, industrial, and intellectual. The old order had to change, but in what way? Leo Tolstoy rightly saw it was not programs but a human heart-change that was key. Love itself, however, could be deceptive in a people whose hearts had been corrupted by modernity.

Tolstoy is a valuable guide in finding that corruption. He shows us most of the errors we're likely to commit in our personal lives, and he spares us nothing. However, he does not seem to believe in any original corruption . . . any sin that cannot be blamed on upbringing or bad personal choices.

Can we really fix ourselves? Can we really see what needs to be seen and do what needs to be done? Tolstoy suggests we can, even though the road will be long and arduous. He is Orthodox enough to see that humans are sinners in need of mercy, but not Orthodox enough to get to the root of the problem.

The prophet does not plunge deeply enough into the human heart.

Tolstoy was Christian enough to see that evil exists but not holy or self-aware enough to know the depths to which a nation or a man could go. His romance is, therefore, more true to life than most of Hollywood's chick flicks, but just as dangerous. Tolstoy can imagine an Anna, but not a Lenin. Many millions of Russians would die after the prophet's failure to see how bad things could really get.

## ⟳ FROM ⟳

# Anna Karenina, Part 4

### Chapter 14

When Kitty had gone and Levin was left alone, he felt such uneasiness without her, and such an impatient longing to get as quickly, as quickly as possible, to tomorrow morning, when he would see her again and be plighted to her forever, that he felt afraid, as though of death, of those fourteen hours that he had to get through without her. It was essential for him to be with someone to talk to, so as not to be left alone, to kill time. Stepan Arkadyevitch would have been the companion most congenial to him, but he was going out, he said, to a *soirèe*, in reality to the ballet. Levin only had time to tell him he was happy, and that he loved him, and would never, never forget what he had done for him. The eyes and the smile of Stepan Arkadyevitch showed Levin that he comprehended that feeling fittingly.

"Oh, so it's not time to die yet?" said Stepan Arkadyevitch, pressing Levin's hand with emotion.

"N-n-no!" said Levin.

Darya Alexandrovna too, as she said good-bye to him, gave him a sort of congratulation, saying, "How glad I am you have met Kitty again! One must value old friends." Levin did not like these words of Darya Alexandrovna's. She could not understand how lofty and beyond her it all was, and she ought not to have dared to allude to it. Levin said good-bye to them, but, not to be left alone, he attached himself to his brother.

"Where are you going?"

"I'm going to a meeting."

"Well, I'll come with you. May I?"

"What for? Yes, come along," said Sergey Ivanovitch, smiling. "What is the matter with you today?"

"With me? Happiness is the matter with me!" said Levin, letting down the window of the carriage they were driving in. "You don't mind?—it's so stifling. It's happiness is the matter with me! Why is it you have never married?"

Sergey Ivanovitch smiled.

"I am very glad, she seems a nice gi . . ." Sergey Ivanovitch was beginning.

"Don't say it! don't say it!" shouted Levin, clutching at the collar of his fur coat with both hands, and muffling him up in it. "She's a nice girl" were such simple, humble words, so out of harmony with his feeling.

Sergey Ivanovitch laughed outright a merry laugh, which was rare with him. "Well, anyway, I may say that I'm very glad of it."

"That you may do tomorrow, tomorrow and nothing more! Nothing, nothing, silence," said Levin, and muffling him once more in his fur coat, he added: "I do like you so! Well, is it possible for me to be present at the meeting?"

"Of course it is."

"What is your discussion about today?" asked Levin, never ceasing smiling.

They arrived at the meeting. Levin heard the secretary hesitatingly read the minutes which he obviously did not himself understand; but Levin saw from this secretary's face what a good, nice, kind-hearted person he was. This was evident from his confusion and embarrassment in reading the minutes. Then the discussion began. They were disputing about the misappropriation of certain sums and the laying of certain pipes, and Sergey Ivanovitch was very cutting to two members, and said something at great length with an air of triumph; and another member, scribbling something on a bit of paper, began timidly at first, but afterwards answered him very viciously and delightfully. And then Sviazhsky (he was there too) said something too, very handsomely and nobly. Levin listened to them, and saw clearly that these missing sums and these pipes were not anything real, and that they were not at all angry, but were all the nicest, kindest people, and everything was as happy and charming as possible among them. They did no harm to anyone, and were all enjoying it. What struck Levin was that he could see through them all today, and from little, almost imperceptible signs knew the soul of each, and saw distinctly that they were all good at heart. And Levin himself in particular they were all extremely fond of that day. That was evident from the way they spoke to him, from the friendly, affectionate way even those he did not know looked at him.

"Well, did you like it?" Sergey Ivanovitch asked him.

"Very much. I never supposed it was so interesting! Capital! Splendid!"

Sviazhsky went up to Levin and invited him to come round to tea with him. Levin was utterly at a loss to comprehend or recall what it was he had disliked in Sviazhsky, what he had failed to find in him. He was a clever and wonderfully good-hearted man.

"Most delighted," he said, and asked after his wife and sister-in-law. And from a queer association of ideas, because in his imagination the idea of Sviazhsky's sister-in-law was connected with marriage, it occurred to him that there was no one to whom he could more suitably speak of his happiness, and he was very glad to go and see them.

Sviazhsky questioned him about his improvements on his estate, presupposing, as he always did, that there was no possibility of doing anything not done already in Europe, and now this did not in the least annoy Levin. On the contrary, he felt that Sviazhsky was right, that the whole business was of little value, and he saw the wonderful softness and consideration with which Sviazhsky avoided fully expressing his correct view. The ladies of the Sviazhsky household were particularly delightful. It seemed to Levin that they knew all about it already and sympathized with him, saying nothing merely from delicacy. He stayed with them one hour, two, three, talking of all sorts of subjects but the one thing that filled his heart, and did not observe that he was boring them dreadfully, and that it was long past their bedtime.

Sviazhsky went with him into the hall, yawning and wondering at the strange humor his friend was in. It was past one o'clock. Levin went back to his hotel, and was dismayed at the thought that all alone now with his impatience he had ten hours still left to get through. The servant, whose turn it was to be up all night, lighted his candles, and would have gone away, but Levin stopped him. This servant, Yegor, whom Levin had noticed before, struck him as a very intelligent, excellent, and, above all, good-hearted man.

"Well, Yegor, it's hard work not sleeping, isn't it?"

"One's got to put up with it! It's part of our work, you see. In a gentleman's house it's easier; but then here one makes more."

It appeared that Yegor had a family, three boys and a daughter, a seamstress, whom he wanted to marry to a cashier in a saddler's shop.

Levin, on hearing this, informed Yegor that, in his opinion, in marriage the great thing was love, and that with love one would always be happy, for happiness rests only on oneself. Yegor listened attentively, and obviously quite took in Levin's idea, but by way of assent to it he enunciated, greatly to Levin's surprise, the observation that when he had lived with good masters he had always been satisfied with his masters, and now was perfectly satisfied with his employer, though he was a Frenchman.

"Wonderfully good-hearted fellow!" thought Levin.

"Well, but you yourself, Yegor, when you got married, did you love your wife?"

"Ay! and why not?" responded Yegor.

And Levin saw that Yegor too was in an excited state and intending to express all his most heartfelt emotions.

"My life, too, has been a wonderful one. From a child up . . ." he was beginning with flashing eyes, apparently catching Levin's enthusiasm, just as people catch yawning.

But at that moment a ring was heard. Yegor departed, and Levin was left alone. He had eaten scarcely anything at dinner, had refused tea and supper at Sviazhsky's, but he was incapable of thinking of supper. He had not slept the previous night, but was incapable of thinking of sleep either. His room was cold, but he was oppressed by heat. He opened both the movable panes in his window and sat down to the table opposite the open panes. Over the snow-covered roofs could be seen a decorated cross with chains, and above it the rising triangle of Charles's Wain with the yellowish light of Capella. He gazed at the cross, then at the stars, drank in the fresh freezing air that flowed evenly into the room, and followed as though in a dream the images and memories that rose in his imagination. At four o'clock he heard steps in the passage and peeped out at the door. It was the gambler Myaskin, whom he knew, coming from the club. He walked gloomily, frowning and coughing. "Poor, unlucky fellow!" thought Levin, and tears came into his eyes from love and pity for this man. He would have talked with him, and tried to comfort him, but remembering that he had nothing but his shirt on, he changed his mind and sat down again at the open pane to bathe in the cold air and gaze at the exquisite lines of the cross, silent, but full of meaning for him, and the mounting lurid yellow star. At seven o'clock there was a noise of people polishing the floors, and bells ringing in some servants' department, and Levin felt that he was beginning to get frozen. He closed the pane, washed, dressed, and went out into the street.

## Chapter 15

The streets were still empty. Levin went to the house of the Shtcherbatskys. The visitors' doors were closed and everything was asleep. He walked back, went into his room again, and asked for coffee. The day servant, not Yegor this time, brought it to him. Levin would have entered into conversation with him, but a bell rang for the servant, and he went out. Levin tried to drink coffee and put some roll in his mouth, but his mouth was quite at a loss what to do with the roll. Levin, rejecting the roll, put on his coat and went out again for a walk. It was nine o'clock when he reached the Shtcherbatskys' steps the second time. In the house they were only just up, and the cook came out to go marketing. He had to get through at least two hours more.

All that night and morning Levin lived perfectly unconsciously, and felt perfectly lifted out of the conditions of material life. He had eaten nothing for a whole day, he had not slept for two nights, had spent several hours undressed in the frozen air, and felt not simply fresher and stronger than ever, but felt utterly independent of his body; he moved without muscular effort, and felt as if he could do anything. He was convinced he could fly upwards or lift the corner of the house, if need be. He spent the remainder of the time in the street, incessantly looking at his watch and gazing about him.

And what he saw then, he never saw again after. The children especially going to school, the bluish doves flying down from the roofs to the pavement, and the little loaves covered with flour, thrust out by an unseen hand, touched him. Those loaves, those doves, and those two boys were not earthly creatures. It all happened at the same time: a boy ran towards a dove and glanced smiling at Levin; the dove, with a whir of her wings, darted away, flashing in the sun, amid grains of snow that quivered in the air, while from a little window there came a smell of fresh-baked bread, and the loaves were put out. All of this together was so extraordinarily nice that Levin laughed and cried with delight. Going a long way round by Gazetny Place and Kislovka, he went back again to the hotel, and putting his watch before him, he sat down to wait for twelve o'clock. In the next room they were talking about some sort of machines, and swindling, and coughing their morning coughs. They did not realize that the hand was near twelve. The hand reached it. Levin went out onto the steps. The sledge-drivers clearly knew all about it. They crowded round Levin with happy faces, quarreling among themselves, and offering their services. Trying not to offend the other sledge drivers, and promising to drive with them too, Levin took one and told him to drive to the Shtcherbatskys'. The sledge-driver was splendid in a white shirt-collar sticking out over his overcoat and into his strong, full-blooded red neck. The sledge was high and comfortable, and altogether such a one as Levin never drove in after, and the horse was a good one, and tried to gallop but didn't seem to move. The driver knew the Shtcherbatskys' house, and drew up at the entrance with a curve of his arm and a "Whoa!" especially indicative of respect for his fare. The Shtcherbatskys' hall-porter certainly knew all about it. This was evident from the smile in his eyes and the way he said:

"Well, it's a long while since you've been to see us, Konstantin Demitrievitch!"

Not only he knew all about it, but he was unmistakably delighted and making efforts to conceal his joy. Looking into his kindly old eyes, Levin realized even something new in his happiness.

"Are they up?"

"Pray walk in! Leave it here," said he, smiling, as Levin would have come back to take his hat. That meant something.

"To whom shall I announce your honor?" asked the footman.

The footman, though a young man, and one of the new school of footmen, a dandy, was a very kind-hearted, good fellow, and he too knew all about it.

"The princess . . . the prince . . . the young princess . . ." said Levin.

The first person he saw was Mademoiselle Linon. She walked across the room, and her ringlets and her face were beaming. He had only just spoken to her, when suddenly he heard the rustle of a skirt at the door, and Mademoiselle Linon vanished from Levin's eyes, and a joyful terror came over him at the nearness of his happiness. Mademoiselle Linon was in great haste, and leaving him, went out at the other door. Directly she had gone out, swift, swift light steps sounded on the parquet, and his bliss, his life, himself—what was best in himself, what he had so long sought and longed for—was quickly, so quickly approaching him. She did not walk, but seemed, by some unseen force, to float to him. He saw nothing but her clear, truthful eyes, frightened by the same bliss of love that flooded his heart. Those eyes were shining nearer and nearer, blinding him with their light of love. She stopped still close to him, touching him. Her hands rose and dropped onto his shoulders.

She had done all she could—she had run up to him and given herself up entirely, shy and happy. He put his arms round her and pressed his lips to her mouth that sought his kiss.

She too had not slept all night, and had been expecting him all the morning.

Her mother and father had consented without demur, and were happy in her happiness. She had been waiting for him. She wanted to be the first to tell him her happiness and his. She had got ready to see him alone, and had been delighted at the idea, and had been shy and ashamed, and did not know herself what she was doing. She had heard his steps and voice, and had waited at the door for Mademoiselle Linon to go. Mademoiselle Linon had gone away. Without thinking, without asking herself how and what, she had gone up to him, and did as she was doing.

"Let us go to mamma!" she said, taking him by the hand. For a long while he could say nothing, not so much because he was afraid of desecrating the loftiness of his emotion by a word, as that every time he tried to say something, instead of words he felt that tears of happiness were welling up. He took her hand and kissed it.

"Can it be true?" he said at last in a choked voice. "I can't believe you love me, dear!"

She smiled at that "dear," and at the timidity with which he glanced at her.

"Yes!" she said significantly, deliberately. "I am so happy!"

Not letting go his hands, she went into the drawing room. The princess, seeing them, breathed quickly, and immediately began to cry and then immediately began to laugh, and with a vigorous step Levin had not expected, ran up to him, and hugging his head, kissed him, wetting his cheeks with her tears.

"So it is all settled! I am glad. Love her. I am glad. . . . Kitty!"

"You've not been long settling things," said the old prince, trying to seem unmoved; but Levin noticed that his eyes were wet when he turned to him.

"I've long, always wished for this!" said the prince, taking Levin by the arm and drawing him towards himself. "Even when this little featherhead fancied . . ."

"Papa!" shrieked Kitty, and shut his mouth with her hands.

"Well, I won't!" he said. "I'm very, very . . . plea . . . Oh, what a fool I am. . . ."

He embraced Kitty, kissed her face, her hand, her face again, and made the sign of the cross over her.

And there came over Levin a new feeling of love for this man, till then so little known to him, when he saw how slowly and tenderly Kitty kissed his muscular hand.

## Chapter 16

The princess sat in her armchair, silent and smiling; the prince sat down beside her. Kitty stood by her father's chair, still holding his hand. All were silent.

The princess was the first to put everything into words, and to translate all thoughts and feelings into practical questions. And all equally felt this strange and painful for the first minute.

"When is it to be? We must have the benediction and announcement. And when's the wedding to be? What do you think, Alexander?"

"Here he is," said the old prince, pointing to Levin—"he's the principal person in the matter."

"When?" said Levin blushing. "Tomorrow; if you ask me, I should say, the benediction today and the wedding tomorrow."

"Come, *mon cher*, that's nonsense!"

"Well, in a week."

"He's quite mad."

"No, why so?"

"Well, upon my word!" said the mother, smiling, delighted at this haste. "How about the trousseau?"

"Will there really be a trousseau and all that?" Levin thought with horror. "But can the trousseau and the benediction and all that—can it spoil my happiness? Nothing can spoil it!" He glanced at Kitty, and noticed that she was not in the least, not in the very least, disturbed by the idea of the trousseau. "Then it must be all right," he thought.

"Oh, I know nothing about it; I only said what I should like," he said apologetically.

"We'll talk it over, then. The benediction and announcement can take place now. That's very well."

The princess went up to her husband, kissed him, and would have gone away, but he kept her, embraced her, and, tenderly as a young lover, kissed her several times, smiling. The old people were obviously muddled for a moment, and did not quite know whether it was they who were in love again or their daughter. When the prince and the princess had gone, Levin went up to his betrothed and took her hand. He was self-possessed now and could speak, and he had a great deal he wanted to tell her. But he said not at all what he had to say.

"How I knew it would be so! I never hoped for it; and yet in my heart I was always sure," he said. "I believe that it was ordained."

"And I!" she said. "Even when. . . ." She stopped and went on again, looking at him resolutely with her truthful eyes, "Even when I thrust from me my happiness. I always loved you alone, but I was carried away. I ought to tell you. . . . Can you forgive that?"

"Perhaps it was for the best. You will have to forgive me so much. I ought to tell you . . ."

This was one of the things he had meant to speak about. He had resolved from the first to tell her two things—that he was not chaste as she was, and that he was not a believer. It was agonizing, but he considered he ought to tell her both these facts.

"No, not now, later!" he said.

"Very well, later, but you must certainly tell me. I'm not afraid of anything. I want to know everything. Now it is settled."

He added: "Settled that you'll take me whatever I may be—you won't give me up? Yes?"

"Yes, yes."

Their conversation was interrupted by Mademoiselle Linon, who with an affected but tender smile came to congratulate her favorite pupil. Before she had gone, the servants came in with their congratulations. Then relations arrived, and there began that state of blissful absurdity from which Levin did not emerge till the day after his wedding. Levin was in a continual state of awkwardness and discomfort, but the intensity of his happiness went on all the while increasing. He felt continually that a great deal was being expected of him—what, he did not know; and he did everything he was told, and it all gave him happiness. He had thought his engagement would have nothing about it like others, that the ordinary conditions of engaged couples would spoil his special happiness; but it ended in his doing exactly as other people did, and his happiness being only increased thereby and becoming more and more special, more and more unlike anything that had ever happened.

"Now we shall have sweetmeats to eat," said Mademoiselle Linon—and Levin drove off to buy sweetmeats.

"Well, I'm very glad," said Sviazhsky. "I advise you to get the bouquets from Fomin's."

"Oh, are they wanted?" And he drove to Fomin's.

His brother offered to lend him money, as he would have so many expenses, presents to give. . . .

"Oh, are presents wanted?" And he galloped to Foulde's.

And at the confectioner's, and at Fomin's, and at Foulde's he saw that he was expected; that they were pleased to see him, and prided themselves on his happiness, just as everyone whom he had to do with during those days. What was extraordinary was that everyone not only liked him, but even people previously unsympathetic, cold, and callous, were enthusiastic over him, gave way to him in everything, treated his feeling with tenderness and delicacy, and shared his conviction that he was the happiest man in the world because his betrothed was beyond perfection. Kitty too felt the same thing. When Countess Nordston ventured to hint that she had hoped for something better, Kitty was so angry and proved so conclusively that nothing in the world could be better than Levin, that Countess Nordston had to admit it, and in Kitty's presence never met Levin without a smile of ecstatic admiration.

The confession he had promised was the one painful incident of this time. He consulted the old prince, and with his sanction gave Kitty his diary, in which there was written the confession that tortured him. He had written this diary at the time with a view to his future wife. Two things caused him anguish: his lack of purity and his lack of faith. His confession of unbelief passed unnoticed. She was religious, had never doubted the truths of religion, but his external unbelief did not affect her in the least. Through love she knew all his soul, and in his soul she saw what she wanted, and that such a state of soul should be called unbelieving was to her a matter of no account. The other confession set her weeping bitterly.

Levin, not without an inner struggle, handed her his diary. He knew that between him and her there could not be, and should not be, secrets, and so he had decided that so it must be. But he had not realized what an effect it would have on her, he had not put himself in her place. It was only when the same evening he came to their house before the theater, went into her room and saw her tear-stained, pitiful, sweet face, miserable with suffering he had caused and nothing could undo, he felt the abyss that separated his shameful past from her dovelike purity, and was appalled at what he had done.

"Take them, take these dreadful books!" she said, pushing away the notebooks lying before her on the table. "Why did you give them me? No, it was better anyway," she added, touched by his despairing face. "But it's awful, awful!"

His head sank, and he was silent. He could say nothing.

"You can't forgive me," he whispered.

"Yes, I forgive you; but it's terrible!"

But his happiness was so immense that this confession did not shatter it, it only added another shade to it. She forgave him; but from that time more than ever he considered himself unworthy of her, morally bowed down lower than ever before her, and prized more highly than ever his undeserved happiness.

## Chapter 17

Unconsciously going over in his memory the conversations that had taken place during and after dinner, Alexey Alexandrovitch returned to his solitary room. Darya Alexandrovna's [that is, Dolly Oblonsky's] words about forgiveness had aroused in him nothing but annoyance. The applicability or non-applicability of the Christian precept to his own case was too difficult a question to be discussed lightly, and this question had long ago been answered by Alexey Alexandrovitch in the negative. Of all that had been said, what stuck most in his memory was the phrase of stupid, good-natured Turovtsin—"Acted like a man, he did! Called him out and shot him!" Everyone had apparently shared this feeling, though from politeness they had not expressed it.

"But the matter is settled, it's useless thinking about it," Alexey Alexandrovitch told himself. And thinking of nothing but the journey before him, and the revision work he had to do, he went into his room and asked the porter who escorted him where his man was. The porter said that the man had only just gone out. Alexey Alexandrovitch ordered tea to be sent him, sat down to the table, and taking the guidebook, began considering the route of his journey.

"Two telegrams," said his manservant, coming into the room. "I beg your pardon, your excellency; I'd only just that minute gone out."

Alexey Alexandrovitch took the telegrams and opened them. The first telegram was the announcement of Stremov's appointment to the very post Karenin had coveted. Alexey Alexandrovitch flung the telegram down, and flushing a little, got up and began to pace up and down the room. "*Quos vult perdere dementat,*" he said, meaning by *quos* the persons responsible for this appointment. He was not so much annoyed that he had not received the post, that he had been conspicuously passed over; but it was incomprehensible, amazing to him that they did not see that the wordy phrase-monger Stremov was the last man fit for it. How could they fail to see how they were ruining themselves, lowering their prestige by this appointment?

"Something else in the same line," he said to himself bitterly, opening the second telegram. The telegram was from his wife. Her name, written in blue pencil, "Anna," was the first thing that caught his eye. "I am dying; I beg, I implore you to come. I shall die easier with your forgiveness," he read. He smiled contemptuously, and flung down the telegram. That this was a trick and a fraud, of that, he thought for the first minute, there could be no doubt.

"There is no deceit she would stick at. She was near her confinement. Perhaps it is the confinement. But what can be their aim? To legitimize the child, to compromise me, and prevent a divorce," he thought. "But something was said in it: I am dying. . . ." He read the telegram again, and suddenly the plain meaning of what was said in it struck him.

"And if it is true?" he said to himself. "If it is true that in the moment of agony and nearness to death she is genuinely penitent, and I, taking it for a trick, refuse to go? That would not only be cruel, and everyone would blame me, but it would be stupid on my part."

"Piotr, call a coach; I am going to Petersburg," he said to his servant.

Alexey Alexandrovitch decided that he would go to Petersburg and see his wife. If her illness was a trick, he would say nothing and go away again. If she was really in danger, and wished to see him before her death, he would forgive her if he found her alive, and pay her the last duties if he came too late.

All the way he thought no more of what he ought to do.

With a sense of weariness and uncleanness from the night spent in the train, in the early fog of Petersburg Alexey Alexandrovitch drove through the deserted Nevsky and stared straight before him, not thinking of what was awaiting him. He could not think about it, because in picturing what would happen, he could not drive away the reflection that her death would at once remove all the difficulty of his position. Bakers, closed shops, night-cabmen, porters sweeping the pavements flashed past his eyes, and he watched it all, trying to smother the thought of what was awaiting him, and what he dared not hope for, and yet was hoping for. He drove up to the steps. A sledge and a carriage with the coachman asleep stood at the entrance. As he went into the entry, Alexey Alexandrovitch, as it were, got out his resolution from the remotest corner of his brain, and mastered it thoroughly. Its meaning ran: "If it's a trick, then calm contempt and departure. If truth, do what is proper."

The porter opened the door before Alexey Alexandrovitch rang. The porter, Kapitonitch, looked queer in an old coat, without a tie, and in slippers.

"How is your mistress?"

"A successful confinement yesterday."

Alexey Alexandrovitch stopped short and turned white. He felt distinctly now how intensely he had longed for her death.

"And how is she?"

Korney in his morning apron ran downstairs.

"Very ill," he answered. "There was a consultation yesterday, and the doctor's here now."

"Take my things," said Alexey Alexandrovitch, and feeling some relief at the news that there was still hope of her death, he went into the hall.

On the hatstand there was a military overcoat. Alexey Alexandrovitch noticed it and asked:

"Who is here?"

"The doctor, the midwife, and Count Vronsky."

Alexey Alexandrovitch went into the inner rooms.

In the drawing room there was no one; at the sound of his steps there came out of her boudoir the midwife in a cap with lilac ribbons.

She went up to Alexey Alexandrovitch, and with the familiarity given by the approach of death took him by the arm and drew him towards the bedroom.

"Thank God you've come! She keeps on about you and nothing but you," she said.

"Make haste with the ice!" the doctor's peremptory voice said from the bedroom.

Alexey Alexandrovitch went into her boudoir.

At the table, sitting sideways in a low chair, was Vronsky, his face hidden in his hands, weeping. He jumped up at the doctor's voice, took his hands from his face, and saw Alexey Alexandrovitch. Seeing the husband, he was so overwhelmed that he sat down again, drawing his head down to his shoulders, as if he wanted to disappear; but he made an effort over himself, got up and said:

"She is dying. The doctors say there is no hope. I am entirely in your power, only let me be here . . . though I am at your disposal. I . . ."

Alexey Alexandrovitch, seeing Vronsky's tears, felt a rush of that nervous emotion always produced in him by the sight of other people's suffering, and turning away his face, he moved hurriedly to the door, without hearing the rest of his words. From the bedroom came the sound of Anna's voice saying something. Her voice was lively, eager, with exceedingly distinct intonations. Alexey Alexandrovitch went into the bedroom, and went up to the bed. She was lying turned with her face towards him. Her cheeks were flushed crimson, her eyes glittered, her little white hands thrust out from the sleeves of her dressing gown were playing with the quilt, twisting it about. It seemed as though she were not only well and blooming, but in the happiest frame of mind. She was talking rapidly, musically, and with exceptionally correct articulation and expressive intonation.

"For Alexey—I am speaking of Alexey Alexandrovitch (what a strange and awful thing that both are Alexey, isn't it?)—Alexey would not refuse me. I should forget, he would forgive. . . . But why doesn't he come? He's so good he doesn't know himself how good he is. Ah, my God, what agony! Give me some water, quick! Oh, that will be bad for her, my little girl! Oh, very well then, give her to a nurse. Yes, I agree, it's better in fact. He'll be coming; it will hurt him to see her. Give her to the nurse."

"Anna Arkadyevna, he has come. Here he is!" said the midwife, trying to attract her attention to Alexey Alexandrovitch.

"Oh, what nonsense!" Anna went on, not seeing her husband. "No, give her to me; give me my little one! He has not come yet. You say he won't forgive me, because you don't know him. No one knows him. I'm the only one, and it was hard for me even. His eyes I ought to know—Seryozha has just the same eyes—and I can't bear to see them because of it. Has Seryozha had his dinner? I know everyone will forget him. He would not forget. Seryozha must be moved into the corner room, and Mariette must be asked to sleep with him."

All of a sudden she shrank back, was silent; and in terror, as though expecting a blow, as though to defend herself, she raised her hands to her face. She had seen her husband.

"No, no!" she began. "I am not afraid of him; I am afraid of death. Alexey, come here. I am in a hurry, because I've no time, I've not long left to live; the fever will begin directly and I shall understand nothing more. Now I understand, I understand it all, I see it all!"

Alexey Alexandrovitch's wrinkled face wore an expression of agony; he took her by the hand and tried to say something, but he could not utter it; his lower lip quivered, but he still went on struggling with his emotion, and only now and then glanced at her. And each time he glanced at her, he saw her eyes gazing at him with such passionate and triumphant tenderness as he had never seen in them.

"Wait a minute, you don't know . . . stay a little, stay! . . ." She stopped, as though collecting her ideas. "Yes," she began; "yes, yes, yes. This is what I wanted to say. Don't be surprised at me. I'm still the same. . . . But there is another woman in me, I'm afraid of her: she loved that man, and I tried to hate you, and could not forget about her that used to be. I'm not that woman. Now I'm my real self, all myself. I'm dying now, I know I shall die, ask him. Even now I feel—see here, the weights on my feet, on my hands, on my fingers. My fingers—see how huge they are! But this will soon all be over. . . . Only one thing I want: forgive me, forgive me quite. I'm terrible, but my nurse used to tell me; the holy martyr—what was her name? She was worse. And I'll go to Rome; there's a wilderness, and there I shall be no trouble to any one, only I'll take Seryozha and the little one. . . . No, you can't forgive me! I know, it can't be forgiven! No, no, go away, you're too good!" She held his hand in one burning hand, while she pushed him away with the other.

The nervous agitation of Alexey Alexandrovitch kept increasing, and had by now reached such a point that he ceased to struggle with it. He suddenly felt that what he had regarded as nervous agitation was on the contrary a blissful spiritual condition that gave him all at once a new happiness he had never known. He did not think that the Christian law that he had been all his life trying to follow, enjoined on him to forgive and love his enemies; but a glad feeling of love and forgiveness for his enemies filled his heart. He knelt down, and laying his head in the curve of her arm, which burned him as with fire through the sleeve, he sobbed like a little child. She put her arm around his head, moved towards him, and with defiant pride lifted up her eyes.

"That is he. I knew him! Now, forgive me, everyone, forgive me! . . . They've come again; why don't they go away? . . . Oh, take these cloaks off me!"

The doctor unloosed her hands, carefully laying her on the pillow, and covered her up to the shoulders. She lay back submissively, and looked before her with beaming eyes.

"Remember one thing, that I needed nothing but forgiveness, and I want nothing more. . . . Why doesn't *he* come?" she said, turning to the door towards Vronsky. "Do come, do come! Give him your hand."

Vronsky came to the side of the bed, and seeing Anna, again hid his face in his hands.

"Uncover your face—look at him! He's a saint," she said. "Oh! uncover your face, do uncover it!" she said angrily. "Alexey Alexandrovitch, do uncover his face! I want to see him."

Alexey Alexandrovitch took Vronsky's hands and drew them away from his face, which was awful with the expression of agony and shame upon it.

"Give him your hand. Forgive him."

Alexey Alexandrovitch gave him his hand, not attempting to restrain the tears that streamed from his eyes.

"Thank God, thank God!" she said, "now everything is ready. Only to stretch my legs a little. There, that's capital. How badly these flowers are done—not a bit like a violet," she said, pointing to the hangings. "My God, my God! when will it end? Give me some morphine. Doctor, give me some morphine! Oh, my God, my God!"

And she tossed about on the bed.

The doctors said that it was puerperal fever, and that it was ninety-nine chances in a hundred it would end in death. The whole day long there was fever, delirium, and unconsciousness. At midnight the patient lay without consciousness, and almost without pulse.

The end was expected every minute.

Vronsky had gone home, but in the morning he came to inquire, and Alexey Alexandrovitch meeting him in the hall, said: "Better stay, she might ask for you," and himself led him to his wife's boudoir. Towards morning, there was a return again of excitement, rapid thought and talk, and again it ended in unconsciousness. On the third day it was the same thing, and the doctors said there was hope. That day Alexey Alexandrovitch went into the boudoir where Vronsky was sitting, and closing the door sat down opposite him.

"Alexey Alexandrovitch," said Vronsky, feeling that a statement of the position was coming, "I can't speak, I can't understand. Spare me! However hard it is for you, believe me, it is more terrible for me."

He would have risen; but Alexey Alexandrovitch took him by the hand and said:

"I beg you to hear me out; it is necessary. I must explain my feelings, the feelings that have guided me and will guide me, so that you may not be in error regarding me. You know I had resolved on a divorce, and had even begun to take proceedings. I won't conceal from you that in beginning this I was in uncertainty, I was in misery; I will confess that I was pursued by a desire to revenge myself on you and on her. When I got the telegram, I came here with the same feelings; I will say more, I longed for her death. But . . ." He paused, pondering whether to disclose or not to disclose his feeling to him. "But I saw her and forgave her. And the happiness of forgiveness has revealed to me my duty. I forgive completely. I would offer the other cheek, I would give my cloak if my coat be taken. I pray to God only not to take from me the bliss of forgiveness!"

Tears stood in his eyes, and the luminous, serene look in them impressed Vronsky.

"This is my position: you can trample me in the mud, make me the laughing-stock of the world, I will not abandon her, and I will never utter a word of reproach to you," Alexey Alexandrovitch went on. "My duty is clearly marked for me; I ought to be with her, and I will be. If she wishes to see you, I will let you know, but now I suppose it would be better for you to go away."

He got up, and sobs cut short his words. Vronsky too was getting up, and in a stooping, not yet erect posture, looked up at him from under his brows. He did not understand Alexey Alexandrovitch's feeling, but he felt that it was something higher and even unattainable for him with his view of life.

*Translated by Constance Garnett, 1917*

## On Anna Karenina

### Frederica Mathewes-Green

If you know anything about *Anna Karenina,* you know that it's the story of a woman who abandons her husband for another man and comes to a bad end. What you might not know is that the novel is about *two* marriages: Anna's, which ends sadly, and Levin's, which, though not without the usual stresses, goes well. The often-quoted first sentence of the book sets up the dichotomy: "All happy families are alike; each unhappy family is unhappy in its own way."

The selection included above comes from the exact center of the book; it's the hinge of the story. It begins with Levin walking around in a lovestricken daze—surely one of the most delightful passages in any novel—because Kitty has just accepted his proposal of marriage. Earlier in the story she had rejected him because, as an innocent young woman newly introduced to society, she was thrilled by the attentions of a handsome, worldly officer, Vronsky. Kitty rejected Levin's suit at a ball where she was expecting Vronsky's proposal—but then she saw Vronsky dancing with another woman, gazing at her with an expression of rapt, headlong love that he had never bestowed on Kitty. That woman was Anna Karenina.

As in most nineteenth-century novels, the characters' families are interwoven. Kitty's sister Dolly is married to Anna's brother, Stiva Oblonsky. The book's first scene depicts a crisis in that marriage: Dolly has just discovered a love note from her husband to the children's French governess, and her pain and fury has thrown the household into disarray. Anna comes for a visit, hoping to talk with Dolly and Stiva and enable a reconciliation.

Anna's sensitive intervention is successful, and she returns home to her husband, Alexei Karenin (a rather dry government official twenty years her senior), and their eight-year-old son.

But during her visit Anna had a disturbing experience. She met Vronsky, and both were instantly aware of a powerful attraction. Vronsky pursued her and, though she initially resisted, her defenses were soon overcome. Their affair became a familiar topic of society gossip, but somehow Karenin managed to ignore the truth until Anna told him bluntly, "I am his mistress, I cannot stand you, I'm afraid of you, I hate you." Karenin, shamed and furious, resolved at least to prevent Anna from getting what she wanted: the freedom to be with Vronsky.

Up to this point, the story of Anna's love affair follows a familiar pattern: two people meet and fall in love, but one of them is already married and the heartless spouse stands in the way. We don't encounter that storyline much anymore, but before the sexual revolution made premarital sex permissible, extramarital sex was often treated sympathetically in fiction, on the premise that one's destined true love might appear after a marriage had already taken place. This storyline gains drama if the resistant spouse is depicted as a bad guy, and that is how Karenin is often seen. In the 1935 film version (starring Greta Garbo), Basil Rathbone portrayed Karenin in the same cold, cruel manner that he did the villainous Mr. Murdstone in the same year's *David Copperfield*.

Thus, true love thwarted by a selfish spouse has been, in some ages, a common-enough story—but that's not the story Tolstoy wrote. In the passage above, Karenin goes to Anna's bedside knowing she has contracted a postpartum infection and secretly hoping she will die. But once he's there, something unexpected happens. A disturbance starts working within him as she clutches his hand and babbles feverishly. It breaks forth, a cascade of love and forgiveness for all who have hurt him. Exhilarating and joyous, it reduces him to sobbing, with his head against Anna's burning arm.

Look at what Tolstoy has done here: He has put a character through a radical transformation and, in the process, reversed our view of that character. We knew Karenin as dull, cold, and overly concerned with his social standing, but a radiance of soul has suddenly blazed out. Everything has been turned upside down. Now he is the noble figure while Vronsky discovers himself cast down and humiliated.

How did Tolstoy accomplish this reversal? We can reread the passage looking for authorial fingerprints, but it's hard to find any clues. It looks as if Tolstoy achieved the transformation simply by telling us that it's what happened. In the hands of other novelists, this turn of events might have sounded manipulative, heavy-handed, and simply unbelievable. But when Tolstoy tells the story, for some reason we believe it. It doesn't feel like we're reading fiction. It's more like watching a documentary.

This reality-effect is the distinctive feature of Tolstoy's writing; readers and critics have been trying to express just what this characteristic is, and how he does it, for over a century. The fashion of "realism" in fiction—that is, building a story from elements of ordinary life—did not originate with Tolstoy; it got its start decades earlier in France and had been well demonstrated by his time by Honoré de Balzac and Gustave Flaubert. But in Tolstoy's hands, reality somehow seems more real.

———

Clifton Fadiman, writing a foreword to Tolstoy's *War and Peace*, says, "It is translucent. It seems to have been composed in the sunlight." Critic Philip Rahv commented, "One might say that in a sense there are no plots in Tolstoy but simply the unquestioned and unalterable process of life itself."

How did he do it? In a review of a new translation of *Anna Karenina* (in the 2/5/01 *New Yorker*), James Wood ferrets out a few of Tolstoy's tricks. For one thing, he continually reverts to descriptions of physical reality. That's hardly a professional secret—every writer learns the rule "Show, don't tell"—but Tolstoy has a way of drawing our attention to those concrete details that keeps us in his characters' world.

Later in the novel, Vronsky is besieged by tormenting, insomniac thoughts, and at the very moment he thinks, "Why do people shoot themselves?" he suddenly notices by his head a pillow embroidered by his sister-in-law. He touches its tassel and tries to think when he saw her last. But it is painful to think of anything beyond his immediate misery, and he tells himself, "No, I must sleep!" Tolstoy does not just tell us that there is a pillow near Vronsky's head; he draws our attention to it by telling us it drew Vronsky's attention. He renders it visible by mentioning concrete details: it is embroidered, it has a tassel, and it causes an image of Varvara to flit across Vronsky's memory.

Furthermore, Wood points out, Tolstoy's "details are almost always propelled by function." The details have dynamic power because they are linked to the character's actions and responses. Vronsky is first surprised to see the pillow, then touches the tassel, pictures its maker, moves the pillow, presses his head to it, makes an effort to keep his eyes closed, then sits up abruptly. The pillow exists in the story as Vronsky interacts with it; it is not there because the omniscient narrator thought it would make a good part of the descriptive background.

So Tolstoy does not tell us how things look to the author; he tells us how they look to the characters. In short, he does not use simile and metaphor. (That astonishing assertion in Wood's review is what got me started reading Tolstoy in the first place. How can anyone write without using metaphor and simile? That would be like—never mind.)

Wood cites for comparison Flaubert's description of the steam rising from a train's funnel, and his authorial suggestion that it looks like an ostrich plume. There is no intrinsic connection between the steam and a plume; when we agree to that image, we are agreeing to see reality through the author's eyes. Tolstoy instead tells us how things look to the characters. These things exist, with the characters, in a present-tense shared reality: "The writer who uses metaphor is describing the world hypothetically, as it might be," Wood writes. "Tolstoy is describing the world as it is."

This is why we get the sensation in Tolstoy's novels, Wood says, that "everything is extraordinarily free" yet "everything is also curiously inevitable." When a surge of love and forgiveness flows through Karenin, we are as surprised as he is; however, it is the only thing that could have happened.

But there may be yet another element to Tolstoy's translucent craftsmanship, one that has to do with love. Mark Van Doren commented, "For Tolstoy . . . anything that human beings do has its glory. . . . I think he can be said to have hated nothing that ever happened." Indeed, Tolstoy appears to love all his characters. Even the reckless playboy Dolokhov, who foments much trouble in *War and Peace*, is later revealed to be a good son and the support of his widowed mother and sisters. Tolstoy didn't have to show us a good side to Dolokhov; he chose to. Every character in his fictional universe can give a reason that he should be loved.

Lionel Trilling points out that this consistent affection for his characters is what sets Tolstoy apart. Flaubert is equally "objective," he says, but "Flaubert's objectivity is charged with irritability and Tolstoy's with affection. For Flaubert everyone and everything is somehow at fault. For Tolstoy everyone and everything has a saving grace." It is "this quality of affection that accounts for the unique illusion of reality that Tolstoy creates. It is when the novelist really loves his characters that he can show them in their completeness and contradictions. . . . What we call Tolstoy's objectivity is simply the power of his love to suffer no abatement from the notice and account it takes of the fact that life usually falls below its ideal of itself." Tolstoy's love for his characters is strong enough to recognize their capacity for evil. He does not need them to maintain a false standard of goodness in order to be loved (as some characters in Dickens might be said to do).

Tolstoy wrote of Pierre, the earnest and bumbling lead character of *War and Peace*, "By loving people without cause, he discovered indubitable causes for loving them." It would be hard to find a more succinct description of the chief work of the Holy Spirit in the human heart.

Trilling believes Tolstoy's expectation—that there is some good in every ordinary person—feels to us like reality because it is the reality we want. We want to be loved like this, believing that we are "not heroic yet not without heroism, not splendid yet not without moments of light," and "managing somehow . . . to maintain a curious dignity." We award Tolstoy praise for achieving a crystalline quality of realism, Trilling claims, because we recognize his reality as the one we most desire.

Life is not sugar-coated in Tolstoy's works; terrible things take place. But it can be argued that he lacks the profound understanding of evil that makes Dostoevsky's works so powerful. Trilling suspects, though, that our age (he was writing in 1952) is inclined to think that the worst things are the truest things, itself a form of blindness. "We may come to assume that evil is equivalent to reality," he warns, "and may even come, in some distant and unconscious way, to honor it as such."

We may come to assume that whatever is dark and edgy is true; and to mistrust joy; or even lose the ability to depict honest joy. "Though many have represented the attenuation or distortion of human relationships, scarcely any have been able to make actual what the normalities of relationships are." Tolstoy shows us family, parenthood, romance in all their ordinary variety, and these images complement more harrowing works of art by reminding us of what there is to lose.

---

*Anna Karenina* has its critics. Some have charged Tolstoy with delivering a formless novel in which Anna's situation dramatically outweighs Levin's, and the two parallel stories barely intersect. A friend of Tolstoy's made that complaint when the book was first published, and Richard Pevear quotes Tolstoy's reply in the introduction to his new translation:

> On the contrary, I am proud of my architecture. But my vaults have been assembled in such a way that the keystone cannot be seen. Most of my effort has gone into that. The cohesion of the structure does not lie in the plot or in the relations (the meetings) of the characters, it is an internal cohesion . . . look well and you will find it.

When thinking in terms of that invisible structure, it's useful to remember that this selection comes in the middle, not at the end. Karenin's flood of divine forgiveness will not necessarily last. He has discovered, through this wrenching experience, that the reason tears had always been upsetting to him was that he was trying to hold back a powerful impulse for compassion. Now, to give free rein to that love, and to forgive from the heart, and to treasure the baby his wife had borne to her lover, all this gives him great joy. But he can see from the surprised looks of those around him, and the joy his acquaintances can barely conceal ("as if delighted, as if they were getting somebody married"), that he will not be permitted to continue in this simplicity of heart. (Karenin's experience was Tolstoy's own; he wrote in his *Confession*, "Every time I tried to display my innermost desires—a wish to be morally good—I met with contempt and scorn, and as soon as I gave in to base desires I was praised and encouraged.")

Levin, like Karenin, is overwhelmed and behaving oddly. Those who know him are surprised and affected by his joy, and they even find wedding talk contagious ("The old folk evidently got confused for a moment and could not quite tell whether it was they who were in love again, or only their daughter."). But Levin will not be permitted to continue his cloud-walking. "Will there really be a trousseau?" He thinks "with horror," but, seeing that it pleases Kitty, he admits that it must be so. Levin's simple, spontaneous effusion of love will be hemmed in and altered by the society that surrounds him.

---

Two roads diverge in this novel, but the more you look, the more you notice similarities. I was struck this time by the image of Kitty's kissing her father's "muscular hand," surely an unappealing note on which to end this most delicate and whimsical section. A few pages later we see Karenin reach out toward Anna as she endures the unhelpful badgering of her friend Princess Tverskoy. Though he has exhibited extraordinary love for Anna, at the sight of "his moist hand with its big, swollen veins" she recoils, taking it "with an obvious effort." We realize that no amount of love on his part will render Anna able to love him. In this poignant juxtaposition of two unattractive hands, we perhaps catch a glimpse of Tolstoy's hidden structure.

But, really, you're going to want to buy the book and search it out yourself, starting from the beginning.


## ON UNFAITHFULNESS

### Amy Obrist


Leo Tolstoy's *Anna Karenina* is commonly understood as an adultery novel. Dolly Oblonsky suffers tremendously throughout on account of her husband Stiva's affair. Kitty and Levin alternately experience deep jealousy and fear of betrayal, each when the other interacts with flirtatious members of Russia's high society. Anna herself is one of the most notorious fallen women in literature, seduced by Alexei Vronsky but herself becoming the primary target of society's wrath. Unfaithfulness is all around; it is only a serious transgression when social conventions governing it are not observed.

Yet while marital infidelity—or the fear of it—is intricately woven into each thread of the plot, it is first and foremost a symbol of other kinds of unfaithfulness. Falseness, deception, and lies are endemic to Russian high society. Worse than being an unfaithful husband, Stiva deceives himself by justifying his unfaithfulness. Similarly, he justifies the graft by which he obtains his government position and his spendthrift squandering of his wife's fortune. He maintains the external image of the perfect society man and follows all the rules of liberal society perfectly—but has no inner life or true self.

If this is the case for Stiva, it also is true for a character the reader may not be ready to judge so hastily, Alexei Karenin. Laying aside Anna's unfaithfulness, it is essential to examine Karenin as Tolstoy presents him. As Dolly welcomes her sister-in-law, perfect society woman and wife of the statesman, a hint is given that something is amiss in Dolly's recollection that "as far as she could remember her impression of the Karenins' house in Petersburg, she had not liked it; there was something false in the whole shape of their family life." She smoothes over this memory as Anna ironically persuades Dolly to stay in her marriage.

Karenin is a politician at the height of his career, living an ordered, proper life in which each minute of his day is accounted for. For him, life is about duty. He moves in a social circle known widely as "the conscience of St. Petersburg." Anna tells herself "he is a good man, truthful, kind and remarkable in his sphere."

Yet here Anna is trying to convince herself. Karenin meets her with a "mocking smile"; she feels a vague dissatisfaction, an "old, familiar feeling, similar to that state of pretence she experienced in her relations with her husband; but previously she had not noticed it." Moreover, his associations with his religious friend, Lydia Ivanovna, now bother Anna for their hypocrisy. "All this was there before, but why didn't I notice it before? . . . In fact it's ridiculous: her goal is virtue, she is a Christian, yet she's angry all the time, and they're all her enemies, and they're all enemies on account of Christianity and virtue."

The hypocrisy and self-deceit endemic to society life drive the plot about Kitty Oblonsky and Konstantin Levin too. Kitty refuses Levin's proposal—although she is certain of his love—because she expects Count Vronsky, an elite society man, to propose to her after the upcoming ball; the narrator hints that this preference is problematic: "It was as if there was some falseness—not in him, he was very simple and nice—but in herself, while with Levin she felt completely simple and clear." Although her father would prefer the simple, serious Levin as a son-in-law, Kitty's mother, Princess Oblonsky, seeks a "brilliant match" for her daughter. Her mother deceives Kitty into preferring Vronsky despite feeling awkwardness about him, a sure sign of self-betrayal in Tolstoy's code.

Anna is different from others in her milieu. Kitty observes of Anna "that there was in her some other, higher world of interests, inaccessible to her, complex and poetic." Kitty later goes further, finding something "alien, demonic, and enchanting" in Anna. Yet Kitty does not yet understand herself or that she has been deceived by the hypocrisy and false values around her. For Kitty to find something otherworldly or alien in Anna and to first call it good and then evil suggests she does not yet understand her own relation to society. However, she points out that Anna is different.

Of what does Anna's difference consist? It takes her a long time to understand this herself. Already a fallen women—but still able to maintain appearances in society—she compares herself with her friend Betsy, exclaiming, "How I wish I knew others as I know myself," and asking herself, "Am I worse than others or better? Worse, I think." Later, when she's cast out from this society irrevocably and barred from seeing her son, Anna articulates her disgust with the pervasive hypocrisy around her, saying of Lydia, "She's worse than I am. At least I don't lie." Anna's special quality is her willingness to look into herself and not deceive about what she finds there.

Anna Karenina is no worse than others. True, she never seems fully to comprehend herself in relation to society. Her misfortune is that she understands the falsehood of high society but is bound tragically to this world by circumstance.

## CHAPTER TWENTY SEVEN

# FYODOR DOSTOEVSKY

## Modern (1821–1881)

**D**espite temptations to belong to other religions, Dostoevsky can only be understood as an Orthodox Christian. He wasn't always orthodox, and his behavior fell short of his ideals, but as a writer, only Dante could equal his profound psychological glimpse of the power of the faith.

Dante lived in a happier age where he knew Christianity was true; Dostoevsky had only hope that sometimes reached faith in the power of the Gospel to save mankind. Dante was the forerunner for a Renaissance; Dostoevsky stood as a revelator before an apocalypse.

Younger readers of *The Brothers Karamazov* would have the chance to die in World War I, the influenza plague, the Russian Civil War, or Lenin's police state.

Unlike Tolstoy, though, Dostoevsky avoided the more fatuous schemes for improving Russia. He understood the depths of the real problem, and he was more willing to consider radical, even revolutionary, ideas. The difference between the two great authors was that Dostoevsky knew the darkness at the heart of humanity; *The Brothers Karamazov* is an accurate picture of flawed but still hopeful human souls. He also knew that even a man as horrid as the Karamazov father was a soul created in God's image.

Dostoevsky knew how to write a saintly character. He did so in his appropriately titled novel *The Idiot*, but none of the Karamazov characters are Christian enough for the rest to think them idiots. Even Alyosha, the most spiritual of the four brothers, is flawed and is as likely to end a demonic revolutionary as a great saint, if he does not grow.

Most of us have such defects, but we resist seeing them just as we resist seeing the goodness in the bad people around us. Dostoevsky was giving Russia the bad news that *Russians* were the problem—not just the socialists or the Tsar. Like Jeremiah, the Old Testament prophet, people heard what he said, but too few acted on it to save either Israel or Russia. Everyone else, they thought, should change; very few saw the dilemma in the soul of even the "best" of men.

The good news of this novel is that a man need not receive justice to change for the good. Even errors and bad times can drive him to God. Dostoevsky never forgot that a justice-defying Roman cross could be used for redemption.

FROM

# The Brothers Karamazov

### "THE GRAND INQUISITOR"

"EVEN this must have a preface—that is, a literary preface," laughed Ivan, "and I am a poor hand at making one. You see, my action takes place in the sixteenth century, and at that time, as you probably learnt at school, it was customary in poetry to bring down heavenly powers on earth. Not to speak of Dante, in France, clerks, as well as the monks in the monasteries, used to give regular performances in which the Madonna, the saints, the angels, Christ, and God Himself were brought on the stage. In those days it was done in all simplicity. In Victor Hugo's *Notre Dame de Paris* an edifying and gratuitous spectacle was provided for the people in the Hotel de Ville of Paris in the reign of Louis XI in honour of the birth of the dauphin. It was called *Le bon jugement de la tres sainte et gracieuse Vierge Marie*, and she appears herself on the stage and pronounces her *bon jugement*. Similar plays, chiefly from the Old Testament, were occasionally performed in Moscow too, up to the times of Peter the Great. But besides plays there were all sorts of legends and ballads scattered about the world, in which the saints and angels and all the powers of Heaven took part when required. In our monasteries the monks busied themselves in translating, copying, and even composing such poems—and even under the Tatars.

"There is, for instance, one such poem (of course, from the Greek), The Wanderings of Our Lady through Hell, with descriptions as bold as Dante's. Our Lady visits hell, and the Archangel Michael leads her through the torments. She sees the sinners and their punishment. There she sees among others one noteworthy set of sinners in a burning lake; some of them sink to the bottom of the lake so that they can't swim out, and 'these God forgets'—an expression of extraordinary depth and force. And so Our Lady, shocked and weeping, falls before the throne of God and begs for mercy for all in hell—for all she has seen there, indiscriminately. Her conversation with God is immensely interesting. She beseeches Him, she will not desist, and when God points to the hands and feet of her Son, nailed to the Cross, and asks, 'How can I forgive His tormentors?' she bids all the saints, all the martyrs, all the angels and archangels to fall down with her and pray for mercy on all without distinction. It ends by her winning from God a respite of suffering every year from Good Friday till Trinity Day, and the sinners at once raise a cry of thankfulness from hell, chanting, 'Thou art just, O Lord, in this judgment.' Well, my poem would have been of that kind if it had appeared at that time. He comes on the scene in my poem, but He says nothing, only appears and passes on. Fifteen centuries have passed since He promised to come in His glory, fifteen centuries since His prophet wrote, 'Behold, I come quickly'; Of that day and that hour knoweth no man, neither the Son, but the Father,' as He Himself predicted on earth. But humanity awaits him with the same faith and with the same love. Oh, with greater faith, for it is fifteen centuries since man has ceased to see signs from heaven.

*No signs from heaven come to-day*
*To add to what the heart doth say.*

"There was nothing left but faith in what the heart doth say. It is true there were many miracles in those days. There were saints who performed miraculous cures; some holy people, according to their biographies, were visited by the Queen of Heaven herself. But the devil did not slumber, and doubts were already arising among men of the truth of these miracles. And just then there appeared in the north of Germany a terrible new heresy. 'A huge star like to a torch' (that is, to a church) 'fell on the sources of the waters and they became bitter.' These heretics began blasphemously denying miracles. But those who remained faithful were all the more ardent in their faith. The tears of humanity rose up to Him as before, awaited His coming, loved Him, hoped for Him, yearned to suffer and die for Him as before. And so many ages mankind had prayed with faith and fervour, 'O Lord our God, hasten Thy coming'; so many ages called upon Him, that in His infinite mercy He deigned to come down to His servants. Before that day He had come down, He had visited some holy men, martyrs, and hermits, as is written in their lives. Among us, Tyutchev, with absolute faith in the truth of his words, bore witness that

*Bearing the Cross, in slavish dress,*
*Weary and worn, the Heavenly King*
*Our mother, Russia, came to bless,*
*And through our land went wandering.*

"And that certainly was so, I assure you.

"And behold, He deigned to appear for a moment to the people, to the tortured, suffering people, sunk in iniquity, but loving Him like children. My story is laid in Spain, in Seville, in the most terrible time of the Inquisition, when fires were lighted every day to the glory of God, and 'in the splendid *auto da fe* the wicked heretics were burnt.' Oh, of course, this was not the coming in which He will appear, according to His promise, at the end of time in all His heavenly glory, and which will be sudden 'as lightning flashing from east to west.' No, He visited His children only for a moment, and there where the flames were crackling round the heretics. In His infinite mercy He came once more among men in that human shape in which He walked among men for thirty-three years fifteen centuries ago. He came down to the 'hot pavements' of the southern town in which on the day before almost a hundred heretics had, *ad majorem gloriam Dei*, been burnt by the cardinal, the Grand Inquisitor, in a magnificent *auto da fe*, in the presence of the king, the court, the knights, the cardinals, the most charming ladies of the court, and the whole population of Seville.

"He came softly, unobserved, and yet, strange to say, everyone recognised Him. That might be one of the best passages in the poem. I mean, why they recognised Him. The people are irresistibly drawn to Him, they surround Him, they flock about Him, follow Him. He moves silently in their midst with a gentle smile of infinite compassion. The sun of love burns in His heart, and power shine from His eyes, and their radiance, shed on the people, stirs their hearts with responsive love. He holds out His hands to them, blesses them, and a healing virtue comes from contact with Him, even with His garments. An old man in the crowd, blind from childhood, cries out, 'O Lord, heal me and I shall see Thee!' and, as it were, scales fall from his eyes and the blind man sees Him. The crowd weeps and kisses the earth under His feet. Children throw flowers before Him, sing, and cry hosannah. 'It is He—it is He!' repeat. 'It must be He, it can be no one but Him!'

"He stops at the steps of the Seville cathedral at the moment when the weeping mourners are bringing in a little open white coffin. In it lies a child of seven, the only daughter of a prominent citizen. The dead child lies hidden in flowers. 'He will raise your child,' the crowd shouts to the weeping mother. The priest, coming to meet the coffin, looks perplexed, and frowns, but the mother of the dead child throws herself at His feet with a wail. 'If it is Thou, raise my child!' she cries, holding out her hands to Him. The procession halts, the coffin is laid on the steps at His feet. He looks with compassion, and His lips once more softly pronounce, 'Maiden, arise!' and the maiden arises. The little girl sits up in the coffin and looks round, smiling with wide-open wondering eyes, holding a bunch of white roses they had put in her hand.

"There are cries, sobs, confusion among the people, and at that moment the cardinal himself, the Grand Inquisitor, passes by the cathedral. He is an old man, almost ninety, tall and erect, with a withered face and sunken eyes, in which there is still a gleam of light. He is not dressed in his gorgeous cardinal's robes, as he was the day before, when he was burning the enemies of the Roman Church—at this moment he is wearing his coarse, old, monk's cassock. At a distance behind him come his gloomy assistants and slaves and the 'holy guard.' He stops at the sight of the crowd and watches it from a distance. He sees everything; he sees them set the coffin down at His feet, sees the child rise up, and his face darkens. He knits his thick grey brows and his eyes gleam with a sinister fire. He holds out his finger and bids the guards take Him.

"And such is his power, so completely are the people cowed into submission and trembling obedience to him, that the crowd immediately makes way for the guards, and in the midst of deathlike silence they lay hands on Him and lead him away. The crowd instantly bows down to the earth, like one man, before the old Inquisitor. He blesses the people in silence and passes on. The guards lead their prisoner to the close, gloomy vaulted prison—in the ancient palace of the Holy Inquisition and shut him in it. The day passes and is followed by the dark, burning, 'breathless' night of Seville. The air is 'fragrant with laurel and lemon.' In the pitch darkness the iron door of the prison is suddenly opened and the Grand Inquisitor himself comes in with a light in his hand. He is alone; the door is closed at once behind him. He stands in the doorway and for a minute or two gazes into His face. At last he goes up slowly, sets the light on the table and speaks.

" 'Is it Thou? Thou?' but receiving no answer, he adds at once. 'Don't answer, be silent. What canst Thou say, indeed? I know too well what Thou wouldst say. And Thou hast no right to add anything to what Thou hadst said of old. Why, then, art Thou come to hinder us? For Thou hast come to hinder us, and Thou knowest that. But dost thou know what will be to-morrow? I know not who Thou art and care not to know whether it is Thou or only a semblance of Him, but to-morrow I shall condemn Thee and burn Thee at the stake as the worst of heretics. And the very people who have to-day kissed Thy feet, to-morrow at the faintest sign from me will rush to heap up the embers of Thy fire. Knowest Thou that? Yes, maybe Thou knowest it,' he added with thoughtful penetration, never for a moment taking his eyes off the Prisoner."

"I don't quite understand, Ivan. What does it mean?" Alyosha, who had been listening in silence, said with a smile. "Is it simply a wild fantasy, or a mistake on the part of the old man—some impossible quid pro quo?"

"Take it as the last," said Ivan, laughing, "if you are so corrupted by modern realism and can't stand anything fantastic. If you like it to be a case of mistaken identity, let it be so. It is true," he went on, laughing, "the old man was ninety, and he might well be crazy over his set idea. He might have been struck by the appearance of the Prisoner. It might, in fact, be simply his ravings, the delusion of an old man of ninety, over-excited by the *auto da fe* of a hundred heretics the day before. But does it matter to us after all whether it was a mistake of identity or a wild fantasy? All that matters is that the old man should speak out, that he should speak openly of what he has thought in silence for ninety years."

"And the Prisoner too is silent? Does He look at him and not say a word?"

"That's inevitable in any case," Ivan laughed again. "The old man has told Him He hasn't the right to add anything to what He has said of old. One may say it is the most fundamental feature of Roman Catholicism, in my opinion at least. 'All has been given by Thee to the Pope,' they say, 'and all, therefore, is still in the Pope's hands, and there is no need for Thee to come now at all. Thou must not meddle for the time, at least.' That's how they speak and write too—the Jesuits, at any rate. I have read it myself in the works of their theologians. 'Hast Thou the right to reveal to us one of the mysteries of that world from which Thou hast come?' my old man asks Him, and answers the question for Him. 'No, Thou hast not; that Thou mayest not add to what has been said of old, and mayest not take from men the freedom which Thou didst exalt when Thou wast on earth. Whatsoever Thou revealest anew will encroach on men's freedom of faith; for it will be manifest as a miracle, and the freedom of their faith was dearer to Thee than anything in those days fifteen hundred years ago. Didst Thou not often say then, "I will make you free"? But now Thou hast seen these "free" men,' the old man adds suddenly, with a pensive smile. 'Yes, we've paid dearly for it,' he goes on, looking sternly at Him, 'but at last we have completed that work in Thy name. For fifteen centuries we have been wrestling with Thy freedom, but now it is ended and over for good. Dost Thou not believe that it's over for good? Thou lookest meekly at me and deignest not even to be wroth with me. But let me tell Thee that now, to-day, people are more persuaded than ever that they have perfect freedom, yet they have brought their freedom to us and laid it humbly at our feet. But that has been our doing. Was this what Thou didst? Was this Thy freedom?' "

"I don't understand again." Alyosha broke in. "Is he ironical, is he jesting?"

"Not a bit of it! He claims it as a merit for himself and his Church that at last they have vanquished freedom and have done so to make men happy. 'For now' (he is speaking of the Inquisition, of course) 'for the first time it has become possible to think of the happiness of men. Man was created a rebel; and how can rebels be happy? Thou wast warned,' he says to Him. 'Thou hast had no lack of admonitions and warnings, but Thou didst not listen to those warnings; Thou didst reject the only way by which men might be made happy. But, fortunately, departing Thou didst hand on the work to us. Thou hast promised, Thou hast established by Thy word, Thou hast given to us the right to bind and to unbind, and now, of course, Thou canst not think of taking it away. Why, then, hast Thou come to hinder us?' "

"And what's the meaning of 'no lack of admonitions and warnings'?" asked Alyosha.

"Why, that's the chief part of what the old man must say.

" 'The wise and dread spirit, the spirit of self-destruction and non-existence,' the old man goes on, 'great spirit talked with Thee in the wilderness, and we are told in the books that he "tempted" Thee. Is that so? And could anything truer be said than what he revealed to Thee in three questions and what Thou didst reject, and what in the books is called "the temptation"? And yet if there has ever been on earth a real stupendous miracle, it took place on that day, on the day of the three temptations. The statement of those three questions was itself the miracle. If it were possible to imagine simply for the sake of argument that those three questions of the dread spirit had perished utterly from the books, and that we had to restore them and to invent them anew, and to do so had gathered together all the wise men of the earth—rulers, chief priests, learned men, philosophers, poets—and had set them the task to invent three questions, such as would not only fit the occasion, but express in three words, three human phrases, the whole future history of the world and of humanity—dost Thou believe that all the wisdom of the earth united could have invented anything in depth and force equal to the three questions which were actually put to Thee then by the wise and mighty spirit in the wilderness?

" 'From those questions alone, from the miracle of their statement, we can see that we have here to do not with the fleeting human intelligence, but with the absolute and eternal. For in those three questions the whole subsequent history of mankind is, as it were, brought together into one whole, and foretold, and in them are united all the unsolved historical contradictions of human nature. At the time it could not be so clear, since the future was unknown; but now that fifteen hundred years have passed, we see that everything in those three questions was so justly divined and foretold, and has been so truly fulfilled, that nothing can be added to them or taken from them.

"'Judge Thyself who was right—Thou or he who questioned Thee then? Remember the first question; its meaning, in other words, was this: "Thou wouldst go into the world, and art going with empty hands, with some promise of freedom which men in their simplicity and their natural unruliness cannot even understand, which they fear and dread—for nothing has ever been more insupportable for a man and a human society than freedom. But seest Thou these stones in this parched and barren wilderness? Turn them into bread, and mankind will run after Thee like a flock of sheep, grateful and obedient, though for ever trembling, lest Thou withdraw Thy hand and deny them Thy bread." But Thou wouldst not deprive man of freedom and didst reject the offer, thinking, what is that freedom worth if obedience is bought with bread? Thou didst reply that man lives not by bread alone. But dost Thou know that for the sake of that earthly bread the spirit of the earth will rise up against Thee and will strive with Thee and overcome Thee, and all will follow him, crying, "Who can compare with this beast? He has given us fire from heaven!" Dost Thou know that the ages will pass, and humanity will proclaim by the lips of their sages that there is no crime, and therefore no sin; there is only hunger?

" ' "Feed men, and then ask of them virtue!" that's what they'll write on the banner, which they will raise against Thee, and with which they will destroy Thy temple. Where Thy temple stood will rise a new building; the terrible tower of Babel will be built again, and though, like the one of old, it will not be finished, yet Thou mightest have prevented that new tower and have cut short the sufferings of men for a thousand years; for they will come back to us after a thousand years of agony with their tower. They will seek us again, hidden underground in the catacombs, for we shall be again persecuted and tortured. They will find us and cry to us, "Feed us, for those who have promised us fire from heaven haven't given it!" And then we shall finish building their tower, for he finishes the building who feeds them. And we alone shall feed them in Thy name, declaring falsely that it is in Thy name.

" 'Oh, never, never can they feed themselves without us! No science will give them bread so long as they remain free. In the end they will lay their freedom at our feet, and say to us, "Make us your slaves, but feed us." They will understand themselves, at last, that freedom and bread enough for all are inconceivable together, for never, never will they be able to share between them! They will be convinced, too, that they can never be free, for they are weak, vicious, worthless, and rebellious. Thou didst promise them the bread of Heaven, but, I repeat again, can it compare with earthly bread in the eyes of the weak, ever sinful and ignoble race of man? And if for the sake of the bread of Heaven thousands shall follow Thee, what is to become of the millions and tens of thousands of millions of creatures who will not have the strength to forego the earthly bread for the sake of the heavenly? Or dost Thou care only for the tens of thousands of the great and strong, while the millions, numerous as the sands of the sea, who are weak but love Thee, must exist only for the sake of the great and strong? No, we care for the weak too. They are sinful and rebellious, but in the end they too will become obedient. They will marvel at us and look on us as gods, because we are ready to endure the freedom which they have found so dreadful and to rule over them—so awful it will seem to them to be free. But we shall tell them that we are Thy servants and rule them in Thy name. We shall deceive them again, for we will not let Thee come to us again. That deception will be our suffering, for we shall be forced to lie.

" 'This is the significance of the first question in the wilderness, and this is what Thou hast rejected for the sake of that freedom which Thou hast exalted above everything. Yet in this question lies hid the great secret of this world. Choosing "bread," Thou wouldst have satisfied the universal and everlasting craving of humanity—to find someone to worship. So long as man remains free he strives for nothing so incessantly and so painfully as to find someone to worship. But man seeks to worship what is established beyond dispute, so that all men would agree at once to worship it. For these pitiful creatures are concerned not only to find what one or the other can worship, but to find community of worship is the chief misery of every man individually and of all humanity from the beginning of time. For the sake of common worship they've slain each other with the sword. They have set up gods and challenged one another, "Put away your gods and come and worship ours, or we will kill you and your gods!" And so it will be to the end of the world, even when gods disappear from the earth; they will fall down before idols just the same.

"'Thou didst know, Thou couldst not but have known, this fundamental secret of human nature, but Thou didst reject the one infallible banner which was offered Thee to make all men bow down to Thee alone—the banner of earthly bread; and Thou hast rejected it for the sake of freedom and the bread of Heaven. Behold what Thou didst further. And all again in the name of freedom! I tell Thee that man is tormented by no greater anxiety than to find someone quickly to whom he can hand over that gift of freedom with which the ill-fated creature is born. But only one who can appease their conscience can take over their freedom. In bread there was offered Thee an invincible banner; give bread, and man will worship thee, for nothing is more certain than bread. But if someone else gains possession of his conscience—Oh! then he will cast away Thy bread and follow after him who has ensnared his conscience. In that Thou wast right. For the secret of man's being is not only to live but to have something to live for. Without a stable conception of the object of life, man would not consent to go on living, and would rather destroy himself than remain on earth, though he had bread in abundance. That is true.

"'But what happened? Instead of taking men's freedom from them, Thou didst make it greater than ever! Didst Thou forget that man prefers peace, and even death, to freedom of choice in the knowledge of good and evil? Nothing is more seductive for man than his freedom of conscience, but nothing is a greater cause of suffering. And behold, instead of giving a firm foundation for setting the conscience of man at rest for ever, Thou didst choose all that is exceptional, vague and enigmatic; Thou didst choose what was utterly beyond the strength of men, acting as though Thou didst not love them at all—Thou who didst come to give Thy life for them! Instead of taking possession of men's freedom, Thou didst increase it, and burdened the spiritual kingdom of mankind with its sufferings for ever. Thou didst desire man's free love, that he should follow Thee freely, enticed and taken captive by Thee. In place of the rigid ancient law, man must hereafter with free heart decide for himself what is good and what is evil, having only Thy image before him as his guide. But didst Thou not know that he would at last reject even Thy image and Thy truth, if he is weighed down with the fearful burden of free choice? They will cry aloud at last that the truth is not in Thee, for they could not have been left in greater confusion and suffering than Thou hast caused, laying upon them so many cares and unanswerable problems.

" 'So that, in truth, Thou didst Thyself lay the foundation for the destruction of Thy kingdom, and no one is more to blame for it. Yet what was offered Thee? There are three powers, three powers alone, able to conquer and to hold captive for ever the conscience of these impotent rebels for their happiness—those forces are miracle, mystery and authority. Thou hast rejected all three and hast set the example for doing so. When the wise and dread spirit set Thee on the pinnacle of the temple and said to Thee, "If Thou wouldst know whether Thou art the Son of God then cast Thyself down, for it is written: the angels shall hold him up lest he fall and bruise himself, and Thou shalt know then whether Thou art the Son of God and shalt prove then how great is Thy faith in Thy Father."

" 'But Thou didst refuse and wouldst not cast Thyself down. Oh, of course, Thou didst proudly and well, like God; but the weak, unruly race of men, are they gods? Oh, Thou didst know then that in taking one step, in making one movement to cast Thyself down, Thou wouldst be tempting God and have lost all Thy faith in Him, and wouldst have been dashed to pieces against that earth which Thou didst come to save. And the wise spirit that tempted Thee would have rejoiced. But I ask again, are there many like Thee? And couldst Thou believe for one moment that men, too, could face such a temptation? Is the nature of men such, that they can reject miracle, and at the great moments of their life, the moments of their deepest, most agonising spiritual difficulties, cling only to the free verdict of the heart? Oh, Thou didst know that Thy deed would be recorded in books, would be handed down to remote times and the utmost ends of the earth, and Thou didst hope that man, following Thee, would cling to God and not ask for a miracle. But Thou didst not know that when man rejects miracle he rejects God too; for man seeks not so much God as the miraculous. And as man cannot bear to be without the miraculous, he will create new miracles of his own for himself, and will worship deeds of sorcery and witchcraft, though he might be a hundred times over a rebel, heretic and infidel.

" 'Thou didst not come down from the Cross when they shouted to Thee, mocking and reviling Thee, "Come down from the cross and we will believe that Thou art He." Thou didst not come down, for again Thou wouldst not enslave man by a miracle, and didst crave faith given freely, not based on miracle. Thou didst crave for free love and not the base raptures of the slave before the might that has overawed him for ever. But Thou didst think too highly of men therein, for they are slaves, of course, though rebellious by nature. Look round and judge; fifteen centuries have passed, look upon them. Whom hast Thou raised up to Thyself? I swear, man is weaker and baser by nature than Thou hast believed him! Can he, can he do what Thou didst? By showing him so much respect, Thou didst, as it were, cease to feel for him, for Thou didst ask far too much from him— Thou who hast loved him more than Thyself! Respecting him less, Thou wouldst have asked less of him. That would have been more like love, for his burden would have been lighter. He is weak and vile. What though he is everywhere now rebelling against our power, and proud of his rebellion? It is the pride of a child and a schoolboy. They are little children rioting and barring out the teacher at school. But their childish delight will end; it will cost them dear.

" 'Mankind as a whole has always striven to organise a universal state. There have been many great nations with great histories, but the more highly they were developed the more unhappy they were, for they felt more acutely than other people the craving for world-wide union. The great conquerors, Timours and Ghenghis-Khans, whirled like hurricanes over the face of the earth striving to subdue its people, and they too were but the unconscious expression of the same craving for universal unity. Hadst Thou taken the world and Caesar's purple, Thou wouldst have founded the universal state and have given universal peace. For who can rule men if not he who holds their conscience and their bread in his hands? We have taken the sword of Caesar, and in taking it, of course, have rejected Thee and followed him. Oh, ages are yet to come of the confusion of free thought, of their science and cannibalism. For having begun to build their tower of Babel without us, they will end, of course, with cannibalism. But then the beast will crawl to us and lick our feet and spatter them with tears of blood. And we shall sit upon the beast and raise the cup, and on it will be written, "Mystery." But then, and only then, the reign of peace and happiness will come for men.

" 'Thou art proud of Thine elect, but Thou hast only the elect, while we give rest to all. And besides, how many of those elect, those mighty ones who could become elect, have grown weary waiting for Thee, and have transferred and will transfer the powers of their spirit and the warmth of their heart to the other camp, and end by raising their free banner against Thee. Thou didst Thyself lift up that banner. But with us all will be happy and will no more rebel nor destroy one another as under Thy freedom. Oh, we shall persuade them that they will only become free when they renounce their freedom to us and submit to us. And shall we be right or shall we be lying? They will be convinced that we are right, for they will remember the horrors of slavery and confusion to which Thy freedom brought them. Freedom, free thought, and science will lead them into such straits and will bring them face to face with such marvels and insoluble mysteries, that some of them, the fierce and rebellious, will destroy themselves, others, rebellious but weak, will destroy one another, while the rest, weak and unhappy, will crawl fawning to our feet and whine to us: "Yes, you were right, you alone possess His mystery, and we come back to you, save us from ourselves!"

" 'Receiving bread from us, they will see clearly that we take the bread made by their hands from them, to give it to them, without any miracle. They will see that we do not change the stones to bread, but in truth they will be more thankful for taking it from our hands than for the bread itself! For they will remember only too well that in old days, without our help, even the bread they made turned to stones in their hands, while since they have come back to us, the very stones have turned to bread in their hands. Too, too well will they know the value of complete submission! And until men know that, they will be unhappy. Who is most to blame for their not knowing it?—speak! Who scattered the flock and sent it astray on unknown paths? But the flock will come together again and will submit once more, and then it will be once for all. Then we shall give them the quiet humble happiness of weak creatures such as they are by nature.

" 'Oh, we shall persuade them at last not to be proud, for Thou didst lift them up and thereby taught them to be proud. We shall show them that they are weak, that they are only pitiful children, but that childlike happiness is the sweetest of all. They will become timid and will look to us and huddle close to us in fear, as chicks to the hen. They will marvel at us and will be awe-stricken before us, and will be proud at our being so powerful and clever that we have been able to subdue such a turbulent flock of thousands of millions. They will tremble impotently before our wrath, their minds will grow fearful, they will be quick to shed tears like women and children, but they will be just as ready at a sign from us to pass to laughter and rejoicing, to happy mirth and childish song. Yes, we shall set them to work, but in their leisure hours we shall make their life like a child's game, with children's songs and innocent dance. Oh, we shall allow them even sin, they are weak and helpless, and they will love us like children because we allow them to sin. We shall tell them that every sin will be expiated, if it is done with our permission, that we allow them to sin because we love them, and the punishment for these sins we take upon ourselves. And we shall take it upon ourselves, and they will adore us as their saviours who have taken on themselves their sins before God. And they will have no secrets from us. We shall allow or forbid them to live with their wives and mistresses, to have or not to have children according to whether they have been obedient or disobedient—and they will submit to us gladly and cheerfully. The most painful secrets of their conscience, all, all they will bring to us, and we shall have an answer for all. And they will be glad to believe our answer, for it will save them from the great anxiety and terrible agony they endure at present in making a free decision for themselves. And all will be happy, all the millions of creatures except the hundred thousand who rule over them. For only we, we who guard the mystery, shall be unhappy. There will be thousands of millions of happy babes, and a hundred thousand sufferers who have taken upon themselves the curse of the knowledge of good and evil. Peacefully they will die, peacefully they will expire in Thy name, and beyond the grave they will find nothing but death. But we shall keep the secret, and for their happiness we shall allure them with the reward of heaven and eternity. Though if there were anything in the other world, it certainly would not be for such as they.

" 'It is prophesied that Thou wilt come again in victory, Thou wilt come with Thy chosen, the proud and strong, but we will say that they have only saved themselves, but we have saved all. We are told that the harlot who sits upon the beast, and holds in her hands the mystery, shall be put to shame, that the weak will rise up again, and will rend her royal purple and will strip naked her loathsome body. But then I will stand up and point out to Thee the thousand millions of happy children who have known no sin. And we who have taken their sins upon us for their happiness will stand up before Thee and say: "Judge us if Thou canst and darest." Know that I fear Thee not. Know that I too have been in the wilderness, I too have lived on roots and locusts, I too prized the freedom with which Thou hast blessed men, and I too was striving to stand among Thy elect, among the strong and powerful, thirsting "to make up the number." But I awakened and would not serve madness. I turned back and joined the ranks of those who have corrected Thy work. I left the proud and went back to the humble, for the happiness of the humble. What I say to Thee will come to pass, and our dominion will be built up. I repeat, to-morrow Thou shalt see that obedient flock who at a sign from me will hasten to heap up the hot cinders about the pile on which I shall burn Thee for coming to hinder us. For if anyone has ever deserved our fires, it is Thou. To-morrow I shall burn Thee. *Dixi.*' "

—————

Ivan stopped. He was carried away as he talked, and spoke with excitement; when he had finished, he suddenly smiled.

Alyosha had listened in silence; towards the end he was greatly moved and seemed several times on the point of interrupting, but restrained himself. Now his words came with a rush.

"But . . . that's absurd!" he cried, flushing. "Your poem is in praise of Jesus, not in blame of Him—as you meant it to be. And who will believe you about freedom? Is that the way to understand it? That's not the idea of it in the Orthodox Church. . . . That's Rome, and not even the whole of Rome, it's false—those are the worst of the Catholics the Inquisitors, the Jesuits! . . . And there could not be such a fantastic creature as your Inquisitor. What are these sins of mankind they take on themselves? Who are these keepers of the mystery who have taken some curse upon themselves for the happiness of mankind? When have they been seen? We know the

Jesuits, they are spoken ill of, but surely they are not what you describe? They are not that at all, not at all. . . . They are simply the Romish army for the earthly sovereignty of the world in the future, with the Pontiff of Rome for Emperor . . . that's their ideal, but there's no sort of mystery or lofty melancholy about it. . . . It's simple lust of power, of filthy earthly gain, of domination—something like a universal serfdom with them as masters—that's all they stand for. They don't even believe in God perhaps. Your suffering Inquisitor is a mere fantasy."

"Stay, stay," laughed Ivan. "How hot you are! A fantasy you say, let it be so! Of course it's a fantasy. But allow me to say: do you really think that the Roman Catholic movement of the last centuries is actually nothing but the lust of power, of filthy earthly gain? Is that Father Paissy's teaching?"

"No, no, on the contrary, Father Paissy did once say something rather the same as you . . . but of course it's not the same, not a bit the same," Alyosha hastily corrected himself.

"A precious admission, in spite of your 'not a bit the same.' I ask you why your Jesuits and Inquisitors have united simply for vile material gain? Why can there not be among them one martyr oppressed by great sorrow and loving humanity? You see, only suppose that there was one such man among all those who desire nothing but filthy material gain—if there's only one like my old Inquisitor, who had himself eaten roots in the desert and made frenzied efforts to subdue his flesh to make himself free and perfect. But yet all his life he loved humanity, and suddenly his eyes were opened, and he saw that it is no great moral blessedness to attain perfection and freedom, if at the same time one gains the conviction that millions of God's creatures have been created as a mockery, that they will never be capable of using their freedom, that these poor rebels can never turn into giants to complete the tower, that it was not for such geese that the great idealist dreamt his dream of harmony. Seeing all that he turned back and joined—the clever people. Surely that could have happened?"

"Joined whom, what clever people?" cried Alyosha, completely carried away. "They have no such great cleverness and no mysteries and secrets. . . . Perhaps nothing but Atheism, that's all their secret. Your Inquisitor does not believe in God, that's his secret!"

"What if it is so! At last you have guessed it. It's perfectly true, it's true that that's the whole secret, but isn't that suffering, at least for a man like that, who has wasted his whole life in the desert and yet could not shake off his incurable love of humanity? In his old age he reached the clear conviction that nothing but the advice of the great dread spirit could build up any tolerable sort of life for the feeble, unruly, 'incomplete, empirical creatures created in jest.' And so, convinced of this, he sees that he must follow the counsel of the wise spirit, the dread spirit of death and destruction, and therefore accept lying and deception, and lead men consciously to death and destruction, and yet deceive them all the way so that they may not notice where they are being led, that the poor blind creatures may at least on the way think themselves happy. And note, the deception is in the name of Him in Whose ideal the old man had so fervently believed all his life long. Is not that tragic? And if only one such stood at the head of the whole army 'filled with the lust of power only for the sake of filthy gain'—would not one such be enough to make a tragedy?

"More than that, one such standing at the head is enough to create the actual leading idea of the Roman Church with all its armies and Jesuits, its highest idea. I tell you frankly that I firmly believe that there has always been such a man among those who stood at the head of the movement. Who knows, there may have been some such even among the Roman Popes. Who knows, perhaps the spirit of that accursed old man who loves mankind so obstinately in his own way, is to be found even now in a whole multitude of such old men, existing not by chance but by agreement, as a secret league formed long ago for the guarding of the mystery, to guard it from the weak and the unhappy, so as to make them happy. No doubt it is so, and so it must be indeed. I fancy that even among the Masons there's something of the same mystery at the bottom, and that that's why the Catholics so detest the Masons as their rivals breaking up the unity of the idea, while it is so essential that there should be one flock and one shepherd. . . . But from the way I defend my idea I might be an author impatient of your criticism. Enough of it."

"You are perhaps a Mason yourself!" broke suddenly from Alyosha. "You don't believe in God," he added, speaking this time very sorrowfully. He fancied besides that his brother was looking at him ironically. "How does your poem end?" he asked, suddenly looking down. "Or was it the end?"

"I meant to end it like this. When the Inquisitor ceased speaking he waited some time for his Prisoner to answer him. His silence weighed down upon him. He saw that the Prisoner had listened intently all the time, looking gently in his face and evidently not wishing to reply. The old man longed for him to say something, however bitter and terrible. But He suddenly approached the old man in silence and softly kissed him on his bloodless aged lips. That was all his answer. The old man shuddered. His lips moved. He went to the door, opened it, and said to Him: 'Go, and come no more . . . come not at all, never, never!' And he let Him out into the dark alleys of the town. The Prisoner went away."

"And the old man?"

"The kiss glows in his heart, but the old man adheres to his idea."

"And you with him, you too?" cried Alyosha, mournfully.

Ivan laughed.

"Why, it's all nonsense, Alyosha. It's only a senseless poem of a senseless student, who could never write two lines of verse. Why do you take it so seriously? Surely you don't suppose I am going straight off to the Jesuits, to join the men who are correcting His work? Good Lord, it's no business of mine. I told you, all I want is to live on to thirty, and then . . . dash the cup to the ground!"

"But the little sticky leaves, and the precious tombs, and the blue sky, and the woman you love! How will you live, how will you love them?" Alyosha cried sorrowfully. "With such a hell in your heart and your head, how can you? No, that's just what you are going away for, to join them . . . if not, you will kill yourself, you can't endure it!"

"There is a strength to endure everything," Ivan said with a cold smile.

"The strength of the Karamazovs—the strength of the Karamazov baseness."

"To sink into debauchery, to stifle your soul with corruption, yes?"

"Possibly even that . . . only perhaps till I am thirty I shall escape it, and then—"

"How will you escape it? By what will you escape it? That's impossible with your ideas."

"In the Karamazov way, again."

"'Everything is lawful,' you mean? Everything is lawful, is that it?"

Ivan scowled, and all at once turned strangely pale.

"Ah, you've caught up yesterday's phrase, which so offended Muisov— and which Dmitri pounced upon so naively and paraphrased!" he smiled queerly. "Yes, if you like, 'everything is lawful' since the word has been said, I won't deny it. And Mitya's version isn't bad."

Alyosha looked at him in silence.

"I thought that going away from here I have you at least," Ivan said suddenly, with unexpected feeling; "but now I see that there is no place for me even in your heart, my dear hermit. The formula, 'all is lawful,' I won't renounce—will you renounce me for that, yes?"

Alyosha got up, went to him and softly kissed him on the lips.

"That's plagiarism," cried Ivan, highly delighted. "You stole that from my poem. Thank you though. Get up, Alyosha, it's time we were going, both of us."

They went out, but stopped when they reached the entrance of the restaurant.

"Listen, Alyosha," Ivan began in a resolute voice, "if I am really able to care for the sticky little leaves I shall only love them, remembering you. It's enough for me that you are somewhere here, and I shan't lose my desire for life yet. Is that enough for you? Take it as a declaration of love if you like. And now you go to the right and I to the left. And it's enough, do you hear, enough. I mean even if I don't go away to-morrow (I think I certainly shall go) and we meet again, don't say a word more on these subjects. I beg that particularly. And about Dmitri too, I ask you specially, never speak to me again," he added, with sudden irritation; "it's all exhausted, it has all been said over and over again, hasn't it? And I'll make you one promise in return for it. When at thirty, I want to 'dash the cup to the ground,' wherever I may be I'll come to have one more talk with you, even though it were from America, you may be sure of that. I'll come on purpose. It will be very interesting to have a look at you, to see what you'll be by that time. It's rather a solemn promise, you see. And we really may be parting for seven years or ten. Come, go now to your *Pater Seraphicus*, he is dying. If he dies without you, you will be angry with me for having kept you. Good-bye, kiss me once more; that's right, now go."

Ivan turned suddenly and went his way without looking back. It was just as Dmitri had left Alyosha the day before, though the parting had been very different. The strange resemblance flashed like an arrow through Alyosha's mind in the distress and dejection of that moment. He waited a little, looking after his brother. He suddenly noticed that Ivan swayed as he walked and that his right shoulder looked lower than his left. He had never noticed it before. But all at once he turned too, and almost ran to the monastery. It was nearly dark, and he felt almost frightened; something new was growing up in him for which he could not account. The wind had risen again as on the previous evening, and the ancient pines murmured gloomily about him when he entered the hermitage copse. He almost ran. "*Pater Seraphicus*—he got that name from somewhere—where from?" Alyosha wondered. "Ivan, poor Ivan, and when shall I see you again? . . . Here is the hermitage. Yes, yes, that he is, *Pater Seraphicus*, he will save me—from him and for ever!"

Several times afterwards he wondered how he could, on leaving Ivan, so completely forget his brother Dmitri, though he had that morning, only a few hours before, so firmly resolved to find him and not to give up doing so, even should he be unable to return to the monastery that night.

*Translated by Constance Garnett, 1912*

# THE STORY WITHIN THE STORY

## John Granger

There is a select set of novels that marks anyone seen carrying them around as "serious" readers and thinkers. Proust's *Remembrance of Things Past*, Tolstoy's *Anna Karenina*, Faulkner's *Absalom, Absalom*, and anything by James Joyce, but especially *Finnegan's Wake,* are all the kind of books that young people on better college campuses carry "cover up and out" so everyone can see the title and understand that "here we have a student wrestling with real ideas and profound artistry." Dostoevsky's *The Brothers Karamazov*, often cited as one of, even just *the* best novel ever written, is certainly in this elite group as well.

Which I think is unfortunate. This is a shame right off the top because folks who don't self-identify as nerds or geeks are unlikely to pick up *Brothers* and give it a shot. It's one of those books that if you do open it up and start, alas, much of the time you spend reading it you're thinking to yourself self-consciously, "Gosh, I'm reading *War and Peace*" rather than really entering into the story.

The funny thing about this is that *Brothers*, compared to, say, Joyce's *Ulysses* or Pynchon's *Gravity's Rainbow*, is not only readable, it's downright engaging and entertaining. It's a murder mystery, after all, and, if it isn't quite as accessible or racy as a Mickey Spillane piece, it's a lot closer to that standard than any of its peers on the "Greatest Ever" short shelf.

The reason that *Brothers* is at or very near the top of literary taxonomy's hierarchy, then, isn't difficult or magisterial language. A Russian friend told me once, when I volunteered the only reason I would learn his language would be to read *Brothers*, that I wouldn't need to study very long: "Dostoevsky writes like a newspaper reporter." What makes *The Brothers Karamazov* a book for everyone's bucket list is that reading it is quite literally a transformative experience *and* we are better people, more human really, after the change.

I think about this masterwork the same way I look at other books I love and reread for greater appreciation. I look at the story's obvious structure, reflect on the predominant symbolism, and hunt for some kind of "key" or "lens" the author imbedded into the book for a serious reader to use for opening up or looking within the surface narrative.

My assumption when reading a classic that resonates powerfully with readers across generations and gender, culture, creedal divides is that it is a Ring Composition. From the book of Genesis to *The Chronicles of Narnia* and *Harry Potter*, the works that capture readers' hearts have been written in a circle, that at the very least have a beginning, middle, and end that are joined. (See Mary Douglas, *Thinking in Circles: An Essay on Ring Composition* [Yale University Press, 2007], for the ubiquity and qualities of this traditional and pervasive story structure.) Sure enough, the epigraph, heart, and final scene of *The Brothers Karamazov*—John 12:24, the Life of Father Zossima, and Alyosha's speech at the Stone—are all about the death of self and ego for the greater life in the inner heart, our shared life in Christ.

The predominant symbolism of *Brothers* is, as you'd guess, in the brothers: passionate Dmitri, coldly rational Ivan, and spiritual Alyosha. Like the three lead characters in the old *Star Wars* and older *Star Trek*; the three hobbits on Mount Doom; and Harry, Ron, and Hermione (the authors of which stories understand Dostoevsky's genius), the trio in his spectacular murder mystery are a "soul triptych."

They act, in effect, as allegorical transparencies for the three faculties or powers of the human soul as represented by Plato in his "Allegory of the Charioteer" in the *Phaedrus*: the desires, the will or reason, and the discerning spirit or heart. In the vernacular we'd say "body, mind, and spirit."(See C. S. Lewis's essay "Men Without Chests" [in *Abolition of Man*] for a longer discussion of this traditional faculty-psychology and triptych.) Dostoevsky gives us pictures of these soul-aspects in the Karamazov brothers as they act out their relationship to one another as well as to right and wrong.

---

The parable quality of the novel is easily overlooked because of the narrative's realism, even grittiness. *Brothers* has the power it has, however, like its three-lead shadows in more recent books, films, and television, because the realism draws us into the story and, as we enter, we suspend our disbelief or critical skepticism. Our souls' faculties then recognize, identify with, and experience the trials of their reflections in the Karamazov family drama. It's an alchemical, transformative experience via imagination.

And the key or story lens through which the anagogical meaning is revealed is in the chapter excerpted above, "The Grand Inquisitor." In it, Ivan tells Alyosha a parable of Christ and a Catholic cardinal—the Inquisitor of the title—in fifteenth-century Spain.

Their conversation in "Inquisitor" and Ivan's story are not a stand-alone piece but the beginning of their relationship and a snapshot of their understanding of themselves, each other, and the world. Coming as it does before Alyosha's crisis of faith and his temporary descents to passion and skepticism (of a sort) consequent to his elder's demise and seeming disgrace, the chapter holds an important place in revealing Alyosha's temptations and decisions in the next books of the novel, as well as Ivan's eventual phrenesis and collapse. It's not the whole play; it's more of a prologue.

Sophisticated Ivan tells Alyosha a fable of his own invention about Christ having returned to earth in Spain at the height of the Catholic Inquisition's executions of unrepentant heretics and infidels, which he dates in the fifteenth century. The people who meet the Son of God in the streets thrill to the miracles He performs—curing the blind, raising a child from the dead on the steps of the cathedral—but, before things get out of hand, the Grand Inquisitor arrests the Messiah and has Him jailed. He speaks that night to the silent Jesus, who never says a word, about how His return cannot be allowed because the people want mystery, miracle, and authority and will gladly exchange their free will, freedom, and conscience in exchange for the peace and happiness to be found in them. The Inquisitor promises to burn Christ at the stake the next day and pledges that those who cried "hosannah" will throw wood on the fire at his instruction.

After the Inquisitor reveals he lost his faith after years in the desert winning his spiritual freedom and realizing men were not equal to this challenge, the Christ responds with a silent kiss. The cardinal releases Him with the instruction never to come again. Ivan tells Alyosha that the "kiss glows in his heart, but the old man adheres to his idea." The younger brother, convinced Ivan is telling him a parable of his own beliefs in the person of the Spanish cleric, confronts him with his atheism, and, to show his love for the lost soul, kisses him. Ivan accuses him of "plagiarism" which, no doubt, is true.

What's going on here, and why should we care?

The Inquisitor's parable is a key to the novel; as "story within a story," the author is giving us a picture of novelist and reader, i.e., his idea of what he wants us to take away from *The Brothers Karamazov*. Alyosha, the inner heart of the Karamazov triptych and a stand-in for the book's readers, naturally identifies with Christ, the Light of the World, in Ivan's story. Ivan, the worldly rationalist and skeptic, is a story transparency for "reason"; if not Dostoevsky, he's the sophisticated reader who identifies with his thoughts rather than heart.

In "Inquisitor," then, we see the same message of death to self for the life in Christ that is in the book's Ring signatures and the parabolic soul-faculty symbolism that is the work's major allegorical structure. I hope on reading or rereading this signature chapter from Dostoevsky's masterpiece that you feel as I always do, namely, invited to reenter this Christian literary crucible and experience again the agony of a dismembered soul and the joy of its final reorientation in Christ.

## CHAPTER TWENTY EIGHT

# FRIEDRICH NIETZSCHE

## Modern (1844–1900)

Nietzsche is a devilishly clever philosopher. He despises much I admire— Jesus, Judaism come to mind—but is witty and brutally logical about it. Besides, if Jesus and Judaism were as Nietzsche says they are, then they would be worthy of contempt.

Reading Nietzsche on any topic one knows much about is likely to produce both bewilderment and recognition. For example, Nietzsche misreads ancient Greek philosophy, sometimes wildly so, but he does not misread the uses that some of his contemporaries made of ancient Greek philosophy. I cannot recognize Christianity in his rants against the church, but I do recognize too much of myself.

At his best, which by any measure is most of the time and in his opinion all the time, Nietzsche provokes dialogue. Does anybody agree with all his conclusions? Can anyone forget the experience of reading him? Nietzsche insists that we follow any argument all the way to its logical end, even if the end is awful. He is right to demand this consistency of us.

A delightful thing about Nietzsche: He has no time for poseurs of any sort. He loathes Christians, but he is equally mocking of the effete atheists of Parisian cafe culture. It has been stimulating to think of the scorn he would've had for a middle-brow "great books" reader such as this one. If one thinks reading "greats" will magically produce wisdom, Nietzsche is a needed slap in the face. He doesn't suffer people who study philosophy to fake their way through happy-hour chatter or a Katie Couric interview.

Evil men would come to take fragments of Nietzsche and then use them as a "philosophical" justification for nearly unimaginable evils such as the Holocaust. Nietzsche was no Nazi, not even in embryo, and he was no more responsible for the Leopold and Loeb murder than Jesus was for Jim Jones' Peoples Temple.

Nietzsche sees the rot in Western liberalism, but he also was made possible by it. If he is a prophet of our inconsistency and decay, he was no holy prophet. A culture is in trouble when the worst men are the most authentic men. Somebody claimed that in modern times the devil has all the best music, and in Nietzsche the devil had the best contemporary philosopher too.

<hr>

&#8269; FROM &#8270;

# Genealogy of Morals

### FIRST ESSAY
### GOOD AND EVIL, GOOD AND BAD

### 7

You will have already guessed how easily the priestly way of evaluating could split from the knightly-aristocratic and then continue to develop into its opposite. Such a development receives a special stimulus every time the priest caste and the warrior caste confront each other jealously and are not willing to agree about the winner. The knightly-aristocratic judgments of value have as their basic assumption a powerful physicality, a blooming, rich, even overflowing health, together with those things which are required to maintain these qualities—war, adventure, hunting, dancing, war games, and in general everything which involves strong, free, happy action. The priestly-noble method of evaluating has, as we saw, other preconditions: these make it difficult enough for them when it comes to war!

As is well known, priests are the most evil of enemies—but why? Because they are the most powerless. From their powerlessness, their hate grows into something immense and terrifying, to the most spiritual and most poisonous manifestations. Those who have been the greatest haters in world history and the most spiritually rich haters have always been the priests—in comparison with the spirit of priestly revenge all the remaining spirits are hardly worth considering. Human history would be a really stupid affair without that spirit which entered it from the powerless.

Let us quickly consider the greatest example. Everything on earth which has been done against "the nobility," "the powerful," "the masters," "the possessors of power" is not worth mentioning in comparison with what the Jews have done against them—the Jews, that priestly people who knew how to get final satisfaction from their enemies and conquerors through a radical transformation of their values, that is, through an act of the most spiritual revenge. This was appropriate only to a priestly people with the most deeply rooted priestly desire for revenge.

In opposition to the aristocratic value equations (good = noble = powerful = beautiful = fortunate = loved by god), the Jews successfully and with a fearsome consistency dared to reverse it and to hang on to that with the teeth of the most profound hatred (the hatred of the powerless), that is, to "only those who suffer are good; only the poor, the powerless, the low are good; only the suffering, those in need, the sick, the ugly are the pious; only they are blessed by God; for them alone there is salvation. By contrast, you privileged and powerful people, you are for all eternity the evil, the cruel, the lecherous, insatiable, the godless—you will also be the unblessed, the cursed, and the damned for all eternity!" We know who inherited this Judaic transformation of values. . . .

In connection with that huge and immeasurably disastrous initiative which the Jews launched with this most fundamental of all declarations of war, I recall the sentence I wrote at another time [in *Beyond Good and Evil*, 118]—namely, that with the Jews the slave condition in morality begins: that condition which has a two-thousand-year-old history behind it and which we nowadays no longer notice because, well, because it has triumphed.

## 8

But you fail to understand that? You have no eye for something that needed two millennia to emerge victorious? . . . That's nothing to wonder at: all lengthy things are hard to see, to assess. However, that's what took place: out of the trunk of that tree of vengeance and hatred, Jewish hatred, the deepest and most sublime hatred, that is, a hatred which creates ideals and transforms values—something whose like has never been seen on earth—from that grew something just as incomparable, a new love, the deepest and most sublime of all the forms of love. From what other trunk could that have grown? . . .

However, you must not make the mistake of thinking that this love arose essentially as the denial of that thirst for vengeance, as the opposite of Jewish hatred. No. The reverse is the truth! This love grew out of that hatred, as its crown, as the victorious crown extending itself wider and wider in the purest brightness and sunshine, which, so to speak, was seeking for the kingdom of light and height, the goal of that hate—aiming for victory, trophies, seduction—with the same urgency with which the roots of that hatred were sinking down ever deeper and more greedily into everything deep and evil.

Take this Jesus of Nazareth, the bodily evangelist of love, the "Saviour," who brought holiness and victory to the poor, to the sick, to the sinners. Was he not in fact seduction in its most terrible and irresistible form, the seduction and detour to exactly those Judaic values and new ideals? Didn't Israel in fact attain, with the detour of this "Saviour," with this apparent enemy to and dissolver of Israel, the final goal of its sublime thirst for vengeance? Isn't it part of the secret black art of a truly great politics of vengeance, a far-sighted, underground, slowly expropriating, and premeditated revenge, that Israel itself had to disown and nail to the cross the tool essential to its revenge before all the world, so that "all the world," that is, all Israel's enemies, could then swallow this bait?

On the other hand, could anyone, using the full subtlety of his mind, imagine a more dangerous bait? Something to match the enticing, intoxicating, narcotizing, corrupting power of that symbol of the "holy cross," that ghastly paradox of a "god on the cross," that mystery of an unimaginable and ultimate cruelty and self-crucifixion of god for the salvation of mankind? . . . At least it is certain that *sub hoc signo [under this sign]* Israel, with its vengeance and revaluation of the worth of all other previous values, has triumphed again and again over all other ideals, over all nobler ideals.

**9**

"But what are you doing still talking about more noble ideals! Let's look at the facts: the people have triumphed—or 'the slaves,' or 'the rabble,' or 'the herd,' or whatever you want to call them—if this has taken place because of the Jews, then good for them! No people had a more world-historical mission. 'The masters' have been disposed of. The morality of the common man has won. We may take this victory as a blood poisoning (it did mix the races up)—I don't deny that. But this intoxication has undoubtedly been successful. The 'Salvation' of the human race (namely, from 'the masters') is well under way. Everything is turning Jewish or Christian or plebeian (what do the words matter!).

"The progress of this poison through the entire body of humanity seems irresistible—although its tempo and pace may seem from now on constantly slower, more delicate, less audible, more circumspect—well, we have time enough. . . . From this point of view, does the church today still have necessary work to do, does it really have a right to exist? Or could we dispense with it? *Quaeritur. [That's a question to be asked]*. It seems that it obstructs and hinders the progress of this poison, instead of speeding it up? Well, that might even be what makes the church useful . . . Certainly the church is something positively gross and vulgar, which a more delicate intelligence, a truly modern taste resists. Should the church at least not be something more sophisticated? . . . Today the church alienates more than it seduces. . . . Who among us would really be a free spirit if the church were not there? The church repels us, not its poison. . . . Apart from the church, we love the poison. . . ."

This is the epilogue of a "free thinker" to my speech, an honest animal, who has revealed himself well—and he's a democrat. He listened to me up to that point and couldn't stand to hear my silence. But for me at this point there is much to be silent about.

## 10

The slave revolt in morality begins when the resentment itself becomes creative and gives birth to values: the resentment of those beings who are prevented from a genuinely active reaction and who compensate for that with a merely imaginary vengeance. While all noble morality grows out of a triumphant self-affirmation, slave morality from the start says No to what is "outside," "other," "a non-self." And this No is its creative act. This transformation of the glance which confers value—this necessary projection towards what is outer instead of back into itself—that is inherent in resentment. In order to arise, slave morality always requires first an opposing world, a world outside itself. Psychologically speaking, it needs external stimuli in order to act at all. Its action is basically reaction.

The reverse is the case with the noble method of valuing: it acts and grows spontaneously. It seeks its opposite only to affirm itself even more thankfully, with even more rejoicing. Its negative concept of "low," "common," "bad" is only a pale contrasting image after the fact in relation to its positive basic concept, intoxicated with life and passion, "We are noble, good, beautiful, and happy!" When the noble way of evaluating makes a mistake and abuses reality, that happens with reference to the sphere which it does not know well enough, indeed, the sphere it has strongly resisted learning the truth about: under certain circumstances it misjudges the sphere it despises—the sphere of the common man, the low people.

On the other hand, we should consider that even assuming that the effect of contempt, of looking down or looking superior, falsifies the image of the person despised, such distortion will fall short by a long way of the distortion with which the repressed hatred and vengeance of the powerless man mistakenly assault his opponent—naturally, in effigy. In fact, in contempt there is too much negligence, too much dismissiveness, too much looking away and impatience, all mixed together, even too much feeling of joy, for it to be capable of converting its object into a truly distorted monster.

We should not fail to hear the almost benevolent nuances which for a Greek noble, for example, lay in all the words with which he set himself above the lower people—how a constant type of pity, consideration, and forbearance is mixed in there, sweetening the words, to the point where almost all words which refer to the common man finally remain as expressions for "unhappy," "worthy of pity" (compare *deilos [cowardly]*, *deilaios [lowly, mean]*, *poneros [oppressed by toil, wretched]*, *mochtheros [suffering, wretched]*—the last two basically designating the common man as a slave worker and beast of burden). On the other hand, for the Greek ear the words "bad," "low," "unhappy" have never stopped echoing a single note, one tone colour, in which "unhappy" predominates. That is the inheritance of the old, noble, aristocratic way of evaluating, which does not betray its principles even in contempt.

(Philologists might recall the sense in which *oizuros [miserable]*, *anolbos [unblessed]*, *tlemon [wretched]*, *dustychein [unfortunate]*, *xymfora [misfortune]* were used). The "well born" felt that they were "the happy ones"; they did not have to construct their happiness artificially first by looking at their enemies, or in some circumstance to talk themselves into it, to lie to themselves (the way all men of resentment habitually do). Similarly they knew, as complete men, overloaded with power and thus necessarily active, they must not separate action from happiness. They considered being active necessarily associated with happiness (that's where the phrase *eu prattein [do well, succeed]* derives its origin)—all this is very much the opposite of "happiness" at the level of the powerless, the oppressed, those festering with poisonous and hostile feelings, among whom happiness comes out essentially as a narcotic, an anesthetic, quiet, peace, "Sabbath," relaxing the soul, stretching one's limbs, in short, as something passive.

While the noble man lives for himself with trust and candour (*gennaios*, meaning "of noble birth" stresses the nuance "upright" and also probably "naïve"), the man of resentment is neither upright nor naïve, nor honest and direct with himself. His soul squints. His spirit loves hiding places, secret paths, and back doors. Everything furtive attracts him as his world, his security, his refreshment. He understands about remaining silent, not forgetting, waiting, temporarily diminishing himself, humiliating himself.

A race of such men will necessarily end up cleverer than any noble race. It will value cleverness to a very different extent, that is, as a condition of existence of the utmost importance; whereas, cleverness among noble men easily acquires a delicate aftertaste of luxury and sophistication about it. Here it is not nearly so important as the complete certainty of the ruling unconscious instincts or even a certain lack of cleverness, something like brave recklessness, whether in the face of danger or of an enemy, or wildly enthusiastic, sudden fits of anger, love, reverence, thankfulness, and vengefulness, by which in all ages noble souls have recognized each other.

The resentment of the noble man himself, if it comes over him, consumes and exhausts itself in an immediate reaction and therefore does not poison. On the other hand, in countless cases it just does not appear, whereas in the case of all weak and powerless people it is unavoidable. The noble man cannot take his enemies, his misfortunes, even his bad deeds seriously for very long—that is the mark of a strong, complete nature, in whom there is a surplus of plastic, creative, healing power, which also can make one forget (a good example for that from the modern world is Mirabeau, who had no memory of the insults and maliciousness people directed at him, and who therefore could not forgive, because he just forgot). Such a man with one shrug throws off him all those worms which eat into other men. Only here is possible (provided that it is at all possible on earth) the real "love for one's enemy." How much respect a noble man already has for his enemies! And such a respect is already a bridge to love. . . . In fact, he demands his enemy for himself, as his mark of honour. Indeed, he has no enemy other than one who has nothing to despise and a great deal to respect! By contrast, imagine for yourself "the enemy" as a man of resentment conceives him—and right here we have his action, his creation: he has conceptualized "the evil enemy," "the evil one," and as a fundamental idea—and from that he now thinks his way to an opposite image and counterpart, a "good man"—himself!

## 11

We see exactly the opposite with the noble man, who conceives the fundamental idea "good" in advance and spontaneously by himself and from there first creates a picture of "bad" for himself. This "bad" originating from the noble man and that "evil" arising out of the stew pot of insatiable hatred—of these the first is a later creation, an afterthought, a complementary colour; whereas the second is the original, the beginning, the essential act of conception in slave morality.

Although the two words "bad" and "evil" both seem opposite to the same idea of "good," how different they are. But it is not the same idea of the "good"; it is much rather a question of who the "evil man" really is, in the sense of the morality of resentment. The strict answer to that is this: precisely the "good man" of the other morality, the noble man himself, the powerful, the ruling man, only coloured over, reinterpreted, and seen through the poisonous eyes of resentment.

Here there is one thing we will be the last to deny: the man who knows these "good men" only as enemies, knows them as nothing but evil enemies, and the same men who are so strongly held bound by custom, honour, habit, thankfulness, even more by mutual suspicion and jealousy *inter pares [among equals]* and who, by contrast, demonstrate in relation to each other such resourceful consideration, self-control, refinement, loyalty, pride, and friendship—these men, once outside where the strange world, the foreign, begins, are not much better than beasts of prey turned loose. There they enjoy freedom from all social constraints. In the wilderness they make up for the tension which a long fenced-in confinement within the peace of the community brings about. They go back to the innocent consciousness of a wild beast of prey, as joyful monsters, who perhaps walk away from a dreadful sequence of murder, arson, rape, and torture with exhilaration and spiritual equilibrium, as if they had merely pulled off a student prank, convinced that the poets now have something more to sing about and praise for a long time.

At the bottom of all these noble races we cannot fail to recognize the beast of prey, the blond beast splendidly roaming around in its lust for loot and victory. This hidden basis from time to time needs to be discharged: the animal must come out again, must go back into the wilderness— Roman, Arab, German, Japanese nobility, Homeric heroes, Scandinavian Vikings—in this need they are all alike.

It was the noble races which left behind the concept of the "barbarian" in all their tracks, wherever they went. A consciousness of and a pride in this fact reveals itself even in their highest culture (for example, when Pericles says to his Athenians, in that famous Funeral Speech, "our audacity has broken a way through to every land and sea, putting up permanent memorials to itself for good and ill"). This "audacity" of the noble races, mad, absurd, sudden in the way it expresses itself, its unpredictability, even the improbability of its undertakings—Pericles emphatically praises the *rayhumia* [*mental balance, freedom from anxiety*] of the Athenians—its indifference to and contempt for safety, body, life, comfort, its fearsome cheerfulness and the depth of its joy in all destruction, in all the physical pleasures of victory and cruelty—everything summed up for those who suffer from such audacity in the image of the "barbarian," the "evil enemy," something like the "Goth" or the "Vandal."

The deep, icy mistrust which the German evokes, as soon as he comes to power—even today—is still an after-effect of that unforgettable terror with which for a century Europe confronted the rage of the blond German beast (although there is hardly any idea linking the old Germanic tribes and we Germans, let alone any blood relationship).

Once before I have remarked on Hesiod's dilemma when he thought up his sequence of cultural periods and sought to express them as Gold, Silver, and Iron. But he didn't know what to do with the contradiction presented to him by the marvelous but, at the same time, so horrifying world of Homer, other than to make two cultural ages out of one, then placing one after the other—first the age of Heroes and Demi-gods from Troy and Thebes, just as that world remained as a memorial for the noble races who had their own ancestors in it, and then the Iron Age, as that same world appeared to the descendants of the downtrodden, exploited, ill treated, those carried off and sold—a metallic age, as mentioned: hard, cold, cruel, empty of feeling and scruples, with everything crushed and covered over in blood.

Assuming as true what in any event is taken as "the truth" nowadays, that it is precisely the purpose of all culture to breed a tame and civilized animal, a domestic pet, out of the beast of prey "man," then we would undoubtedly have to consider the essential instruments of culture all those instinctive reactions and resentments by means of which the noble races with all their ideals were finally disgraced and overpowered—but that would not be to claim that the bearers of these instincts also in themselves represented culture. It would much rather be the case that the opposite is not only probable—no! nowadays it is visibly apparent. These people carrying instincts for oppression and a lust for revenge, the descendants of all European and non-European slavery, and all pre-Aryan populations in particular, represent the regression of mankind! These "instruments of culture" are a disgrace to humanity, more a reason to be suspicious of or a counterargument against "culture" in general!

We may well be right when we hang onto our fear of the blond beast at the base of all noble races and keep up our guard. But who would not find it a hundred times better to fear if he could at the same time be allowed to admire, rather than not fear and no longer be able to rid himself of the disgusting sight of the failures, the stunted, the emaciated, the poisoned? Is not that our fate? Today what is it that constitutes our aversion to "man"? For we suffer from man—there's no doubt of that. It's not a matter of fear, rather it's the fact that we have nothing more to fear from men, that the maggot "man" is in the foreground swarming around, that the "tame man," the hopelessly mediocre and unpleasant man, has already learned to feel that he is the goal, the pinnacle, the meaning of history, "the higher man,"—yes indeed, he even has a certain right to feel that about himself, insofar as he feels separate from the excess of failed, sick, tired, spent people, who are nowadays beginning to make Europe stink, and feels at least somewhat successful, at least still capable of life, at least able to say "yes" to life.

## 12

At this point I won't suppress a sigh and a final hope. What is it exactly that I find so totally unbearable? Something which I cannot deal with on my own, which makes me choke and feel faint? Bad air! Bad air! It's when something which has failed comes close to me, when I have to smell the entrails of a failed soul! Apart from that what can we not endure by way of need, deprivation, bad weather, infirmity, hardship, loneliness? Basically we can deal with all the other things, born as we are to an underground and struggling existence. We come back again and again into the light, we live over and over our golden hour of victory—and then we stand there, just as we were born, unbreakable, tense, ready for something new, for something even more difficult, more distant, like a bow which all trouble only serves to pull more tight.

But if there are heavenly goddesses who are our patrons, beyond good and evil, then from time to time grant me a glimpse, grant me a single glimpse into something perfect, something completely developed, something happy, powerful, triumphant, from which there is still something to fear! A glimpse of a man who justifies humanity, of a complementary and redeeming stroke-of-luck of a man, for whose sake we can hang onto a faith in humanity! . . .

For matters stand like this: the diminution and levelling of European man hides our greatest danger, for the sight of him makes us tired. We don't see anything today which wants to be greater. We suspect that things are constantly going down and down into something thinner, more good-natured, more prudent, more comfortable, more mediocre, more indifferent, more Chinese, more Christian—humanity, there is no doubt, is becoming constantly "better" . . . Europe's fate lies right here. With our fear of mankind we also have lost our love for mankind, our reverence for mankind, our hopes for mankind, even our will to be mankind. A glimpse at man makes us tired—what is today's nihilism, if it is not that? . . . We are weary of man.

## 13

But let's go back: the problem with the other origin of the "good," of the good as the man of resentment has imagined it for himself, demands some conclusion. That lambs are annoyed at the great predatory birds is not a strange thing, and it provides no reason for holding anything against these large birds of prey, because they snatch away small lambs. And if the lambs say among themselves "These predatory birds are evil—and whoever is least like a predatory bird—and especially who is like its opposite, a lamb—shouldn't that animal be good?" there is nothing to find fault with in this setting up of an ideal, except for the fact that the birds of prey might look down with a little mockery and perhaps say to themselves "We are not at all annoyed with these good lambs—we even love them. Nothing is tastier than a tender lamb."

To demand that strength does not express itself as strength, that it must not consist of a will to overpower, a will to throw down, a will to rule, a thirst for enemies and opposition and triumph—that is as unreasonable as to demand that weakness express itself as strength. A quantum of force is just such a quantum of drive, will, action—indeed, it is nothing but these drives, willing, and actions in themselves—and it cannot appear as anything else except through the seduction of language (and the fundamental errors of reason petrified in it), which understands and misunderstands all action as conditioned by something which causes actions, by a "Subject."

In fact, in just the same way as people separate lightning from its flash and take the latter as an action, as the effect of a subject, which is called lightning, so popular morality separates strength from the manifestations of that strength, as if behind the strong person there is an indifferent substrate, which is free to manifest strength or not. But there is no such substrate, there is no "being" behind the doing, acting, becoming. "The doer" is merely invented after the fact—the act is everything. People basically duplicate the event: when they see lightning, well, that is an action of an action: they set up the same event first as the cause and then again as its effect.

Natural scientists are no better when they say "Force moves, force causes" and so on—our entire scientific knowledge, for all its coolness, its freedom from feelings, still remains exposed to the seductions of language and has not gotten rid of the changelings foisted on it, the "Subject" (the atom, for example, is such a changeling, like the Kantian "Thing in itself"): it's no wonder that the repressed, secretly smouldering feelings of rage and hate use this belief for themselves and, in fact, maintain a faith in nothing more strongly than in the idea that the strong are free to be weak and predatory birds are free to be lambs—and in so doing, they arrogate to themselves the right to blame the birds of prey for being birds of prey. . . .

When the oppressed, the downtrodden, the conquered say to each other, with the vengeful cunning of the powerless, "Let us be different from evil people, namely, good! And that man is good who does not overpower, who hurts no one, who does not attack, who does not retaliate, who hands revenge over to God, who keeps himself hidden, as we do, who avoids all evil and demands little from life in general—like us, the patient, humble, and upright"—what that amounts to, coolly expressed and without bias, is essentially nothing more than "We weak people are merely weak. It's good if we do nothing, because we are not strong enough."

But this bitter state, this shrewdness of the lowest ranks, which even insects possess (for in great danger they stand as if they were dead in order not to do "too much"), has, thanks to the counterfeiting and self-deception of powerlessness, dressed itself in the splendour of a self-denying, still, patient virtue, just as if the weakness of the weak man himself—that means his essence, his actions, his entire single, inevitable, and irredeemable reality—is a voluntary achievement, something willed, chosen, an act, something of merit. This kind of man needs to believe in the disinterested, freely choosing "subject" out of his instinct for self-preservation, self-approval, in which every falsehood is habitually sanctified. The subject (or, to use a more popular style, the soul) has up to now probably been the best principle for belief on earth, because, for the majority of the dying, the weak, and the downtrodden of all sorts, it makes possible a sublime self-deception which establishes weakness itself as freedom and their being like this or that as something meritorious.

## 14

Is there anyone who would like to take a little look down on and under that secret how man fabricates an ideal on earth? Who has the courage for that? Come on, now! Here is an open glimpse into this dark workshop. Just wait a moment, my dear Mr. Presumptuous and Nosy: your eye must first get used to this artificial flickering light. . . . So, enough! Now speak! What's going on down there? Speak up. Say what you see, man of the most dangerous curiosity—now I'm the one who's listening.—

"I see nothing, but I hear all the more. It is a careful and crafty light rumour-mongering and whispering from every nook and cranny. It seems to me that people are lying; a sugary mildness clings to every sound. Weakness is going to be falsified into something of merit. There's no doubt about it—things are just as you said they were."

—Keep talking!

"And powerlessness which does not retaliate is being falsified into 'goodness,' anxious baseness into 'humility,' submission before those one hates to 'obedience' (of course, obedience to the one who, they say, commands this submission—they call him God). The inoffensiveness of the weak man, even cowardice, in which he is rich, his standing at the door, his inevitable need to wait around—here these acquire good names, like 'patience' and are called virtue. That incapacity for revenge is called the lack of desire for revenge, perhaps even forgiveness ('for they know not what they do—only we know what they do!'). And people are talking about 'love for one's enemy'—and sweating as they say it."

—Keep talking!

"They are miserable—there's no doubt about that—all these rumour mongers and counterfeiters in the corners, although crouched down beside each other in the warmth—but they are telling me that their misery is God's choice, His sign. One beats the dog one loves the most. Perhaps this misery may be a preparation, a test, an education, perhaps it is even more—something that will one day be rewarded and paid out with huge interest in gold, no, in happiness. They call that 'blessedness.'"

—Go on!

"Now they are telling me that they are not only better than the powerful, the masters of the earth, whose spit they have to lick (not out of fear, certainly not out of fear, but because God commands that they honour those in authority)—they are not only better than these but they also are 'better off,' or at any rate will one day have it better. But enough! Enough! I can't endure it any more. Bad air! Bad air! This workshop where man fabricates ideals—it seems to me it stinks from nothing but lies."

—No! Just wait a minute more! So far you haven't said anything about the masterpiece of these black magicians who know how to make whiteness, milk, and innocence out of every blackness. Have you not noticed the perfection of their sophistication, their most daring, refined, most spiritual, most fallacious artistic attempt. Pay attention! These cellar animals full of vengeance and hatred—what are they making right now out of that vengeance and hatred? Have you ever heard these words? If you heard only their words, would you suspect that you were completely among men of resentment?

"I understand. Once again I'll open my ears (oh! oh! oh! and hold my nose). Now I'm hearing for the first time what they've been saying so often: 'We good men—we are the righteous'—what they demand they don't call repayment but 'the triumph of righteousness.' What they hate is not their enemy. No! They hate 'injustice,' 'godlessness.' What they believe and hope is not a hope for revenge, the intoxication of sweet vengeance (something Homer called 'sweeter than honey') but the victory of God, the righteous God, over the godless. What remains for them to love on earth are not their brothers in hatred but their 'brothers in love,' as they say, all the good and righteous people on the earth."

—And what do they call what serves them as a consolation for all the suffering of life—their phantasmagoria of future blessedness which they are expecting?

"What that? Am I hearing correctly? They call that 'the last judgment,' the coming to their kingdom, the coming of 'God's kingdom'—but in the meanwhile they live 'in faith,' 'in love,' 'in hope.'"

—Enough! Enough!

*Translated by Ian C. Johnston, 2009*


# ON GENEALOGY OF MORALS

## Fred Sanders


God was dead, to begin with. If you want to understand the philosophy of Friedrich Nietzsche, you have to start where he started, with the premise that there is no God and that Christian monotheism had all been a big mistake. As far as Nietzsche was concerned, the best thinkers of the mid-nineteenth century had altogether undermined Christian truth claims: Strauss's *Life of Jesus Critically Examined* (1846) and Feuerbach's *Essence of Christianity* (1855) were among the important books that had settled things (two books, by the way, that novelist George Eliot made sure to translate so they could have their effect for English readers). By the 1880s, anybody who still clung to Christianity was either not paying attention or was fooling themselves. The master of melodrama and bombast in the intellectual life, Nietzsche looked back on recent Western thought and said, "We have become God's murderers."

So God was dead as a coffin-nail, and Nietzsche knew it. He also knew that the educated people of his day knew it. But what bothered him was that they didn't act like it. Though sound scholarship had demolished Christian theology, Christian morality was still alive and well. So Nietzsche appointed himself the official whistle-blower on the death of God, and like many of the radicals of the late nineteenth century, he insisted that we should follow out the logic of godlessness to its conclusions.

The very people who had spent the nineteenth century driving God out of their worldviews were failing to draw the necessary conclusions about their morality. Even without God, they held on to absolute truth, to reason, to the binding claims of right and wrong. Worst of all, the godless moderns still had a conscience, and it continued to condemn them when they violated its dictates. Nietzsche spent half his time reminding them that they had no right to hold on to the benefits of monotheism after murdering God, and the other half of his time rejoicing that there was no longer any ground on which conscience could stand.

---

"If God is dead, anything is possible," mused Dostoevsky's Grand Inquisitor in *The Brothers Karamazov*, and it was Friedrich Nietzsche who set himself to the task of showing what that meant for ethics. Since morals didn't come from a God, where did they come from? He answered that question in 1887 with his *Genealogy of Morals*, which is the best, and by far clearest, introduction to his overall project.

In short, the first essay in the three-part *Genealogy* argues that morality itself, the whole idea of good versus evil, came about when weak people figured out a way to make strong people feel bad about being strong. The reason we feel we should take pity on the weak, or feel bad for imposing our wills on others, is that long ago, in some dark, underground workshop of the spirit, the weak had invented "morals" to compensate for their weakness. Instead of just straightforwardly hating their enemies, they declared that their superiors stood under the judgment of a higher authority—God— whose law condemned them. And then, amazingly, they had convinced the strong to accept these twisted ideals as "the way things ought to be."

This was the slave-revolt at the beginning of the epoch of morality, and the slaves have been in charge ever since.

Until Nietzsche, that is, who claimed to be writing with a prophetic voice that announced a new, natural way of valuing things: Whatever affirms and perpetuates life is good, and whatever denies or suppresses life is bad. All of this has to be read in Nietzsche's own words, though, because they are so powerful ("I can write in letters which make even the blind see," he said).

Christian readers have trouble engaging Nietzsche because, to state the obvious, they don't share his presupposition that the arguments of Victorian atheism were in fact conclusive. They would like to reserve the right to go back and have those debates about truth. But as hard as he is to engage, Nietzsche is well worth coming to terms with for several reasons. He pioneered the strategy of discrediting Christianity by ignoring the question of its truth, in order to cut straight to his major complaint: Christianity is bad for human beings and other living things like the mind, the arts, and freedom. That attitude is probably the dominant tone of popular atheism in our time.

Nietzsche is also the one whose systematic, genealogical suspicion toward the whole vocabulary of Christian virtue (love, joy, peace, patience, kindness, goodness, faithfulness, gentleness, self-control) has burned away so much of the faith's credibility. Christianity has always been called into question by the bad conduct of its adherents. But Nietzsche (who grew up in a pastor's home and maintained a commitment to Christ well into his teens) transformed that anecdotal criticism into a wholesale deconstruction. *Genealogy of Morals* is the book where he did so, and if this book is right, then every word of the New Testament is a mendacious lie. At least, all the significant nouns.

## CHAPTER TWENTY NINE

# G. K. CHESTERTON

## Modern (1874–1936)

Gilbert Keith Chesterton is aware he is in this compendium, but fortunately he cannot comment on the inclusion. If he could, he'd almost certainly say he does not belong in it, humiliate the editor for including him at the expense of some better writer, and, as usual, he would be more or less right.

Chesterton was not a great philosopher like Aquinas or a sublime poet like Dante. His fiction lacks the polish of Austen or the passion of either of the Brontë sisters. He's decidedly second-rate compared to Plato or Shakespeare, but that's an amazing thing to be.

Chesterton is here as our ambassador to the Great Conversation. He's bright enough to sit at the High Table with the Masters *and* witty enough to explain them to us who sit below.

In the meantime, his work is a delight.

Rare is the man or woman who reads Homer for fun, but once you start reading Chesterton it's hard to stop. He could explain Shakespeare or Aquinas in new ways so interesting that scholars would pause to consider and amateurs would learn. Chesterton sometimes got details wrong, yet he often captured the essential nature of a writer or problem.

Chesterton does not argue so much as live on a page . . . and he is always jolly. Reading Chesterton is simply jollification, and nobody in this book does "jolly" better. As a result, G. K. Chesterton is a genius we can enjoy and an eccentric who can see what less wild men might miss.

———

Humankind will read Chaucer in two hundred years. Will we read Chesterton? Perhaps not, but in this century Chesterton is needed. He is a near contemporary chronologically, but of all the writers in this book he comes closest to being a man of no age, because he is a man of all the ages that come before him.

Chesterton exhales as a subject of Christendom. Most of us don't think enough about that kingdom, and to read a robust and brilliant treatment of the subject in readable prose is a rare treat. Perhaps, after all, being world-class at jollification is enough, and Chesterton is fully worthy of inclusion here.

See for yourself.

 FROM

# *Orthodoxy*

### IV. The Ethics of Elfland

When the business man rebukes the idealism of his office-boy, it is commonly in some such speech as this: "Ah, yes, when one is young, one has these ideals in the abstract and these castles in the air; but in middle age they all break up like clouds, and one comes down to a belief in practical politics, to using the machinery one has and getting on with the world as it is." Thus, at least, venerable and philanthropic old men now in their honoured graves used to talk to me when I was a boy. But since then I have grown up and have discovered that these philanthropic old men were telling lies. What has really happened is exactly the opposite of what they said would happen. They said that I should lose my ideals and begin to believe in the methods of practical politicians. Now, I have not lost my ideals in the least; my faith in fundamentals is exactly what it always was. What I have lost is my old childlike faith in practical politics. I am still as much concerned as ever about the Battle of Armageddon; but I am not so much concerned about the General Election. As a babe I leapt up on my mother's knee at the mere mention of it. No; the vision is always solid and reliable. The vision is always a fact. It is the reality that is often a fraud. As much as I ever did, more than I ever did, I believe in Liberalism. But there was a rosy time of innocence when I believed in Liberals.

. . .

In fairyland we avoid the word "law"; but in the land of science they are singularly fond of it. Thus they will call some interesting conjecture about how forgotten folks pronounced the alphabet, Grimm's Law. But Grimm's Law is far less intellectual than Grimm's Fairy Tales. The tales are, at any rate, certainly tales; while the law is not a law. A law implies that we know the nature of the generalisation and enactment; not merely that we have noticed some of the effects. If there is a law that pick-pockets shall go to prison, it implies that there is an imaginable mental connection between the idea of prison and the idea of picking pockets. And we know what the idea is. We can say why we take liberty from a man who takes liberties. But we cannot say why an egg can turn into a chicken any more than we can say why a bear could turn into a fairy prince. As IDEAS, the egg and the chicken are further off from each other than the bear and the prince; for no egg in itself suggests a chicken, whereas some princes do suggest bears.

Granted, then, that certain transformations do happen, it is essential that we should regard them in the philosophic manner of fairy tales, not in the unphilosophic manner of science and the "Laws of Nature." When we are asked why eggs turn to birds or fruits fall in autumn, we must answer exactly as the fairy godmother would answer if Cinderella asked her why mice turned to horses or her clothes fell from her at twelve o'clock. We must answer that it is MAGIC. It is not a "law," for we do not understand its general formula. It is not a necessity, for though we can count on it happening practically, we have no right to say that it must always happen.

It is no argument for unalterable law (as Huxley fancied) that we count on the ordinary course of things. We do not count on it; we bet on it. We risk the remote possibility of a miracle as we do that of a poisoned pancake or a world-destroying comet. We leave it out of account, not because it is a miracle, and therefore an impossibility, but because it is a miracle, and therefore an exception. All the terms used in the science books, "law," "necessity," "order," "tendency," and so on, are really unintellectual, because they assume an inner synthesis, which we do not possess. The only words that ever satisfied me as describing Nature are the terms used in the fairy books, "charm," "spell," "enchantment." They express the arbitrariness of the fact and its mystery. A tree grows fruit because it is a MAGIC tree. Water runs downhill because it is bewitched. The sun shines because it is bewitched.

I deny altogether that this is fantastic or even mystical. We may have some mysticism later on; but this fairy-tale language about things is simply rational and agnostic. It is the only way I can express in words my clear and definite perception that one thing is quite distinct from another; that there is no logical connection between flying and laying eggs. It is the man who talks about "a law" that he has never seen who is the mystic. Nay, the ordinary scientific man is strictly a sentimentalist. He is a sentimentalist in this essential sense, that he is soaked and swept away by mere associations. He has so often seen birds fly and lay eggs that he feels as if there must be some dreamy, tender connection between the two ideas, whereas there is none. A forlorn lover might be unable to dissociate the moon from lost love; so the materialist is unable to dissociate the moon from the tide. In both cases there is no connection, except that one has seen them together. A sentimentalist might shed tears at the smell of apple-blossom, because, by a dark association of his own, it reminded him of his boyhood. So the materialist professor (though he conceals his tears) is yet a sentimentalist, because, by a dark association of his own, apple-blossoms remind him of apples. But the cool rationalist from fairyland does not see why, in the abstract, the apple tree should not grow crimson tulips; it sometimes does in his country.

This elementary wonder, however, is not a mere fancy derived from the fairy tales; on the contrary, all the fire of the fairy tales is derived from this. Just as we all like love tales because there is an instinct of sex, we all like astonishing tales because they touch the nerve of the ancient instinct of astonishment. This is proved by the fact that when we are very young children we do not need fairy tales: we only need tales. Mere life is interesting enough. A child of seven is excited by being told that Tommy opened a door and saw a dragon. But a child of three is excited by being told that Tommy opened a door. Boys like romantic tales; but babies like realistic tales—because they find them romantic.

In fact, a baby is about the only person, I should think, to whom a modern realistic novel could be read without boring him. This proves that even nursery tales only echo an almost pre-natal leap of interest and amazement. These tales say that apples were golden only to refresh the forgotten moment when we found that they were green. They make rivers run with wine only to make us remember, for one wild moment, that they run with water. I have said that this is wholly reasonable and even agnostic. And, indeed, on this point I am all for the higher agnosticism; its better name is Ignorance. We have all read in scientific books, and, indeed, in all romances, the story of the man who has forgotten his name. This man walks about the streets and can see and appreciate everything; only he cannot remember who he is. Well, every man is that man in the story. Every man has forgotten who he is. One may understand the cosmos, but never the ego; the self more distant than any star. Thou shalt love the Lord thy God; but thou shalt not know thyself. We are all under the same mental calamity; we have all forgotten our names. We have all forgotten what we really are. All that we call common sense and rationality and practicality and positivism only means that for certain dead levels of our life we forget that we have forgotten. All that we call spirit and art and ecstacy only means that for one awful instant we remember that we forget.

. . .

The modern world as I found it was solid for modern Calvinism, for the necessity of things being as they are. But when I came to ask them I found they had really no proof of this unavoidable repetition in things except the fact that the things were repeated. Now, the mere repetition made the things to me rather more weird than more rational. It was as if, having seen a curiously shaped nose in the street and dismissed it as an accident, I had then seen six other noses of the same astonishing shape. I should have fancied for a moment that it must be some local secret society. So one elephant having a trunk was odd; but all elephants having trunks looked like a plot. I speak here only of an emotion, and of an emotion at once stubborn and subtle. But the repetition in Nature seemed sometimes to be an excited repetition, like that of an angry schoolmaster saying the same thing over and over again. The grass seemed signalling to me with all its fingers at once; the crowded stars seemed bent upon being understood. The sun would make me see him if he rose a thousand times. The recurrences of the universe rose to the maddening rhythm of an incantation, and I began to see an idea.

All the towering materialism which dominates the modern mind rests ultimately upon one assumption; a false assumption. It is supposed that if a thing goes on repeating itself it is probably dead; a piece of clockwork. People feel that if the universe was personal it would vary; if the sun were alive it would dance. This is a fallacy even in relation to known fact. For the variation in human affairs is generally brought into them, not by life, but by death; by the dying down or breaking off of their strength or desire. A man varies his movements because of some slight element of failure or fatigue. He gets into an omnibus because he is tired of walking; or he walks because he is tired of sitting still. But if his life and joy were so gigantic that he never tired of going to Islington, he might go to Islington as regularly as the Thames goes to Sheerness. The very speed and ecstacy of his life would have the stillness of death. The sun rises every morning. I do not rise every morning; but the variation is due not to my activity, but to my inaction. Now, to put the matter in a popular phrase, it might be true that the sun rises regularly because he never gets tired of rising. His routine might be due, not to a lifelessness, but to a rush of life.

The thing I mean can be seen, for instance, in children, when they find some game or joke that they specially enjoy. A child kicks his legs rhythmically through excess, not absence, of life. Because children have abounding vitality, because they are in spirit fierce and free, therefore they want things repeated and unchanged. They always say, "Do it again"; and the grown-up person does it again until he is nearly dead. For grown-up people are not strong enough to exult in monotony. But perhaps God is strong enough to exult in monotony. It is possible that God says every morning, "Do it again" to the sun; and every evening, "Do it again" to the moon. It may not be automatic necessity that makes all daisies alike; it may be that God makes every daisy separately, but has never got tired of making them. It may be that He has the eternal appetite of infancy; for we have sinned and grown old, and our Father is younger than we. The repetition in Nature may not be a mere recurrence; it may be a theatrical ENCORE. Heaven may ENCORE the bird who laid an egg. If the human being conceives and brings forth a human child instead of bringing forth a fish, or a bat, or a griffin, the reason may not be that we are fixed in an animal fate without life or purpose. It may be that our little tragedy has touched the gods, that they admire it from their starry galleries, and that at the end of every human drama man is called again and again before the curtain. Repetition may go on for millions of years, by mere choice, and at any instant it may stop. Man may stand on the earth generation after generation, and yet each birth be his positively last appearance.

This was my first conviction; made by the shock of my childish emotions meeting the modern creed in mid-career. I had always vaguely felt facts to be miracles in the sense that they are wonderful: now I began to think them miracles in the stricter sense that they were WILLFUL. I mean that they were, or might be, repeated exercises of some will. In short, I had always believed that the world involved magic: now I thought that perhaps it involved a magician. And this pointed a profound emotion always present and sub-conscious; that this world of ours has some purpose; and if there is a purpose, there is a person. I had always felt life first as a story: and if there is a story there is a story-teller.

But modern thought also hit my second human tradition. It went against the fairy feeling about strict limits and conditions. The one thing it loved to talk about was expansion and largeness. Herbert Spencer would have been greatly annoyed if any one had called him an imperialist, and therefore it is highly regrettable that nobody did. But he was an imperialist of the lowest type. He popularized this contemptible notion that the size of the solar system ought to over-awe the spiritual dogma of man. Why should a man surrender his dignity to the solar system any more than to a whale? If mere size proves that man is not the image of God, then a whale may be the image of God; a somewhat formless image; what one might call an impressionist portrait. It is quite futile to argue that man is small compared to the cosmos; for man was always small compared to the nearest tree. But Herbert Spencer, in his headlong imperialism, would insist that we had in some way been conquered and annexed by the astronomical universe. He spoke about men and their ideals exactly as the most insolent Unionist talks about the Irish and their ideals. He turned mankind into a small nationality. And his evil influence can be seen even in the most spirited and honourable of later scientific authors; notably in the early romances of Mr. H. G. Wells. Many moralists have in an exaggerated way represented the earth as wicked. But Mr. Wells and his school made the heavens wicked. We should lift up our eyes to the stars from whence would come our ruin.

But the expansion of which I speak was much more evil than all this. I have remarked that the materialist, like the madman, is in prison; in the prison of one thought. These people seemed to think it singularly inspiring to keep on saying that the prison was very large. The size of this scientific universe gave one no novelty, no relief. The cosmos went on for ever, but not in its wildest constellation could there be anything really interesting; anything, for instance, such as forgiveness or free will. The grandeur or infinity of the secret of its cosmos added nothing to it. It was like telling a prisoner in Reading gaol that he would be glad to hear that the gaol now covered half the county. The warder would have nothing to show the man except more and more long corridors of stone lit by ghastly lights and empty of all that is human. So these expanders of the universe had nothing to show us except more and more infinite corridors of space lit by ghastly suns and empty of all that is divine.

In fairyland there had been a real law; a law that could be broken, for the definition of a law is something that can be broken. But the machinery of this cosmic prison was something that could not be broken; for we ourselves were only a part of its machinery. We were either unable to do things or we were destined to do them. The idea of the mystical condition quite disappeared; one can neither have the firmness of keeping laws nor the fun of breaking them. The largeness of this universe had nothing of that freshness and airy outbreak which we have praised in the universe of the poet. This modern universe is literally an empire; that is, it was vast, but it is not free. One went into larger and larger windowless rooms, rooms big with Babylonian perspective; but one never found the smallest window or a whisper of outer air.

...

Thus ends, in unavoidable inadequacy, the attempt to utter the unutterable things. These are my ultimate attitudes towards life; the soils for the seeds of doctrine. These in some dark way I thought before I could write, and felt before I could think: that we may proceed more easily afterwards, I will roughly recapitulate them now. I felt in my bones; first, that the world does not explain itself. It may be miracle with a supernatural explanation; it may be a conjuring trick, with a natural explanation. But the explanation of the conjuring trick, if it is to satisfy me, will have to be better than the natural explanations I have heard. The thing is magic, true or false. Second, I came to feel as if magic must have a meaning, and meaning must have some one to mean it. There was something personal in the world, as in a work of art; whatever it meant it meant violently. Third, I thought this purpose beautiful in its old design, in spite of its defects, such as dragons. Fourth, that the proper form of thanks to it is some form of humility and restraint: we should thank God for beer and Burgundy by not drinking too much of them. We owed, also, an obedience to whatever made us. And last, and strangest, there had come into my mind a vague and vast impression that in some way all good was a remnant to be stored and held sacred out of some primordial ruin. Man had saved his good as Crusoe saved his goods: he had saved them from a wreck. All this I felt and the age gave me no encouragement to feel it. And all this time I had not even thought of Christian theology.

...

VIII. The Romance of Orthodoxy

...

Students of popular science, like Mr. Blatchford, are always insisting that Christianity and Buddhism are very much alike, especially Buddhism. This is generally believed, and I believed it myself until I read a book giving the reasons for it. The reasons were of two kinds: resemblances that meant nothing because they were common to all humanity, and resemblances which were not resemblances at all. The author solemnly explained that the two creeds were alike in things in which all creeds are alike, or else he described them as alike in some point in which they are quite obviously different. Thus, as a case of the first class, he said that both Christ and Buddha were called by the divine voice coming out of the sky, as if you would expect the divine voice to come out of the coal-cellar. Or, again, it was gravely urged that these two Eastern teachers, by a singular coincidence, both had to do with the washing of feet. You might as well say that it was a remarkable coincidence that they both had feet to wash. And the other class of similarities were those which simply were not similar. Thus this reconciler of the two religions draws earnest attention to the fact that at certain religious feasts the robe of the Lama is rent in pieces out of respect, and the remnants highly valued. But this is the reverse of a resemblance, for the garments of Christ were not rent in pieces out of respect, but out of derision; and the remnants were not highly valued except for what they would fetch in the rag shops. It is rather like alluding to the obvious con-nection between the two ceremonies of the sword: when it taps a man's shoulder, and when it cuts off his head. It is not at all similar for the man. These scraps of puerile pedantry would indeed matter little if it were not also true that the alleged philosophical resemblances are also of these two kinds, either proving too much or not proving anything. That Buddhism approves of mercy or of self-restraint is not to say that it is specially like Christianity; it is only to say that it is not utterly unlike all human exis-tence. Buddhists disapprove in theory of cruelty or excess because all sane human beings disapprove in theory of cruelty or excess. But to say that Buddhism and Christianity give the same philosophy of these things is simply false. All humanity does agree that we are in a net of sin. Most of humanity agrees that there is some way out. But as to what is the way out, I do not think that there are two institutions in the universe which contradict each other so flatly as Buddhism and Christianity.

Even when I thought, with most other well-informed, though unschol-arly, people, that Buddhism and Christianity were alike, there was one thing about them that always perplexed me; I mean the startling difference in their type of religious art. I do not mean in its technical style of representa-tion, but in the things that it was manifestly meant to represent. No two ideals could be more opposite than a Christian saint in a Gothic cathedral and a Buddhist saint in a Chinese temple. The opposition exists at every point; but perhaps the shortest statement of it is that the Buddhist saint always has his eyes shut, while the Christian saint always has them very wide open. The Buddhist saint has a sleek and harmonious body, but his eyes are heavy and sealed with sleep. The mediaeval saint's body is wasted to its crazy bones, but his eyes are frightfully alive. There cannot be any real community of spirit between forces that produced symbols so different as that. Granted that both images are extravagances, are perversions of the pure creed, it must be a real divergence which could produce such opposite extravagances. The Buddhist is looking with a peculiar intentness inwards. The Christian is staring with a frantic intentness outwards. If we follow that clue steadily we shall find some interesting things.

A short time ago Mrs. Besant, in an interesting essay, announced that there was only one religion in the world, that all faiths were only versions or perversions of it, and that she was quite prepared to say what it was. According to Mrs. Besant this universal Church is simply the universal self. It is the doctrine that we are really all one person; that there are no real walls of individuality between man and man. If I may put it so, she does not tell us to love our neighbours; she tells us to be our neighbours. That is Mrs. Besant's thoughtful and suggestive description of the religion in which all men must find themselves in agreement. And I never heard of any suggestion in my life with which I more violently disagree. I want to love my neighbour not because he is I, but precisely because he is not I. I want to adore the world, not as one likes a looking-glass, because it is one's self, but as one loves a woman, because she is entirely different. If souls are separate love is possible. If souls are united love is obviously impossible. A man may be said loosely to love himself, but he can hardly fall in love with himself, or, if he does, it must be a monotonous courtship. If the world is full of real selves, they can be really unselfish selves. But upon Mrs. Besant's principle the whole cosmos is only one enormously selfish person.

It is just here that Buddhism is on the side of modern pantheism and immanence. And it is just here that Christianity is on the side of humanity and liberty and love. Love desires personality; therefore love desires division. It is the instinct of Christianity to be glad that God has broken the universe into little pieces, because they are living pieces. It is her instinct to say "little children love one another" rather than to tell one large person to love himself. This is the intellectual abyss between

Buddhism and Christianity; that for the Buddhist or Theosophist personality is the fall of man, for the Christian it is the purpose of God, the whole point of his cosmic idea. The world-soul of the Theosophists asks man to love it only in order that man may throw himself into it. But the divine centre of Christianity actually threw man out of it in order that he might love it. The oriental deity is like a giant who should have lost his leg or hand and be always seeking to find it; but the Christian power is like some giant who in a strange generosity should cut off his right hand, so that it might of its own accord shake hands with him. We come back to the same tireless note touching the nature of Christianity; all modern philosophies are chains which connect and fetter; Christianity is a sword which separates and sets free. No other philosophy makes God actually rejoice in the separation of the universe into living souls. But according to orthodox Christianity this separation between God and man is sacred, because this is eternal. That a man may love God it is necessary that there should be not only a God to be loved, but a man to love him.

All those vague theosophical minds for whom the universe is an immense melting-pot are exactly the minds which shrink instinctively from that earthquake saying of our Gospels, which declare that the Son of God came not with peace but with a sundering sword. The saying rings entirely true even considered as what it obviously is; the statement that any man who preaches real love is bound to beget hate. It is as true of democratic fraternity as a divine love; sham love ends in compromise and common philosophy; but real love has always ended in bloodshed. Yet there is another and yet more awful truth behind the obvious meaning of this utterance of our Lord. According to Himself the Son was a sword separating brother and brother that they should for an aeon hate each other. But the Father also was a sword, which in the black beginning separated brother and brother, so that they should love each other at last.

This is the meaning of that almost insane happiness in the eyes of the mediaeval saint in the picture. This is the meaning of the sealed eyes of the superb Buddhist image. The Christian saint is happy because he has verily been cut off from the world; he is separate from things and is staring at them in astonishment. But why should the Buddhist saint be astonished at things?—since there is really only one thing, and that being impersonal can hardly be astonished at itself. There have been many pantheist poems suggesting wonder, but no really successful ones. The pantheist cannot wonder, for he cannot praise God or praise anything as really distinct from himself. Our immediate business here, however, is with the effect of this Christian admiration (which strikes outwards, towards a deity distinct from the worshipper) upon the general need for ethical activity and social reform. And surely its effect is sufficiently obvious. There is no real possibility of getting out of pantheism, any special impulse to moral action. For pantheism implies in its nature that one thing is as good as another; whereas action implies in its nature that one thing is greatly preferable to another. Swinburne in the high summer of his scepticism tried in vain to wrestle with this difficulty. In "Songs before Sunrise," written under the inspiration of Garibaldi and the revolt of Italy he proclaimed the newer religion and the purer God which should wither up all the priests of the world:

> *What doest thou now*
> *Looking Godward to cry*
> *I am I, thou art thou,*
> *I am low, thou art high,*
> *I am thou that thou seekest to find him, find thou but*
> *thyself, thou art I.*

All Christianity concentrates on the man at the cross-roads. The vast and shallow philosophies, the huge syntheses of humbug, all talk about ages and evolution and ultimate developments. The true philosophy is concerned with the instant. Will a man take this road or that?—that is the only thing to think about, if you enjoy thinking. The aeons are easy enough to think about, any one can think about them. The instant is really awful: and it is because our religion has intensely felt the instant, that it has in literature dealt much with battle and in theology dealt much with hell. It is full of DANGER, like a boy's book: it is at an immortal crisis. There is a great deal of real similarity between popular fiction and the religion of the western people. If you say that popular fiction is vulgar and tawdry, you only say what the dreary and well-informed say also about the images in the Catholic churches. Life (according to the faith) is very like a serial story in a magazine: life ends with the promise (or menace) "to be continued in our next." Also, with a noble vulgarity, life imitates the serial and leaves off at the exciting moment. For death is distinctly an exciting moment.

But the point is that a story is exciting because it has in it so strong an element of will, of what theology calls free-will. You cannot finish a sum how you like. But you can finish a story how you like. When somebody discovered the Differential Calculus there was only one Differential Calculus he could discover. But when Shakespeare killed Romeo he might have married him to Juliet's old nurse if he had felt inclined. And Christendom has excelled in the narrative romance exactly because it has insisted on the theological free-will. It is a large matter and too much to one side of the road to be discussed adequately here; but this is the real objection to that torrent of modern talk about treating crime as disease, about making a prison merely a hygienic environment like a hospital, of healing sin by slow scientific methods. The fallacy of the whole thing is that evil is a matter of active choice whereas disease is not. If you say that you are going to cure a profligate as you cure an asthmatic, my cheap and obvious answer is, "Produce the people who want to be asthmatics as many people want to be profligates." A man may lie still and be cured of a malady. But he must not lie still if he wants to be cured of a sin; on the contrary, he must get up and jump about violently. The whole point indeed is perfectly expressed in the very word which we use for a man in hospital; "patient" is in the passive mood; "sinner" is in the active. If a man is to be saved from influenza, he may be a patient. But if he is to be saved from forging, he must be not a patient but an IMPATIENT. He must be personally impatient with forgery. All moral reform must start in the active not the passive will.

Here again we reach the same substantial conclusion. In so far as we desire the definite reconstructions and the dangerous revolutions which have distinguished European civilization, we shall not discourage the thought of possible ruin; we shall rather encourage it. If we want, like the Eastern saints, merely to contemplate how right things are, of course we shall only say that they must go right. But if we particularly want to MAKE them go right, we must insist that they may go wrong.

Lastly, this truth is yet again true in the case of the common modern attempts to diminish or to explain away the divinity of Christ. The thing may be true or not; that I shall deal with before I end. But if the divinity is true it is certainly terribly revolutionary. That a good man may have his back to the wall is no more than we knew already; but that God could have his back to the wall is a boast for all insurgents for ever. Christianity is the only religion on earth that has felt that omnipotence made God incomplete. Christianity alone has felt that God, to be wholly God, must have been a rebel as well as a king. Alone of all creeds, Christianity has added courage to the virtues of the Creator. For the only courage worth calling courage must necessarily mean that the soul passes a breaking point and does not break.

In this indeed I approach a matter more dark and awful than it is easy to discuss; and I apologise in advance if any of my phrases fall wrong or seem irreverent touching a matter which the greatest saints and thinkers have justly feared to approach. But in that terrific tale of the Passion there is a distinct emotional suggestion that the author of all things (in some unthinkable way) went not only through agony, but through doubt. It is written, "Thou shalt not tempt the Lord thy God." No; but the Lord thy God may tempt Himself; and it seems as if this was what happened in Gethsemane. In a garden Satan tempted man: and in a garden God tempted God. He passed in some superhuman manner through our human horror of pessimism. When the world shook and the sun was wiped out of heaven, it was not at the crucifixion, but at the cry from the cross: the cry which confessed that God was forsaken of God. And now let the revolutionists choose a creed from all the creeds and a god from all the gods of the world, carefully weighing all the gods of inevitable recurrence and of unalterable power. They will not find another god who has himself been in revolt. Nay, (the matter grows too difficult for human speech,) but let the atheists themselves choose a god. They will find only one divinity who ever uttered their isolation; only one religion in which God seemed for an instant to be an atheist.

These can be called the essentials of the old orthodoxy, of which the chief merit is that it is the natural fountain of revolution and reform; and of which the chief defect is that it is obviously only an abstract assertion. Its main advantage is that it is the most adventurous and manly of all theologies. Its chief disadvantage is simply that it is a theology. It can always be urged against it that it is in its nature arbitrary and in the air. But it is not so high in the air but that great archers spend their whole lives in shooting arrows at it—yes, and their last arrows; there are men who will ruin themselves and ruin their civilization if they may ruin also this old fantastic tale.

This is the last and most astounding fact about this faith; that its enemies will use any weapon against it, the swords that cut their own fingers, and the firebrands that burn their own homes. Men who begin to fight the Church for the sake of freedom and humanity end by flinging away freedom and humanity if only they may fight the Church. This is no exaggeration; I could fill a book with the instances of it. Mr. Blatchford set out, as an ordinary Bible-smasher, to prove that Adam was guiltless of sin against God; in manoeuvring so as to maintain this he admitted, as a mere side issue, that all the tyrants, from Nero to King Leopold, were guiltless of any sin against humanity. I know a man who has such a passion for proving that he will have no personal existence after death that he falls back on the position that he has no personal existence now. He invokes Buddhism and says that all souls fade into each other; in order to prove that he cannot go to heaven he proves that he cannot go to Hartlepool. I have known people who protested against religious education with arguments against any education, saying that the child's mind must grow freely or that the old must not teach the young. I have known people who showed that there could be no divine judgment by showing that there can be no human judgment, even for practical purposes. They burned their own corn to set fire to the church; they smashed their own tools to smash it; any stick was good enough to beat it with, though it were the last stick of their own dismembered furniture. We do not admire, we hardly excuse, the fanatic who wrecks this world for love of the other. But what are we to say of the fanatic who wrecks this world out of hatred of the other? He sacrifices the very existence of humanity to the non-existence of God. He offers his victims not to the altar, but merely to assert the idleness of the altar and the emptiness of the throne. He is ready to ruin even that primary ethic by which all things live, for his strange and eternal vengeance upon some one who never lived at all.

And yet the thing hangs in the heavens unhurt. Its opponents only succeed in destroying all that they themselves justly hold dear. They do not destroy orthodoxy; they only destroy political courage and common sense. They do not prove that Adam was not responsible to God; how could they prove it? They only prove (from their premises) that the Czar is not responsible to Russia. They do not prove that Adam should not have been punished by God; they only prove that the nearest sweater should not be punished by men. With their oriental doubts about personality they do not make certain that we shall have no personal life hereafter; they only make certain that we shall not have a very jolly or complete one here. With their paralysing hints of all conclusions coming out wrong they do not tear the book of the Recording Angel; they only make it a little harder to keep the books of Marshall & Snelgrove. Not only is the faith the mother of all worldly energies, but its foes are the fathers of all worldly confusion. The secularists have not wrecked divine things; but the secularists have wrecked secular things, if that is any comfort to them. The Titans did not scale heaven; but they laid waste the world.

## ON ORTHODOXY

### Dale Ahlquist

**W**hen people read *Orthodoxy* for the first time, they generally discover that their pens run out of ink from underlining almost every sentence in the book. The relentless and irresistible quotable quotes also make for a rather disjointed reading experience. So they finish the book and, in spite of it being almost entirely underlined, they wonder, *What was that about, anyway?* Then they reread the book and are quite bewildered to discover it is an entirely different work, giving them the odd sensation of reading it for the first time, in spite of the obvious evidence of their very own underlinings from the previous read. The third time is generally the charm, as Chesterton's thesis suddenly bursts through his dazzling rhetoric and imaginative arguments.

    *Fresh* is a fitting word. *Orthodoxy* is a lively, creative, and unique approach to defending the Christian faith. Yet Chesterton insists that it is not a book of apologetics; he claims it's simply his account of how he came to embrace Christianity for himself. His journey, however, is not typical, for he did not study the arguments in favor of but rather the arguments against Christianity. He did not study classic Christian philosophy but rather a variety of modern anti-Christian philosophies. He thought he was forming a new heresy, but when he put on the finishing touches, he found it was orthodoxy. He thought he'd come up with a new religion and was embarrassed to discover that someone else had come up with it almost two thousand years earlier.

The heart of the book is found, first, in the coherent morality of fairy tales, or the "Ethics of Elfland," where logic is still logical and still capable of teaching science a few lessons. Then he hands us the surprising and seemingly contradictory truths of the faith, the "Paradoxes of Christianity," where logic gets put to the test.

It is a theme throughout Chesterton's writings that faith does not contradict reason, but reason often appears to contradict itself. Reason requires faith as a starting point. As he says elsewhere, "You cannot prove your first statement. Otherwise it would not be your first statement."

And, a lush portrait of the faith, which always has attracted both the strongest of devotion and the fiercest of opposition wherever it appears, is known as the "Romance of Orthodoxy."

In preceding chapters, Chesterton has examined the narrowness of modern philosophies, each "sharpened to a narrow point," ending in madness, or what he calls "the clean well-lit prison of one idea." In chapters following he will show how in art, literature, politics, and worship, Christianity not only provides satisfaction but sanity.

Chesterton is defending not only the Christian church but also the essence of Western society, a product of Hebrew monotheism, Greek philosophy, and Roman civilization, all brought together when Christ steps onto history's stage. Chesterton draws a striking contrast between East and West, summed up in differences between the circle and the cross, the symbols representing Buddhism and Christianity. The circle is centripetal, spinning inward toward madness and self-destruction, like a snake eating its own tail; the cross is centrifugal, spreading its arms to the four winds, "a signpost for free travelers."

The other principle Chesterton defends in *Orthodoxy* is the value of solid tradition against the flakiness of fads and fashions. The modern world is obsessed with being modern. Therefore, old things that were carefully created for a purpose are suddenly discarded thoughtlessly with no sense of their importance. Then, of course, the new things that replace them are quickly discarded as well.

Thus, the modern world is a mess. Chesterton saw it coming. He also saw the solution. As with any prophet, his warnings are timely, but so are his exhortations. He is encouraging, not discouraging. We know he's right when he tells us we must hate the world enough to change it, yet love it enough to think it worth changing.

**John Mark Reynolds,** PhD, is the director and founder of the Torrey Honors Institute and associate professor of Philosophy at Biola University. He has authored and coauthored several books, including *When Athens Met Jerusalem: An Introduction to Classical and Christian Thought.*

# TRANSLATION CREDITS

Preferred Editions in the Torrey Honors Institute

Homer. *The Odyssey of Homer.* Translated by Richmond Alexander Lattimore. New York: Harper Perennial, 1999.

Plato. *Plato Complete Works.* Edited by John M. Cooper and D.S. Hutchinson. Indianapolis, IN: Hackett Pub., 1997.

Plato. *The Republic of Plato.* Translated by Allan David Bloom. New York: Basic, 1991.

Aristotle. *Nicomachean Ethics.* Translated by Terence Irwin. Indianapolis, IN: Hackett Pub., 1999.

Virgil. *The Aeneid.* Translated by Robert Fitzgerald. New York: Vintage, 1990.

Augustine. *Confessions.* Translated by Henry Chadwick. Oxford: Oxford UP, 1998.

Boethius. *The Consolation of Philosophy.* Translated by V.E. Watts. London: Penguin, 1999.

Aquinas, Thomas. *Summa Theologica of St. Thomas Aquinas.* Translated by Fathers of the English Dominican Province. Notre Dame: Ave Maria, 1997.

Chaucer, Geoffery. *The Canterbury Tales*. Translated by Nevill Coghill. London: Penguin, 2003.

Dante, Alighieri. *Inferno*. Translated by Anthony M. Esolen. New York: Modern Library, 2002.

Calvin, John. *Calvin: Institutes of the Christian Religion*. Edited by John T. McNeill. Translated by Ford Lewis Battles. Philadelphia: Westminster John Knox, 1960.

Spenser, Edmund. *The Faerie Queene*. Edited by Thomas P. Roche Jr. and C. Patrick O'Donnell Jr. London: Penguin, 1979.

Erasmus. *Praise of Folly*. Translated by Betty Radice. London: Penguin Classics, 1971.

Locke, John. *The Works of John Locke in Nine Volumes*. London: British Library, 1794.

Cervantes, Miguel De. *Don Quixote*. Translated by Charles Jarvis. New York: Oxford World's Classics, 1992.

Shakespeare, William. *The Norton Shakespeare*. Edited by Stephen Greenblatt, Walter Cohen, Jean E. Howard, and Katharine Eisaman Maus. New York: W.W. Norton, 2008.

Descartes, René. *Meditations on First Philosophy: With Selections From the Objections and Replies*. Edited by John Cottingham. New York: Cambridge University Press, 1996.

Milton, John. *The Major Works*. Edited by Jonathan Goldberg and Stephen Orgel. New York: Oxford University Press, 2008.

Pascal, Blaise. *Pensées and Other Writings*. Translated by Honor Levi. Edited by Anthony Levi. New York: Oxford UP, 2008.

Locke, John. *Second Treatise of Government*. Edited by C.B. Macpherson. Indianapolis: Hackett Pub., 1980.

Newton, Isaac. *Isaac Newton: Philosophical Writings*. Edited by Andrew Janiak. Cambridge: Cambridge UP, 2004.

Wesley, John. *Wesley's Doctrinal Standards: The Sermons With Introductions, Analysis, and Notes*. Edited by Rev. N. Burwash. Salem, OH: Schmul Pub., 1988.

Tolstoy, Leo. *Anna Karenina*. Translated by Richard Pevear and Larissa Volokhonsky. New York: Penguin, 2004.

Dostoyevsky, Fyodor. *The Brothers Karamazov*. Translated by Richard

Pevear and Larissa Volokhonsky. New York: Farrar, Straus and Giroux, 2002.

Nietzsche, Friedrich. *On the Genealogy of Morals and Ecce Homo.* Edited by Walter Kaufmann. Translated by Walter Kaufmann and R.J. Hollingdale. New York: Vintage, 1989.

Tocqueville, Alexis de. *Democracy in America.* Translated by Harvey C. Mansfield and Delba Winthrop. Edited by Harvey C. Mansfield and Delba Winthrop. Chicago: University of Chicago, 2002.

Austen, Jane. *Pride and Prejudice.* Edited by James Kinsley. New York: Oxford UP, 2008.

Marx, Karl, and Friedrich Engels. *The Communist Manifesto.* Translated by Samuel Moore. Edited by David McLellan. New York: Oxford UP, 2008.

Darwin, Charles. *The Origin of Species.* New York: Signet Classics, 2003.

Chesterton, G.K. *Orthodoxy.* New York: Doubleday, 2001.

# CONTRIBUTORS

Dale Ahlquist is the president and co-founder of the American Chesterton Society and one of the world's leading experts on G. K. Chesterton. He created and hosts the EWTN television series *G. K. Chesterton: The Apostle of Common Sense,* publishes *Gilbert Magazine,* and is a frequent guest lecturer at various universities.

Hunter Baker, JD, is the associate dean of Arts and Sciences and associate professor of Political Science at Union University. He authored *The End of Secularism,* has contributed to *First Things* and *Touchstone* magazines, and is a contributing editor for *Salvo* magazine. He is the winner of the 2011 Michael Novak Award from the Acton Institute.

Jamie Y. Whitaker Campbell, JD, is an assistant professor of Humanities and Law in the Torrey Honors Institute at Biola University; she also teaches American Constitutional Law, focusing on the development of individual liberties within the American justice system.

William Dembski, PhD, is a professor of Philosophy and the director of the Center for Cultural Engagement at Southwestern Baptist Theological Seminary. He is an advocate for Intelligent Design and the author of numerous books on the topic including *Intelligent Design Uncensored* and *The Design of Life: Discovering Signs of Intelligence in Biological Systems.*

Anthony Esolen, PhD, is a professor of Literature at Providence College and a senior editor of *Touchstone* magazine. In addition to authoring several books, he is well-known for his translations of classical works of literature, including Dante's *Divine Comedy.*

Michael Fatigati is the assistant to the director and adjunct professor at Biola University's Torrey Honors Institute.

Al Geier, PhD, is an associate professor of Classics at the University of Rochester and is the author of *Plato's Erotic Thought: The Tree of the Unknown.*

John Granger is a Christian literary critic most famous for his writing regarding the artistry and meaning of the *Harry Potter* novels. Dubbed "The Dean of Harry Potter Scholars" by *Time* magazine, Granger is a frequent guest speaker at academic and Harry Potter fan conferences, talk shows, and universities.

Gary Hartenburg is a doctoral candidate at the University of California, Irvine, and an assistant professor of Philosophy at St. Katherine College.

Joe Henderson, PhD, is an assistant professor of Old Testament and Hermeneutics at Biola University's Torrey Honors Institute.

Hugh Hewitt, JD, is a professor of Law at Chapman University and host of the nationally syndicated *Hugh Hewitt Show.* He is a prolific contributor to various new media outlets and has authored dozens of books on faith and politics, and the intersection of the two.

Philip Johnson, JD, is a professor emeritus of Law at Berkeley Law School and is considered one of the founders of the modern Intelligent Design movement. He is the author of many books, including *Darwin on Trial, Defeating Darwinism by Opening Minds,* and *The Wedge of Truth.*

Janelle Klapausak is an assistant professor at Biola University's Torrey Honors Institute and is currently a doctoral candidate at Baylor University.

Peter Kreeft, PhD, is a professor of Philosophy at Boston College and The King's College, New York. He is an acclaimed author and speaker on many philosophical and theological topics.

Jeffrey S. Lehman is a tutor at Thomas Aquinas College in Santa Paula, California. He is also a fellow of the Center for Thomas More Studies and holds a PhD in philosophy from the Institute of Philosophic Studies at the University of Dallas.

Robert Llizo, PhD, is a lecturer in Medieval History at Biola University's Torrey Honors Institute.

Frederica Mathewes-Green is a noted Christian author and speaker. She has written several books, including *The Jesus Prayer: The Ancient Desert Prayer That Tunes the Heart to God* and *The Illumined Heart: The Ancient Christian Path of Transformation*. She is a frequent contributor to Christian and religious publications such as *Christianity Today* and *Beliefnet*.

Russell Moore, PhD, is the dean of the School of Theology and senior vice-president for Academic Administration at Southern Baptist Theology Seminary. He is also a senior editor at *Touchstone* magazine and author of several books, including *Adopted for Life* and *A Theology for the Church*.

Amy Obrist, PhD, is an assistant professor of Russian and German Language and chair of the Modern Languages Department at Biola University.

Greg Peters, PhD, is an associate professor of Medieval Theology at Biola University's Torrey Honors Institute.

John Mark Reynolds, PhD, is the director and founder of the Torrey Honors Institute and associate professor of Philosophy at Biola University. He has authored and coauthored several books, including *When Athens Met Jerusalem: An Introduction to Classical and Christian Thought*.

Fred Sanders, PhD, is an associate professor of Systematic Theology at Biola University's Torrey Honors Institute. He lectures frequently on the Trinity and Christian art, and is the author of several books, including *The Deep Things of God: How the Trinity Changes Everything.*

Melissa Schubert is an assistant professor of English Literature at Biola University's Torrey Honors Institute. She is currently a doctoral candidate at Claremont Graduate University.

Diane Vincent, PhD, is an assistant professor of Medieval Literature at Biola University's Torrey Honors Institute.

Thomas Ward is currently a doctoral candidate in UCLA's Department of Philosophy and holds an MPhil from the University of Oxford.